MILK STREET

365

MILK STREET

365

THE ALL-PURPOSE COOKBOOK FOR EVERY DAY OF THE YEAR

CHRISTOPHER KIMBALL

WRITING AND EDITING

J. M. Hirsch, Michelle Locke and Dawn Yanagihara

RECIPES

Wes Martin, Courtney Hill, Diane Unger and the
Milk Street Kitchen Cooks and Recipe Contributors

ART DIRECTION

Jennifer Baldino Cox

VORACIOUS

LITTLE, BROWN AND COMPANY

NEW YORK   BOSTON   LONDON

Little, Brown and Company
Hachette Book Group
1290 Avenue of the Americas, New York, NY 10104
littlebrown.com

First Edition: April 2024

Voracious is an imprint of Little, Brown and Company, a division of Hachette Book Group, Inc.

The Voracious name and logo are trademarks of Hachette Book Group, Inc.

The publisher is not responsible for websites (or their content) that are not owned by the publisher.

The Hachette Speakers Bureau provides a wide range of authors for speaking events. To find out more, go to hachettespeakersbureau.com or call (866) 376-6591.

PHOTOGRAPHY AND STYLING CREDITS:

Photographs by Connie Miller of CB Creatives except as noted. Channing Johnson: IX. Joe Murphy: 5 (bottom left), 7, 9, 14, 16 (bottom right), 21 (bottom right), 30-31, 43, 50 (bottom left), 52 (bottom right), 57, 64, 66, 74, 77 (bottom right), 79, 108, 113, 114, 115, 124, 136 (bottom left), 145 (bottom right), 146, 148, 158, 160 (bottom left), 163, 164 (bottom left), 166, 180, 187 (top left), 195, 198 (bottom left), 199, 200, 203 (bottom right), 206, 207, 224-225 (thumbnails), 241 (bottom right), 254-255 (thumbnails), 262-263, 276, 277, 282, 290 (bottom left), 298-299, 304, 311 (top left), 318, 337 (bottom right), 352, 359, 361, 372 (bottom right), 375 (bottom right), 386, 406, 408, 417, 420, 431 (bottom right), 439, 442-443, 445, 453, 454, 457, 461 (bottom right), 463 (bottom right), 472, 480 (right), 492, 500, 501, 510, 520, 524 (bottom left), 542 (bottom left), 548, 549 (bottom right), 556 (top left), 558, 568-569, 578-579, 587 (bottom right), 590-591, 594, 603 (right), 604, 605, 610 (top left), 613 (bottom right), 614 (left); Brianna Coleman: 2, 545. Erik Bernstein 5 (top right), 11, 16 (top left), 27, 29, 34 (bottom left), 40, 44, 46, 47 (bottom right), 59 (top left), 60, 69, 89 (bottom right), 91, 139, 175, 185, 190, 191, 194, 215, 228 (top left), 229, 253 (bottom right), 269, 273 (bottom right), 290 (right), 301, 305, 306, 307, 309, 314, 315 (bottom right), 319, 376, 388, 395, 414, 415 (bottom right), 449, 460, 462, 463 (bottom left), 517, 526, 542 (top right), 552, 561, 585 (left), 588, 595, 598 (top left), 612 (bottom right), 613 (top left). Brian Samuels: 6, 254 (lead photo), 345, 347, 464, 543, 563, 574, 585 (bottom). Erika LaPresto: V, 15, 56, 68, 104, 220 (top right), 248, 300, 344, 357, 421, 426, 458, 476, 490, 525, 537, 559 (top left), 581. Joyelle West: 24, 294, 592. Michael Piazza: 105. Kristin Teig: 208.

Food styling by Christine Tobin except as noted. Wes Martin: V, 5 (bottom left), 7, 9, 14, 15, 16 (bottom right), 21 (bottom right), 43, 50 (bottom left), 52 (bottom right), 56, 57, 64, 66, 68, 74, 77 (bottom right), 79, 104, 108, 111, 113, 114, 115, 124, 136 (bottom left), 145 (bottom right), 146, 148, 158, 160 (bottom left), 161, 163, 164 (bottom left), 166, 180, 187 (top left), 195, 198 (bottom left), 199, 200, 203 (bottom right), 206, 207, 220 (top right), 224-225 (thumbnails), 241 (bottom right), 248, 254-255 (thumbnails), 262-263, 276, 277, 281, 282, 290 (bottom left), 298-299, 300, 304, 311 (top left), 318, 334, 337 (bottom right), 344, 352, 357, 359, 361, 372 (bottom right), 375 (bottom right), 386, 406, 408, 417, 420, 421, 426, 431 (bottom right), 438, 439, 442-443, 445, 453, 454, 457, 458, 461 (bottom right), 463 (bottom right), 472, 476, 480 (right), 490, 492, 500, 501, 510, 520, 524 (bottom left), 525, 537, 542 (bottom left), 548, 549 (bottom right), 550, 556 (top left), 558, 559 (top left), 568-569, 572, 578-579, 581, 587 (bottom right), 590-591, 594, 598 (bottom right), 599, 603 (right), 604, 605, 610 (top left), 613 (bottom right), 614 (left). Catrine Kelty: 10 (bottom right), 19, 61 (top left), 85, 105, 120, 156-157, 184, 188, 193, 205 (bottom left), 208, 226, 228 (bottom right), 231 (bottom left), 232, 233, 236-237, 238, 240, 241 (top left), 242, 243, 244, 245, 246-247, 249 (bottom right), 253 (top left), 256, 258, 259, 265, 272, 275 (top left), 278, 280, 284, 285 (bottom right), 292, 296, 297, 327 (bottom left), 329, 333, 339, 341, 351, 380, 381, 382, 404-405, 424, 440, 441, 452, 455, 459, 467, 474, 483, 488, 497, 514, 540-541, 547, 559 (bottom right), 564, 612 (top left). Erika Joyce: 5 (top right), 11, 16 (top left), 27, 29, 34 (bottom left), 40, 44, 46, 47 (bottom right), 59 (top left), 60, 69, 89 (bottom right), 91, 139, 161, 175, 185, 190, 191, 194, 215, 228 (top left), 229, 253 (bottom right), 269, 273 (bottom right), 290 (right), 301, 305, 306, 307, 309, 314, 315 (bottom right), 319, 376, 388, 395, 414, 415 (bottom right), 438, 449, 460, 462, 463 (bottom left), 517, 526, (top right), 552, 561, 585 (left), 588, 595, 598 (top left), 612 (bottom right), 613 (top left). Catherine Smart: 129, 160 (top right), 162, 202, (top right), 257, 346, 366-367, 377, 379, 383, 446 (right), 461 (top left), 493, 533, 571, 576. Monica Mariano: 18, 103, 270, 358. Gabriella Rinaldo: 119, 267, 313, 363, 370, 391. Molly Shuster: 603 (top left).

ISBN 978-0-316-53868-8
LCCN 2023939613

10 9 8 7 6 5 4 3 2 1

IM

Print book interior design by Gary Tooth / Empire Design Studio
Printed in China

CONTENTS

INTRODUCTION

Growing up, our kitchen had *The Joy of Cooking,* Irma S. Rombauer's paean to the cooking of America, especially the Midwest. We also had Fannie Farmer, *The Settlement Cook Book* and one or two other "big" books that housed most of what one needed to know to feed the family. Later, there was Julia Child's *Mastering the Art of French Cooking*, Jacques Pepin's illustrated books on technique, *James Beard's American Cookery, The Silver Palate Cookbook*, which was to the '70s what Fannie Farmer was to the turn of the century. Then cookbooks tuned to more specific themes: Paula Wolfert on Morocco, Diana Kennedy on Mexico, Julia Sahni on India, Marcella Hazan on Italy, and quirkier offerings, such as Moosewood or books by Vincent Price.

Then suddenly, it seemed America had tired of the big books. We became a more diverse cookbook audience, hungering for information about other cultures and cuisines. Recipes no longer evolved from one generation to the next; they were abandoned in favor of whatever struck our fancy at the time. (Mollie Katzen's *The Enchanted Broccoli Forest* anyone?) Like cable television, the culinary world broke into a thousand different pieces, each with its own promoters and defenders, then blossomed on the internet where everyone had access to a large audience.

All of this leads to the question: Why do a big cookbook such as *365*? A good question with a good answer. After a revolution comes consolidation, a new normal establishes itself until the next upheaval. I have seen our everyday repertoire rebuild itself, mostly from global influence, into a fresh collection of recipes that redefines American home cooking. Few cookbooks today omit a recipe for hummus, or

shakshuka or kebabs or flatbread or pho or tagine. A fried chicken dish from South Korea no longer is headline news. Pasta dishes that most of us had never heard of a generation ago – gricia or trapanese – are now common. Mexican cuisine no longer is guacamole and burritos, but tlayudas, esquites and calabacitas. As for ingredients, pomegranate molasses, za'atar, harissa and fish sauce no longer are exotic; they are pantry staples.

Having spent the last seven years traveling the world to help introduce home cooks to this expanded culinary universe, we humbly offer *365* as a fresh take on the big book, the one that can be a helpful guide to the new home cooking, to the process of changing the way you cook. We are not experts on any particular cuisine. Instead, we are reporters and translators who provide a competent easy-to-digest overview to the world of choices at your fingertips. The recipes work. They have been passed through our kitchen with an eye to time, money and convenience, but, we hope, with a deep conviction in the original point of a recipe, its flavors, textures and soul. We have traveled to home kitchens around the world to ground our culinary work in original recipes, though we are quick to add that authenticity is in the eye of the beholder. No two homes make the same recipe alike, whether it is hummus or three-cup chicken. The culinary world is fast and furious in its need for change, innovation and cultural mashups. Nothing is written in stone.

So, if you want one book to help change the way you cook, to help change the way you think about food and cooking, *365* is that book. From there, you can drill more deeply into whatever passions excite you, but we hope that *365* will always be a trusted guide.

salads

The Vinaigrette Manifesto

There's nothing wrong with the classic French vinaigrette, often defined as little more than a 3:1 ratio of oil to vinegar seasoned with a bit of salt and pepper. But the rest of the world doesn't feel beholden to that basic dressing paradigm.

In the Middle East, a dressing may be tahini and lemon juice on chopped tomatoes and cucumber. In Morocco, roasted vegetables are dressed with chermoula, a bold puree of copious parsley, cilantro, olive oil and lemon.

We were reminded of this by Diane Kochilas, a Greek-American chef whose cookbook, "My Greek Table," includes a guide to that country's way with dressings. And their way is far more freewheeling than most of us are accustomed to.

Their way is citrus juice instead of vinegar. It is yogurt, mustard and honey whipped in. It is crumbled feta cheese, chopped olives, fresh oregano and even ouzo, Greece's anise-flavored aperitif. And it's about flavor more than following exacting ratios.

Kochilas inspired us to play with these fresh combinations, remembering that almost anything goes. For a base, we liked a 2:1 ratio of extra-virgin olive oil to acid, though use whatever mix tastes best to you. And we liked her preference for citrus juices—both lemon and orange—over vinegar.

Lesson learned: The classic French vinaigrette is fine. But it's just the start. Here is a basic citrus-oil dressing with two variations.

Lemon–Olive Oil Vinaigrette

Start to finish: 5 minutes
Makes 1 cup

If the dressing separates, simply shake again. Each can be refrigerated up to one week. Bring to room temperature before using.

Don't hesitate to use these beyond salads. They're also great on grains, chicken and seafood.

⅔ cup extra-virgin olive oil

⅓ cup lemon juice

1 teaspoon dried oregano

Kosher salt and ground black pepper

In a small jar with a tight-fitting lid, combine the oil, lemon juice, oregano and ½ teaspoon each salt and pepper. Seal the jar, then shake vigorously. Taste and season with salt and pepper.

For Orange, Garlic and Olive Vinaigrette:

Use ⅔ cup extra-virgin olive oil, 1 teaspoon grated orange zest plus ¼ cup orange juice, 2 tablespoons lemon juice, 2 tablespoons finely chopped pitted green olives, 1 medium garlic clove (finely grated), ¼ teaspoon kosher salt and ¼ teaspoon black pepper.

For Feta-Herb Vinaigrette:

Use ⅔ cup extra-virgin olive oil, ⅓ cup lemon juice, 1 ounce crumbled feta cheese (¼ cup), 1 tablespoon fresh oregano (minced), 1 medium garlic clove (finely grated), ¼ teaspoon kosher salt and ¼ teaspoon black pepper.

GREEK CABBAGE SALAD WITH CARROTS AND OLIVES

Start to finish: 45 minutes (15 minutes active)
Servings: 4

Cabbage-based politiki salata may be a dish for fall and winter in Greece, but the bright flavors and crisp textures are great any time of the year. We were introduced to it at the Avissinia Café in Athens and find it is an excellent accompaniment to grilled meats and fish. The salad is best eaten the day it is made, but it can be refrigerated for up to four hours in advance; hold off on adding the feta and olives until just before serving.

½ medium head green cabbage, cored and thinly sliced (about 4 cups)

3 medium carrots, peeled and coarsely shredded (about 1¼ cups)

5 tablespoons lemon juice, divided

Kosher salt

3 tablespoons extra-virgin olive oil

½ teaspoon white sugar

1 medium garlic clove, finely grated

3 medium celery stalks, thinly sliced on the diagonal (about 1 cup)

1 small or ½ large red bell pepper, stemmed, seeded and cut into rough matchsticks

4 ounces feta cheese, crumbled (1 cup)

½ cup chopped pitted green olives

In a large bowl, combine the cabbage, carrots, 3 tablespoons of lemon juice and ¼ teaspoon salt. Toss gently, just until the vegetables begin to wilt, about 1 minute. Let stand at room temperature 30 minutes, or until the cabbage softens slightly. Alternatively, cover and refrigerate for up to 4 hours.

In a small bowl, whisk together the olive oil, sugar, garlic, remaining 2 tablespoons lemon juice and ¾ teaspoon salt.

Add the celery and bell pepper to the cabbage mixture. Drizzle with the dressing and toss. Using tongs, transfer the salad to a serving bowl, leaving behind any accumulated liquid. Top with feta and olives.

SHAVED BRUSSELS SPROUTS WITH BROWNED BUTTER VINAIGRETTE

Start to finish: 30 minutes
Servings: 8

Most slaws are an uninspiring mashup of raw cabbage and sweet mayonnaise. We wanted tender texture and more nuanced taste, and got that by using browned butter in the vinaigrette instead of the traditional oil. We also opt for flavorful Brussels sprouts over cabbage. For speed, shred the sprouts with a food processor fitted with a thin slicing disk (4 millimeters or thinner). Otherwise, halve, then thinly slice them by hand using a chef's knife. We further tenderize the sprouts by salting them before adding the dressing. Whole-grain mustard adds flavor as well as a bit of texture to the vinaigrette.

1 pound Brussels sprouts, trimmed and finely shredded (see headnote)

Kosher salt and ground black pepper

⅔ cup sherry vinegar

4 teaspoons whole-grain mustard

8 tablespoons (1 stick) salted butter

⅓ cup finely chopped fresh dill

1 cup smoked almonds, chopped

½ cup dried cranberries

In a large bowl, toss the shredded sprouts with ¾ teaspoon salt. Let stand for 15 minutes.

Meanwhile, in a medium bowl, whisk together the vinegar, mustard and ½ teaspoon salt. In a small saucepan over medium-low, melt the butter, then cook, swirling the pan, until the milk solids at the bottom are golden brown and the butter has a nutty aroma, 5 to 6 minutes.

While whisking, gradually add the browned butter to the vinegar mixture, then continue to whisk to cool the mixture slightly, about 20 seconds. Stir in the dill and ½ teaspoon pepper.

Add the smoked almonds and cranberries to the sprouts, then pour the dressing over the mixture and toss well. Let stand at room temperature for at least 15 minutes to thoroughly season the sprouts, or cover and let stand for up to 1 hour. Taste and season with salt and pepper, then transfer to a serving bowl.

FRISÉE SALAD WITH BACON AND POACHED EGGS

Start to finish: 30 minutes
Servings: 4

Frisée aux lardons—a salad of frilly frisée dressed with wine-vinegar vinaigrette and embellished bits of crisp, salty bacon and a runny-yolked poached egg—is a French bistro classic. Our recipe is inspired by the version we had at Le Maquis in Paris' 18th arrondissement. There, chef Paul Boudier included toasted croutons, a delicious addition that complements the other ingredients. To find the simplest and best poaching method, we cooked dozens of eggs. We learned that abundant water is needed so the temperature doesn't plummet when the eggs are dropped in; this is why we use 3 quarts of water in a large Dutch oven. Also, spiking the poaching water with vinegar helps the proteins set quickly, reducing the "feathering" of the whites and resulting in neater-looking eggs. As for the greens, if you're not a fan of frisée, substitute an equal amount by volume of torn escarole, endive or radicchio.

2 ounces country-style bread, crusts removed, torn into rough ¼-inch pieces (about 1½ cups)

1 tablespoon plus ⅓ cup extra-virgin olive oil, divided

Kosher salt and ground black pepper

8 ounces thick-cut bacon, cut crosswise in ¼-inch pieces

1 medium shallot, halved and thinly sliced

¼ cup white wine vinegar

2 teaspoons Dijon mustard

1 teaspoon honey

¼ cup white vinegar

2 medium heads frisée, trimmed and torn into rough 1-inch pieces (about 8 cups)

4 large eggs

In a large Dutch oven, toss together the bread, 1 tablespoon oil and a sprinkle each of salt and pepper. Set over medium and toast, stirring occasionally, until golden brown, 4 to 5 minutes. Transfer to a plate and set aside. Wipe out the pot.

In the same pot over medium, cook the bacon, stirring, until browned and crisp, 6 to 7 minutes. Using a slotted spoon, transfer to a paper towel-lined plate. Pour off and discard all but 1 tablespoon fat. Add the shallot to the pot; cook over medium, stirring, until softened, 1 to 2 minutes. Remove from the heat, add the wine vinegar and scrape up any browned bits. Transfer the mixture to a large bowl; rinse out the pot and return it to the burner. To the shallots, whisk in the remaining ⅓ cup oil, the mustard, honey, ¼ teaspoon salt and ½ teaspoon pepper.

In the same pot over medium-high, combine 3 quarts water and the white vinegar; bring to a boil. Break 1 egg into a small bowl, ramekin or teacup. Add the egg to the water by holding the bowl just above the surface, tilting it and letting the egg slide in; the egg will sink. Repeat with the remaining eggs, spacing them evenly and noting the order added. Simmer gently, uncovered and without stirring, until the whites are set but the yolks are still soft, 3 to 4 minutes; do not boil.

Using a slotted spoon, remove the eggs one at a time in the order they were added, allowing excess water to drain off, and place on a plate. Whisk the shallot mixture to recombine. Add the frisée, toasted bread and three-quarters of the bacon; toss. Taste and season with salt and pepper. Divide among 4 serving plates or shallow bowls. Top each with a poached egg. Sprinkle with additional pepper and the remaining bacon.

ESCAROLE AND FENNEL SALAD WITH CAPERS AND GOLDEN RAISINS

Start to finish: 20 minutes
Servings: 4

We combine pleasantly bitter greens with crisp, anise-y fennel and a punchy vinaigrette for a light, leafy salad with a terrific contrast of flavors and textures. Capers bring brininess to the vinaigrette, while golden raisins add a touch of chewy sweetness. We first soak the raisins and shallot in vinegar to plump the fruit and mellow the allium's bite. Escarole or frisée are a great choice for the greens, as their frilly leaves catch and hold the capers and raisins. If your fennel bulb still has the fronds attached, trim them off and chop for a colorful garnish.

⅓ cup golden raisins

1 small shallot, halved and thinly sliced

2½ tablespoons white balsamic vinegar OR white wine vinegar

Kosher salt and ground black pepper

1 medium fennel bulb, trimmed, halved lengthwise and cored

3 tablespoons extra-virgin olive oil

2 tablespoons drained capers, roughly chopped

1 medium head escarole, tough outer leaves removed and discarded OR 2 small heads frisée OR a combination, torn into bite-size pieces

In a large bowl, stir together the raisins, shallot, vinegar and ¼ teaspoon each salt and pepper. Let stand, stirring occasionally, to plump the raisins and lightly pickle the shallot, about 15 minutes.

Meanwhile, use a mandoline or sharp chef's knife to slice the fennel ¹⁄₁₆ inch thick. To do so with the mandoline, hold each fennel half by the base and slice crosswise as far as is safe; discard the base. Set aside.

Into the bowl with the raisins and shallots, stir in the oil and capers. Add the fennel and escarole, then toss. Taste and season with salt and pepper.

Optional garnish: Chopped fennel fronds OR fresh tarragon OR fresh dill

GREEN SALAD WITH NORI VINAIGRETTE

Start to finish: 30 minutes, plus cooling and chilling
Servings: 6

This is our adaptation of a salad created by Eventide Oyster Co. in Portland, Maine. Roasted seaweed (also called nori) is pulverized to a coarse powder and added to the dressing, lending the dish deep, umami-rich flavor notes reinforced with soy sauce and mirin. Instead of using full-sized sheets of plain nori (the variety used for sushi), we opted for the convenience of an individual package of seasoned seaweed snacks that are available in most grocery stores. Quick-pickled veggies give the salad lots of texture and bright flavor, but keep in mind that they need to pickle for at least two hours before they're ready to use. To shave the carrot, run a sharp vegetable peeler down the length of the vegetable.

4 ounces red radishes, sliced into thin rounds

1 medium carrot, peeled and shaved into long, thin strips (see headnote)

½ small red onion, thinly sliced

1½ cups plus 2 tablespoons unseasoned rice vinegar, divided

⅓ cup white sugar

¼-ounce (7-gram) package roasted seaweed snacks, torn into small pieces (about 1 cup packed)

2 tablespoons soy sauce

2 tablespoons mirin

2 tablespoons grapeseed or other neutral oil

10 ounces spring mix or other delicate greens

Kosher salt

In a medium heatproof bowl, combine the radishes, carrot and onion. In a small saucepan over medium-high, combine 1½ cups vinegar, the sugar and ¾ cup water. Bring to a rapid boil, stirring to dissolve the sugar, then pour over the vegetables. Cool to room temperature, then cover and refrigerate for at least 2 hours or for up to 1 week.

In a spice grinder, process the seaweed until finely chopped, gently shaking the grinder, about 30 seconds; check under the blade for clumps and break up any. You should have about 2 tablespoons pulverized seaweed. In a large bowl, whisk together the seaweed, soy sauce, mirin, oil and the remaining 2 tablespoons vinegar; the dressing will thicken slightly.

Drain the pickles in a fine-mesh strainer. Add half of the drained pickles to the bowl with the dressing along with the salad greens. Toss to combine, then taste and season with salt. Transfer to a platter or bowl and top with the remaining drained pickles.

Understanding Acids

From the bright freshness of a just-squeezed lemon to the savory tang of aged balsamic vinegar, acids are a quick way to boost, brighten and balance flavors. We use them in dressings and marinades and often take a one-two approach, starting a dish with acid or an acid-based sauce, then adding a final squirt or drizzle at the end to revive the flavors.

Cider Vinegar

The mildly acidic, lightly fruity flavor of cider vinegar is neutral vinegar we turn to often. The flavor varies by brand; we prefer Bragg Organic Raw Unfiltered Apple Cider Vinegar.

Citrus

The zest and juice of lemons, limes and oranges are excellent for balancing the flavors of other ingredients, especially anything heavy or fatty. Look for round, plump fruit that feel heavy for their size. They should also give when squeezed; hard fruit won't produce much juice. Citrus should be stored in the crisper drawer of your refrigerator. Use a wand-style grater for zesting citrus. It produces light, feathery shreds that blend easily into dishes. Make sure to avoid the white pith beneath the zest, which can be bitter. There are countless ways to juice citrus fruits (juicer, reamer, fork, tong tips), though we do recommend squeezing it over a small mesh strainer to catch seeds. For recipes calling for both zest and juice, it's easier to zest before juicing.

Pomegranate Molasses

Intensely sweet and sour, pomegranate molasses is used throughout the Middle East in both sweet and savory dishes. It's essentially boiled-down pomegranate juice that is rounded out with a bit of sugar and acid. We like it drizzled over grilled or roasted meats or vegetables just before serving, mixed with Greek-style yogurt for a simple dip, or added to vinaigrettes. It pairs particularly well with Aleppo pepper. Refrigerated, an open bottle will last indefinitely, though it may need to be warmed in hot water or the microwave before it will flow freely.

Sherry Vinegar

Used liberally in Spanish and French cooking, sherry vinegar has a complex, slightly nutty flavor. The best sherry vinegars have a little age on them, which softens the harsh edges. Look for labels indicating the vinegar is at least 3 years old. It will cost a little more than unaged vinegar, but the difference in flavor is worth it.

Unseasoned Rice Vinegar

Rice vinegar is a staple of Japanese cooking and packs a mild, neutral acidity well suited to vegetables, seafood and poultry. It can also add kick to citrus juice. Be sure to purchase unseasoned rice vinegar; seasoned rice vinegar is used for making sushi rice and already contains salt and sugar, which can make it difficult to balance in dressings.

Verjus

Verjus is the cooking wine substitute you've been searching for. While fruit juices or vinegar can work, verjus—made from the juice of unripe wine grapes—adds a gentle mineral tang and a wine-like body. Verjus can be tricky to find and may require purchasing online. Refrigerate after opening to prevent spoilage. It will last for two to three months.

White Balsamic Vinegar

White balsamic has little to do with the dark, sweet, long-aged stuff most people are familiar with. But its light, neutral flavor and mild sweetness make it an acid we use often. White balsamic is perfect for when we want a clean flavor that highlights, but doesn't compete with, other flavors.

SALADS

7

BITTER GREENS AND ORANGE SALAD WITH WALNUTS AND GOAT CHEESE

Start to finish: 15 minutes
Servings: 4

This salad is full of bold flavors, a mixture of bitter, sweet, briny and creamy. Navel oranges do well here, but colorful Cara Cara or blood oranges are great if they are in season. As for greens, use a combination of sturdy varieties so the leaves can stand up to the other ingredients. Our favorite was a mixture of endive, radicchio and frisée; you'll need one head of each to get the 12 cups needed for this salad.

3 medium oranges (see headnote)

¼ cup red wine vinegar

2 tablespoons fresh oregano, finely chopped

Kosher salt and ground black pepper

1 medium shallot, halved and thinly sliced

½ cup pitted Kalamata olives, finely chopped

⅓ cup walnuts, toasted and finely chopped

¼ cup extra-virgin olive oil

4 ounces fresh goat cheese (chèvre), crumbled

12 cups lightly packed mixed bitter greens (see headnote), in bite-size pieces

Cut ½ inch off the top and bottom of each orange. One at a time, stand each on a cut end and, slicing from top to bottom, cut away the peel and pith following the contour of the fruit. Cut the oranges vertically into quarters, then trim away the seedy core from each. Cut each quarter crosswise into ½-inch-thick slices.

In a large bowl, combine the vinegar, oregano, ¼ teaspoon salt and ½ teaspoon pepper. Add the shallot and oranges, along with their juice, and toss. Let stand for 10 minutes.

To the oranges, add the olives, walnuts, oil and all but 3 tablespoons of the goat cheese, then stir gently until combined and the cheese begins to break down and become creamy. Add the greens and toss. Taste and season with salt and pepper, then transfer to a serving platter. Sprinkle with the remaining goat cheese.

TOMATO, BREAD AND CHORIZO SALAD WITH SHERRY VINAIGRETTE

Start to finish: 40 minutes

Servings: 4

Think of this as a mashup of panzanella, or Italian bread salad, and Spanish migas, which combines toasted stale bread and chorizo. Ripe, in-season tomatoes are best, but in non-summer months, Campari (also called cocktail) tomatoes are a good alternative, as they tend to be juicy and sweet year round. (Camparis tend to be smaller, so simply cut them into 1-inch wedges; no need to halve the wedges crosswise.) Tossing the prepped tomatoes with a little salt and sugar slightly softens them while drawing out some of their juices, which help soften and flavor the bread. Sourdough works especially well, but any loaf with a chewy, sturdy crumb does nicely.

1 pound ripe medium tomatoes, cored, cut into 1-inch wedges and halved crosswise

1 teaspoon white sugar

Kosher salt and ground black pepper

4 ounces Spanish chorizo, thinly sliced and roughly chopped

6 tablespoons extra-virgin olive oil, divided

6 ounces rustic sourdough bread, cut into 1-inch cubes (about 5 cups)

3 tablespoons sherry vinegar

1 teaspoon dried oregano

¾ cup jarred roasted red peppers, patted dry and roughly chopped

½ cup roughly chopped fresh flat-leaf parsley

1 ounce manchego cheese

In a large bowl, toss the tomatoes, sugar and 1 teaspoon salt. Let stand, tossing occasionally, while you prepare the salad. In a 12-inch skillet over medium, cook the chorizo, stirring, until lightly browned, 3 to 5 minutes. Using a slotted spoon, transfer to a paper towel-lined plate; set aside.

To the fat in the skillet, add 2 tablespoons oil and the bread. Cook over medium, stirring, until browned and crisp, 3 to 5 minutes. Remove from the heat and cool. Meanwhile, in a small bowl, whisk together the remaining 4 tablespoons oil, the vinegar, oregano and ½ teaspoon each salt and pepper.

To the tomatoes and their juices, add the roasted peppers, parsley, chorizo and bread. Re-whisk the dressing, then add it to the tomato-bread mixture; toss. Let stand until the bread softens slightly, about 10 minutes, tossing once or twice. Taste and season with salt and pepper, then transfer to a platter. Using a vegetable peeler, shave the manchego over the top.

ROMAINE AND RADICCHIO SALAD WITH OLIVES, EGGS AND POMEGRANATE VINAIGRETTE

Start to finish: 20 minutes

Servings: 4 to 6

This crisp, colorful salad gets meaty, briny flavor from oil-cured olives and fruity tang from pomegranate molasses. We supplement sweet romaine lettuce with pleasantly bitter radicchio and also toss in some parsley (or mint, or a combination of the two) for added aroma and herbal notes. Hard-cooked eggs cut into wedges lend substance to the salad, making it hearty enough to serve as a light main. Either whole-grain or Dijon mustard works nicely in the dressing, balancing the sweetness of the pomegranate molasses, so use whichever you prefer or what you have on hand.

3 tablespoons orange juice OR white wine vinegar

2 tablespoons pomegranate molasses

2 tablespoons extra-virgin olive oil

4 teaspoons whole-grain mustard
OR 1 tablespoon Dijon mustard

Kosher salt and ground black pepper

1 small head romaine lettuce (about 12 ounces),
cut crosswise into 2- to 3-inch pieces

1 small head radicchio (about 8 ounces), quartered
lengthwise, then cut crosswise into 1-inch pieces

½ cup lightly packed fresh parsley OR mint
OR a combination, torn if large

⅓ cup pitted oil-cured black olives, chopped

2 hard-cooked eggs, peeled, each cut into 6 wedges

In a large bowl, whisk together the orange juice, molasses, oil, mustard, ½ teaspoon salt and ¼ teaspoon pepper.

To the bowl, add the romaine, radicchio, parsley and olives; toss until well combined. Taste and season with salt and pepper. Transfer to a serving platter and top with the eggs.

Optional garnish: Pomegranate seeds

The Sweet Science of Shredding

Shredding or grating root vegetables such as carrots makes them taste sweeter and fresher than chopping or slicing.

When a root vegetable is cut, its cells rupture and release sugars and volatile hydrocarbons, the sources of the vegetable's sweetness and aroma. The more cells you rupture, the better the taste.

Shredding ruptures cells and also changes how the vegetable interacts with the dressing, it also creates a more porous surface on the pieces of vegetable and exposes more of that surface. That means more dressing comes into contact with the vegetable and is better absorbed—a minimal and simple dressing has an outsized effect on the finished dish.

We often use a box grater to shred carrots, or a food processor fitted with the medium shredding disk. To balance sweet, earthy root vegetables, we look for dressings with a little kick. Jalapeños go into the dressing for our shredded carrot salad with cumin and cashews (recipe p. 11). The cumin is bloomed in hot fat to boost its fragrance and flavor. Peppery horseradish livens up our shredded beet and carrot salad (recipe p. 12). And our take on classic Moroccan carrot salad (recipe p. 12), is paired with a spice-infused dressing that includes sweet-tart pomegranate molasses.

Shredded Carrot Salad with Cumin and Cashews

Start to finish: 20 minutes
Servings: 4

This recipe transforms ho-hum carrots into a delicious, eye-catching salad. **The key is to shred carrots to minimize fibrousness and enhance sweetness; use the large holes on a box grater or a food processor fitted with the medium shredding disk.** We add a final layer of flavor to the finished dish with a tarka, made by blooming spices and/or aromatics in hot fat to release their fragrance and flavor, a technique that comes from the Indian kitchen. Cilantro lends herbaceousness, while jalapeños bring a kick of heat. For a milder version, remove the seeds from the chilies.

1 pound medium carrots, peeled and shredded (see headnote)

2 jalapeño chilies, stemmed and thinly sliced

2 tablespoons lemon juice

Kosher salt and ground black pepper

3 tablespoons neutral oil

2 teaspoons cumin seeds OR brown mustard seeds OR a combination

½ cup roughly chopped unsalted OR salted cashews

½ cup roughly chopped fresh cilantro OR mint

In a large bowl, toss together the carrots, two-thirds of the chilies, lemon juice and ¼ teaspoon salt; set aside.

To make the tarka, in an 8-inch skillet over medium-high, combine the oil and cumin seeds. Cook, swirling the pan, until the seeds begin to sizzle, 30 to 60 seconds. Add the cashews, then cook, stirring often, until fragrant and once again beginning to sizzle, about 1 minute.

Pour the tarka over the carrot mixture and toss. Cool slightly, then add the cilantro and toss again. Taste and season with salt and pepper. Serve sprinkled with the remaining chilies.

SALADS

11

In a large bowl, whisk together the oil, lemon juice, horse-radish and ½ teaspoon each salt and pepper; set aside.

Using the large holes of a box grater, shred the carrots, followed by the beets; reserve separately.

Add the shredded vegetables, dill and caraway to the dressing. Toss to combine, then taste and season with salt and pepper. Transfer to a serving bowl and sprinkle with additional chopped dill. Serve with a dollop of sour cream (if using).

BEET AND CARROT SALAD WITH HORSERADISH AND DILL

Start to finish: 30 minutes
Servings: 4 to 6

Shredded red beets and carrots tossed with lemon juice, horseradish and a good measure of fresh dill make a salad that's vibrant in flavor and color. Crush the caraway seeds in a mortar with a pestle, or pulse them a few times in a spice grinder (don't pulverize them until powdery). We shred the carrots before the beets so the carrots aren't immediately stained by the beets. That said, after tossing, the entire salad eventually will turn bright red.

¼ cup extra-virgin olive oil

3 tablespoons lemon juice

2 tablespoons prepared horseradish

Kosher salt and ground black pepper

2 medium carrots (about 8 ounces total), peeled

2 medium red beets (about 8 ounces total), peeled

⅓ cup lightly packed fresh dill, roughly chopped, plus more to serve

1 tablespoon caraway seeds, crushed

Sour cream, to serve (optional)

MOROCCAN CARROT SALAD

Start to finish: 20 minutes
Servings: 4

Our take on the classic Moroccan carrot salad transforms average grocery-store carrots into a delicious side dish. Shredding both minimizes the fibrousness of the carrots and increases their sweetness. We then dress the carrots with a fruity, tangy-sweet dressing infused with spices. Dried apricots, toasted pistachios and fresh mint are perfect accents. Pomegranate molasses, often used in Middle Eastern cooking, is a dark, thick syrup with a sweet-sour flavor; look for it in the international aisle of the grocery store or in Middle Eastern markets.

2 tablespoons lemon juice

1 tablespoon pomegranate molasses

½ teaspoon ground turmeric

Kosher salt and ground black pepper

¼ cup extra-virgin olive oil

⅓ cup dried apricots, thinly sliced

1½ teaspoons cumin seeds, toasted

1 pound carrots, peeled and shredded

½ cup shelled roasted pistachios, toasted and chopped

¾ cup pitted green olives, chopped

½ cup roughly chopped fresh mint, plus more to serve

In a large bowl, whisk together the lemon juice, molasses, turmeric and ¼ teaspoon salt. While whisking, slowly pour in the oil. Add the apricots and cumin, then let stand for 5 minutes to allow the apricots to soften.

Add the carrots and stir until evenly coated. Stir in the pistachios, olives and mint. Taste and season with salt and pepper, then transfer to a serving bowl. Sprinkle with additional mint.

KALE SALAD WITH SMOKED ALMONDS AND PICADA CRUMBS

Start to finish: 15 minutes

Servings: 6

Flavorful and seasonal, kale is a prime candidate for a winter salad. But when eaten raw, the hardy leaves can be unpleasantly tough. We start with lacinato kale, also known as dinosaur or Tuscan kale. Its long blue-green leaves are sweeter and more tender than curly kale. Thinly slicing the greens makes them more salad-friendly. Then we massage the leaves with chopped smoked almonds that act as an abrasive to further soften their structure. An acidic shallot-sherry vinaigrette also helps to tenderize and brighten the kale (look for a sherry vinegar aged at least three years). Intensely flavorful paprika breadcrumbs, inspired by the Catalan sauce picada, tie everything together.

2 medium shallots, halved and thinly sliced

5 tablespoons sherry vinegar

Kosher salt and ground black pepper

2 tablespoons honey

8 tablespoons extra-virgin olive oil

1 cup smoked almonds

4 ounces chewy white bread, cut into 1-inch cubes

2 teaspoons fresh thyme

1 tablespoon sweet paprika

2 bunches lacinato kale, stemmed, washed, spun dry and thinly sliced crosswise (10 cups)

1 cup lightly packed fresh mint, chopped

In a small bowl, whisk together the shallots, vinegar and ¼ teaspoon salt. Let stand for 10 minutes. Whisk in the honey, 5 tablespoons of the oil and ½ teaspoon pepper; set aside.

In a food processor, process the almonds until roughly chopped, about 8 pulses; transfer to a large bowl. Add the bread to the processor and process to rough crumbs, about 20 seconds. Add the thyme, the remaining 3 tablespoons oil, paprika, ¼ teaspoon salt and ½ teaspoon pepper. Process until incorporated, about 10 seconds.

Transfer the crumb mixture to a 12-inch skillet. Cook over medium, stirring often, until the mixture is crisp and browned, 8 to 10 minutes. Transfer to a plate and let cool.

Add the kale and mint to the bowl with the almonds. Massage the greens until the kale softens and darkens, 10 to 20 seconds. Add the dressing and crumbs, then toss to combine. Taste and season with salt and pepper.

Getting Greens Right

It's not always easy buying greens.

As simple as it is to throw together a salad, there's often one major challenge: buying the right amount of greens. While recipes usually call for greens by volume in cups, they tend to be sold in other forms: by weight or by the bunch, head, bag or box. Plus, many recipes call for already-prepped greens. Since there's a drastic difference in volume between whole and prepped greens, it's especially difficult to gauge the amount you need by sight alone.

To make shopping simpler, we measured 15 varieties of greens—from frisée to collards—first prepping them, if needed, in the way they're commonly used. We found that with loose greens, 1 ounce of greens is equivalent to roughly 1¼ cups. By comparison, lettuce heads yield approximately ½ cup chopped greens per ounce once prepped. And cabbages and endives produce roughly ⅓ cup per ounce once prepped.

Greens	Starting Amount	Prepped Size	Prepped Volume
Baby Arugula	5-ounce container	Loosely packed	6 cups
Baby Spinach	5-ounce container	Loosely packed	6 cups
Cabbage, Napa	2-pound head	½-inch strips	12 cups
Cabbage, Red/Green (Medium)	2-pound head	Shredded	12 cups
Cabbage, Savoy	1½-pound head	2-inch pieces	12 cups
Collard Greens	8-ounce bunch	Stems stripped, 2-inch pieces	8 cups
Endive	5-ounce head	¼-inch crosswise slice	1½ cups
Frisée	8-ounce head	2-inch pieces	8 cups
Kale, Curly	8-ounce bunch	Stems stripped, 2-inch pieces	6 cups
Kale, Lacinato	8-ounce bunch	Stems stripped, 2-inch pieces	6 cups
Lettuce, Green/Red Leaf	8-ounce head	2-inch pieces	5 cups
Lettuce, Iceberg (Medium)	1½-pound head	2-inch pieces	12 cups
Lettuce, Romaine Heart	12-ounce heart	2-inch pieces	6 cups
Lettuce, Romaine	1-pound head	2-inch pieces	8 cups
Mesclun Greens Mix	5-ounce container	Loosely packed	6 cups

CHICKEN SALAD WITH ROMAINE AND TAHINI-HERB DRESSING

Start to finish: 30 minutes
Servings: 4

For this main-course chicken salad, we make a creamy-herbal dressing by blending rich, nutty tahini with handfuls of fresh parsley and cilantro, lime juice, garlic and olive oil. Apple, celery and romaine bring light, fresh notes and lots of texture. We especially like a firm, snappy apple such as Honeycrisp or Granny Smith, but use whatever variety you prefer. You will need 3 cups of shredded cooked chicken for the salad; an average-size rotisserie bird should yield just enough meat. If you have walnuts on hand, toast some and sprinkle them on before serving.

1¼ cups lightly packed fresh flat-leaf parsley

⅓ cup lightly packed fresh cilantro

½ cup tahini

½ cup lime juice

¼ cup extra-virgin olive oil

1 tablespoon honey

1 large garlic clove, roughly chopped

Kosher salt and ground black pepper

3 cups shredded cooked chicken

2 medium celery stalks, thinly sliced on the diagonal

1 medium apple, quartered, cored and thinly sliced

1 small head romaine lettuce (about 12 ounces), cut crosswise into rough 1-inch pieces

In a blender, combine ⅓ cup water, the parsley, cilantro, tahini, lime juice, oil, honey, garlic and ½ teaspoon each salt and pepper. Blend until smooth, about 1 minute, scraping the jar as needed.

In a large bowl, toss together the chicken, celery and apple. Add the herb-tahini puree; fold until well combined. Add the romaine and toss to combine. Taste and season with salt and pepper.

TOMATO SALAD WITH PEANUTS, CILANTRO AND CHIPOTLE-SESAME DRESSING

Start to finish: 35 minutes
Servings: 4 to 6

This robustly seasoned, almost meaty tomato salad was inspired by Mexican salsa macha, a savory-spicy condiment made with dried chilies, garlic, nuts and seeds that are fried in oil, then pureed. We enhance the texture and flavor of the tomatoes by salting them and letting them stand for a bit before combining with the other ingredients.

2 tablespoons neutral oil

¼ cup roasted peanuts

2 tablespoons sesame seeds OR
1 medium garlic clove, thinly sliced OR both

1 chipotle chili in adobo sauce, minced,
plus 1 teaspoon adobo sauce

3 tablespoons cider vinegar

Kosher salt and ground black pepper

2 pounds ripe tomatoes, cored and cut
into ½-inch wedges (see headnote)

1½ cups lightly packed fresh cilantro
OR basil OR flat-leaf parsley OR a combination,
torn if large

In a small saucepan over medium, combine the oil and peanuts. Cook, stirring occasionally, until fragrant and browned, 4 to 6 minutes. Using a slotted spoon, transfer the peanuts to a paper towel-lined plate.

To the same saucepan over medium, add the sesame seeds. Cook, stirring, until lightly golden, about 2 minutes. Remove from the heat, then stir in the chipotle and adobo sauce, vinegar and ¼ teaspoon each salt and pepper. Cool to room temperature. Meanwhile, in a serving bowl, toss the tomatoes with ½ teaspoon salt; let stand for about 10 minutes. Chop the peanuts.

Spoon the chipotle-sesame mixture over the tomatoes. Add the cilantro and peanuts, then stir gently. Taste and season with salt and pepper.

Optional garnish: Flaky salt **OR** crumbled cotija cheese **OR** both

CHANGE THE WAY YOU COOK

Tomato Tips

Tomatoes at their best are fantastic, sweet-savory, juicy and colorful. At their worst—and this too often is the case—they're mealy and flavorless. Here are two ways to get a better tomato.

At the Market

For an especially colorful salad, look for heirloom tomatoes of different hues. Out of season, supermarket tomatoes tend to be flavorless and dull. A better choice are cherry and grape tomatoes, which are reliably sweet all year. You also can combine tomato varieties and sizes for more varied texture and appearance.

At Home

Lightly salting watery produce such as tomatoes before adding it to a recipe enhances flavor and texture. It ensures even seasoning, draws out moisture for a meatier texture and concentrates flavors. For most vegetables, the water is discarded; let the produce stand in a strainer. Kosher salt is best for salting tomatoes; the large granules distribute more evenly and won't clump the way table salt can when tossed with moist ingredients. Use ¼ to ½ teaspoon kosher salt per pound. When using smaller tomatoes, be sure to halve them so the salt can season the flesh.

Tomato, Arugula and Bread Salad with Fresh Corn and Mozzarella

Start to finish: 20 minutes
Servings: 4 to 6

This vibrant, summery salad includes elements of Italian panzanella (bread salad). **For best flavor and texture, we mix the tomato wedges and onion slices with the vinaigrette and allow them to marinate briefly before tossing in the leafy greens, herb, cheese and toasted bread and corn.** Crisp, juicy kernels cut from cobs of peak-season corn are, of course, ideal, but in a pinch or during winter months, frozen corn that has been thawed and patted dry is fine. Fresh mozzarella is sold in orbs of different sizes; smallish bocconcini and even smaller ciliegine are great for this salad because they're easily torn into bite-size pieces.

6 ounces crusty white bread, sliced ½-inch thick and torn into bite-size pieces (about 6 cups)

6 tablespoons extra-virgin olive oil, divided

Kosher salt and ground black pepper

2 tablespoons white balsamic vinegar OR sherry vinegar

1 pound ripe tomatoes, cored and cut into ½-inch-thick wedges

1 small red onion, halved and thinly sliced

1½ cups corn kernels (from 2 ears corn)

2 cups lightly packed baby arugula OR watercress OR mixed greens

4 ounces fresh mozzarella cheese (see headnote), torn into bite-size pieces

½ cup lightly packed fresh basil OR mint, torn

Heat the oven to 450°F with a rack in the middle position. In a large bowl, toss the bread with 3 tablespoons of oil, ½ teaspoon salt and 1 teaspoon pepper. Distribute in a single layer on a rimmed baking sheet; reserve the bowl. Bake for 5 minutes. Meanwhile, in the same bowl, whisk together the remaining 3 tablespoons oil, the vinegar and ½ teaspoon each salt and pepper. Add the tomatoes and onion, then toss; set aside.

After the bread has toasted for 5 minutes, add the corn to the baking sheet and stir to combine. Bake until the croutons are golden brown, 5 to 7 minutes, stirring once about halfway through. Cool to room temperature. To the tomato-onion mixture, add the bread-corn mixture, the arugula, mozzarella and basil, then toss to combine. Taste and season with salt and pepper. Transfer to a serving bowl.

SALADS

4 medium shallots, peeled and thinly
sliced into rounds, divided

¼ cup grapeseed or other neutral oil

1½ pounds firm, ripe tomatoes, stemmed,
seeded and cut into ½-inch wedges

1 pint cherry or grape tomatoes, halved

3 tablespoons roasted peanuts, roughly chopped

2 serrano chilies, stemmed and sliced into thin rounds

2 teaspoons toasted chickpea flour
(optional, see headnote)

¼ teaspoon red pepper flakes (optional)

½ cup lightly packed fresh cilantro

2 tablespoons fish sauce

1 teaspoon grated lime zest, plus
2 tablespoons lime juice

Kosher salt and ground black pepper

Fill a small bowl with ice water and stir in half the sliced
shallots; set aside until ready to use. In a small saucepan
over medium-high, combine the oil and remaining shallots.
Cook, stirring occasionally and reducing the heat as the
shallots begin to color, until light golden brown, 7 to 10
minutes. Drain in a fine-mesh sieve set over a small heatproof bowl. Transfer the fried shallots to a paper towel-lined
plate; they will crisp as they cool. Discard the oil or reserve
for another use.

In a serving bowl, combine both types of tomatoes, the
peanuts, chilies, chickpea flour (if using) and pepper flakes
(if using). Thoroughly drain the soaked shallots and add to
the bowl, along with the cilantro, fish sauce, lime zest and
juice and ¼ teaspoon salt. Gently toss. Taste and season
with salt and black pepper. Sprinkle with the fried shallots.

BURMESE TOMATO SALAD WITH SHALLOTS AND PEANUTS

Start to finish: 30 minutes
Servings: 4

Burmese tomato salad is a bold, bright toss of complemen-
tary colors and shapes with lively, vibrant flavors to match
its appearance. Its tastes are sweet, salty, tangy, nutty,
herbal and spicy—and the dish is a fantastic way to use
garden-ripe tomatoes. Our version of the salad is an
adaptation of a recipe from "The Rangoon Sisters" by
London-based supper-club hosts and authors Amy Chung
and Emily Chung. In numerous Burmese dishes, toasted
chickpea flour brings its unique earthy, nutty flavor and
adds some starchiness; it's optional in our salad, but it
lends a little richness while also helping to tie the elements
together. If you wish to include it, toast the flour in a small,
dry skillet over medium, stirring, until browned and
fragrant, about two minutes, then transfer to a small bowl
and cool. We use a mix of round tomatoes and cherry (or
grape) tomatoes for varied shapes and textures.

AVOCADO, PINEAPPLE AND ARUGULA SALAD WITH FRESH CHILI AND LIME

Start to finish: 30 minutes
Servings: 6 to 8

This bright, beautifully balanced salad of creamy avocado,
fruity pineapple and peppery greens is our version of Cuban
ensalada de aguacate, berro y piña, a dish we learned about
from Cuba-born Maricel Presilla, chef, food historian and
author of "Gran Cocina Latina." In our recipe, we use both

lime zest and juice for citrusy notes, plus white vinegar for an extra shot of acidity. Steeping the sliced red onion and grated garlic in the vinegar for a few minutes mellows their bite so their flavors don't dominate. For efficiency, you can use that time to prep other ingredients. And for ease, purchase an already peeled and cored pineapple from the refrigerator case in the produce section of the supermarket, but be sure to drain the pineapple of any juice and pat it dry, as extra moisture will dilute the flavors and turn the salad soggy. We think a little chili heat is a nice counterpoint to the sweet-sour pineapple and rich avocado, but if you wish to minimize the spiciness, seed the chili before slicing it.

1 small red onion, halved and thinly sliced

1 medium garlic clove, finely grated

2 tablespoons white vinegar

Kosher salt and ground black pepper

**3 cups (1 pound) fresh pineapple chunks
(½- to 1-inch pieces), drained and patted dry**

**1 serrano or Fresno chili, stemmed, seeded
(if desired) and thinly sliced**

1 tablespoon extra-virgin olive oil

**½ teaspoon smoked paprika, plus
extra to serve**

**2 teaspoons finely grated lime zest, plus
2 tablespoons lime juice**

**2 ripe avocados, halved, pitted and
cut into ½- to 1-inch chunks**

**4 cups lightly packed baby arugula
(about 2½ ounces)**

In a small bowl, stir together the onion, garlic, vinegar and ¼ teaspoon salt; set aside for about 10 minutes. In a large bowl, toss together the pineapple, chili, oil, paprika, lime zest and juice, ½ teaspoon salt and ¼ teaspoon pepper.

Using tongs or a fork, transfer the onion slices to the bowl with the pineapple mixture, reserving the vinegar. Add the avocado, then gently toss. Add the arugula and gently toss again. Taste and season with salt, pepper and some of the reserved vinegar mixture, if needed. Transfer to a serving bowl and sprinkle with additional smoked paprika.

CABBAGE AND CHICKEN SALAD WITH GOCHUJANG AND SESAME

Start to finish: 30 minutes
Servings: 4 to 6

Gochujang, ginger, scallions and sesame—core ingredients in the Korean kitchen—inject loads of flavor to a simple cabbage and shredded chicken salad. Gochujang, one of our pantry go-tos, is a fermented chili paste that packs spiciness, subtle sweetness, lots of umami and rich color in a single spoonful. Look for it in the international aisle of the supermarket or in Asian grocery stores. For convenience, use the meat from a rotisserie chicken; an average-size bird yields about 3 cups, the amount needed for this recipe.

3 tablespoons gochujang

2 tablespoons grapeseed or other neutral oil

1 tablespoon white sugar

1 tablespoon finely grated fresh ginger

2 teaspoons toasted sesame oil, plus more to serve

¼ cup unseasoned rice vinegar OR cider vinegar

Kosher salt and ground black pepper

1 pound green cabbage, cored and thinly sliced (about 4 cups)

3 cups shredded cooked chicken

1 bunch scallions, thinly sliced on the diagonal OR 1 large grated carrot OR both

In a large bowl, whisk together the gochujang, neutral oil, sugar, ginger, sesame oil, vinegar, ¼ teaspoon salt and ½ teaspoon pepper. Add the cabbage, chicken and half of the scallions; toss. Taste and season with salt and pepper.

Transfer to a serving dish, drizzle with additional sesame oil and sprinkle with the remaining scallions.

Optional garnish: Toasted sesame seeds OR toasted walnuts

PITA, CHICKPEA AND HERB SALAD WITH TAHINI YOGURT

Start to finish: 35 minutes
Servings: 4

Known as fatteh in the Levant, this dish is a way to turn stale pita bread into a meal. We, however, start with fresh pita, brush it with olive oil and crisp it in the oven, then break it into shards before topping the pieces with warmed chickpeas. Yogurt spiked with garlic, tahini and lemon ties everything together. Za'atar, a Middle Eastern spice blend that usually includes sesame seeds, sumac, thyme and oregano, adds complex flavor while pistachios add richness. Fatteh typically is served for breakfast but with so many textures and flavors, we think it also makes a light yet satisfying dinner.

Two 8-inch pita breads, each split into 2 rounds

2 tablespoons extra-virgin olive oil, plus more to serve

2½ teaspoons ground cumin, divided

1 cup plain whole-milk yogurt

¼ cup tahini

2 medium garlic cloves, finely grated

1 teaspoon grated lemon zest, plus 2 tablespoons lemon juice

Kosher salt and ground black pepper

Two 15½-ounce cans chickpeas, 3 tablespoons liquid reserved, then drained

1½ teaspoons za'atar, plus more to serve

1½ cups lightly packed fresh mint, dill, parsley or a combination, torn if large

⅓ cup roasted pistachios

Heat the oven to 400°F with a rack in the middle position. On a rimmed baking sheet, brush both sides of the pita rounds with the oil, then sprinkle evenly with 2 teaspoons cumin. Bake until browned and crisp, about 10 minutes total, flipping once about halfway through. Cool to room temperature.

While the pita cools, in a small bowl, whisk together the yogurt, tahini, garlic, lemon zest and juice, the remaining ½ teaspoon cumin and ¼ teaspoon each salt and pepper; set aside. In a medium microwave-safe bowl, toss the chickpeas and 3 tablespoons liquid with the za'atar and ½ teaspoon salt. Cover and microwave on high until hot, 3 to 3½ minutes, stirring once halfway through.

Break the cooled pita into bite-size pieces and place in a wide, shallow serving bowl or divide among 4 individual bowls. Using a slotted spoon, arrange the warm chickpeas on top. Spoon on the yogurt mixture, then top with the herbs, pistachios and a generous drizzle of oil. Sprinkle with additional za'atar.

CHANGE THE WAY YOU COOK

Use Your Herbs by the Handful

We use fresh herbs with reckless abandon to add bold, bright flavor to many of our recipes. Instead of scant tablespoons, think in terms of handfuls.

It's important to wash and dry herbs well. Any moisture clinging to them can turn them mushy during chopping and dilute the flavors of the dishes to which they are added. Salad spinners work best. Herbs can also be dried by rolling them in a towel and gently squeezing. With a little care, most fresh herbs can be refrigerated in the crisper drawer for a week or more. Wrap loosely in paper towels, then place in a plastic bag.

Some fresh herbs, such as cilantro, mint and parsley, have edible stems. We like to use them to flavor stocks, soups and stews.

As for dried herbs, we find they aren't always appropriate because they require long, steady cooking to coax out their flavors. Exceptions to that rule include oregano (both Mexican and Turkish varieties, which offer different flavors) and mint, which packs a deeper, earthier flavor than fresh

SMASHED CUCUMBER SALAD WITH PEANUTS, SCALLIONS AND CILANTRO

Start to finish: 25 minutes
Servings: 4

This refreshing, boldly textured and flavored salad is from southern China's Yunnan province. Smashing cucumbers helps release the seeds, which are the source of much of the vegetables' wateriness. It also creates craggy surfaces that are better at absorbing flavor. Salting the cucumbers draws out excess moisture, preventing it from diluting the other flavors. Serve with grilled meats or seafood along with jasmine rice.

2 medium garlic cloves, finely grated

2 teaspoons finely grated fresh ginger

¼ cup lime juice

1½ teaspoons Sriracha

½ teaspoon white sugar

Kosher salt and ground black pepper

3 English cucumbers, trimmed and peeled

½ cup roasted unsalted peanuts, finely chopped

4 scallions, thinly sliced

1 serrano chili, stemmed, halved, seeded and thinly sliced

½ cup lightly packed fresh cilantro, finely chopped

In a small bowl, stir together the garlic, ginger, lime juice, Sriracha, sugar and ¼ teaspoon salt. Set aside. Place the cucumbers on a cutting board. With the flat side of a chef's knife or a rolling pin, hit the cucumbers until they split and crack.

Slice the cucumbers ½-inch thick on the diagonal and transfer to a large colander set over a large bowl. Add 1 teaspoon salt and toss. Top with a plate smaller than the diameter of the colander; weigh down the plate with 2 or 3 cans. Let stand until liquid has pooled in the bowl, about 15 minutes. Discard the liquid, then rinse and dry the bowl.

In the same large bowl, combine the cucumbers, peanuts, scallions, chili and cilantro. Add the dressing and toss to coat. Taste and season with salt and pepper.

THAI-STYLE COLESLAW WITH MINT AND CILANTRO

Start to finish: 25 minutes
Servings: 6

Looking for a brighter, fresher, cabbage slaw than the mayonnaise-rich American version, we were inspired by a recipe from San Antonio chef Quealy Watson that featured Southeast Asian flavors. Coconut milk in the dressing, instead of mayonnaise, has just the right amount of richness and body. Fish sauce adds savory pungency, while sugar balances with sweetness. For heat, we like fresh chili "cooked" in lime juice, which mellows the bite and helps disperse the heat more evenly. For vegetables, we use tender yet crunchy napa cabbage along with sliced red radishes and snap peas for vivid color and even more texture.

3 tablespoons lime juice

4 teaspoons white sugar

1 tablespoon fish sauce, plus more as needed

1 medium serrano chili, stemmed,
seeded and minced

⅓ cup coconut milk

1 pound napa cabbage (1 small head),
thinly sliced crosswise (about 8 cups)

6 radishes, trimmed, halved and thinly sliced

4 ounces sugar snap peas, strings removed,
thinly sliced on the diagonal

½ cup roughly chopped fresh cilantro

½ cup roughly chopped fresh mint

½ cup roasted, salted cashews,
roughly chopped

In a liquid measuring cup or small bowl, mix together
the lime juice, sugar, fish sauce and chili. Let stand for 10
minutes. Whisk in the coconut milk, then taste and adjust
seasoning with additional fish sauce if desired.

In a large bowl, combine the cabbage, radishes, peas,
cilantro and mint. Add the dressing and toss until evenly
coated. Stir in the cashews and transfer to a serving bowl.

SHAVED FENNEL, MUSHROOM
AND PARMESAN SALAD

Start to finish: 15 minutes

Servings: 4

This is an elegant take on an American favorite: the Italian
deli salad. We dressed thinly sliced vegetables, cheese and
salami with a lemony vinaigrette that keeps the flavors bright
and fresh. The salad tastes best the day it's made, but still is
delicious if refrigerated overnight; bring to room temperature before serving.

⅓ cup lemon juice

⅓ cup extra-virgin olive oil

3 medium garlic cloves, minced

6 peperoncini, stemmed, seeded and sliced
into thin rings, plus 1 tablespoon brine

Kosher salt

1 large fennel bulb, trimmed and halved

8 ounces white button mushrooms, stemmed

3-ounce chunk Parmesan cheese (without rind)

2 ounces thinly sliced salami, chopped

¾ cup lightly packed flat-leaf parsley leaves,
finely chopped

In a small bowl, whisk together the lemon juice, oil, garlic,
peperoncini brine and 1 teaspoon salt. Set aside.

Adjust the blade of your mandoline to slice 1/16 inch thick. One at a time, hold each fennel half by the base and slice against the grain as far as is safe; discard the base. Transfer to a large bowl. Next, slice each mushroom cap on the mandoline and add to the bowl. Finally, slice the Parmesan on the mandoline, roughly crumbling any large slices, and add to the fennel-mushroom mixture.

Add the peperoncini, salami and parsley to the bowl, then toss. Drizzle with the dressing and toss again.

SHAVED ZUCCHINI AND HERB SALAD WITH PARMESAN

Start to finish: 20 minutes
Servings: 4

We adopt the Italian technique of slicing raw zucchini into thin ribbons for this vibrant salad. The zucchini really shines, balanced with the clean, sharp flavors of a lemony dressing along with Parmesan and hazelnuts. Inspiration for our bright lemon dressing came from The River Cafe in London and its spare, lemony, arugula-studded zucchini carpaccio. And we also took note of the hazelnut accents in zucchini salad recipes from Francis Mallmann and Yotam Ottolenghi. The hazelnuts—or almonds, if that's what you have on hand—gave the salad crunch and a slightly buttery note. A Y-style peeler makes it easy to shave zucchini into ribbons. Don't worry if the ribbons vary in width; this adds to the visual appeal of the dish. Toasted sliced, slivered or chopped whole almonds can be used in place of the hazelnuts.

1 teaspoon grated lemon zest, plus
3 tablespoons juice (1 lemon)

3 tablespoons extra-virgin olive oil

¼ teaspoon honey

Kosher salt and ground black pepper

1 pound zucchini (2 medium)

1 ounce Parmesan cheese, finely grated
(about ½ cup), plus shaved to serve

½ cup lightly packed mint, torn

½ cup lightly packed fresh basil, torn

¼ cup hazelnuts, toasted, skinned and
roughly chopped

In a large bowl, whisk together the lemon zest and juice, oil, honey, and ¼ teaspoon each salt and pepper. Set aside. Use a Y-style peeler or mandoline to shave the zucchini from top to bottom into ribbons; rotating as you go. Stop shaving when you reach the seedy core. Discard the cores.

To the dressing, add the shaved zucchini, grated cheese, mint and basil, then toss until evenly coated. Transfer to a serving plate and sprinkle with shaved Parmesan and hazelnuts.

The Mandoline: A Better Way to Slice

When it comes to even cuts, no kitchen tool can rival the mandoline, the paddle-like slicing blade that can quickly reduce fruits and vegetables to slices, slivers, rounds, ribbons and shreds. Even a food processor's slicing disk can't compete; in our testing, a mandoline yields slices that are four times thinner than a processor's results.

At one time, the only mandolines available to cooks were large French stainless-steel varieties that sold for $200 or more. Today, quality mandolines can cost well under $100, making them an affordable addition to one's kitchen. This means home cooks can prep fruits and vegetables with ease, speed and precision. Not only do the uniform cuts created by a mandoline yield dishes with restaurant-quality looks, they also result in dishes that cook more evenly.

At Milk Street, we spent a few weeks working with our favorite mandoline—the no-frills Benriner—while developing recipes for shaved salads. In the process, we noted several tips that helped us make better use of our mandoline, including safety practices and ways to make slicing simpler.

First and foremost, safety. The sharp blade of a mandoline can be intimidating. Rather than rely on hand guards as a safety measure, we prefer using a cut-resistant glove. Look for one with a snug fit. Though it may sound obvious, it's important to keep your fingers away from the blade. Don't apply a lot of pressure; it can make slicing more difficult. Use firm, even pressure to allow the food to slide smoothly against the blade. Also, know when to stop—don't attempt to slice until there is no more to slice.

A few more practices make slicing easier and safer. For rounded fruits and vegetables, first create a flat edge by cutting off a small piece before slicing. Look for a natural handle—the stem end of a radish or the root end of radicchio, for instance—to hold when slicing.

Prep Work: To slice large vegetables like celery root or cabbage, the item must first be cut down to size—it needs to be narrower than the width of your mandoline's blade. Start by trimming the uneven surfaces, then cut the vegetable into smaller pieces—halves or quarters—that will easily fit on your mandoline.

Set Up: For models without blade settings, to set the desired cut thickness, use a ruler to measure between the blade and the edge of the mandoline, then make a test slice and measure its thickness.

Diagonal Cut: To slice something on the diagonal, first cut the item in half at a 45-degree angle on a cutting board, then slice both halves on the mandoline.

Shreds: To shred firm heads of leafy vegetables, first evaluate whether it's necessary to cut the head into halves or quarters. Hold the piece by its base, then slice against the vegetable's grain to create fine shreds.

Matchsticks: We found the julienne blades included with some models work best on items with significant water content, such as apples or onions. Avoid firm vegetables like celery root and carrots.

Planking: Even for models without julienne blades, the mandoline can make matchsticks easy. Slice the vegetable into thin planks, then stack the planks and use a chef's knife to cut them lengthwise into matchsticks.

Shaved Carrot Salad with Poppy Seeds and Parsley

Start to finish: 30 minutes (15 minutes active)
Servings: 4

This colorful salad is our version of one we sampled in Buenos Aires at a tapas stall that reflects Spain's lingering influence in Argentina. **Shaving carrots into long, thin strips transforms the typically sturdy, fibrous vegetable into a tender salad base with ample surface area to soak up seasonings.** Chef Diego Fernandez of De Lucía Tapas at the Mercado San Telmo showed us how the dressing ingredients are heated briefly in a skillet, then the carrot shavings are added and cooked just until barely tender. We further simplified by microwaving the carrots. A sharp Y-style vegetable peeler works well for shaving the carrots into ribbons, but you also can use a mandoline. Either way, choose large, thick carrots—not the slender variety that are sold in bunches—because they're easier to shave. And stop shaving once you reach the fibrous cores. Carrots vary in sweetness, so you may need to add a little extra sugar, lemon juice and/or salt at the end.

4 or 5 large carrots (about 1½ pounds), peeled

Kosher salt

1 tablespoon poppy seeds

¼ cup extra-virgin olive oil

2 medium garlic cloves, smashed and peeled

2 star anise pods

¼ cup lemon juice, plus more as needed

1 teaspoon white sugar, plus more as needed

½ cup lightly packed fresh flat-leaf parsley, torn if large

Use a Y-style peeler or a mandoline to shave the carrots from top to bottom into long, wide ribbons, rotating as you go. Stop shaving when you reach the core; discard the cores. Put the ribbons in a large, microwave-safe bowl and toss with ½ teaspoon salt. Cover and microwave on high until wilted but still crisp-tender, 3 to 5 minutes, stirring once halfway through; set aside, uncovered, leaving any liquid in the bowl.

In a small saucepan over medium, toast the poppy seeds, stirring often, until fragrant and slightly darker in color, about 2 minutes. Transfer to a small bowl. In the same saucepan over medium, heat the oil, garlic and star anise, stirring occasionally, until the garlic begins to brown at the edges, 1 to 2 minutes. Reduce to low, add the lemon juice and sugar, then whisk until the sugar dissolves. Bring to a simmer and cook, whisking occasionally, for 3 minutes. Remove and discard the garlic and star anise.

Pour the warm dressing over the carrots and toss. Let stand for 15 minutes. Add the poppy seeds and parsley, then toss again. Taste and season with salt, lemon juice and/or sugar, then transfer to a serving dish.

HARISSA POTATO SALAD WITH MINT AND LEMON

Start to finish: 50 minutes
Servings: 4 to 6

Harissa—a chili paste from North Africa that is a Milk Street pantry staple—brings earthy spice, heat and bold flavor to an otherwise basic potato salad. Harissa varies in spiciness brand to brand, so start with 2 tablespoons and taste, then add more if you like. Before tossing the potatoes with the mayo, we combine them while warm with lemon zest, lemon juice and black pepper so they better absorb the seasonings. Fresh mint balances the heat, while red onion brings a refreshing bite.

2 pounds russet potatoes, peeled and cut into ¾-inch pieces

Kosher salt and ground black pepper

1 tablespoon grated lemon zest, plus 4 tablespoons lemon juice, divided

⅓ cup mayonnaise

2 to 2½ tablespoons harissa paste

1 small red onion, halved and thinly sliced OR 3 medium radishes, halved and thinly sliced

¾ cup lightly packed fresh mint OR cilantro OR a combination, roughly chopped

In a large saucepan, combine the potatoes and 1½ tablespoons salt, then add enough water to cover by 1 inch. Bring to a boil over medium-high, then reduce to medium and simmer, uncovered and stirring occasionally, until a skewer inserted into the potatoes meets no resistance, 8 to 10 minutes.

Drain the potatoes in a colander, then transfer to a large bowl. Add the lemon zest, 2 tablespoons lemon juice and ½ teaspoon pepper; toss. Cool to room temperature, about 20 minutes, stirring occasionally. Meanwhile, in a small bowl, stir together the mayonnaise, harissa and the remaining 2 tablespoons lemon juice.

Into the cooled potatoes, stir in the onion and mayonnaise mixture, followed by the mint. Taste and season with salt and pepper.

AUSTRIAN POTATO SALAD

Start to finish: 30 minutes
Servings: 4

Austrian cooks add flavor and creaminess to their potato salad by cooking the potatoes in chicken broth, then using the starchy cooking liquid as the base for the dressing. That means you can skip the mayonnaise. Cornichon brine, red wine vinegar and Dijon mustard provide sharp notes; celery and fresh dill add crunch and bright flavor. Many recipes call for waxy potatoes, but we chose Yukon Golds for their rich flavor and creamy texture. If your potatoes are quite large, quarter them instead of halving before slicing.

2 pounds Yukon Gold potatoes, peeled, halved and sliced ¼-inch thick

2 cups low-sodium chicken broth

Kosher salt and ground black pepper

¼ cup finely chopped cornichons, plus 1 tablespoon brine

2 tablespoons red wine vinegar, divided

½ medium red onion, finely chopped (about ½ cup)

½ teaspoon caraway seeds

¼ cup grapeseed or other neutral oil

1 tablespoon Dijon mustard

2 medium celery stalks, finely chopped (about ½ cup)

2 hard-cooked eggs, peeled and chopped (optional)

¼ cup chopped fresh dill

In a large saucepan, combine the potatoes, broth and 1 teaspoon salt. Add enough water to just cover the potatoes. Bring to a boil over medium-high, then reduce to medium-low and cook until a skewer inserted into the potatoes meets no resistance, 8 to 10 minutes. Reserve ½ cup of the cooking liquid, then drain the potatoes and transfer them to a large bowl. Sprinkle with the cornichon brine, 1 tablespoon of the vinegar and ½ teaspoon pepper.

In the same saucepan, combine the reserved cooking liquid with the onion and caraway seed, then bring to a simmer over medium-high. Pour the mixture over the potatoes and stir well. Let stand, stirring occasionally, until the liquid has been absorbed, about 10 minutes.

In a liquid measuring cup or small bowl, whisk together the oil, mustard, the remaining 1 tablespoon vinegar, ¼ teaspoon salt and ½ teaspoon pepper until emulsified. Pour the mixture over the potatoes and add the celery, cornichons, dill and eggs (if using), then fold until well combined. Taste and season with salt and pepper. Serve at room temperature.

SOUTHEAST ASIAN CHICKEN SALAD WITH CASHEWS AND COCONUT

Start to finish: 25 minutes
Servings: 6 to 8

At Chin Chin restaurant in Sydney, Australia, we were particularly taken by a complexly textured and highly aromatic chicken salad made with lemon grass, coconut and fistfuls of fresh Southeast Asian herbs. Store-bought rotisserie chicken gets the salad on the table in minutes. To cook your own, in a medium saucepan combine 1 pound boneless, skinless chicken breasts with 1 quart low-sodium chicken broth and 1 teaspoon kosher salt. Bring to a simmer over medium-high, then cover, reduce to low and cook, adjusting the heat to maintain a bare simmer, until the thickest part of the breasts reaches 160°F, 15 to 20 minutes. Let the chicken cool in the liquid until just warm, then remove and shred the meat. An equal amount of low-sodium soy sauce can be substituted for the fish sauce.

⅓ cup unsweetened wide-flake coconut

2 Fresno or jalapeño chilies, stemmed, seeded and thinly sliced

3 medium garlic cloves, smashed and peeled

⅓ cup lime juice

¼ cup fish sauce (see headnote)

2½ teaspoons white sugar

2 medium shallots, halved and thinly sliced

3 cups shredded cooked chicken (see headnote)

¼ medium head green or red cabbage, cored and shredded (about 2 cups)

½ cup roasted cashews, roughly chopped

2 cups lightly packed fresh basil, torn

2 cups lightly packed fresh cilantro leaves

In a small skillet over medium, toast the coconut, stirring frequently, until light golden brown, 2 to 3 minutes. Transfer to a small bowl and set aside.

In a blender, combine half of the sliced chilies, the garlic, lime juice, fish sauce and sugar. Blend until smooth, about 1 minute. Transfer to a large bowl, add the shallots and chicken and let stand for 10 minutes.

Add the cabbage and toss with your hands to combine, gently rubbing the dressing into the shreds. Add the remaining sliced chilies, the cashews and coconut, then toss. Add the basil and cilantro and gently toss again.

CUCUMBER SALAD WITH SOUR CREAM AND DILL

Start to finish: 45 minutes (15 minutes active)
Servings: 4 to 6

To create this creamy, crunchy dish, we looked to the Polish salad known as mizeria, which features cucumbers, sour cream, dill and sometimes red onion. Though it's not traditional, we also added prepared horseradish for a spicy kick. Be sure to salt the cucumbers first and let them stand for 15 minutes, then squeeze them before dressing to remove excess moisture. This produces a crisp texture and a drier surface to which the dressing and seasonings can adhere. Cool and refreshing, this makes a great accompaniment to seared or roasted salmon or crisp-crusted chicken or pork cutlets.

2 English cucumbers, peeled, halved lengthwise and cut on the diagonal into ¼-inch slices

Kosher salt and ground black pepper

½ medium red onion, thinly sliced

¼ cup white vinegar

½ cup sour cream

¼ cup prepared horseradish

1 cup lightly packed fresh dill, roughly chopped

In a large colander set over a large bowl, toss the cucumbers with 1 teaspoon salt. In a small bowl, stir together the onion, vinegar and ¼ teaspoon salt. Let both the cucumbers and the onion mixture stand for 15 minutes; occasionally toss the cucumbers to encourage the liquid to drain.

In a medium bowl, stir together the sour cream and horseradish. Using your hands, firmly squeeze the cucumbers to remove as much water as possible; discard the liquid. Add the cucumbers to the sour cream mixture and stir. Drain the onion in the now-empty colander, then add it to the cucumber mixture; discard the liquid. Stir in the dill. Taste and season with salt and pepper. Serve immediately or cover, refrigerate for about 1 hour and serve chilled.

Know the Knives You Need

Watching pro chefs chopping rapid fire with an arsenal of high-priced knives can make the task of assembling your own kitchen knife set seem daunting. Fortunately, the needs of the average home cook are far more modest. Step No. 1 is to consider your style of cooking. Are you the sort of cook who enjoys breaking down large cuts of meat? Or is vegetarian cooking more your style? Maybe something in the middle? Step No. 2 is to match a few select knives to your needs, comfort and price point.

Most kitchen knives in the U.S. can be divided into European and Japanese styles. European knives typically are heavier and have thicker blades ground with broader angles. They are built more for durability than nimbleness. Japanese knives feature thinner blades ground with more acute blade angles, which cut more easily because there's less metal to push through the item being cut.

SOME COMMON JAPANESE STYLES TO CONSIDER:

Santoku: Translated as "three virtues," the santoku is a hybrid blade designed for all-purpose cooking (in contrast to most Japanese knives, which are task dependent). The blade, which typically is lighter, shorter and taller than Western-style chef's knives, usually is flat at the edge for maximum board contact to ensure clean, crisp slicing.

Bunka: Considered the precursor to the santoku, the bunka is another all-purpose Japanese knife. It features a more angular blade and an acute tip that is ideal for all manner of cuts and tight detail work, from julienning vegetables to prepping meats.

Nakiri: This simple, rectangular blade—usually 6 to 7 inches long and 2 inches tall—is the ultimate tool for preparing vegetables. It features a thin, lightweight blade and flat edge to allow full contact with the cutting board. Look for a nakiri with a slightly rounded blade tip, which allows for rock chopping and mincing.

Gyuto: The truest Japanese analog of a Western chef's knife is the gyuto, which translates to "cow sword." Gyutos come in varying lengths, blade designs and weights. The lighter, thinner blade of the gyuto makes it an appealing style for those accustomed to a European chef's knife but looking for something more nimble.

Petty: A bit longer than a Western paring knife, the petty knife excels at small detail work, such as peeling and prepping vegetables, mincing garlic or shallots, and preparing sandwiches. Choose a length that's comfortable for you; a smaller knife is easier to control, but has limitations.

Chuka Bocho: These Chinese-style vegetable cleavers have large, thin, rectangular blades that lack a bolster (the thick junction between blade and handle), making them lighter than Western-style cleavers. Finished with a stubby, barrel-shaped handle, these cleavers are best used for delicate work. To use, pinch the blade between your thumb and forefinger while the rest of your fingers wrap around the handle. Works best with a chopping—not rocking—motion.

SOME WESTERN STYLES TO CONSIDER:

Chef's Knife: The traditional European-style chef's knife is good for all-purpose prep. We recommend thinner, lighter models. The longer the blade, the better it is for smooth slicing, but it can feel unwieldy for close work. Test the handle and bolster for comfort when choking up tight for a secure pinch grip.

Paring Knife: Paring knives come in many shapes, sizes and price points. We favor blades between 3 and 3½ inches long for best control. Look for larger handles that fit securely in the palm; many paring knives have narrow handles that turn and twist during use, especially if wet or greasy.

SALADS

31

Lebanese-Style Tabbouleh

Start to finish: 15 minutes
Servings: 4

Israeli-born British chef Yotam Ottolenghi is clear about tabbouleh. It should be "all about the parsley." But **in the U.S., the Middle Eastern salad often goes heavy on the bulgur, a wheat that has been cooked, dried and cracked. The result is a salad that is mealy, bland and stubbornly soggy. That's because the bulgur sponges up all the juices from the tomatoes. Our solution was to barely cook the bulgur—essentially underhydrating it—allowing it to soak up those juices without becoming waterlogged.** We added generous helpings of herbs, livening up the parsley with some mint. Wet herbs will dilute the dressing and make the bulgur gummy. Be sure to dry them thoroughly with a spinner and paper towels before mincing. Some type of onion is traditional; we used shallots, preferring their gentler bite, and soaked them in lemon juice to soften their flavor and texture. While the sumac is optional, we loved its fruity complexity and light acidity.

½ cup boiling water

⅓ cup fine bulgur

1 teaspoon ground sumac (optional)

½ teaspoon ground allspice

Kosher salt and ground black pepper

3 tablespoons lemon juice

1 small shallot, minced

¼ teaspoon white sugar

¼ cup extra-virgin olive oil

2 or 3 small ripe tomatoes, cored and chopped

4 cups lightly packed fresh flat-leaf parsley, finely chopped

1 cup lightly packed fresh mint, finely chopped

In a medium bowl, combine the water, bulgur, sumac (if using), allspice and ¼ teaspoon salt. Cover with plastic wrap and let sit for 10 minutes. In a large bowl, stir together the lemon juice, shallot, sugar and ½ teaspoon of salt; let sit for 10 minutes.

Whisk the oil into the lemon juice mixture. Fluff the bulgur with a fork and add to the dressing along with the tomatoes; mix well. Fold the parsley and mint into the tabbouleh, then taste and season with salt, pepper and additional sumac, if needed. Tabbouleh will keep refrigerated for up to 24 hours.

TOASTED FARRO AND APPLE SALAD WITH MUSTARD VINAIGRETTE

Start to finish: 1 hour (30 minutes active)
Servings: 4 to 6

Farro, a type of wheat, has a satisfyingly tender-chewy texture and a nutty flavor that's accentuated by toasting the grains before they're simmered. This autumnal salad matches toothsome farro with tangy-sweet apple, crisp celery and pungent onion that's mellowed by briefly steeping it in the mustard vinaigrette. Be sure the farro is still warm when it's dressed. As it cools, the grains absorb flavor. The salad is delicious served cold or at room temperature.

1 cup pearled farro

Kosher salt and ground black pepper

3 tablespoons cider vinegar
OR white wine vinegar

2 teaspoons Dijon mustard
OR whole-grain mustard

3 tablespoons extra-virgin olive oil

½ small red OR yellow onion,
finely chopped

1 large apple, cored and cut in
½-inch cubes

2 medium celery stalks, chopped

1 cup lightly packed fresh flat-leaf parsley
OR mint OR dill OR a combination,
roughly chopped

In a large saucepan over medium, toast the farro, stirring, until lightly browned and fragrant, about 3 minutes. Add 1 quart water and 1 teaspoon salt; stir. Bring to a simmer over medium-high, then reduce to medium and simmer, uncovered and stirring once or twice, until the farro is tender with a little chew, 25 to 30 minutes.

Meanwhile, in a large bowl, whisk together the vinegar, mustard, oil and ½ teaspoon each salt and pepper. Stir in the onion; set aside. When the farro is done, drain in a colander; cool for 5 to 10 minutes.

Add the still-warm farro to the dressing mixture and toss. Let stand until cooled to room temperature, tossing once or twice. Add the apple, celery and parsley; toss to combine. Taste and season with salt and pepper.

Optional garnish: Sliced radishes **OR** crumbled fresh goat cheese (chèvre) **OR** toasted walnuts **OR** a combination

PISTACHIO-ORANGE BULGUR SALAD WITH MINT

Start to finish: 30 minutes
Servings: 4

A fresh orange does double duty in this colorful side dish: Grated zest gives a flavor boost to quick-pickled red onions, which provide a bright, tangy contrast to the nutty bulgur, while the chopped fruit adds sweetness and juiciness. We use red wine vinegar in the pickling liquid to tame the onion. Pistachios bring crunch and mint lends freshness. Feel free to swap in other nuts, such as pecans or almonds. We call for coarse bulgur rather than finely ground (the type used in tabbouleh) because the coarse variety holds up well when cooked. Serve alongside hearty braises and roasted meats.

1 cup coarse bulgur

Kosher salt and ground black pepper

½ small red onion, halved and thinly sliced

3 tablespoons red wine vinegar

1 medium orange

3 tablespoons extra-virgin olive oil

⅓ cup roughly chopped pistachios
OR pecans OR sliced almonds

½ cup lightly packed fresh mint OR cilantro,
roughly chopped

In a medium saucepan, combine the bulgur, ½ teaspoon salt and 1½ cups water. Bring to a boil over medium-high, then cover, reduce to medium-low and cook without stirring until the liquid has been absorbed, 15 to 18 minutes. Remove from the heat and let stand, covered, for 5 minutes.

Meanwhile, in a large bowl, stir together the onion, vinegar, ½ teaspoon salt and ¼ teaspoon pepper. Grate 1 tablespoon zest from the orange, then stir it into the onion-vinegar mixture. Using a sharp knife, slice about ½ inch off the top and bottom of the orange. Stand the orange on a cut end and cut from top to bottom following the contours of the fruit to remove the peel and white pith. Quarter the orange lengthwise, then thinly slice crosswise.

Using a fork, fluff the bulgur and add to the bowl. Stir in the oil, then fold in the orange pieces. Cool slightly, about 10 minutes, then stir in the pistachios and mint. Taste and season with salt and pepper.

QUINOA AND AVOCADO SALAD WITH ALMONDS AND MINT

Start to finish: 30 minutes
Servings: 4

White, red or rainbow (tricolor) quinoa works in this recipe, so use whichever type you prefer. Most quinoa sold in grocery stores is pre-rinsed to rid the seeds of the naturally occurring, bitter-tasting saponin coating; check the package and if it does not indicate, rinse and drain the quinoa first. The simplest way to remove the seedy cores from the zucchini halves is to scrape them out with a spoon; this keeps the moisture of the seeds from diluting the dish. Serve as a vegetarian main course or as a side to grilled or seared fish or shrimp.

1 cup quinoa (see headnote)

1½ teaspoons ground cinnamon

Kosher salt and ground black pepper

2 ripe avocados, pitted, peeled and thinly sliced

1 medium zucchini or yellow summer squash
(about 8 ounces), halved lengthwise, seeded
(see headnote) and thinly sliced

⅓ cup white balsamic vinegar

¼ cup extra-virgin olive oil

⅓ cup golden raisins

1 cup chopped fresh mint

½ cup salted roasted almonds, chopped

In a large saucepan over medium-high, stir together the quinoa, cinnamon, ½ teaspoon each salt and pepper and 1¼ cups water. Bring to a boil, then cover and simmer on low until the quinoa absorbs the liquid, 13 to 15 minutes.

Meanwhile, in a large bowl, toss the avocados and zucchini with the vinegar, oil and ¼ teaspoon salt.

When the quinoa is done, remove the pan from heat. Scatter the raisins over the quinoa, then drape a kitchen towel across the pan and re-cover. Let stand for 10 minutes.

Using a fork, fluff the quinoa. Transfer to the bowl with the avocados and zucchini, then gently fold to evenly distribute. Gently stir in the mint and almonds, then taste and season with salt and pepper.

BULGUR-TOMATO SALAD WITH HERBS AND POMEGRANATE MOLASSES

Start to finish: 30 minutes
Servings: 4

This Armenian salad, known as eetch, is reminiscent of tabbouleh but because it's grain-centric rather than herb-focused, it's heartier and more substantial. Instead of soaking the bulgur in water—as is done for tabbouleh—the bulgur is hydrated in a mixture of tomato paste and water, so the grains take on tangy-sweet flavor and a red-orange hue. If you want to make the salad more tart and tangy, mix in a splash of lemon juice. For a more substantial meal, add blanched green beans and crumbled feta cheese.

3 tablespoons tomato paste

2 tablespoons extra-virgin olive oil

1 medium red bell pepper, stemmed, seeded and finely chopped

6 scallions (4 finely chopped, 2 thinly sliced, reserved separately)

Kosher salt and ground black pepper

3 medium garlic cloves, finely chopped

1½ teaspoons ground cumin

1 teaspoon Aleppo pepper or ¼ teaspoon red pepper flakes

1 cup coarse bulgur

1 tablespoon pomegranate molasses, plus more if needed

1 pint grape tomatoes, halved

¾ cup chopped fresh mint or flat-leaf parsley

In a small bowl, whisk together 1⅓ cups water and the tomato paste. Set aside. In a 10-inch skillet over medium, heat the oil until shimmering. Add the bell pepper, chopped scallions and ¼ teaspoon salt. Cover and cook, stirring occasionally, until the pepper is tender, about 5 minutes. Stir in the garlic, cumin and Aleppo pepper, then cook until fragrant, about 1 minute.

Stir in the bulgur, tomato paste mixture and ½ teaspoon salt. Bring to a boil over medium-high. Cover, reduce to low and simmer until the bulgur has absorbed the liquid, 12 to 15 minutes. Remove from the heat and let stand, covered, for 5 minutes.

Transfer to a wide, shallow bowl and let cool until warm, about 5 minutes. Drizzle the pomegranate molasses over the bulgur, then fold until combined. Fold in the tomatoes, mint and the sliced scallions. Taste and season with salt, pepper and additional molasses.

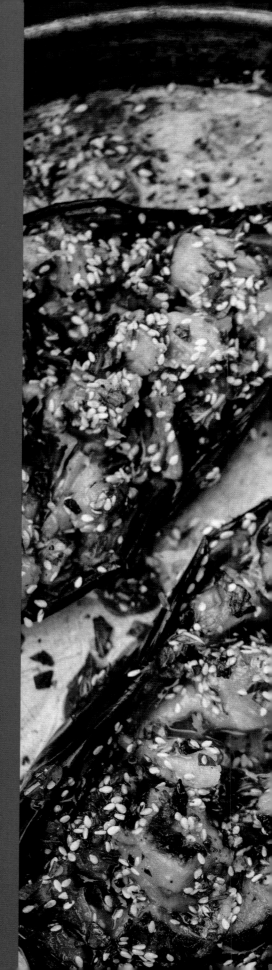

Vegetables

The Basics of Blanching Vegetables

Blanching vegetables is a quick way to cook them to a tender-crisp texture while preserving their freshness. The technique is simple—briefly plunge vegetables into boiling water, then shock them immediately in ice water—but timing is important. Boil too long and they turn mushy. Chill too long and they become waterlogged.

Blanched vegetables are great in salads, pastas and sandwiches. They also store well for up to three days—wrapped in a kitchen towel and sealed in a plastic bag. Vegetables intended for later cooking in stir-fries or sautés should be blanched slightly less than those for immediate use. To determine the best times for each preparation, we blanched various vegetables, starting the clock as soon as they went in. Most blanched faster than suggested by many of the sources we consulted.

Before blanching, cut large, firm vegetables (like broccoli or cauliflower) into smaller pieces. More tender produce, such as green beans, can be blanched whole. Hearty greens like kale and chard should be stemmed. After shocking, always drain blanched vegetables and dry them on towels or in a salad spinner to remove excess water.

Be sure to blanch in ample water—we prefer 4 quarts seasoned with 1 tablespoon kosher salt. For best flavor, we also salt the shocking water—3 quarts cold water mixed with 1 tablespoon kosher salt and 1 quart ice. A mesh spider or long-handled tongs are best for transferring vegetables to the ice bath.

Item	Size Pieces	Time to Blanch for Storage	Time to Blanch to Crisp-Tender	Time in Ice Bath
Green beans	Whole, trimmed	2 minutes	3 minutes	1 minute
Haricots verts	Whole	1½ minutes	2 minutes	1 minute
Broccoli	1-inch florets	1 minute	1½ minutes	1 minute
Cauliflower	1-inch florets	1½ minutes	2 minutes	1 minute
Swiss chard	Stemmed	20 seconds	30 seconds	30 seconds
Lacinato kale	Stemmed	30 seconds	40 seconds	30 seconds
Curly kale	Stemmed	30 seconds	40 seconds	30 seconds
Asparagus-small to medium	Whole, trimmed	30 seconds	1 minute	1 minute
Asparagus-large	Whole, trimmed	1 minute	2 minutes	1 minute
Snap peas	Whole, trimmed and stringed	1 minute	1½ minutes	1 minute
Broccoli rabe	2-inch pieces	30 seconds	40 seconds	30 seconds
Corn	Whole ear	5 minutes	7 minutes	1 minute

SKILLET-ROASTED ASPARAGUS

Start to finish: 15 minutes
Servings: 4

In this quick and easy method for basic skillet-roasted asparagus, an initial blast over high heat gives the spears a light char to develop sweet, nutty flavor, then covered cooking with a little water renders the spears perfectly crisp-tender. Serve the asparagus unadorned straight from the pan, or add the following embellishment to dress it up. You will need a 12-inch skillet with a lid for this recipe.

2 tablespoons grapeseed or other neutral oil

2 pounds asparagus, trimmed

Kosher salt

In a 12-inch skillet over high, heat the oil until shimmering. Add the asparagus, sprinkle with ¼ teaspoon salt and cook, tossing once or twice, until lightly charred in spots, 2 to 4 minutes.

Add 1 tablespoon water, immediately cover and reduce to medium. Cook until the asparagus is crisp-tender, 1 to 2 minutes. Using tongs, transfer to a platter, leaving any remaining water in the skillet.

SKILLET-ROASTED ASPARAGUS WITH SESAME-LIME DRESSING

In a small bowl, stir together 3 **tablespoons lime juice** and **1 medium shallot** (minced). Set aside, then prepare skillet-roasted asparagus. After transferring the asparagus to a platter, to the lime juice–shallot mixture, stir in **1 teaspoon grated lime zest, 1 tablespoon toasted sesame oil, 2 teaspoons honey** and **¼ teaspoon red pepper flakes.** Drizzle over the asparagus, then sprinkle with **1 tablespoon toasted sesame seeds.**

BROCCOLI WITH SMOKED PAPRIKA AND TOASTED GARLIC BREADCRUMBS

Start to finish: 20 minutes

Servings: 4

In this texture-packed dish, a combination of browned garlic, smoky paprika and crisp breadcrumbs—inspired by the Catalan sauce picada—enhances skillet-cooked broccoli. After being seared in a hot pan, the broccoli is combined with water, quickly covered and steamed until tender-crisp. Added just before serving, a good dose of fresh thyme and a splash of woodsy-sweet sherry vinegar bring bright, fresh notes.

4 tablespoons extra-virgin olive oil, divided

⅓ cup panko breadcrumbs

3 medium garlic cloves, minced

½ teaspoon smoked paprika

1 pound broccoli crowns, cut into 1- to 1½-inch florets

Kosher salt and ground black pepper

1 tablespoon fresh thyme, chopped

1 tablespoon sherry vinegar

In a 12-inch skillet over medium, heat 2 tablespoons oil until shimmering. Add the panko and cook, stirring occasionally, until lightly golden, about 2 minutes. Stir in the garlic and smoked paprika; cook until the panko is deep golden brown and the garlic no longer is raw, about 1 minute. Transfer to a small bowl and set aside; wipe out the skillet.

In the same skillet over medium-high, heat the remaining 2 tablespoons oil until barely smoking. Add the broccoli and stir to coat, then sprinkle with ¼ teaspoon salt and ½ teaspoon pepper and distribute in an even layer. Cook, stirring only a few times, until lightly charred, about 4 minutes. Add ¼ cup water, then immediately cover. Reduce to medium and cook, occasionally shaking the pan, until the water has cooked off and the broccoli is tender-crisp, about 4 minutes.

Off heat, stir in the thyme and vinegar. Taste and season with salt and pepper. Transfer to a serving dish and sprinkle with the panko mixture.

Optional garnish: Toasted sliced or slivered almonds **OR** shaved manchego cheese **OR** both

BROCCOLI WITH LEMON, TOASTED GARLIC AND SMOKED ALMONDS

Start to finish: 30 minutes

Servings: 4 to 6

In this recipe, simple steamed broccoli gets big, bold flavor when it's tossed after cooking with a lemony, nutty, toasted-garlic dressing. We double up on the smokiness by using both smoked almonds and Spanish smoked paprika; the nuts also add a welcome texture that plays off the tender-crisp broccoli. Mint, with its menthol freshness, lightens up all the deep, earthy notes in the dish.

¼ cup extra-virgin olive oil

4 medium garlic cloves, thinly sliced

2 tablespoons grated lemon zest, plus 3 tablespoons lemon juice

¼ teaspoon smoked paprika

½ cup smoked almonds, chopped

Kosher salt and ground black pepper

1½ pounds broccoli, stems peeled and cut into 1½-inch pieces, florets cut into 1-inch pieces

⅓ cup lightly packed fresh mint

In a 10-inch skillet over medium, heat the oil and garlic, stirring, until the garlic is golden brown, 1 to 2 minutes. Scrape the mixture into a large bowl. Whisk in the lemon zest and juice, smoked paprika, almonds and ½ teaspoon each salt and pepper; set aside.

Fill a large Dutch oven with about 1 inch of water, cover and bring to a simmer over medium-high. Distribute the broccoli in an even layer in a steamer basket, then carefully place the basket in the pot. Cover, reduce to medium and cook until the broccoli is tender-crisp, 8 to 10 minutes.

Transfer the broccoli to the bowl with the dressing, add the mint and toss. Taste and season with salt and pepper.

Steaming Vegetables

Done properly, steaming is one of the best ways to cook vegetables. Its gentle but speedy heat preserves flavors and nutrients. But those results aren't a given. Ignore a few simple guidelines and you can just as easily end up with the sort of mushy produce that helped give cafeteria food a bad reputation. Luckily, we have some easy tips for ensuring perfectly tender-crisp steamed vegetables every time.

For equipment, all you need is a pot and a steamer basket. Whether stainless steel or bamboo, all steamer baskets work the same: suspending food over hot water and allowing steam to gently cook the food above.

But it's important to gauge the water level. Too much water will swamp the steamer; too little boils off too soon. So before cooking, place the empty basket in the pot and add enough water to reach just below the level of the basket. Then bring the water to a simmer over medium-high before adding the vegetables. Prep is important, too. Vegetables should be cut into uniform sizes so all pieces cook at the same rate.

Finally, pay attention to timing. We tested our most frequently steamed vegetables to find the optimal cooking times. This chart is especially helpful if you're planning to steam a mixture of vegetables. Start steaming the denser, longer-cooking vegetables first, then add the more delicate produce later, to ensure they all finish at the same time. Steaming, solved.

VEGETABLE STEAMING TIME TO TENDER-CRISP

Vegetable	Unit	Time
Asparagus	8 ounces pencil-thick spears, trimmed	2 mins
Broccoli	2 cups florets (about 1½ inches)	4 mins
Carrots	2 medium carrots, sliced into ¼-inch rounds (about 2 cups)	5 mins
Cauliflower	2 cups florets (about 1½ inches)	4 mins
Corn on the cob	4-inch-long pieces	4 mins
Green beans	8 ounces, trimmed	3½-4 mins

VEGETABLES

41

CHARRED BROCCOLI WITH JAPANESE-STYLE TOASTED SESAME SAUCE

Start to finish: 30 minutes

Servings: 4

The nutty, salty-sweet flavor of the Japanese sesame mixture known as gomae pairs perfectly with the roasted notes of charred broccoli. To maximize flavorful browning, distribute the broccoli evenly in the skillet and pat down the pieces so they make contact with the pan's hot surface. You will need a 12-inch cast-iron skillet for this recipe.

⅓ cup sesame seeds

4 teaspoons mirin

4 teaspoons soy sauce

4 teaspoons sake

1 tablespoon white sugar

⅛ to ¼ teaspoon cayenne pepper (optional)

1¼ pounds broccoli, florets cut into 1-inch pieces, stems peeled, halved and sliced ½-inch thick

2 tablespoons grapeseed or other neutral oil

Kosher salt

In a small skillet over medium, toast the sesame seeds until fragrant and golden brown, about 4 minutes. Transfer to a plate and cool to room temperature. In a spice grinder, pulse the seeds until coarsely ground, about 3 pulses. Transfer to a small bowl and stir in the mirin, soy sauce, sake, sugar and cayenne (if using).

In a large bowl, toss the broccoli with the oil and ½ teaspoon salt. Heat a 12-inch cast-iron skillet over high for 3 minutes, or until a drop of water evaporates in 1 to 2 seconds. Add the broccoli and use a wooden spoon to pat it in a snug, even layer; reserve the bowl.

Cook without stirring until deeply browned in spots, about 4 minutes. Stir, turn the broccoli, and continue to cook until charred and crisp-tender, another 4 to 5 minutes. Return the broccoli to the bowl and spoon the sesame sauce on top. Stir to coat, then taste and season with salt.

GRILLED BROCCOLI WITH HARISSA VINAIGRETTE AND PICKLED SHALLOT

Start to finish: 35 minutes, plus grill prep

Servings: 4

Smoky, deeply charred broccoli is delicious, but grilling the vegetable can be tricky because the dense stems cook more slowly than the florets. Peeling the stalks, then cutting the broccoli into spears helps, but grilling still tends to dry out the vegetable before it's fully cooked. The solution? We parcook the broccoli in the microwave. (Alternatively, you could blanch the broccoli in boiling water for 2 minutes, plunge into ice water just until cool, then pat dry.) Charred broccoli requires robust seasonings that can stand up to the brassica's boldness. We borrowed a flavor combination from "Berber & Q: On Vegetables" by London chef Josh Katz and threw together a citrus and harissa vinaigrette. We toss some of the dressing with the broccoli before grilling, then some at the end for a jolt of brightness. Quick-pickled shallot and raisins, plus a handful of dill (or mint), are fantastic finishing touches.

1½ pounds broccoli, trimmed, stalks peeled

Kosher salt and ground black pepper

2½ tablespoons white vinegar

2 medium shallots, halved and thinly sliced

3 tablespoons golden raisins

⅓ cup extra-virgin olive oil

1 to 1½ tablespoons harissa paste

3 tablespoons lime juice

2 teaspoons honey

½ cup lightly packed fresh dill
or mint, torn

Slice the broccoli heads lengthwise into halves or quarters, depending on size, then into spears with stems about ½ inch thick. In a large microwave-safe bowl, mix ½ teaspoon salt in ¼ cup water. Add the broccoli and toss; cover and microwave on high for 2 minutes. Toss, cover and microwave until bright green and just shy of tender-crisp, another 2 minutes. Remove from the bowl. Discard the water, wipe out the bowl and reserve it. (The broccoli can be cooled and refrigerated for 1 day.)

In a small bowl, mix ½ teaspoon salt with the vinegar and 2 tablespoons water. Stir in the shallots and raisins. Set aside, tossing occasionally, until needed. In the reserved

large bowl, whisk together the oil, harissa, lime juice, honey and ½ teaspoon each salt and pepper. Measure out ¼ cup and set aside. Add the broccoli to the bowl with the remaining dressing and toss until coated.

Prepare a charcoal or gas grill. For a charcoal grill, spread a large chimney of hot coals evenly over one side of the grill bed; open the bottom grill vents and the lid vent. Heat the grill, covered, for 5 minutes, then clean and oil the cooking grate. For a gas grill, turn all burners to high and heat, covered, for 10 to 15 minutes, then clean and oil the grate.

Place the broccoli on the grill (on the hot side, if using charcoal); reserve the bowl. Cook, occasionally turning the broccoli, until well charred and tender-crisp, 6 to 8 minutes. Return the broccoli to the bowl. Immediately add the reserved dressing (while the broccoli is hot) and toss. Taste and season with salt and pepper.

Transfer the broccoli to a platter. Using a slotted spoon, lift the pickled shallots and raisins out of their liquid and scatter over the broccoli; discard the liquid. Sprinkle with the dill.

43

Pan-Seared Brussels Sprouts with Feta and Honey

Start to finish: 25 minutes
Servings: 4

These skillet-charred Brussels sprouts are dressed with salty feta, sweet honey, spicy red pepper flakes and a dose of lemon juice for layers of contrasting flavors. **Cooking the sprouts in a searing-hot skillet creates a deep caramelization of natural sugars that counters the vegetable's tendency to bitterness.** Chopped almonds contribute a rich, nutty crunch; pomegranate seeds, if in season, also work nicely, adding pops of color and fruity freshness. Be sure to reduce the heat to medium once you've added the sprouts; this ensures they char and become tender but don't burn. And choose Brussels sprouts that are similarly sized. Small to medium ones work best.

1 pound small to medium Brussels sprouts, trimmed and halved

1 tablespoon neutral oil

2 teaspoons plus 2 tablespoons honey, divided, plus more to serve

Kosher salt and ground black pepper

½ to ¾ teaspoon red pepper flakes

1 ounce feta cheese, crumbled (¼ cup)

¼ cup roasted almonds, roughly chopped OR pomegranate seeds OR a combination

1 tablespoon lemon juice

In a medium bowl, toss the sprouts with the oil, 2 teaspoons honey, ½ teaspoon salt and ¼ teaspoon black pepper. Heat a 12-inch cast-iron skillet over medium-high until water flicked onto the surface immediately sizzles and evaporates. Place the sprouts cut side down in the pan, then reduce to medium; reserve the bowl. Cook without stirring until deeply browned on the bottoms, 5 to 7 minutes.

Using tongs, flip the sprouts and cook, stirring occasionally, until a skewer inserted into the largest sprout meets just a little resistance, 4 to 6 minutes; lower the heat if the sprouts brown too quickly. Return the sprouts to the bowl, then immediately add the remaining 2 tablespoons honey and pepper flakes; toss. Add the feta, almonds and lemon juice;

toss again. Taste and season with salt and black pepper. Transfer to a serving dish and, if desired, drizzle with additional honey.

Optional garnish: Chopped fresh flat-leaf parsley **OR** chopped fresh chives

Roasting Vegetables 101

Roasting is one of the easiest ways to cook vegetables. The dry heat encourages browning, creating aromatic compounds and toasted flavors. A toss with oil and salt before roasting is sometimes all that's needed to round out the results.

But while it seems simple, there are a surprising number of variables to roasting vegetables. From cauliflower to carrots, each has a different form, water content and density—meaning each can require different prep, roasting time and temperature. We wanted a singular go-to reference for perfectly roasted vegetables.

So we prepared nine common vegetables, measuring everything from time and temperature to the right amount of oil and salt. We started with common weights—a medium butternut squash, for instance, weighs about 2 pounds—and basic cuts, using 1-inch chunks in most cases. Some items needed only trimming. We tossed all the vegetables with varying amounts of olive oil and salt, then roasted them on low-rimmed baking sheets. We gauged tenderness and browning to determine the right timings.

While the results were fairly straightforward—producing roasted vegetables our kitchen was happy to snack on—we did make some crucial notes along the way. For pan prep, we skipped kitchen parchment or foil. The former can burn at high temperatures, and the latter tended to cause sticking. A metal spatula was the best tool for flipping and stirring, which prevents scorching the pan. But stirring didn't benefit all the vegetables. Leaving some undistrubed actually led to better browning, as with the sprouts.

Minding the vegetables' structure was important. Sturdier items like broccoli developed better color at higher temperatures; they also required less attention under the high heat. More delicate vegetables such as asparagus and green beans fared better at slightly lower heat and required closer monitoring.

Finally, when determining doneness, insert a paring knife into large pieces to check for tenderness, but be sure the vegetables have browned as well. Some items, like potatoes, soften early on but aren't truly done until they're brown and crispy.

Vegetable	Weight	Preparation	Roasting Temp	Extra-Virgin Olive Oil	Kosher Salt	Cook Time	Stir Halfway Through?
Asparagus	1 pound	Tough bottoms trimmed, about 1-inch removed	475°F	1 tablespoon	¼ teaspoon	7 to 12 mins	No
Broccoli	1½ pounds	1-inch wide florets, stems peeled and in ¼-inch coins	500°F	3 tablespoons	½ teaspoon	15 to 20 mins	Yes
Brussels Sprouts	1½ pounds	Trimmed, halved	475°F	2 tablespoons	½ teaspoon	15 to 20 mins	No
Butternut Squash	2 pounds (about 1 med. squash)	Peeled, seeded, 1-inch pieces	500°F	1½ tablespoons	½ teaspoon	35 to 40 mins	Yes
Carrots	2 pounds	Peeled, 1-inch pieces	500°F	2 tablespoons	¾ teaspoon	20 to 25 mins	Yes
Cauliflower	2 pounds (about 1 med. head)	Core removed, 1-inch florets	500°F	4 tablespoons	¾ teaspoon	10 to 15 mins	No
Green Beans	1 pound	Trimmed, left whole	475°F	2 tablespoons	¼ teaspoon	12 to 17 mins	No
Sweet Potatoes	2 pounds	Peeled, 1-inch pieces	500°F	2 tablespoons	1 teaspoon	30 to 35 mins	Yes
Yukon Gold Potatoes	3 pounds	Peeled, 1-inch pieces	500°F	4 tablespoons	1 teaspoon	45 to 50 mins	Yes

VEGETABLES

In a food processor fitted with the medium (3-mm) slicing disk, slice the sprouts, emptying into a large bowl as needed. Add the vinegar, soy sauce and ¼ teaspoon each salt and pepper. Using your hands, massage the sprouts until they wilt, 10 to 20 seconds. Let stand for 10 minutes. Transfer the mixture to a serving bowl. Distribute the ginger and chilies evenly over the top; do not stir or toss.

In an 8-inch skillet over medium-high, combine the oil and sesame seeds. Cook, stirring occasionally, until golden brown, 1 to 2 minutes. Drizzle the oil-seed mixture onto the sprouts and aromatics, then immediately toss. Taste and season with additional soy sauce and pepper.

Optional garnish: Chopped fresh cilantro

HOT-OIL BRUSSELS SPROUTS WITH GINGER AND SESAME

Start to finish: 25 minutes
Servings: 4

Earthy and subtly sweet with pleasant hints of bitterness, shredded raw Brussels sprouts make excellent slaw-style salads. We massage shredded sprouts with rice vinegar and soy sauce, tenderizing the sprouts and tempering their cabbage-like qualities. We add fresh ginger and chilies, then we draw fragrance and flavor from the aromatics by pouring a mixture of sizzling oil and sesame seeds on top. The sprouts are lightly cooked, each bite imbued with nutty, toasty notes.

1 pound Brussels sprouts, trimmed

3 tablespoons unseasoned rice vinegar

2 tablespoons soy sauce, plus more as needed

Kosher salt and ground black pepper

1 tablespoon finely grated fresh ginger

1 or 2 Fresno OR serrano OR jalapeño chilies, stemmed and thinly sliced OR 2 scallions, thinly sliced OR both

3 tablespoons neutral oil

2 tablespoons sesame seeds

AFGHAN-STYLE BRAISED BUTTERNUT SQUASH WITH GARLIC-MINT YOGURT

Start to finish: 50 minutes (25 minutes active)
Servings: 4 to 6

This is our version of the Afghan pumpkin dish called borani kadoo. We use butternut squash instead of pumpkin since it is readily available throughout the year, and swap tomato paste for the fresh tomatoes called for in many versions. The garlicky, minty yogurt is an excellent foil for the stewed squash—don't omit it, as it really elevates and completes the dish.

4 tablespoons grapeseed or other neutral oil, divided

2-pound butternut squash, peeled, seeded and cut into 1½-inch chunks

1 medium yellow onion, chopped

Kosher salt and ground black pepper

2 medium garlic cloves, minced

1¼ teaspoons ground coriander

½ teaspoon ground turmeric

½ teaspoon ground cinnamon

1 tablespoon tomato paste

1 tablespoon white sugar

1 cup plain whole-milk yogurt

¼ cup lightly packed fresh mint, chopped

In a large Dutch oven over medium-high, heat 2 tablespoons oil until shimmering. Add the squash and cook, stirring often, until golden brown, 6 to 8 minutes. Transfer to a medium bowl.

To the pot, add the remaining 2 tablespoons oil along with the onion and ½ teaspoon salt. Cook over medium-high, stirring often, until lightly browned, about 3 minutes. Add half of the garlic, the coriander, turmeric and cinnamon; cook, stirring, until fragrant, about 30 seconds. Stir in the tomato paste and return the squash to the pot. Add the sugar and 1 cup water, then bring to a simmer, scraping up any browned bits. Cover, reduce to medium-low and cook, stirring occasionally and adding water 2 tablespoons at a time as needed if the mixture looks dry, until a skewer inserted into the squash meets no resistance, 25 to 30 minutes; there should be a little lightly thickened liquid remaining in the pot.

While the squash cooks, in a small bowl, stir together the yogurt, mint, the remaining garlic and ¼ teaspoon each salt and pepper; set aside until ready to serve. When the squash is done, taste and season with salt and pepper. Transfer to a serving dish and serve with the yogurt mixture.

BUTTER-ROASTED CARROTS WITH ZA'ATAR AND POMEGRANATE MOLASSES

Start to finish: 40 minutes (20 minutes active)
Servings: 6

Carrots roasted in a moderately hot oven for almost an hour become super-sweet and almost meltingly tender. We start them coated with olive oil but drizzle them with melted butter partway through roasting. The milk solids in the butter caramelize in the oven, adding a rich, nutty fragrance and flavor. Za'atar, a Middle Eastern seed and spice blend, and orange zest and juice bring complexity to the dish. Pistachios and sweet-tart pomegranate molasses are finishing touches that make this dish special. Bunch carrots—the type sold with their greens attached—are especially good here because they're slender and fresh. After halving them, if any of the upper portions are especially thick, cut them in half lengthwise.

2½ pounds long, slender carrots (see headnote), peeled and halved crosswise on a sharp diagonal

1 tablespoon extra-virgin olive oil

Kosher salt and ground black pepper

1 orange

4 tablespoons salted butter, melted

2 teaspoons za'atar OR ground coriander OR Aleppo pepper, divided

2 tablespoons raw OR roasted pistachios, finely chopped

2 teaspoons pomegranate molasses

Heat the oven to 350°F with a rack in the middle position. On a rimmed baking sheet, toss the carrots with the oil, ¾ teaspoon salt and ¼ teaspoon pepper, then distribute evenly. Roast for 30 minutes. Meanwhile, grate 1 teaspoon zest from the orange, then cut the orange into quarters.

Drizzle the carrots with the butter and sprinkle with the za'atar and zest. Toss, then redistribute evenly. Place the orange quarters cut sides up on the baking sheet. Roast until a skewer inserted into the largest carrot meets no resistance, another 15 to 20 minutes, stirring once about halfway through.

Squeeze the juice from 1 orange quarter over the carrots. Using a wide metal spatula, transfer to a platter, scraping up any browned bits. Taste the carrots and season with salt and pepper. Sprinkle with the pistachios and drizzle with the pomegranate molasses. Serve the remaining orange quarters on the side.

POTATO AND CAULIFLOWER CURRY

Start to finish: 45 minutes

Servings: 4

In traditional recipes for aloo gobi, the vegetables often are fried before being simmered. But we wanted a simpler, neater cooking method as well as a lighter, fresher flavor. So we opted instead to roast the cauliflower and potatoes in a high-heat oven. Before roasting, we tossed the vegetables with a little cornstarch, which assists with browning and crispness, and also helps thicken the curry when the ingredients are later simmered.

2- to 2½-pound head cauliflower, trimmed, cored and cut into 1½-inch florets

1 pound russet potatoes, peeled and cut into 1-inch chunks

5 tablespoons grapeseed or other neutral oil, divided

1 tablespoon cornstarch

Kosher salt and ground black pepper

2 tablespoons cumin seeds

1 tablespoon finely grated fresh ginger

1 tablespoon ground turmeric

1 tablespoon sweet paprika

1 tablespoon ground coriander

¼ teaspoon cayenne pepper

2 teaspoons packed brown sugar

¼ cup finely chopped fresh cilantro

1 tablespoon lime juice

Heat the oven to 500°F with a rack in the middle position. Spray a rimmed baking sheet with cooking spray. In a large bowl, combine the cauliflower and potatoes with 3 tablespoons of oil. Sprinkle the cornstarch, ½ teaspoon salt and 1 teaspoon pepper over the vegetables, then toss well. Distribute in an even layer on the prepared baking sheet and roast without stirring until lightly browned and a knife inserted into a piece meets just a little resistance, about 15 minutes.

In a large Dutch oven over medium, heat the remaining 2 tablespoons oil until shimmering. Add the cumin seeds and cook, stirring, until fragrant, about 1 minute. Stir in the ginger and cook until fragrant, about 30 seconds. Stir in the turmeric, paprika, coriander, cayenne, sugar and ¾ teaspoon salt. Add the cauliflower-potato mixture and toss to coat. Stir in 2 cups water, cover and cook, stirring often, until the liquid has thickened and the vegetables are fully tender, 5 to 7 minutes. Off heat, stir in the cilantro and lime juice. Taste and season with salt and pepper.

Chermoula-Roasted
Whole Cauliflower

Start to finish: 1 hour 10 minutes (10 minutes active)
Servings: 4

The simplest, most fuss-free way to cook cauliflower is to put a whole head in the oven to roast. After about an hour, the cauliflower emerges tender and caramelized and needs only to be cut into wedges for serving. The flavorings here are drawn from North African chermoula, an aromatic spice and herb relish that's used as a condiment as well as a marinade.

2-pound head cauliflower, trimmed

¼ cup neutral oil

1½ tablespoons coriander seeds

1½ tablespoons cumin seeds

1 tablespoon sweet paprika

2 teaspoons granulated garlic

Kosher salt and ground black pepper

⅓ cup lightly packed fresh mint
OR fresh flat-leaf parsley, chopped

Lemon wedges, to serve

Heat the oven to 425°F with a rack in the middle position. Place the cauliflower on a rimmed baking sheet.

In a small bowl, stir together the oil, coriander, cumin, paprika, garlic and 1 teaspoon salt and 2 teaspoons pepper. Brush the mixture onto the cauliflower, then roast until deeply browned and a skewer inserted into the center meets no resistance, 55 to 70 minutes.

Cut the cauliflower into wedges. Serve sprinkled with the mint and with lemon wedges on the side.

VEGETABLES

49

CHANGE THE WAY YOU COOK

Use Cornstarch for Crispy "Fried" Vegetables

So-called oven-frying is a great shortcut for saving the fuss and mess of deep-frying. But with vegetables, the results too often are disappointingly limp. The exception is potatoes, the natural starches of which crisp under high heat. But it turns out that replicating that effect with less starchy vegetables, such as cauliflower or sweet potatoes, is easy if you give them a light coating of cornstarch before roasting.

That's because cornstarch is composed of nearly one-third amylose starch, which crisps when exposed to oil and high heat. The technique (which works best on low-moisture produce) is simple, yielding wonderfully crisp, browned results. Start by heating an oiled baking sheet at 425°F. The hot pan helps the vegetables brown and crisp immediately and evenly. Next, toss the produce (which should be cut into small chunks or thin slices) with oil, then with cornstarch; the coating should be light, almost just a dusting, not clumped or thick. Be sure to shake off any excess.

When you arrange the vegetables on the baking sheet, don't overcrowd, which promotes steaming. Cook in batches if you must. Finally, flip the vegetables only once, halfway through cooking, so they develop more of a crust.

This also is an excellent way to add flavor; seasoning the cornstarch with any finely ground spice ensures bold, even flavor. In addition to cauliflower and sweet potatoes, this technique works well with carrots, rings of red onion and cubes of winter squash.

CAULIFLOWER STEAKS WITH PICKLED PEPPERS, CAPERS AND PARMESAN

Start to finish: 45 minutes
Servings: 4

To make a satisfying vegetarian main, we cut thick cauliflower "steaks" from the center section of the whole head; you'll get two steaks per head. The ends that are left over tend to fall apart because they're detached from the core, but don't discard them—use them to make cauliflower rice, roast them separately or make them into soup. The savory-sweet topping for these cauliflower steaks riffs on a recipe in "Six Seasons" by Joshua McFadden.

Two 2- to 2½-pound cauliflower heads, trimmed

6 tablespoons extra-virgin olive oil, divided

Kosher salt and ground black pepper

½ cup Peppadew peppers OR sweet cherry peppers, patted dry and finely chopped

½ cup lightly packed fresh flat-leaf parsley, chopped

1 ounce Parmesan cheese, finely grated
(½ cup)

¼ cup drained capers, patted dry
and roughly chopped

Heat the oven to 500°F with a rack in the middle position. Mist a rimmed baking sheet with cooking spray. Halve each cauliflower top to bottom. From the cut side of each half, slice off a 1½-inch-thick slab to make a total of 4 "steaks"; reserve the ends for another use. Brush the steaks on all sides with 4 tablespoons of oil and season with salt and pepper. Roast on the prepared baking sheet until browned on the bottoms, about 20 minutes. Meanwhile, in a small bowl, stir together the Peppadews, parsley, Parmesan, capers and the remaining 2 tablespoons oil.

After the cauliflower has roasted for 20 minutes, spread the Peppadew mixture onto the steaks. Continue to roast until the topping is well browned and the steaks are tender, another 8 to 10 minutes.

CHILI-GARLIC ROASTED WHOLE CAULIFLOWER

Start to finish: 1 hour 10 minutes (10 minutes active)
Servings: 4

Gobi Manchurian, an Indo-Chinese dish of deep-fried and seasoned cauliflower, is widely popular partly for its crisp-saucy quality, but also for its addictive savory-sweet spiciness. For this recipe, we've applied a similar flavor profile to roasted whole cauliflower.

2-pound head cauliflower, trimmed

¼ cup neutral oil

2 tablespoons chili-garlic sauce

2 tablespoons ketchup

1 tablespoon garam masala

Kosher salt and ground black pepper

2 scallions, thinly sliced

Heat the oven to 425°F with a rack in the middle position. Place the cauliflower on a rimmed baking sheet.

In a small bowl, stir together the oil, chili-garlic sauce, ketchup, garam masala, 1 teaspoon salt and 2 teaspoons pepper. Brush half the mixture onto the cauliflower, then

roast until deeply browned and a skewer inserted into the center meets just a little resistance, 40 to 55 minutes. Brush on the remaining mixture and roast for another 10 minutes. Cut the cauliflower into wedges. Serve sprinkled with the scallions.

ARMENIAN SWISS CHARD WITH TOMATOES AND CHICKPEAS

Start to finish: 35 minutes
Servings: 4 to 6

Greens and chickpeas are a pairing in many cuisines, and this is our version of the Armenian dish called nivik (sometimes spelled "nivig"). Spinach and chard are the typical choices for nivik; we chose the latter, as chard leaves are sturdier and the stems offer added texture, taste and substance. Onion, garlic and tomatoes are trusty flavor accents, and lemon, stirred in at the very end, brightens things. For convenience, we use canned chickpeas so the dish can be on the table in well under an hour. It's hearty enough to be a vegetarian main, especially if sprinkled with the optional garnish of toasted almonds, but is equally good as a side to fish, chicken or pork.

3 tablespoons extra-virgin olive oil

1 bunch Swiss chard (about 1 pound), stems chopped, leaves cut crosswise into rough ¾-inch ribbons, reserved separately

1 medium yellow onion, chopped

Kosher salt and ground black pepper

2 medium garlic cloves, minced

2 ripe tomatoes, cored and chopped

15½-ounce can chickpeas, rinsed and drained

2 tablespoons lemon juice

In a 12-inch skillet over medium, heat the oil until shimmering. Add the chard stems, onion and ½ teaspoon each salt and pepper. Cook, stirring occasionally, until softened and golden brown, 10 to 12 minutes. Increase to medium-high, add the garlic and cook, stirring, until fragrant, about 30 seconds. Stir in the tomatoes and chickpeas, then cook, stirring occasionally, until the tomatoes begin to break down, 3 to 4 minutes.

Add the chard leaves and cook, stirring occasionally, until wilted, 2 to 3 minutes. Off heat, stir in the lemon juice, then taste and season with salt and pepper. Transfer to a serving dish.

Optional Garnish: Toasted slivered almonds

CHANGE THE WAY YOU COOK

Better Knife Care

With proper care, knives actually require only infrequent sharpening. Kitchen knives always should be washed by hand and dried. The high heat and detergents of a dishwasher can damage a knife's handle and dull the edge.

Hone: To maintain a knife's sharp edge, it's important to steel it—or hone it—frequently. Steeling isn't sharpening: it's straightening and realigning the edge of the blade. Consistent steeling greatly prolongs the time between sharpenings. We recommend ceramic steels, which are harder than metal versions. To use a steel, with a gentle hand swipe each side of the blade down the length of the rod at a roughly 17-degree angle a few times; wipe the blade clean before use.

Sharpen: When honing fails to bring back a knife's edge, it's time to sharpen. This can be done with a simple pull-through sharpener (there are dozens of affordable designs), an electric sharpener (we like those from Worksharp), or with a sharpening stone (easy, but takes practice). Or leave it to the experts and find a local sharpener or a mail-order service.

Crisp Oven-Fried Cauliflower with Tahini-Yogurt Sauce

Start to finish: 45 minutes (15 minutes active)
Servings: 4 to 6

We love the crisp exterior and creamy interior of arnabeet mekleh, or Lebanese fried cauliflower, but cooking the florets in a pot of oil on the stovetop is not our favorite kitchen activity. Luckily, roasting well-oiled, starch-coated cauliflower in a hot oven yields delicious results that come incredibly close to the real deal. We add a few spices here to layer in flavor and aroma. If the tahini-yogurt sauce isn't for you, try serving the cauliflower with mango chutney or aioli.

½ cup cornstarch

1 tablespoon ground cumin

2 teaspoons ground fennel seed
OR curry powder

1 teaspoon ground coriander

Kosher salt and ground black pepper

3-pound head cauliflower, trimmed
and cut into 1-inch florets

½ cup grapeseed or other neutral oil

1 cup whole-milk plain yogurt

2 tablespoons tahini

2 tablespoons finely chopped fresh mint

1 tablespoon lemon juice

1 small garlic clove, finely grated

Heat the oven to 475°F with a rack in the middle position. In a small bowl, whisk together the cornstarch, cumin, fennel, coriander, 1 teaspoon salt and 2 teaspoons pepper. In a large bowl, toss the cauliflower with the oil, using your hands to rub the oil into the florets. Sprinkle with the cornstarch mixture and toss until evenly coated. Transfer the florets to a rimmed baking sheet, shaking off excess cornstarch mixture and turning the pieces cut side down as much as possible. Roast for 15 minutes.

Using a metal spatula, flip the florets, then continue to roast until deep golden brown, another 15 to 20 minutes. Meanwhile, in a small bowl, whisk together the yogurt, tahini, mint, lemon juice, garlic and ⅛ teaspoon salt. Serve the cauliflower with the yogurt-tahini sauce.

Optional garnish: Thinly sliced scallions OR lemon wedges OR both

VEGETABLES

53

ETHIOPIAN STEWED COLLARD GREENS

Start to finish: 1 hour (20 minutes active)

Servings: 4

Gomen wat translates as "collard greens stew." In Ethiopia, we tasted multiple versions of the hardy greens braised with beef (in which case, the dish is called gomen besiga), but we prefer the lighter, brighter, more flavorful version in which the greens are cooked without meat. Ethiopian butter, made from fermented milk, infuses dishes to which it's added—including the gomen wat we sampled—with a unique depth of flavor and appealing funkiness, not unlike a fragrant cheese. Indian ghee, which is easier to find, is a reasonably good substitute. Look for ghee in either the refrigerator section near the butter or in the grocery aisle near the coconut oil. If you cannot find it, use salted butter in its place but also add 1 teaspoon white miso along with the broth to subtly boost flavor. If collard greens are not available, curly kale will work, but reduce the greens' cooking time to 15 to 20 minutes.

3 tablespoons ghee (see headnote)

1 medium yellow onion, halved and thinly sliced

6 medium garlic cloves, minced

3 tablespoons minced fresh ginger, divided

¾ teaspoon ground cardamom

½ teaspoon ground turmeric

1 bunch (about 1 pound) collard greens, stemmed and roughly chopped

1½ cups low-sodium beef, chicken or vegetable broth

Kosher salt and ground black pepper

1 or 2 Fresno or serrano chilies, stemmed, seeded and thinly sliced

1 tablespoon lemon juice

In a large pot over medium, melt the ghee. Add the onion and cook, stirring occasionally, until lightly browned, 5 to 10 minutes. Stir in the garlic, 2 tablespoons of ginger, the cardamom and turmeric. Cook, stirring occasionally, until fragrant and lightly toasted, about 1 minute.

Add about half of the collards and cook, stirring, until slightly wilted, then add the remaining collards. Stir in the broth and ½ teaspoon pepper. Cover and cook, stirring occasionally, until the collards are tender, 20 to 30 minutes.

Off heat, stir in the chili(es), lemon juice and remaining 1 tablespoon ginger. Taste and season with salt and pepper, then transfer to a serving dish.

GRILLED EGGPLANT WITH SESAME AND HERBS

Start to finish: 1 hour

Servings: 6

This recipe is our adaptation of an eggplant dish taught to us by Irit Aharon, who runs a small eatery in Tel Aviv. We swapped her technique of charring whole eggplants on the burner of a gas stove for grilling halved ones over a charcoal or gas fire. We like serving the eggplant in the charred skins, but the cooked flesh also can be scooped into a bowl, mashed and mixed with the herb mixture, then finished with olive oil and lemon juice. Leave the stems on the eggplants when halving them. If you prefer to cook the eggplant indoors, heat the broiler with a rack about 6 inches from the heat. Place the oil-brushed eggplant halves cut side up on a wire rack set on a broiler-safe rimmed baking sheet. Broil until golden brown, about 10 minutes, then reduce the oven to 475°F and roast until soft throughout, another 30 to 40 minutes.

2 medium eggplants (1 to 1½ pounds each), halved lengthwise

½ cup extra-virgin olive oil, divided, plus extra to serve

Kosher salt and ground black pepper

6 medium garlic cloves, finely grated

½ cup finely chopped fresh parsley

½ cup finely chopped fresh mint

6 tablespoons sesame seeds, toasted

1 tablespoon grated lemon zest, plus 2 tablespoons lemon juice

Prepare a charcoal or gas grill. For a charcoal grill, spread a large chimney of hot coals evenly over one side of the grill bed; open the bottom grill vents. Heat the grill, covered, for 5 minutes, then clean and oil the cooking grate. For a gas grill, turn half of the burners to high and heat, covered, for 5 to 10 minutes, then clean and oil the grate.

Using a paring knife, carefully score the flesh of each eggplant half in a crosshatch pattern, spacing the cuts about ¾ inch apart. Be careful not to cut through the skin. Use ¼ cup of the oil to brush the eggplant flesh evenly, then season with salt and pepper. In a small bowl, stir together the remaining ¼ cup oil and the garlic.

Grill the eggplant halves cut side down on the hot side of the grill until well browned, 5 to 10 minutes. Flip the halves cut side up and move to the cooler side of the grill. Brush the garlic-oil mixture onto the flesh, using the brush to push the garlic into the cuts. Cover and cook until a skewer inserted at the narrow end of the largest eggplant half meets no resistance, 30 to 40 minutes.

In a small bowl, stir together the parsley, mint, sesame seeds, lemon zest and ½ teaspoon each salt and pepper. Use a spoon to carefully separate the flesh from the skin of each half, but leave it in place. Sprinkle each half with the herb mixture, then carefully stir it into the flesh to combine. Drizzle with olive oil and the lemon juice. Serve warm or at room temperature.

NO-FRY NEAPOLITAN EGGPLANT PARMESAN

Start to finish: 1¾ hours, plus cooling
Servings: 6 to 8

At the family-owned trattoria La Tavernetta Vittozzi in Naples, Anna Vittozzi taught us to make a lighter, brighter eggplant Parmesan that still was rich with cheese and tangy with tomato sauce. The secret? Skip the breading. Though the Vittozzi version involved pan-frying eggplant, we found we could achieve similar results by roasting olive oil-brushed slices in the oven. This easier, more hands-off approach yields golden-brown, silky-textured eggplant, perfect for layering with a simple tomato sauce and fresh basil, plus plenty of cheese. In addition to umami-packed Parmesan, Vittozzi used smoked provolone, which added a delicious depth and savoriness to the dish. Smoked mozzarella might be easier to find in the U.S., and it's a fine stand-in, as is scamorza cheese. If none of those are options, opt for low-moisture mozzarella cheese but avoid fresh mozzarella, which contains too much water.

7 tablespoons extra-virgin olive oil, divided

Five 1-pound globe eggplants

Kosher salt and ground black pepper

1 medium yellow onion, finely chopped

28-ounce can crushed tomatoes

3 tablespoons salted butter, cut into 3 pieces

8 ounces smoked provolone, smoked mozzarella or smoked scamorza cheese, shredded (2 cups), divided

2 ounces Parmesan cheese, finely grated (1 cup), divided

1 cup lightly packed fresh basil, torn

Heat the oven to 425°F with racks in the upper- and lower-middle positions. Brush 2 rimmed baking sheets with 2 tablespoons oil each.

Remove half of the skin from each eggplant. To do this, using a vegetable peeler and working from top to bottom, peel off strips of skin about 1 inch apart. Cut the eggplants crosswise into ¼-inch-thick rounds, then arrange in a single layer on the prepared baking sheets, slightly overlapping.

Brush the eggplant with 2 tablespoons of the remaining oil, then sprinkle lightly with salt and pepper. Roast until the slices are spottily browned, the edges are slightly crisped and the moisture has cooked off, 35 to 40 minutes; halfway through, use a wide metal spatula to flip the slices, then switch the positions of the baking sheets. Remove from the oven; leave the oven on.

Meanwhile, in a large saucepan over medium-low, heat the remaining 1 tablespoon oil until shimmering. Add the onion and ½ teaspoon salt; cover and cook, stirring occasionally, until the onion is translucent, 4 to 5 minutes. Stir in the tomatoes, butter, ½ teaspoon pepper and ½ cup water. Bring to a simmer, then reduce to medium-low and cook, stirring occasionally, until the sauce is slightly thickened, 15 to 20 minutes. Remove from the heat and cool for 15 minutes. Taste and season with salt and pepper.

Measure 1 cup of the tomato sauce into a 9-by-13-inch baking dish and spread to cover the bottom. Arrange one-third of the eggplant on top of the tomato sauce, overlapping the slices if needed, then sprinkle evenly with 1 cup provolone, ¼ cup Parmesan and about half of the basil. Spoon on another ¾ cup tomato sauce and spread evenly. Layer on half of the remaining eggplant, followed by the remaining provolone, ¼ cup of the remaining Parmesan and the remaining basil. Spoon on another ¾ cup sauce and layer on the remaining eggplant. Cover with the remaining sauce, spreading it evenly, then sprinkle with the remaining Parmesan.

Bake on the lower rack until the edges are bubbling and the cheese is melted, 15 to 20 minutes. Cool for about 10 minutes before serving.

7 Essential Knife Skills

Chopping Onions

Trim off the sprout end, then stand the onion on the trimmed end. Cut the onion in half through the root end, then peel each half. Place one half broad side down on the cutting board with the root end farthest from you. Holding the onion in place with your fingers, curling your fingertips inward, push the blade down through the onion to the cutting board, without cutting through the root end; make about six or seven vertical slices across the onion, keeping the root intact. Turn the onion and cut crosswise toward the root end to create rough squares.

Coring Bell Peppers

To easily remove the seeds and ribs from bell peppers, stand the pepper upright and slice downward on each side of the core, creating planks of pepper. The ribs and seeds will remain attached to the stem and dimpled bottom.

Smashing Ginger and Garlic

To mash garlic cloves or thin coins of fresh ginger to a pulp, place the blade of a cleaver or chef's knife flat on top and give it a firm whack or two with the palm of your hand. If necessary, work the blade back and forth across the pulp a few times for a finer texture.

Cutting Scallions on the Diagonal

To create thin ribbons of scallion greens, position scallions—several if thin, one if large—on your cutting board at a 45-degree angle to your knife and slice crosswise as thinly as possible.

Safely Chopping Round Vegetables

To prevent vegetables such as zucchini, squash or eggplant from rolling, make a thin slice down the length of one side of the vegetable to create a flat edge it can rest on.

Cutting Carrot Sticks

To cut carrots into even pieces, halve them crosswise between the thick and thin portions. Now halve each piece lengthwise, then follow the arc of the vegetable to slice into long, even pieces.

Coring and Slicing Cabbage

To remove the tough core from green and red cabbages, cut the cabbage into quarters, then slice out the core at an angle (it's easy to see demarcation between core and leaves). Shred the leaves by cutting crosswise as thinly as possible.

VEGETABLES

57

SLOW-ROASTED FENNEL AND RED ONIONS WITH TAHINI AND SPICES

Start to finish: 1¾ hours (15 minutes active)
Servings: 4 to 6

Slow-roasting fennel and onions is one of the best ways to coax out their inherent sweetness. We start them in a covered baking dish, mixed with olive oil, tahini and seasonings, as well as water that creates steam to help them tenderize. They finish roasting uncovered to cook off any remaining moisture and develop deep, rich, flavorful caramelization. The vegetables are delicious warm or at room temperature (but hold off adding the mint until ready to serve).

⅓ cup extra-virgin olive oil

2 tablespoons tahini

1½ teaspoons ground cumin

1 teaspoon hot paprika OR 1¾ teaspoons sweet paprika, plus ¼ teaspoon cayenne pepper

1 teaspoon ground coriander

½ teaspoon ground cinnamon

1 tablespoon grated lemon zest, plus 2 tablespoons lemon juice

Kosher salt and ground black pepper

2 large fennel bulbs, trimmed, halved lengthwise and cut into 1-inch wedges

2 medium red onions, sliced into ½-inch rounds

1 cup lightly packed fresh mint, chopped

Heat the oven to 450°F with a rack in the middle position. In a 9-by-13-inch baking dish, stir together the oil, tahini, cumin, paprika, coriander, cinnamon, lemon juice, 1 teaspoon salt, 2 teaspoons pepper and ½ cup water. Add the fennel and onions; toss until well coated, then distribute in an even layer, making sure the onions are evenly dispersed amongst the fennel wedges. Cover tightly with foil and bake for 1 hour.

Uncover and bake until the liquid has cooked off and the vegetables are browned and very tender, about another 15 minutes. Cool on a wire rack for about 15 minutes. Sprinkle the lemon zest and mint over the top and serve.

Optional garnish: Chopped fennel fronds

GREEN BEANS WITH CHIPOTLE CHILI AND PEANUTS

Start to finish: 20 minutes
Servings: 4

Inspired by the smoky, nutty notes of Mexican salsa macha, this green bean dish employs our sear-and-steam technique. We sear the beans in a hot skillet until charred, then add water and a tight-fitting lid, allowing them to steam through. The result is deep flavor from browning and a pleasing tender-crisp texture. Sesame seeds and peanuts add plenty of crunch, while chipotle chili in adobo and fresh lime juice contribute smokiness and bright, citrusy flavor.

4 tablespoons extra-virgin olive oil, divided

3 medium garlic cloves, thinly sliced

½ cup roasted peanuts, chopped

2 tablespoons sesame seeds

1 pound green beans, trimmed

Kosher salt and ground black pepper

1 chipotle chili in adobo sauce, minced

2 tablespoons lime juice

In a 12-inch skillet over medium, combine 2 tablespoons oil and the garlic. Cook, stirring, until the garlic begins to brown, about 1 minute. Add the peanuts and sesame seeds; cook, stirring, until the mixture is golden brown, about 1 minute. Transfer to a small bowl and set aside; wipe out the skillet.

In the same skillet over medium-high, heat the remaining 2 tablespoons oil until barely smoking. Add the green beans and stir to coat, then sprinkle with ¼ teaspoon salt and ½ teaspoon pepper and distribute in an even layer. Cook, stirring only a few times, until the beans are lightly charred, about 4 minutes. Add ¼ cup water, then immediately cover. Reduce to medium and cook, occasionally shaking the pan, until the water has cooked off and the beans have become tender-crisp, about 3 minutes.

Off heat, stir in the chipotle chili and lime juice. Taste and season with salt and pepper. Transfer to a serving dish and sprinkle with the peanut-sesame mixture.

LEBANESE BRAISED GREEN BEANS

Start to finish: 40 minutes
Servings: 4

The Lebanese dish called loubieh bi zeit, or green beans in olive oil, typically is prepared with flat, sturdy runner beans. The beans are braised until tender in a tomato sauce that's sometimes seasoned with a mix of spices but always enriched with a glug of olive oil. For our version, we opted for easier-to-find standard green beans, and made a seasoning blend with a few common spices. We got the most flavor out of canned whole tomatoes by crushing and cooking them until thick and jammy, and using some of their juices as the cooking liquid for the beans.

1 teaspoon ground cumin

1 teaspoon ground coriander

½ teaspoon grated nutmeg

¼ teaspoon ground cardamom

¼ teaspoon ground cinnamon

Kosher salt and ground black pepper

¼ cup extra-virgin olive oil

2 medium shallots, halved and thinly sliced

1½ pounds green beans, trimmed

28-ounce can whole peeled tomatoes, drained, 1 cup juices reserved, tomatoes crushed by hand and reserved separately

In a small bowl, stir together the cumin, coriander, nutmeg, cardamom, cinnamon and 1 teaspoon pepper.

In a large Dutch oven over medium-high, heat the oil until shimmering. Add the shallots and cook, stirring occasionally, until golden brown, 2 to 3 minutes. Add the beans and spice mixture, then stir to coat. Stir in the tomatoes (not the reserved juices) and ¾ teaspoon salt. Cook, stirring occasionally, until the tomatoes begin to brown, 5 to 8 minutes.

Add the reserved juices, cover and reduce to medium-low. Cook until the beans are tender, 15 to 18 minutes, stirring only once or twice. Taste and season with salt and pepper, then transfer to a serving bowl.

BAHARAT MUSHROOMS WITH TAHINI-LEMON SAUCE

Start to finish: 50 minutes (25 minutes active)
Servings: 4

Jerusalem mixed grill is a popular Israeli street food. It includes an assortment of meats griddled with onions and spices. It inspired this recipe that roasts mushrooms until meaty and well browned—and that bears a surprising resemblance to the real deal. Baharat is a Middle Eastern blend of earthy, warm spices. If not available, replace with 1¼ teaspoons each ground coriander and ground cumin. Don't use a bowl to toss the mushrooms, oil and seasonings. Instead, toss the ingredients directly on the baking sheet; this leaves the pan slicked with oil for better caramelization. Serve as a side to chicken or beef, or make it into a vegetarian main with rice pilaf alongside.

¼ cup plus 2 tablespoons olive oil

2½ teaspoons baharat (see headnote), divided

Kosher salt and ground black pepper

1½ pounds cremini OR button mushrooms
OR a combination, trimmed, quartered if large,
halved if medium or small

1 medium red onion, halved and sliced
about ¼ inch thick

¼ cup tahini

3 tablespoons lemon juice, plus lemon wedges,
to serve

1 tablespoon finely chopped fresh chives
OR fresh flat-leaf parsley

Heat the oven to 450°F with a rack in the middle position. On a rimmed baking sheet, stir together the oil, 2 teaspoons baharat, ½ teaspoon salt and ¼ teaspoon pepper. Add the mushrooms and onion; toss to coat, then distribute in an even layer. Roast until the mushrooms are tender and well browned, about 30 minutes, stirring once about halfway through.

Meanwhile, in a small bowl, whisk together the tahini, lemon juice, 2 tablespoons hot water, ¼ teaspoon salt and the remaining ½ teaspoon baharat, adding additional hot water 1 teaspoon at a time as needed to thin to the desired consistency.

Transfer the mushrooms to a serving dish. Taste and season with salt and pepper. Spoon on the tahini sauce or serve on the side. Sprinkle the mushrooms with the chives and serve with lemon wedges.

PAN-ROASTED WINTER VEGETABLES WITH MISO, GINGER AND HONEY

Start to finish: 45 minutes
Servings: 4 to 6

A cast-iron skillet, with its steady, even heat, works beautifully for pan-roasting vegetables and achieving flavorful caramelization. This wintry combination of carrots, parsnips, Brussels sprouts and shallots starts on the stovetop, covered for a portion of the time to facilitate cooking. Cast-iron skillets often do not have lids, so if needed, borrow one from a similarly sized pot or simply set a baking sheet on top. After a toss with butter and a savory-sweet mixture of umami-rich miso, ginger and honey, the vegetables finish in a moderately hot oven, where the even heat renders them fully tender and nicely browned. Serve as a side to roasted chicken, turkey, duck, pork or lamb, or offer it as part of a vegetarian meal.

2 tablespoons white miso

2 teaspoons honey, plus more to serve

2 teaspoons finely grated fresh ginger

Kosher salt and ground black pepper

8 ounces carrots, peeled, trimmed, halved
lengthwise and cut into 3- to 4-inch pieces

8 ounces parsnips, peeled, trimmed, halved

lengthwise and cut into 3- to 4-inch pieces

1 pound medium Brussels sprouts, trimmed and halved

3 medium shallots, root end intact, halved

2 tablespoons grapeseed or other neutral oil

2 tablespoons salted butter, cut into 2 pieces

Heat the oven to 425°F with a rack in the upper-middle position. In a small bowl, whisk together the miso, honey, ginger and ½ teaspoon pepper; set aside.

In a 12-inch cast-iron skillet, toss the carrots, parsnips, Brussels sprouts, shallots, oil and ½ teaspoon salt. Distribute in an even layer with the cut sides against the pan as much as possible. Set over medium-high and cook, stirring only once or twice, until the vegetables begin to brown, 5 to 7 minutes. Cover, reduce to medium and cook, stirring occasionally, until the carrots and parsnips begin to soften, 4 to 5 minutes.

Add the butter and toss until melted, then add the miso mixture and toss until the vegetables are evenly coated. Transfer the skillet, uncovered, to the oven and roast until the vegetables are tender and nicely charred, 10 to 15 minutes; stir once about halfway through.

Remove the skillet from the oven (the handle will be hot), then taste and season with salt and pepper. Serve directly from the skillet, drizzled with additional honey, or transfer to a serving dish, then drizzle with additional honey.

GREEK PEAS WITH POTATOES AND HERBS

Start to finish: 35 minutes

Servings: 4

The Greek name for this dish, arakas kokkinistos, translates as "reddened peas." The version taught to us by Greek cooking instructor Argiro Barbarigou included tomato paste, and that's what we call for here. Whereas traditional arakas kokkinistos is pea-centric, we've included a generous amount of potatoes and some carrots to give the stew-like dish enough substance and heft that it can be served as a vegetarian main. Lemon zest and juice added at the end, along with a generous dose of fresh herbs, brightens the flavors.

6 tablespoons extra-virgin olive oil, divided, plus more to serve

1 medium red onion, finely chopped

4 medium garlic cloves, minced

2 tablespoons tomato paste

2 medium carrots, peeled, halved lengthwise and cut into ½-inch pieces

1½ pounds Yukon Gold potatoes, unpeeled, cut into ½-inch pieces

Kosher salt and ground black pepper

2½ cups frozen peas

1 tablespoon finely grated lemon zest, plus 1 tablespoon lemon juice

¾ cup chopped fresh dill

½ cup chopped fresh mint

3 ounces feta cheese, crumbled (3 ounces)

In a large Dutch oven over medium-high, heat 3 tablespoons of the oil until shimmering. Add the onion and garlic, then cook, stirring occasionally, until the onion begins to turn translucent, about 3 minutes. Add the tomato paste and cook, stirring constantly, until the onion is well coated and the tomato paste is fragrant, 1 to 2 minutes. Add the carrots, potatoes, 2½ cups water, 1½ teaspoons salt and ¾ teaspoon pepper, then bring to a simmer. Cover, reduce to medium and cook until a knife inserted into a potato meets no resistance, 15 to 18 minutes.

Off heat, stir in the peas. Cover and let stand until the peas are warmed through, about 2 minutes. Stir in the remaining 3 tablespoons oil and the lemon zest and juice. Taste and season with salt and pepper. Stir in ½ of the dill and mint. Transfer to a serving bowl, sprinkle with the remaining herbs and feta, then drizzle with additional oil.

GREEK BAKED VEGETABLES

Start to finish: 50 minutes

Servings: 6

The Greek baked vegetable dish known as briam is an example of lathera (also spelled ladera)—vegetable-centric dishes that feature a generous amount of olive oil (lathi in Greek). In briam, potatoes give the dish weight and sub-stance, but it's the summer produce—such as zucchini, tomatoes, garlic and herbs—that are the main attraction. Because potatoes take longer to cook than juicier, less starchy vegetables, we give them a head start by parcooking them in the microwave. Crumbled feta cheese scattered on after baking provides salty, briny notes that play off the sweetness of the tender vegetables. Briam is excellent warm, but also delicious at room temperature.

2 pounds Yukon Gold potatoes, unpeeled, sliced ¼ inch thick

2 medium zucchini (about 8 ounces each), sliced into ½-inch-thick rounds

1 medium red onion, halved and thinly sliced

4 medium garlic cloves, thinly sliced

6 ripe plum tomatoes, 4 cored and chopped, 2 cored and sliced crosswise into ¼-inch-thick rounds

1 tablespoon plus ½ teaspoon dried oregano

¼ cup plus 2 teaspoons extra-virgin olive oil, plus more to serve

Kosher salt and ground black pepper

2 ounces feta cheese, crumbled (½ cup)

¼ cup lightly packed fresh basil, torn, or 3 tablespoons chopped fresh flat-leaf parsley or dill (or a combination)

Heat the oven to 475°F with a rack in the middle position. In a large microwave-safe bowl, combine the potatoes and ¼ cup water. Cover and microwave on high until the potatoes are just shy of tender, about 10 minutes, stirring once halfway through.

Pour off and discard any liquid in the bottom of the bowl. Add the zucchini, onion, garlic, the chopped tomatoes, the 1 tablespoon oregano, the ¼ cup oil, 1½ teaspoons salt and 1 teaspoon pepper. Toss well, then distribute evenly in a 9-by-13-inch broiler-safe baking pan. Lay the tomato slices on top, spacing them evenly. Drizzle with the remaining 2 teaspoons oil, then sprinkle with the remaining ½ tea-spoon oregano and ¼ teaspoon each salt and pepper. Bake until a skewer inserted into the vegetables meets no resistance, about 25 minutes.

Turn the oven to broil and broil until well browned, about 5 minutes. Remove from the oven and sprinkle with the feta. Let rest for about 10 minutes, then sprinkle with the basil and drizzle with additional oil.

Smashed Potatoes with Chili-Lemon Vinaigrette

Start to finish: 1 hour 20 minutes (25 minutes active)
Servings: 4

To make creamy-inside, crispy-outside potatoes, we first boil whole fingerlings or small Yukon Golds, then flatten and roast them in a very hot oven. We took a cue from Mokonuts, a popular Parisian café, and dressed the smashed potatoes with a tangy-spicy vinaigrette that nicely accents the potatoes' starchy, mildly sweet flavor. When boiling the potatoes, begin timing as soon as they're added to the water. To make ahead, the potatoes can be boiled, smashed, cooled and refrigerated a day in advance; to finish, brush with oil and roast as directed. The vinaigrette can be made in advance except for the chilies, then covered and refrigerated until ready to use; bring to room temperature and add the chilies.

2½ pounds fingerling potatoes or small (1- to 1½-inch) Yukon Gold potatoes

4 medium garlic cloves, peeled

3 rosemary sprigs

Kosher salt

¼ cup lemon juice

6 tablespoons extra-virgin olive oil, divided

1 small jalapeño or Fresno chili, stemmed and sliced into thin rings

¼ cup lightly packed fresh flat-leaf parsley, chopped

Heat the oven to 500°F with a rack in the middle position. In a large pot over high, bring 2 quarts water to boil. Add the potatoes, garlic, rosemary and ½ cup salt, then cook, uncovered and stirring occasionally, until a skewer inserted into the largest potato meets no resistance, 18 to 22 minutes.

Using a slotted spoon, transfer the potatoes to a wire rack set in a rimmed baking sheet (leaving the rosemary behind); place the garlic in a small bowl. Let the potatoes cool for about 10 minutes. Meanwhile, using a fork, mash

the garlic to a paste, then stir in the lemon juice and 2 tablespoons of oil, followed by the chilies; set aside.

After the potatoes have cooled slightly, carefully remove the rack from the baking sheet. Wipe away any moisture on the baking sheet and place the potatoes in an even layer directly on the sheet. Using the bottom of a dry measuring cup or ramekin, press down on each potato so it is slightly flattened and splits open but remains intact. Brush the tops of the potatoes with the remaining 4 tablespoons oil.

Roast the potatoes without turning them until browned and crisp, 35 to 40 minutes. Using a wide metal spatula, transfer to a serving platter, then sprinkle with the parsley and drizzle with the vinaigrette.

CHANGE THE WAY YOU COOK

Know Your Salts

We use kosher salt in our cooking because the larger granules are easier to measure and sprinkle with your fingers. **The two most common brands are Diamond Crystal Kosher Salt and Morton Coarse Kosher Salt; we use Morton.** Grains of Diamond Crystal are slightly larger and fluffier than those of Morton, which are dense and compact, so the same volume of Diamond is less salty than Morton. **If you use Diamond Crystal in our recipes, increase the amount called for to roughly double.** Flaky finishing salts, such as Maldon Sea Salt Flakes, add a delicious crunch and salty pop but should be used only at the table, not during cooking.

Type of salt	Grams per teaspoon	Grams per tablespoon	Grams per ¼ cup	Blanching vegetables or Salting Pasta Water (per 4 quarts water)
Table salt	6	20	80	1 tablespoon
Diamond Crystal kosher salt	3	10	40	2 tablespoons
Morton coarse kosher salt	5	15	70	1 heaping tablespoon
Fine sea salt	6	20	75	1 heaping tablespoon
Flaky sea salt (Maldon)	2	10	30	--

PATATAS BRAVAS

Start to finish: 1¾ hours (40 minutes active)

Servings: 6

Patatas bravas is a popular Spanish tapa, and for good reason. Potatoes fried until perfectly crisp and served piping hot with alioli (the Spanish version of aioli) and a smoked paprika sauce (called bravas sauce) have universal appeal. To avoid having to fry the potatoes—the classic preparation—we first parcook chunked russets in the microwave, then coat them with cornstarch and finish them on a well-oiled baking sheet in a hot oven. This technique delivers fluffy-creamy interiors and ultra crisp exteriors without the hassle and mess of deep-frying.

FOR THE POTATOES:

⅓ cup plus 1 tablespoon extra-virgin oil

3 pounds russet potatoes, peeled and cut into 1½- to 2-inch chunks

2 tablespoons cornstarch

Kosher salt

FOR THE ALIOLI:

2 medium garlic cloves, finely grated

2 tablespoons lemon juice or sherry vinegar

½ cup mayonnaise

2 tablespoons extra-virgin olive oil

Kosher salt

FOR THE BRAVAS SAUCE:

3 tablespoons extra-virgin olive oil, divided

1 medium shallot, minced

1 tablespoon all-purpose flour

½ to 1 teaspoon cayenne pepper

Kosher salt and ground black pepper

¼ cup sweet vermouth

2 teaspoons sherry vinegar

1 tablespoon smoked sweet paprika

FOR SERVING:

Kosher salt and ground black pepper

1 tablespoon smoked sweet paprika

To make the potatoes, heat the oven to 450°F with a rack in the middle position. Pour ⅓ cup oil onto a rimmed baking sheet and tilt to coat; set aside. In a large microwave-safe bowl, combine the potatoes and ¼ cup water. Cover loosely and microwave on high until just shy of tender, about 8 minutes, stirring once about halfway through.

Drain the potatoes, spread them on a kitchen towel and pat dry. Dry the bowl and return the potatoes to the bowl. Sprinkle with the cornstarch and ¾ teaspoon salt, then toss until evenly coated. Drizzle with the remaining 1 table-spoon oil and toss again. Distribute in an even layer on the prepared baking sheet and roast until deeply browned and well crisped, about 40 minutes, flipping with a metal spatula once halfway through.

While the potatoes roast, make the alioli and bravas sauce. To make the alioli, in a small bowl, mix the garlic and lemon juice, then let stand for 5 minutes. Whisk in the

mayonnaise, oil and ¼ teaspoon salt, then set aside until ready to serve.

To make the bravas sauce, in an 8-inch skillet over medium, heat 2 tablespoons of oil until shimmering. Add the shallot and cook, stirring, until just beginning to soften, about 2 minutes. Whisk in the flour, cayenne and ¼ teaspoon salt, then cook, whisking constantly, until the flour is very lightly browned, 1 to 2 minutes. Gradually whisk in the vermouth and ¼ cup water followed by the vinegar. Whisking con-stantly, bring to a full simmer, then remove from the heat. Whisk in the paprika and the remaining 1 tablespoon oil. Taste and season with salt and pepper, then transfer to a serving bowl; cover and set aside at room temperature until ready to serve.

When the potatoes are done, use a slotted spoon to transfer them to a serving dish. Sprinkle with paprika and salt and black pepper to taste, then toss. Serve with the alioli and bravas sauce.

MILK-SIMMERED MASHED POTATOES

Start to finish: 45 minutes

Servings: 4

These simple mashed potatoes are silky-smooth and rich, no heavy cream required. To achieve this, we simmer potatoes in milk, allowing them to absorb the dairy's flavor while retaining their starch, as opposed to washing it away with boiling water. We tested the technique with russets but found their texture too mealy. Yukon Golds, on the other hand, had the perfect amount of starch, yielding buttery mashed potatoes with a naturally creamy texture.

2 pounds Yukon Gold potatoes, peeled and cut into ½-inch chunks

2½ cups whole milk, plus more as needed

Kosher salt and ground black pepper

4 tablespoons salted butter, cut into 4 pieces

In a large saucepan, combine the potatoes, milk and 1 teaspoon salt. Bring to a simmer over medium, then reduce to low and cook, uncovered and stirring often, until the potatoes are beginning to fall apart and most of the milk has been absorbed, 30 to 40 minutes.

Remove the pan from the heat. Add the butter and, using a potato masher, mash the potatoes into an almost-smooth puree. If desired, thin with additional milk. Taste and season with salt and pepper.

GOCHUJANG-GLAZED POTATOES

Start to finish: 30 minutes

Servings: 4

Gamja jorim, or salty-sweet soy-simmered potatoes, is a common banchan (small plate) on the Korean table. For our version, we added gochujang (Korean fermented chili paste) for a little heat and extra umami. Yukon Gold potatoes 1½ to 2 inches in diameter worked best, but creamier potatoes were good, too. If your potatoes are very small (about 1 inch in diameter), cut them in half; if larger than 2 inches, cut them into eighths. Depending on the sugar content of your potatoes, they may or may not brown lightly as they cook before the soy mixture is added. This is a great side dish to grilled meats and seafood.

3 tablespoons plus 2 teaspoons soy sauce

¼ cup mirin

1 tablespoon gochujang

1 tablespoon white sugar

2 large garlic cloves, finely grated

Kosher salt and ground black pepper

1 tablespoon grapeseed or other neutral oil

2 pounds small Yukon Gold potatoes (1½ to 2 inches in diameter), quartered

2 teaspoons toasted sesame oil

2 teaspoons unseasoned rice vinegar

2 teaspoons sesame seeds, toasted

2 scallions, thinly sliced

In a small bowl, whisk together ½ cup water, 3 tablespoons of the soy sauce, the mirin, gochujang, sugar, garlic and ½ teaspoon each salt and pepper.

In a 12-inch nonstick skillet over medium, heat the oil until shimmering. Add the potatoes and stir to coat. Cover and cook, stirring occasionally, until the edges of the potatoes are translucent, 10 to 12 minutes.

Stir in the soy sauce mixture. Bring to a simmer over medium-high, then reduce to medium, cover and cook, stirring occasionally, until the tip of a knife inserted into the largest piece meets no resistance, about 10 minutes.

Uncover and cook over medium-high, stirring gently but frequently, until the liquid completely evaporates and the potatoes are glazed, about 5 minutes.

Off heat, stir in the remaining 2 teaspoons soy sauce, the sesame oil, vinegar and sesame seeds. Taste and season with salt and pepper. Transfer to a platter and sprinkle with scallions.

SUYA-SPICED ROASTED POTATOES WITH TOMATO-CHILI RELISH

Start to finish: 40 minutes
Servings: 4 to 6

Suya is a Nigerian street food of spiced meat threaded on skewers and grilled. We make our suya spice mix by processing peanuts, paprika, ginger, garlic and a touch of brown sugar and use it to add flavor and crunch to potatoes. We add a bit of oil and toss the mixture onto halved potatoes before roasting. A simple fresh tomato relish with chili and lime served on the side brightens up the dish.

½ cup unsalted dry-roasted peanuts

2 teaspoons sweet OR hot paprika

2 teaspoons ground ginger

2 teaspoons granulated garlic

1 teaspoon packed light brown sugar

Kosher salt and ground black pepper

3 tablespoons grapeseed or other neutral oil, divided

1½ pounds small (1½ to 2 inches) Yukon Gold OR red potatoes, halved

3 plum tomatoes, cored and finely chopped

1 medium shallot, finely chopped

1 serrano chili, stemmed, seeded and finely chopped

½ cup lightly packed fresh flat-leaf parsley, chopped

2 tablespoons lime juice

Heat the oven to 475°F with a rack in the middle position. Mist a rimmed baking sheet with cooking spray. In a food processor, combine the peanuts, paprika, ginger, garlic, sugar, ½ teaspoon salt and 1 teaspoon pepper. Process until finely ground, about 20 seconds. Add 2 tablespoons of the oil and pulse until evenly combined, 3 to 5 times, scraping the bowl as needed.

In a large bowl, toss the potatoes with the remaining 1 tablespoon oil and ¼ teaspoon salt. Add the nut-spice mixture and use your hands to toss and press the seasoning onto the potatoes so it sticks. Scrape the potatoes and any residual seasoning onto the prepared baking sheet, then distribute in an even layer. Roast until well browned all around and a skewer inserted into the potatoes meets no resistance, 20 to 25 minutes; use a metal spatula to turn the potatoes about halfway through.

While the potatoes roast, in a small bowl, stir together the tomatoes, shallot, chili, parsley, lime juice, and ½ teaspoon each salt and pepper. When the potatoes are done, transfer to a serving dish and sprinkle with salt. Serve with the tomato relish on the side.

INDIAN-SPICED SMASHED POTATOES

Start to finish: 1 hour 20 minutes (30 minutes active)
Servings: 4 to 6

These crisp on the outside, dense and creamy on the inside smashed potatoes are our riff on the gunpowder potatoes we loved at Dishoom, an Indian restaurant with multiple locations in the U.K. We simmer then drain skin-on potatoes, smash them until they crack open, then roast them on a baking sheet until the exteriors brown and crisp. Sliced jalapeños bring chili heat, and a trio of coarsely ground spices—cumin, coriander and fennel—add texture and warm, earthy flavor. We also like to include fenugreek, which has distinctive maple-like notes. If you cannot find it, simply omit. Blooming the spices in butter just before tossing with the smashed potatoes draws out their character while also infusing the fat for better distribution of flavor. Dishoom serves a cooling raita alongside the potatoes (recipe p. 69), but if you prefer a simpler accompaniment, offer lime wedges for squeezing.

**2½ pounds small (1- to 1½-inch) Yukon Gold,
red or fingerling potatoes**

Kosher salt and ground black pepper

3 tablespoons grapeseed or other neutral oil

**2 jalapeño chilies, stemmed and sliced
into thin rings**

2 teaspoons cumin seeds

2 teaspoons coriander seeds

2 teaspoons fennel seeds

4 tablespoons salted butter, cut into 4 pieces

¾ teaspoon ground fenugreek (optional)

3 scallions, thinly sliced

¼ cup finely chopped fresh cilantro

Lime wedges or raita, to serve

In a large pot, combine the potatoes, 3 tablespoons salt and 2 quarts water. Bring to a boil and cook, stirring occasionally, until a skewer inserted into the potatoes meets no resistance, about 25 minutes. Meanwhile, heat the oven to 500°F with a rack in the middle position.

Drain the potatoes in a colander. Transfer to a rimmed baking sheet and toss with the oil. Using the bottom of a dry measuring cup or ramekin, press down on each potato so it flattens slightly and splits open but remains intact. Roast without stirring for 20 minutes, then sprinkle evenly with the chilies. Continue to roast without stirring until the potatoes are crisp and well browned, another 10 to 15 minutes.

Meanwhile, in a spice grinder, combine the cumin, coriander and fennel seeds; pulse until coarsely ground. In a small saucepan over medium, melt the butter. Add the ground seeds and fenugreek (if using) and cook, swirling the pan, until fragrant, 2 to 3 minutes; set aside off heat.

When the potatoes are done, use a wide metal spatula to transfer them to a large bowl. Add the spiced butter; toss to coat. Fold in the scallions and cilantro. Taste and season with salt and pepper. Serve with lime wedges.

RAITA

Start to finish: 20 minutes
Makes about 1 cup

In a small bowl, stir together ¾ **cup plain whole-milk Greek yogurt, 3 tablespoons finely chopped fresh cilantro, 2 tablespoons lime juice, 2 tablespoons water, 1 jalapeño chili** (stemmed and minced), **1 scallion** (thinly sliced) and **kosher salt** and **ground black pepper,** to taste.

TAHINI-ROASTED SWEET POTATOES WITH ZA'ATAR

Start to finish: 50 minutes (20 minutes active)
Servings: 4

Two Middle Eastern pantry staples, tahini and za'atar, the seed and spice blend, boost the flavor of sweet potatoes. First we coat the potato wedges with tahini, za'atar and cornstarch, then roast them in a hot oven until golden brown and meltingly tender. The cornstarch helps bind the fatty tahini and produces a deliciously crisp coating. For the finishing sauce, we stir more tahini and za'atar into creamy yogurt, then add lime juice for a refreshing tang.

⅓ cup plus 3 tablespoons tahini, divided

2 tablespoons extra-virgin olive oil

2 tablespoons cornstarch

1 tablespoon plus 1 teaspoon za'atar, divided

Kosher salt and ground black pepper

2 pounds orange-fleshed sweet potatoes, peeled and cut into 1- to 1½-inch wedges

¾ cup plain whole-milk yogurt

1 teaspoon grated lime zest OR lemon zest, plus 2 tablespoons lime juice OR lemon juice

Heat the oven to 450°F with a rack in the lower-middle position. Line a rimmed baking sheet with kitchen parchment. In a small bowl, whisk together the ⅓ cup tahini and oil; set aside.

In a large bowl, whisk together the cornstarch, 1 tablespoon za'atar, 1 teaspoon salt and ½ teaspoon pepper. Add the sweet potatoes and toss to coat. Pour in the tahini mixture and rub the mixture into the potatoes; reserve the small bowl. Distribute in an even layer on the prepared baking sheet.

Roast until the potatoes are lightly browned on the bottom, about 15 minutes, rotating the baking sheet about halfway through. Remove from the oven and, using a thin metal spatula, flip each wedge. Roast until golden brown and a skewer inserted into the potatoes meets no resistance, about another 15 minutes, once again flipping the wedges and rotating the sheet halfway through.

Meanwhile, in the reserved bowl, whisk together the yogurt, lime zest and juice, the remaining 3 tablespoons tahini, the remaining 1 teaspoon za'atar and ¼ teaspoon each salt and pepper. Transfer the potatoes to a platter. Serve with the yogurt-lime sauce.

Optional garnish: Ground sumac OR Aleppo pepper OR chopped fresh flat-leaf parsley OR a combination

SUMMER TOMATO TIAN

Start to finish: 1¾ hours (15 minutes active), plus cooling
Servings: 4

In Provence, France, a tian is a casserole of sliced vegetables as well as the round, shallow earthenware vessel in which the dish is baked. A classic tian showcases an assortment of summer produce, but here the focus is on tomatoes seasoned with garlic and herbs. We opt exclusively for plum tomatoes, which are firmer and drier than regular round tomatoes, because they withstand long baking and yield deep, rich, concentrated flavor. Ripe, in-season tomatoes are best, of course, but even less-than-stellar fruits are good. We love this served warm with crusty bread and cheese, but the tomatoes can be refrigerated for up to a week and tucked into sandwiches or offered alongside grilled or roasted meats and seafood.

6 tablespoons extra-virgin olive oil, divided

4 medium garlic cloves, minced

2 pounds ripe plum tomatoes, cored and cut crosswise into ¼- to ½-inch slices

Kosher salt and ground black pepper

6 sprigs fresh basil OR 4 sprigs fresh rosemary

Crusty bread, to serve

Heat the oven to 425°F with a rack in the middle position. Coat the bottom and sides of a 9-inch pie plate with 2 tablespoons of oil. Sprinkle half of the garlic over the bottom. Arrange the tomatoes in concentric rings in the pie plate, shingling and tightly packing the slices.

Sprinkle with salt and pepper, then tuck the herb sprigs into the tomatoes and scatter on the remaining garlic. Drizzle evenly with the remaining 4 tablespoons oil. Bake until the tomatoes are browned, bubbling and meltingly tender, about 1½ hours. Cool for about 15 minutes. Serve with crusty bread.

Optional garnish: Burrata cheese OR fresh mozzarella cheese OR flaky sea salt

Soups

Homemade Vegetable Broth

Start to finish: 1¾ hours (35 minutes active), plus cooling
Makes about 2 quarts

Store-bought vegetable broth tends to be watery, sweet and lacking freshness. This homemade version has savoriness and depth of flavor, as well as body. In addition to the aromatics that are foundational, we coax umami out of cremini mushrooms and tomato paste by sautéing them until well-browned. We also add Yukon Gold potatoes, which soften and break down, lending the broth earthy flavor, richness and substance. A narrowish stockpot with about an 8-quart capacity is ideal, as liquid will not evaporate as quickly as it would in a Dutch oven. If a Dutch oven is the only option, partially cover the pot during simmering to prevent over-reduction.

2 tablespoons extra-virgin olive oil

8 ounces cremini mushrooms, sliced about ¼ inch thick

Kosher salt

1 tablespoon tomato paste

1 large yellow onion, halved and sliced

2 medium carrots, peeled and cut into rough 1-inch pieces

2 medium celery stalks, cut into rough 1-inch pieces

1 pound plum tomatoes, quartered

8 ounces Yukon Gold potatoes, unpeeled, sliced about about ¼ inch thick

1 bunch flat-leaf parsley

4 bay leaves

2 thyme sprigs or ½ teaspoon dried thyme

2 teaspoons black peppercorns

In a large (about 8-quart) pot, heat the oil over medium-high until just shimmering. Add the mushrooms and 1 teaspoon salt; cook, stirring occasionally, until well browned, about 5 minutes. Add the tomato paste and cook, stirring, until it begins to brown and stick to the pot, about 1 minute. Add 14 cups water, scraping up any browned bits. Add the onion,

carrots, celery, tomatoes, potatoes, parsley, bay, thyme and peppercorns. Bring to a boil over high, then reduce to medium-low and simmer, uncovered and stirring occasionally, for 1 hour.

Remove the pot from the heat. Cool for 15 minutes, then strain through a fine-mesh strainer set over a large bowl; press firmly on the solids to extract as much liquid as possible; discard the solids. You should have 2 quarts strained broth; if you have less, add water to reach that amount. Let the broth cool completely, then cover and refrigerate for up to 5 days or transfer to an airtight container and freeze for a few months.

SOUPE AU PISTOU

Start to finish: 35 minutes
Servings: 4

Soupe au pistou is a humble, hearty vegetable, bean and pasta soup from Provence. We learned our version from home cook Agnes Daragon, a Harley-driving nurse who teaches country dancing and grew up in her mother's restaurant. The soup takes its name from the pistou—a heady, pesto-like puree of basil, garlic, cheese and olive oil—that garnishes individual bowlfuls. To get the soup on the table fast, we opt for canned cannellini beans as well as store-bought pesto, but feel free to use homemade, if you like. We've found that supermarket refrigerated pesto sold near the fresh pasta typically has brighter, fresher flavor than shelf-stable jarred brands. Serve the soup with hunks of crusty bread.

**2 tablespoons extra-virgin olive oil,
plus more to serve**

1 medium yellow onion, chopped

1 pint cherry tomatoes

2 medium garlic cloves, finely chopped

1 quart low-sodium chicken broth

2 bay leaves

1 teaspoon dried thyme

Kosher salt and ground black pepper

4 ounces small pasta, such as ditalini or elbows

**1 medium (about 8 ounces) zucchini,
cut into ½-inch cubes**

**Two 15½-ounce cans cannellini beans,
rinsed and drained**

**4 tablespoons basil pesto, divided,
plus more to serve**

In a large pot over medium-high, heat the oil until shimmering. Add the onion and tomatoes, then cook, stirring occasionally, until the onion begins to brown and the tomatoes begin to break down, 5 to 7 minutes.

Add the garlic and cook, stirring, until fragrant, about 45 seconds. Add the broth, bay, thyme, 1 teaspoon each salt and pepper and 2 cups water, then bring to a simmer. Stir in the pasta and zucchini. Cook, uncovered and stirring occasionally, until the zucchini is almost tender, 5 to 6 minutes.

Add the beans and cook, stirring occasionally, until the pasta is al dente, the zucchini is completely tender and the beans are warmed through, 3 to 4 minutes. Remove and discard the bay. Using tongs, gently squeeze any tomatoes that are still whole so they burst.

Taste and season with salt and pepper. Ladle into bowls, then swirl 1 tablespoon pesto into each serving and drizzle with additional oil. Serve with additional pesto on the side.

INDIAN-SPICED BUTTERNUT SQUASH SOUP WITH YOGURT

Start to finish: 1 hour
Servings: 4

In his book "Bollywood Kitchen," filmmaker Sri Rao offers a pureed butternut squash soup with flavors that are bold and vibrant, yet comforting. Our adaptation, like his, includes fresh ginger and warm spices to complement the natural sweetness of squash. But because butternut often has a one-note flavor, we include carrots for earthiness and depth. A spoonful of yogurt and some spiced pumpkin seeds adds color and texture.

75

Stir in the ginger, cumin, coriander, ¼ teaspoon of cayenne and ½ teaspoon salt, then cook until fragrant, about 30 seconds. Pour in 5 cups water and bring to a simmer. Cover, reduce to medium-low and cook, stirring occasionally, until a skewer inserted into the squash meets no resistance, 10 to 15 minutes. Remove from the heat and let cool, uncovered, for about 15 minutes.

Meanwhile, in a 10-inch skillet over medium, stir together the remaining 1 teaspoon oil, the remaining ¼ to ½ teaspoon cayenne, the pumpkin seeds and ¼ teaspoon salt. Cook, stirring frequently, until toasted and fragrant, 3 to 5 minutes. Transfer to a small bowl and set aside.

Using a blender and working in 2 or 3 batches to avoid overfilling the jar, puree the squash mixture and its cooking liquid, processing until mostly smooth, 15 to 30 seconds. Return the pureed soup to the pot. Whisk in the yogurt and heat over low, stirring occasionally, just until warmed; do not allow the soup to simmer. (Alternatively, puree the soup directly in the pot with an immersion blender, then stir in the yogurt; the soup won't need reheating.) Taste and season with salt. Ladle the soup into serving bowls and top with additional yogurt and spiced pumpkin seeds just before serving.

- -

TOMATO-RICE SOUP WITH CARAMELIZED ONION

Start to finish: 45 minutes
Servings: 4

To deepen the flavor of this pantry staple soup, we caramelize an onion and simmer some of it into the soup; the rest is reserved for garnish. Though our preference is long-grain white rice (regular, jasmine or basmati), even starchy Arborio rice works. Long-grain brown rice is good, too, but be sure to increase the simmering time to 35 to 40 minutes. No matter what type of rice you use, rinse and drain it before adding it to the pot.

1 tablespoon extra-virgin olive oil, plus more to serve

1 large yellow onion, halved and thinly sliced

1 teaspoon white sugar

Kosher salt and ground black pepper

1 teaspoon dried thyme

---

2 tablespoons plus 1 teaspoon extra-virgin olive oil, divided

2-pound butternut squash, peeled, seeded and cut into ½-inch chunks (4 cups)

2 medium carrots, peeled and cut into ½-inch chunks

Kosher salt

1 medium yellow onion, chopped

1 tablespoon finely grated fresh ginger

1½ teaspoons ground cumin

1 teaspoon ground coriander

½ to ¾ teaspoon cayenne pepper, divided

½ cup pumpkin seeds

½ cup plain whole-milk yogurt, plus more to serve

In a large pot over medium-high, heat 2 tablespoons oil until barely smoking. Add the squash, carrots and 1 teaspoon salt, then cook, stirring occasionally, until the squash begins to brown, about 4 minutes. Add the onion and continue to cook, stirring occasionally, until the onion has softened, 3 to 4 minutes.

½ cup long-grain white rice, rinsed and drained
(see headnote)

14½-ounce can whole peeled tomatoes, crushed by hand

1 quart low-sodium chicken broth OR vegetable broth

½ cup lightly packed fresh flat-leaf parsley OR basil
leaves, chopped

In a large saucepan over medium, heat the oil until shimmering. Add the onion, sugar and ½ teaspoon each salt and pepper. Cook, stirring occasionally, until the onion is well browned, 12 to 15 minutes. Transfer half to a small bowl; set aside.

Add the thyme to the remaining onion in the pan and cook, stirring, until fragrant, about 30 seconds. Add the rice, tomatoes with juices and broth. Bring to a simmer over medium-high, then cover, reduce to medium and simmer, stirring occasionally, until the rice is tender, 18 to 20 minutes.

Off heat, stir in the parsley, then taste and season with salt and pepper. Garnish with the reserved onion and a drizzle of additional oil.

Optional garnish: Basil pesto **OR** finely grated Parmesan cheese **OR** both

Skip the Cream, Keep the Creaminess

We often enrich soups, stews and even some sauces by pureeing a portion of the vegetables or legumes with a bit of the cooking liquid.

For an especially creamy consistency, use a conventional blender or an immersion blender to puree about 1 cup cooked vegetables or beans with a bit of the cooking liquid, then return it to the pot.

For chunkier results, instead of using a blender, transfer the solids and liquid to a bowl and mash with a fork.

SOUPS

CREAM-FREE TOMATO BISQUE WITH PARMESAN CROUTONS

Start to finish: 40 minutes (20 minutes active)
Servings: 4

In our grown-up twist on that childhood favorite—a bowl of creamy tomato soup with grilled cheese for dipping—we created a silky bisque and serve it topped with crisp Parmesan croutons in place of a sandwich. Rather than thicken the soup with heavy cream, we simmer pieces of torn bread in the tomato broth, then blend everything to produce a satisfying soup with a velvety texture. Canned crushed tomatoes keep prep time to a minimum.

4 tablespoons salted butter, cut into 1-tablespoon pieces, divided

5 tablespoons extra-virgin olive oil, divided

8 ounces country-style white bread, crusts removed, torn into bite-size pieces (about 6 cups), divided

¾ teaspoon dried thyme OR dried oregano, divided

Kosher salt and ground black pepper

¼ teaspoon red pepper flakes (optional)

1 ounce Parmesan OR pecorino Romano cheese, finely grated (½ cup), plus more to serve

1 medium yellow onion, finely chopped

2 medium garlic cloves, smashed and peeled

28-ounce can crushed tomatoes

In a large pot over medium-high, melt 2 tablespoons butter with 2 tablespoons oil. Set aside 1½ cups torn bread for thickening the soup. Add the remaining bread, ½ teaspoon thyme, ¼ teaspoon each salt and black pepper, and the pepper flakes (if using) to the pot. Cook, stirring occasionally and lowering the heat as needed to prevent the seasonings from burning, until the bread is golden brown, 2 to 4 minutes. Transfer to a large plate, toss with the Parmesan and spread in a single layer. Set aside to cool and crisp.

In the same pot over medium, melt the remaining 2 tablespoons butter. Add the onion, garlic, ½ teaspoon salt and the remaining ¼ teaspoon thyme; cook, stirring occasionally, until the onion is translucent but not browned, 5 to 7 minutes. Stir in the tomatoes, the 1½ cups reserved bread and 4 cups water. Cook, uncovered and stirring occasionally, until the bread is completely soft and the broth is slightly

thickened, about 10 minutes. Remove from the heat and cool for about 5 minutes.

Using a blender and working in batches so the jar is never more than half full, puree the tomato mixture, streaming in the remaining 3 tablespoons oil, until smooth. Return the soup to the pot. (Alternatively, if you own an immersion blender, puree the soup directly in the pot; when almost smooth, slowly stream in the remaining 3 tablespoons oil while blending.) Cook over medium-low, stirring often, until heated through, 2 to 5 minutes. Thin the soup with water, if needed, to reach the desired consistency.

Off heat, taste and season with salt and black pepper. Serve topped with the croutons and sprinkled with additional Parmesan.

Optional garnish: Basil pesto

CORN CHOWDER WITH MISO AND SCALLIONS

Start to finish: 45 minutes
Servings: 4 to 6

This corn chowder, inspired by a corn side dish in "The Gaijin Cookbook" by Ivan Orkin and Chris Ying, is unconventional in a couple of ways. Instead of relying on an abundance of dairy for creaminess, we puree a portion of the cooked vegetables. This gives the soup body without blunting the delicate sweet, grassy notes of the corn, nor the earthiness of the potatoes. Secondly, white miso lends deep, umami-rich flavor, so there's no need for the salt pork or bacon typically used in corn chowder, nor even for chicken broth, so this soup is vegetarian-friendly. Fresh in-season corn is, of course, best—we cut the kernels from the ears and simmer the cobs right in the mix, which infuses the broth with maximum flavor. Out of season, frozen corn kernels are a decent stand-in. You won't have cobs for simmering, but the chowder still will be good. if you wish the chowder to have golden hue, stir in a pinch or two of ground turmeric.

3 tablespoons salted butter, cut into 2 or 3 pieces

1 bunch scallions, thinly sliced, white and green parts reserved separately

Kosher salt and ground black pepper

¼ cup white miso

¼ cup mirin

4 ears corn, husked, kernels cut from cobs (about 3 cups), cobs reserved

1 pound Yukon Gold potatoes, unpeeled, cut into ½-inch cubes

In a large Dutch oven over medium, melt the butter. Add the scallion whites and ½ teaspoon salt; cook, stirring occasionally, until softened but not browned, 3 to 5 minutes. Add the miso and cook, stirring to incorporate it into the scallion, until the miso is lightly browned, about 1 minute. Add the mirin and cook, stirring, until the liquid has mostly evaporated, about 1 minute. Stir in 6 cups water, then add the reserved corn cobs. Bring to a boil over medium-high, then stir in the corn kernels and potatoes. Return to a boil, then reduce to medium and simmer, uncovered and stirring occasionally, until the potatoes are tender, about 15 minutes.

Remove from the heat and cool for 5 to 10 minutes. Remove and discard the corn cobs. Transfer 1½ cups of the solids to a blender along with about ½ cup of the liquid. Puree until the mixture is smooth, about 1 minute.

Return the blended portion to the pot and stir. Bring to a simmer over medium, stirring occasionally. Remove from the heat, then taste and season with salt and pepper. Ladle into bowls and sprinkle with the scallion greens.

Optional garnish: Chili oil

CAULIFLOWER SOUP WITH HARISSA BUTTER

Start to finish: 45 minutes (20 minutes active)
Servings: 4 to 6

This soup gets a burst of bold, rich flavor as well as stunning color from a drizzle of harissa bloomed in browned butter. Look for harissa, a North African spice paste, in well-stocked supermarkets and Middle Eastern markets. Spiciness varies by brand so we suggest a range. We prefer to puree this soup in a conventional jar blender for a perfectly smooth, silky texture. If you own an immersion blender, though, you can puree it directly in the pot after the mixture has cooled for a few minutes; the texture will be a little chunkier. Pita chips served on the side offer contrasting crunchiness.

6 tablespoons salted butter, cut into 1-tablespoon pieces, divided

1 to 2 tablespoons harissa paste (see headnote)

1 large yellow onion, halved and thinly sliced

Kosher salt and ground black pepper

3-pound head cauliflower, trimmed and cut into 1-inch florets

1 quart low-sodium chicken OR vegetable broth

Chopped fresh dill, to serve

Pita chips, to serve

In a large pot over medium-high, melt 4 tablespoons of butter and cook, stirring often, until browned, 2 to 3 minutes. Add the harissa and cook, stirring, until fragrant, about 30 seconds, then transfer to a small bowl; set aside. In the same pot over medium, melt the remaining 2 tablespoons butter. Add the onion and ½ teaspoon salt, then cover and cook, stirring occasionally, until softened but not browned, 6 to 8 minutes. Add the cauliflower, broth and 3½ cups water. Bring to a simmer, cover and cook until the cauliflower is fully tender, 15 to 20 minutes. Cool uncovered for about 5 minutes.

Using a blender and working in 2 or 3 batches to avoid overfilling the jar, puree the mixture until smooth. Return the soup to the pot and reheat over medium, stirring, adding water as needed to thin. Taste and season with salt and pepper. Serve drizzled with the harissa butter, sprinkled with dill and with pita chips on the side.

CARROT AND ALMOND SOUP WITH MINT-SAFFRON YOGURT

Start to finish: 50 minutes
Servings: 4 to 6

This rich, creamy, elegant soup gets its velvety texture from pureeing carrots that are simmered until tender along with a small measure of smooth almond butter. Tangy yogurt mixed with lemon, mint and saffron is a colorful finishing touch on each bowlful that brightens the carrots' flavor and balances their natural sweetness. If you own an immersion blender, you can use it to puree the soup directly in the pot.

¼ teaspoon saffron threads, crumbled

1 tablespoon boiling water

2 tablespoons extra-virgin olive oil

1 medium yellow onion, chopped

¼ cup smooth almond butter

1 teaspoon ground coriander

Kosher salt and ground black pepper

1 pound carrots, peeled and chopped into 1½-inch pieces

1 quart low-sodium chicken broth OR vegetable broth

1 cup plain whole-milk yogurt

2 tablespoons lemon juice

¼ cup finely chopped fresh mint

In a small bowl, stir together the saffron and boiling water, then set aside to cool and allow the water to infuse.

Meanwhile, in a large saucepan over medium, heat the oil until shimmering. Add the onion and cook, stirring occasionally, until softened but not browned, about 5 minutes. Add the almond butter, coriander and 1 teaspoon each salt and pepper; cook, stirring, until fragrant, about 30 seconds. Add the carrots, broth and ½ cup water. Bring to a simmer, then reduce to medium-low and cook, uncovered and stirring occasionally, adjusting the heat as needed to maintain a gentle simmer, until a skewer inserted into the carrots meets no resistance, 20 to 25 minutes.

While the carrot mixture is simmering, in a small bowl, stir together the yogurt, lemon juice, mint and ¼ teaspoon each salt and pepper. Set a fine-mesh strainer over the bowl and pour the saffron water into the strainer; discard the solids in the strainer. Stir the yogurt mixture until well combined.

When the carrots are tender, remove the pan from the heat and cool for about 5 minutes. Using a blender and working in 2 or 3 batches to avoid overfilling the jar, puree the mixture until smooth. Return the soup to the pan and reheat over medium, stirring occasionally. Taste and season with salt and pepper. Serve topped with some of the yogurt mixture.

CREAMY ZUCCHINI AND PUMPKIN SEED SOUP

Start to finish: 45 minutes
Servings: 4

At Restoran August in Varaždin, Croatia, chef Goran Jelušić taught us this simple soup, called krem juha od tikvica sa bučinim košticama. "Krem" means cream, but the soup has no dairy in it. Instead, it gets its richness from toasted pumpkin seeds that are simmered then pureed with tender slices of zucchini; together they yield a silky, velvety texture. Fresh dill and lemon zest lift and brighten the flavors. Our inspiration recipe used pumpkin seed oil; if you can find it, use it in place of the olive oil—it will heighten the nuttiness of the toasted seeds. Vegetable broth and chicken broth work equally well here, so use whichever you prefer.

3 tablespoons extra-virgin olive oil or pumpkin seed oil

1 cup raw pumpkin seeds

1 medium yellow onion, halved and thinly sliced

Kosher salt and ground black pepper

2 tablespoons all-purpose flour

2 pounds zucchini, trimmed, halved lengthwise and cut into ½-inch pieces (7 cups)

1 bunch fresh dill, stems and leaves chopped, reserved separately

1 quart low-sodium vegetable or chicken broth

**1 teaspoon grated lemon zest, plus
1 lemon cut into wedges**

Crème fraîche, to serve (optional)

In a large Dutch oven over medium, combine the oil and pumpkin seeds. Cook, stirring often, until fragrant and lightly toasted, about 5 minutes. Using a slotted spoon, transfer to a small bowl; set aside.

To the pot over medium, add the onion and ½ teaspoon salt. Cook, stirring occasionally, until softened but not browned, 5 to 8 minutes. Add the flour and cook, stirring constantly, until evenly moistened, about 1 minute. Add the zucchini and dill stems, stirring well, then stir in the broth and ⅔ cup of the toasted pumpkin seeds. Bring to a boil over medium-high, then reduce to medium and cook, uncovered and stirring, at a vigorous simmer, until the zucchini is translucent, 5 to 10 minutes.

Remove the pot from the heat and cool for 5 minutes. Using a blender and working in batches so the jar is never more than half full, puree until smooth; transfer each batch to a large bowl.

Wipe out the pot, then pour in the puree. Cook over low, stirring often, until heated through, about 5 minutes. Off heat, stir in the dill leaves and lemon zest, then taste and season with salt and pepper. Ladle the soup into bowls, dollop with crème fraîche (if using) and sprinkle with the remaining ⅓ cup pumpkin seeds. Serve with lemon wedges.

CREAMY PINTO BEAN AND TOMATO SOUP

Start to finish: 35 minutes
Servings: 4 to 6

A Tarascan soup from the state of Michoacán in central Mexico inspired this satisfying pantry-centric soup that can be on the table in under 45 minutes. Fire-roasted tomatoes add a subtle smokiness and the lime juice stirred in at the end adds brightness. Finish the smooth, velvety soup with a garnish or two to add contrasting colors, flavors and textures; see below for suggestions.

½ medium white OR yellow onion, halved

3 medium garlic cloves, smashed and peeled

14½-ounce can diced fire-roasted tomatoes

1 tablespoon chili powder

Kosher salt and ground black pepper

2 tablespoons extra-virgin olive oil

Two 15½-ounce cans pinto beans, rinsed and drained

2 cups low-sodium chicken broth OR vegetable broth

1 teaspoon dried oregano, preferably Mexican oregano

2 tablespoons lime juice, plus lime wedges to serve

In a blender, combine the onion, garlic, tomatoes with juices, chili powder and ½ teaspoon each salt and pepper. Blend until smooth, about 1 minute, scraping the jar as needed.

In a large saucepan over medium, heat the oil and the tomato puree until it comes to a simmer; reserve the blender jar. Cook, stirring occasionally and reducing the heat if the mixture begins to spatter, until slightly thickened, 4 to 5 minutes. Meanwhile, add the beans and broth to the blender and blend until smooth, 1 minute.

Add the bean puree to the pan along with the oregano. Bring to a simmer over medium and cook, stirring occasionally, until the soup is lightly thickened, 5 to 6 minutes.

Off heat, stir in the lime juice. Taste and season with salt and pepper. Serve with lime wedges.

Optional garnish: Diced avocado OR chopped fresh cilantro OR sour cream (or Mexican crema) OR crumbled queso fresco OR crumbled tortilla chips OR a combination

SPICY BLACK BEAN AND COCONUT SOUP

Start to finish: 50 minutes
Servings: 4 to 6

Nigerian frejon, a smooth puree of beans and coconut milk, inspired this rich, flavorful soup that happens to be vegetarian (even vegan). We blend only a portion of the bean mixture so the soup is lightly thickened, not a heavy puree, with lots of texture from creamy whole beans. If you have coconut oil in the pantry, use it in place of the neutral oil—it will add extra coconut flavor and aroma.

2 tablespoons grapeseed or other neutral oil (see headnote), divided

½ medium red onion, finely chopped, plus more to serve

3 medium garlic cloves, chopped

14½-ounce can coconut milk

2 jalapeño chilies, stemmed, halved and seeded

¼ teaspoon ground allspice

½ teaspoon dried thyme OR 1 teaspoon minced fresh thyme

Kosher salt

Four 15½-ounce cans black beans, rinsed and drained

1½ tablespoons lime juice, plus lime wedges to serve

In a large pot over medium-high, heat 2 tablespoons oil until shimmering. Add the onion and cook, stirring occasionally, until translucent, 5 to 7 minutes. Add the garlic and cook, stirring, until fragrant, about 1 minute. Add 2½ cups water, the coconut milk, jalapeños, allspice, thyme and ¾ teaspoon salt, then bring to a simmer. Add the beans and simmer, uncovered and stirring occasionally, for 20 minutes.

Remove the pot from the heat and cool for 10 minutes. Transfer 3 cups of the bean mixture to a blender along with the jalapeños and puree until smooth. Return the puree to the pot and bring to a simmer over medium.

Off heat, stir in the lime juice, then taste and season with salt. Ladle into bowls and garnish with chopped onion; serve with lime wedges.

Optional garnish: Chopped plum tomatoes

83

Miso-Based Broths

Start to finish: 10 minutes
Makes 1 quart

Miso, a savory-salty fermented bean paste, is a building block of countless Japanese soups. It's also an excellent shortcut for making a quick batch of broth that tastes long-simmered. Miso is made from soybeans that have been fermented with a grain. White miso uses rice and it is slightly sweet. Red miso uses more soybeans, plus barley and often undergoes a longer fermentation; it is better for heartier applications such as stews. These broths can be cooled and stored in the refrigerator for up to five days. The miso will settle upon standing, so stir to recombine before using.

Red Miso Broth

In a large saucepan over medium, combine **4 medium garlic cloves** and **2 tablespoons tomato paste**. Cook until the tomato paste has browned, 2 to 3 minutes. Add **4 cups water**, then whisk in **½ cup red miso**. Bring to a simmer, then reduce to medium-low and cook for 5 minutes. Strain through a fine-mesh strainer.

White Miso Broth

In a large saucepan over medium, cook **4 medium garlic cloves**, **1 ounce fresh ginger**, peeled and smashed, and **1 medium shallot**, roughly chopped until beginning to brown, about 2 minutes. Add **4 cups water**, then whisk in the miso. Bring to a gentle simmer, then reduce to medium-low and cook for 5 minutes. Strain through a fine-mesh strainer.

MISO RAMEN

Start to finish: 35 minutes
Servings: 4

Rich, umami-packed miso ramen originates in Sapporo in northern Japan, where hearty, soul-warming fare is welcomed during the cold winter months. Our much-simplified rendition of the classic noodle soup may raise eyebrows among ramen purists, but we think the recipe delivers solid flavor with minimal effort. Miso supplies flavor, color and character to the broth; we prefer red (or aka) miso for its assertiveness, but milder, sweeter white (shiro) miso works, too. Dashi, an umami-rich stock and a building block in the Japanese kitchen, is essential here. You can make your own (recipe p. 85) or use instant dashi that requires only water for dissolving or steeping. Look for instant dashi in Asian grocery stores or the international aisle of the supermarket. We've kept the garnishes minimal, but as an extra flourish, you could add a halved soft-cooked egg to each bowl.

8 ounces ground pork

1½ tablespoons finely grated fresh ginger

6 medium garlic cloves, finely grated

1 tablespoon soy sauce

1 tablespoon toasted sesame oil

1 tablespoon mirin

4 scallions, thinly sliced (about 1 cup), divided

½ cup red miso or white miso (see headnote)

1 quart low-sodium chicken broth

1 quart dashi (see headnote)

Kosher salt

1 pound non-instant dried ramen noodles

¾ cup frozen corn kernels, thawed and patted dry

4 thin slices salted butter (optional)

Shichimi togarashi or chili oil, to serve (optional)

In a large saucepan, combine the pork, ginger, garlic, soy sauce, sesame oil, mirin and 2 tablespoons water. Mix with your hands until well combined.

Set the pan over medium-high and cook, stirring often and breaking the meat into small pieces, until the meat is no longer pink, 2 to 3 minutes. Add ½ cup of the scallions and

the miso; cook, stirring, until the ingredients are well combined and the mixture is heated through, about 1 minute. Stir in the broth and dashi, then bring to a simmer. Reduce to medium and cook, uncovered and stirring occasionally, for 15 minutes.

When the broth is nearly done, in a large pot, bring 4 quarts water to a boil. Add the ramen and cook, stirring occasionally, until tender. Drain in a colander, rinse under warm water and drain again, shaking the colander to remove as much water as possible. Divide the noodles among 4 serving bowls.

Taste the broth and season with salt. Ladle the broth over the noodles. Top each bowlful with the remaining scallions, corn and a slice of butter (if using). Serve with shichimi togarashi or chili oil (if desired).

HOMEMADE DASHI

Start to finish: 20 minutes
Makes about 4½ cups

Japanese dashi is an umami-rich stock and a building block for countless dishes. This recipe for basic dashi is based on Sonoko Sakai's kombu and bonito dashi formula in "Japanese Home Cooking." The recipe can easily be halved or doubled. The dashi will keep well in the refrigerator in an airtight container for a couple days.

4-inch square (about ½ ounce) kombu

3½ to 4 cups (about 1 ounce) lightly packed bonito flakes (katsuobushi)

In a medium saucepan over medium, heat the kombu and 6 cups water to just below a simmer. Remove the kombu (discard it or reserve it for another use) and bring the liquid to a boil over medium-high. Turn off the heat, add the bonito flakes (katsuobushi) and steep for about 2 minutes.

Pour the broth through a fine-mesh strainer set over a medium bowl. Discard the bonito. Use the dashi right away or cool, cover and refrigerate for up to 2 days.

TOFU AND KIMCHI SOUP

Start to finish: 40 minutes
Servings: 4

This flavorful soup is a much-simplified version of Korean kimchi jjigae. It comes together quickly, but has loads of flavor thanks to a few high-impact ingredients, namely soy sauce, kimchi and gochujang, a fermented chili paste that we consider a staple. Bacon takes the place of the pork that's commonly used in kimchi jjigae; its smokiness works perfectly with the spiciness and fermented notes of both kimchi and gochujang, and its fat lends the soup just enough richness. Be sure to reserve the juices that drain from the kimchi, as they're great for adding salty tang to the soup at the end, if needed. Serve with steamed rice on the side.

2 slices bacon, finely chopped

1 bunch scallions, white parts thinly sliced, green parts cut into 1-inch pieces, reserved separately

6 cups low-sodium chicken broth

1½ tablespoons soy sauce, plus more if needed

3 to 4 tablespoons gochujang

2 tablespoons mirin

14-ounce container firm OR extra-firm tofu, drained, patted dry and cut into ½-inch cubes

2 cups cabbage kimchi, drained (juices reserved) and roughly chopped

In a large saucepan over medium, cook the bacon, stirring, until lightly browned, about 2 minutes. Pour off and discard all but 1 tablespoon of the fat. Add the scallion whites and cook, stirring, until softened, about 1 minute. Add the broth and bring to a simmer, scraping up any browned bits. Whisk in the soy sauce, gochujang and mirin. Bring to a simmer and cook uncovered for 15 minutes.

Pour off and discard any water released by the tofu, then add the tofu and kimchi to the saucepan; stir to combine. Return to a simmer and cook, stirring occasionally, until heated through, about 10 minutes. Off heat, stir in the scallion greens; let stand for about 5 minutes. Taste and, if desired, stir in additional soy sauce and some or all of the reserved kimchi juices.

Optional garnish: Toasted sesame oil **OR** toasted sesame seeds **OR** halved soft-cooked eggs **OR** a combination

PORTUGUESE-STYLE POTATO, KALE AND SAUSAGE SOUP

Start to finish: 50 minutes (20 minutes active)
Servings: 4

Known as caldo verde in Portugal, this hearty soup traditionally is made with linguiça or chouriço, but just about any type of smoked, spiced sausage, including kielbasa or Cajun andouille, yields a flavorful potful. Often, water is used as the base for the soup, though chicken broth, which we call for here, deepens the flavor. Some versions are brothy, with the potatoes left in chunks, while others are pureed and thick. We chose to puree, including some of the sausage, which yields a rich, well-seasoned soup. Then the kale is added at the end and cooked briefly so it offers textural contrast and vibrant color.

3 tablespoons extra-virgin olive oil, plus more to serve

8 ounces kielbasa OR linguiça sausage, quartered lengthwise and sliced ½ inch thick

1 medium yellow onion, chopped

4 medium garlic cloves, smashed and peeled

1 pound russet OR Yukon Gold potatoes, peeled and cut into 1-inch chunks

1 quart low-sodium chicken broth

3 bay leaves

1 small bunch lacinato kale OR curly kale, stemmed and finely chopped (about 6 cups)

1 tablespoon white wine vinegar

Kosher salt and ground black pepper

In a large pot over medium, combine the oil and sausage. Cook, stirring occasionally, until lightly browned, 3 to 4 minutes. Using a slotted spoon, transfer to a plate; set aside.

To the fat in the pot, add the onion and garlic, then cook over medium, stirring occasionally, until golden brown, 4 to 6 minutes. Add the potatoes, stirring to coat with the fat, then add half of the sausage, the broth, bay and 3 cups water. Bring to a simmer over medium-high, then reduce to medium-low and simmer, uncovered and stirring occasionally, until the potatoes are tender, 10 to 15 minutes. Remove the pot from the heat and let the soup cool for about 5 minutes. Remove and discard the bay.

Using a blender and working in batches so the jar is never more than half full, puree the soup until smooth, 1 to 2 minutes, then return the soup to the pot. Add the kale and the remaining sausage; cook, uncovered, over medium-high, stirring often and scraping along the bottom to prevent scorching, until the soup has thickened slightly and the kale is just tender, 3 to 5 minutes.

Off heat, stir in the vinegar, then taste and season with salt. Serve with a generous grinding of pepper and a drizzle of additional oil.

FARRO SOUP WITH CELERY AND PARMESAN

Start to finish: 1 hour (25 minutes active)

Servings: 4

This soup is remarkably flavorful, though it's made with just a handful of basic ingredients. It features farro, an ancient wheat grain that boasts a pleasantly chewy texture and nutty taste. Be sure to use pearled farro; the grains have had the bran removed, which speeds up the cooking. Quick-cooking barley is a great alternative to farro. To boost the umami, we first brown tomato paste, then finish the soup with a shower of grated Parmesan. If you have a Parmesan rind on hand, add it to the simmering soup to deepen the flavor.

3 tablespoons extra-virgin olive oil

1 medium yellow onion, halved and thinly sliced

4 medium celery stalks, thinly sliced

1 teaspoon dried rosemary OR dried thyme

Kosher salt and ground black pepper

2 tablespoons tomato paste

1 cup pearled farro OR quick-cooking barley

1-inch piece Parmesan rind (optional), plus 2 ounces Parmesan cheese, finely grated (1 cup)

2 quarts low-sodium chicken broth OR vegetable broth

In a large saucepan over medium-high, heat the oil until shimmering. Add the onion, celery, rosemary, ¼ teaspoon salt and ½ teaspoon pepper. Reduce to medium and cook, stirring often, until the vegetables begin to release their moisture, about 2 minutes. Reduce to medium-low, cover and cook, stirring occasionally, until the vegetables are softened but not browned, 10 to 15 minutes.

Add the tomato paste and cook over medium-high, stirring, until the paste browns and slightly sticks to the pan, about 2 minutes. Add the farro and stir until the grains are well combined with the paste. Add the Parmesan rind (if using) and the broth. Bring to a simmer, then reduce to medium and simmer, uncovered, stirring once or twice, until the farro is tender with a little chew, 25 to 30 minutes.

Off heat, remove and discard the Parmesan rind (if used). Taste and season with salt and pepper. Serve sprinkled with Parmesan and a generous grind of pepper.

Optional garnish: Basil pesto

SOUPY RICE WITH CHICKEN, BOK CHOY AND MUSHROOMS

Start to finish: 30 minutes
Servings: 4

Soupy rice, a classic Chinese dish, is a way to turn leftover cooked rice into a meal. Our version, however, starts with uncooked rice and simmers it in a blend of chicken broth and water before a simple stir-fry of shiitake mushrooms, chicken and bok choy is stirred in. Partially freezing the chicken thighs makes them easier to cut into bits.

8 ounces boneless, skinless chicken thighs, cut into rough ¼-inch pieces

1½ tablespoons oyster sauce

Kosher salt and ground white pepper

1 quart low-sodium chicken broth

1½ cups jasmine rice, rinsed and drained

1 tablespoon grapeseed or other neutral oil

8 ounces fresh shiitake mushrooms, stems removed and caps thinly sliced

1 tablespoon grated fresh ginger

1 pound baby bok choy, trimmed and cut crosswise into ½-inch pieces

5 scallions, thinly sliced

Toasted sesame oil or chili oil, to serve

In a small bowl, stir together the chicken, oyster sauce and ¼ teaspoon white pepper. Set aside. In a large Dutch oven over medium-high, combine 4 cups water, the broth, rice and 1 teaspoon salt. Bring to a boil, stirring occasionally. Reduce to low, cover and simmer, stirring once or twice, until the rice is tender, about 8 minutes.

While the rice cooks, in a 12-inch nonstick skillet over medium-high, heat the neutral oil until barely smoking. Add the mushrooms and ¼ teaspoon salt and cook, stirring, until softened and shrunken in size, 3 to 4 minutes. Add the chicken and cook, stirring, until no longer pink, about 3 minutes. Stir in the ginger. Turn off the heat, stir in the bok choy and set aside until the rice is ready.

When the rice is tender, quickly stir in the bok choy–chicken mixture. Turn off the heat, cover and let stand until the bok choy stems are crisp-tender, about 3 minutes. Taste and season with salt and white pepper. Ladle the rice into bowls. Sprinkle with additional white pepper and scallions, then drizzle with sesame oil.

CHICKPEA AND HARISSA SOUP

Start to finish: 1 hour, plus soaking the chickpeas
Servings: 8

This brothy-bready Tunisian chickpea soup, called lablabi, gets punches of flavor from garlic, tomato paste, harissa paste and cumin. Instead of using stale bread—as is common in Tunisia—we got better texture by toasting chunks of crusty bread in olive oil. Toasted ground cumin is used in the soup as well as on it. To be efficient, toast all 4 tablespoons at once in a small, dry skillet over medium, stirring constantly until fragrant, about one minute.

FOR THE SOUP:

2 cups dried chickpeas

Kosher salt and ground black pepper

5 tablespoons extra-virgin olive oil, divided

1 large yellow onion, chopped

6 medium garlic cloves, minced

2 tablespoons tomato paste

2 tablespoons ground cumin, toasted

6 tablespoons harissa paste

3 quarts low-sodium chicken broth or water

8 ounces crusty white bread, sliced ½-inch-thick and torn into bite-size pieces

2 tablespoons lemon juice

FOR SERVING:

8 soft-cooked eggs, peeled and halved

½ cup drained capers

½ cup chopped pitted green olives

½ cup chopped fresh flat-leaf parsley

½ cup chopped fresh cilantro

Extra-virgin olive oil

Harissa paste

2 tablespoons ground cumin, toasted

Lemon wedges

First, soak the chickpeas. In a large bowl, combine 2 quarts water, the chickpeas and 1 tablespoon salt. Let soak at room temperature for at least 12 hours or up to 24 hours. Drain the chickpeas and set aside.

To make the soup, in a large Dutch oven, heat 2 tablespoons of the oil until shimmering. Add the onion and cook, stirring occasionally, until lightly golden, about 5 minutes. Stir in the garlic and cook until fragrant, about 30 seconds. Add the tomato paste and cook, stirring, until it browns, about 2 minutes. Stir in the cumin and harissa, then cook until fragrant, about 1 minute. Add the chickpeas and broth, then bring to a boil over high. Reduce to medium and simmer, uncovered, until the chickpeas are tender, stirring occasionally, about 1 hour.

Meanwhile, in a 12-inch nonstick skillet over medium, combine the bread, the remaining 3 tablespoons oil and ½ teaspoon salt. Cook, stirring occasionally, until the bread is crisp and light golden brown, 4 to 6 minutes. Remove from the heat and let the croutons cool in the pan, then transfer to a bowl.

When the chickpeas are tender, remove the pot from the heat and stir in the lemon juice. Taste and season with salt and pepper.

To serve, place 2 to 3 tablespoons of croutons in each serving bowl. Ladle chickpeas and broth around them, then top each portion with soft-cooked egg halves and 1 tablespoon each capers, olives, parsley and cilantro, or as desired. Drizzle with oil and garnish to taste with harissa and cumin. Serve with lemon wedges.

WHITE BEAN SOUP WITH BROCCOLI RABE AND PARMESAN

Start to finish: 1 hour
Servings: 4 to 6

This quick soup stars hearty greens and creamy white beans. Browned garlic and tomato paste, as well as an optional Parmesan rind, enhance store-bought broth, adding depth, umami and richness. Poaching a whole head of garlic in the broth mellows its flavor; the result is reminiscent of roasted garlic. We squeeze out the softened cloves and mash them with some beans to mix into the broth, adding body to the soup. Warm crusty bread is the perfect accompaniment.

3 tablespoons extra-virgin olive oil, divided, plus more to serve

1 head garlic, top third cut off and discarded

2 tablespoons tomato paste

Two 15½-ounce cans cannellini OR great northern beans, rinsed and drained

Kosher salt and ground black pepper

1 quart low-sodium chicken broth OR vegetable broth

1-inch piece Parmesan rind (optional), plus finely grated Parmesan cheese, to serve

1-pound bunch broccoli rabe, trimmed and roughly chopped OR 1 large head escarole, chopped

In a large pot over medium, heat 2 tablespoons oil until shimmering. Add the garlic head cut side down and cook until well browned, 2 to 3 minutes. Transfer to a small plate; set aside.

To the same pot over medium, add the tomato paste and cook, stirring, until it browns and slightly sticks, 2 to 3 minutes. Stir in the beans, 3 cups water and ½ teaspoon each salt and pepper, scraping up any browned bits. Return the garlic to the pot, then add the broth and Parmesan rind (if using). Bring to a simmer over medium-high, then reduce to medium, cover partially, and cook, stirring, until a skewer inserted into the largest garlic clove meets no resistance, 25 to 30 minutes.

Using tongs, remove the garlic head and squeeze the cloves onto a large plate; discard the skins. Using a slotted spoon, transfer about ½ cup beans to the plate with the garlic. Drizzle the garlic and beans with the remaining 1 tablespoon oil, then use a fork to mash them to a smooth paste.

Stir the garlic-bean mixture into the pot. Add the rabe and simmer, stirring, until tender, 5 to 6 minutes. Off heat, remove and discard the Parmesan rind (if used). Taste and season with salt and pepper. Serve sprinkled with grated Parmesan and drizzled with additional oil.

Optional garnish: Red pepper flakes

CHANGE THE WAY YOU COOK

Broth Boosters

Store-bought broth is one of our shelf stalwarts; it can really help get a weeknight supper going. But while convenient, it can be a bit one-note and bland. Here are some ways we add flavor to ready-made broth without adding a lot of work.

Browned tomato paste is one of our umami standbys and it works for broth, too. At the start of the recipe, add 1 to 2 tablespoons of tomato paste to the pot with an equal amount of olive oil. Cook, stirring constantly, until browned and coating the pan, about 2 minutes. Add chicken or vegetable broth, scraping the bottom of the pan and stirring the paste into the liquid. We use this technique for our garlicky white bean soup (recipe p. 89), and paprika-pinto bean soup (recipe p. 91).

Don't throw away the **rinds from your Parmesan cheese.** Instead, save them and add one or two chunks to brothy soups and stews. For a medium to large potful, aim for a couple inches of rind in total, but even just a small piece will improve flavor. As the liquid simmers, the rind softens and releases tons of richness. Be sure to taste the dish before seasoning with salt; the Parmesan adds plenty of that, too. And don't forget to discard the rind before serving.

In Greece, we learned that **extra-virgin olive oil** gives soup body and fruity richness. We often use it at the start of the recipe—as the fat to soften or lightly brown vegetables, for example—then again just before serving. Depending on the soup, we might whisk additional oil into the pot or simply drizzle more onto individual bowlfuls to reinforce the peppery richness.

Poached garlic is another easy way to add flavor to a broth. When simmering soups and stews, we often cut off the top third of a whole head of garlic. We then add it directly to the liquid and simmer it along with the other ingredients. By the time the dish is done, the garlic cloves are tender and can be squeezed out (tongs are ideal for this) and mashed or whisked into the liquid. For added depth, we sometimes brown the cut side of the head in olive oil before adding it to the liquid.

PAPRIKA-PINTO BEAN SOUP
WITH COLLARD GREENS

Start to finish: 50 minutes
Servings: 6 to 8

This recipe was loosely inspired by Portuguese feijoada, a rustic stew of beans, cabbage, sausage and multiple cuts of pork. Tomato paste is browned early in the cooking process to bring depth and umami to this hearty dish. For the meat, we opted for chorizo, a flavor-packed sausage that boasts a robust, smoky taste. Be sure to use Spanish chorizo, a dry-cured sausage with a firm, sliceable texture, not fresh Mexican chorizo. Canned beans streamline prep. Collards simmer low and slow for about half an hour, becoming meltingly tender.

2 tablespoons extra-virgin olive oil, plus more to serve

2 medium yellow onions, finely chopped

Kosher salt and ground black pepper

4 ounces Spanish chorizo, quartered lengthwise and cut into ½-inch pieces

¼ cup tomato paste

2 tablespoons sweet paprika

Two 15½-ounce cans pinto beans OR pink beans, rinsed and drained

1 bunch collard greens OR lacinato kale, stemmed, leaves chopped

In a large Dutch oven over medium, heat 2 tablespoons oil until shimmering. Add the onions and ½ teaspoon salt; cook, stirring occasionally, until lightly browned, about 10 minutes. Add the chorizo and tomato paste, then cook, stirring often, until the paste browns and slightly sticks to the pan, about 2 minutes.

Add the paprika, beans, collard greens and 8 cups water. Bring to a boil over medium-high, then cover, reduce to low and simmer, stirring occasionally, until the greens are very tender, about 30 minutes. Off heat, taste and season with salt and pepper. Serve drizzled with additional oil.

GREEK WHITE BEAN SOUP

Start to finish: 1½ hours, plus soaking time for beans
Servings: 6

Carrots lend sweetness to this soup that's balanced by briny olives and salty feta cheese. Half are added at the start and the rest at the end to preserve their taste and texture. Dried cannellini beans that are soaked before cooking yield a full-flavored soup. To soak the beans, in a large bowl, stir together 2 quarts water and 1 tablespoon kosher salt. Add the beans, soak at room temperature for at least 12 hours or up to 24 hours, then drain well. Canned beans work in a pinch; see instructions below. We use extra-virgin olive oil to give the soup a little body and fruity, peppery richness throughout, as we were shown by Argiro Barbarigou, one of Greece's leading voices on classic cooking. We vigorously whisk in a few tablespoons just before serving. Refrigerate leftovers in an airtight container for up to two days; reheat in a saucepan over low, adding water as needed to thin the consistency.

6 tablespoons extra-virgin olive oil, divided,
plus more to serve

1 large red onion, chopped

3 medium celery stalks, chopped

3 medium carrots, peeled and chopped, divided

Kosher salt and ground black pepper

4 medium garlic cloves, minced

½ teaspoon red pepper flakes

3 tablespoons tomato paste

1 pound dried cannellini beans, soaked and
drained (see headnote)

2½ quarts low-sodium chicken broth

4 teaspoons red wine vinegar

½ cup finely chopped fresh flat-leaf parsley

½ cup pitted Kalamata olives, chopped

2 ounces feta cheese, crumbled (½ cup)

In a large pot over medium, heat 3 tablespoons of oil until shimmering. Add the onion, celery, half the carrots and ¼ teaspoon salt, then cook, stirring occasionally, until the vegetables begin to brown, about 5 minutes. Add the garlic and red pepper flakes, then cook, stirring, until fragrant, about 30 seconds. Add the tomato paste and cook, stirring, until the paste begins to brown, about 2 minutes. Stir in the beans and the broth, then bring to a simmer over medium-high. Cover partially, reduce to low and simmer, stirring occasionally, until the beans are tender, about 1 hour.

Using a slotted spoon, transfer 1 cup of the beans to a medium bowl. Using a potato masher or fork, mash the beans to a paste, then whisk the mixture back into the soup. Add the remaining carrots, bring to a simmer over medium and cook, stirring occasionally, until the carrots are just tender, about 10 minutes.

Off heat, stir in the vinegar, then vigorously whisk in the remaining 3 tablespoons oil. Taste and season with salt and pepper. Ladle into bowls and top with the parsley, olives and cheese.

GREEK WHITE BEAN SOUP (FASOLADA) WITH CANNED BEANS:

Rinse and drain **four 15½-ounce cans cannellini beans**; measure 1 cup of the beans into a medium bowl, then use a potato masher or fork to mash to a paste. Follow the recipe as written, making the following changes: Add all of the carrots at once; reduce the broth to 1½ quarts; and add both the whole and mashed beans at once. After bringing to a simmer over medium-high, reduce to medium-low, cover and cook, stirring occasionally and maintaining a gentle simmer, until the carrots are just tender, about 20 minutes. Finish the soup off heat as directed.

TURKISH RED LENTIL SOUP

Start to finish: 45 minutes
Servings: 4

Kırmızı mercİmek çorbası is a traditional Turkish soup made with red lentils, which soften and break down during cooking, adding a rustic texture that's creamy but not starchy or heavy. Some versions include vegetables such as potatoes, carrots or fresh tomatoes, but ours lets the lentils take the lead. The Aleppo pepper brings gentle heat to the dish. If you can't find it, order online or substitute with an additional teaspoon of paprika and ½ teaspoon red pepper flakes. The soup can be made vegan by substituting olive oil for the butter.

3 tablespoons salted butter

**1 medium yellow onion cut into
½-inch dice (about 1 cup)**

1 medium garlic clove, finely grated

1 tablespoon tomato paste

1 tablespoon sweet paprika

½ teaspoon ground cumin

1 cup red lentils

2 tablespoons long-grain white rice

Kosher salt

3 tablespoons extra-virgin olive oil

2 teaspoons Aleppo pepper (see headnote)

Chopped fresh mint, to serve (optional)

Lemon wedges, to serve

In a large saucepan over medium, melt the butter. Add the onion and cook, stirring occasionally, until softened and translucent, about 5 minutes. Add the garlic and cook until fragrant, about 30 seconds. Stir in the tomato paste, paprika and cumin, then cook for about 1 minute.

Add the lentils, rice, 5 cups of water and 1 teaspoon salt. Stir to combine then bring to a boil over medium-high. Reduce the heat to maintain a lively simmer, cover and cook, stirring occasionally, until the lentils and rice are tender and broken down, about 30 minutes. Season to taste.

Meanwhile, in a small skillet over medium, heat the oil, swirling to coat the pan. Add the Aleppo pepper and cook until a few bubbles appear and the oil is bright red. Remove from heat and set aside.

Serve the soup with Aleppo pepper oil drizzled over each serving. Serve with mint, if using, and lemon wedges on the side.

UMBRIAN LENTIL SOUP

Start to finish: 1 hour

Servings: 4 to 6

In her kitchen in Perugia, Italy, home cook Silvia Buitoni taught us how to make brothy but hearty Umbrian lentil soup, or zuppa di lenticchie, a regional classic and a fine example of rustic Italian cooking. Of utmost importance, of course, are the lentils. Golden in tone with a pale green cast, Castelluccio lentils, which are grown in the Umbrian village of the same name, are the backbone of this simple but satisfying dish. Their flavor is nutty, earthy and subtly sweet, and though they become tender and plump with cooking, they still retain their shape beautifully and don't break down as they cook. Castelluccio lentils are worth seeking out in Italian markets or online—but if you can't find them, opt instead for French lentils du Puy, which are green-gray in color and have similar texture and flavor characteristics. Puy lentils may take a little longer to cook, so be sure to taste them for doneness.

3 tablespoons extra-virgin olive oil, plus more to serve

1 medium yellow onion, chopped

2 medium celery stalks, halved lengthwise and chopped

2 medium carrots, peeled, halved lengthwise and cut into ¼-inch pieces

Kosher salt and ground black pepper

2 medium garlic cloves, finely grated

3 tablespoons tomato paste

1¼ cups Castelluccio lentils (see headnote) or lentils du Puy, rinsed and drained

1 tablespoon minced fresh rosemary

¼ to ½ teaspoon red pepper flakes

Finely grated Parmesan cheese, to serve

In a Dutch oven over medium-high, heat the oil until shimmering. Add the onion, celery, carrots and ½ teaspoon salt; cook, stirring occasionally, until the vegetables are lightly browned, about 5 minutes. Add the garlic and cook, stirring, until fragrant, about 30 seconds. Add the tomato paste and cook, stirring often, until the paste begins to brown and stick to the bottom of the pot, about 2 minutes.

Add 6 cups water and scrape up any browned bits. Stir in the lentils, rosemary and pepper flakes. Bring to a simmer, stirring often, then cover and reduce to medium-low and simmer, stirring occasionally, until the lentils are just shy of tender, about 40 minutes.

Uncover, increase the heat to medium and cook, stirring occasionally, until the lentils are fully tender and the soup has thickened slightly, 8 to 10 minutes. Taste and season with salt and black pepper. Serve drizzled with additional oil and sprinkled with Parmesan.

POLENTA SOUP WITH CRISPY PANCETTA AND KALE

Start to finish: 40 minutes (15 minutes active)

Servings: 4

This is our take on polentina, a traditional Italian peasant soup that's not much more than brothy polenta. We add pancetta, leeks and rosemary to give the dish complexity and round out the flavor of the corn. Topped with broth-blanched kale laced with sweet-tart pickled peppers, this soup is a light but satisfying meal in a bowl.

1 tablespoon extra-virgin olive oil, plus more to serve

3 ounces thinly sliced pancetta

2 leeks, white and light green parts only, halved lengthwise and thinly sliced

Return the broth to a simmer over medium-high, then gradually whisk in the cornmeal. Reduce to medium-low and cook uncovered until the polenta is tender, about 20 minutes, stirring frequently and adjusting the heat as needed to maintain a slow simmer. Taste and season with salt and pepper.

Stir the Peppadew peppers and remaining 1 teaspoon rosemary into the kale. Ladle the soup into serving bowls, then top with the kale. Crumble the pancetta over the top, drizzle with additional oil and sprinkle with Parmesan.

GREEK-INSPIRED FISH SOUP WITH RICE AND LEMON

Start to finish: 45 minutes

Servings: 4

The Greek fish soup called psarosoupa traditionally is made with homemade fish broth. It typically is chunky with vegetables and sometimes rich and creamy with tempered egg, but it's always brightened with a generous amount of lemon juice and enriched with fruity olive oil. Our much-simplified version is easy enough for a weeknight dinner. We use store-bought chicken (or vegetable) broth as the primary liquid, but we boost the umami factor and seafood flavor with a couple tablespoons of Asian fish sauce. Just before serving, drizzle individual bowlfuls with olive oil as a finishing touch.

4 teaspoons minced fresh rosemary, divided

2 quarts low-sodium chicken broth

Kosher salt and ground black pepper

1 bunch lacinato kale, stemmed, leaves torn into 1-inch pieces

½ cup coarse stone-ground yellow cornmeal

⅓ cup drained Peppadew Sweet Picanté Peppers, chopped

Finely grated Parmesan cheese, to serve

In a large pot over medium, add the oil and pancetta. Cook, stirring occasionally, until crisp, 6 to 10 minutes. Using a slotted spoon, transfer the pancetta to a paper towel-lined plate.

To the pot, add the leeks and 3 teaspoons of rosemary, then cook, stirring occasionally, until the leeks are golden brown and tender, 3 to 5 minutes. Add the broth, ¾ teaspoon salt and ½ teaspoon pepper, then stir to scrape up any browned bits. Bring to a simmer over medium-high, stir in the kale and cook until tender, 2 to 4 minutes. Using a slotted spoon, transfer the kale to a medium bowl (it's fine if some of the leeks come with the kale); set aside.

2 tablespoons extra-virgin olive oil, plus more to serve

3 medium celery stalks, roughly chopped

2 medium carrots, peeled and roughly chopped

Kosher salt and ground black pepper

2 tablespoons fish sauce

½ cup long-grain white rice, rinsed and drained

1 quart low-sodium chicken broth OR vegetable broth

1 teaspoon dried oregano

1 pound skinless cod fillets, cut into 2-inch pieces

¼ cup lemon juice

In a large Dutch oven over medium, heat the olive oil until shimmering. Add the celery, carrots and ¼ teaspoon each salt and pepper. Cook, stirring occasionally, until the vegetables are slightly softened, about 5 minutes. Stir in the fish sauce, followed by the rice, broth, oregano and 2 cups water. Bring to a boil over medium-high, then reduce to medium and simmer, uncovered and stirring occasionally, until the rice is tender and the broth has thickened slightly, 15 to 18 minutes.

Remove the pot from the heat. Add the fish, then quickly cover and let stand until the fish is opaque throughout and flakes easily, 6 to 8 minutes. Gently stir in the lemon juice, then taste and season with salt and pepper. Serve drizzled with additional oil.

Optional garnish: Chopped fresh flat-leaf parsley OR chopped fresh dill

VIETNAMESE-STYLE HOT-AND-SOUR SOUP WITH SHRIMP

Start to finish: 35 minutes
Servings: 4

Vietnamese hot-and-sour soup with shrimp, called canh chua tôm, bursts with fresh, bright, contrasting flavors. This is our pantry-friendly version of that dish. Jalapeño chili provides the "hot" and lime juice brings the "sour." Canned, frozen or fresh pineapple works well, so use whichever is most convenient or that you happen to have. Cilantro or bean sprouts added as a garnish really enhance this soup; top bowls with one or, even better, both.

1 tablespoon grapeseed or other neutral oil

1 medium yellow onion, halved and thinly sliced

6 cups low-sodium chicken broth

2 teaspoons grated lime zest, plus 2 tablespoons lime juice, plus lime wedges to serve

1 pint cherry OR grape tomatoes, halved

1 cup drained juice-packed canned pineapple chunks OR chopped slices OR thawed frozen pineapple chunks OR chopped fresh pineapple

1 jalapeño chili, stemmed and sliced into thin rounds, plus more to serve

3 tablespoons fish sauce, plus more if needed

12 ounces extra-large (21/25 per pound) shrimp, peeled and deveined

In a large pot over medium-high, heat the oil until shimmering. Add the onion and cook, stirring occasionally, until starting to brown, about 5 minutes. Add the broth and lime zest, then bring to a boil over medium-high. Stir in the tomatoes, pineapple, jalapeño and fish sauce; cook at a vigorous simmer, uncovered and stirring occasionally, until the tomatoes begin to soften, about 5 minutes.

Add the shrimp, cover and remove from the heat. Let stand until the shrimp are opaque throughout, 4 to 5 minutes. Stir in the lime juice. Taste and stir in additional fish sauce, if needed. Serve garnished with additional jalapeño slices and lime wedges on the side.

Optional garnish: Chopped fresh cilantro OR bean sprouts OR both

One-Hour Homemade Chicken Broth

Start to finish: 1 hour
Makes 2 quarts

Instead of the hours of simmering that classic chicken broths call for, our five-ingredient version delivers rich flavor and body in just under an hour, start to finish. We simmer chicken wings or drumsticks until they give up most of their flavor and collagen, yet the meat remains good enough to be put to another use (see What to Do with Leftover Drumsticks or Wings, below). It's a good idea to leave the broth salt-free or only lightly seasoned; if it's paired with salty ingredients or used in a recipe that calls for reduction, the dish won't end up overseasoned. Refrigerate the broth in an airtight container for up to five days or freeze for up to a month.

1 large yellow onion, chopped

6 large garlic cloves, smashed and peeled

2 bay leaves

2 teaspoons black peppercorns

3 pounds chicken drumsticks or wings

Kosher salt (optional)

In a large pot over high, combine 2½ quarts water, the onion, garlic, bay and peppercorns. While the water heats, use a sharp knife to make several slashes in the skin and flesh on both sides of each drumstick or wing, cutting all the way to the bone. Add the pieces to the pot as they are prepped.

When all the chicken is in the pot, cover and bring to a boil. Uncover, reduce to medium, and cook at a vigorous simmer for 35 minutes. Strain through a fine-mesh strainer set over a large bowl; discard the solids or, if desired, remove the chicken and reserve for another use. If desired, season with salt.

What to Do With Leftover Drumsticks or Wings

If you used drumsticks, remove the meat, discarding the skin and bones; you'll have about 3 cups meat for making chicken salad or adding to soups. If you used wings, discard the tips (if present), toss the drumettes and flats with about 1 cup

barbecue sauce and arrange in an even layer on a foil-lined rimmed baking sheet; broil about 4 inches from the element until well browned on both sides, 8 to 10 minutes total, flipping the wings about halfway through

SOUPS

97

Instant Pot Chicken Broth

The Instant Pot takes the effort out of homemade broth; our version takes just 10 minutes hands-on time. Chicken wings, which contain ample collagen, yield a rich, full-bodied broth. Store in an airtight container in the refrigerator for up to five days or freeze for up to a month.

Start to finish: 1½ hours, plus cooling (10 minutes active)
Makes about 10 cups

3½ to 4 pounds chicken wings

1 large yellow onion, halved and thinly sliced

2 bay leaves

Kosher salt

In a 6-quart Instant Pot, combine the chicken, onion, bay, ½ teaspoon salt and 2 quarts water.

Lock the lid in place and move the pressure valve to **Sealing.** Select **Pressure Cook** or **Manual**; make sure the pressure level is set to **High.** Set the cooking time for 1 hour. When pressure cooking is complete, let the pressure release naturally for 20 minutes, then release any remaining steam by moving the pressure valve to **Venting.** Press **Cancel,** then carefully open the pot.

Cool for about 30 minutes. Strain the broth through a fine-mesh strainer set over a large bowl. Cool to room temperature, then use a wide spoon to skim off and discard any fat on the surface. (Alternatively, once the broth has cooled, cover and refrigerate until cold, then scrape the congealed fat off the surface.)

SPANISH GARLIC SOUP

Start to Finish: 45 minutes
Servings: 4

José Andrés taught us this "end of month" recipe—the sort of meal to make quickly with whatever is on hand and money is tight. His approach: garlic cooked in copious amounts of olive oil with handfuls of thinly sliced stale bread and several tablespoons of smoked paprika. Add some water and simmer, then off heat stir in four or five whisked eggs. Supper is served. For our version, we realized the leftover bread, garlic and smoked paprika we had in our cupboards weren't up to Andrés' standards. So we needed to tweak. We boosted flavor by using low-sodium chicken broth instead of plain water, and we sautéed both sweet and smoked paprika with garlic and scallions. We actually didn't have stale bread, so we turned a loaf of rustic sourdough (a baguette or any crusty loaf will do) into delicious croutons. To serve, the soup and croutons are married in the serving bowls, allowing each person to adjust the ratio of soup to bread, as well as how long they soak.

6 scallions, trimmed and thinly sliced, whites and greens separated

6 medium garlic cloves, thinly sliced

6 tablespoons extra-virgin olive oil, divided, plus extra

4 teaspoons sweet paprika

1½ teaspoons smoked paprika

6 ounces sourdough or other rustic bread, cut into ½-inch cubes (about 4 cups), divided

1½ quarts low-sodium chicken broth

Kosher salt and ground black pepper

4 large egg yolks

2 tablespoons sherry vinegar (optional)

In a medium saucepan over medium-low, combine the scallion whites, garlic and 3 tablespoons of the oil. Cook, stirring occasionally, until beginning to color, 8 to 10 minutes. Add both paprikas and cook, stirring, until fragrant and darkened, 30 seconds.

Add 1 cup of the bread cubes and stir well. Whisk in the broth, increase heat to medium-high and bring to a simmer. Reduce heat to medium-low and simmer, whisking occa-

sionally to break up the bread, for 15 minutes. Whisk vigorously to ensure the bread is thoroughly broken up.

Meanwhile, in a 12-inch skillet over medium, combine the remaining 3 tablespoons oil, the remaining 3 cups bread, the scallion greens, and ½ teaspoon each salt and pepper. Cook, stirring occasionally, until browned and crisp, 8 to 10 minutes.

In a medium bowl, whisk the egg yolks. Slowly whisk in 1 cup of the hot broth. Remove the soup from the heat. Off heat, vigorously whisk the egg yolks into the soup, then whisk in the vinegar, if using. Taste and season with salt and pepper. To serve, fill individual bowls with the crouton mixture, then ladle the soup over them. Drizzle with additional oil, if desired.

CHICKEN SOUP WITH RICOTTA DUMPLINGS

Start to finish: 2 hours (1 hour active), plus chilling
Servings: 4

Polpette di ricotta, or ricotta "meatballs" (named only for their round shape, not because they contain meat), are from Calabria in southern Italy. In the humble soup known as polpette di ricotta in brodo, the "meatballs" are gently poached in hot broth, where they turn into light, tender dumplings. The mildness of the ricotta allows the savory, pleasantly funky flavor of pecorino to come to the fore. For our version, we enhance store-bought chicken broth by simmering in a few aromatic vegetables plus bone-in chicken thighs that later provide shredded meat to make the soup more substantial. The dumpling mixture needs at least an hour or up to 24 to chill and hydrate before shaping, and the formed dumplings require at least 30 minutes in the refrigerator to firm up before cooking, so plan accordingly. If convenient, the broth can be made in advance and refrigerated in an airtight container for up to three days. But if making ahead, it's best to wait to shred the chicken until just before serving.

3 slices (5 ounces) hearty white sandwich bread, crusts removed, torn into pieces

1½ ounces (without rind) pecorino Romano cheese, cut into rough ½-inch chunks, plus finely grated pecorino Romano cheese, to serve

1 cup whole-milk ricotta cheese

2 large egg yolks

¼ teaspoon grated nutmeg

Kosher salt and ground black pepper

2 quarts low-sodium chicken broth

2 pounds bone-in, skin-on chicken thighs, trimmed

1 large yellow onion, cut into large chunks

2 medium carrots, peeled and cut into thirds or fourths

2 medium celery stalks, cut into thirds or fourths ½ cup all-purpose flour

¼ cup finely chopped fresh flat-leaf parsley

In a food processor, combine the bread and pecorino chunks; process until finely ground, about 30 seconds. Add the ricotta, egg yolks, nutmeg, and ½ teaspoon each salt and pepper; process until smooth, about 1 minute, scraping the bowl as needed. Transfer to a medium bowl, cover and refrigerate for at least 1 hour or up to 24 hours.

In a large Dutch oven, combine the broth, chicken thighs, onion, carrots and celery. Bring to a simmer over medium-high, then reduce to low, cover and simmer until a skewer inserted into the chicken meets no resistance, about 45 minutes. Remove the pot from the heat.

Using tongs, transfer the chicken to a medium bowl; set aside until cool enough to handle. Meanwhile, using a slotted spoon, remove and discard the vegetables from the broth. Taste the broth and season with salt and pepper; set aside. Using 2 forks or your hands, shred the chicken into bite-size pieces; discard the skin and bones. Cover and set aside until ready to use.

Line a rimmed baking sheet with kitchen parchment. Have ready the flour in a pie plate or other shallow dish. Scoop the chilled ricotta mixture into 16 portions, each about a generous tablespoon, onto the prepared baking sheet. Using your hands, form the portions into balls, drop them into the flour and toss to coat. Shake off the excess and return the dumplings to the baking sheet. Refrigerate uncovered for at least 30 minutes or up to 1 hour.

Return the broth to a simmer over medium. Gently add the dumplings and return the broth to a simmer. Cover and cook, adjusting the heat as needed to maintain a simmer (do not allow the broth to boil), for 10 minutes; the dumplings will rise to the surface and expand.

Using a slotted spoon, divide the dumplings among individual bowls. Let rest for about 5 minutes to allow the dumplings to firm up; they will slump slightly as they cool. Divide the shredded chicken among the bowls and sprinkle each portion with parsley. Ladle in the hot broth and sprinkle with grated pecorino.

SOMALI CHICKEN SOUP

Start to finish: 50 minutes
Servings: 4

This is our take on maraq cad, the Somali soup known for its finishing touches, which are added at the last moment so they retain bright bold flavor and texture. We were taught how to make it by Somalia native and Massachusetts food consultant Nimco Mahamud-Hassan. Serve this soup family style: Bring the pot to the table along with the radishes, cabbage and lime wedges, then have diners fill and garnish their bowls as they like. Offer a simple homemade or storebought hot sauce alongside. Hot steamed rice, added to bowls before the soup is ladled in, is a satisfying addition.

1 tablespoon grapeseed or other neutral oil

2 large yellow onions, chopped

Kosher salt and ground white pepper

2 serrano chilies, stemmed and sliced into thin rounds

4 medium garlic cloves, smashed and peeled

4 teaspoons ground coriander

2 teaspoons ground cardamom

1 bunch fresh cilantro, stems chopped, leaves finely chopped, reserved separately

4 plum tomatoes, cored, seeded and chopped, divided

1½ quarts low-sodium chicken broth or water

Four 12-ounce bone-in, skin-on chicken breasts

1½ cups jasmine or basmati rice, rinsed and drained

2 tablespoons lime juice, plus lime wedges, to serve

Thinly sliced radishes and/or chopped red cabbage, to serve (optional)

Green chili sauce, berbere sauce or other hot sauce, to serve (see recipes p. 102)

In a large Dutch oven over medium, heat the oil until shimmering. Add the onions and ¼ teaspoon salt and cook, stirring, until beginning to brown, about 5 minutes. Add the chilies, garlic, coriander, cardamom, cilantro stems and half of the tomatoes. Cook, stirring constantly, until fragrant, about 30 seconds.

Add the broth and bring to a simmer over high. Submerge the chicken breasts, cover and cook over low until the chicken registers 160°F and is no longer pink at the thickest part, about 30 minutes.

Meanwhile, in a medium saucepan, combine the rice, 2 cups water and ½ teaspoon salt. Bring to a simmer over medium-high, then reduce to low and cook, covered, until the liquid is absorbed and the rice is tender, 15 to 20 minutes. Off heat, remove the lid, lay a clean dish towel over the pot, replace the cover and let stand for about 10 minutes or until ready to serve.

Using tongs, transfer the chicken to a large plate and set aside to cool. Pour the broth through a fine-mesh strainer set over a large heatproof bowl; discard the solids. Return the broth to the pot. When the chicken is cool enough to handle, shred the meat into bite-size pieces, discarding the skin and bones.

Add the chicken to the broth and bring to a simmer over medium-high. Remove from the heat and stir in the remaining tomatoes, the cilantro leaves and lime juice. Taste and season with salt and pepper.

To serve, fluff the rice with a fork, then mound a portion into each serving bowl. Ladle the soup over the rice, then top each portion with radishes and/or cabbage (if using) and the hot sauces. Serve with lime wedges.

GREEN CHILI SAUCE

Start to finish: 5 minutes
Makes about 1 cup

This sauce is spicy and sharp on its own, but a spoonful stirred into a serving of soup provides the perfect flavor accent. Store leftovers in an airtight container in the refrigerator for up to a week.

1 plum tomato, cored and quartered

5 serrano chilies, stemmed

3 tablespoons lime juice

2 large garlic cloves, smashed and peeled

¾ teaspoon kosher salt

In a blender, combine all ingredients and process until smooth, 1 to 2 minutes, scraping the sides as needed.

BERBERE SAUCE

Start to finish: 15 minutes
Makes about ¼ cup

For this bold, paste-like sauce, macerating the onion in lime juice tempers its harsh bite. For a brighter flavor, substitute sweet paprika instead of smoked. This sauce is best used the day it is made.

3 tablespoons lime juice

1 tablespoon minced red onion

¼ teaspoon kosher salt

1 tablespoon smoked paprika

1 teaspoon ground coriander

1 teaspoon ground ginger

½ teaspoon cayenne pepper

¼ teaspoon ground cardamom

In a small bowl, stir together the lime juice, onion and salt. Let stand for 10 minutes. Meanwhile, in a small skillet over medium-low, toast the paprika, coriander, ginger, cayenne and cardamom, stirring constantly, until fragrant, 1 to 2 minutes. Remove from the heat and let cool for 10 minutes. Stir the spices into the lime juice-onion mixture.

CHICKEN AND VEGETABLE SOUP WITH CHIPOTLE CHILIES

Start to finish: 1 hour
Servings: 6

In Mexico City, Josefina López Méndez, chef at Chapulín restaurant, taught us to make a chicken and vegetable soup brimming with layers of delicious flavors. Called caldo tlalpeño, Mendez' soup was boldly seasoned with aromatics and was subtly smoky and spicy with chipotle chilies. Chickpeas, we later learned, are a common ingredient in classic caldo tlalpeño, but Méndez favors rice—she ladled the finished soup over already cooked rice that had been divided among individual bowls. We slightly streamlined the process, using some of the broth that becomes the soup to steam the rice. Last-minute garnishes—avocado, cheese and cilantro—soften with the heat of the broth, their flavors and aromas mixing and mingling. Méndez offered a charred habanero salsa on the side to be stirred in to taste. The spicy, tangy, bitter notes made the soup even more dynamic. Our version of her salsa follows; we highly recommend making a batch if you can, though the soup is terrific even without.

1 pound ripe tomatoes, cored and quartered

1 large white onion, quartered

2 chipotle chilies in adobo sauce, plus 1 tablespoon adobo sauce

6 medium garlic cloves, smashed and peeled

1 bunch cilantro, stems roughly chopped, leaves chopped, reserved separately

2 tablespoons grapeseed or other neutral oil

2 pounds bone-in, skin-on chicken thighs, trimmed and patted dry

2 quarts low-sodium chicken broth

1½ cups long-grain white rice, rinsed and drained

2 medium zucchini, quartered lengthwise and sliced about ¼ inch thick

12 ounces green beans, trimmed and cut on the diagonal into ½-inch pieces

Kosher salt and ground black pepper

1 ripe avocado, halved, pitted, peeled and chopped

2 ounces (½ cup) queso fresco cheese, crumbled, or queso Oaxaca cheese, shredded

Charred habanero salsa (see following recipe), to serve

Lime wedges, to serve

In a blender, combine the tomatoes, onion, chipotle chilies and adobo sauce, garlic and cilantro stems. Blend until smooth, scraping the blender jar as needed, about 2 minutes; set aside.

In a large Dutch oven over medium-high, heat the oil until barely smoking. Add the chicken skin side down and cook, without disturbing, until well browned, about 10 minutes. Transfer to a large plate. Add the tomato-onion puree to the pot and cook, scraping up any browned bits, until a spatula drawn through the mixture leaves a trail, 6 to 8 minutes. Stir in the broth, return the chicken to the pot and pour in any accumulated juices. Bring to a simmer, then cover, reduce to medium and cook, stirring occasionally and adjusting the heat as needed to maintain a simmer, until a skewer inserted into the largest thigh meets no resistance, about 30 minutes. Remove the pot from the heat. Using tongs, transfer the chicken to a clean plate; set aside.

Measure 2¼ cups of the hot broth into a large saucepan and add the rice. Bring to a simmer over medium-high, then cover, reduce to low and cook without stirring until the rice has absorbed the liquid, about 18 minutes. Remove from the heat, uncover, drape a kitchen towel across the pan and re-cover. Let stand until ready to serve.

While the rice cooks, use 2 forks or your hands to shred the chicken into bite-size pieces; discard the skin and bones. Set the shredded meat aside.

Bring the broth in the Dutch oven to a simmer over medium. Add the zucchini and green beans; cook, stirring occasionally, until the beans are tender-crisp, about 5 minutes. Remove the pot from the heat, then stir in the chicken and about half of the cilantro leaves. Taste and season with salt and pepper.

Using a fork, fluff the rice, then divide it among individual bowls. Ladle the soup over the rice. Top each serving with avocado, cheese and the remaining cilantro leaves. Serve with the salsa and lime wedges.

CHARRED HABANERO SALSA

Start to finish: 30 minutes
Makes about ½ cup

This salsa, known as salsa de habanero tatemado, is at once fruity, spicy, bitter, tangy and subtly sweet—owing mostly to the intense charring of the chilies and alliums. (Due to the stovetop charring, you may wish to turn on the hood and/or open a window during cooking.) We adapted the recipe taught to us by Josefina López Méndez. The habaneros are kept whole for easier turning. For more timid palates, remove some or all of the seeds. A little of this fiery salsa goes a long way.

5 habanero chilies, whole

2 medium garlic cloves, unpeeled

½ medium red onion, cut into ½-inch wedges, layers separated

2 tablespoons lime juice

Kosher salt

Heat a 10-inch cast-iron skillet over medium-high until water flicked onto the surface immediately sizzles and evaporates. Add the chilies, garlic and onion; cook, occasionally turning each item, until completely blackened, about 20 minutes. If charring at different rates, transfer each item to a plate when done. The chilies and garlic cloves should be softened and the onions should be crisp. Set aside until cool enough to handle.

Peel the garlic. Trim off and discard the stems from the habaneros; if desired, seed some or all of the chilies. In a blender, combine the garlic, chilies, onion, lime juice, ¼ cup water and ¼ teaspoon salt. Process until almost smooth, about 15 seconds, scraping the blender jar as needed. Taste and season with salt. If serving right away, transfer to a small bowl; if storing, transfer to an airtight container and refrigerate for up to 1 week.

THAI HOT-AND-SOUR SOUP WITH CHICKEN AND MUSHROOMS

Start to finish: 1 hour (30 minutes active)
Servings: 4

Tom yum is a classic Thai soup that is spicy, sour and savory. It also is intensely fragrant and flavorful with Southeast Asian aromatics, including lemon grass, galangal and makrut lime leaves. On a trip to Bangkok, we learned to make tom yum gai—the chicken version—from home cook and food blogger Rawadee Yenchujit. Back home, we needed to substitute ginger and lime zest for the harder-to-find galangal and makrut lime leaves. If you can find fresh galangal, use an equal amount in place of the ginger. And if you're able to get fresh makrut, use 10 sets of leaves (they grow in pairs) in place of the lime zest. The chili paste, sometimes referred to as chili "jam"—nam prik pao in Thai—is a common addition to tom yum. Made by blending shallots, garlic, dried chilies, shrimp paste, tamarind, oil and other ingredients, the paste brings complexity and color to the soup, along with a touch of fat that helps carry the flavors. Thai Kitchen roasted chili paste is sold in small jars in the international aisle of most supermarkets. If you like, serve the soup with steamed jasmine rice.

2 limes (see headnote)

4 stalks lemon grass, trimmed to the bottom
6 inches, dry outer layers discarded, bruised

4 Fresno or jalapeño chilies, stemmed,
2 halved and seeded, 2 sliced into thin rings

3 medium shallots, halved

3 medium garlic cloves, smashed and peeled

2-inch piece fresh ginger (see headnote), cut into
4 or 5 coins and bruised

2 tablespoons Thai chili paste (see headnote)

Kosher salt and ground white pepper

1½ pounds bone-in, skin-on chicken breasts, trimmed

12 ounces button or cremini mushrooms, quartered if
small or medium, cut into sixths if large

¼ cup fish sauce, plus more as needed

⅓ cup chopped fresh cilantro

Using a vegetable peeler, remove the zest from the limes in strips; remove only the colored portion, not the white pith underneath. You will need a total of 8 strips, each 2 to 3 inches long. Juice the limes; set aside.

In a large saucepan, combine 6 cups water, the zest strips, lemon grass, 2 halved chilies, shallots, garlic, ginger, Thai chili paste, 1 teaspoon salt and ¼ teaspoon white pepper. Add the chicken, cover and bring to a gentle simmer over medium-low; simmer until the thickest part of the breast reaches 160°F, 25 to 30 minutes. Using tongs or a slotted spoon, transfer the chicken to a medium bowl; set aside to cool. Remove and discard the solids from the broth.

Return the broth, covered, to a simmer over medium. Add the mushrooms, re-cover and cook until tender, 10 to 15 minutes. Meanwhile, shred the chicken into bite-size pieces, discarding the skin and bones.

When the mushrooms are tender, return the chicken and any accumulated juices to the pan. Stir in the sliced chilies, ⅓ cup of the reserved lime juice, the fish sauce and ¼ teaspoon white pepper. Taste and season with additional lime juice, fish sauce and pepper. Serve sprinkled with the cilantro.

GEORGIAN CHICKEN SOUP

Start to finish: 1¾ hours (45 minutes active)
Servings: 6

We wanted a chicken soup that tastes fresh and light, yet also robust and satisfying. We found our answer in chik-hirtma, a traditional soup from Georgia, the Eurasian country that bridges Türkiye and Russia. Georgian cuisine often marries Western techniques with Eastern flavors. We used a recipe from Darra Goldstein, author of "The Georgian Feast," as our starting point. Her chikhirtma calls for a whole chicken, but that much meat made the soup feel heavy, so we used just chicken legs. We built flavor with bunches of dill and cilantro stems and a head of garlic, as well as coriander, cinnamon and bay leaves.

FOR THE BROTH AND CHICKEN:

1 bunch fresh cilantro

1 bunch fresh dill

1 garlic head

2½ to 3 pounds bone-in, skin-on chicken legs

10 cups water

1 large yellow onion, quartered

1 teaspoon kosher salt

1 teaspoon black peppercorns

½ teaspoon coriander seeds

½ teaspoon red pepper flakes (optional)

3-inch cinnamon stick

2 bay leaves

FOR THE SOUP:

1 pound carrots (about 5 medium), peeled, halved lengthwise and cut into ½-inch pieces

1 large yellow onion, coarsely chopped (about 1½ cups)

3 tablespoons salted butter

¼ teaspoon kosher salt

½ cup dry vermouth

1 tablespoon all-purpose flour

6 large egg yolks

¼ cup lemon juice (1 to 2 lemons)

Ground black pepper

To make the broth, tie the stems of the cilantro and dill into bundles, then trim off the leaves, reserving ¼ cup of each for garnish. Cut off and discard the top third of the garlic head, leaving the head intact. In a large pot, combine both sets of stems, the garlic, the chicken and the remaining broth ingredients. Bring to a boil, then reduce heat to medium-low and simmer for 45 minutes. Remove and set aside the garlic head. Transfer the chicken to a plate and cool until easily handled. Shred the chicken into bite-size pieces, discarding the skin, bones and cartilage. Set aside.

To make the soup, strain the broth into another pot or bowl, discarding the solids. Using tongs, squeeze the garlic head into the broth; the tender cloves should easily pop out of their skins. Whisk into the broth. Wipe out the empty pot, then add the carrots, onion, butter and salt. Set over medium-high and cook, stirring occasionally, until the onion is browned, 10 to 12 minutes. Add the vermouth, scraping up any browned bits, and cook until evaporated, 1 to 2 minutes. Add the flour and cook, stirring constantly, for 1 minute. Add 2 cups of the broth and stir until smooth, then add the remaining broth and bring to a simmer. In a medium bowl, whisk the yolks. Continue whisking while slowly adding 1 cup of hot broth from the pot. Whisk in the lemon juice, then return the mixture to the pot and whisk to combine. Add the chicken and any accumulated juices and cook until just heated through (do not simmer). Taste and season with salt and pepper. Serve with chopped cilantro and dill leaves.

TURKISH-STYLE CHICKEN SOUP WITH YOGURT, CHICKPEAS AND BULGUR

Start to finish: 35 minutes

Servings: 4

There are many different versions of düğün çorbası, or Turkish wedding soup, and a good number of them are made with lamb. But a chicken-based recipe from "Anatolia" by Somer Sivrioglu and David Dale inspired this soup, which is rich and satisfying but not at all heavy. We opted out of the egg and flour that enriches and thickens classic düğün çorbası, but we include both chickpeas and bulgur for substance and texture. Butter infused with Aleppo pepper finishes individual bowlfuls, adding color, aroma and depth of flavor. Aleppo pepper is mildly spicy, with a touch of fruitiness and smoke.

1 pound boneless, skinless chicken breasts, trimmed and cut into ¾-inch chunks

Kosher salt and ground black pepper

6 tablespoons (¾ stick) salted butter, cut into 1-tablespoon pieces, divided

1 medium yellow onion, chopped

¾ cup coarse bulgur

4 medium garlic cloves, minced

1 quart low-sodium chicken broth

15½-ounce can chickpeas, drained (do not rinse)

1 tablespoon Aleppo pepper OR 2 teaspoons sweet paprika plus ½ teaspoon red pepper flakes

1 cup whole-milk yogurt

½ cup chopped fresh dill

In a medium bowl, toss the chicken with ¼ teaspoon each salt and black pepper; set aside. In a large pot over medium-high, melt 2 tablespoons of butter. Add the onion, bulgur and ½ teaspoon salt, then cook, stirring occasionally, until the onion browns and the bulgur darkens in color, 5 to 8 minutes.

Add the garlic and cook, stirring, until fragrant, about 30 seconds. Add the broth, 1 cup water and ¾ teaspoon black pepper, then bring to a boil. Reduce to medium, and simmer, uncovered and stirring occasionally, until the bulgur is softened, about 15 minutes. Stir in the chicken and chickpeas, then cook, uncovered and stirring occasionally, until the chicken no longer is pink at the center and the bulgur is very soft, about 5 minutes.

Meanwhile, in a small skillet over medium, heat the remaining 4 tablespoons butter until bubbling. Add the Aleppo pepper and cook, swirling the pan, until the butter is bright red and fragrant, about 1 minute. Set aside off heat.

When the chicken and bulgur are done, remove the pot from the heat. Whisk in the yogurt and dill, then taste and season with salt and pepper. Ladle the soup into serving bowls, then drizzle 1 tablespoon of the Aleppo butter over each.

SARDINIAN HERB SOUP WITH FREGOLA AND WHITE BEANS

Start to finish: 45 minutes
Servings: 4

Traditionally, the Sardinian soup called s'erbuzzu is jammed with wild herbs and greens—sometimes more than 17 varieties. And with both fregola (a pea-shaped Sardinian pasta) and white beans in the mix, the soup—taught to us by chef Luigi Crisponi at Santa Rughe restaurant in Gavoi— is as hearty and starchy as it is herbal. For our version, we narrowed the list of herbs and greens to those we felt had the most impact: parsley for grassiness, tarragon for sweet anise notes and arugula for pepperiness. We also used pancetta to build a savory backbone and ricotta salata cheese, as Sardinians do, for complexity. If you can't find fregola, substitute an equal amount of pearl couscous, but cook it for only 5 minutes before adding the beans, parsley and garlic. And if ricotta salata is not available, finely grated pecorino Romano is a reasonable swap, but halve the amount.

2 tablespoons extra-virgin olive oil, plus more to serve

3 to 4 ounces pancetta, chopped

1 bunch flat-leaf parsley, stems minced, leaves roughly chopped, reserved separately

1½ teaspoons fennel seeds

½ cup dry white wine

Kosher salt and ground black pepper

2 quarts low-sodium chicken broth

¾ cup fregola (see headnote)

15½-ounce can large white beans, such as butter beans, rinsed and drained

3 medium garlic cloves, minced

4 ounces ricotta salata cheese (see headnote), crumbled (¾ cup)

4 ounces baby arugula (about 6 cups lightly packed), roughly chopped

½ cup lightly packed fresh tarragon, chopped

In a large pot over medium, heat the oil and pancetta. Cook, stirring occasionally, until the pancetta is browned, 6 to 8 minutes. Stir in the parsley stems and fennel seeds, then add the wine and 1 teaspoon pepper, scraping up any browned bits. Bring to a simmer over medium-high and cook, stirring, until most of the moisture has evaporated, 2 to 3 minutes.

Add the broth and bring to a boil over high. Stir in the fregola and cook, stirring occasionally and adjusting the heat to maintain a simmer, until the fregola is just shy of tender, about 10 minutes. Add the beans, garlic, parsley leaves and half of the ricotta salata, then continue to cook, stirring occasionally and adjusting the heat to maintain a bare simmer, until the fregola is fully tender, about another 10 minutes.

Off heat, stir in the arugula and tarragon, then taste and season with salt and pepper. Serve sprinkled with the remaining ricotta salata and drizzled with additional oil.

Big Flavor from Slender Stems

Don't trash your cilantro stems—they are full of flavor. After trimming off the leaves to use elsewhere, we frequently puree the stems into sauces, salsas and moles. We also use them to flavor rice dishes and soups. This also works with parsley stems, which we use to infuse broths with herbal, minerally flavor.

We use tender herb stems in a number of our recipes, including our Peruvian chicken soup (recipe follows), Sardinian soup (recipe p. 107), and cod fillets with zhoug, a spicy pesto-like condiment popular in the Middle East (recipe p. 392).

When pureeing stems for use this way, start by discarding any tough, woody specimens, then wash and dry them carefully (wet stems will create soggy sauces), then blitz in the food processor.

Parsley and cilantro stems also can be chopped and added without pureeing to soups and stews. We often combine them with the leaves for a double dose of fresh, herbal flavor. We often add the stems earlier in cooking so they have time to soften, then finish the dish with the more tender leaves. Adding the leaves just before serving preserves their freshness and color.

PERUVIAN CHICKEN, RICE AND CILANTRO SOUP

Start to finish: 1 hour 10 minutes (30 minutes active)

Servings: 4

Chicken soup too often turns out blandly insipid—or a muddle of flavors with too many seasonings added to compensate. We avoid that trap in this version, inspired by Peru's aguadito de pollo. Bright, green seasonings take center stage with a full bunch of cilantro, stems and all, and a cup of peas; we use frozen for convenience. Traditional aguadito includes starchy Peruvian corn. Rather than substitute sweet corn, which is far more sugary, we opted to omit it. The soup gets mild spiciness from ají amarillo, an orange-yellow chili with a fruity yet earthy flavor that is ubiquitous in Peruvian cuisine. In fresh form, the chilies are difficult to find in the U.S., but ají amarillo paste, sold in jars, is available in some well-stocked markets and specialty stores, as well as online. If you can't find it, use 2 or 3 seeded and finely minced jalapeños.

1 tablespoon grapeseed or other neutral oil

4 medium garlic cloves, minced

1 medium white onion, finely chopped

1 bunch fresh cilantro, stems minced, leaves left whole, reserved separately

¼ cup ají amarillo paste (see headnote)

Kosher salt and ground black pepper

1½ pounds bone-in, skin-on chicken breasts, thighs or legs

1 cup long-grain white rice, rinsed and drained

3 medium carrots, peeled and cut crosswise into ½-inch pieces

1 medium red or yellow bell pepper, stemmed and cut into ½-inch pieces

1 cup frozen peas

2 tablespoons lime juice

In a large pot over medium-high, heat the oil until shimmering. Add the garlic, onion, cilantro stems, aji amarillo paste and 1 teaspoon salt. Cook, stirring occasionally, until the paste begins to brown on the bottom of the pot, about 8 minutes. Add 7 cups water and bring to a simmer, scraping up the browned bits. Add the chicken in an even layer, then return to a simmer. Cover and cook, adjusting heat to

maintain a simmer, until a skewer inserted at the thickest part of the meat meets no resistance, about 40 minutes. Transfer the chicken to a plate and set aside until cool enough to handle.

In a blender, combine the cilantro leaves, a pinch of salt and ⅓ cup water. Blend, scraping the sides as needed, until smooth, about 1 minute. You should have about ½ cup puree. Set aside.

To the pot, stir in the rice, carrots, bell pepper, ¼ teaspoon salt and ½ teaspoon pepper. Bring to a simmer over medium-high, then cover, reduce to low and cook without stirring until the rice and vegetables are tender, about 10 minutes. Meanwhile, shred the chicken into bite-size pieces, discarding the skin and bones.

When the rice and vegetables are tender, stir the shredded chicken and peas into the soup. Cook until the peas are heated through, about 1 minute. Off-heat, stir in the cilantro puree and lime juice, then taste and season with salt and pepper.

PERSIAN-STYLE CHICKEN, MUSHROOM AND BARLEY SOUP

Start to finish: 1 hour
Servings: 6

This satisfying soup is a riff on the Persian dish called soup-e jo. Though barley's natural starch lends the soup body, béchamel, a mixture of butter, flour and milk, also is traditional for added richness and thickening. For ease, we skip the béchamel and instead simply mix a tablespoon of flour into the sautéed onion and mushrooms, then swirl in a little cream at the very end. Fragrant spices give the soup color and complexity, and fresh herbs (we like a combination of mint and dill, though just one does nicely) lift and brighten the flavors.

2 tablespoons extra-virgin olive oil

1 medium yellow onion, chopped

12 ounces cremini mushrooms, trimmed and quartered if small or medium, cut into eighths if large

2 teaspoons ground cumin

1 teaspoon ground turmeric

1 tablespoon all-purpose flour

Kosher salt and ground black pepper

1 cup pearled barley

2 pounds boneless, skinless chicken thighs, trimmed and cut into 1-inch chunks

2 quarts low-sodium chicken broth

½ cup heavy cream

1 cup lightly packed fresh mint, dill or a combination, chopped

In a large pot over medium-high, heat the oil until shimmering. Add the onion and mushrooms; cook, stirring occasionally, until the onion is softened and the mushrooms release moisture, 6 to 8 minutes.

Add the cumin, turmeric, flour, 1 teaspoon salt and ½ teaspoon pepper; cook, stirring, until well combined, about 30 seconds. Stir in the barley and chicken, followed by the broth. Bring to a simmer over medium-high, then reduce to medium-low and simmer, uncovered and stirring occasionally, until the barley is tender, about 40 minutes.

Off heat, stir in the cream and half of the herbs. Taste and season with salt and pepper. Ladle into bowls and sprinkle with the remaining herbs.

GREEK EGG-LEMON SOUP

Start to finish: 45 minutes (20 minutes active)
Servings: 4

This Greek soup gets its name, avgolemono, from the egg-lemon mixture used to thicken the broth. Some versions are simply broth that's thickened and seasoned, while others are more substantial and include rice and chicken, as we've done here. To boost the flavor of store-bought chicken broth, we poach bone-in chicken breasts in it, then shred the meat and add it to the soup just before serving. Grated carrots lend sweetness and color, while lemon zest deepens the citrus notes. To prevent the eggs from curdling, keep these tips in mind: Temper the eggs first by slowly adding a small amount of the hot broth to the bowl before whisking the mixture into the pan. And after adding the mixture, don't let the soup reach a boil or even a simmer.

1 quart low-sodium chicken broth

12-ounce bone-in, skin-on chicken breast, halved crosswise

Three 2-inch strips lemon zest, plus 3 tablespoons lemon juice

2 medium carrots, peeled and shredded on the large holes of a box grater

1 medium yellow onion, chopped

¾ cup long-grain white rice, rinsed and drained

Kosher salt and ground black pepper

3 large eggs

In a large saucepan, combine the broth, chicken, 2 cups water, the lemon zest strips, carrots and onion. Bring to a simmer over medium-high, then reduce to low, cover and cook until the thickest part of the chicken reaches 160°F, 15 to 18 minutes.

Using tongs, remove and discard the zest strips; transfer the chicken to a plate and set aside. Return the broth to a simmer over medium, then stir in the rice, ¾ teaspoon salt and ¼ teaspoon pepper. Reduce to low, cover and cook, stirring once halfway through, until the rice is tender, 12 to 15 minutes. Meanwhile, remove and discard the skin and bones from the chicken and shred the meat; set aside.

When the rice is done, remove the pan from the heat and uncover. In a medium bowl, whisk together the eggs and lemon juice. While whisking constantly, slowly ladle about 1 cup of the hot rice-broth mixture into the egg mixture, then slowly whisk this mixture into the pan. Stir in the shredded chicken.

Return the pan to low and cook, stirring constantly, until the soup is warm and lightly thickened, 2 to 4 minutes; do not allow the soup to simmer. Off heat, taste and season with salt and pepper.

Optional garnish: Chopped fresh dill OR chives

ROMANIAN PORK AND WHITE BEAN SOUP WITH VINEGAR AND CARAWAY

Start to finish: 2¾ hours, plus soaking time for the beans
Servings: 4 to 6

This soup, called ciorbă de porc, was inspired by a recipe from "Carpathia: Food from the Heart of Romania" by Irina Georgescu. It's hearty, subtly smoky pork and beans in a tomatoey broth scented with caraway and finished with dill. Beans and smoked meat are a common pairing, and we've included both. The defining characteristic of ciorbă is a distinct tanginess. We use white wine vinegar, but according to Georgescu, other options include pickle brine, sauerkraut liquid, even the juice of sour plums. Make the punchy, quick-pickled red onion garnish while the soup simmers.

Kosher salt and ground black pepper

1 pound dried great northern beans

2 tablespoons grapeseed or other neutral oil

2 medium yellow onions, chopped

2 medium celery stalks, chopped

2 medium carrots, peeled and chopped

1 medium red bell pepper, seeded and chopped

1-pound smoked ham hock

1½ pounds pork baby back ribs (½ rack),
cut between the bones into 3 sections

28-ounce can whole tomatoes, finely
crushed by hand

2 teaspoons caraway seeds

1 quart low-sodium chicken broth

3 tablespoons finely chopped fresh dill

¼ cup white wine vinegar

Pickled red onion (recipe follows), to serve

First, soak the beans. In a large bowl, combine 2 quarts water, 1 tablespoon salt and the beans. Stir until the salt dissolves, then soak at room temperature for at least 12 hours or up to 24 hours. Drain the beans and set aside.

In a large pot over medium-high, heat the oil until shimmering. Add the onions, celery, carrots and bell pepper, then cook, stirring often, until the vegetables begin to brown, 5 to 8 minutes. Add the beans, ham hock, ribs, tomatoes

with juices, caraway, broth and 1 quart water; stir to combine. Bring to a boil over high, then cover, reduce to medium and cook, stirring occasionally and adjusting the heat as needed to maintain a simmer, until the beans are tender and a paring knife inserted into the meat between the rib bones meets no resistance, about 2 hours.

Remove the pot from the heat. Using tongs, transfer the ham hock and ribs to a large plate. When cool enough to handle, remove the meat from both and shred into bite-size pieces; discard the bones, fat and gristle.

Return the meat to the pot and bring to a simmer over medium, stirring occasionally. Remove from the heat, then stir in the dill and vinegar. Taste and season with salt and pepper. Serve with pickled red onion.

PICKLED RED ONION

In a medium bowl, combine **1 medium red onion** (halved and thinly sliced), **½ cup white wine vinegar**, **1 tablespoon white sugar** and **1 teaspoon kosher salt**. Stir until the sugar and salt dissolve. Cover and refrigerate until ready to serve.

1 pound ground pork

6 scallions, white parts finely chopped, green parts thinly sliced, reserved separately

1 large egg white, lightly beaten

3 tablespoons fish sauce, divided

4 teaspoons grated fresh ginger, divided

Kosher salt and ground white pepper

2 tablespoons grapeseed or other neutral oil

1 medium yellow onion, chopped

4 medium garlic cloves, thinly sliced

2 quarts low-sodium chicken broth (8 cups)

1 bunch watercress, cut into 1½-inch lengths (4 cups lightly packed)

2 tablespoons lime juice

VIETNAMESE MEATBALL AND WATERCRESS SOUP

Start to finish: 40 minutes
Servings: 4

This refreshing supper is a take on canh, a type of quick, brothy Vietnamese soup. The soups can be sour, rich with vegetables, or loaded with seafood. But whatever variety, the unifying factor is simplicity. Our version stays true to the simplicity, but scales up the ingredients so it can serve as a satisfying meal on its own. Watercress adds a peppery note; look for "live" watercress, which is packaged with its roots attached. It stays fresher longer and is easier to clean. To prep it, trim off and discard the roots, rinse and drain the greens, then cut them into 1½-inch lengths, discarding any stems that are thick or tough. If you prefer, substitute an equal amount of baby spinach for the watercress, but roughly chop the leaves before using. We also liked this soup made with chicken bouillon paste instead of chicken broth; use 2 tablespoons of paste dissolved in 2 quarts of water.

Line a rimmed baking sheet with kitchen parchment and mist with cooking spray. In a medium bowl, combine the pork, scallion whites, egg white, 1 tablespoon of the fish sauce, 2 teaspoons of the ginger, ¾ teaspoon salt and 1 teaspoon white pepper. Mix with your hands. Lightly moisten your hands with water and form into 20 balls, each about a generous tablespoon. Set on the prepared baking sheet, cover and refrigerate.

In a large Dutch oven over medium, heat the oil until shimmering. Add the onion and cook, stirring occasionally, until beginning to soften, about 5 minutes. Stir in the remaining 2 teaspoons ginger and the garlic, then cook until fragrant, about 30 seconds. Add the broth and bring to a boil over high. Reduce to medium-low and simmer, uncovered, until the onion is fully softened, about 10 minutes.

Add the meatballs, then bring to a simmer over medium-high. Reduce the heat to maintain a gentle simmer and cook without stirring until the meatballs are cooked through, 8 to 10 minutes. They should reach 160°F at the center.

Off heat, stir in the watercress and the remaining 2 table-spoons fish sauce. Let stand until the greens are wilted and tender, about 1 minute. Stir in the lime juice. Taste and season with salt and pepper, then stir in the scallion greens.

Homemade Beef Broth

Start to finish: 5½ hours (30 minutes active), plus cooling
Makes about 2 quarts

This robust beef broth gets rich color and deep flavor by first roasting beef shanks and vegetables before slowly simmering on the stovetop. Dried shiitake mushrooms lend loads of umami to the broth; they're optional, so feel free to skip them, or just toss in a couple if you don't want to use a full ounce. A tall, narrowish stockpot with a capacity of about 8 quarts works best because it allows less evaporation than a wider Dutch oven. If you only have a wide Dutch oven, partially cover the pot during simmering so the broth does not over-reduce. After simmering, the meat on the shanks will be fall-off-the-bone tender; it won't have much flavor, but it can be repurposed. If using the broth right away, after straining make sure to use a spoon to skim off the fat on the surface. If making ahead, however, the easiest way to defat the broth is to refrigerate it until fully chilled, then scrape off the congealed fat.

3 pounds bone-in beef shanks (about 1 inch thick)

8 ounces cremini mushrooms, left whole if small or medium, halved if large

2 medium celery stalks, cut into rough 1-inch pieces

1 large yellow onion, quartered lengthwise

1 medium carrot, peeled and cut into rough 1-inch pieces

1 tablespoon extra-virgin olive oil

Kosher salt

1 tablespoon tomato paste

4 bay leaves

3 or 4 thyme sprigs OR 1 teaspoon dried thyme

1 tablespoon black peppercorns

1 ounce (12 to 14) dried shiitake mushrooms (optional; see headnote)

Heat the oven to 475°F with a rack in the middle position. Arrange the beef shanks in a single layer on one side of a large roasting pan. On the other side, toss the cremini

mushrooms, celery, onion and carrot with the oil and 1 teaspoon salt. Roast, without stirring, until well browned, about 1 hour.

Transfer the vegetables and meat to a large (about 8-quart) pot. Add 1 cup water to the now-empty pan and scrape up any browned bits. Add the liquid to the pot along with another 13 cups water, the tomato paste, bay, thyme, peppercorns and shiitake mushrooms (if using). Bring to a boil over high, then reduce to medium-low and simmer, uncovered, for 4 hours. Remove the pot from the heat and cool for about 15 minutes.

Strain the broth through a fine-mesh strainer set over a large bowl; discard the solids. You should have 2 quarts strained broth; if you have less, add water to attain that amount. If using right away, skim off and discard any fat from the surface with a wide, shallow spoon. If making ahead, cool completely, then cover and refrigerate up to 3 days. Before use, skim off and discard the hardened fat on the surface. (At this point, the broth can be frozen for up to a few months).

Speedy Pressure-Cooked Beef Broth

Start to finish: 2½ hours (30 minutes active), plus cooling
Makes about 2 quarts

For pressure-cooked beef broth, beef shanks and vegetables still are roasted in a hot oven before going into the Instant Pot. But don't worry, the cooking still takes less than half the time doing it on the stovetop. Dried shiitake mushrooms bring extra meatiness to the broth, but the flavor is full and rich even without them, so leave them out if you prefer. Or add only a few.

3 pounds bone-in beef shanks (about 1 inch thick)

8 ounces cremini mushrooms, left whole if small or medium, halved if large

2 medium celery stalks, cut into rough 1-inch pieces

1 large yellow onion, quartered lengthwise

1 medium carrot, peeled and cut into rough 1-inch pieces

1 tablespoon extra-virgin olive oil

Kosher salt

1 tablespoon tomato paste

4 bay leaves

3 or 4 thyme sprigs OR 1 teaspoon dried thyme

1 tablespoon black peppercorns

1 ounce (12 to 14) dried shiitake mushrooms (optional; see headnote)

Heat the oven to 475°F with a rack in the middle position. Arrange the beef shanks in a single layer on one side of a large roasting pan. On the other side, toss the cremini mushrooms, celery, onion and carrot with the oil and 1 teaspoon salt. Roast, without stirring, until well browned, about 1 hour.

Transfer the vegetables and meat to a 6-quart Instant Pot. Add 1 cup water to the now-empty pan and scrape up any browned bits. Add the liquid to the pot along with another 10 cups water, the tomato paste, bay, thyme, peppercorns and shiitake mushrooms (if using). Lock the lid in place and move the pressure valve to **Sealing.** Select **Pressure Cook** or

Manual; make sure the pressure level is set to **High.** Set the cooking time to 1 hour. When pressure cooking is complete, allow the pressure to release naturally for 15 minutes, then release the remaining steam by moving the pressure valve to **Venting.** Press **Cancel,** then carefully open the pot.

Strain the broth through a fine-mesh strainer set over a large bowl; discard the solids. You should have 2 quarts strained broth; if you have less, add water to attain that amount. If using right away, skim off and discard any fat from the surface with a wide, shallow spoon. If making ahead, cool completely, then cover and refrigerate up to 3 days. Before use, skim off and discard the hardened fat on the surface. (At this point, the broth can be frozen for up to a few months).

UKRAINIAN BORSCH

Start to finish: 2½ hours (1 hour active)
Servings: 6 to 8

More than merely a meat and beet soup, Ukrainian borsch is a chunky, vividly hued dish that unites the country. Every household or cook has their own way of making borsch, but the flavor always is savory-sweet, with a touch of acidity that makes the flavors sparkle. Based on what we gleaned from chef Ievgen Klopotenko as well as from home cooks, we developed a borsch recipe that can be made either with beef or pork. Klopotenko explained the dish traditionally was cooked in a wood-fired oven, which infused the broth with smokiness. He suggested we add smoked paprika to mimic that woodsiness. Home cook Stas Kotz included star anise and caraway in his version, spices that complement the earthy-sweet and meaty flavors. The addition of white beans comes from Katerana Ilyasevich, who simmered some in her borsch for added heartiness and texture. This recipe requires two cooking vessels, as is customary: a pot for simmering the meat and a skillet for sautéing the aromatics. This makes it easy to brown the aromatics and build flavor. Sour cream and dill are key finishing flavors that are stirred into individual bowls, so don't skip them.

2 pounds boneless beef chuck roast or boneless pork shoulder, trimmed and cut into 1½-inch chunks

2 star anise pods

2 bay leaves

Kosher salt and ground black pepper

4 tablespoons grapeseed or other neutral oil, divided

1 medium yellow onion, finely chopped

12 ounces red beets, peeled and shredded on the large holes of a box grater (3 cups)

2 medium carrots, peeled and shredded on the large holes of a box grater (1½ cups)

3 tablespoons tomato paste

2 medium garlic cloves, minced

1½ teaspoons caraway seeds

14½-ounce can (1½ cups) tomato puree

1 tablespoon smoked paprika

8 ounces Yukon Gold potatoes, peeled and cut into ½-inch cubes

8 ounces Savoy cabbage or green cabbage, thinly sliced (about 4 cups)

15½-ounce can great northern beans, rinsed and drained

1½ tablespoons red wine vinegar, plus more as needed

Sour cream, to serve

Chopped fresh dill, to serve

In a large pot, combine the beef, star anise, bay, 1 teaspoon salt and 3 quarts water. Bring to a boil over medium-high, then reduce to medium and simmer, uncovered, until a skewer inserted into the meat meets no resistance, 1½ to 2 hours; occasionally skim off and discard the foam that rises to the surface.

Meanwhile, in a 12-inch skillet over medium-high, heat 3 tablespoons oil until shimmering. Add the onion and ½ teaspoon salt; cook, stirring occasionally, until lightly browned, about 3 minutes. Add half of the beets, the carrots, tomato paste, ½ teaspoon salt and ¾ teaspoon pepper; cook, stirring, until the mixture browns and sticks to the skillet, 3 to 5 minutes.

Push the vegetables to the edge of the pan and add the remaining 1 tablespoon oil to the clearing. Add the garlic and caraway; cook, stirring, until fragrant, about 1 minute. Remove the pan from the heat and stir the garlic-caraway mixture into the vegetables. Stir in the tomato puree and paprika, then ladle in 1 cup of the liquid from the large pot. Scrape up any browned bits, then set the skillet aside.

When the meat is tender, remove and discard the star anise and bay from the broth. Add the contents of the skillet to the pot along with the remaining beets and the potato. Simmer, uncovered and stirring occasionally, until the potatoes are tender, about 20 minutes.

Stir in the cabbage and beans. Cook, stirring occasionally, until the cabbage is tender, 5 to 8 minutes. Off heat, stir in the vinegar. Taste and season with salt, pepper and additional vinegar, if needed. Ladle into bowls, top each with a dollop of sour cream and sprinkle with dill.

HAITIAN-STYLE PUMPKIN AND BEEF SOUP

Start to finish: 3½ hours

Servings: 8

Our version of Haiti's pumpkin and beef soup, joumou, is rich yet light, with a flavorful pumpkin-based broth and tender pieces of beef, butternut squash and potato. Two Scotch bonnet peppers give this soup a spicy backdrop; we studded ours with cloves, a tip we took from Haiti-born cook Sophia Sanon who now resides in Montreal. If you can't find Scotch bonnets, habaneros work well, too. You should end up with about 2 pounds of meat after trimming a 3-pound boneless beef chuck roast; trim as much visible fat as possible. The beef for the soup can be cooked up to 24 hours ahead of time; cover and refrigerate for up to three days.

8 whole cloves

2 Scotch bonnet or habanero chilies

3 pounds boneless beef chuck roast, trimmed and cut into ½- to ¾-inch pieces

Kosher salt and ground black pepper

3 tablespoons extra-virgin olive oil, divided

3½ quarts (14 cups) low-sodium chicken broth, divided

3 bay leaves

3 medium leeks, white and light green parts sliced into ¼-inch rings, rinsed and drained

12 medium garlic cloves, smashed and peeled

15-ounce can pumpkin puree

1 pound butternut squash, peeled, seeded and cut into ½-inch cubes

1 pound Yukon Gold potatoes, cut into ½-inch cubes

1 cup finely chopped fresh cilantro

3 tablespoons lime juice, plus lime wedges to serve

Hot sauce, to serve

Press 4 cloves into each of the chilies, then set aside. Use paper towels to pat the meat dry, then season with salt and pepper.

In a large saucepan over medium-high, heat 1 tablespoon of the oil until just smoking. Add half of the beef and cook, stirring occasionally, until well browned, about 5 minutes. Add the remaining beef, 2 cups of the broth, the bay leaves and 1 clove-studded chili. Bring to a simmer, cover and reduce to low. Cook, stirring occasionally, until the beef is very tender, about 2 hours.

Using a slotted spoon, transfer the beef to a medium bowl and set aside to cool. Simmer the broth over medium-high until reduced to about 1 cup, about 20 minutes. Meanwhile, when the beef is cool enough to handle, shred any larger pieces into bite-size chunks. Set aside. Remove and discard the bay leaves and chili from the broth and pour over the beef. Cover and refrigerate until needed.

Meanwhile, in a large Dutch oven over medium, heat the remaining 2 tablespoons oil. Add the leeks and garlic and cook, stirring occasionally, until the leeks are wilted, about 5 minutes. Stir in the pumpkin puree and cook until the mixture looks dry, about 2 minutes. Add the remaining 3 quarts broth and the remaining clove-studded chili. Bring to a boil over medium-high. Cover, reduce to medium and cook, stirring occasionally, until the leeks are tender, about 30 minutes.

Set a fine-mesh strainer over a large bowl. Pour the pumpkin-broth mixture through the strainer and firmly press on the solids to extract as much liquid as possible. Discard the solids, return the liquid to the Dutch oven and bring to a simmer over medium-high. Stir in the squash and potatoes, return to a simmer on medium, and cook, uncovered, stirring occasionally, until the vegetables are just tender, 20 to 30 minutes. Add the reserved beef and its liquid and cook, stirring occasionally, until the beef is heated through, 5 to 10 minutes. Off heat, stir in the cilantro and lime juice. Taste and season with salt and pepper. Serve with lime wedges and hot sauce.

TAIWANESE BEEF NOODLE SOUP

Start to finish: 2¾ hours (45 minutes active)
Servings: 6

Niu rou mian, or beef noodle soup, is one of Taiwan's signature dishes. Chuang Pao-hua, founder of the Chung-Hua Culinary Teaching Center, in Taipei's Datong District, taught us how to make the hearty meal the labor-intensive, traditional way. For our much-simplified version, we use beef shanks, which yield full-bodied broth and tender, shreddable beef in a couple hours. Our flavorings include toban djan, a spicy, fermented chili-bean paste. sold in most Asian markets. If you can't find it, substitute 2 tablespoons white miso mixed with 4 teaspoons chili-garlic sauce and

2 teaspoons soy sauce. The soup is lightly spicy; add more toban djan and/or some ground Sichuan pepper at the table for more heat. Chinese wheat noodles of any thickness worked, as did Japanese udon and long Italian pasta, such as spaghetti.

1 tablespoon grapeseed or other neutral oil

6 garlic cloves, smashed and peeled

4-inch piece fresh ginger, peeled, cut into 6 to 8 pieces and smashed

6 scallions, whites roughly chopped, greens thinly sliced, reserved separately

3 star anise pods

1 tablespoon Sichuan peppercorns

3 tablespoons chili bean sauce (toban djan, see headnote)

2 tablespoons tomato paste

2 tablespoons packed dark brown sugar

⅓ cup soy sauce

⅓ cup sake

2 to 2½ pounds bone-in beef shanks (about 1 inch thick), trimmed

Kosher salt

1 pound baby bok choy, trimmed and cut crosswise into 1-inch pieces

8 ounces dried wheat noodles

In a large Dutch oven over medium, combine the oil, garlic, ginger and the white scallion parts. Cook, stirring, until sizzling, about 3 minutes. Stir in the star anise and peppercorns, then cook until fragrant, about 30 seconds. Stir in the chili-bean sauce, tomato paste, brown sugar, soy sauce, sake and 2½ quarts water. Bring to a boil over high.

Add the beef shanks and return to a simmer. Cover, reduce to low and cook, adjusting as needed to maintain a gentle simmer, until the beef is tender and beginning to fall apart, about 2 hours.

Use a slotted spoon to transfer the beef shanks to a bowl and set aside. Pour the cooking liquid through a fine-mesh strainer set over a large bowl; discard the solids. Reserve the pot. Skim off and discard the fat from the surface of the liquid, then return to the pot. When cool enough to handle, shred the meat into bite-size pieces, discarding the bones, fat and gristle. Add the meat to the pot and bring to a simmer over medium-high, then reduce to low and cover to keep warm.

In a large pot, bring 4 quarts water to a boil. Add 1 tablespoon salt and the bok choy. Cook until the stems are crisp-tender, about 3 minutes. Use a slotted spoon to transfer the bok choy to a large plate and set aside. Add the noodles to the water and cook until tender. Drain, rinse under lukewarm water, then drain again.

Divide the noodles and bok choy among serving bowls then ladle in the soup and sprinkle with scallion greens.

ITALIAN WEDDING SOUP

Start to finish: 2¾ hours (45 minutes active)
Servings: 6

The name of the dish on which this recipe is based is minestra maritata, which translates from the Italian as "married soup." It is not the Italian wedding soup of meatballs, greens and pasta that's popular in the U.S., though the two do share similarities. At the family-owned restaurant La Tavernetta Vittozzi in Naples, we were taught how to make the Campanian version of the classic dish, and we used the lessons learned for our own adaptation. As in Naples, the meats in our recipe are bone-in cuts of beef and pork that give the broth richness and body. But for easier eating, after cooking we shred the meat and discard the bones. Pancetta also simmers in the mix along with a piece of Parmesan rind, each lending even more savoriness to the broth. La Tavernetta Vittozzi uses three different varieties of wintry greens in their minestra maritata—cabbage, broccoli rabe and escarole, the latter two blanched separately before they are added to the soup. (This "marriage" of cooked greens and broth is what gives the dish its name.) To streamline, we opt for rabe or escarole (or a combination, if it suits you) and we simmer the vegetable directly in the broth. Rabe offers an assertive bitterness that nicely balances the richness of the soup; escarole is milder and cooks down to a silky, supple texture. Warm, crusty bread is the perfect accompaniment.

8 ounces pancetta, chopped

2 tablespoons extra-virgin olive oil

1 large yellow onion, roughly chopped

2 medium carrots, peeled and roughly chopped

1 medium celery stalk, roughly chopped

4 medium garlic cloves, smashed and peeled

3 tablespoons tomato paste

½ to ¾ teaspoon red pepper flakes

Kosher salt and ground black pepper

4 bay leaves

2½-pound rack pork baby back ribs, cut into 3 sections between the ribs

1-pound bone-in beef shank (1 to 1½ inches thick)

2-inch piece Parmesan cheese rind, plus finely grated Parmesan, to serve

1 bunch broccoli rabe, trimmed and roughly chopped, or 1 large head escarole, chopped, or a combination

½ cup lightly packed fresh basil, chopped

In a large Dutch oven, combine the pancetta and oil. Cook over medium-low, stirring occasionally, until the pancetta begins to brown, about 10 minutes. Increase to medium, stir in the onion, carrots and celery, then cook, stirring occasionally, until the vegetables begin to soften, about 10 minutes.

Add the garlic, tomato paste, pepper flakes and 1 teaspoon salt; cook, stirring, until the tomato paste begins to stick to the pot and brown, 1 to 2 minutes. Add 10 cups water and the bay, then bring to a boil over medium-high, scraping up

any browned bits. Add the ribs, beef shank and Parmesan rind. Return to a simmer, then cover, reduce to medium-low and cook, stirring occasionally, until a skewer inserted between the pork ribs and into the meat on the shank meets no resistance, about 2 hours. Remove from the heat.

Using tongs, transfer the ribs and shank to a large bowl; set aside to cool. Meanwhile, using a slotted spoon, remove and discard the solids from the broth. Tilt the pan to pool the liquid to one side, then use a wide spoon to remove and discard as much fat as possible from the surface of the liquid.

When the meats are cool enough to handle, shred the beef into bite-size pieces, discarding the fat, bone and gristle.

Using a paring knife, cut the pork ribs between the bones to separate into individual ribs. Remove the meat from the bones and shred into bite-size pieces; discard the fat, bones and gristle. Set both meats aside.

Bring the broth to a simmer over medium-high. Add the rabe to the pot and cook, stirring often, until tender, 5 to 7 minutes. Stir in the shredded meats and cook, stirring, until heated through, about 2 minutes. Off heat, stir in the basil, then taste and season with salt and black pepper. Serve with grated Parmesan on the side.

HARISSA-SPICED BEEF AND PASTA SOUP

Start to finish: 1¼ hours

Servings: 4 to 6

On any given evening during the month of Ramadan, a soup similar to this graces many Libyan tables. Packed with fork-tender meat, plump orzo, warming spices and bright herbs, the comforting meal is adored nationwide—so much so that it's called "shorba," meaning, quite simply, soup, with no confusion as to which soup is being referred to. For a more traditional flavor profile, replace the beef with boneless leg of lamb. Seasoning the dish with dried mint is a must; its citrusy notes balance the harissa, a smoky North African pepper paste that brings both chili heat and complex spicing to the soup. Our favorite brand of harissa is DEA, sold in a yellow tube. Look for it in the international aisle of the supermarket. Though optional, we love incorporating Aleppo pepper for additional layers of bright yet earthy heat.

2 tablespoons extra-virgin olive oil, plus more to serve

1 pound boneless beef short ribs, trimmed and cut into ½-inch cubes

Kosher salt and ground black pepper

2 tablespoons harissa paste

½ teaspoon ground turmeric

¼ teaspoon ground cinnamon

6-ounce can tomato paste (⅔ cup)

15½-ounce can chickpeas, rinsed and drained

¾ cup orzo pasta

1 large ripe tomato, cored and finely chopped

1 cup lightly packed fresh flat-leaf parsley, finely chopped

2 tablespoons lemon juice

1 tablespoon dried mint

1 teaspoon Aleppo pepper, plus more to serve (optional)

In a large Dutch oven over medium-high, heat the oil until shimmering. Add the beef in an even layer and season with ½ teaspoon salt and ¼ teaspoon black pepper. Cook, without stirring, until browned on the bottom, about 4 minutes. Continue to cook, stirring occasionally, until the beef is browned all over, 4 to 6 minutes.

Add the harissa, turmeric and cinnamon; cook, stirring, until fragrant, about 30 seconds. Add the tomato paste and cook, stirring, until the paste begins to brown and stick to the pot, 2 to 3 minutes. Stir in the chickpeas and 8 cups water. Bring to a simmer, uncovered, over medium-high; reduce to medium and cook, stirring occasionally, for 25 minutes.

Stir in the orzo and cook, uncovered and stirring often to prevent sticking, until the orzo and beef are tender, 15 to 20 minutes.

Off heat, stir in the tomato, parsley, lemon juice, mint and Aleppo pepper (if using). If desired, thin the soup by adding up to 1 cup hot water. Taste and season with salt and black pepper. Serve drizzled with additional oil and sprinkled with additional Aleppo pepper (if using).

SYRIAN-STYLE MEATBALL SOUP WITH RICE AND TOMATOES

Start to finish: 40 minutes
Servings: 4

This rustic meatball and rice soup is pure comfort food. The recipe is our adaptation of one from "Aromas of Aleppo" by Poopa Dweck. Made with canned tomatoes, rice and boxed broth, plus a few warming spices, onion and garlic, the soup requires only one refrigerated ingredient: ground beef (ground turkey works well, too). And the prep is easy. We grate both the onion and garlic so no knifework is required. What's more, there's no need to pre-shape or brown the meatballs. As you form them, simply drop them into the simmering broth.

1 pound ground beef OR turkey

4 tablespoons extra-virgin olive oil, divided

1 large yellow onion, grated on the large holes of a box grater, divided

5 medium garlic cloves, finely grated

2 teaspoons ground allspice OR ground cumin, divided

¼ teaspoon red pepper flakes OR ground cinnamon OR both

Kosher salt and ground black pepper

28-ounce can diced tomatoes

1 quart low-sodium beef OR chicken broth

½ cup long-grain white rice OR basmati rice, rinsed and drained

In a medium bowl, combine the beef, 2 tablespoons oil, ¼ cup of the grated onion, half of the garlic, 1½ teaspoons of the allspice, the red pepper flakes, 1 teaspoon salt and ½ teaspoon black pepper. Mix with your hands until well combined; set aside.

In a large pot, combine the remaining 2 tablespoons oil, the remaining onion, the remaining garlic, the remaining ½ teaspoon allspice and ½ teaspoon salt. Cook over medium-high, stirring occasionally, until the mixture is browned and sticks to the pot, about 5 minutes.

Add the tomatoes with juices, the broth and 2 cups water. Bring to a simmer, scraping up any browned bits, then stir in the rice. Reduce to medium and cook, uncovered and

stirring occasionally, for 8 minutes; the rice will not be fully cooked.

Using dampened hands, pinch off a 1-tablespoon portion of the meat mixture, form it into a ball and drop it into the broth. Shape the remaining meat mixture and add to the pot in the same way; it's fine if the meatballs are not completely uniform. Simmer, uncovered and stirring occasionally, until the soup is slightly thickened and the center of the meatballs reach 160°F, 10 to 15 minutes. Off heat, taste and season with salt and black pepper.

Optional garnish: Chopped fresh flat-leaf parsley **OR** chopped fresh cilantro **OR** pomegranate molasses **OR** a combination

Beans & Lentils

How to Cook Dried Beans

Start to finish: 35 to 70 minutes, depending on bean variety (10 minutes active), plus soaking
Makes 6 to 7 cups

Dried beans cooked on the stovetop can be inconsistent. After much testing, we learned that oven-cooking is more reliable and easier. We start with an overnight soak in salted water. The salt softens the skins, allowing water to better penetrate, producing tender beans. Drained and combined with fresh water and more salt, the beans are brought to a boil on the stovetop, then transferred to the oven for low-and-slow cooking. Once in the oven, the cooking is hands off.

Some varieties of beans can be trickier to cook. Calcium, which varies by type of bean and also by where they are grown, is a major factor. Higher-calcium beans hold their shape better; lower-calcium beans are more likely to blow out. Kidney beans tend to be particularly prone to blowouts; we adapted to account for that. Older beans take longer to tenderize so begin checking for doneness on the low end of the time range, but don't be surprised if they require longer than suggested. Store the cooked beans in their cooking liquid.

1 pound (2 cups) dried beans (see chart)

Kosher salt

In a large bowl, stir together 2 quarts water, the beans and 1 tablespoon salt. Soak at room temperature for at least 12 hours or up to 24 hours.

Heat the oven to 275°F with a rack in the lower-middle position. Drain the beans and place them in a Dutch oven. Add 6 cups water and 1½ teaspoons salt. Bring to a rolling boil over medium-high; as the mixture heats, use a wide, flat spoon to skim off and discard the scum that rises to the surface. Once boiling, stir, then cover and transfer to the oven. Cook until the beans are tender but still retain their shape (see chart; for kidney beans cook as instructed for 40 minutes, then remove the pot from the heat and let stand, covered, for 20 to 30 minutes, until the beans become fully tender).

Remove the pot from the oven. Cool the beans in the liquid in the pot. If using right away, drain, reserving the liquid if desired. If storing, transfer the beans and liquid to a container, cover and refrigerate up to 5 days.

Type	Cook Time	Yield
Chickpeas	45 to 70 minutes	7 cups
Black beans	45 to 60 minutes	6 cups
Pinto beans	35 to 50 minutes	7 cups
Kidney beans	40 minutes* *Plus 20-30 minutes off heat	6 cups
Cannellini beans	50 to 60 minutes	6 cups
Great northern beans	35 to 45 minutes	6 cups
Navy beans	45 to 60 minutes	6 cups

FALAFEL

Start to finish: 2 hours (50 minutes active), plus soaking
Makes about 25 falafel

Across Amman, Jordan, we tasted numerous versions of falafel and concluded that perfection entails a combination of three things: a crisp, beautifully burnished crust without any greasiness; an interior that has a light and tender texture; and bold but well-balanced seasonings that complement the earthiness of the chickpeas. To develop our own recipe, we borrowed techniques from home cooks as well as professionals who taught us their methods and formulas, but we also came up with a few tricks of our own. Namely, we add both salt and baking soda to the water for soaking the dried chickpeas to help tenderize both the interiors and exteriors of the legumes. For varied texture in the processed chickpea mixture, we finely grind half in the food processor before tossing in the remainder and pulsing only until the second addition is finely nubby. This results in fried falafel that hold together but have crisp, lacy exteriors. Additional baking soda plus baking powder provides leavening, yielding falafel that are practically airy. Parsley and cilantro bring fresh herbal flavor, and baharat, an all-purpose Middle Eastern seasoning blend, lends complex spiciness. Baharat can be purchased at larger supermarkets or use our recipe to make your own (recipe p. 126). To form the falafel and drop them into the oil, you will need a 1¾-inch (2-tablespoon) spring-loaded ice cream/dough scoop. Our favorite way to eat falafel is to stuff them into fresh pita bread with thin slices of ripe tomato, then drizzle on lemony tahini sauce. Sliced cucumber and onion are great, too.

12 ounces dried chickpeas

Kosher salt and ground black pepper

2 teaspoons baking soda, divided

2 teaspoons baking powder

1 tablespoon baharat (see headnote)

**1 bunch flat-leaf parsley, leaves and
tender stems roughly chopped (about 1¼ cups)**

**1 bunch cilantro, leaves and stems
roughly chopped (about 1¼ cups)**

2 tablespoons lemon juice

6 to 8 cups grapeseed or other neutral oil

Tahini-yogurt sauce (recipe p. 126)

Warm pita bread, to serve

Thin tomato wedges, to serve

In a large bowl, stir together the chickpeas, 2 quarts water, 1 tablespoon salt and 1 teaspoon of the baking soda. Let soak at room temperature for at least 12 hours, or up to 24 hours.

Drain the chickpeas in a colander, rinse them and drain again. In a food processor, combine half of the chickpeas (about 2 cups), 2½ teaspoons salt, ½ teaspoon of the remaining baking soda, the baking powder, baharat and 1 teaspoon pepper. Process, scraping the bowl as needed, until the mixture is roughly chopped, about 1 minute. Add 1 cup water and continue to process until the mixture is mostly smooth, scraping the bowl as needed, about 2 minutes. Add the remaining chickpeas, parsley and cilantro. Pulse, occasionally scraping the bowl, until the mixture resembles very coarse sand; this will require about 60 pulses. Transfer the mixture to a medium bowl. Cover and refrigerate for at least 1 hour or up to 3 hours.

When you are ready to fry the falafel, set a wire rack in a rimmed baking sheet. Into a large (7- to 8-quart) Dutch oven over medium-high, add oil to a depth of about 1½ inches and heat to 325°F. When the oil is nearly to temperature, remove the chickpea mixture from the refrigerator. Add the lemon juice and remaining ½ teaspoon baking soda to the chickpea mixture; stir until well combined.

When the oil reaches 325°F, use a 1¾-inch (2-tablespoon) spring-loaded scoop to scoop up a portion of the chickpea mixture, lightly compacting the mixture into it against the side of the bowl. Holding the scoop just above the surface of the oil to prevent splashing, carefully release the portion into the oil. Working quickly, scoop an additional 8 or so portions into the pot. Fry, occasionally rotating the falafel, until deep golden brown, about 5 minutes; adjust the heat as needed to maintain an oil temperature of 300°F to 325°F. Using a slotted spoon, transfer the falafel to the prepared rack. Cook the remaining chickpea mixture in the same way, stirring the mixture as needed to reincorporate any liquid that separates out and allowing the oil to come back up to temperature before adding subsequent batches.

Serve the falafel with the tahini-yogurt sauce, pita and tomatoes.

TAHINI-YOGURT SAUCE

Start to finish: 10 minutes
Makes about 2 cups

This simple tahini sauce is a creamy, cooling counterpoint to crisp, freshly fried falafel. It can be made a day or two in advance and stored in an airtight container in the refrigerator, but bring to room temperature before serving.

½ cup tahini

¾ cup boiling water

½ cup plain whole-milk Greek yogurt

3 tablespoons lemon juice

Kosher salt

1 tablespoon sesame seeds, toasted

Put the tahini in a medium bowl. Gradually whisk in the water, followed by the yogurt, lemon juice and ½ teaspoon salt. Whisk in the sesame seeds.

BAHARAT

Start to finish: 5 minutes
Makes about ½ cup

Baharat, which simply translates as "spices" from Arabic, is a versatile Middle Eastern spice blend. It's sold in well-stocked supermarkets, spice shops and Middle Eastern grocery stores. But it is easy to mix your own, especially if you start with ground spices. There's no right or wrong way of making baharat—each cook usually has their own formula. This recipe is our favorite mix. It includes some brown sugar to balance the spices. Stored in an airtight container, the baharat will keep for a few months. But if you don't think you'll use it up before it begins to stale, the recipe can easily be halved.

2 tablespoons packed brown sugar

1 tablespoon ground cardamom

1 tablespoon ground coriander

1 tablespoon ground cumin

1 tablespoon kosher salt

1 tablespoon ground sumac

1 teaspoon ground black pepper

1 teaspoon ground cinnamon

1 teaspoon granulated garlic

In a small bowl, whisk together all ingredients. Transfer to an airtight container and store in a cool, dry place for up to a few months.

CHICKPEA AND CUCUMBER SALAD

Start to finish: 15 minutes
Servings: 6

Chaat is a style of savory South Asian street snack with dozens of varieties. All combine a mix of contrasting flavors and textures—sweet, tart and spicy, as well as creamy and crunchy. This is our version of chickpea (chana) chaat; it's a good appetizer or side to grilled meats or seafood. We toast curry powder in a dry skillet over medium for 1 minute, stirring constantly, to deepen its flavors and cook out any raw notes. To mimic the crunch of fried samosa wrappers that are sometimes used in chaat, we used the fried wonton strips sold near the croutons in the supermarket. For convenience, we used store-bought tamarind chutney (look in the international aisle) and spiked it with brown sugar, lime juice and hot sauce. We preferred the acidic heat of Tabasco or Frank's Red Hot sauce. Feel free to substitute chopped tomato and/or mango for all or some of the cucumber. And if you like, drizzle with whole-milk plain yogurt.

Two 15½-ounce cans chickpeas, drained, rinsed and patted dry

1 small red onion, finely chopped

2 teaspoons curry powder, toasted (see headnote)

Kosher salt and ground black pepper

⅓ cup tamarind chutney

1½ tablespoons hot sauce, plus more as needed

3 tablespoons lime juice, plus lime wedges, to serve

2 tablespoons packed light brown sugar

3 cups (4 ounces) fried wonton strips

1 English cucumber, quartered lengthwise and cut crosswise into ¼-inch pieces

1 cup lightly packed cilantro leaves, finely chopped

In a large bowl, toss the chickpeas, onion, curry powder and 1 teaspoon each salt and pepper. Set aside.

In a small bowl, whisk together the chutney, hot sauce, lime juice and sugar. Taste and season with more hot sauce, if desired. Pour ¼ cup of this mixture over the chickpeas and toss. Cover and let stand for 15 minutes.

To the chickpea mixture, mix in the wonton strips, cucumber and half the cilantro. Taste and season with salt and pepper. Drizzle with half the remaining chutney mixture and sprinkle with the remaining cilantro. Serve with the extra chutney mixture and lime wedges.

CHICKPEA AND FETA MEATBALLS

Start to finish: 45 minutes (30 minutes active)
Servings: 4

Keftedes are Greek meatballs, and this recipe is our vegetarian interpretation of the chickpea and sardine keftedes from "Smashing Plates" by London chef Maria Elia. Instead of cooking the chickpea mixture as balls, we flatten the portions into patties directly in the skillet. This creates more surface area for browning and speeds the cooking. These chickpea patties are great with a simple salad, or tuck them into pita with veggies such as onions, tomatoes, cucumber and/or radishes.

½ cup whole-milk plain yogurt

¼ cup tahini

6 teaspoons lemon juice, divided,
plus lemon wedges to serve

1½ teaspoons ground cumin, divided

Kosher salt and ground black pepper

1 large egg

1½ teaspoons sweet paprika

½ teaspoon ground cinnamon

Two 15½-ounce cans chickpeas, rinsed and drained

2 ounces feta cheese, crumbled (½ cup)

½ cup finely chopped fresh mint, flat-leaf parsley or a
combination, plus whole or torn leaves to serve

2 tablespoons grapeseed or other neutral oil, divided

In a small bowl, stir together the yogurt, tahini, 4 teaspoons
of lemon juice and 1 teaspoon of cumin. Transfer ⅓ cup
of the mixture to a large bowl. Into the remaining yogurt
mixture, stir the remaining 2 teaspoons lemon juice and
¼ teaspoon each salt and pepper; set aside for serving.

To the large bowl, add the egg, paprika, cinnamon, the
remaining ½ teaspoon cumin, ¾ teaspoon salt and 1 teaspoon pepper, then whisk to combine. Add the chickpeas
and mash with a potato masher until broken down but not
completely smooth. Add the feta and herb(s), then mix well.

Form into 12 evenly sized balls (each about a scant ¼ cup);
place on a plate and refrigerate for about 15 minutes.

In a 12-inch nonstick skillet over medium, heat 1 tablespoon of oil until shimmering. Add 6 of the balls, spacing
them evenly apart (return the remainder to the refrigerator),
then flatten each with a metal spatula into a 2- to 2½-inch
patty. Cook until golden brown on both sides, 3 to 4 minutes
per side, gently flipping them once. Transfer to a platter and
tent with foil. Wipe out the skillet and repeat with the
remaining oil and patties. Top the keftedes with whole or
torn herb(s) and serve with the yogurt-tahini sauce and
lemon wedges.

HOT-AND-SOUR CURRIED CHICKPEAS

Start to finish: 25 minutes
Servings: 4

Khatte chole, or Indian sour chickpeas, was our starting
point for this quick-and-easy vegetarian curry. Amchoor,
or dried green mango powder, usually supplies the dish's
characteristic tartness, but instead we steep chopped onion
and jalapeño in lemon juice to make a quick pickle that
adds crunch as well as acidity. For less heat, remove the
seeds from the jalapeño before chopping. A box grater
makes quick work of reducing the onions and tomatoes
to a pulp—no food processor or blender needed. Serve the
chickpeas with naan or basmati rice.

2 medium red onions, halved

1 jalapeño chili, stemmed and finely chopped

¼ cup lemon juice

2 teaspoons finely grated fresh ginger, divided

3 large plum tomatoes, halved lengthwise
and cored

3 tablespoons salted butter, divided

2 teaspoons garam masala

1½ teaspoons curry powder

Kosher salt

Two 15½-ounce cans chickpeas, rinsed
and drained

¼ cup chopped fresh cilantro, plus
more to serve

ETHIOPIAN CHICKPEA STEW WITH BERBERE SPICE BLEND

Start to finish: 45 minutes

Servings: 4

Shiro wat is an Ethiopian stew made with ground dried legumes mixed with spices (a blend known as mitten shiro), along with aromatics, tomatoes and the spice blend called berbere (recipe p. 337). Meant to be served with injera (Ethiopian flatbread) and other dishes to comprise a complete meal, shiro wat is a thick, rustic puree. We loved the flavors, but wanted them as a stew hearty enough to be a vegetarian main, so we opted to use canned whole chickpeas and flavored them with many of the traditional seasonings and ingredients. Ground red lentils give our stew added earthiness while also acting as a thickener. As a cooking fat, we use Indian ghee, which approximates the flavor of Ethiopian fermented butter but is easier to find. Look for ghee in the supermarket grocery aisle near the coconut oil or in the refrigerator aisle next to the butter. If you cannot find it, use salted butter in its place but also add 1 teaspoon white miso when adding the water.

2 tablespoons red lentils

3 tablespoons ghee (see headnote)

1 medium yellow onion, chopped

1 pint cherry or grape tomatoes, halved

8 medium garlic cloves, minced

2 tablespoons minced fresh ginger

2 tablespoons berbere (see headnote)

Two 15½-ounce cans chickpeas, rinsed and drained

Kosher salt and ground black pepper

1 cup lightly packed fresh flat-leaf parsley, chopped

1 jalapeño or Fresno chili, stemmed and chopped (optional)

In a spice grinder, pulse the lentils until finely ground, about 10 pulses; set aside. In a large saucepan over medium, melt the ghee. Add the onion and cook, stirring occasionally, until golden brown, 8 to 10 minutes. Stir in the tomatoes, garlic, ginger and berbere. Cook, stirring occasionally, until the tomatoes have given up their liquid and the mixture is beginning to brown, 3 to 5 minutes.

Finely chop 1 onion half, then in a small bowl combine it with the jalapeño, lemon juice and 1 teaspoon of ginger. Set aside. On the large holes of a box grater set over a large bowl, grate the remaining 3 onion halves. Next, grate the tomato halves starting on the cut sides and grating down to the skin; discard the skins.

In a large saucepan over medium, heat 2 tablespoons of butter, the garam masala and curry powder, stirring, until fragrant, about 30 seconds. Add the onion-tomato pulp, the remaining 1 teaspoon ginger and ½ teaspoon salt. Increase to medium-high and cook, stirring occasionally, until a spoon leaves about a 5-second trail when drawn through the mixture, 8 to 10 minutes.

Add the chickpeas and cook, stirring, until the chickpeas are warmed through, 1 to 2 minutes. Remove the pan from the heat. Measure out and reserve about ⅓ cup of the onion-jalapeño pickle, then add the remainder to the pan along with the cilantro, the remaining 1 tablespoon butter and ¼ teaspoon salt. Stir to combine, then taste and adjust the seasoning with salt. Transfer to a serving dish and sprinkle with the reserved onion-jalapeño pickle and additional cilantro.

Add the chickpeas, ground lentils, 2 cups water and ½ teaspoon each salt and pepper. Boil over medium-high, then reduce to medium and cook at a simmer, uncovered and stirring often, until the sauce clings to the chickpeas, about 15 minutes. Off heat, stir in the parsley and chili (if using). Taste and season with salt and pepper.

GREEK BRAISED CHICKPEAS WITH TOMATOES AND ORANGE

Start to finish: 45 minutes

Servings: 4

On the Greek island of Ikaria, Diane Kochilas introduced us to an ultrasimple yet remarkably delicious dish of chickpeas layered with tomatoes, herbs, orange and honey that is baked for a couple hours to meld and concentrate the flavors. Our version simmers canned chickpeas on the stovetop with many of the same ingredients and is ready in under an hour, yet the flavors are equally rich and complex. We liked this dish made with a strong, dark honey, such as buckwheat, but a milder variety works, too. Orange blossom honey is a good option, as it echoes the citrus notes of the orange zest and juice. Serve with crusty bread, and perhaps some briny feta alongside.

¼ cup extra-virgin olive oil, plus more to serve

2 tablespoons tomato paste

2 tablespoons honey (see headnote), divided

Three 15½-ounce cans chickpeas, drained, ¼ cup liquid reserved

28-ounce can diced tomatoes

1 medium red onion, halved and thinly sliced

3 medium garlic cloves, thinly sliced

5 bay leaves

1 sprig fresh rosemary

1 teaspoon grated orange zest, plus ¼ cup orange juice

Kosher salt and ground black pepper

1 tablespoon chopped fresh oregano

½ cup lightly packed fresh flat-leaf parsley, chopped

In a large Dutch oven over medium, combine the oil, tomato paste and 1 tablespoon of the honey. Cook, stirring often, until the tomato paste begins to brown, 6 to 7 min-

utes. Stir in the chickpeas, then stir in the tomatoes with their juices. Bring to a simmer over medium-high and cook, stirring occasionally, until the liquid has evaporated, 10 to 12 minutes.

Stir in the onion, garlic, bay, rosemary, orange juice, ¾ teaspoon each salt and pepper, and the reserved chickpea liquid. Bring to a simmer, then cover and cook over medium-low, stirring occasionally, until the onion has softened, 12 to 15 minutes.

Remove from the heat, then taste and season with salt and pepper. Stir in the oregano and orange zest. Transfer to a serving bowl. Sprinkle with parsley, then drizzle with the remaining honey and additional oil.

TUNISIAN CHICKPEAS WITH SWISS CHARD

Start to finish: 35 minutes
Servings: 4

This wholesome but hearty dish was inspired by a recipe in "Mediterranean Cooking" by Paula Wolfert, an expert on North African and Mediterranean cuisines. Browned tomato paste, onion and garlic create a flavor base that complements the earthiness of Swiss chard. Use rainbow chard if you can find it—the vibrant stems add color to the dish. Roughly mashing the tomatoes and chickpeas creates a chunky, rustic broth that's perfect with crusty bread, warmed flatbread or couscous, but the dish also is an excellent side to roasted or grilled chicken or lamb.

2 tablespoons extra-virgin olive oil, plus more to serve

1 medium red onion, chopped

4 medium garlic cloves, smashed and peeled

2 tablespoons tomato paste

2 teaspoons ground coriander

2 teaspoons ground cumin

Two 15½-ounce cans chickpeas, rinsed and drained

28-ounce can whole peeled tomatoes

1 large bunch Swiss chard (about 1 pound), stems finely chopped, leaves roughly chopped, reserved separately

Kosher salt and ground black pepper

Lemon wedges, to serve

In a large Dutch oven over medium, heat the oil until shimmering. Add the onion, garlic, tomato paste, coriander and cumin, then cook, stirring occasionally, until the tomato paste has browned, 2 to 4 minutes. Add the chickpeas, tomatoes with their juice, chard stems, ¾ teaspoon salt, ½ teaspoon pepper and 1 cup water, scraping up any browned bits.

Bring to a simmer, then cover, reduce to medium-low and cook, stirring occasionally, until the onion and chard stems have softened, 10 to 14 minutes. With the pot still on medium-low, use a potato masher or the back of a large spoon to roughly mash the mixture; it's fine if many of the chickpeas remain whole.

Return to a simmer over medium-high, then add the chard leaves. Cook, stirring, until they are wilted, 2 to 3 minutes. Taste and season with salt and pepper. Serve with a drizzle of oil and lemon wedges on the side.

131

FRIED WHITE BEANS WITH BACON, GARLIC AND SPINACH

Start to finish: 25 minutes
Servings: 4

This simple recipe takes full advantage of the starchiness of cannellini beans. Frying the beans in the fat rendered from bacon combined with some fruity olive oil blisters, browns and crisps their exteriors, creating a pleasing contrast to the soft, creamy interiors. Garlic, smoked paprika and lemon juice are perfect flavor accents, and baby spinach wilted into the mix at the end of cooking rounds out the dish. For best crisping and to minimize splatter, pat the beans dry after draining them. And when frying, stir the beans only every minute or so. With some crusty bread alongside, this makes a great light main.

4 ounces bacon, chopped

1 tablespoon extra-virgin olive oil, plus more to serve

4 medium garlic cloves, minced

½ teaspoon smoked paprika

Kosher salt and ground black pepper

Two 15½-ounce cans cannellini beans, rinsed, drained and patted dry

5-ounce container baby spinach

2 tablespoons lemon juice, plus lemon wedges to serve

In a 12-inch skillet combine the bacon and 1 tablespoon oil. Cook over medium, stirring occasionally, until the bacon is crisp, 5 to 6 minutes. Using a slotted spoon, transfer to a paper towel-lined plate; set aside.

To the fat remaining in the skillet, add the garlic, paprika and 1 teaspoon pepper. Cook over medium-high, stirring, until fragrant, about 30 seconds. Add the beans and cook, stirring only about once every minute or so, until the skins begin to split and crisp and are lightly browned, 5 to 6 minutes.

Add the spinach and stir just until wilted. Remove the pan from the heat and stir in the lemon juice, then taste and season with salt and pepper. Transfer to a serving dish, drizzle with additional oil and sprinkle with the bacon. Serve with lemon wedges.

WHITE BEANS WITH SAGE, GARLIC AND FENNEL

Start to finish: 45 minutes
Servings: 4

This is a simplified version of classic Tuscan fagioli uccellet-to. For complexity, we flavor the beans with three layers of sage—finely chopped leaves, sage-infused oil and crumbled fried leaves. Any variety of canned white beans will work, though great northern and navy beans held their shape better than cannellini. This dish is hearty enough to serve as a main—it's excellent with grilled rustic bread—but is also a good accompaniment to roasted chicken or pork.

6 tablespoons extra-virgin olive oil, divided

1 large fennel bulb, trimmed and finely chopped

1 medium yellow onion, finely chopped

4 large garlic cloves, finely chopped

3 tablespoons finely chopped fresh sage, plus 20 whole leaves

¼ teaspoon red pepper flakes

Kosher salt and ground black pepper

14½-ounce can diced tomatoes

Two 15½-ounce cans white beans (see headnote),
1 can rinsed and drained

Shaved or grated Parmesan cheese, to serve

In a large Dutch oven over medium, heat 3 tablespoons
of the oil until shimmering. Add the fennel, onion, garlic,
chopped sage, red pepper flakes and ½ teaspoon salt. Cover
and cook, stirring occasionally, until the vegetables have
softened, about 15 minutes.

Stir in the tomatoes and the beans. Cook, uncovered,
stirring occasionally and adjusting the heat as needed to
maintain a gentle simmer, for 10 minutes. Taste and season
with salt and pepper.

Meanwhile, line a plate with paper towels. In a 12-inch
skillet over medium-high, heat the remaining 3 tablespoons
oil until shimmering. Add the sage leaves and cook, flipping
the leaves once, until the edges begin to curl, about 1 minute.
Transfer to the prepared plate; reserve the oil.

Transfer the beans to a serving bowl, then drizzle with the
sage oil. Coarsely crumble the sage leaves over the beans.
Top with Parmesan.

TURKISH BEANS WITH PICKLED TOMATOES

Start to finish: 3 hours (15 minutes active)
Servings: 6

This hearty white bean stew was inspired by the Turkish
dish kuru fasulye, basically beans stewed in a spicy tomato
sauce. We also borrowed a bit of flavor from the Middle
Eastern pantry, using pomegranate molasses, a syrup
of boiled pomegranate juice, to add a unique and fruity
sweetness. You'll find it in the grocer's international section
or near the honey, maple syrup and molasses. This dish
calls for dried beans, which means an overnight soak for
evenly cooked beans. The creamy texture of dried cannellini
beans, soaked overnight, were best, but great northern
beans worked well, too. We maximized meaty flavor—
without using a lot of meat—by using a collagen-rich beef
or lamb shank. Serve these beans as is or with a drizzle of
extra-virgin olive oil and a spoonful of whole-milk yogurt.
We also loved the bright contrast provided by pickled
tomatoes (recipe p. 134). The beans can be made up to two
days ahead. Reheat over low, adding water to reach your
desired consistency.

1 pound dried cannellini beans

Kosher salt and ground black pepper

12- to 16-ounce lamb shank

1 large yellow onion, chopped
(about 2 cups)

4 tablespoons (½ stick) salted butter

8 garlic cloves, peeled and smashed

4 thyme sprigs

2 bay leaves

1 teaspoon paprika

1 teaspoon red pepper flakes

14½-ounce can diced tomatoes, drained

½ cup chopped fresh parsley

2 tablespoons chopped fresh dill,
plus more to serve

2 tablespoons pomegranate molasses,
plus more to serve

Whole-milk yogurt and extra-virgin olive oil,
to serve

Pickled tomatoes (recipe p. 134), to serve

In a large bowl, combine 3 quarts water, the beans and 2 teaspoons salt. Let soak at room temperature for at least 12 hours, or up to 24 hours. Drain and rinse the beans.

Heat the oven to 325°F with a rack in the middle position. In a large oven-safe pot or Dutch oven over high heat, combine 5½ cups water, the beans, shank, onion, butter, garlic, thyme, bay leaves, paprika and red pepper flakes. Bring to a boil, then cover and transfer to the oven. Bake for 1 hour 15 minutes.

Remove the pot from the oven. Stir in the tomatoes and 1 teaspoon salt. Return, uncovered, to the oven and bake until the beans are fully tender and creamy and the liquid is slightly thickened, another 1 hour 15 minutes. Transfer the pot to a rack. Remove the shank and set aside. Discard the thyme sprigs and bay leaves.

When cool enough to handle, remove the meat from the bone, discarding fat, gristle and bone. Finely chop the meat and stir into the beans. Stir in the parsley, dill and molasses. Taste and season with salt and pepper. Serve with yogurt, olive oil, pomegranate molasses and dill.

PICKLED TOMATOES

Start to finish: 5 minutes, plus chilling
Makes 1½ cups

These pickled tomatoes are delicious with our Turkish beans but can also be used on sandwiches or in hearty soups. Be sure to seed the tomatoes. If you can't find Aleppo pepper, substitute with a slightly smaller amount of red pepper flakes.

3 plum tomatoes (12 ounces), cored, seeded and diced

3 tablespoons cider vinegar

1 tablespoon chopped fresh dill

1 teaspoon crushed Aleppo pepper

1 teaspoon white sugar

¼ teaspoon kosher salt

In a medium bowl, stir together all of the ingredients. Refrigerate for at least 1 hour.

OAXACAN REFRIED BLACK BEANS

Start to finish: 2¾ hours (35 minutes active)
Servings: 6

In Oaxaca, black beans are a part of almost every meal. Though they sometimes are served whole, we especially liked the balanced, complex flavor and smooth, velvety consistency of refried black beans. We got a lesson in the importance of the daily basic from Rodolfo Castellanos, Oaxaca native and winner of Top Chef Mexico, and his mother. Lard gives these beans a rich meatiness, but coconut oil is a good vegetarian substitute. The beans can be stored in an airtight container in the refrigerator for up to a week. We liked this topped with cotija and fresh cilantro.

4 tablespoons lard or refined coconut oil, divided

1 large white onion, chopped

1 pint grape or cherry tomatoes

5 guajillo chilies, stemmed and seeded

1 pound dried black beans, rinsed

10 medium garlic cloves, peeled and kept whole, plus 5 medium garlic cloves, minced

3 bay leaves

1 teaspoon aniseed

Kosher salt and ground black pepper

4 teaspoons ground cumin

4 teaspoons ground coriander

1 tablespoon ancho chili powder

1 teaspoon dried oregano

In a large pot over medium-high, heat 1 tablespoon of lard until barely smoking. Add the onion, tomatoes and guajillo chilies, then cook, stirring occasionally, until the onion is well browned, 5 to 7 minutes. Add the beans, whole garlic cloves, bay and aniseed, then stir in 10 cups water. Bring to a boil, then cover partially and reduce to low. Cook, stirring occasionally, until the beans are completely tender, 1½ hours to 2 hours.

Stir in 1 teaspoon salt. Set a colander in a large bowl and drain the beans, reserving the cooking liquid. Remove and discard the bay leaves from the beans. Transfer the drained beans to a food processor and pulse a few times to break up the beans. With the machine running, add 1½ cups of the reserved cooking liquid and process until smooth, 2 to 3 minutes, scraping the bowl as needed. Taste and season with salt, then set aside.

In a 12-inch nonstick skillet over medium, heat 2 tablespoons of the remaining lard until shimmering. Add the minced garlic, cumin, coriander, chili powder and oregano, then cook, stirring, until fragrant, about 30 seconds.

Stir in the pureed beans and cook, stirring frequently, until beginning to brown on the bottom, 8 to 10 minutes. Continue to cook and stir, adding reserved cooking water as needed, until the mixture has the consistency of mashed potatoes, 5 to 7 minutes. Off heat, stir in the remaining 1 tablespoon lard, then taste and season with salt and pepper.

135

CHANGE THE WAY YOU COOK

Heat Beans for Better Flavor

A canned bean salad delivers a speedy, nutritious and all-around convenient supper, but it needs a nudge on the flavor factor. That's why we bring the heat.

Turns out warming beans before tossing them with aromatics or other high-impact ingredients is a simple and effective way to season them. The heat makes the beans expand; as the surfaces cool and contract they more easily absorb flavor.

We use the microwave to warm the beans—it takes just a few minutes—then add seasonings ranging from a Greek-inspired mix of garlic, onion, red wine vinegar and oil to a Caribbean medley of oil, lime, jalapeño and coconut.

CUBAN-STYLE BLACK BEANS AND RICE

Start to finish: 45 minutes
Servings: 4 to 6

This is a classic Cuban combination of black beans and rice that uses sautéed onion, green bell pepper and garlic as foundational flavors. The beans usually are cooked from dried, but with canned black beans, the dish is a breeze to prepare and can be thrown together at a moment's notice. Some versions are made with pork—and indeed, smoky, salty bacon is a delicious addition. If you wish to include bacon, begin by cooking 4 ounces, chopped, in the saucepan over medium-high until crisp, 6 to 7 minutes; add the onion and bell pepper to the bacon and its rendered fat, omitting the oil, then proceed with the recipe.

3 tablespoons grapeseed or other neutral oil

1 medium yellow onion, chopped

1 medium green bell pepper, stemmed, seeded and chopped

Kosher salt and ground black pepper

4 medium garlic cloves, chopped

1 teaspoon ground cumin

¾ teaspoon dried oregano OR 2 bay leaves
OR both

1 cup long-grain white rice, rinsed and drained

1½ cups low-sodium chicken broth

Two 15½-ounce cans black beans,
rinsed and drained

In a large saucepan over medium-high, heat the oil until shimmering. Add the onion, bell pepper and ¼ teaspoon salt, then cook, stirring occasionally, until softened, 7 to 9 minutes. Add the garlic, cumin and oregano; cook, stirring, until fragrant, about 1 minute. Stir in the rice, then add the broth, beans and ¼ teaspoon pepper. Bring to a simmer, then cover, reduce to low and cook until the rice has absorbed the liquid, 20 to 25 minutes.

Remove the pot from the heat. Let stand, covered, for 10 minutes. Fluff the mixture with a fork, then remove and discard the bay. Taste and season with salt and pepper.

GREEK BEAN SALAD

Start to finish: 45 minutes (15 minutes active)
Servings: 6

This bean salad was inspired by one we tasted in Greece. White beans, crunchy red onion, lush avocado and a tangle of herbs—all dressed with just lemon juice and oil—added up to complex flavor that was much more than the sum of the simple parts. We swapped the large, flat butter beans typically used by Greek cooks for easier-to-find cannellini, and we opted for the convenience of canned. We boosted their flavor by heating them before adding the dressing. This can be done a day in advance and the beans can be refrigerated until ready to serve. If you like, bring the beans to room temperature before tossing with the avocado, herbs and lemon, but even cold the salad is delicious.

Four 15½-ounce cans cannellini beans,
rinsed and drained

Kosher salt and ground black pepper

2 medium garlic cloves, finely grated

1 small red onion, halved and thinly sliced

⅓ cup red wine vinegar

3 tablespoons extra-virgin olive oil,
plus more, to serve

1 ripe avocado, halved, pitted, peeled
and cut into ½-inch pieces

1 cup lightly packed fresh flat-leaf parsley,
torn if large

½ cup lightly packed fresh dill, chopped

1 teaspoon grated lemon zest, plus
1 teaspoon lemon juice

In a large microwave-safe bowl, toss the beans with ½ teaspoon salt. Cover and microwave on high until hot, 3 to 3½ minutes, stirring once halfway through.

To the hot beans, add the garlic, onion, vinegar, oil, 1 teaspoon salt and ¾ teaspoon pepper; toss to combine. Let stand until cooled to room temperature, about 30 minutes, stirring once or twice.

Stir the beans once again, then stir in the avocado, parsley, dill and lemon zest and juice. Taste and season with salt and pepper. Transfer to a serving bowl and drizzle with additional oil.

137

BLACK BEAN–BELL PEPPER SALAD WITH COCONUT AND LIME

Start to finish: 20 minutes
Servings: 4

This simple Caribbean-inspired black bean salad has a spicy-sweet brightness to match its festive appearance. Heating the beans so they're piping hot when dressed helps them absorb seasonings as they cool so each forkful is flavorful. For ease, we use the microwave to heat the beans. If you happen to have fresh mango or pineapple on hand, dice some and toss it into the salad just before serving. This is a perfect side to grilled seafood, pork or chicken.

Two 15½-ounce cans black beans, rinsed and drained

Kosher salt and ground black pepper

2 tablespoons extra-virgin olive oil

1 teaspoon grated lime zest, plus ¼ cup lime juice

½ medium red onion, finely chopped

1 jalapeño chili, stemmed, seeded and finely chopped

1 medium orange bell pepper OR red bell pepper, stemmed, seeded and finely chopped

½ cup unsweetened wide-flake coconut

In a large microwave-safe bowl, toss the beans with ½ teaspoon salt. Cover and microwave on high until hot, 1½ to 2 minutes, stirring once about halfway through.

To the hot beans add the oil and lime zest and juice; toss to combine. While the beans are still warm, stir in the onion, jalapeño, bell pepper and coconut. Cool to room temperature, then taste and season with salt and pepper.

KIDNEY BEAN AND RICE SALAD WITH BACON AND CIDER VINEGAR

Start to finish: 25 minutes
Servings: 4 to 6

Red beans and rice, a Louisiana classic, inspired this salad. Smoky bacon, fruity cider vinegar and an entire bunch of scallions add loads of flavor, while red bell pepper and celery bring sweetness and crunch. Straight from the can, beans are bland, but heating them with seasonings ensures tastiness on the inside as well as on the outside because as the beans cool, they soak up lots of flavor. Serve the salad at room temperature.

4 ounces bacon, chopped

1 tablespoon extra-virgin olive oil

1 bunch scallions, thinly sliced on the diagonal, whites and greens reserved separately

⅓ cup cider vinegar

Kosher salt and ground black pepper

Two 15½-ounce cans kidney beans, rinsed and drained

2 cups cooked white rice

2 medium celery stalks, thinly sliced

1 medium red bell pepper, stemmed,
seeded and chopped

In a 12-inch skillet over medium-high, cook the bacon, stirring occasionally, until browned and crisp, 5 to 6 minutes. Using a slotted spoon, transfer the bacon to a paper towel-lined plate; set aside. Pour off and discard all but 2 tablespoons of the fat from the skillet.

Return the skillet to medium-high, add the oil, scallion whites, vinegar and ½ teaspoon each salt and pepper. Bring to a simmer, scraping up any browned bits. Add the beans and cook, uncovered and stirring occasionally, until heated through, 3 to 5 minutes.

Transfer the bean mixture to a medium bowl. Add the rice, celery, bell pepper, scallion greens and bacon; toss to combine. Taste and season with salt and pepper. Serve at room temperature.

BLACK-EYED PEA AND
TOMATO SALAD

Start to finish: 1 hour (20 minutes active)
Servings: 4

This simple salad of earthy-sweet black-eyed peas, crisp vegetables and fragrant herbs stars a smooth, rich garlicky dressing. We simmer a whole head of garlic with the beans, softening and mellowing its flavor, to make the dressing, and we add it to the black-eyed peas while they're still warm, allowing them to absorb ample flavor as they cool. It's important to gently incorporate the ingredients; aggressive stirring will turn the black-eyed peas to mush.

1 head garlic, top third cut off
and discarded

8 ounces (1½ cups) dried black-eyed peas,
rinsed and drained

1 pint cherry OR grape tomatoes, halved

3 tablespoons white wine vinegar
OR red wine vinegar

3 tablespoons extra-virgin olive oil,
plus more to serve

Kosher salt and ground black pepper

2 medium celery stalks, chopped

1 cup lightly packed fresh flat-leaf parsley
OR basil, roughly chopped

In a large saucepan, combine the garlic head and black-eyed peas. Add 6 cups water and bring to a boil over medium-high. Boil for 5 minutes, then reduce to medium-low and simmer, uncovered and stirring occasionally, until the peas are fully tender but still hold their shape, 20 to 25 minutes. Meanwhile, in a medium bowl, toss the tomatoes with ½ teaspoon salt; set aside.

When the peas are done, drain them in a colander. Using tongs, remove the garlic head and squeeze the cloves into a small bowl; discard the skins. Using a fork, mash the garlic cloves until mostly smooth. Stir in the vinegar, oil and ¼ teaspoon pepper.

Transfer the still-warm peas to the tomatoes, then add the dressing and gently stir to combine. Stir in the celery and parsley, then taste and season with salt and pepper. Serve warm or at room temperature, drizzled with additional oil.

Canned Bean Conversions

Beans are a Milk Street pantry staple. For convenience, we often reach for canned. But we almost always prefer the taste, texture and economy of dried beans. There's only one problem: Recipes that call for canned beans—and most do—can leave us puzzled trying to figure out how to adjust the quantities for dried beans.

So we wanted to come up with equivalents for canned and dried beans. We tested 11 common varieties, comparing the weights and volumes of canned and their cooked-from-dry equivalents. For the dried beans, we soaked 1 cup of beans overnight in 4 cups water and 1½ teaspoons kosher salt. All of our beans were cooked over medium heat in 6 cups unsalted water. Cooking time begins at the point of simmer.

As we tested, a formula emerged: Most 15-ounce cans of beans, once drained, yielded roughly 1½ cups (9½ ounces) of beans. Each cup of dried beans produced between 2½ and 3¼ cups (or about 1 pound) of cooked beans. So for every can of beans a recipe calls for, you'll want to start with roughly ½ cup of dried beans.

Type	Volume Dry	Volume Cooked	Cooking Time
Chickpeas	1 cup	2¾ cups	15 mins
Cannellini Beans	1 cup	3¼ cups	25 mins
Black Beans	1 cup	2½ cups	35 mins
Pinto Beans	1 cup	2¾ cups	30 mins
Kidney Beans	1 cup	3 cups	30 mins
Navy Beans	1 cup	2¾ cups	20 mins
Great Northern Beans	1 cup	3 cups	15 mins
Pink Beans	1 cup	3 cups	20 mins
Black-Eyed Peas	1 cup	3 cups	30 mins
Cranberry Beans	1 cup	2½ cups	15 mins
Butter Beans	1 cup	3¼ cups	20 mins

TURKISH WHITE BEAN SALAD

Start to finish: 40 minutes (10 minutes active)
Servings: 4 to 6

Fasülye piyazi, a simple white bean salad with tomatoes, herbs, olives and eggs, is a classic in Türkiye. To infuse the beans with flavor, we toss them with salt and optional dried mint, then heat them in the microwave before combining them while hot with onion, vinegar and pepper. As the beans cool, they absorb the seasonings. Chopped hard-cooked eggs often accompany this salad, so feel free to add some as a garnish. If you have Aleppo pepper in your pantry, a sprinkling will lend mild, smoky heat to the finished salad.

Two 15½-ounce cans great northern beans
OR navy beans, rinsed and drained

½ teaspoon dried mint (optional)

Kosher salt and ground black pepper

1 small red onion, halved and thinly sliced

3 tablespoons red wine vinegar

1 cup cherry OR grape tomatoes, halved

½ cup pitted green OR black olives
OR a combination, roughly chopped

1 or 2 Fresno OR serrano chilies, stemmed
and sliced into thin rings

1 teaspoon grated lemon zest
OR ground sumac

Extra-virgin olive oil, to serve

In a large microwave-safe bowl, toss the beans with the dried mint (if using) and ½ teaspoon salt. Cover and microwave on high until hot, 3 to 3½ minutes, stirring once halfway through. Add the onion, vinegar and ¾ teaspoon pepper to the hot beans, toss, then let stand for about 30 minutes, stirring once or twice.

Stir in the tomatoes, olives, chilies and lemon zest. Taste and season with salt and pepper, then transfer to a serving dish. Serve drizzled with oil.

Optional garnish: Chopped hard-cooked eggs **OR** Aleppo pepper **OR** torn fresh mint **OR** a combination

PINTO BEANS WITH BACON AND CHIPOTLE

Start to finish: 40 minutes
Servings: 4 to 6

Mexican frijoles charros, or "cowboy beans," often are made by simmering pinto beans and fresh tomatoes with multiple varieties of pork, including sausage, ham, pork rind, and shoulder or foot. In our pantry-centric riff on frijoles charros, we keep things simple—but make them smoky—by using bacon. We add spiciness and even more smoky notes with chipotle chili in adobo sauce. Serve these hearty, stewy beans with warm tortillas.

6 ounces bacon, chopped

1 medium red onion, ¾ chopped,
¼ finely chopped, reserved separately

3 medium garlic cloves, finely chopped

1 chipotle chili in adobo, chopped,
plus 2 teaspoons adobo sauce

2 teaspoons ground cumin

2 teaspoons chili powder

Two 15½-ounce cans pinto beans,
rinsed and drained

3 cups low-sodium chicken broth

14½-ounce can crushed tomatoes

Kosher salt and ground black pepper

In a large pot over medium, cook the bacon, stirring occasionally, until lightly browned and beginning to crisp, 4 to 6 minutes. Add the chopped onion; cook, stirring occasionally, until softened and beginning to brown, 4 to 5 minutes.

Add the garlic, chipotle and adobo sauce, cumin and chili powder; cook, stirring, until fragrant, 1 to 2 minutes. Add the beans, broth and tomatoes. Bring to a simmer, scraping up any browned bits, then reduce to medium-low and cook, stirring occasionally, until the mixture is slightly thickened, about 20 minutes.

Off heat, taste and season with salt and pepper. Serve sprinkled with the finely chopped onion.

Optional garnish: Chopped fresh cilantro OR sliced radishes OR both

BUTTER BEANS IN TOMATO SAUCE WITH DILL AND FETA

Start to finish: 40 minutes
Servings: 4

Gigantes plaki is a much-loved Greek dish that bakes gigantes beans (extra-large white beans) in a savory tomato sauce. For ease and speed, our version uses canned butter beans and briefly simmers them on the stovetop in a simple yet flavorful sauce made with canned crushed tomatoes and tomato paste for added depth. Fresh herbs and feta cheese add brightness and brininess to round out the dish. If you like, offer the feta on the side at the table; added to individual portions, the cheese has a firmer texture and a sharper bite. To round out the meal, serve with a simple leafy salad and crusty bread for mopping up the sauce.

¼ cup extra-virgin olive oil, plus more to serve

1 medium sweet onion or red onion, chopped

Kosher salt and ground black pepper

2 medium garlic cloves, thinly sliced

2 tablespoons tomato paste

¼ teaspoon red pepper flakes

14½-ounce can crushed tomatoes

Two 15-ounce cans butter beans, rinsed and drained

5 tablespoons chopped fresh dill or 2½ tablespoons chopped fresh marjoram, divided

3 ounces feta cheese, crumbled (¾ cup)

In a 12-inch skillet over medium, heat the oil until shimmering. Add the onion and ¼ teaspoon salt, then cook, stirring occasionally, until softened and translucent, 5 to 7 minutes.

Add the garlic, tomato paste and pepper flakes, then cook, stirring, until the tomato paste darkens slightly and begins to stick to the pan, about 2 minutes. Stir in the crushed tomatoes, ½ cup water, ½ teaspoon salt and ¼ teaspoon black pepper. Bring to a simmer, then reduce to medium-low and cook, stirring occasionally, until slightly thickened, 7 to 10 minutes.

Add the beans and bring to a simmer over medium, stirring occasionally. Off heat, stir in 4 tablespoons of dill (or 2 tablespoons of marjoram), then taste and season with salt

and black pepper. Transfer to a serving dish, sprinkle with the feta and remaining dill (or marjoram), then drizzle with additional oil.

PINTO BEANS WITH SAUSAGE, KALE AND EGGS

Start to finish: 30 minutes
Servings: 4 to 6

During the era of Portuguese colonization of Brazil, feijão tropeiro, or cattlemen's beans, was born out of a need to create sustenance from ingredients that didn't require refrigeration, such as dried meats, dried beans and cassava flour. Modern versions, however, typically are made with vegetables and sometimes eggs, and they inspired this hearty one-pan meal that's a terrific option for breakfast, lunch or dinner. Any type of smoked sausage—kielbasa, linguiça or even andouille—works well in this dish.

3 large eggs

3 tablespoons extra-virgin olive oil

6 ounces kielbasa OR linguiça sausage, halved lengthwise, then sliced ¼ inch thick

½ medium yellow onion, chopped

½ medium red bell pepper, stemmed, seeded and chopped

2 medium garlic cloves, finely chopped

1 bunch lacinato OR curly kale, stemmed and sliced ¼ inch thick

15½-ounce can pinto beans, rinsed and drained

Kosher salt and ground black pepper

In a small bowl, whisk the eggs until well combined; set aside. In a 12-inch nonstick skillet over medium-high, heat the oil until shimmering. Add the kielbasa and cook, stirring occasionally, until beginning to brown, 2 to 3 minutes. Add the onion and bell pepper; cook, stirring occasionally, until the vegetables are softened and beginning to brown, 3 to 4 minutes. Add the garlic and cook, stirring, until fragrant, 30 to 60 seconds.

Using a silicone spatula, push the sausage-vegetable mixture to one side of the skillet. Pour the eggs into the other side of the pan and cook, stirring constantly, until just set, 1 to 2 minutes. Stir the eggs into the sausage-vegetable mixture, breaking apart any large curds.

Add the kale and cook, stirring, until the leaves are wilted and tender-crisp, 2 to 3 minutes. Add the beans and cook, stirring occasionally, until heated through, 3 to 4 minutes. Off heat, taste and season with salt and pepper.

Optional garnish: Thinly sliced scallions

143

BLACK-EYED PEA AND TOMATO STEW

Start to finish: 30 minutes
Servings: 4

Heady with ginger and chilies, Ghana's "red-red" stew gets its namesake color from a combination of red palm oil and tomatoes. We found the more widely available refined coconut oil was a good substitute for red palm oil. For the legumes, we preferred Whole Foods' 365 Everyday Value canned black-eyed peas for their soft, creamy texture. Goya brand, sold in slightly larger cans, also yielded good results, but the texture was a bit firmer. Red-red typically is paired with thick slabs of fried plantain; we opted for the simplicity and crunch of store-bought plantain chips. If you like, garnish the stew with cilantro leaves, and for added spice, offer hot sauce on the side.

¼ cup refined coconut oil

1 large yellow onion, quartered lengthwise and thinly sliced

2 jalapeño chilies, stemmed, halved, seeded and thinly sliced

3-ounce piece fresh ginger, cut into 4 to 6 chunks

1 tablespoon tomato paste

1 tablespoon curry powder

1 teaspoon chipotle chili powder

Four 15½-ounce cans black-eyed peas, rinsed and drained

2 tablespoons soy sauce

1 pint cherry or grape tomatoes, halved

Kosher salt and ground black pepper

Lime wedges, to serve

Plantain chips, to serve

In a large Dutch oven over medium-high, heat the coconut oil until shimmering. Add the onion and cook, stirring occasionally, until beginning to brown, about 5 minutes. Stir in the jalapeños, ginger, tomato paste, curry powder and chipotle powder. Cook until fragrant, about 1 minute.

Add the black-eyed peas and stir well. Stir in 1½ cups water, the soy sauce and tomatoes, then bring to a simmer. Reduce to medium-low and cook, uncovered, stirring occasionally

and adjusting the heat to maintain a gentle but steady simmer, until slightly thickened, about 20 minutes.

Remove and discard the ginger chunks, then taste and season with salt and pepper. Let cool for 5 minutes. Serve with lime wedges and plantain chips.

AFGHAN-STYLE BEAN CURRY

Start to finish: 25 minutes
Servings: 4

The Afghan dish called lubya (sometimes spelled lobia) is a simple curry made with kidney beans. In our version, we use Roman or pinto beans, which have a creamier, more yielding texture than kidneys. The ingredients are few and the cooking time is brief, but the flavors in this vegetarian dish are rich, aromatic and satisfying. Serve with warmed flatbread to scoop up the beans or with basmati rice.

3 tablespoons ghee OR salted butter

1 medium yellow onion, chopped

4 medium garlic cloves, minced

1 tablespoon ground coriander

1 teaspoon ground cumin

Kosher salt and ground black pepper

Two 15½-ounce cans Roman beans
OR pinto beans, rinsed and drained

14½-ounce can tomato puree (1½ cups)

Finely chopped red onion, to serve

Chopped fresh mint OR cilantro, to serve

In a large saucepan over medium, melt the ghee. Add the yellow onion, garlic, coriander, cumin and 1 teaspoon each salt and pepper; cook, stirring occasionally, until the onion is translucent, about 10 minutes.

Stir in the beans, tomato puree and 1 cup water, then bring to a simmer. Reduce to medium-low and cook, uncovered and stirring occasionally, until the mixture is creamy and thick, about 15 minutes. Taste and season with salt and pepper. Serve sprinkled with chopped red onion and mint.

MILK STREET BASIC

Spiced Fried Chickpeas

Start to finish: 10 minutes
Makes about 1 cup

Chickpeas dusted with cornstarch and toasted in a skillet become crisp outside while remaining creamy inside.
These crunchy chickpeas are perfect on top of hummus, soups and salads, or on their own as a satisfying snack. We season them with two Mediterranean mainstays: smoked paprika and cumin. The recipe is highly adaptable, though, so feel free to change up the spices. We love making these with curry powder, Chinese five-spice, Ethiopian berbere or zesty za'atar—use 2 teaspoons in place of the cumin and smoked paprika (always include the sugar; it really enhances the flavors).

15½-ounce can chickpeas, rinsed, drained and patted dry

2 tablespoons cornstarch

¼ cup extra-virgin olive oil

1 teaspoon ground cumin

1 teaspoon smoked paprika

¼ teaspoon white sugar

Kosher salt and ground black pepper

In a medium bowl, toss the chickpeas with the cornstarch. Transfer to a fine-mesh strainer and shake to remove excess cornstarch.

In a 10-inch skillet over medium-high, heat the oil until shimmering. Add the chickpeas and cook, stirring occasionally, until golden brown and crisp, about 5 minutes. Remove from the heat and stir in the cumin, paprika, sugar, ½ teaspoon salt and ¼ teaspoon pepper.

BAKED WHITE BEANS AND SAUSAGES WITH PAPRIKA, ONIONS AND SWEET PEPPERS

Start to finish: 1 hour 50 minutes (20 minutes active)
Servings: 6

Tavče gravče, which translates as "beans in a pan," is a Macedonian classic. Traditionally, large dried white beans called tetovac, named after a city in northwestern Macedonia, are the star of the rustic dish, while onions, garlic, peppers and paprika provide deep, rich flavor and color. We opted for the convenience of canned butter beans, which are plump, creamy and the best widely available alternative to tetovac beans. (If butter beans are difficult to find, cannellini beans work, too.) Combined with sautéed aromatics and baked for an hour with smoked sausages, the beans turn silky-soft and deeply flavorful. Serve with crusty bread on the side.

4 tablespoons grapeseed or other neutral oil, divided

2 medium yellow onions, chopped

2 medium red bell peppers, stemmed, seeded and chopped

Kosher salt and ground black pepper

6 medium garlic cloves, thinly sliced

4 teaspoons sweet paprika

1½ teaspoons dried mint (optional)

Three 15½-ounce cans butter beans (1½ cups liquid reserved), rinsed and drained

2 dried árbol chilies OR ¼ teaspoon red pepper flakes

1 to 1¼ pounds smoked sausage, such as kielbasa or bratwurst

¼ cup lightly packed fresh flat-leaf parsley, chopped

Heat the oven to 400°F with a rack in the lower-middle position. In a large Dutch oven over medium-high, heat 3 tablespoons of the oil until shimmering. Add the onions, bell peppers and 1 teaspoon salt; cook, stirring occasionally, until lightly browned, 8 to 10 minutes.

Add the garlic, paprika, mint (if using) and ½ teaspoon pepper; cook, stirring, until fragrant, about 1 minute. Stir in the beans and the reserved liquid, the árbol chilies and 1½ cups water. Bring to a simmer, stirring occasionally, then nestle the sausages into the pot and drizzle the surface with the remaining 1 tablespoon oil. Transfer to the oven and bake, without stirring, until the sausages are browned and the beans on the surface are slightly crisped, 1 to 1¼ hours.

Remove the pot from the oven and let stand, uncovered, for about 15 minutes; the bean mixture will thicken as it cools. Transfer the sausages to a cutting board. Cut them into pieces, return them to the pot and stir into the beans. Remove and discard the árbol chilies (if used). Taste and season with salt and pepper, then sprinkle with parsley. Serve from the pot.

ROMAN BEANS WITH PANCETTA AND SEARED RADICCHIO

Start to finish: 25 minutes
Servings: 4 to 6

In the Veneto region of northeastern Italy, the combination of beans and radicchio is classic. For this warm salad-like dish, we cut radicchio into wedges and sear it to mellow its bitterness and soften its texture so the leaves meld nicely with tender, creamy beans. Fried sage rounds out the flavors

with herbal notes and a garlic-lemon vinaigrette adds pungency and brightness while tying everything together. Roman beans also are known as borlotti or cranberry beans (pink kidney beans are a fine substitute); we use canned for weeknight convenience. Try to purchase pancetta in a chunk rather than thinly sliced so it can be chopped into small pieces that fry up with a crisp-chewy texture.

4 tablespoons extra-virgin olive oil, divided

1 teaspoon grated lemon zest, plus
2 tablespoons lemon juice

4 ounces pancetta (see headnote), chopped

5 fresh sage leaves

1 medium garlic clove, smashed and peeled

10-ounce head radicchio, tough outer
leaves removed, cut into 8 wedges, core
trimmed from each piece

Kosher salt and ground black pepper

Two 15½-ounce cans Roman beans or
pink kidney beans (see headnote), rinsed
and drained

¼ cup walnuts, toasted and roughly chopped

In a small bowl, whisk together 3 tablespoons of oil and the lemon zest and juice; set aside. In a 12-inch skillet over medium-high, heat the remaining 1 tablespoon oil until shimmering. Add the pancetta, sage and garlic, then cook, stirring occasionally, until the pancetta is crisped and browned, 4 to 5 minutes. Remove the pan from the heat.

Using a slotted spoon, transfer the pancetta and sage to a paper towel-lined plate; transfer the garlic to the oil-lemon mixture. Mash the garlic to a paste with a fork; set aside. Pour off and discard all but 1 tablespoon of fat from the skillet. Return the pan to medium-high and heat until the fat is shimmering. Add the radicchio in an even layer, sprinkle with ¼ teaspoon salt and cook without stirring until lightly charred on the bottom, 3 to 4 minutes.

Using tongs, turn the radicchio and continue to cook until the leaves are translucent and fully wilted, 5 to 6 minutes. Reduce to medium and add the beans, pancetta, sage, 1 tablespoon water and the lemon-garlic dressing. Cook, stirring, until the beans are heated through, 1 to 2 minutes. Remove from the heat, then taste and season with salt and pepper. Transfer to a serving dish and sprinkle with the walnuts.

147

A Lesson in Lentils

Lentils, one of the oldest cultivated legumes, vary from creamy to firm, with flavors that range from delicate and earthy to peppery and bold. Unlike dried beans, lentils need no soaking before cooking. Simply rinse them and remove any debris, then add them to seasoned cooking liquid (5 cups liquid to 1 cup lentils), simmer until tender, then drain. For most lentils, 1 cup dry yields 2 to 2½ cups cooked.

Brown

Brown lentils—the most common variety—have a mild, earthy flavor and can range in color from khaki to nearly black. Because they hold their shape well during cooking, they're ideal for pilafs, soups and stews, or even as a vegetable taco filling. Cook time: 20 to 30 minutes. To serve with roasted lamb or beef, simmer **5 cups water, 1 cup brown lentils, 4 medium garlic cloves, 4 bay leaves, 2½ teaspoons ground cumin, ½ teaspoon ground allspice** and **¼ teaspoon kosher salt**, uncovered and stirring occasionally, until the lentils are tender, 20 to 25 minutes. Remove and discard the bay, then stir in 4 scallions (thinly sliced). Season with salt and pepper. Serve with **plain whole-milk yogurt**.

Green

Green lentils have a firm texture and robust flavor, making them a good addition to salads with bold flavors, such as garlic and blue cheese. Cook time: about 45 minutes. To serve as a salad, in a large saucepan heat **1 tablespoon extra-virgin olive oil** over medium. Add **8 ounces cremini mushrooms** (thinly sliced), **¼ teaspoon kosher salt** and **½ teaspoon black pepper**. Cook, stirring, until softened. Stir in **1 cup green lentils, 2 medium garlic cloves** (smashed and peeled), **½ teaspoon red pepper flakes, ¼ teaspoon kosher salt** and **5 cups water**. Simmer, uncovered and stirring, until just tender, 20 to 25 minutes. Season with salt and pepper, then stir in **⅓ cup chopped fresh dill**. Toss with **bitter greens** and **orange segments.**

Lentils Du Puy

Dark green lentils du Puy (aka French green lentils) have a robustly earthy, mineral-rich flavor and firm, texture, making them ideal for salads and other dishes where a discrete shape is important. To serve with grilled pork, simmer **5 cups water, 1 cup Puy lentils, 2 medium shallots** (halved and thinly sliced), **2 tablespoons whole-grain mustard** and **¼ teaspoon kosher salt** uncovered and stirring occasionally, until just tender, 20 to 25 minutes. Drain, then stir in **1 teaspoon fresh thyme** (minced) and **4 teaspoons cider vinegar**. Season to taste.

Black/Beluga

Earthy-tasting black lentils pair well with braises and other rich dishes. Cook time: 25 to 30 minutes. For a side to salmon or chicken, simmer **5 cups water, 1 cup black lentils** and **¼ teaspoon kosher salt**, uncovered and stirring occasionally, until tender, 20 to 25 minutes. Whisk together **6 tablespoons extra-virgin olive oil, 3 tablespoons white wine vinegar, 2 teaspoons Dijon mustard, ¼ teaspoon kosher salt** and **½ teaspoon black pepper**. Stir in **2 scallions** (thinly sliced) and **1 celery stalk** (finely chopped). Drain and add the lentils, then stir in **3 tablespoons chopped mint**.

Red

Red lentils cook fast and break down easily, making them best for pureeing for rustic soups or hearty sides. Cook time: 15 to 20 minutes. To serve as a curry, simmer **2½ cups water, 1 cup red lentils, 1 ounce fresh ginger** (peeled and thinly sliced) and **¼ teaspoon kosher salt**, uncovered and stirring, until the lentils have broken down into a coarse puree, 15 to 20 minutes. Discard the ginger, then transfer to a serving bowl. In a small saucepan over medium-high, melt **4 tablespoons salted butter**. Add **1½ teaspoons cumin seeds** (lightly crushed), **1 teaspoon curry powder, 1 teaspoon fennel seeds** (lightly crushed) and **¼ teaspoon cayenne pepper**. Cook, swirling, until fragrant, 30 to 45 seconds. Pour over the lentils.

wine and 1 cup water; bring to a simmer, scraping up any browned bits. Cook, uncovered and stirring occasionally, until just a little liquid remains and the beans begin to split, 10 to 15 minutes.

Off heat, stir in the parsley and half the bacon, then taste and season with salt and pepper. Serve sprinkled with the remaining bacon.

LENTIL SALAD WITH GORGONZOLA

Start to finish: 1½ hours (30 minutes active)
Servings: 6

Green lentils du Puy, also known as French lentils, cook quickly, hold their shape well and do a great job at soaking up flavors in a rich broth or stew. But it can be a bit of a race to develop that flavor before the lentils overcook and become mushy. Our solution: Simmer vegetables and aromatics in advance, then add lentils. To really punch up the flavor we turned to one of our favorite seasoning shortcuts and simmered a whole head of garlic with the herbs until it was mellow and tender; the cloves became soft enough to be mashed and formed the basis of a richly savory dressing. Pungent Gorgonzola cheese gave the salad sharp contrast, while toasted walnuts added crunch.

½ cup white balsamic vinegar

2 medium shallots, peeled, halved lengthwise, thinly sliced

Kosher salt and ground black pepper

1 garlic head, outer papery skin removed

2 medium carrots, halved crosswise

1 celery rib, halved crosswise

1 tablespoon yellow mustard seeds

6 sprigs fresh thyme, tied together

2 bay leaves

1½ cups (10 ounces) French green lentils, rinsed and drained

1 tablespoon extra-virgin olive oil

2 ounces Gorgonzola cheese, crumbled (about ¾ cup)

½ cup chopped fresh parsley

½ cup walnuts, toasted and chopped

BACON AND RED WINE–BRAISED KIDNEY BEANS

Start to finish: 45 minutes (15 minutes active)
Servings: 4

The rustic French dish called haricots rouges à la vigneronne, or winemaker's red beans, boasts rich, bold, beef bourguignon-like flavors. Our version, made with canned kidney beans, is quick and easy. Carrots and onion add sweetness to balance the tannins of the red wine, while bacon contributes a smoky, long-cooked flavor. This is the perfect accompaniment to roasted pork or chicken. Or make it the center of a meal with a bright arugula salad and crusty bread alongside.

4 ounces bacon, chopped

2 medium carrots, peeled, halved lengthwise and thinly sliced

1 medium yellow onion, finely chopped

Two 15½-ounce cans red kidney beans, rinsed and drained

1 cup dry red wine

1 cup lightly packed fresh flat-leaf parsley, chopped

Kosher salt and ground black pepper

In a large saucepan over medium-high, cook the bacon, stirring, until browned and crisp, 5 to 8 minutes. Using a slotted spoon, transfer to a plate; set aside.

To the fat in the pot, add the carrots and onion. Cook over medium-high, stirring occasionally, until the vegetables are lightly browned, about 7 minutes. Add the beans,

In a liquid measuring cup, combine the vinegar, shallots and ½ teaspoon salt. Set aside. Meanwhile, cut off and discard the top third of the garlic head, leaving the head intact. In a 2-quart saucepan over medium-high, combine the garlic, 6 cups water, carrots, celery, mustard seeds, thyme, bay leaves and ½ teaspoon salt. Bring to a boil, then cover, reduce heat to low and simmer for 30 minutes. Remove and discard the carrot, celery, thyme and bay leaves.

Return the pot to medium-high and stir in the lentils. Return to a boil, then cover and reduce heat to low. Simmer until the lentils are tender but still hold their shape, 30 to 35 minutes. Remove the garlic and set aside. Drain the lentils, reserving the liquid, and transfer to a large bowl. Stir in the vinegar-shallot mixture and let cool to room temperature.

Squeeze the pulp from the garlic into a bowl and mash with a fork. Stir in ¼ cup of the reserved cooking water, the oil and ¼ teaspoon salt. Stir the garlic mixture, half of the cheese, the parsley and half the walnuts into the lentils. Taste and season with salt and pepper. Transfer to a platter and top with the remaining cheese and walnuts.

LENTIL SALAD WITH TAHINI, ALMONDS AND POMEGRANATE MOLASSES

Start to finish: 1 hour (15 minutes active)
Servings: 4

Made with creamy tahini, toasted almonds and sweet-and-sour pomegranate molasses, this lentil salad boasts layers of complex flavor. Spice cabinet staples like smoked paprika or cumin work beautifully to enhance the earthiness of the lentils. If you have baharat in your pantry, by all means, use it instead. This blend of warm and savory spices, popular in Middle Eastern cooking, usually includes cardamom, coriander, cloves and cumin; you'll find baharat in many supermarkets (recipe p. 126). We dress the salad while still warm and let it stand so the lentils absorb the seasonings.

¼ cup extra-virgin olive oil

½ medium yellow onion OR 2 medium shallots, halved and thinly sliced

¼ cup sliced almonds

Kosher salt and ground black pepper

1 teaspoon smoked paprika OR ground cumin OR baharat

1 cup brown lentils OR green lentils, rinsed and drained

3 tablespoons tahini

2 tablespoons lemon juice

1 tablespoon pomegranate molasses,
plus more to serve

¾ cup chopped fresh flat-leaf parsley
OR chopped fresh cilantro OR thinly sliced
scallions OR a combination

In a large saucepan over medium-high, heat the oil until shimmering. Add the onion and cook, stirring often, until browned at the edges, about 3 minutes. Add the almonds and a pinch each of salt and pepper, then cook, stirring often, until the almonds are lightly browned, about 2 minutes. Add the paprika and cook, stirring, until fragrant, about 30 seconds. Using a slotted spoon, transfer the onion-almond mixture to a paper towel-lined plate. Pour the spiced oil into a medium bowl; set aside.

In the same saucepan, combine the lentils, ½ teaspoon salt, 1 teaspoon pepper and 5 cups water. Bring to a simmer over medium-high, then reduce to medium and simmer, uncovered and stirring occasionally, until the lentils are tender but still hold their shape, 15 to 20 minutes; drain.

To the spiced oil, whisk in the tahini and 2 tablespoons water until smooth. Whisk in the lemon juice and pomegranate molasses, then stir in the lentils. Let stand for at least 15 minutes.

Stir in half each of the parsley and onion-almond mixture, then taste and season with salt and pepper. Garnish with the remaining parsley, onion-almond mixture and a drizzle of additional pomegranate molasses.

Optional garnish: Seeded and minced jalapeño chili **OR** pomegranate seeds **OR** both

SPANISH-STYLE LENTIL STEW WITH GARLIC AND SMOKED PAPRIKA

Start to finish: 1½ hours (20 minutes active)
Servings: 4 to 6

Warming lentil stews are common throughout Spain, where they're often enriched with chorizo, a spiced dry-cured sausage. In this recipe, we mimic chorizo's smoky, savory flavor with a combination of bacon and smoked paprika. We also simmer a whole head of garlic in the mix—it mellows and sweetens with long, slow cooking, infusing the stew with a subtle garlicky flavor that complements the earthy lentils. Round out the meal with a salad of bitter greens and a loaf of crusty bread.

4 ounces bacon, chopped

1 tablespoon extra-virgin olive oil

1 medium yellow onion, chopped

2 teaspoons smoked paprika, plus more to serve

Kosher salt and ground black pepper

14½-ounce can diced tomatoes, drained,
juices reserved

1¼ cups brown OR green lentils, rinsed
and drained

1 head garlic, outer papery skins removed,
top third cut off and discarded

1 medium red OR orange bell pepper, stemmed,
seeded and chopped OR 2 medium carrots, peeled
and thinly sliced

1 cup lightly packed fresh flat-leaf parsley, chopped

In a large pot over medium-high, cook the bacon, stirring occasionally, until browned and crisp, 3 to 5 minutes. Using a slotted spoon, transfer to a paper towel-lined plate; set aside. Pour off and discard all but 1 tablespoon of the fat in the pot.

Return the pot to medium-high, add the oil and heat until shimmering. Add the onion, paprika, ½ teaspoon salt and ¼ teaspoon pepper. Cook, stirring often, until the onion begins to brown and soften, about 3 minutes. Add the tomato juices and scrape up the browned bits, then cook, stirring, until the juices are reduced and syrupy, about 2 minutes.

Stir in the lentils, the drained tomatoes, garlic and 6 cups water. Bring to a simmer, then reduce to medium and cook, uncovered and stirring occasionally, until the lentils are tender but not falling apart, about 25 minutes. Add the bell pepper and simmer, uncovered and stirring occasionally, until the lentils are fully softened and beginning to break down, 20 to 25 minutes.

Off heat, using tongs, squeeze the garlic cloves from the head into the lentil mixture; discard the empty skins. Stir the stew, mashing some of the garlic and lentils against the side of the pot to thicken slightly. Stir in half each of the parsley and bacon. Taste and season with salt and pepper. Serve sprinkled with the remaining parsley and bacon and additional paprika (if desired).

LENTILS AND BULGUR WITH FRIED ONIONS

Start to finish: 45 minutes
Servings: 4

Mujaddara is comfort food in many Middle Eastern countries. It often is made with lentils and rice, but this version combines lentils and bulgur. For ease, we cook them in the same pot, with the lentils getting a head start so they finish at the same time. Lots of scallions and deeply caramelized onions—almost burnt, really—finish the dish for layers of complex flavor. Served hot, warm or at room temperature, mujaddara is hearty enough to be a vegetarian main, but it's also a delicious accompaniment to grilled or roasted meats.

4 medium garlic cloves, smashed and peeled

4 bay leaves

2½ teaspoons ground cumin

½ teaspoon ground allspice

Kosher salt and ground black pepper

1 cup brown lentils, rinsed and drained

⅓ cup extra-virgin olive oil

2 medium yellow onions, halved and thinly sliced

1 cup coarse bulgur

1 bunch scallions, thinly sliced

Plain whole-milk yogurt, to serve

In a large saucepan over medium-high, combine 3½ cups water, the garlic, bay, cumin, allspice, 1½ teaspoons salt and 1 teaspoon pepper. Bring to a boil, then stir in the lentils and reduce to medium. Cover and cook, stirring occasionally and adjusting the heat to maintain a simmer, until the lentils are tender but not falling apart, about 25 minutes.

Meanwhile, in a 12-inch skillet over medium-high, heat the oil until shimmering. Add the onions and cook, stirring only occasionally at the start then more often once browning begins at the edges of the pan, until deeply caramelized and crisped, 10 to 15 minutes; adjust the heat if the onions brown too quickly. Using a slotted spoon, transfer the onions to a paper towel-lined plate and spread evenly. Sprinkle with ¼ teaspoon salt and set aside.

When the lentils are tender, stir the bulgur into the pot. Cover, reduce to low and cook without stirring until the liquid has been absorbed and the bulgur is tender, 10 to 14 minutes. Remove the pot from the heat. Using a fork, fluff the lentils and bulgur, removing and discarding the bay and roughly mashing the garlic. Taste and season with salt and pepper. Stir in half the scallions, then transfer to a serving bowl. Top with the fried onions and the remaining scallions. Serve hot, warm or at room temperature, with yogurt on the side.

BERBERE-SPICED RED LENTILS

Start to finish: 30 minutes
Servings: 4 to 6

This lentil stew is our spin on the Ethiopian dish misir wat. It's seasoned with berbere, a rich, complex, aromatic Ethiopian blend of warm spices, savory dried alliums and red chilies. Look for berbere in spice shops or in well-stocked grocery stores (recipe p. 337). We garnish the lentils with a mix of chopped tomatoes, jalapeño and grated ginger, a non-traditional touch that brings bright flavor and color to the dish. If you can get the Ethiopian flatbread called injera, serve some alongside, though warm naan and/or rice are also excellent accompaniments.

4 tablespoons ghee or salted butter, divided

1 large yellow onion, chopped

2 tablespoons tomato paste

4 medium garlic cloves, finely grated

4 teaspoons finely grated fresh ginger, divided

1 tablespoon berbere

1 cup red lentils, rinsed and drained

1 quart low-sodium chicken broth
or vegetable broth

Kosher salt and ground black pepper

3 ripe plum tomatoes, cored, seeded
and roughly chopped

1 jalapeño chili, stemmed, seeded and chopped

In a large saucepan over medium, heat 2 tablespoons of the ghee until shimmering. Add the onion and cook, stirring occasionally, until lightly browned, 5 to 7 minutes.

Add the tomato paste and cook, stirring, until lightly browned and beginning to stick to the pan, about 2 minutes. Add the garlic, 3 teaspoons of the ginger and the berbere; cook, stirring, until fragrant, about 30 seconds. Stir in the lentils and broth, then bring to a simmer over medium-high. Reduce to medium-low and simmer, uncovered and stirring often, until the lentils are fully tender and the mixture is creamy, 20 to 25 minutes.

Meanwhile, in a medium bowl, toss together the tomatoes, jalapeño, remaining 1 teaspoon ginger and ¼ teaspoon each salt and pepper; set aside.

When the lentils are done, remove the pan from the heat. Stir in the remaining 2 tablespoons ghee. Taste and season with salt and pepper. Transfer to a serving bowl and top with the tomato mixture.

DAL TARKA

Start to finish: 1¼ hours (20 minutes active)
Servings: 4

Dal tarka, or stewed lentils finished with spice-infused butter, is a ubiquitous Indian dish, though some versions are more elaborate than others. Different varieties of lentils can be used to make dal, but we opted for split yellow lentils (toor dal) to recreate the dal tarka we had in Mumbai. (Note: Yellow lentils and yellow split peas are not the same.) If you're able to find ghee, a type of clarified butter, we highly recommend using it to make the tarka because its full, round, slightly nutty flavor lends depth to the dish. If ghee is not available, salted butter works well.

1 cup split yellow lentils, rinsed and drained

2 teaspoons ground turmeric, divided

Kosher salt

3 tablespoons ghee (see headnote) or salted butter,
cut into 3 pieces

1 tablespoon cumin seeds

4 medium garlic cloves, thinly sliced

1 small red onion, finely chopped

1 medium tomato, cored and chopped

½ teaspoon cayenne pepper

½ cup lightly packed fresh cilantro, chopped

In a medium saucepan, combine the lentils, 1 teaspoon of the turmeric and 5½ cups water. Bring to a boil, then cook, uncovered and stirring occasionally and adjusting the heat to maintain a simmer, until the lentils are thick and have broken down, 1 to 1¼ hours; stir more often as the mixture thickens. Stir in 1 teaspoon salt; cover to keep warm and set aside.

In a small saucepan over medium-high, cook the ghee and cumin seeds, stirring, until sizzling, 1 to 1½ minutes. Add the garlic and onion, then cook, stirring often and swirling the pan, until the onion is tender and translucent, 3 to 5 minutes. Add the tomato and cook, stirring, until the tomato has released its moisture but the pieces maintain some shape, about 2 minutes.

Off heat, stir in the remaining 1 teaspoon turmeric and the cayenne. Spoon the lentils into individual serving bowls, then top each portion with some of the tomato mixture. Sprinkle with cilantro.

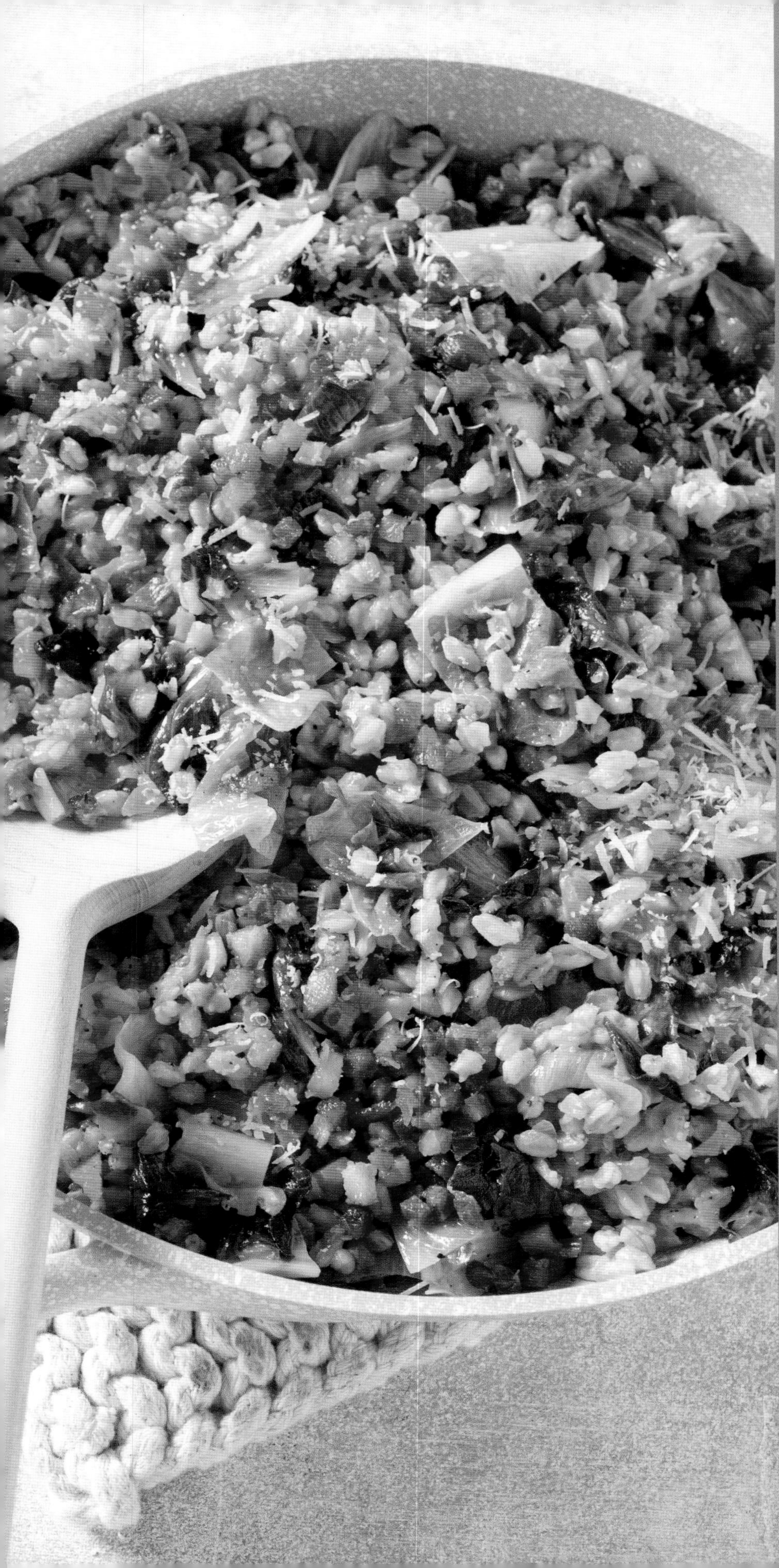

Grains

How to Cook Long-Grain Rice

Long-Grain White Rice

In a fine-mesh strainer, rinse and drain **1½ cups long-grain white rice.** In a large saucepan, stir together the rice, **½ teaspoon kosher salt** and **2¼ cups water.** Bring to a boil over medium-high, then reduce to low. Immediately cover and cook until the rice is tender, about 15 minutes. Remove the pan from the heat and let stand, covered, for 10 minutes. Using a fork, fluff the grains. Makes 4 cups.

White Basmati Rice

In a fine-mesh strainer, rinse and drain **1½ cups basmati rice.** In a large saucepan, stir together the rice, **½ teaspoon kosher salt** and **2¼ cups water.** Bring to a boil over medium-high, then reduce to low. Immediately cover and cook until the rice is tender, 15 to 17 minutes. Remove the pan from the heat and let stand, covered, for 10 minutes. Using a fork, fluff the grains. Makes 4 cups.

White Jasmine Rice

In a fine-mesh strainer, rinse and drain **1½ cups jasmine rice.** In a large saucepan, stir together the rice, **½ teaspoon kosher salt** (optional) and **2 cups water.** Bring to a boil over medium-high, then reduce to low. Immediately cover and cook until the rice is tender, 15 to 17 minutes. Remove the pan from the heat and let stand, covered, for 10 minutes. Using a fork, fluff the grains. Makes 4 cups.

Garlic Fried Rice with Chicken

Start to finish: 35 minutes
Servings: 4

Crisp garlic chips are a great way to embolden dishes, a technique we use in our take on the Filipino dish known as sinangag. We brown sliced garlic, creating golden garlic chips to mix into the rice at the end, along with a flavorful oil that infuses the entire dish. Sinangag typically is served as a side, but we add chicken to transform it into a main. For best texture, use cooked rice that's been refrigerated until firm. To make enough rice for this recipe, in a large saucepan, combine 2 cups water and 1½ cups jasmine rice (or regular long-grain white rice), rinsed and drained. Bring to a simmer over medium-high, then reduce to low, cover and cook for 15 to 18 minutes. Let stand, covered, for 10 minutes, then transfer to a wide, shallow bowl. Cool to room temperature, then cover and refrigerate until well chilled.

8 ounces boneless, skinless chicken thighs, trimmed and cut into ½- to ¾-inch pieces

2 tablespoons soy sauce, divided

½ teaspoon white sugar

Kosher salt and ground black pepper

3 tablespoons grapeseed or other neutral oil, divided

8 medium garlic cloves, thinly sliced

3 scallions, thinly sliced, white and green parts reserved separately

4 cups cooked and chilled long-grain white rice, preferably jasmine rice (see headnote)

In a medium bowl, stir together the chicken, 1 tablespoon soy sauce, the sugar and ¼ teaspoon salt. In a 12-inch nonstick skillet over medium-high, heat 1 tablespoon oil until shimmering. Add the chicken in an even layer and cook without stirring until browned on the bottom, 2 to 3 minutes. Stir the chicken, then cook, stirring occasionally, until well browned all over and cooked through, another 2 to 3 minutes. Transfer the chicken to a plate; set aside.

Wash and dry the skillet. Set it over medium-low and add the remaining 2 tablespoons oil and the garlic. Cook,

stirring only occasionally at first then more often once the garlic begins to color, until some of the slices are light golden brown, about 5 minutes. Add the scallion whites and cook, stirring, until most of the garlic is golden brown, about 2 minutes.

Add the rice, breaking up any clumps, followed by the remaining 1 tablespoon soy sauce and ¼ teaspoon salt. Cook over medium-high, stirring and scraping the bottom of the pan to incorporate the garlic and any browned bits, until the rice is heated through, about 2 minutes. Add the chicken and any accumulated juices; cook, stirring, until warmed through, about 1 minute.

Off heat, taste and season with salt. Transfer to a serving dish, then sprinkle with the scallion greens and pepper.

Pressure-Cooked Long-Grain Rice

Start to finish: 25 to 40 minutes
Makes 3 cups (4 servings)

The pressure-cooker function on an Instant Pot offers a dead-easy way to prepare rice, as there is no need to babysit the saucepan and there is zero threat of boiling over or scorching on the bottom. This method works for both white and brown long-grain rice, but note that brown rice requires longer cooking. We tested regular, basmati and jasmine rice; for jasmine, you may wish to omit the salt, as this variety typically is cooked without seasoning. The recipe can be increased by 50 percent or even doubled for a 6-quart Instant Pot. Just be sure to use a 1 to 1 rice to water ratio.

1 cup long-grain white or brown rice (see headnote), rinsed and drained

Kosher salt

In a 6-quart Instant Pot, combine the rice, 1 cup water and ½ teaspoon salt. Stir, then distribute in an even layer.

Lock the lid in place and move the pressure valve to **Sealing.** Select **Pressure Cook** or **Manual**; adjust the pressure level to **High.** Set the cooking time for 6 minutes for white rice or 22 minutes for brown rice. When pressure cooking is complete, allow the pressure to release naturally for 10 minutes, then release the remaining steam by moving the pressure valve to **Venting.** Press **Cancel,** then carefully open the pot.

Using potholders, carefully remove the insert from the housing. Fluff the rice with a fork.

ARROZ VERDE

Start to finish: 25 minutes
Servings: 4

Arroz verde, or green rice, is a flavorful Mexican side dish that pairs well with almost any type of main, from Indian curries to simple roasted chicken. It often is made by adding pureed cilantro and chilies to the liquid at the start of cooking, but this produces rice that's army green and dull in taste. To keep the color and flavor fresh, we cook our rice with just the hardier flavorings—garlic, scallion and half of the chilies—then stir in the puree after cooking. Seeding all the jalapeños keeps this dish mild; if you want some heat, leave the seeds in one or more of the chilies.

1 tablespoon grapeseed or other neutral oil

1½ cups long-grain white rice, rinsed and drained

½ teaspoon ground cumin

3 scallions, thinly sliced

4 jalapeño chilies, stemmed, seeded, 2 finely chopped, 2 roughly chopped

4 medium garlic cloves, finely chopped

Kosher salt

2 cups lightly packed fresh cilantro stems and leaves, roughly chopped

In a large saucepan over medium, heat the oil until shimmering. Add the rice and cumin, then cook, stirring, until the grains are translucent and the cumin is fragrant, about 2 minutes. Stir in the scallions, the finely chopped jalapeños, three-fourths of the garlic, 2 cups water and 1 teaspoon salt. Bring to a simmer over high, then cover, reduce to low and cook until the rice absorbs the liquid, 10 to 15 minutes.

While the rice cooks, in a blender, combine ¼ cup water, the cilantro, the roughly chopped jalapeños, the remaining garlic and ½ teaspoon salt. Blend until smooth, about 1 minute, scraping the blender as needed.

When the rice is done, remove the pan from the heat. Uncover, then drape a kitchen towel across the top of the pan. Replace the lid and let stand for 5 minutes.

Using a fork, gently fluff the rice. Transfer to a large bowl, then add the cilantro puree and fold with a silicone spatula until fully incorporated.

KIMCHI FRIED RICE WITH SUNNY-SIDE-UP EGGS

Start to finish: 40 minutes
Servings: 4 to 6

There are countless ways to make kimchi fried rice, or kimchi bokkeum bap, as it's called in Korea. During a visit to Seoul, we had a few lessons. Chef Sung Min Lee started his kimchi fried rice by lightly caramelizing a sliced onion, which added sweetness and texture. He also used equal amounts of kimchi and rice, a ratio that we, too, found optimal. Chef Dong Mae Choi added bold flavor by seasoning the mix with dadaegi, a spicy sauce often stirred into noodles and soups. Choi pureed nearly a dozen ingredients in her dadaegi; we simplified the blend, but kept the Asian pear, which brought sweetness and fruity notes. Asian pears are seasonal; if not available, use a regular pear. We were surprised to learn that freshly cooked medium- or long-grain rice is typically used for kimchi fried rice. But we find cooked and chilled rice stir-fries into a lighter, fluffier texture. If you own a 12- to 14-inch wok, feel free to use it in place of a nonstick skillet. It provides more space for tossing and slightly speeds the cooking.

8 ounces Asian pear (see headnote), peeled, cored and roughly chopped

1 bunch scallions, whites roughly chopped, greens thinly sliced, reserved separately

2 medium garlic cloves, smashed and peeled

½-inch piece fresh ginger, peeled and roughly chopped

2½ tablespoons gochujang

2 tablespoons soy sauce

Kosher salt and ground black pepper

8 ounces ground pork

3 tablespoons grapeseed or other neutral oil, divided

1 medium yellow onion, halved and thinly sliced

2 to 2½ cups napa cabbage kimchi (from a 1-pound jar), squeezed of excess liquid and chopped, plus 2 tablespoons kimchi juice

¾ cup frozen corn kernels, thawed

2½ cups cooked and chilled long- or medium-grain white rice

4 to 6 sunny-side-up fried eggs

Sesame seeds, toasted, to serve

Toasted sesame oil or chili oil, to serve

161

In a blender, combine the pear, scallion whites, garlic, ginger, gochujang, soy sauce, ¼ teaspoon salt and ½ teaspoon pepper. Blend, scraping the blender jar as needed, until smooth, 1 to 2 minutes. In a small bowl, combine 2 tablespoons of the puree and the pork; mix until well combined.

In a 12-inch nonstick skillet over medium-high, heat 1 tablespoon oil until shimmering. Add the pork and cook, stirring and breaking the meat into small bits, until lightly browned, 2 to 3 minutes. Scrape the pork onto a plate; set aside.

In the same skillet over medium-high, heat the remaining 2 tablespoons oil until shimmering. Add the onion and ¼ teaspoon salt, then cook, stirring occasionally, until golden brown, 5 to 7 minutes. Stir in the kimchi and corn, then distribute in an even layer; cook, stirring only once or twice, until the kimchi begins to brown, about 5 minutes.

Stir in the puree, scraping up any browned bits. Add the rice, pork and kimchi juice; cook, stirring, until the mixture is well combined and the rice is heated through, about 2 minutes. Off heat, stir in most of the scallion greens, then taste and season with salt and pepper. Serve topped with the eggs, sprinkled with the remaining scallion greens and sesame seeds and drizzled with sesame oil.

THAI FRIED RICE

Start to finish: 20 minutes
Servings: 4

Cooked in under five minutes in the open-air kitchen of his home in Thailand, chef Andy Ricker's fried rice was speedy, simple—and delicious. Pork belly, shallot and garlic added bold flavors. Soy and fish sauces added savory depth. Fresh herbs kept everything bright and light. We returned to Milk Street and got to work deconstructing Thai cooking. Ricker prefers to use a wok because it allows him to move food away from the hot oil at the center to the cooler sides of the pan. In a nod to the Western kitchen, we began with a large nonstick skillet, though you can use a wok if you have one. Pork belly can be hard to find in the U.S. Looking for a substitute we found ground pork too greasy and bacon too smoky. Pancetta—if culturally odd—was just right, which makes sense since it's cured pork belly. In a skillet, we had

to reverse-engineer the process and move foods in and out, starting with the eggs, then the pancetta. We liked the aromatic flavor of jasmine rice, but long-grain white or basmati work, too. Thai restaurants offer condiments for fried rice, including sliced green chilies in white vinegar. We came up with our own (recipe p. 608). Use it with the fried rice or any dish that needs a hit of gentle heat and acid.

1 tablespoon Thai fish sauce

1 teaspoon soy sauce

1 teaspoon white sugar

4 cups cooked and chilled jasmine rice

1 tablespoon peanut or vegetable oil

2 eggs, lightly beaten

4 ounces thinly sliced pancetta, chopped

4 scallions, white and green parts sliced thin, reserved separately

1 large shallot, minced

1 garlic clove, minced

¼ cup minced fresh cilantro

Sliced cucumber and lime wedges, to serve

In a bowl, stir together the fish sauce, soy sauce, 1 teaspoon water and sugar. Set aside. Use your hands to break up the rice so no clumps remain. Set aside.

In a 12-inch nonstick skillet over medium-high, heat the oil until just smoking. Pour in the eggs and cook, stirring, until just set. Transfer the eggs to a plate. Add the pancetta to the skillet and cook over medium until crisp. Using a slotted spoon, transfer to the plate with the eggs.

Pour off all but 1 tablespoon of the fat from the skillet and return to medium-high. Add the scallion whites, shallot and garlic and cook until softened, about 30 seconds. Add the rice and cook, stirring occasionally, until heated through, about 1 minute.

Stir the fish sauce mixture, then pour over the rice. Cook, stirring, until well mixed. Stir in the pancetta and egg, breaking up the egg. Transfer to a large platter and sprinkle with cilantro and scallion greens. Serve with cucumber, lime wedges and pickled chilies (recipe p. 608), if desired.

CURRIED CHICKEN FRIED RICE WITH CHILIES

Start to finish: 40 minutes
Servings: 4

Nigerian fried rice, seasoned with curry powder, dried thyme and a handful of aromatics, inspired this meal-in-a-skillet. Beef liver and an assortment of vegetables are classic ingredients, but we opted for chicken thighs and green beans. Instead of using just-cooked rice, which results in a softer, moisture texture in the finished dish, we start with plain cooked rice that's been chilled so the grains "fry" up light and fluffy. Fragrant basmati is especially good, but any type of long-grain white rice works.

3 tablespoons neutral oil or refined coconut oil, divided

1 pound boneless, skinless chicken thighs, trimmed and cut into 1-inch pieces

2 teaspoons curry powder, divided

Kosher salt and ground black pepper

4 scallions, thinly sliced, whites and greens reserved separately

2 tablespoons minced fresh ginger

4 ounces green beans, trimmed and cut into 1-inch pieces

1 teaspoon dried thyme

1 Fresno or jalapeño chili, stemmed, seeded and thinly sliced

4 cups cooked and chilled long-grain white rice, preferably basmati

1 cup low-sodium chicken broth

In a 12-inch skillet over medium-high, heat 2 tablespoons oil until barely smoking. Add the chicken and sprinkle with ½ teaspoon curry powder, ½ teaspoon salt and ¼ teaspoon pepper. Cook, stirring occasionally, until evenly browned, 4 to 6 minutes.

Push the chicken to the perimeter of the pan. To the center, add the remaining 1 tablespoon oil, the scallion whites and ginger; cook, stirring, until lightly browned, about 1½ minutes. Into the scallion mixture, stir the beans, thyme, half the chili, the remaining 1½ teaspoons curry powder and ¼ teaspoon each salt and pepper. Stir the chicken into the bean mixture; cook, stirring occasionally, until the beans are bright green, about 2 minutes. Stir in the rice, then add the broth and scrape up any browned bits. Cook, stirring, until the liquid is absorbed, 3 to 5 minutes.

Off heat, taste and season with salt and pepper. Serve sprinkled with the scallion greens and remaining chili.

163

Chilled Rice for Fried Rice

Start to finish: 20 minutes, plus cooling
Makes 4 cups

Fried rice is fast but it is best when made with rice that has been cooked and cooled in advance. Warm, freshly cooked rice won't deliver light, fluffy texture; it sticks to the pan and turns heavy and gummy. Regular long-grain white rice works well in most fried-rice recipes, so it's a good variety to have cooked, cooled and on hand. Make sure to allow two hours minimum to adequately chill the rice so the grains are firm; it can also be prepared up to three days in advance and kept refrigerated. For real make-ahead convenience, the rice also can be frozen. Make a batch or two, then freeze in zip-close plastic bags.

1½ cups long-grain white rice, rinsed and drained

½ teaspoon kosher salt

In a large saucepan, stir together the rice, salt and 2¼ cups water. Bring to a boil over medium-high, then reduce to low. Immediately cover and cook until tender, about 15 minutes. Remove the pan from the heat and let stand, covered, for 10 minutes. Using a fork, fluff the grains. Transfer to a wide, shallow bowl; cool to room temperature, then cover and refrigerate until well chilled, at least 2 hours or for up to 3 days.

JAPANESE-STYLE RICE WITH CORN, BUTTER AND SOY SAUCE

Start to finish: 50 minutes (10 minutes active)
Servings: 4 to 6

Frozen corn kernels add color and sweetness to Japanese-style short-grain rice, with a little butter bringing richness and soy sauce adding umami. If you want to up the nutrition, substitute ¼ cup rinsed and drained quinoa or pearled barley for an equal amount of the rice. Whether you use only rice or mix your grains, don't skip the soak or rest before or after steaming, respectively, as they are essential for even cooking.

1½ cups Japanese-style short-grain white rice, rinsed and drained

1 tablespoon soy sauce

Kosher salt and ground black OR white pepper

1½ cups frozen corn kernels, thawed and patted dry

2 tablespoons salted butter, cut into 6 pieces

4 scallion greens, cut on the diagonal into ¼-inch slices (about ¼ cup)

In a large saucepan, stir together the rice, 2 cups water, the soy sauce and ½ teaspoon salt. Scatter the corn evenly over the top; do not stir. Cover and let stand for 30 minutes.

Set the pan over medium-high and bring to a boil. Reduce to low and cook, covered and without stirring, until the rice has absorbed the water, about 18 minutes. Remove the pan from the heat and let stand, covered, for 10 minutes.

Uncover, scatter the butter on top, then fluff the rice with a fork, combining the rice and corn, until the butter is melted. Transfer to a serving dish and top with the scallions and a few grindings of pepper.

Optional garnish: Toasted sesame seeds OR lemon wedges OR both

JOLLOF RICE

Start to finish: 45 minutes
Servings: 6

For our take on jollof, a one-pot rice dish popular in West Africa, we use nutty, fragrant basmati rice seasoned with paprika, curry powder and thyme. To ensure the rice cooks evenly, use a large skillet with a tight-fitting lid. A 14½-ounce can of diced tomatoes can be used in place of the plum tomatoes; no need to drain the juices.

1 pound plum tomatoes, cored
and quartered

1 red bell pepper, stemmed, seeded
and cut into quarters

2 medium garlic cloves, peeled

Kosher salt and ground black pepper

¼ cup extra-virgin olive oil

1 medium yellow onion, chopped

1½ cups basmati rice, rinsed and drained

3 medium carrots, peeled and chopped
into ¼-inch pieces

1 tablespoon curry powder

1½ teaspoons smoked paprika

1 teaspoon dried thyme

1 cup frozen green peas

In a food processor, combine the tomatoes, bell pepper, garlic and ½ teaspoon salt. Process until smooth, about 1 minute. Set aside.

In a large skillet over medium, heat the oil until shimmering. Add the onion and cook, stirring, until beginning to brown, 6 to 8 minutes. Stir in the rice, then the carrots, curry powder, paprika, thyme, ¾ teaspoon salt and ½ teaspoon pepper. Cook, stirring, until the rice is fragrant, 1 to 2 minutes. Stir in 1½ cups water, bring to a simmer and cook, stirring occasionally, until most of the water has been absorbed, about 2 minutes.

Stir in the tomato puree and return to a simmer, then reduce to medium-low. Cover and cook until almost dry and the rice is tender, 12 to 15 minutes.

Scatter the peas over the rice, then cover the pan. Remove from the heat and let stand until the remaining moisture has been absorbed and the peas are heated through, about 5 minutes. Stir the peas into the rice. Taste and season with salt and pepper.

165

The Rice Rundown

Some 40,000 varieties of rice grow around the world, each differing in flavor, aroma and texture. And each can require a nuanced cooking method influenced by the length of the grains and how they are milled. Here, we offer instructions for cooking six common varieties. For each, start by rinsing and thoroughly draining the rice, then cook it in a large saucepan over medium-high heat. Each recipe yields 4 cups of cooked rice.

Only the tough hull is removed from **long-grain brown rice,** leaving the fiber-rich bran and germ intact, giving the rice more nutrients, a nutty flavor and a slightly chewy texture. Because it has oil in its bran layer, brown rice can spoil faster than white rice; uncooked rice keeps for six months stored in a cool, dry place. In a fine-mesh strainer, rinse and drain **1½ cups long-grain brown rice, brown basmati rice or brown jasmine rice**. In a large saucepan, bring **3 quarts water** to a boil. Stir in the rice and **2 teaspoons kosher salt** (optional if using jasmine rice), then return to a boil. Cook until the rice is tender but with a slight chew, about 25 minutes. Drain in a fine-mesh strainer, then return the rice to the pan. Immediately cover and let stand for 10 minutes. Using a fork, fluff the grains.

Long-grain white rice has had its bran and germ removed, making it quicker-cooking and milder in flavor than brown. Before it is packaged, it may be polished to remove any impurities and give the grain a glossy appearance. In a fine-mesh strainer, rinse and drain **1½ cups long-grain white rice**. In a large saucepan, stir together the rice, **½ teaspoon kosher salt** and **2¼ cups water**. Bring to a boil over medium-high, then reduce to low. Immediately cover and cook until the rice is tender, about 15 minutes. Remove the pan from the heat and let stand, covered, for 10 minutes. Using a fork, fluff the grains.

Long-grained, fragrant and nutty, **basmati rice** is primarily grown in India and Pakistan. When cooked properly, the grains should stay distinct and fluffy. In a fine-mesh strainer, rinse and drain **1½ cups basmati rice**. In a large sauce-pan, stir together the rice, **½ teaspoon kosher salt** and **2¼ cups water**. Bring to a boil over medium-high, then reduce to low. Immediately cover and cook until the rice is tender, 15 to 17 minutes. Remove the pan from the heat and let stand, covered, for 10 minutes. Using a fork, fluff the grains.

Jasmine rice is shorter, softer and plumper than basmati, but just as aromatic (and still a long-grained rice). Grown in Thailand, jasmine rice cooks up somewhat sticky and slightly sweet. In a fine-mesh strainer, rinse and drain **1½ cups jasmine rice**. In a large saucepan, stir together the rice, **½ teaspoon kosher salt** (optional) and **2 cups water**. Bring to a boil over medium-high, then reduce to low. Immediately cover and cook until the rice is tender, 15 to 17 minutes. Remove the pan from the heat and let stand, covered, for 10 minutes. Using a fork, fluff the grains.

Japanese-style medium- and short-grain white rice is plump and stubby. Most of what's available in the U.S is grown domestically. When cooked, the grains become sticky but remain distinct, and take on a shiny, slightly translucent quality. In a fine-mesh strainer, rinse and drain **1½ cups Japanese-style medium- or short-grain white rice**. In a large saucepan, stir together the rice and **1¾ cups water**. Bring to a boil over medium-high, then reduce to low. Immediately cover and cook until the rice is tender, about 12 minutes. Remove the pan from the heat and let stand, covered, for 10 to 15 minutes. Using a fork, fluff the grains.

Native to North America, **wild rice** is a semi-aquatic grass that is nutty, woody and toothsome. In a fine-mesh strainer, rinse and drain **1½ cups wild rice**. In a large saucepan, stir together the rice, **1 teaspoon kosher salt** and **5 cups water**. Bring to a boil over medium-high, then reduce to medium-low. Simmer, stirring occasionally, until the rice is tender-chewy and about half of the grains split open and curl, about 45 minutes. Drain in a fine-mesh strainer.

PERSIAN JEWELED RICE

Start to finish: 55 minutes (20 minutes active)
Servings: 4

This rice pilaf is named for the colorful dried fruits and nuts that embellish the saffron-tinted basmati rice. The bright color of raw pistachios is best here. Traditionally, jeweled rice is a labor-intensive dish; we've created a simplified version that's visually stunning as well as richly, deeply flavorful. We almost always toast nuts to enhance their flavor and texture, but here raw pistachios are best, as they are more vivid in color and subtler in flavor than toasted or roasted.

1 teaspoon saffron threads

4 tablespoons (½ stick) salted butter

2 medium yellow onions, halved and thinly sliced

Kosher salt and ground black pepper

2 cups basmati rice, rinsed and drained

2 teaspoons ground cumin

1¾ teaspoons ground cardamom

2 medium carrots, peeled and shredded on the large holes of a box grater (about 1 cup)

1 cup dried cranberries

1 teaspoon finely grated orange zest

½ cup shelled pistachios, chopped, divided

In a microwave-safe bowl, combine the saffron with 2⅔ cups water. Microwave on high until the water has a yellow hue, about 1 minute; set aside.

In a 12-inch skillet over medium, melt the butter. Add the onions and 1 teaspoon salt, then cook, stirring occasionally, until softened and light golden brown, 10 to 12 minutes. Stir in the rice, cumin, cardamom and ½ teaspoon each salt and pepper. Cook, stirring, until the grains are lightly browned and no longer translucent, 4 to 7 minutes. Stir in the saffron water, carrots and cranberries. Bring to a boil over medium-high, then cover, reduce to low, and cook until the rice has absorbed the liquid and the carrots are tender, 25 to 30 minutes.

Fluff the rice with a fork, then stir in the orange zest and ¼ cup of pistachios. Taste and season with salt and pepper. Transfer to a shallow bowl and sprinkle with the remaining ¼ cup pistachios.

UZBEK RICE WITH BEEF AND CARROTS

Start to finish: 2 hours (35 minutes active)
Servings: 8

Plov, a hearty pilaf-like mélange of rice, onion, carrots, meat, spices and sometimes other ingredients such as lentils or chickpeas, is widely regarded as the national dish of Uzbekistan. It can be a humble, everyday offering or an elaborate celebratory one, but plov is always intended to be a shared dish. Our streamlined recipe uses boneless beef short ribs, which are rich in meaty flavor because they're not shy of fat, and a whole head of garlic, as is traditional. Golden raisins stud the rice, bringing bursts of sweetness that balance the richness of the beef. The spicing in our plov is minimal, but the finished dish is still abundantly flavorful and deeply aromatic. Fresh parsley, though not traditional, adds fresh, grassy notes and bright color.

2 cups basmati rice

Kosher salt and ground black pepper

3 tablespoons grapeseed or other neutral oil

1½ pounds boneless beef short ribs,
trimmed and cut into ¾- to 1-inch chunks

2 medium yellow onions, halved and
sliced ½ inch thick

3 bay leaves

1 tablespoon plus ½ teaspoon ground cumin, divided

2½ teaspoons ground coriander, divided

½ to ¾ teaspoon cayenne pepper

3 medium carrots, peeled, halved lengthwise
and thinly sliced on the diagonal

1 head garlic, outer papery skins removed,
top third cut off and discarded

½ cup golden raisins

½ cup chopped fresh flat-leaf parsley

Pomegranate seeds, to serve (optional)

In a large bowl, combine the rice and 1 tablespoon salt. Add water to cover by 1 inch, then stir and set aside.

In a large Dutch oven over medium-high, heat the oil until shimmering. Add the beef and cook, stirring occasionally, until brown all over, about 7 minutes. Add the onions, bay, 1 tablespoon of the cumin, 2 teaspoons of the coriander, the cayenne, 1½ teaspoons salt and ½ teaspoon black pepper. Cook, stirring occasionally, until the onions are slightly wilted, 3 to 5 minutes.

Add 1 cup water and bring to a simmer, scraping up any browned bits. Add the garlic head, cut side down. Reduce to medium-low, cover and cook, stirring occasionally and adjusting the heat as needed to maintain a simmer, until the beef is almost tender, 30 to 35 minutes.

Stir in the carrots and return the mixture to a simmer over medium. Cover, reduce to medium-low and cook until both the meat and carrots are tender, 10 to 15 minutes. Using tongs, remove the garlic head; set aside. Remove the pot from the heat and stir in the raisins.

Drain the rice in a fine-mesh sieve, then rinse under cool running water and drain again. Sprinkle the rice in an even layer over the beef mixture. Using tongs, squeeze the garlic cloves from the head directly onto the rice. Sprinkle with the remaining ½ teaspoon each cumin and coriander,

½ teaspoon salt and ¼ teaspoon black pepper. Add 3 cups water, being careful not to disturb the rice. Bring to a boil over medium-high, then cover, reduce to low and cook without stirring until the water is absorbed, 30 to 35 minutes.

Remove the pot from the heat and let stand, covered, for 10 minutes. Using a fork, fluff the rice. Add the parsley and stir to integrate the layers; remove and discard the bay. Taste and season with salt and black pepper. Serve the plov directly from the pot, or, if desired, transfer to a serving dish; sprinkle with pomegranate seeds (if using).

INDIAN TOMATO RICE

Start to finish: 35 minutes (15 minutes active)
Servings: 4

Robust tomato flavor is key to this popular southern Indian dish, typically prepared when there is an abundance of ripe, red tomatoes and leftover basmati rice. It can be eaten as a light meal with a dollop of yogurt or pairs well with seafood, poultry or even a simple fried egg. We needed a year-round recipe, so we concentrated on finding the best way to impart deep tomato flavor. A combination of cherry or grape tomatoes and tomato paste was best. We also focused on making sure the rice was cooked properly, fluffy and tender with each grain separate. We were inspired by Madhur Jaffrey's tomato rice recipe in "Vegetarian India," though we upped the intensity of both the spices and tomato flavor. We preferred brown or black mustard seeds for their pungency; if you substitute yellow mustard seeds, increase the volume to 1½ teaspoons. Serrano chilies can be used in place of bird's eye chilies, also called Thai bird or Thai chilies. Or you can leave them out entirely. If your pan does not have a tight-fitting lid, cover it with foil before putting the lid in place.

1 cup white basmati rice, rinsed

2 tablespoons tomato paste

2 tablespoons grapeseed or other neutral oil

1 teaspoon cumin seeds

1 teaspoon coriander seeds

1 teaspoon brown or black mustard seeds

2 bird's eye chilies, stemmed and halved lengthwise (optional)

1 garlic clove, finely grated

1 teaspoon finely grated fresh ginger

Kosher salt

½ pound cherry or grape tomatoes, quartered

¼ cup lightly packed chopped fresh cilantro

In a bowl, combine the rinsed rice with enough cold water to cover by 1 inch and let soak for 15 minutes. Drain the rice very well. In a 2-cup liquid measuring cup, combine 1¼ cups water and the tomato paste and whisk until dissolved.

In a large saucepan over medium, combine the oil, cumin, coriander, mustard seeds, chilies (if using), garlic and ginger. Cook until the seeds begin to pop and the mixture is fragrant, about 1 minute.

Stir in the rice and ¾ teaspoon salt and cook until the rice is coated with oil, about 30 seconds. Stir in the water-tomato paste mixture and bring to a simmer. Cover, reduce the heat to low and cook until the water has been absorbed, about 15 minutes. Remove from the heat, add the tomatoes and let sit, covered, for 5 minutes. Stir in the cilantro, fluffing the rice with a fork.

PALESTINIAN UPSIDE-DOWN CHICKEN AND RICE

Start to finish: 2 hours (30 minutes active), plus resting

Servings: 8

Reem Kassis, author of "The Palestinian Table," showed us how to make this multilayered rice dish on a trip to Galilee. It's important to use a pot 9½ to 11 inches in diameter and 4 to 6 inches deep. After searing and removing the chicken, we line the pot with a parchment round to guarantee that the rice, which forms a crisp, browned bottom layer, does not stick when the pot is inverted for serving. If you prefer, you can serve directly from the pot, but we still recommend lining the bottom.

Risotto with Fresh Herbs

Start to finish: 25 minutes
Servings: 4

We learned the principles of risotto from two chefs in Milan, Max Masuelli (and his son, Andrea) at Trattoria Masuelli San Marco, who use neither chicken broth nor onion, and Diego Rossi, of Trippa, who showed us that skipping the traditional wine and adding a splash of sherry vinegar at the end produced bright flavor (we used white balsamic). **Contrary to popular belief, risotto does not require vigilance and uninterrupted stirring. Our method adds half the liquid early and depends on brisk intermittent stirring to agitate the rice grains and release their starch, thickening the cooking liquid and producing the creamy consistency that's the hallmark of great risotto.** Arborio rice is the most common choice for risotto in the U.S., but cooks in Milan—and at Milk Street—preferred carnaroli. However, Arborio works well with careful cooking. Serve in warmed, shallow bowls.

3½ cups vegetable broth (recipe follows)

6 tablespoons (¾ stick) salted butter, cut into 1-tablespoon pieces, divided

1 cup carnaroli or Arborio rice

1 ounce Parmesan cheese, finely grated (½ cup)

2 teaspoons minced fresh thyme

⅓ cup thinly sliced scallions

¼ cup finely chopped parsley

½ teaspoon grated lemon zest

Kosher salt

4 teaspoons white balsamic vinegar

In a small saucepan over medium, bring the broth, covered, to a simmer. Reduce to low to keep warm.

In a large saucepan over medium-high, melt 2 tablespoons of butter. Add the rice and cook, stirring, until translucent at the edges, 1 to 2 minutes. Add 2½ cups of the hot broth and bring to a boil, then reduce to medium and cook, stirring frequently, until the grains are almost tender but still quite firm at the core (it will be quite soupy), 8 to 10 minutes; adjust the heat as needed to maintain a vigorous simmer.

Add ½ cup broth and cook, stirring frequently and briskly, until the rice is just shy of al dente but still soupy, 3 to 5 minutes. If the rice is thick and dry but the grains are still too firm, add the remaining hot broth in ¼-cup increments and continue to cook, stirring, until the rice is just shy of al dente.

Off heat, stir in the Parmesan, thyme, scallions, parsley, lemon zest, ¼ teaspoon salt and the remaining 4 tablespoons butter, 1 piece at a time. Taste and season with salt, then stir in the vinegar. Serve immediately.

Easy Vegetable-Broth

Start to finish: 30 minutes
Makes about 1 quart

One 1-ounce chunk of Parmesan rind

2 large celery stalks, chopped

1 medium yellow onion, chopped

1 medium tomato, roughly chopped

3 large garlic cloves, smashed and peeled

1 cup lightly packed fresh flat-leaf parsley

In a large saucepan over high, combine all ingredients with 5 cups water and bring to a boil. Partially cover, then reduce to medium and cook for 20 minutes, adjusting the heat to maintain a lively simmer.

Pour the broth through a fine-mesh strainer into a large bowl; discard the solids. You should have about 1 quart of broth.

2 cups basmati rice

Kosher salt and ground black pepper

1½ pounds bone-in, skin-on chicken thighs, trimmed

4 tablespoons extra-virgin olive oil, divided

⅓ cup slivered almonds

8 ounces cauliflower florets (1-inch pieces)

8 medium garlic cloves, chopped

4 tablespoons (½ stick) salted butter, melted

4 teaspoons ground cumin

1 tablespoon ground allspice

2 teaspoons ground turmeric

1 teaspoon grated nutmeg

8 ounces eggplant (½ medium), sliced into ¼-inch-thick rounds

1 quart low-sodium chicken broth

In a large bowl, combine the rice and 1 tablespoon salt. Add water to cover by 1 inch, then set aside. Have ready a lidded pot that measures 9½ to 11 inches in diameter and 4 to 6 inches deep. Cut 2 rounds of kitchen parchment the same diameter as the pot.

Season the chicken with salt and pepper. Set the pot over medium and heat 1 tablespoon of the oil until shimmering. Add the chicken skin down and cook until browned, about 10 minutes. Transfer to a plate and set aside. Remove the pot from the heat. Place 1 parchment round on the bottom, then turn to coat with fat.

Add the remaining 3 tablespoons oil to the parchment-lined pot, then sprinkle evenly with the almonds. Drain the rice in a fine-mesh strainer, then rinse under cool running water and drain again. Scatter 1 cup of the rice in a thin, even layer over the almonds. In a medium bowl, mix the remaining rice with the cauliflower, garlic, butter, cumin, allspice, turmeric, nutmeg, ¾ teaspoon salt and 1¾ teaspoons pepper. Reserve ½ cup of this mixture, then distribute the remainder in an even layer.

Place the chicken in the pot, slightly nestling the pieces into the rice-cauliflower layer; discard any accumulated juices. Shingle the eggplant slices over the chicken in an even layer. Sprinkle with the reserved ½ cup rice.

Pour the broth into the pot (it will not fully cover the eggplant), then bring to a boil over medium-high. Lay the second parchment round against the surface, then cover with the lid. Cook for 5 minutes, reduce to low and cook, undisturbed, for 35 minutes.

Remove the pot from the heat, uncover and let stand for 15 minutes. Remove the parchment, then invert a serving platter onto the pot. Holding the platter against the pot, carefully invert the two together; leave the pot overturned on the platter and let rest for about 10 minutes. Slowly lift off the pot and, if needed, remove and discard the parchment.

VENETIAN RICE AND PEAS

Start to finish: 1¼ hours
Servings: 4 to 6

Rice and peas, or risi e bisi, is a classic Venetian dish, traditionally eaten on April 25, St. Mark's Day. Sweet peas stud the dish, and in the version taught to us by Michela Tasca, owner of Ca' de Memi farm and bed and breakfast in Piombino Dese outside of Venice, the al dente grains were bathed in beautiful pale green broth, a result of peas pureed into the cooking liquid. For our version, we puree peas plus fresh parsley with a small amount of a broth infused with aromatics. To keep the flavors and color vibrant, we hold off on adding the puree, along with additional whole peas, until

the rice has finished cooking. Vialone nano is the preferred variety of Italian medium-grain rice for risi e bisi, but Arborio works just as well.

1 medium carrot, peeled and thinly sliced

1 large white onion, half thinly sliced, half finely chopped

1 medium celery stalk, thinly sliced

2 teaspoons fennel seeds

1 quart low-sodium chicken broth

2 cups frozen peas, divided (1 cup still frozen, 1 cup thawed and at room temperature)

2 cups lightly packed fresh flat-leaf parsley

3 to 4 ounces pancetta, finely chopped

4 tablespoons salted butter, cut into 1-tablespoon pieces, divided

1 cup vialone nano or Arborio rice

Ground black pepper

2 ounces Parmesan cheese, finely grated (1 cup), plus more to serve

In a large pot, combine the carrot, the sliced onion, celery, fennel seeds, broth and 2 cups water. Bring to a boil over medium-high, then cover, reduce to medium-low and simmer until the vegetables have softened, 10 to 12 minutes.

Remove the pot from the heat and, using a slotted spoon, transfer the solids to a blender, draining off as much liquid as possible. Add 1 cup of the broth to the blender along with the still-frozen peas and the parsley; leave the remaining broth in the pot so it remains warm. Blend until the mixture is smooth, 1½ to 2 minutes; you should have about 3 cups puree. Set aside in the blender jar.

In a large saucepan over medium, combine the chopped onion, pancetta and 2 tablespoons butter. Cook, stirring occasionally, until the onion is lightly browned and the pancetta is rendered and lightly browned, 6 to 8 minutes. Add the rice and stir until the grains are coated with fat, then stir in 1 cup of the broth. Cook, stirring, until the liquid is mostly absorbed, about 5 minutes. Ladle in additional broth to barely cover the rice and simmer, stirring often, until the broth is mostly absorbed. Repeat the addition of broth and simmering until mostly absorbed 4 or 5 times, until the rice is al dente and most of the broth has been used; this process should take 25 to 30 minutes.

Remove the pan from the heat and let stand uncovered for 5 minutes. Add the thawed peas and the puree, then stir until heated through, about 1 minute. Add the remaining 2 tablespoons butter and stir until melted. Stir in the Parmesan, then taste and season with salt and pepper. Serve sprinkled with additional Parmesan.

LEMON AND SHRIMP RISOTTO WITH FRESH BASIL

Start to finish: 45 minutes
Servings: 4

This is our version of the risotto di limone Giovanna Aceto taught us to make in Amalfi, Italy. The risotto is finished with an egg yolk and some cream, giving the rice velvety taste and texture. For a flavorful broth, we steep shrimp shells and strips of lemon zest in water, and stir in lemon juice and grated zest just before serving. If you buy peeled shrimp, bottled clam juice is a fine substitute. Bring two 8-ounce bottles clam juice, 3 cups water, ½ teaspoon salt and the zest strips to a simmer in the saucepan and cook, covered, for 10 minutes to infuse, then strain as directed.

In a **medium saucepan** over medium, heat 2 teaspoons oil until shimmering. Add the shrimp shells and cook, stirring constantly, until pink, 1 to 2 minutes. Add 5 cups water, the zest strips and ½ teaspoon salt, then bring to a simmer. Cover, reduce to low and cook for 10 minutes. Pour the broth through a strainer set over a medium bowl; rinse out the pan. Press on the solids to extract as much liquid as possible, then discard. Return the broth to the pan, cover and set over low to keep warm.

In a **large Dutch oven** over medium-high, heat 1 tablespoon of oil until shimmering. Add the onion and ¼ teaspoon salt, then cook, stirring occasionally, until softened, 6 to 7 minutes. Add the rice and cook, stirring, until the grains are translucent at the edges, 1 to 2 minutes. Add the wine and cook, stirring occasionally, until the pan is almost dry, about 3 minutes. Add 3 cups of the hot broth and cook, stirring often and briskly, until a spoon drawn through the mixture leaves a trail, 10 to 12 minutes.

Add the remaining broth and cook, stirring, until the rice is tender, 8 to 10 minutes. Remove from the heat; stir in the shrimp. Cover and let stand 5 to 7 minutes.

Stir in the remaining 1 tablespoon oil, the lemon juice, egg yolk, cream, basil, and the grated zest. The risotto should be loose but not soupy; if needed, stir in water 1 tablespoon at a time to achieve the proper consistency. Taste and season with salt. Serve drizzled with additional oil.

2 lemons

2 teaspoons plus 2 tablespoons
extra-virgin olive oil, divided, plus more to serve

12 ounces extra-large (21/25 per pound)
shrimp, peeled (shells reserved), deveined
and patted dry

Kosher salt

1 small yellow onion, finely chopped

1 cup carnaroli or Arborio rice

½ cup dry white wine

1 large egg yolk

2 tablespoons heavy cream

½ cup loosely packed fresh basil, roughly chopped

Using a vegetable peeler (preferably a Y-style peeler), remove the zest from 1 of the lemons in long, wide strips; try to remove only the colored portion of the peel, not the bitter white pith just underneath. Using a rasp-style grater, grate the zest from the remaining lemon; set aside separately. Halve the lemons and squeeze ¼ cup juice; set the juice aside.

RISOTTO WITH SAUSAGE AND SUN-DRIED TOMATOES

Start to finish: 40 minutes

Servings: 4

Creamy risotto doesn't require uninterrupted stirring. Instead we add half the liquid early and then depend on brisk intermittent stirring to agitate the rice grains and release their starch, thickening the cooking liquid and producing the creamy consistency of great risotto. This version is rich with bits of sausage—use sweet or hot, depending on your preference. Sun-dried tomatoes are added at the end for a splash of color and tangy sweetness, while Parmesan cheese lends umami.

1 quart low-sodium chicken broth

2 tablespoons extra-virgin olive oil, divided

8 ounces sweet OR hot Italian sausage, casing removed

1 small yellow onion, finely chopped

Kosher salt and ground black pepper

1 cup Arborio rice

¼ cup drained oil-packed sun-dried tomatoes, chopped

⅓ cup finely chopped fresh flat-leaf parsley OR basil

1 ounce Parmesan cheese, finely grated (½ cup), plus more to serve

In a medium saucepan over medium, bring the broth and 2 cups water, covered, to a simmer. Reduce to low to keep warm.

In a large saucepan over medium, heat 1 tablespoon oil until shimmering. Add the sausage and cook, breaking it into small pieces, until no longer pink and starting to

brown, 5 to 6 minutes. Using a slotted spoon, transfer the sausage to a small bowl; set aside.

To the same large saucepan over medium, add the remaining 1 tablespoon oil and heat until shimmering. Add the onion and ¼ teaspoon salt; cook, stirring occasionally, until softened, about 5 minutes. Add the rice and cook, stirring constantly, until the grains are translucent at the edges, 1 to 2 minutes. Add 3 cups of the hot broth mixture and bring to a boil over medium-high. Reduce to medium and cook, stirring often and briskly, until most of the liquid is absorbed, 10 to 12 minutes; adjust the heat as needed to maintain a vigorous simmer.

Cook, adding ¼ cup of the broth at a time, until the rice is al dente and loose but not soupy, another 8 to 10 minutes. You may not need all of the broth. Stir in the sausage and accumulated juices along with the sun-dried tomatoes; cook, stirring occasionally, until heated through, about 1 minute.

Off heat, stir in the parsley and Parmesan, then taste and season with salt and pepper. Serve sprinkled with additional Parmesan.

BROWN RICE AND MUSHROOM RISOTTO WITH MISO AND SCALLIONS

Start to finish: 1 hour 10 minutes

Servings: 4 to 6

We've given Italian risotto Japanese flair in a few ways. We swapped out the traditional Arborio rice for short-grain brown rice, which we first toast to bring out its nutty taste. We also replaced the usual wine with sake, which lends subtly sweet, mellow flavor, and the Parmesan with white miso for umami and salty savoriness. Cooked with earthy mushrooms, this hearty dish makes a satisfying main course that happens to be vegan.

1 cup short-grain brown rice

2 tablespoons neutral oil

1 bunch scallions, white parts minced, green parts thinly sliced, reserved separately

8 ounces cremini mushrooms, thinly sliced OR shiitake mushrooms (stemmed), thinly sliced OR a combination

Kosher salt and ground black pepper

3 tablespoons white miso

¼ cup sake OR dry white wine

In a large saucepan over medium, toast the rice, stirring, until fragrant and nutty, about 2 minutes. Transfer to a small bowl; set aside. In the same saucepan over medium-high, heat the oil until shimmering. Add the scallion whites, mushrooms, ½ teaspoon salt and 1 teaspoon pepper. Cook, stirring occasionally, until the mushrooms are soft and the moisture they release has mostly evaporated, 4 to 5 minutes.

Add the miso and cook, stirring, until it starts to brown and stick to the bottom of the pan, about 2 minutes. Add the sake and cook, scraping up any browned bits, until slightly thickened, about 2 minutes. Stir in the rice, then add 3 cups water. Bring to a simmer over medium-high, then reduce to low, cover and cook, stirring occasionally and briskly, until the rice is creamy and the grains are tender but with a little chewiness, 50 to 55 minutes; if at any point, the rice looks dry, stir in ¼ to ½ cup water and continue to cook.

Off heat, taste and season with salt and pepper. Serve sprinkled with the scallion greens.

Optional garnish: Toasted sesame oil OR toasted sesame seeds OR furikake OR shichimi togarashi

SAFFRON RISOTTO

Start to finish: 25 minutes

Servings: 4

Saffron-rich risotto is a specialty of Milan. Medium-grain Italian rice is essential for achieving a rich, creamy consistency, as it has the ideal starch content. Arborio rice is the most common choice for risotto in the U.S., but cooks in Milan—and at Milk Street—preferred carnaroli. We found that the grains better retained their structure and resisted overcooking. With careful cooking, however, Arborio will yield delicious results. A quick five-ingredient homemade vegetable broth is the best cooking liquid for this risotto; its fresh, clean flavor won't compete with the other ingredients (recipe follows). Serve in warmed, shallow bowls to prevent the rice from cooling too quickly. If the flavor and aroma of saffron don't appeal to you, try one of our variations; the techniques we learned in Milan also worked well for other flavors.

3½ cups vegetable broth (see recipe below)

1 teaspoon saffron threads

6 tablespoons (¾ stick) salted butter,
cut into 1-tablespoon pieces, divided

1 cup carnaroli or Arborio rice

1 ounce Parmesan cheese, finely grated (½ cup)

Kosher salt

4 teaspoons white balsamic vinegar

In a small saucepan over medium, bring the broth, covered, to a simmer. Reduce to low to keep warm. In a small bowl or measuring cup, combine ½ cup of the hot broth and the saffron. Set aside.

In a large saucepan over medium-high, melt 2 tablespoons of butter. Add the rice and cook, stirring constantly, until translucent at the edges, 1 to 2 minutes. Add 2½ cups of the remaining hot broth and bring to a boil, then reduce to medium and cook, stirring frequently and briskly, until the grains are almost tender but still quite firm at the core (it will be quite soupy), 8 to 10 minutes; adjust the heat to maintain a vigorous simmer.

Add the saffron broth and cook, stirring frequently and briskly, until the rice is just shy of al dente but still soupy, 3 to 5 minutes. If the rice is thick and dry but the grains are still too firm, add the remaining hot broth in ¼-cup increments and continue to cook, stirring, until the rice is just shy of al dente.

Off heat, stir in the Parmesan, ¼ teaspoon salt and the remaining 4 tablespoons butter, 1 piece at a time. Taste and season with salt, then stir in the vinegar. Serve immediately.

FIVE-INGREDIENT VEGETABLE BROTH

Start to finish: 30 minutes
Makes about 1 quart

This simple vegetarian broth can be made in about 30 minutes. Use immediately after straining or cool to room temperature, cover and refrigerate for up to five days.

2 medium carrots, peeled and chopped

2 large celery stalks, chopped

1 medium yellow onion, chopped

1 medium tomato, roughly chopped

1 large garlic clove, smashed and peeled

In a large saucepan over high, combine all ingredients with 5 cups water and bring to a boil. Partially cover, then reduce to medium and cook for 20 minutes, adjusting the heat to maintain a lively simmer.

Pour the broth through a fine-mesh strainer into a large bowl; discard the solids. You should have about 1 quart of broth.

LOMBARDY-STYLE RICE WITH CHICKEN

Start to finish: 45 minutes
Servings: 4

This humble dish from the Lombardy region of northern Italy is known as riso alla pitocca. With familiar flavors and a creamy consistency from the starchiness of Arborio rice, it's pure comfort food, Italian style. Riso alla pitocca is in some ways similar to risotto, but is simpler to cook because there's no need to add liquid in multiple additions, nor for careful or continuous stirring. We do, however, stir the rice vigorously at the end, after the grains are tender, to help create a richer, thicker, more velvety consistency.

Stir in the hot broth, the rice and chicken. Bring to a simmer, then cover, reduce to low and cook until the rice is tender, about 15 minutes. Remove from the heat and quickly stir, then re-cover and let stand for 5 minutes.

Add the chives, butter, and about three-fourths of the cheese, then stir vigorously until the butter is melted and the rice is creamy. Taste and season with salt and pepper. Serve sprinkled with the remaining cheese.

1 pound boneless, skinless chicken thighs, trimmed and cut into 1-inch pieces

Kosher salt and ground black pepper

2½ cups low-sodium chicken broth

2 tablespoons extra-virgin olive oil

1 medium yellow onion, chopped

2 medium carrots, chopped

2 medium garlic cloves, thinly sliced

½ cup dry white wine

1 cup Arborio rice

¼ cup chopped fresh chives

2 tablespoons salted butter, cut into 4 pieces

2 ounces Parmesan cheese, finely grated (1 cup)

Season the chicken with ½ teaspoon each salt and pepper. In a 1-quart liquid measuring cup or medium microwave-safe bowl, heat the broth, covered, until simmering, 2 to 3 minutes; set aside, covered.

In a large Dutch oven over medium-high, heat the oil until shimmering. Add the onion, carrots and ¼ teaspoon salt, then cook, stirring occasionally, until the onion is translucent, about 3 minutes. Add the garlic and cook, stirring, until fragrant, about 30 seconds. Add the wine and cook, scraping up any browned bits, until the wine has mostly evaporated, 2 to 3 minutes.

TOMATO RICE WITH OREGANO AND FETA

Start to finish: 25 minutes

Servings: 4

On the Greek island of Ikaria, Diane Kochilas, authority on the cuisine of her native Greece, taught us to make a risotto-esque tomato rice in which the grains are cooked until al dente (the centers are still slightly firm) and the consistency is a little soupy. Instead of the regular round tomatoes that Kochilas grated to a pulp before use, we opt for grape or cherry tomatoes, halved, because they tend to be dependably good no matter the season. She also used ouzo, the Greek anise-flavored liqueur, as seasoning in the rice, and we do so as well. However, if you prefer, substitute an equal amount of white wine plus 1 teaspoon fennel seeds. To avoid a flare-up, take the skillet off the heat when adding the ouzo (this step is not necessary if using wine instead of ouzo).

3 tablespoons extra-virgin olive oil, plus more to serve

1 tablespoon salted butter

1 small red onion, finely chopped

1 pint grape or cherry tomatoes, halved

Kosher salt and ground black pepper

1 tablespoon tomato paste

3 medium garlic cloves, finely grated

1 cup Arborio rice

⅓ cup ouzo (see headnote)

4 cups hot water, divided

¼ cup minced fresh oregano

2 tablespoons lemon juice

2 ounces feta cheese, crumbled (½ cup)

In a 12-inch skillet over medium-high, heat the oil and butter until the butter melts. Add the onion, tomatoes and ½ teaspoon salt, then cook, stirring occasionally, until the onion has softened and the tomatoes begin to release their juice, about 5 minutes.

Add the tomato paste and cook, stirring, until the tomato paste begins to brown, about 1 minute. Stir in the garlic and cook until fragrant, about 30 seconds. Add the rice and cook, stirring constantly, until the grains are translucent at the edges, 1 to 2 minutes. Remove the pan from the heat and stir in the ouzo. Return to medium-high and bring to a simmer, then cook, stirring, until most of the moisture has been absorbed, about 1 minute.

Stir in 3 cups of the hot water and ¾ teaspoon salt. Bring to a boil, then reduce to medium and cook uncovered, stirring often and briskly, until the rice is al dente (tender but with some firmness at the center) and the consistency is creamy but still rather loose, 8 to 10 minutes; adjust the heat as needed to maintain a vigorous simmer. If the rice is thick and dry but the grains are still too firm, add the remaining 1 cup hot water and continue to cook, stirring, until the rice is al dente.

Off heat, stir in the oregano and lemon juice, then taste and season with salt and pepper. Transfer to a serving bowl and sprinkle with the feta. Serve with oil for drizzling.

CHICKEN AND BEAN PAELLA

Start to finish: 1½ hours
Servings: 4

Outside of Spain, paella is considered a luxurious dish, loaded with seafood, scented with pricy saffron and served as an event in and of itself. Its beginnings, however, are more humble. The one-pan dish was prepared by Valencian farm workers as a midday meal. This type of paella, called paella Valenciana, still is made today. For our version—adapted for a nonstick 12-inch skillet with a lid—we opted for chicken thighs, canned white beans, fresh green beans and grape or cherry tomatoes; saffron is a nice addition, but optional. Using the right rice is key to getting the proper subtly creamy but not overly starchy consistency. Look for Bomba rice, sometimes labeled simply as "Valencian rice." Calasparra rice from Murcia, Spain, is another good option. If neither is available, substitute an equal amount of Arborio rice, but before cooking, rinse it well and drain, and also reduce the amount of broth to 2½ cups. To be efficient, during the 30 minutes that the chicken marinates, prepare the remaining ingredients.

2 teaspoons sweet paprika

1½ teaspoons smoked paprika, divided

Kosher salt and ground black pepper

1 pound boneless, skinless chicken thighs, trimmed, cut into 1-inch pieces and patted dry

4 tablespoons extra-virgin olive oil, divided

15½-ounce can cannellini beans, rinsed and drained

1 pint grape or cherry tomatoes, halved

1 tablespoon tomato paste

6 medium garlic cloves, minced

½ cup dry sherry

3 cups low-sodium chicken broth

4 bay leaves

2 teaspoons minced fresh rosemary

½ teaspoon saffron threads (optional)

1 cup Valencian rice (see headnote)

8 ounces green beans, trimmed and cut into 1-inch pieces

Lemon wedges, to serve

1 teaspoon smoked paprika, then cook until fragrant, about 30 seconds. Add the sherry and cook, stirring occasionally, until most of the liquid has evaporated and the mixture begins to sizzle, 2 to 4 minutes.

Stir in the broth, bay, rosemary and saffron (if using), then bring to a boil over medium-high. Stir in the green beans and the cannellini bean-chicken mixture along with any accumulated juices. Sprinkle the rice into the skillet, then stir to combine and evenly distribute the grains, pressing down to ensure they are fully submerged. Return to a boil, then reduce to medium and cook, uncovered, until most of the liquid is absorbed and craters appear in the rice, 16 to 18 minutes. Increase to medium-high and continue to cook, without stirring but rotating the pan every 10 seconds or so, until you hear sizzling and smell a toasty aroma, 1 to 2 minutes.

Remove the pan from the heat. Drape a clean kitchen towel across the top, then cover with a lid and let rest for 10 minutes. Use a wooden spoon or silicone spatula to scoop the paella onto individual plates, scraping along the pan to loosen the bottom crust (socarrat). Serve with lemon wedges.

In a medium bowl, combine the sweet paprika, ½ teaspoon of smoked paprika, ½ teaspoon salt and 1 teaspoon pepper. Add the chicken and toss until coated. Cover and refrigerate for at least 30 minutes.

In a 12-inch nonstick skillet over medium-high, heat 2 tablespoons of oil until barely smoking. Add the chicken in an even layer and cook without stirring until well-browned, about 3 minutes. Using tongs, flip the pieces and cook until the second sides are well-browned, another 1 to 2 minutes. Using the tongs, return the chicken to the bowl, leaving the fat in the pan.

To the same skillet over medium, add the beans and cook, stirring, until the beans are fragrant and coated with oil, about 30 seconds. Transfer to the bowl with the chicken.

Set the skillet over medium-high, then stir in the tomatoes and ½ teaspoon salt. Cover and cook, stirring occasionally, until the tomatoes are browned, the liquid they released has evaporated and the mixture begins to sizzle, 5 to 7 minutes. Stir in the remaining 2 tablespoons oil and the tomato paste and cook, stirring, until the mixture is beginning to brown, about 2 minutes. Stir in the garlic and the remaining

COCONUT RICE

Start to finish: 30 minutes
Servings: 4 to 6

This coconut rice is rich with tropical notes that work especially well with the floral quality of jasmine rice. Coconut milk adds richness, but too much can weigh down the delicate grains. So for a light, fluffy texture, we mostly use unsweetened coconut water and supplement it with a small amount of coconut milk. A bit of sugar and salt accentuate the flavors. The bottom of the rice may caramelize a little during cooking; this is normal and depends on the saucepan as well as heat output of the burner.

2 cups jasmine rice, rinsed and drained

1⅔ cups unsweetened coconut water

¾ cup coconut milk

½ teaspoon white sugar

½ teaspoon kosher salt

In a **medium** saucepan, stir together all of the ingredients. Bring to a simmer over medium-high, stirring occasionally, then cover, reduce to low and cook without stirring until the rice has absorbed the liquid, 10 to 12 minutes.

Remove from the heat and let stand, covered, for 10 minutes. Fluff with a fork.

PUERTO RICAN-STYLE ARROZ CON POLLO

Start to finish: 1 hour 10 minutes (30 minutes active)
Servings: 6 to 8

Arroz con pollo, or chicken and rice, is a much-loved dish in many Latin American countries. Pieces of chicken cooked directly in rice seasoned with aromatics and herbs, the grains soaking up the juices from the bird—it's comfort food at its best. In his book "Cocina Tropical," chef Jose Santaella includes the recipe for the arroz con pollo he serves at his restaurant, Santaella, in San Juan, Puerto Rico. As with most versions of arroz con pollo, the flavor foundation is sofrito, a cooked mixture of aromatic vegetables, herbs, ham and capers, so you will need to make a batch of sofrito (recipe p. 181) as the first step. Santaella cuts up a

whole chicken, but for ease we use bone-in, skin-on chicken breasts. We do, however, cut each one in half so the chicken cooks on par with the rice. Medium-grain rice, starchier than long-grain but less so than short-grain, is the right type of rice to use here. Italian Arborio is a widely available option; Spanish Valencia and bomba rice, used for paella, work, too. A combination of chicken broth and beer is the cooking liquid; the beer's hoppiness provides flavor balance and helps lighten the dish. Look for a light, quaffable pilsner, such as Corona Extra.

1 teaspoon dried oregano

1 teaspoon onion powder

1 teaspoon granulated garlic or garlic powder

Kosher salt and ground black pepper

3 pounds bone-in, skin-on chicken breasts, trimmed and halved crosswise

2 tablespoons grapeseed or other neutral oil or annatto oil (recipe p. 181)

1 cup sofrito (recipe p. 181)

¼ cup tomato paste

1 cup pimento-stuffed green olives, chopped

1½ cups medium-grain white rice (see headnote), rinsed and drained

12-ounce bottle or can pilsner-style beer (see headnote)

1 cup low-sodium chicken broth

1 cup drained roasted red peppers, chopped

¼ cup chopped fresh cilantro

2 tablespoons extra-virgin olive oil

In a small bowl, stir together the oregano, onion powder, granulated garlic and ½ teaspoon each salt and pepper. Season the chicken on all sides with the mixture.

In a large Dutch oven over medium-high, heat the grapeseed oil until shimmering. Add the chicken and cook, turning once or twice, until browned on both sides, about 5 minutes. Transfer to a large plate and set aside. Pour off and discard the fat from the pot.

Return the pot to medium-high and add the sofrito, tomato paste and olives. Cook, stirring constantly, until fragrant and the mixture begins to brown, about 3 minutes. Stir in the rice and cook, stirring often, until the mixture begins to stick to the pot, 2 to 3 minutes.

Add the beer and scrape up any browned bits, then add the broth. Return the chicken and accumulated juices to the pot, nestling the pieces skin side up in the rice mixture. Bring to a simmer and simmer, uncovered and stirring occasionally and scraping the bottom of the pot, until the rice has absorbed some of the liquid and the mixture has thickened slightly, about 5 minutes. Reduce to medium-low, cover and cook without stirring until the rice is tender and the center of the thickest piece of chicken reaches about 155°F, about 30 minutes.

Remove the pot from the heat. Stir in the roasted peppers, cilantro and olive oil. Re-cover and let stand for 5 to 10 minutes, then stir again, being sure to scrape the bottom of the pot. Taste and season with salt and pepper.

SOFRITO

Start to finish: 30 minutes
Makes about 2 cups

Sofrito, a cooked mixture of aromatic vegetables and other ingredients, is the flavor base for countless Latin American dishes. We adapted José Santaella's formula, making a few changes based on ingredient availability. Annatto oil is optional for lending the sofrito a reddish hue; you can purchase it in grocery stores or make your own, see following recipe. The sofrito will keep in an airtight container in the refrigerator for up to one week.

½ cup extra-virgin olive oil

2 medium yellow onions, finely chopped

10 medium garlic cloves, minced

1 tablespoon tomato paste

¼ cup finely chopped smoked ham

8 ounces ripe tomatoes, cored and chopped

1 large cubanelle pepper or 1 medium red, yellow or orange bell pepper, stemmed, seeded and chopped

3 tablespoons drained capers

2 bay leaves

1 tablespoon dried oregano

1 tablespoon annatto oil (optional; see sidebar)

In a 12-inch skillet over medium-high, heat the olive oil until shimmering. Add the onions and cook, stirring often, until beginning to brown, 2 to 4 minutes. Add the garlic and tomato paste; cook, stirring, until fragrant, about 1 minute. Add the ham and cook, stirring, for about 1 minute. Add the tomatoes, pepper, capers, bay, oregano and annatto oil (if using). Cook, stirring often, until the mixture begins to stick to the pan, 6 to 8 minutes; reduce the heat if it begins to brown. Transfer to a small bowl.

ANNATTO OIL

Start to finish: 15 minutes
Makes ½ cup

Annatto is the seed from the achiote tree; it has a mild flavor and vivid red color. It's easy to make your own annatto oil by warming the seeds in neutral oil.

1 tablespoon annatto seeds

½ cup grapeseed or other neutral oil

In a small saucepan, combine the annatto and oil. Heat over low, occasionally swirling the pan, until the oil is red, about 10 minutes. Cool completely, then pour through a fine-mesh strainer set over a jar. Cover and store at room temperature for several months.

A Guide to Cooking Grains

Most supermarkets today offer a bewildering variety of formerly obscure grains, expanding our options far beyond the days of basic white rice. But this presents a fresh challenge: sorting out the best way to cook each. Individual grains require specific timing and liquid volumes, factors further influenced by whether they're refined and whether you rinse them.

To simplify this, we tested the 12 most widely available grains, cooking up many batches of each to determine optimal timing and liquid volume. We standardized the cooking process wherever possible, aiming for a yield of 4 cups cooked grains per variety. We rinsed and drained each grain before cooking (to remove lingering debris and excess starch) and for most grains we seasoned the cooking water with ½ teaspoon kosher salt.

To cook, we combined the grain, water and salt in a saucepan, then brought it to a boil before covering, reducing the heat to medium-low and cooking. Timing begins when the cover goes on the pot. Some grains had the best taste and texture when left to steam off heat after cooking.

Grain	Quantity	Liquid	Cook time (in mins)	Rest time (in mins)
Long-Grain White Rice	1½ cups	2¼ cups	15	–
Jasmine Rice	1½ cups	2 cups	15–17	–
Basmati Rice	1½ cups	2¼ cups	15–17	–
Short- or Medium-Grain Japanese White Rice	1½ cups	1¾ cups	12	10–15
Long-Grain Brown Rice	1½ cups	2¼ cups	25	10
Short-Grain Brown Rice	1¼ cups	2 cups	35–40	10
Wild Rice	1½ cups	5 cups	45	–
Quinoa	1¼ cups	2¼ cups	15–20	5
Millet	1¼ cups	2¼ cups	15–20	10
Farro*	1½ cups	4 cups	15	–
Barley	1½ cups	4 cups	25–30	–
Coarse Bulgur	1¼ cups	2½ cups	15–20	5

*Strain if water remains in the pan after cooking

TOASTED BULGUR WITH WALNUTS AND PICKLED GRAPES

Start to finish: 40 minutes
Servings: 4 to 6

Grains are a go-to pantry staple—they work well in everything from soups and salads to main courses and side dishes. Here, we combine bulgur with quick-pickled grapes and red onion for pops of sweet-tart flavor, plus some walnuts for umami and buttery crispness. Both the bulgur and the walnuts are toasted to bring out their nutty taste. The recipe calls for coarse bulgur, which has a pleasantly chewy bite. Serve at room temperature alongside roasted or grilled chicken, meat or fish.

8 ounces seedless red OR green grapes, halved (1½ cups)

1 small red OR yellow onion, halved and thinly sliced

3 tablespoons cider vinegar

Kosher salt and ground black pepper

½ cup walnuts OR pecans OR almonds

1 cup coarse bulgur

2 tablespoons extra-virgin olive oil

2 cups lightly packed fresh flat-leaf parsley OR mint, roughly chopped

In a large bowl, stir together the grapes, onion, vinegar and ½ teaspoon each salt and pepper; set aside.

In a large saucepan over medium, toast the walnuts, stirring often, until fragrant and lightly browned, 2 to 3 minutes. Transfer to a cutting board; reserve the saucepan. Let the nuts cool slightly, then roughly chop; set aside.

In the same saucepan over medium, toast the bulgur, stirring often, until fragrant, about 1 minute. Add 2 cups water and bring to a simmer over medium-high, stirring occasionally. Cover, reduce to low and cook until all of the water has been absorbed, 12 to 15 minutes. Remove the pan from the heat, uncover and let the bulgur cool slightly, stirring occasionally, for 10 to 15 minutes.

Add the bulgur to the bowl with the grapes and onion; toss to combine. Stir in the oil, parsley and half of the walnuts. Taste and season with salt and pepper. Serve sprinkled with the remaining walnuts.

Optional garnish: Crumbled feta cheese **OR** blue cheese **OR** fresh goat cheese (chèvre)

BULGUR AND VERMICELLI PILAF WITH TOMATOES, YOGURT AND HERBS

Start to finish: 45 minutes
Servings: 4 to 6

This hearty grain-and-noodle pilaf is based on a classic Cypriot dish called pilafi pourgouri. Nutty, nubby bulgur and bits of toasted vermicelli find delicious flavor companions in caramelized onion and tomatoes (we use canned for convenience) that have cooked down until jammy and concentrated. A portion of the onion-tomato mixture simmers into the grain and noodles so the pilaf is seasoned throughout. The rest is spooned on as a garnish, along with yogurt for a little creaminess and parsley and mint for fresh, grassy notes. If you cannot find vermicelli (it's sometimes sold in nests), capellini or even angel hair pasta work well. Serve this as a light main or as a side to grilled or roasted lamb.

Into the remaining tomato mixture in the skillet, stir the bulgur and the remaining 1 tablespoon oil. Return to medium-high and add 2¼ cups water, scraping up any browned bits, then stir in the pasta and ¼ teaspoon each salt and pepper. Bring to a simmer, then cover, reduce to low and cook undisturbed until the liquid has been absorbed, 12 to 15 minutes.

Remove the pan from the heat and let stand, covered, for 5 minutes. Using a fork, fluff the pilaf, then taste and season with salt and pepper. Transfer to a serving bowl and spoon on the yogurt, followed by the reserved tomato mixture. Sprinkle with the herbs and drizzle with additional oil.

CARAMELIZED ONION BULGUR WITH GREENS AND POMEGRANATE MOLASSES

Start to finish: 1 hour (30 minutes active)
Servings: 4

Inspired by a dish we had in Galilee, this recipe combines hearty bulgur with silky greens and bittersweet caramelized onions. Instead of slowly caramelizing the onions to a jammy consistency, we cook them over higher heat so they retain some crispy texture. We season the dish with baharat and allspice, cooking them briefly in oil to bloom the flavors. Baharat is a Middle Eastern blend of black pepper, cardamom and other warm spices, though you can substitute cumin plus cinnamon instead. Coarse bulgur, rather than fine, is toasted in the spices to enhance the grains' nutty taste and infuse them with the seasonings. Pomegranate molasses brings a sweet, tart pop to the finished dish.

4 tablespoons extra-virgin olive oil, divided

2 medium yellow onions, halved and thinly sliced

Kosher salt and ground black pepper

1 cup coarse bulgur

1½ teaspoons baharat (see headnote)
OR 2 teaspoons ground cumin plus
¼ teaspoon ground cinnamon

½ teaspoon ground allspice

1 bunch collard greens OR lacinato kale
OR curly kale, stemmed and chopped

Pomegranate molasses, to serve

---

4 tablespoons extra-virgin olive oil, divided, plus more to serve

2 ounces vermicelli or capellini, broken into rough 1-inch pieces (about 1 cup)

1 medium yellow onion, finely chopped

Kosher salt and ground black pepper

14½-ounce can diced tomatoes

1 cup coarse bulgur

½ cup whole-milk plain yogurt

2 tablespoons chopped fresh flat-leaf parsley

1 tablespoon chopped fresh mint

In a 12-inch skillet, combine 2 tablespoons oil and the pasta. Cook over medium-high, stirring occasionally, until lightly browned, about 2 minutes. Transfer to a small bowl.

In the same skillet, combine 1 tablespoon of the remaining oil, the onion, ½ teaspoon salt and ¼ teaspoon pepper; cook over medium-high, stirring occasionally, until the onion is browned, 4 to 6 minutes. Add the tomatoes with juices, reduce to medium and cook, stirring occasionally, until all of the liquid has evaporated and the mixture resembles jam, about 4 minutes. Remove the pan from the heat, then transfer about half (1 cup) of the tomato mixture to a small bowl and set aside.

In a 12-inch skillet over medium-high, heat 3 tablespoons oil until shimmering. Add the onions and cook, stirring occasionally at the start then more frequently once beginning to brown, until deeply caramelized and crisped, 10 to 15 minutes; reduce the heat if the onions brown too quickly. Transfer to a paper towel-lined plate and sprinkle with a pinch of salt; set aside.

In the same skillet over medium, toast the bulgur, stirring occasionally, until lightly browned and fragrant, 2 to 3 minutes. Add the remaining 1 tablespoon oil, the baharat, allspice and ½ teaspoon pepper; cook, stirring, until fragrant, about 1 minute. Add the greens 1 large handful at a time, stirring to slightly wilt before adding more. Add 2 cups water and 1 teaspoon salt, then scrape up the browned bits. Bring to a simmer over medium-high, then cover, reduce to medium-low and cook without stirring until the liquid has been absorbed, about 15 minutes.

Remove the skillet from the heat and let stand, covered, for 10 minutes. Using a fork, fluff the bulgur mixture, then stir in half of the caramelized onions. Taste and season with salt and pepper. Transfer to a serving dish, top with the remaining onions and drizzle with pomegranate molasses.

Optional garnish: Pomegranate seeds OR thinly sliced scallions OR both

CHANGE THE WAY YOU COOK

Weigh Your Grains!

Cooking the perfect pot of grains is all a matter of using the proper ratio of liquid to grains. Getting it right is the difference between light, fluffy forkfuls or a pile of glop.

Carefully measuring the liquid is key: Too much makes grains (especially rice) mushy. Too little, and they won't cook through. For the water, use a liquid measuring cup, observing it at eye level.

But for the grains, we found measuring by volume imprecise, often resulting in surprising variations.

We solve for this by measuring dry ingredients by weight, not volume. It's more precise—and more convenient, too, as you can measure grains directly into the pot before adding water. Simply set the pot on a digital scale, hit tare (zeroing out the pot's weight), then add the desired weight of grains. And to rinse your rice, it can be weighed in the pot, rinsed, strained and returned to the pot.

For our chart, we tested 14 common grains to find their weight in grams per cup.

1 Level Cup of...	Weight in Grams
Bulgar	195
Farro	200
Oats, Rolled	100
Oats, Steel-cut	190
Pearled Barley	195
Quinoa	185
Rice, Arborio	220
Rice, Basmati	210
Rice, Brown, Long Grain	205
Rice, Brown, Short Grain	195
Rice, Jasmine	215
Rice, White, Long Grain	195
Rice, White, Medium Grain	215
Rice, White, Short Grain	220

JAPANESE-STYLE MIXED-GRAIN RICE

Start to finish: 1 hour (5 minutes active)
Makes about 4 cups

Japanese-style white rice has a satisfying chew and a clean, subtly sweet flavor that pairs well with many foods. Sometimes other grains are mixed into the rice before cooking for added flavor and texture, as well as for a nutritional boost. The amount typically is small so the rice retains its characteristic stickiness. Based on Sonoko Sakai's suggestion in her book, "Japanese Home Cooking," we tested a variety of widely available grains and found that barley, farro, oats, quinoa, millet and amaranth all worked nicely. But avoid ones such as wild rice and black rice, as these grains require longer cooking than the white rice itself.

1¼ cups Japanese-style short- or medium-grain white rice

¼ cup pearled barley, pearled farro, old-fashioned oats, quinoa, millet, amaranth or a combination (see headnote)

In a fine-mesh sieve, rinse the rice and grains under cool running water, stirring, until the water runs almost clear, about 30 seconds. Drain well, shaking the sieve to remove excess water, then transfer to a large saucepan. Add 1¾ cups water, cover and let stand for 30 minutes.

Uncover and bring to a simmer over medium-high. Re-cover, reduce to low and cook, undisturbed, until the grains have absorbed the water, 18 to 20 minutes. Remove from the heat and let stand, covered, for 10 minutes. Fluff with a fork.

TOASTED FARRO WITH PISTACHIOS, GREEN OLIVES AND JALAPEÑOS

Start to finish: 40 minutes, plus cooling
Servings: 4 to 6

This grain-based salad was inspired by Israeli salatim, the wide variety of small plates, ranging from dips to salads to crunchy pickles, that are offered at the start of a meal. It combines the earthy flavor and bouncy texture of farro, a type of wheat, with the colors and contrasting notes of Moroccan carrot salad. We toast the farro to enhance its nuttiness before simmering the grains until tender, and we shred the carrots to heighten their sweetness and soften their texture. Grassy parsley adds freshness, buttery green olives bring briny kick and a bright, lemony dressing ties everything together. The salad is a great accompaniment to everything from grilled fish to roasted chicken and beef or lamb kebabs.

4 tablespoons extra-virgin olive oil, divided

1 cup pearled farro

1 teaspoon ground cumin, divided

3 medium garlic cloves, smashed and peeled

Kosher salt and ground black pepper

1 medium shallot, halved and thinly sliced

¼ cup lemon juice

2 small carrots, peeled and shredded on the large holes of a box grater (about 2 cups)

2 jalapeño chilies, stemmed, seeded and thinly sliced

1½ cups lightly packed fresh flat-leaf parsley, chopped

1 cup pitted green olives, chopped

2 tablespoons chopped roasted pistachios

In a medium saucepan over medium, combine 1 tablespoon oil, the farro and ½ teaspoon cumin. Toast, stirring occasionally, until fragrant and lightly browned, about 3 minutes. Add 5 cups water, the garlic and ¾ teaspoon salt. Bring to a simmer over medium-high, then reduce to medium and simmer, uncovered and stirring occasionally, until the grains are tender with a little chew, 25 to 30 minutes. Meanwhile, in a large bowl, stir together the shallot, lemon juice and ¼ teaspoon salt.

When the farro is done, drain in a colander. Remove the garlic cloves and add them to the shallot mixture. Using a

fork, mash the garlic to a smooth paste. Stir in the remaining 3 tablespoons oil, the remaining ½ teaspoon cumin and ½ teaspoon pepper, then add the carrots and chilies, followed by the still-warm farro. Toss, then let stand, tossing occasionally, until cooled to room temperature.

Stir in the parsley and olives, then taste and season with salt and pepper. Transfer to a serving dish and sprinkle with the pistachios.

TWO-CHEESE BAKED FARRO WITH KALE AND TOMATOES

Start to finish: 1 hour 10 minutes (20 minutes active),
plus cooling / Servings: 6 to 8

Though it's typically simmered with liquid on the stovetop, farro also does well in the oven—a mostly hands-off approach that's easy on the cook. First, we toast the grains to enhance their nutty taste, then bake them until tender in a tomato sauce seasoned with red pepper flakes and dried herbs. Kale lends earthy flavor to the mix. For lots of cheesy goodness, this one-pot dish is topped with mozzarella and Parmesan.

1½ cups pearled farro

4 tablespoons extra-virgin olive oil, divided

1 bunch lacinato kale OR curly kale, stemmed and chopped into rough 1-inch pieces (8 cups) OR 8 ounces Brussels sprouts, trimmed and sliced (4 cups)

4 medium garlic cloves, thinly sliced

Kosher salt and ground black pepper

28-ounce can crushed tomatoes

1 teaspoon dried oregano OR dried thyme OR 2 bay leaves

¼ to ½ teaspoon red pepper flakes

8 ounces mozzarella OR Swiss OR provolone cheese, shredded (2 cups)

2 ounces Parmesan OR Asiago cheese, finely grated (1 cup)

Heat the oven to 425°F with a rack in the lower-middle position. In a large Dutch oven over medium-high, combine the farro and 2 tablespoons oil. Cook, stirring often, until toasted, 3 to 5 minutes. Add the kale, garlic and ½ teaspoon each salt and pepper. Cook, stirring occasionally, until the kale is bright green and slightly wilted, about 2 minutes. Stir in the tomatoes, oregano, pepper flakes and 3 cups water, then bring to a boil. Cover and transfer to the oven.

Bake for 30 minutes, then remove from the oven and uncover. The mixture will have thickened slightly but still will be soupy. Stir, then sprinkle evenly with the mozzarella and Parmesan. Drizzle with the remaining 2 tablespoons oil. Return to the oven, uncovered, and bake until browned and bubbling and the farro is very tender, about 20 minutes; the mixture will be slightly stewy but will thicken as it cools. Cool for about 10 minutes before serving.

FARRO WITH PANCETTA, ESCAROLE AND PARMESAN

Start to finish: 50 minutes
Servings: 4 to 6

Farro, an ancient grain and type of wheat, has a satisfyingly tender-chewy texture and a deliciously nutty flavor. Here, we match it with pancetta and escarole, then finish the dish as if it were risotto, by stirring in butter and Parmesan cheese. Leafy, frilly escarole—which looks like lettuce but actually is a member of the chicory family—has a pleasantly bitter flavor. If you prefer, use lacinato kale (also called Tuscan or dinosaur kale) in its place. Serve as a first course, a light vegetarian main or as a side to grilled or roasted meats, chicken or sausages.

1 tablespoon extra-virgin olive oil

4 ounces pancetta, finely chopped

1 medium shallot, minced

1 large carrot, peeled and finely chopped

½ cup dry white wine

1½ cups pearled farro

Kosher salt and ground black pepper

1 head escarole, chopped in rough
1-inch pieces or 1 large bunch lacinato kale,
stemmed and chopped into rough 1-inch pieces

2 tablespoons salted butter

1 ounce Parmesan cheese, finely grated
(½ cup), plus more to serve

In a 12-inch skillet over medium, cook the oil and the pancetta, stirring occasionally, until the pancetta is browned and crisp, 3 to 5 minutes. Using a slotted spoon, transfer the pancetta to a small bowl, then pour off and discard all but 2 tablespoons fat from the pan.

Return the pan to medium, add the shallot and carrot, then cook, stirring occasionally, until beginning to soften, 1 to 2 minutes. Add the wine and cook, stirring, until most of the liquid has evaporated, about 3 minutes. Stir in the farro and ½ teaspoon each salt and pepper, followed by 3 cups water.

Bring to a simmer over medium-high, then cover, reduce to medium-low and simmer, stirring occasionally, until most of the liquid has been absorbed and the grains are tender with a little chew, about 25 minutes. Add the escarole and

stir just to incorporate, then cover and cook until the escarole begins to soften, about 2 minutes. Stir again, then re-cover and cook, stirring occasionally, until the escarole is tender, 4 to 5 minutes.

Stir in the butter and cheese, then taste and season with salt and pepper. Serve sprinkled with the pancetta and additional cheese.

Soft Polenta

Start to finish: 1¾ hours (10 minutes active)
Servings: 6

Polenta, a savory cornmeal porridge, can be a disappoint-ment in the U.S., tasting mostly of the cheese and fat that weigh it down. Not to mention it requires near-constant whisking to get a lump-free consistency. But in Cossano Belbo, Italy, we learned a better way from Maria Teresa Marino, whose family has run a grain mill for centuries: No cheese, no butter, not much stirring. The porridge was light and fresh and the taste of the corn shined through. We followed that lead, using more water than called for in conventional recipes—11 cups. Combining the cornmeal with cold, not boiling, water, then bringing the entire pot to a simmer, prevented clumping. We finished cooking the polenta in the oven rather than the stovetop for more consistent, gentle heat. For the best flavor and texture, use coarse stone-ground cornmeal. The finished polenta should be pourable; if it's too thick, thin it with water as needed.

2 cups coarse stone-ground yellow cornmeal (see headnote)

Kosher salt and ground black pepper

Heat the oven to 375°F with a rack in the lower-middle position. In a large Dutch oven, whisk together the cornmeal, 1½ teaspoons salt and 11 cups water. Bring to a gentle simmer over medium-high, stirring frequently to prevent clumping. Transfer the pot, uncovered, to the oven and bake for 1 hour.

Remove the pot from the oven. Carefully whisk until smooth, then use a wooden spoon to scrape along the bottom and into the corners of the pot to loosen any stuck bits. Return the pot, uncovered, to the oven and cook until the cornmeal is thick and creamy and the granules are tender, another 10 to 30 minutes, depending on the cornmeal used.

Remove the pot from the oven. Vigorously whisk the polenta until smooth and use the wooden spoon to scrape the bottom, sides and corners. Let stand for 5 minutes. The polenta should thicken just enough for a spoon to leave a brief trail when dragged through; whisk in additional water, if needed, to thin the consistency. Taste and season with salt and pepper. Serve immediately.

Spicy Tomato Sauce with Garlic and Anchovies

Start to finish: 20 minutes
Makes 2 cups

This garlicky sauce is also delicious tossed with pasta. Don't bother chopping the anchovies; they disintegrate as they cook.

4 tablespoons extra-virgin olive oil, divided

5 anchovy fillets

5 medium garlic cloves, minced

½ teaspoon red pepper flakes

2 pints grape tomatoes, 1 pint halved

3 tablespoons red wine vinegar

Kosher salt and ground black pepper

¼ cup lightly packed chopped fresh basil

In a 12-inch nonstick skillet over medium, combine 2 table-spoons of the oil, the anchovies and garlic. Cook, stirring and breaking up the anchovies, until the garlic is light golden brown, 2 to 3 minutes. Add the pepper flakes and tomatoes, then cover and cook, stirring occasionally, until most of the whole tomatoes have burst, 5 to 7 minutes.

Use a fork to gently mash the sauce. Off heat, stir in the vinegar and remaining 2 tablespoons olive oil. Taste and season with salt and pepper, then stir in the basil.

GRAINS

BACON AND BARLEY PILAF WITH CELERY ROOT

Start to finish: 1 hour

Servings: 4

We give barley pilaf-style treatment in this recipe, which adds earthy celery root, sweet leeks and salty-smoky bacon. To tie everything together, the barley is tossed with a tangy mustard vinaigrette, which the grains absorb beautifully. Toasting barley before simmering is the key to enhancing the grain's naturally nutty taste. Be sure to use pearled barley, which has been polished, or "pearled," to remove the outer husk and bran layers; this reduces the cooking time. Serve this hearty, autumnal dish warm or at room temperature, garnished with fresh dill if you like.

1 tablespoon Dijon mustard

1 teaspoon cider vinegar

1 tablespoon extra-virgin olive oil

1 cup pearled barley

4 ounces bacon OR pancetta, chopped

1 medium leek, white and light green parts thinly sliced, rinsed and drained OR 2 medium shallots, finely chopped

8 ounces celery root, peeled and cut into ½-inch pieces

Kosher salt and ground black pepper

In a small bowl, whisk together the mustard, vinegar, oil and 1 tablespoon water; set aside. In a medium saucepan over medium-high, toast the barley, stirring occasionally, until lightly browned and fragrant, 3 to 4 minutes. Transfer to another small bowl; set aside.

In the same saucepan over medium-low, cook the bacon, stirring occasionally, until browned and crisp, 5 to 7 minutes. Add the leek, then cook, stirring occasionally, until softened, about 2 minutes. Add the celery root and ¼ cup water, then scrape up the browned bits. Stir in the barley, 2¾ cups water and ½ teaspoon each salt and pepper. Bring to a simmer over medium-high, stirring occasionally, then cover, reduce to low and cook without stirring until the water is absorbed and the barley and celery root are tender, about 40 minutes.

Off heat, use a fork to fluff the mixture, then gently stir in the vinaigrette. Taste and season with salt and pepper. Serve warm or at room temperature.

Optional garnish: Chopped fresh dill

TOASTED BARLEY WITH SHIITAKE MUSHROOMS AND KIMCHI

Start to finish: 1¼ hours (20 minutes active)

Servings: 4 to 6

This umami-packed barley dish was inspired by Korean boribap, a mix of rice and barley that's steamed and served with banchan (small plates) and soup. We first toast the barley, which brings out a richness and depth of flavor in the grain so it holds its own amidst meaty mushrooms, aromatic sesame oil and tangy, fiery kimchi. If your kimchi is dryish and doesn't have 2 tablespoons of juice for stirring into the barley, use 1 tablespoon water plus 1 tablespoon soy sauce instead. Topping this with runny-yolked fried eggs will transform the barley into a satisfying meal.

1 cup pearled barley

2 tablespoons neutral oil

8 ounces shiitake mushrooms, stemmed, caps sliced about ¼ inch thick

Kosher salt and ground black pepper

1 tablespoon gochujang

1½ teaspoons finely grated fresh ginger

1 cup cabbage kimchi, chopped, plus
2 tablespoons kimchi juice

1½ teaspoons toasted sesame oil

In a large saucepan over medium-high, toast the barley, stirring occasionally, until lightly browned, 4 to 5 minutes. Transfer to a small bowl; set aside.

In the same pan over medium-high, heat the neutral oil until shimmering. Add the mushrooms and ¼ teaspoon salt; cook, stirring occasionally, until softened and lightly browned, about 3 minutes. Return the barley to the pan, add the gochujang and ginger and stir until incorporated. Add 2¾ cups water, scraping up any browned bits. Bring

to a boil, then reduce to low, cover and simmer, stirring occasionally, until the barley has absorbed the liquid and is tender, 40 to 45 minutes. Remove from the heat, drape a kitchen towel across the pan and re-cover. Let stand for about 10 minutes.

Using a fork, fluff the barley mixture. Add the kimchi plus kimchi juice and the sesame oil; stir until well combined and the barley has absorbed the liquid. Taste and season with salt and pepper.

Optional garnish: Cucumber matchsticks **OR** toasted sesame seeds **OR** crumbled nori snacks **OR** thinly sliced scallions **OR** a combination

BARLEY "RISOTTO" WITH MUSHROOMS, KALE AND GORGONZOLA

Start to finish: 45 minutes
Servings: 4

Barley, though not commonly used in Mediterranean cuisine, makes a nutty, toothsome risotto-like dish when cooked with the right amount of liquid. For flavor and to make the grain into a satisfying meal, we use sautéed cremini mushrooms as a base, wilt in baby kale (or spinach or arugula) at the end, then top it all off with a pungent cheese. To make prep go a little quicker, look for already sliced cremini mushrooms in the supermarket. We think the butteriness of Gorgonzola dolce, which is softer and milder than regular Gorgonzola, is an especially good match for the risotto; other delicious cheese options are Taleggio (cut into thin slices with the rind) and Italian fontina (trimmed of rind and cut into small cubes).

¼ cup extra-virgin olive oil, plus
more to serve (optional)

2 medium shallots, chopped

4 medium garlic cloves, minced

Kosher salt and ground black pepper

12 ounces cremini mushrooms, sliced

½ cup dry white wine

1 cup quick-cooking barley

2 cups boiling water

1 small sprig rosemary

5-ounce container baby kale, spinach
or arugula

2 ounces Gorgonzola dolce cheese,
crumbled (½ cup)

In a large saucepan over medium-high, heat the oil until shimmering. Add the shallots, garlic, ½ teaspoon salt and ½ teaspoon pepper, then cook, stirring occasionally, until the shallots are translucent, about 3 minutes. Add the mushrooms and cook, stirring occasionally, until the moisture they release has evaporated and they begin to brown, 7 to 9 minutes.

Add the wine and cook, stirring occasionally, until most of the liquid has evaporated, about 3 minutes. Add the barley, boiling water and rosemary, then bring to a simmer. Cover, reduce to low and cook, stirring occasionally, until most of the liquid has been absorbed and the barley is tender, 10 to 12 minutes.

Off heat, remove and discard the rosemary, then add the kale and stir until wilted. Taste and season with salt and pepper. Transfer to a serving dish and top with the cheese. If desired, drizzle with additional oil.

QUINOTTO WITH GREEN CHILI, CORN AND GOAT CHEESE

Start to finish: 45 minutes
Servings: 4

Quinotto is a dish in which quinoa—which actually is a seed, not a grain—is cooked in a manner similar to the rice-cooking method used to make risotto. Because the starch content of quinoa differs from that of Arborio rice, the consistency of quinotto isn't quite as creamy and luxurious as risotto, but it still is satisfyingly thick. Here we pair quinoa with earthy green poblano chili and kernels of sweet corn (fresh is best, but thawed frozen is good, too), then add richness plus a little tang by stirring in fresh goat cheese. Scallion greens and cilantro finish the dish with allium and herbal freshness. We prefer the look of the dish made with white quinoa, but quinoa of any color will work. Serve as a vegetarian main or as a side to grilled or roasted chicken, beef, pork or lamb.

2 tablespoons extra-virgin olive oil

1 poblano chili, stemmed, seeded and
finely chopped

1 cup fresh or thawed frozen corn kernels

4 scallions, white parts minced, green parts thinly
sliced on the diagonal, reserved separately

Kosher salt and ground black pepper

½ teaspoon ground cumin

1 cup quinoa, preferably white (see headnote),
rinsed and drained

3 cups low-sodium chicken broth
or vegetable broth

4 ounces fresh goat cheese (chèvre),
crumbled (1 cup)

1 cup lightly packed fresh cilantro,
chopped, divided

Lime wedges, to serve

In a 12-inch skillet over medium, heat the oil until shimmering. Add the poblano chili, corn, the scallion whites and ½ teaspoon each salt and pepper. Cook, stirring occasionally, until the vegetables begin to soften, about 5 minutes. Add the cumin and cook, stirring, until fragrant, about 30 seconds.

Stir in the quinoa followed by the broth, then bring to a simmer over medium-high. Cover, reduce to low and cook, stirring occasionally and adjusting the heat as needed to maintain a simmer, until the quinoa is tender and the liquid is almost fully absorbed, 15 to 20 minutes.

Off heat, add half of the goat cheese and half of the cilantro, then stir until the cheese has melted into the quinoa mixture. Taste and season with salt and pepper. If desired, transfer to a serving dish. Sprinkle with the remaining goat cheese, the remaining cilantro and the scallion greens; serve with lime wedges.

LEMON QUINOA WITH TOASTED MUSTARD SEEDS AND PEANUTS

Start to finish: 30 minutes
Servings: 4

Spicy, tangy and nutty, this recipe was inspired by lemon rice, a traditional South Indian dish, but we swapped out the usual white rice for nutrient-rich quinoa. Peanuts, mustard seeds (or cumin seeds) and turmeric are first cooked in hot oil, a technique called blooming, or tempering, to release their fragrance and flavor. A portion of this mixture is reserved for garnish, then the quinoa is cooked in the remaining nut-spice mixture so it's infused with seasoning and aroma. Adding lemon juice at the very end keeps the flavors bright. This is an excellent side to grilled or roasted chicken or seafood; it's also an excellent base for a grain bowl.

¼ cup extra-virgin olive oil

½ cup roasted peanuts OR cashews, roughly chopped

1 tablespoon brown OR yellow mustard seeds OR cumin
seeds OR a combination

½ teaspoon ground turmeric

Kosher salt and ground black pepper

1 cup white quinoa, rinsed and drained

2 tablespoons lemon juice

In a medium saucepan over medium, heat the oil until shimmering. Add the peanuts, mustard seeds, turmeric, 1 teaspoon salt and ¼ teaspoon pepper. Cook, stirring occasionally, until fragrant and the peanuts begin to brown, 1 to 2 minutes. Transfer ¼ cup of the peanut mixture to a small bowl; set aside for garnish.

Add the quinoa to the remaining peanut mixture in the saucepan, then cook, stirring, until the mixture begins to crackle, about 30 seconds. Add 2 cups water and bring to a simmer over medium-high, then cover, reduce to medium-low and cook, without stirring, until the quinoa has absorbed the water, about 15 minutes.

Remove from the heat and let stand, covered, for 10 minutes. Drizzle with the lemon juice, then fluff with a fork. Transfer to a serving dish and spoon on the reserved nut mixture.

Optional garnish: Fresh cilantro **OR** red pepper flakes **OR** both

A Citrus Finish

Save your citrus for the finish. Many dishes benefit from a finishing squeeze of lemon or lime juice, the sharp, acidic notes adding bright, tangy flavor that balances rich flavors. But adding citrus earlier during cooking will dull its impact. Save it for the end, when a squeeze of fresh juice will have plenty of impact.

We do this in our Provençal-inspired beef, orange and olive stew (recipe p. 360), stirring in orange juice toward the end of cooking and reinforcing the sweet, tangy zing with orange zest added off-heat. Similarly, our lemon quinoa based on traditional South Indian lemon rice (recipe p. 194) gets a finishing drizzle of lemon juice. And our rich and hearty Moroccan chicken tagine (recipe p. 339) ends with an off-heat infusion of lemon juice.

We often offer lemon or lime wedges on the side at the table. Dishes of all sorts—from grilled fish to stir-fried noodles to braised beans—benefit from a last-minute squirt of citrus. The acidity not only perks up flavors, the essential oils released when a wedge is squeezed adds bright, fresh aroma.

Eggs

MILK STREET BASIC

Hard-Cooked Eggs

Start to finish: 20 minutes
Makes 6 to 8 eggs

There are many ways to hard-cook an egg, but after much testing, we found no better method than the one used by Chris Edwards, chef at Le Saint Sebastien in Paris' 11th arrondissement and vice-champion of the 2021 Oeuf Mayo World Championship (oeuf mayo is a classic French bistro hors d'oeuvre of hard-cooked eggs garnished with mayonnaise). **Added to boiling water, simmered vigorously, then shocked in icy water, eggs emerge not only perfectly cooked, the shells peel away cleanly and easily.** This approach worked for softer-cooked eggs, too. Boiling for 6 to 6½ minutes gave us perfectly just-runny yolks; 8½ to 9 minutes for medium yolks; and 12½ to 13 minutes for hard-cooked yolks.

6 to 8 cold whole large eggs in their shells

Fill a large saucepan with 3 inches of water; bring to a boil over medium-high. Using a slotted spoon, lower the eggs into the water. Cook, adjusting the heat as needed to maintain a vigorous simmer but not a hard boil, 12½ to 13 minutes for hard-cooked yolks. While the eggs cook, fill a large bowl with about 4 cups ice and 2 cups water; set near the stove.

When the eggs are done, use the slotted spoon to quickly transfer them to the ice bath; cool for 3 minutes, then remove (if left in the ice bath for longer, the eggs may be more difficult to peel). Gently tap each egg against the counter, turning it so the shell cracks all around. Peel away the shell along with the thin membrane underneath.

DEVILED EGGS WITH TUNA, OLIVES AND CAPERS

Start to finish: 2½ hours (20 minutes active)
Makes 12 deviled eggs

The star ingredient in this version of deviled eggs is tuna. Look for tuna packed in olive oil, not water, which is richer and more flavorful. Mixed together with the egg yolks, capers, mustard, olives and roasted red pepper, it becomes a bold filling for a classic hors d'oeuvre. If you want to get ahead, the eggs can be cooked and peeled up to two days in advance.

6 hard-cooked large eggs, peeled and chilled

2 tablespoons extra-virgin olive oil, plus more to serve

1½ tablespoons lemon juice

1 teaspoon Dijon mustard

5-ounce can olive oil–packed tuna, well drained and finely flaked

2 tablespoons finely chopped fresh flat-leaf parsley OR chives, plus more to serve

2 tablespoons finely chopped pitted
black olives, plus more to serve

2 tablespoons finely chopped roasted
red pepper, plus more to serve

1 tablespoon drained capers, finely chopped

Kosher salt and ground black pepper

Slice each egg in half lengthwise. Carefully remove the yolks and place in a medium bowl. Add the oil, lemon juice and mustard to the yolks, then mash to a smooth paste. Add the flaked tuna, parsley, olives, roasted red pepper and capers; stir until well combined. Taste and season with salt, pepper and hot sauce (if using).

Using a spoon, mound the filling onto the egg white halves. Garnish with parsley, olives and roasted red pepper, then drizzle with additional oil.

Optional garnish: Hot sauce

SOY SAUCE EGGS

Start to finish: 30 minutes, plus marinating
Makes 6 eggs

Eggs that are soft-cooked, peeled and marinated in soy sauce are a delicious way to finish a salad, rice bowl or noodle soup. They also are great on avocado toast or as snack on their own. The soy tints the eggs brown, while salt and sugar (we like the floral notes of honey) gently cure the eggs, so over time, they gradually become firmer. Our recipe marinates for a minimum of 4 hours, but the eggs will keep for up to a week, at which point only the very center of the yolks will be soft and slightly gooey. Korean-style soy eggs typically include punchy aromatics in the marinade. If you like, stir 2 teaspoons toasted sesame seeds, 2 thinly sliced scallions, 1 thinly sliced fresh chili and 1 minced garlic clove into the soy mixture before adding the peeled eggs. These ingredients do lose their freshness, though, so consume the eggs within three days.

⅓ cup warm water

¼ cup honey

½ star anise pod (optional)

½ cup soy sauce

⅓ cup sake

6 cold whole large eggs in their shells

In a large saucepan over medium-high, bring to a boil 3 inches of water. Meanwhile, in a tall quart-size container, combine the warm water, honey and star anise (if using); stir until the honey dissolves. Stir in the soy sauce and sake; set aside.

When the water reaches a boil, use a slotted spoon to lower in the eggs. Simmer for 7 minutes. Meanwhile, fill a large bowl with about 4 cups ice and 2 cups water; set near the stove.

When the eggs are done, use the slotted spoon to transfer them to the ice bath. Cool for 3 minutes, then remove. Gently tap each egg on the counter, turning to crack all around, then peel, including the thin membrane beneath the shell.

Add the eggs to the soy mixture. Fold a paper towel so it fits in the container, dampen it with the marinade and place it on top of the eggs to keep them fully submerged. Cover and refrigerate at least 4 hours or up to 7 days. To serve, remove the eggs from the marinade; let stand at room temperature for 20 to 30 minutes, then halve lengthwise.

EGG SALAD WITH HARISSA, OLIVES AND ALMONDS

Start to finish: 20 minutes
Makes about 2 cups

This egg salad features a North African flavor profile. Harissa paste, which we always have on hand to use as a one-stroke way to add bold flavor and complexity, brings a chili kick plus garlickiness and warm, earthy spices to balance the richness of mayonnaise and eggs. Olives and toasted almonds bring pops of briny flavor and contrasting texture.

2 tablespoons mayonnaise

2 tablespoons harissa paste

1 tablespoon lemon juice

Kosher salt and ground black pepper

8 hard-cooked large eggs, peeled and chopped

2 tablespoons chopped pitted green olives

2 tablespoons slivered almonds,
toasted and chopped

1 tablespoon finely chopped fresh
flat-leaf parsley OR cilantro

In a medium bowl, whisk together the mayonnaise, harissa, lemon juice, ½ teaspoon salt and ¼ teaspoon pepper. Add the eggs, olives, almonds and parsley. Using a silicone spatula, fold until just combined. Taste and season with salt and pepper. Serve at room temperature or chilled.

EGG SALAD WITH GOCHUJANG, SESAME AND SCALLIONS

Start to finish: 30 minutes
Makes about 2 cups

Gochujang is a fermented chili paste with deep-red color and slightly gooey consistency. It's a staple of Korean cooking and lends this egg salad mild spiciness along with a good dose of umami. To toast the sesame seeds, stir them in a dry skillet over medium heat until fragrant and light golden brown, 2 to 3 minutes. Allow the seeds to cool before mixing into the salad.

2 tablespoons mayonnaise

2 tablespoons gochujang

1 teaspoon toasted sesame oil

Kosher salt and ground black pepper

8 hard-cooked large eggs, peeled and chopped

¼ cup frozen peas, thawed and patted dry

1 tablespoon sesame seeds, toasted

3 scallions, thinly sliced

In a medium bowl, whisk together the mayonnaise, gochujang, sesame oil, ½ teaspoon salt and ¼ teaspoon pepper. Add the eggs, peas, sesame seeds and scallions. Using a silicone spatula, fold until just combined. Taste and season with salt and pepper. Serve at room temperature or chilled.

TURKISH EGG SALAD WITH ARUGULA AND HERBS

Start to finish: 35 minutes

Servings: 4 to 6

The Turkish egg salad called nergisleme is named after the daffodil (nergis in Turkish) because its colors are white, yellow and green, like the springtime flower. Typically, herbs are tossed into the chopped eggs, the whole mixture seasoned with little more than olive oil and spicy chili. We took a slightly different approach, dressing a mixture of arugula and herbs with a lemon vinaigrette spiked with both sumac and Aleppo pepper (or paprika mixed with cayenne), which we then use as a bed for the eggs. Chopped toasted walnuts add texture but are optional. Serve with warm flatbread.

¼ cup extra-virgin olive oil

2 tablespoons lemon juice

1 teaspoon ground sumac

1 teaspoon Aleppo pepper or ¾ teaspoon sweet paprika plus ¼ teaspoon cayenne pepper

Kosher salt

5-ounce container baby arugula

1 bunch scallions, thinly sliced

1 cup lightly packed fresh dill, finely chopped

8 hard-cooked large eggs, peeled and chopped

2 tablespoons roughly chopped walnuts, toasted (optional)

In a large bowl, whisk together the oil, lemon juice, sumac, Aleppo pepper and ¼ teaspoon salt. Measure 2 tablespoons of the dressing into a small bowl.

Whisk the dressing in the large bowl to recombine. Add the arugula, scallions and dill; toss until combined and evenly coated. Transfer to a serving platter, creating a bed of greens, then top with the eggs. Drizzle the reserved dressing onto the eggs, then sprinkle with the walnuts (if using).

TURKISH POACHED EGGS WITH YOGURT

Start to finish: 30 minutes

Servings: 4

This classic Turkish dish, called çilbir, nestles runny-yolked poached eggs in a creamy, garlic-spiked yogurt, then finishes the dish with a spice-infused butter. We also add a handful of herbs for fresh flavor and bright color. Aleppo pepper gives the infused butter a vibrant red hue and subtle heat. If you can't find it, use 2 teaspoons sweet paprika plus ½ teaspoon red pepper flakes. If you're hesitant to poach eggs, fear not. This method is straightforward. We use 3 quarts of water in a Dutch oven so the temperature doesn't fall precipitously when the eggs are added. And a little vinegar in the water helps the proteins set quickly, resulting in eggs with less "feathering" of the whites. Serve warmed bread alongside, either a crusty, country-style loaf or soft, tender flatbread.

2 small garlic cloves, finely grated

1¼ teaspoons lemon juice

4 tablespoons salted butter, cut into 3 or 4 pieces

1 tablespoon Aleppo pepper (see headnote)

2 cups plain whole-milk or low-fat Greek yogurt

Kosher salt

2 tablespoons lightly packed fresh cilantro

2 tablespoons lightly packed fresh mint, torn if large

1 tablespoon lightly packed fresh dill

¼ cup white vinegar

4 large eggs

Flaky sea salt, to serve (optional)

In a medium bowl, stir together the garlic and lemon juice; set aside for 10 minutes. Meanwhile, in an 8-inch skillet over medium, heat the butter until bubbling. Add the Aleppo pepper and cook, swirling, until bright red and fragrant, about 1 minute. Remove from the heat and set aside.

To the garlic-lemon mixture, stir in the yogurt and ¼ teaspoon salt. Divide among 4 serving bowls, then set aside at room temperature. In a small bowl, toss together the cilantro, mint and dill; set aside.

In a large Dutch oven over medium-high, combine 3 quarts water and the vinegar; bring to a boil. Break 1 egg into a small bowl, ramekin or teacup. Add the egg to the water by holding the bowl just above the surface, tilting it and letting the egg slide in; the egg will sink. Repeat with the remaining eggs, spacing them evenly and noting the order added. Simmer gently, uncovered and without stirring, until the whites are set but the yolks are still soft, 3 to 4 minutes; do not boil.

Using a slotted spoon, remove the eggs one at a time in the order they were added, allowing excess water to drain off, and place on a plate. Let drain for a few minutes, then place 1 egg in each bowl, setting it on the yogurt. Drizzle each serving with 1 tablespoon of the Aleppo butter and top with the herbs, dividing it evenly. Sprinkle with sea salt (if using).

SHAKSHUKA

Start to finish: 30 minutes
Servings: 4 to 6

Shakshuka, or eggs poached in a spicy tomato sauce, is said to be North African in origin and was brought to Israel by Maghrebi Jews. This is a classic version. We use harissa, a North African spice paste and a must-have ingredient in our pantry, to lend bold, rich flavor. Serve with warm, crusty bread.

2 tablespoons extra-virgin olive oil, plus more to serve

1 medium red bell pepper, stemmed, seeded and thinly sliced OR ½ cup drained and thinly sliced roasted red peppers

1 medium red onion, halved and thinly sliced

Kosher salt and ground black pepper

28-ounce can whole peeled tomatoes, crushed by hand

2 tablespoons harissa paste

6 large eggs

¼ cup finely chopped fresh flat-leaf parsley OR cilantro

In a 12-inch nonstick skillet over medium-high, heat the oil until shimmering. Add the bell pepper, onion and ½ teaspoon each salt and pepper. Cook, stirring occasionally, until the onion is light golden brown, about 5 minutes.

Stir in the tomatoes with juices, the harissa and ½ cup water. Bring to a simmer and cook, uncovered, stirring occasionally, until the pepper and onion are fully softened, 6 to 8 minutes. Taste and season with salt and pepper.

Reduce to medium-low, then use the back of a large spoon to make 6 evenly spaced indentations in the tomatoes and sauce, each about 2 inches in diameter. Crack 1 egg into each well, then sprinkle with salt and pepper. Cover and cook until the egg whites are set but the yolks are still runny, 5 to 8 minutes, rotating the skillet halfway through for even cooking. Remove from the heat, sprinkle with parsley and drizzle with additional oil.

Optional garnish: Crumbled feta cheese OR plain yogurt OR chopped pitted black or green olives OR a combination

Poached Eggs

Start to finish: 10 minutes
Makes 4 eggs

To find the simplest and best poaching method, we cooked dozens of eggs. **We learned that abundant water is needed so the temperature doesn't plummet when the eggs are dropped in; this is why we use 3 quarts in a large Dutch oven. Also, spiking the poaching water with vinegar helps the proteins set quickly, reducing the "feathering" of the whites for neater-looking eggs.** When adding the eggs to the simmering water, space them apart so they cook evenly. Also, track the order in which you add them to the pan so you can remove them in the same order, ensuring even doneness across all four yolks.

¼ cup white vinegar

4 large eggs

In a large Dutch oven over medium-high, combine 3 quarts water and the vinegar; bring to a boil. Break 1 egg into a small bowl, ramekin or teacup. Add the egg to the water by holding the bowl just above the surface, tilting it and letting the egg slide in; the egg will sink. Repeat with the remaining eggs, spacing them evenly and noting the order added. Simmer gently, uncovered and without stirring, until the whites are set but the yolks are still soft, 3 to 4 minutes; do not boil.

Using a slotted spoon, remove the eggs one at a time in the order they were added, allowing excess water to drain off, and place on a plate.

TURKISH-STYLE EGGS AND SPINACH

Start to finish: 30 minutes
Servings: 4 to 6

The Turkish spinach and egg dish known as ispanakli yumurta resembles Middle Eastern shakshuka, but spinach takes the place of a tomato-based sauce. Prepackaged baby spinach makes the recipe quick to prepare—the key is to cook it very briefly so it doesn't become watery. Frozen spinach also works well; just thaw it, drain it in a colander and, if it's still very wet, pat it dry with paper towels. This dish often is served with yogurt. We stir some in with the spinach to create a rich, creamy sauce that won't break under moderate heat. Serve flatbread alongside.

2 tablespoons salted butter

1 tablespoon extra-virgin olive oil, plus more to serve

1 medium yellow OR red onion, finely chopped

Kosher salt and ground black pepper

2 medium garlic cloves, minced

½ teaspoon ground cumin

¼ teaspoon red pepper flakes OR ½ teaspoon Aleppo pepper

1-pound container baby spinach OR 1-pound bag frozen chopped spinach, thawed, drained in a colander and patted dry (see headnote)

½ cup plain whole-milk Greek yogurt

6 large eggs

In a large Dutch oven over medium-high, heat the butter and oil until the butter melts. Add the onion and ½ teaspoon each salt and black pepper. Cook, stirring often, until softened but not brown, 5 to 7 minutes. Add the garlic, cumin and pepper flakes; cook, stirring, until fragrant, about 30 seconds.

If using fresh spinach, add it a large handful at a time, stirring to slightly wilt before each addition. Add the yogurt and ½ teaspoon salt. Cook until the spinach is just wilted and deep green and the yogurt is mostly incorporated, about 2 minutes. If using frozen spinach, add it to the pot, along with the yogurt and salt, and stir until combined.

Reduce to medium and use the back of a spoon to form 6 evenly spaced wells in the spinach, each about 2 inches wide and deep enough that the bottom of the pot is visible.

Crack 1 egg into each, then sprinkle with salt and black pepper. Cover and cook until the egg whites are set but the yolks are still runny, 3 to 5 minutes, rotating the pot about halfway through for even cooking. Serve drizzled with additional oil.

Optional garnish: Crumbled feta cheese **OR** hot sauce **OR** both

PERSIAN EGGS WITH SPICED BEEF AND TOMATOES

Start to finish: 35 minutes
Servings: 4

This is an adaptation of a recipe for vaavishkaa from "The Saffron Tales" by Yasmin Khan. The dish is similar to Middle Eastern shakshuka, which also poaches eggs in a spiced tomato sauce, but the addition of ground beef makes for a more substantial meal. We prefer the subtle smokiness that canned fire-roasted tomatoes lend the sauce, but regular diced tomatoes work, too. Warmed flatbread is an excellent accompaniment.

2 tablespoons extra-virgin olive oil, plus more to serve

8 ounces 90 percent lean ground beef

Kosher salt and ground black pepper

1 small red onion, halved and thinly sliced

2 medium garlic cloves, finely chopped

4 teaspoons ground coriander

1 teaspoon ground turmeric

¼ to ½ teaspoon cayenne pepper

28-ounce can diced fire-roasted tomatoes

6 large eggs

3 scallions, thinly sliced

In a 12-inch skillet over medium-high, heat the oil until shimmering. Add the beef, 1½ teaspoons salt and 1 teaspoon black pepper. Cook, stirring and breaking up the meat, until no longer pink, 3 to 4 minutes. Add the onion and garlic, then cook, stirring occasionally, until the onion begins to soften, 3 to 4 minutes.

Stir in the coriander, turmeric and cayenne, followed by the tomatoes with juices. Bring to a simmer, cover and cook, stirring occasionally, until the sauce is slightly thickened, about 10 minutes. Taste and season with salt and black pepper.

With the pan over medium-low, use the back of a spoon to form 6 evenly spaced wells in the sauce, each about 2 inches wide and deep enough that the bottom of the pan is visible. Crack 1 egg into each, then sprinkle with salt and black pepper. Cover and cook until the egg whites are set but the yolks are still runny, 5 to 8 minutes, rotating the skillet about halfway through for even cooking. Off heat, sprinkle with the scallions and drizzle with additional oil.

Fried Eggs

Start to finish: 5 minutes
Makes 4 eggs

For the best fried eggs, we cook them covered so the surface of the whites sets quickly and without risk of overcooking the yolks. Runny-yolked fried eggs can make a complete meal out of a simple salad. They also are excellent over fried rice, soft polenta, root vegetable hash, stir-fried vegetables, avocado toast, a grain bowl or even a burger or pizza. To make just two eggs, use an 8-inch nonstick skillet and 2 teaspoons of butter.

1 tablespoon salted butter

4 large eggs in their shells

Kosher salt and ground black pepper

In a 12-inch nonstick skillet over medium, melt the butter, swirling to coat the pan. When the butter stops foaming, crack an egg into each quadrant of the pan. Use a silicone spatula to gently push the edges of the egg whites toward the yolks to keep the eggs separate. Cover and cook until the whites are set but the yolks are still runny, about 1½ minutes. Season with salt and pepper, then slide the eggs onto individual plates.

EGGS

FRIED EGGS WITH SPINACH AND CUMIN-JALAPEÑO TARKA

Start to finish: 20 minutes

Servings: 2

The Indian technique of making tarka involves blooming spices and other aromatics in hot fat. We use sweet, rich butter to heighten the flavor and aroma of mustard and cumin seeds and tame the bite of fresh garlic, ginger and jalapeño. This recipe can be doubled to make four servings, but the eggs will need to be fried in two batches; the doubled tarka, however, can be made all at once after the second round of eggs is out of the skillet.

2 cups lightly packed baby spinach

1 tablespoon lemon juice

3 tablespoons salted butter, cut into 1-tablespoon pieces, divided

4 large eggs in their shells

½ teaspoon mustard seeds

¼ teaspoon cumin seeds

1 medium garlic clove, minced

½ jalapeño chili, stemmed, seeded and minced

2 teaspoons finely grated fresh ginger

Kosher salt and ground black pepper

In a medium bowl, toss the spinach with the lemon juice, then divide evenly between 2 serving plates, creating a bed for the fried eggs.

In a 12-inch nonstick skillet over medium, melt 1 tablespoon of the butter, swirling to coat the pan. When the butter stops foaming, crack an egg into each quadrant of the pan. Use a silicone spatula to gently push the edges of the egg whites toward the yolks to keep the eggs separate. Cover and cook until the whites are set but the yolks are still runny, about 1½ minutes. Slide 2 eggs onto the spinach on each plate.

In the same skillet over medium-high, heat the remaining 2 tablespoons butter and the mustard and cumin seeds until the butter is melted and gently sizzling, about 1 minute, occasionally swirling the pan. Add the garlic, jalapeño and ginger; cook, stirring, until fragrant, 30 to 60 seconds. Pour the mixture over the eggs, dividing it evenly. Season with salt and pepper.

FRIED EGGS WITH ARUGULA AND BUTTER-BLOOMED DUKKAH

Start to finish: 15 minutes
Servings: 2

The Egyptian nut, seed and spice blend known as dukkah is an excellent embellishment for simple fried eggs. We bloom it in butter before drizzling over fried eggs on a bed of baby arugula. The recipe can be doubled to make four servings; cook the eggs in two batches, but bloom the dukkah all at once after frying the second batch of eggs.

2 cups lightly packed baby arugula

1 tablespoon lemon juice

3 tablespoons salted butter, cut into 1-tablespoon pieces, divided

4 large eggs in their shells

2 tablespoons dukkah

Kosher salt and ground black pepper

In a medium bowl, toss the arugula with the lemon juice, then divide evenly on 2 serving plates, creating a bed for the fried eggs.

In a 12-inch nonstick skillet over medium, melt 1 tablespoon of the butter, swirling to coat the pan. When the butter stops foaming, crack an egg into each quadrant of the pan. Use a silicone spatula to gently push the edges of the egg whites toward the yolks to keep the eggs separate. Cover and cook until the whites are set but the yolks are still runny, about 1½ minutes. Slide 2 eggs onto the arugula on each plate.

Add the remaining 2 tablespoons butter to the still-hot skillet and let melt with the pan's residual heat. Stir in the

dukkah, then drizzle the mixture over the eggs and arugula on each plate. Season with salt and pepper.

DUKKAH

Start to finish: 15 minutes
Makes about 1 cup

In a large skillet over medium, toast ½ **cup raw cashews**, stirring, until beginning to brown, 3 to 4 minutes. Add **2 tablespoons sesame seeds**; continue to toast, stirring, until golden, 1 to 2 minutes. Add **2 tablespoons coriander seeds, 2 tablespoons cumin seeds** and **1 tablespoon caraway seed**. Continue to toast, stirring, until fragrant, about 1 minute. Transfer to a food processor and let cool for about 5 minutes. Add **1 teaspoon dried oregano, ¼ teaspoon kosher salt** and ½ **teaspoon ground black pepper**. Pulse until coarsely ground, 12 to 15 pulses. Store in an airtight container at room temperature for up to a week or for a few months.

Fluffy Olive Oil–Scrambled Eggs

Start to finish: 10 minutes

Serves 4

We've been told the best fat for cooking eggs is butter. But then we noticed that the Chinese cook their well-seasoned, well-browned omelets in oil; the Italians favor oil for their frittatas, and there are plenty of Middle Eastern recipes for puffy deep-fried eggs. To test the method on scrambled eggs, we poured a bit too much olive oil into a non-stick skillet, heated it until just smoking, then poured in whisked eggs. Whoosh! In a quick puff of steam, the eggs were almost instantly cooked in rolling, variegated waves. Why? **Oil gets hotter than butter faster because butter is 20 percent water and can only exceed 212°F once the water has evaporated. Result: Quicker, bigger puffs and more impressive scrambled eggs.** The oil needed a full 3 minutes at medium heat to get hot enough. Higher temperatures cooked the eggs too fast, toughening them. Two tablespoons of oil was enough to coat the bottom of the skillet and flavor the eggs without making them greasy. We like our scrambled eggs particularly wet and not entirely cooked through, which takes just 30 seconds. Leave them a little longer for drier eggs. Either way, take them off the heat before they are fully cooked and let them rest on a warm plate for 30 seconds. They finish cooking off the heat. Mixing the salt into the eggs before cooking is the best way to season them.

2 tablespoons extra-virgin olive oil

8 large eggs

Kosher salt and ground black pepper

In a 12-inch nonstick or seasoned carbon-steel skillet over medium heat, heat the oil until just beginning to smoke, about 3 minutes. While the oil heats, in a bowl use a fork to whisk the eggs and ¼ teaspoon salt until blended and foamy. Pour the eggs into the center of the pan.

Using a silicone spatula, continuously stir the eggs, pushing them toward the middle as they begin to set at the edges and folding the cooked egg over on itself. Cook until the eggs are just set, 60 to 90 seconds. The curds should be shiny, wet and soft, but not translucent or runny. Immediately transfer to warmed plates and season with salt and pepper.

SPANISH SCRAMBLED EGGS WITH SHRIMP AND ASPARAGUS

Start to finish: 25 minutes
Servings: 4 to 6

Spanish huevos revueltos, or scrambled eggs, can be made with various combinations of vegetables, seafood or cured meats. It's a delicious way to put a satisfying meal on the table in under 30 minutes. We pair shrimp and asparagus to make revuelto de espárragos y gambas. To simplify prep, purchase shrimp that already have been shelled and deveined. If you're able to find medium (41/50 per pound) shrimp, they don't need to be halved before cooking. Look for asparagus that are about the size of a pencil or slightly larger, but pass on thin, wiry spears, as they will end up overcooked. Serve with toasted bread.

8 large eggs

Kosher salt and ground black pepper

12 ounces extra-large (21/25 per pound) shrimp, peeled (tails removed), deveined, halved crosswise and patted dry

2 tablespoons extra-virgin olive oil, divided

2 tablespoons sherry vinegar

8 ounces asparagus (see headnote), trimmed and cut into 1-inch pieces

2 medium garlic cloves, thinly sliced

¼ teaspoon smoked paprika, plus more to serve

1 tablespoon chopped fresh flat-leaf parsley

In a large bowl, lightly beat the eggs with ¼ teaspoon salt and ¼ teaspoon pepper; set aside. Season the shrimp with ¼ teaspoon salt and ½ teaspoon pepper. In a 12-inch non-stick skillet over medium-high, heat 1 tablespoon of oil until barely smoking. Add the shrimp in an even layer and cook without stirring until deep golden brown, about 2 minutes.

Remove the pan from the heat, add the vinegar and stir until the vinegar has reduced and the shrimp are opaque throughout, another 20 to 30 seconds. Transfer the shrimp to a plate.

In the same skillet over medium-high, heat the remaining 1 tablespoon oil until shimmering. Add the asparagus and a pinch of salt, then cook, stirring often, until crisp-tender, about 2 minutes. Add the garlic and cook, stirring, until fragrant, about 30 seconds. Reduce to medium and pour the eggs into the center of the skillet. Cook, using a silicone spatula to stir continuously, pushing the egg mixture toward the middle as the edges begin to set, until the eggs are shiny and softly set, about 2 minutes; the curds should not be runny.

Remove the pan from the heat. Pour off and discard the accumulated shrimp juices, then add the shrimp and paprika to the skillet. Fold until the shrimp are evenly distributed, then taste and season with salt and pepper. Transfer to a serving dish and sprinkle with additional paprika and the parsley.

CHEESY TEX-MEX MIGAS

Start to finish: 20 minutes
Servings: 4 to 6

Migas is a Tex-Mex favorite of tortilla chips mixed into scrambled eggs that are flavored with sautéed aromatic vegetables. The chips soften slightly, taking on a satisfying crunchy-chewy texture. This version includes melty cheese folded in at the end to give the migas rich flavor and gooey-ness. If you can, finish the dish with at least one of the optional garnishes listed below, and serve it with warmed tortillas. Refried beans also are great alongside.

8 large eggs

Kosher salt and ground black pepper

2 tablespoons extra-virgin olive oil

1 medium green OR red bell pepper, stemmed, seeded and chopped

1 large ripe tomato, cored and chopped OR 1 cup cherry or grape tomatoes, halved

1 medium yellow onion, chopped

1 teaspoon chili powder OR ground cumin

3 ounces tortilla chips (4 cups), roughly crushed

2 ounces cheddar OR Monterey Jack cheese, shredded (½ cup)

In a large bowl, whisk together the eggs and ½ teaspoon salt; set aside. In a 12-inch nonstick skillet over medium-high, heat the oil until shimmering. Add the bell pepper, tomato, onion, chili powder and ¼ teaspoon salt; cook, stirring occasionally, until the vegetables are softened and lightly browned, 7 to 9 minutes.

Reduce to medium and add about ½ cup of the crushed tortilla chips. Cook, stirring, until any moisture from the vegetables is absorbed, about 30 seconds. Pour the egg mixture into the center of the skillet and cook, using a silicone spatula to stir continuously, pushing the egg mixture toward the middle as the edges begin to set, until the eggs are partially set but still a bit runny, about 2 minutes.

Scatter on the cheese and cook, stirring, until the cheese melts and the eggs are mostly set, about 30 seconds. Remove the pan from the heat, add the remaining tortilla chips and fold just until combined. Taste and season with salt and pepper.

Optional garnish: Chopped fresh cilantro OR diced or sliced avocado OR salsa OR pickled jalapeños OR hot sauce OR a combination

OMELET WITH MUSHROOMS, MUSTARD AND GRUYÈRE

Start to finish: 30 minutes
Servings: 4

Earthy cremini mushrooms, sautéed until lightly browned, are brightened with white wine and mustard. Gruyère cheese and fresh chives pair perfectly with the creminis, adding gooey richness and savory allium notes. A simple vinaigrette-dressed salad and warm crusty bread are ideal accompaniments.

8 large eggs

4 tablespoons finely chopped fresh chives, divided

Kosher salt and ground black pepper

4 tablespoons salted butter, cut into 1-tablespoon pieces, divided

8 ounces cremini mushrooms, trimmed and quartered

⅓ cup dry white wine

3 tablespoons whole-grain Dijon mustard

4 ounces Gruyère cheese, shredded (1 cup)

In a medium bowl, whisk together the eggs, 2 tablespoons of chives, ¼ teaspoon salt and ½ teaspoon pepper. In a 12-inch nonstick skillet over medium, melt 2 tablespoons of butter. Add the mushrooms and cook, stirring occasionally, until well browned, 5 to 8 minutes. Stir in the wine and mustard, then cook, stirring, until the liquid has evaporated, about 2 minutes. Transfer to a small bowl and wipe out the skillet.

In the same skillet over medium, melt the remaining 2 tablespoons butter, then swirl the pan to coat. Pour in the egg mixture and, using a silicone spatula, draw the edges toward the center and gently stir, working your way around the perimeter of the pan. Cook the eggs this way until they form soft, pillowy curds but are still runny enough to pool on the surface of the pan, 1 to 2 minutes.

Spread the eggs in an even layer, then remove from the heat and sprinkle the cheese evenly over the eggs. Cover and let stand until the cheese is melted and the omelet is set, about 5 minutes. Run the spatula around the edge and under the omelet to loosen, then slide it onto a plate. Scatter the mushrooms over one half of the omelet. Using the spatula, fold the omelet in half to enclose the filling. Cut into 4 wedges, then sprinkle with the remaining 2 tablespoons chives.

ZUCCHINI AND GOAT CHEESE OMELET

Start to finish: 25 minutes
Servings: 4

In this simple omelet, lightly caramelized shallots and tender sautéed zucchini pair nicely with creamy, tangy fresh goat cheese. Rather than sprinkle crumbled goat cheese into the omelet, we mix it into the still-hot shallot-zucchini sauté so the cheese binds the filling and each bite is rich and flavorful.

8 large eggs

Kosher salt and ground black pepper

3 tablespoons salted butter, cut into 1-tablespoon pieces, divided

2 medium shallots, halved and thinly sliced

1 medium zucchini (about 8 ounces), quartered lengthwise, seedy core removed, cut into ½-inch pieces

4 ounces fresh goat cheese (chèvre), crumbled

1 tablespoon finely chopped fresh chives

3 tablespoons finely chopped fresh flat-leaf parsley

211

In a medium bowl, whisk together the eggs and ½ teaspoon salt. In a 12-inch nonstick skillet over medium, melt 1 tablespoon of butter. Add the shallots and ¼ teaspoon salt. Cover and cook, stirring occasionally, until lightly browned, about 5 minutes. Add the zucchini and cook, stirring often, until quite tender, 4 to 6 minutes. Transfer to a medium bowl and wipe out the pan. Add ½ teaspoon pepper and the goat cheese to the zucchini and stir until the cheese softens and the mixture is well combined; set aside.

In the same skillet over medium, melt the remaining 2 tablespoons butter, then swirl the pan to coat. Pour in the egg mixture and, using a silicone spatula, draw the edges toward the center and gently stir, working your way around the perimeter of the pan. Cook the eggs until they form soft, pillowy curds but are still runny enough to pool on the surface, 1 to 2 minutes. Spread the eggs in an even layer, then cover, remove from the heat and let stand until the omelet is set, about 5 minutes.

Run the spatula around the edge and under the omelet to loosen it, then slide it onto a plate. Spread the zucchini mixture over half of the omelet, then sprinkle with half of the chives and parsley. Using the spatula, fold the omelet in half to enclose the filling. Cut into 4 wedges, then sprinkle with the remaining chives and parsley.

SPANISH TORTILLA WITH POTATO CHIPS

Start to finish: 35 minutes
Servings: 4 to 6

Spanish chef Ferran Adrià, father of the molecular gastronomy movement, came up with a genius shortcut for making tortilla española, using potato chips instead of slowly cooking sliced raw potatoes in olive oil. Borrowing his time-saving technique, we keep our version of this egg and potato tortilla simple, adding some softened onions and a dash of smoked paprika.

10 large eggs

Kosher salt and ground black pepper

3½ ounces (5 cups) kettle-style potato chips, lightly crushed

3 tablespoons extra-virgin olive oil

2 medium yellow onions, halved and thinly sliced

1 teaspoon smoked paprika, plus more to serve

⅓ cup lightly packed fresh flat-leaf parsley, chopped

Heat the oven to 350°F with a rack in the middle position. In a large bowl, whisk together the eggs and ½ teaspoon salt. Add the potato chips and stir to coat; set aside.

In a 10-inch oven-safe nonstick skillet over medium-high, heat the oil until shimmering. Add the onions, paprika and ¼ teaspoon each salt and pepper. Cover and cook, stirring often, until the onions are softened and lightly browned, 12 to 15 minutes. Reduce to medium-low, then add the egg mixture and quickly stir with a silicone spatula to combine with the onions. Cook undisturbed until the eggs are set and opaque at the edges, 1 to 2 minutes.

Place the skillet in the oven and bake until the eggs are just set on the surface, about 12 minutes. Remove the skillet from the oven (the handle will be hot). Run the spatula around the edges of the tortilla and underneath it to loosen, then carefully slide onto a cutting board. Serve warm or at room temperature, garnished with the parsley, sprinkled with additional paprika and cut into wedges.

Optional garnish: Chopped fresh chives OR flaky salt OR both

VIETNAMESE PORK AND SCALLION OMELET

Start to finish: 20 minutes
Servings: 4 to 6

The Vietnamese omelet called chả trứng chiên is a great way to get a simple and speedy flavor-packed dinner on the table using just five ingredients (not including black pepper and neutral oil). Pork is the classic choice of ground meat for the dish, but ground turkey also works well. You will need an oven-safe 12-inch skillet for this recipe. Serve with steamed jasmine rice and, if you like, a simple salad.

6 large eggs

1 bunch scallions, thinly sliced

8 ounces ground pork OR turkey

3 medium garlic cloves, minced

4 teaspoons fish sauce

Ground black pepper

2 tablespoons grapeseed or other neutral oil

Heat the oven to 425°F with a rack in the middle position. In a medium bowl, whisk the eggs. Reserve a couple tablespoons scallions for garnish.

In a large bowl, use your hands to thoroughly mix the pork, the remaining scallions, garlic, fish sauce and ¼ teaspoon pepper. Add the eggs and mix with a silicone spatula, breaking the pork mixture into bits, until the ingredients are well combined and no large clumps of meat remain.

In a 12-inch nonstick oven-safe skillet over medium-high, heat the oil until barely smoking. Add the pork-egg mixture; using the silicone spatula, break up any large bits of pork and evenly distribute the meat. Cook until the bottom is browned and set enough that you can lift an edge of the omelet with the spatula, about 3 minutes. Transfer the skillet to the oven and cook until the omelet is set in the center, 3 to 4 minutes.

Remove the skillet from the oven (the handle will be hot). Run the spatula around the edges of the omelet and underneath it to loosen, then carefully slide onto a platter. Alternatively, to serve the omelet browned side up, carefully invert it onto a platter. Serve warm or at room temperature, sprinkled with the reserved scallions and cut into wedges.

Optional garnish: Chopped fresh cilantro **OR** Sriracha **OR** lime wedges **OR** a combination

CHANGE THE WAY YOU COOK

The Best Bet for Omelets

Thicker, hearty omelets with substantial fillings make a terrific weeknight supper, but they pose more of a cooking challenge. Leaving them on the heat, as we do with thin, flat omelets, won't work since the bottom will be overcooked before the middle is done. And flipping omelets is something we're just not up for any day of the week.

So, we let the oven do the work for us.

We turn the oven up to high, start our omelet in an oven-safe skillet on the stovetop, then slide the pan into the oven. The eggs finish cooking gently and evenly and we're left with nothing more arduous than whipping the finished dish out of the oven with a flourish.

CURRIED POTATO AND GREEN PEA FRITTATA

Start to finish: 30 minutes

Servings: 4 to 6

This simple frittata, studded with warmly spiced peas and potatoes, takes inspiration from Indian samosas. We bloom curry powder and whole cumin seeds in oil, creating a flavor-rich base for cooking the vegetables. We start the cooking on the stovetop and finish in the oven to make sure the frittata is thick, flat and perfectly baked. You will need a 10-inch oven-safe nonstick skillet. Serve with toasted bread, a leafy salad or both.

8 large eggs

¼ cup half-and-half

Kosher salt and ground black pepper

1 tablespoon extra-virgin olive oil

2 teaspoons curry powder

2 teaspoons cumin seeds

12 ounces Yukon Gold potatoes, peeled and cut into ½-inch cubes

1 cup frozen peas, thawed

Heat the oven to 400°F with a rack in the middle position. In a medium bowl, whisk together the eggs, half-and-half and ½ teaspoon salt; set aside.

In an oven-safe 10-inch nonstick skillet over medium, heat the oil, curry powder and cumin seeds, swirling, until sizzling and fragrant, about 1 minute. Stir in the potatoes, then distribute in an even layer. Cook, stirring occasionally, until the potatoes begin to brown, about 3 minutes. Add in 1½ cups water and ½ teaspoon each salt and pepper; bring to a simmer and cook, uncovered and stirring occasionally, until the potatoes are tender and the water has evaporated, about 12 minutes.

215

Add the peas and cook, stirring, until heated through, about 1 minute. Add the egg mixture and cook, stirring constantly, just until large curds begin to form, about 1 minute. Transfer the skillet to the oven and bake until the center is set, 5 to 7 minutes. Remove from the oven (the handle will be hot), then run a silicone spatula around the edge and under the frittata to loosen. Slide it onto a platter and cut into wedges.

Optional garnish: Finely chopped fresh chives **OR** chopped fresh cilantro **OR** green chutney **OR** chili oil **OR** hot sauce **OR** a combination

CAULIFLOWER-SCALLION FRITTATA WITH HARISSA AND FETA

Start to finish: 45 minutes
Servings: 6

Tunisian tajine (sometimes spelled tajin, and not to be confused with a stewy Moroccan tagine) is similar to a frittata. It's what gave us the idea to season eggs with harissa (a North African spice paste), along with dill and feta before pouring the mixture over a sauté of cauliflower and scallions. This is equally delicious served at room temperature as it is warm, and it makes a good breakfast, lunch or dinner. You will need an oven-safe 12-inch non-stick skillet for this recipe.

10 large eggs

3 tablespoons harissa paste, plus more to serve

4 ounces feta cheese, crumbled (1 cup)

⅔ cup chopped fresh dill

Kosher salt and ground black pepper

2 tablespoons extra-virgin olive oil

2- to 2½-pound head cauliflower, trimmed, cored and cut into ½-inch pieces

1 bunch scallions, thinly sliced

Heat the oven to 375°F with a rack in the middle position. In a large bowl, whisk together the eggs, harissa, feta, all but 2 tablespoons of the dill, ⅛ teaspoon salt and ¼ teaspoon pepper. In an oven-safe 12-inch nonstick skillet over medium-high, heat the oil until shimmering. Add the cauliflower and scallions, then cook, stirring occasionally, until the cauliflower is browned and just shy of tender, about 8 minutes. Add the egg mixture and cook, stirring constantly, until large curds begin to form, about 1 minute. Place in the oven and bake until the center of the frittata is set, about 15 minutes.

Run a silicone spatula around the edges to loosen, then slide the frittata onto a cutting board. Sprinkle with the remaining dill and serve with additional harissa.

SPANISH TORTILLA WITH ROASTED RED PEPPERS

Start to finish: 50 minutes (20 minutes active)

Servings: 4

In Spain, a tortilla is a thick, hearty, frittata-like omelet made with potatoes, onions and plenty of olive oil. We whisk a little smoked paprika into the eggs, and also add some roasted red peppers for pops of color. If you prefer to stick with the simple and classic version, simply omit the paprika and roasted peppers. And for an added Spanish touch, serve the tortilla with garlicky mayonnaise or aioli on the side. This recipe starts on the stovetop but finishes in the oven, so you will need an oven-safe nonstick 10-inch skillet.

8 large eggs

¾ teaspoon smoked paprika

Kosher salt and ground black pepper

4 tablespoons extra-virgin olive oil, divided

1 medium yellow onion, chopped

1½ pounds Yukon Gold potatoes, peeled, halved and sliced ¼ inch thick

1 cup drained roasted red peppers, patted dry and chopped

Heat the oven to 350°F with a rack in the middle position. In a large bowl, whisk together the eggs, paprika and ¾ teaspoon salt. In an oven-safe 10-inch nonstick skillet over medium, heat 3 tablespoons of oil until shimmering. Stir in the onion, potatoes, 1 teaspoon salt and ½ teaspoon pepper. Cover and cook, stirring occasionally, until a fork inserted into the potatoes meets no resistance, 10 to 12 minutes. Stir in the roasted red peppers and cook, stirring, until the peppers are heated through, 1 to 2 minutes.

Fold the hot vegetables into the eggs, separating any potato slices that stick together. Add the remaining 1 tablespoon oil to the same skillet and heat over medium until shimmering. Pour in the egg-potato mixture and distribute in an even layer. Transfer to the oven and bake until the tortilla is set at the center, 25 to 30 minutes.

Transfer the pan to a wire rack (the handle will be hot) and let cool for about 10 minutes. Run a silicone spatula around the edge and under the tortilla to loosen it, then invert a large plate over the skillet. Invert both the skillet and plate, holding them together, then lift off the skillet. Serve the tortilla warm or at room temperature.

FRITTATA WITH TOASTED BREAD, CHEESE AND CARAMELIZED ONIONS

Start to finish: 40 minutes

Servings: 4 to 6

This recipe takes a handful of basic ingredients and turns them into a rich, satisfying breakfast, lunch or dinner. Each element plays an essential role. Crusty bread toasted in butter and olive oil gives the frittata substance and texture, onions cooked until sweet and caramelized add depth, cheese brings umami and gooeyness, and the eggs provide richness and tie everything together. Cooking starts on the stovetop but finishes at 425°F, so you will need a 10-inch nonstick skillet that's oven-safe. Serve a crisp green salad alongside as a counterpoint to the frittata's richness.

10 large eggs

4 ounces cheddar OR Gouda
OR Gruyère cheese, shredded (1 cup)

3 tablespoons salted butter, cut into
1-tablespoon pieces, divided

2 tablespoons extra-virgin olive oil,
divided

3 ounces rustic bread, cut into 1-inch cubes
(about 3 cups)

2 medium yellow onions, finely chopped

Chopped fresh flat-leaf parsley
OR fresh chives, to serve

Heat the oven to 425°F with a rack in the middle position. In a medium bowl, whisk the eggs with ½ teaspoon each salt and pepper, then stir in two-thirds of the cheese; set aside.

In a 10-inch nonstick oven-safe skillet over medium, heat 1 tablespoon butter and 1 tablespoon oil until the butter melts. Add the bread and cook, stirring occasionally, until golden brown, about 3 minutes. Transfer to a medium bowl; set aside.

In the same skillet over medium, heat the remaining 1 tablespoon oil until shimmering. Add the onions and ¼ teaspoon each salt and pepper. Cover and cook, stirring often and adjusting the heat as needed to prevent scorching, until the onions are lightly browned, 10 to 12 minutes. Transfer to the bowl with the bread and wipe out the skillet.

In the same skillet over medium, melt the remaining 2 tablespoons butter. Add the egg mixture, then quickly add the bread and onions; stir just to combine the ingredients and distribute them in an even layer. Cook without stirring for 5 minutes; the edges should be set. Run a silicone spatula around the edges to ensure the eggs are not sticking. Sprinkle evenly with the remaining cheese and place the skillet in the oven. Bake until the frittata is set on the surface and the cheese is lightly browned, 10 to 12 minutes.

Remove the skillet from the oven (the handle will be hot). Run the spatula around the edges of the frittata and underneath it to loosen, then carefully slide onto a cutting board. Let rest for at least 10 minutes. Serve warm or at room temperature, sprinkled with parsley and cut into wedges.

PALESTINIAN CRISPY HERB OMELET

Start to finish: 25 minutes

Servings: 4

Middle Eastern ijee inspired these herb-packed, crisp-crusted omelets. Most of the work is in the herb prep; once you're at the stove, the cooking is done in a matter of minutes. These omelets are meant to be thin, so we developed the recipe to make two 12-inch omelets that are folded in half. Sliced tomatoes and pita bread complete the meal.

1 cup plain whole-milk Greek yogurt

Kosher salt

1¼ cups lightly packed flat-leaf parsley, finely chopped, divided

1 cup lightly packed fresh mint, finely chopped, divided

1 cup lightly packed fresh dill, finely chopped, divided

1 teaspoon plus 4 tablespoons extra-virgin olive oil, divided

½ teaspoon lemon juice, plus lemon wedges to serve

8 large eggs

1 bunch scallions, thinly sliced

3 serrano chilies, stemmed, seeded and minced

1 tablespoon cornstarch

Sliced tomatoes, to serve

Warmed pita bread, to serve

CHANGE THE WAY YOU COOK

Egg Weights

Cracking the code of great baking often means also cracking plenty of eggs. Whether in a dense cheesecake, an airy meringue or a rich pound cake, eggs deliver a critical dose of protein, fat and moisture that plays a key role in the structure, texture and taste of baked goods. And that means misjudging the volume of eggs can lead to disappointing results.

Trouble is, eggs come in a wide variety of sizes, which can present a measurement challenge. If a recipe calls for large eggs (as many recipes do), and you only have jumbos or mediums, adjusting can be a guessing game.

In our baking, we find we get the best and most consistent results by measuring ingredients by weight. So we set out to find a way to apply this approach to eggs, as well. First, we surveyed the weight of cracked eggs (the yolk and white without the shell) for all egg sizes: On average, medium cracked eggs weigh 44 grams; large, 50 grams; extra-large, 56 grams; and jumbo, 63 grams.

From there, we worked out a handy conversion table for different egg sizes. Using our chart, you can see that, for example, a recipe calling for 6 large eggs will require 7 medium eggs or 5 jumbo eggs. For best results, we found that the most accurate way to portion the eggs is to whisk them first, then weigh them, using only the total liquified amount needed.

EGGS - CONVERSIONS BY SIZE AND WEIGHT

If your recipe calls for...	You will need at least...			
Large	Medium	X-Large	Jumbo	Grams
2	3	2	2	100
3	4	3	3	150
4	5	4	4	200
5	6	5	4	250
6	7	6	5	300
7	8	7	6	350
8	9	7	7	400

In a small bowl, stir together the yogurt, ¼ teaspoon salt, ¼ cup of the parsley, 2 tablespoons of the mint, 2 tablespoons of the dill, the 1 teaspoon oil and the lemon juice. In a medium bowl, whisk together the eggs, scallions, chilies, cornstarch, ½ teaspoon salt and all remaining herbs.

In a 12-inch nonstick skillet over medium-high, heat 2 tablespoons of the remaining oil until shimmering. Pour in half of the egg mixture and, using a silicone spatula, gently spread to cover the surface of the skillet. Cook until the bottom is browned and crisp and the top is no longer runny, about 3 minutes.

Remove the pan from the heat, cover and let stand until the eggs are set on top, 30 to 60 seconds. Slide the omelet onto a platter, folding it in half with the spatula. Tent with foil to keep warm.

Pour the remaining 2 tablespoons oil into the pan and heat over medium-high until shimmering. Cook the remaining egg mixture in the same way to make a second omelet. Transfer to the platter, folding in half. Serve with the herbed yogurt, lemon wedges, tomatoes and pita bread.

VELVETY TURKISH SCRAMBLED EGGS WITH YOGURT

Start to finish: 10 minutes
Servings: 4

Made with plenty of olive oil and a thick, salted yogurt called tuzlu, this creamy-rich egg dish traditionally is served as part of a Turkish breakfast spread. The mixture is seasoned with fruity, mildly hot Aleppo pepper and paired with morning meze staples—think sesame bread, salty cheese, olives and fresh vegetables. To ensure the eggs are as velvety as possible, beat them well with the yogurt, taking care to incorporate any streaks. The recipe can easily be halved and cooked in a 10-inch nonstick skillet.

8 large eggs

½ cup plain whole-milk Greek yogurt

Kosher salt and ground black pepper

¼ cup extra-virgin olive oil

4 tablespoons salted butter, cut into 4 pieces

Aleppo pepper, to serve (optional)

In a large bowl, whisk the eggs, yogurt and ½ teaspoon each salt and black pepper until well combined and no yogurt streaks remain. Set aside.

In a 12-inch nonstick skillet over medium-high, heat the oil and butter until the butter melts. Add the egg mixture and cook, without stirring, until beginning to set at the edges, about 15 seconds. Using a silicone spatula, continuously stir, pushing the edges toward the middle as the mixture begins to set and folding the cooked egg over on itself. Cook until the curds are soft, moist and just set but not translucent or runny, 1 to 1½ minutes. Transfer to warmed plates and serve sprinkled with Aleppo pepper (if using).

INDIAN-STYLE SCRAMBLED EGGS WITH TOMATOES AND CHILIES

Start to finish: 25 minutes
Servings: 4

The Indian dish called anda bhurji consists of eggs scrambled with spices and aromatics. We include fresh green chilies and tomatoes in this version, and also mix in some garam masala for warm, subtly sweet spiciness. Ghee, a type of clarified butter with rich, nutty notes, adds to the flavor of the eggs, but neutral oil works, too. For a milder version, remove the seeds from the chilies before chopping. In India, bhurji often is sold by street vendors as a late-night snack, piled on a piece of warm naan or rolled in a paratha, but these eggs are good any time of day.

8 large eggs

2 tablespoons ghee or neutral oil

½ small red onion, thinly sliced

1 tablespoon finely grated fresh ginger

1 or 2 jalapeño chilies, stemmed, halved lengthwise, seeded, and thinly sliced crosswise

2 ripe medium tomatoes, cored, seeded and roughly chopped

1 teaspoon garam masala

Kosher salt and ground black pepper

Chopped fresh cilantro, to serve

In a medium bowl, whisk the eggs until well combined. In a 12-inch nonstick skillet over medium-high, heat the ghee until barely smoking. Add the onion and ginger, then cook, stirring often, until golden brown, about 3 minutes. Add the jalapeño(s), tomatoes, garam masala and ¼ teaspoon salt; cook, stirring, until fragrant, about 2 minutes.

Pour the eggs into the center of the pan. Using a silicone spatula, continuously stir the eggs, pushing them toward the middle as they begin to set at the edges and folding the cooked egg onto itself. Cook until just set, 45 to 60 seconds. Remove the pan from the heat, then taste and season with salt and pepper. Serve sprinkled with cilantro.

Noodles

Pasta Primer

Italian dried pasta is made with durum semolina and generally is designed to be cooked to al dente texture, literally "to the tooth," meaning still with a bit of bite to it. In dishes where the pasta finishes cooking in a sauce, we often stop the pasta cooking just short of al dente. The final simmer in the sauce finishes the pasta while giving it a chance to absorb flavor, rather than just water.

SMALL PASTA

Ditalini

Small and tubular, this is an excellent soup noodle, though it also fares well in salads.

Orecchiette

Orecchiette means "little ears," and this pasta's cup-like shape is ideal for catching sauce with small bits of meat or vegetable.

Orzo

Orzo means barley in Italian, and this small pasta looks like rice. Confusing nomenclature aside, this pasta (not made of barley) is a good addition to soups, adding a bit—but not too much—heft. It's also good toasted and used in salads.

SHORT PASTA

Farfalle

Also known as bow-tie pasta, the name comes from the Italian word for butterflies. The shape makes this pasta a fun addition to salads and the ruffled edges make farfalle good at catching bits of sauce.

Fusilli

This cork-screw-shaped short pasta is excellent at catching bits of sauce. We like to use it in just about any recipe calling for short pasta.

Penne

Penne translates from the Italian as "feather." The short tubes are cut at an angle, resulting in points that resemble a quill nib. Regular penne is smooth; penne rigate has a ridged exterior. Either works especially well with chunky sauces.

Ziti

Short and hollow, tube-like ziti typically is used in baked pasta dishes.

LONG PASTA

Bucatini

Looks like fat spaghetti, but has a hole in the center, the better for sucking up sauces. This is a good noodle to use when the dish is all about the sauce.

Capellini

Also known as angel hair. Long and thin, this cooks quickly and is good with light sauces and in soups.

Fettuccine

Literally named "little ribbons," this long, flat pasta is popular in Tuscan and Roman cooking and is great with smooth, creamy sauces, such as fettuccine Alfredo.

Linguine

Italian for "little tongues," linguine is a long, flattish pasta. It does well with smooth or creamy sauces, but its surface area also makes it a good choice for meat sauces that aren't too chunky. Linguine is an excellent substitute for lo mein and can sometimes even take the place of udon.

Pappardelle

These broad, flat, ribbon-like noodles are often made with egg, which gives them a golden hue and a texture that is more delicate than egg-free semolina pasta. Dried pappardelle typically is sold coiled into nests.

Spaghetti

Spaghetti's long, round strands combine well with smooth or creamy sauces, but also are a good match for chunkier ragùs. It can be a stand-in for some types of Asian noodles.

OTHERS

Gnocchi

Gnocchi is more of a dumpling than a noodle, depending on how it's made. Potato gnocchi falls in dumpling territory, made simply of mashed potato with a little flour and egg with herbs or other seasonings mixed in. There's also gnocchi di farina, made of just flour, water and salt.

Lasagna

Wide and flat, lasagna (plural lasagne) may be one of the older forms of pasta; it is referenced in medieval writings. Today, it's the centerpiece of the layered dish known as lasagna.

Pasta with Tomato, Onion and Butter

Start to finish: 35 minutes
Servings: 4 to 6

Marcella Hazan's famous tomato sauce with onion and butter, from her book "The Essentials of Classic Italian Cooking," transforms three simple ingredients into a luscious sauce. Our pantry-focused version replaces the fresh tomatoes with a can of tomato paste to create a dish that can be on the table in minutes. To enhance the sweetness and umami, we finish the sauce with a splash of balsamic vinegar (white balsamic also is great) and nutty Parmesan cheese. If you don't have spaghetti, use another type of pasta, such as fettuccine or linguine. Fresh basil is a great addition; if you have it on hand, toss some into the pasta just before serving.

1 pound spaghetti

Kosher salt and ground black pepper

4 tablespoons salted butter, cut into 1-tablespoon pieces, divided

1 small yellow onion, chopped

6-ounce can tomato paste

1 tablespoon balsamic vinegar

1 ounce Parmesan cheese, finely grated (½ cup), plus more to serve

In a large pot, bring 4 quarts water to a boil. Add the pasta and 1 tablespoon salt, then cook, stirring occasionally, until al dente. Reserve 2 cups of the cooking water, then drain; set aside.

In the same pot over medium, melt 2 tablespoons butter. Add the onion, reduce to low, cover and cook, stirring occasionally, until the onion has softened, 12 to 14 minutes.

Add the tomato paste, ½ teaspoon pepper and 1½ cups of the reserved cooking water, then whisk until smooth. Add the pasta, the remaining 2 tablespoons butter and the vinegar. Using tongs, toss until the sauce clings to the pasta, the pasta is heated through and the butter is melted, adding more cooking water if needed so the noodles are lightly sauced.

Off heat, toss in the Parmesan, then taste and season with salt and pepper. Serve sprinkled with additional Parmesan.

FARFALLE WITH CREAMY CARROTS AND PANCETTA

Start to finish: 40 minutes
Servings: 4 to 6

This one-pot pasta dish is a riff on a unique recipe from "Thirty Minute Pasta" by Giuliano Hazan. A full pound of carrots plus a knob of butter, a shot of cream and a good dose of Parmesan combine to make a sauce that's flavorful and rich without being heavy. Salty pancetta and briny capers balance the natural sweetness of the carrots. To make quick work of carrot prep, you can use a food processor fitted with the shredding disk instead of a box grater.

4 ounces pancetta, finely chopped

1 pound carrots, peeled and shredded on the large holes of a box grater

2 tablespoons salted butter, cut into 2 pieces, divided

Kosher salt and ground black pepper

1 pound farfalle

1 cup lightly packed fresh flat-leaf parsley, finely chopped

1 ounce Parmesan cheese, finely grated (½ cup), plus more to serve

¼ cup heavy cream

2 tablespoons drained capers, minced

¼ teaspoon freshly grated nutmeg

In a large Dutch oven over medium, cook the pancetta, stirring occasionally, until lightly browned, about 5 minutes. Using a slotted spoon, transfer to a paper towel-lined plate; set aside. Add the carrots to the pot along with 1 tablespoon butter, 1 teaspoon salt and ½ teaspoon pepper. Cook, uncovered and stirring often, until the carrots begin to soften, 3 to 5 minutes.

Stir in 5 cups water and 1 teaspoon salt; bring to a simmer over medium-high. Add the pasta, submerging it in the water as much as possible. Cover and cook, stirring occasionally, until the pasta is al dente and almost dry; if the mixture is dry before the pasta is done, add about ½ cup water as needed.

Off heat, add the remaining 1 tablespoon butter, parsley, Parmesan, cream, capers and nutmeg. Toss, adding additional water as needed so the pasta is lightly sauced. Taste

and season with salt and pepper. Serve sprinkled with the pancetta and additional cheese.

TOMATO SAUCE WITH BROWNED BUTTER AND CUMIN

Start to finish: 20 minutes
Makes 1¼ cups

Deeply savory and packed with umami, browned tomato paste makes an excellent base for this Turkish-inspired sauce, enhanced by butter and spices. Dried mint has a distinct menthol-like tang that balances the mixture's richness, but dried oregano works well, too. This recipe yields enough sauce to coat 1 pound of pasta—also toss in a dollop of plain whole-milk yogurt for a play on Turkish dumplings called manti. The sauce also complements hearty grains, such as bulgur or freekeh, and is delicious over lamb chops or salmon. We recommend finishing dishes featuring this sauce with a sprinkle of chopped fresh flat-leaf parsley or mint, adding bright, herbal notes.

4 tablespoons salted butter, cut into 4 pieces

1 teaspoon cumin seeds

6-ounce can tomato paste (⅔ cup)

Kosher salt and ground black pepper

1 teaspoon Aleppo pepper OR ½ teaspoon
sweet paprika plus ¼ teaspoon red pepper flakes

2 medium garlic cloves, finely grated

1 teaspoon dried mint OR dried oregano

In a 12-inch skillet over medium, melt the butter. Add the cumin seeds and cook, stirring often, until the seeds are sizzling and the butter is golden brown with a nutty aroma, 1 to 2 minutes.

Add the tomato paste, 1 teaspoon salt and ½ teaspoon black pepper; cook, stirring often, until the paste browns and slightly sticks to the pan, 1 to 3 minutes. Add the Aleppo pepper, garlic and mint; cook, stirring, until fragrant, about 30 seconds. Add 1 cup water and bring to a simmer over medium-high, scraping up any browned bits. Reduce to medium-low and cook, stirring, until slightly thickened, about 2 minutes. Off heat, taste and season with salt and black pepper.

PASTA WITH CAULIFLOWER, GARLIC AND TOASTED BREADCRUMBS

Start to finish: 25 minutes

Servings: 4

This pasta dish is a true one-pot dinner. We don't boil the noodles separately—rather, we add them to the pot along with the cauliflower and just enough water to cook both through. Toasted breadcrumbs sprinkled on just before serving offer a welcome textural contrast. We prefer Japanese-style panko over standard dry breadcrumbs for their light, airy texture that, when toasted, takes on a remarkable crispness.

4 tablespoons extra-virgin olive oil, divided

1 cup panko breadcrumbs

4 ounces pancetta, chopped

6 medium garlic cloves, minced

¼ cup tomato paste

½ teaspoon red pepper flakes

1½-pound head cauliflower, trimmed and cut into ½-inch pieces

8 ounces campanelle or orecchiette pasta

Kosher salt and ground black pepper

1 cup lightly packed fresh basil, chopped

Finely grated pecorino Romano cheese, to serve

228

In a large pot over medium, heat 2 tablespoons of oil until shimmering. Add the panko and cook, stirring occasionally, until golden brown, about 3 minutes; transfer to a small bowl.

In the same pot over medium, combine the remaining 2 tablespoons oil, the pancetta and garlic, then cook, stirring, until the garlic is lightly browned, about 2 minutes. Add the tomato paste and pepper flakes; cook, stirring, until the paste begins to brown, about 2 minutes. Pour in 4 cups water and scrape up any browned bits, then stir in the cauliflower, pasta and 1½ teaspoons salt. Bring to a simmer, then cover and cook, stirring occasionally, until the pasta is al dente and the cauliflower is tender, 10 to 12 minutes.

Off heat, taste and season with salt and pepper, then let stand for a few minutes to allow the pasta to absorb some of the sauce. Serve sprinkled with the panko, basil and Pecorino.

ORECCHIETTE WITH CHERRY TOMATOES AND MOZZARELLA

Start to finish: 30 minutes
Servings: 4 to 6

This creamy, sweet-tart orecchiette dish takes inspiration from pasta alla Sorrentina, a southern Italian classic featuring fresh, quick-cooked tomatoes, mozzarella and aromatic basil. To make it, we quickly infuse oil with garlic, then stir in whole cherry or grape tomatoes—no slicing or chopping necessary—and red pepper flakes. Orecchiette and a few cups of water are added to the mix, creating a silky-smooth sauce as they cook together. Fresh mozzarella can become stringy and rubbery if over-mixed, so take care to stir just until it starts to melt.

¼ cup extra-virgin olive oil, plus more to serve

2 medium garlic cloves, thinly sliced

2 pints cherry OR grape tomatoes

½ to 1 teaspoon red pepper flakes

Kosher salt and ground black pepper

1 pound orecchiette

8 ounces fresh mozzarella cheese OR mozzarella di bufala OR burrata cheese, cut into rough ½-inch cubes or torn into small pieces

1 cup lightly packed fresh basil, torn

In a large pot over medium, heat the oil until shimmering. Add the garlic and cook, stirring, until fragrant, about 30 seconds. Add the tomatoes, pepper flakes and 1 teaspoon salt; stir to combine. Add 4 cups water and the pasta; stir to combine. Bring to a boil over medium-high, then reduce to medium and cook, uncovered and stirring occasionally, until the pasta is al dente. If needed, stir in additional water a few tablespoons at a time if the mixture looks dry.

Off heat, taste and season with salt and black pepper. Add half of the mozzarella, stirring just until beginning to melt. Serve topped with the remaining mozzarella and the basil and drizzled with additional oil.

Optional garnish: Finely grated Parmesan cheese OR flaky sea salt OR both

ROMAN SPAGHETTI CARBONARA

Start to finish: 25 minutes
Servings: 4

This brighter take on carbonara came from Pipero Roma in Rome. Chef David Puleio whisked the egg yolks until cooked and slightly foamy, creating a sauce that is much lighter in texture than most carbonara recipes. Mixing the yolks with water and cornstarch ensures the cheese won't clump up when tossed with the pasta.

3 ounces thinly sliced pancetta, chopped

6 large egg yolks

2 teaspoons cornstarch

6 ounces pecorino Romano cheese, finely grated
(3 cups), plus more to serve

12 ounces spaghetti

Kosher salt and ground black pepper

In a 10-inch skillet over medium, cook the pancetta, stirring, until crisp, about 5 minutes. Using a slotted spoon, transfer to a paper towel-lined plate. Measure out and reserve 3 tablespoons of the rendered fat; if needed, supplement with olive oil. Set the pancetta and fat aside.

In a large pot, bring 4 quarts water to a boil. Meanwhile, in a large saucepan, whisk 1¾ cups water, the egg yolks and cornstarch until smooth. Add the cheese and stir until evenly moistened. Set the pan over medium-low and cook, whisking constantly, until the mixture comes to a gentle simmer and is airy and thickened, 5 to 7 minutes; use a silicone spatula to occasionally get into the corners of the pan. Off heat, whisk in the reserved pancetta fat. Remove from the heat and set aside.

Stir the pasta and 1 tablespoon salt into the boiling water and cook until al dente. Reserve about ½ cup of the cooking water, then drain the pasta very well. Return the pasta to the pot and let cool for about 1 minute.

Pour the pecorino-egg mixture over the pasta and toss with tongs until well combined, then toss in the pepper. Let stand, tossing the pasta two or three times, until most of the

liquid has been absorbed, about 3 minutes. Crumble in the pancetta, then toss again. The pasta should be creamy but not loose. If needed, toss in up to 2 tablespoons reserved pasta water to adjust the consistency. Transfer to a warmed serving bowl and serve, passing more pecorino and pepper on the side.

FETTUCCINE ALFREDO

Start to finish: 30 minutes
Servings: 4 to 6

Made the Italian way, fettuccine Alfredo bears little resemblance to the cream-based pasta dish that's popular in the U.S. We scoured Italy for the best versions, and our favorite was prepared by home cook Francesca Guccione in Castelnuovo di Porto, just outside Rome. Rich, luxurious and elegant but neither heavy nor cloying, Guccione's fettuccine Alfredo, like other Roman recipes for the dish, consists of only fresh pasta, Parmigiano Reggiano cheese, butter and salt. The secret lies in using high-quality ingredients and combining them in just the right way, and in just the right volumes. We adapted her winning formula but incorporated a technique we saw employed at a couple restaurants of putting softened butter (rather than melted) into the bowl in which the hot pasta will be tossed. Of utmost importance is the cheese. Purchase a hefty chunk of true Parmigiano Reggiano—not the pre-shredded stuff—trim off the rind (save it for simmering into soups and stews), cut 6 ounces into rough ½-inch pieces and whir them in a food processor until very finely ground. This helps ensure the cheese melts readily. High-fat butter also is key. In Europe, butter typically has a fat content of around 85 percent; standard American butter is only about 80 percent fat. That 5 percent difference has a big impact on the flavor and consistency of the finished dish. At the grocery store, some types of high-fat butter are labeled "European-style"; Plugrá and Kerrygold are two widely available brands.

8 tablespoons salted European-style butter
(see headnote), sliced about ½ inch thick

6 ounces Parmigiano Reggiano cheese
(without rind), cut into rough ½-inch chunks

16 to 18 ounces fresh fettuccine,
homemade (recipe p. 236) or store-bought

Kosher salt

Line a large bowl with the butter slices, placing them in a single layer along the bottom and up the sides of the bowl; let stand at room temperature until the butter is softened.

Meanwhile, in a food processor, process the cheese until very finely ground, about 40 seconds; transfer to a medium bowl (you should have about 1½ cups).

In a large pot, bring 2 quarts water to a boil. Add the pasta and 1½ teaspoons salt, then cook, stirring often, until the pasta is al dente. Remove the pot from the heat. Using tongs, transfer the pasta from the pot, with ample water clinging to it, to the butter-lined bowl. Using the tongs, quickly stir and toss the pasta, incorporating the butter, until the butter is fully melted. Add ½ cup pasta water and toss until the water has been absorbed.

Add 1 cup of the cheese, tossing, ⅓ cup at a time, tossing and adding the next addition only after the previous one has been incorporated. Next, toss in ½ to 1 cup more pasta water, adding about ¼ cup at a time, until the sauce clings to the pasta and only a small amount pools at the bottom of the bowl.

Let stand for 2 minutes to allow the sauce to thicken slightly. If needed, toss in additional pasta water a little at a time until the sauce once again clings to the pasta and only a small amount pools at the bottom of the bowl. Taste and season with salt. Divide among warmed serving bowls and serve immediately with the remaining cheese on the side for sprinkling at the table.

Twirl It to Serve It

In Rome, we encountered pasta dishes that were a study in simplicity—pillowy pasta perfectly coated in sauces that were rich without heft.

The pasta may be carelessly tossed together or carefully executed, or both, but the presentation isn't slapdash. Pasta isn't piled on the plate, it is twirled into neat mounds.

To get this effect at home, place a ladle into the pot of pasta, then use a long fork to gather and twist the pasta into a neat mound in the ladle. Slide the mound out onto a serving plate and lift out the fork.

SKILLET CACIO E PEPE

Start to finish: 20 minutes
Servings: 4

The name of this classic Roman pasta dish translates as "cheese and pepper." We cook the pasta in a 12-inch skillet with a minimal amount of water into which a small amount of all-purpose flour has been whisked. The starchy cooking water becomes the base for making a cheesy sauce that won't break and has a silky and creamy, but not at all heavy, consistency. For this recipe, we found it best to avoid high-end spaghetti, the type with a rough, floury appearance, as the pasta tends to release a large amount of starch during cooking, making the sauce too thick. Widely available brands such as De Cecco and Barilla work well. Use true pecorino Romano cheese purchased in a chunk and grate it finely with a wand-style grater or grind it finely in a food processor.

5 ounces (without rind) pecorino Romano cheese, plus finely grated cheese to serve

2 teaspoons all-purpose flour

Kosher salt

12 ounces spaghetti

3 tablespoons extra-virgin olive oil

2 teaspoons coarsely ground black pepper, plus more to serve

Hot water, if needed

If grating the pecorino by hand, grate it finely using a wand-style grater. If using a food processor, cut the cheese into rough ½-inch pieces and process until finely ground, 30 to 45 seconds. Transfer to a bowl and set aside.

In a 12-inch skillet, combine 5 cups water, the flour and ½ teaspoon salt; whisk until no lumps of flour remain. Bring to a boil over high, stirring occasionally. Add the pasta and cook, uncovered, stirring often and pushing the noodles into the water to keep them submerged, until the spaghetti is al dente and about ½ cup of starchy liquid remains, 10 to 12 minutes.

Remove the pan from the heat and let the pasta cool, tossing with tongs once or twice, for 1 minute. With the pan still off heat, gradually add the cheese while tossing. Once all the cheese has been added, continue tossing until fully

melted. Add the oil and pepper; toss to combine. If the mixture is dry, add hot water 1 tablespoon at a time until the pasta is lightly sauced. Serve in warmed bowls sprinkled with additional pepper and cheese.

"ORZOTTO" WITH ASPARAGUS, LEMON AND PARMESAN

Start to finish: 30 minutes
Servings: 4

Traditionally made with medium-grain Italian rice, risotto gets its creaminess from a unique cooking method: adding liquid slowly and stirring vigorously to release the rice's starch. We've found that applying the technique to other "grains" yields a similarly rich, silky texture—no milk or cream required. So we cook orzo risotto-style in a 12-inch skillet to allow the broth to reduce quickly while providing plenty of room for stirring. The finished dish is a supple, velvety "orzotto." We love the combination of floral basil with grassy-sweet asparagus and tangy lemon, but parsley, dill or chives would be delicious as well.

2 tablespoons extra-virgin olive oil

1 medium shallot, minced

about 5 minutes. Add 1 cup of the remaining broth and simmer vigorously, still stirring often and briskly, until the liquid is again absorbed, about 5 minutes.

Add the asparagus stalks and the remaining 1 cup broth; cook, stirring occasionally, until the asparagus is just shy of tender-crisp, about for 3 minutes. Add the asparagus tips and cook, stirring, until almost all the liquid has been absorbed and the asparagus is tender, another 2 minutes.

Off heat, stir in the lemon zest and juice, Parmesan and about half the basil. Taste and season with salt and pepper. Serve sprinkled with the remaining basil and additional Parmesan.

Kosher salt and ground black pepper

3 medium garlic cloves, peeled and thinly sliced

1 cup orzo

2 tablespoons dry white wine or vermouth

4 cups low-sodium chicken broth or vegetable broth, divided

1 pound asparagus, trimmed and cut into ½-inch pieces on the diagonal; stalks and tips reserved separately

1 teaspoon grated lemon zest, plus 2 tablespoons lemon juice

1 ounce finely grated Parmesan cheese (½ cup), plus more to serve

¼ cup lightly packed fresh basil, thinly sliced

In a 12-inch skillet over medium-high, heat the oil until shimmering. Add the shallot and ½ teaspoon salt; cook, stirring occasionally, until just beginning to soften, about 3 minutes. Add the garlic and cook, stirring, until fragrant, about 30 seconds. Stir in the orzo and cook, stirring often, until the shallot and garlic begin to brown, about 2 minutes.

Add the wine and cook, stirring, until fully evaporated. Stir in 2 cups broth and bring to a vigorous simmer. Cook, stirring often and briskly, making sure to scrape along the edges and sides of the pan, until the liquid is absorbed,

PASTA WITH PESTO ROSSO

Start to finish: 30 minutes

Servings: 4 to 6

This rich, intensely flavored red pesto gets savoriness from pecorino and garlic, sweetness from roasted peppers and sun-dried tomatoes, and richness from nuts and olive oil. Though great tossed with pasta, also try stirring it into risotto or other cooked grains. You can make the pesto in advance and store it in an airtight container in the refrigerator for up to two days.

1 pound farfalle OR fusilli OR other short pasta shape

Kosher salt and ground black pepper

1½ cups roasted red peppers, patted dry and roughly chopped

2 ounces (without rind) pecorino Romano cheese, cut into rough 1-inch pieces, plus finely grated pecorino Romano to serve

1 medium garlic clove, smashed and peeled

½ cup extra-virgin olive oil, plus more to serve

½ cup pine nuts OR slivered almonds

¼ cup drained oil-packed sun-dried tomatoes, roughly chopped

½ teaspoon red pepper flakes

In a large pot, bring 4 quarts water to a boil. Stir in the pasta and 1 tablespoon salt, then cook, stirring occasionally, until al dente. Reserve about ½ cup of the cooking water, then drain and return the pasta to the pot.

While the pasta cooks, in a food processor, combine the roasted peppers, pecorino, garlic, oil, pine nuts, sun-dried tomatoes, red pepper flakes and ¼ teaspoon each salt and black pepper. Process until almost completely smooth, scraping the bowl as needed, about 30 seconds.

Add the pesto to the pasta in the pot along with ¼ cup of the reserved pasta water, then toss; add more reserved pasta water as needed so the pesto coats the noodles. Taste and season with salt and black pepper. Serve drizzled with additional oil and sprinkled with grated pecorino.

Optional garnish: Chopped or shredded fresh basil

SPAGHETTI WITH LEMON PESTO

Start to finish: 25 minutes
Servings: 4

This pasta dish is modeled on the spaghetti al pesto di limone that Giovanna Aceto made for us on her family's farm in Amalfi, Italy. The lemons commonly available in the U.S. are more acidic than Amalfi's lemons, so to make a lemon pesto that approximates the original, we use a little sugar to temper the flavor. For extra citrus complexity, we add lemon zest to the pasta cooking water; the oils from the zest lightly perfume the spaghetti, reinforcing the lemony notes of the pesto.

4 lemons

Kosher salt and ground black pepper

1½ teaspoons white sugar, divided

1 pound spaghetti

½ cup slivered almonds

1 ounce (without rind) Parmesan cheese, cut into rough 1-inch pieces, plus finely grated Parmesan to serve

⅓ cup extra-virgin olive oil, plus more to serve

2 tablespoons finely chopped fresh chives

Using a vegetable peeler (preferably a Y-style peeler), remove the zest from the lemons in long, wide strips; try to remove only the colored portion of the peel, not the bitter white pith just underneath. You should have about ⅔ cup zest strips.

In a large pot, combine 2 quarts water, 1½ teaspoons salt, 1 teaspoon of sugar and half of the zest strips. Bring to a boil and cook for 2 minutes, then remove and discard the zest. Add the spaghetti and cook until al dente. Reserve 1½ cups of the cooking water, then drain the pasta and return it to the pot.

Meanwhile, in a food processor, combine the remaining zest strips, the almonds, Parmesan, the remaining ½ teaspoon sugar and ¼ teaspoon each salt and pepper. Process until the mixture resembles coarse sand, 10 to 20 seconds. Add the oil and process just until the oil is incorporated (the mixture will not be smooth), about another 10 seconds; set aside until the pasta is ready.

To the spaghetti in the pot, add the pesto and ¾ cup of the reserved pasta water, then toss to combine; add more reserved pasta water as needed so the pesto coats the noodles. Toss in the chives. Taste and season with salt and pepper. Serve drizzled with additional oil and with additional grated Parmesan on the side.

Pasta with Pesto alla Genovese

Start to finish: 30 minutes

Makes about 1 cup

We were taught to make pesto alla Genovese in its birth-place—Genoa, Italy, by chef Roberto Panizza. **Pesto traditionally is made in a mortar and pestle of nothing more than basil, pine nuts, cheese, garlic, salt and olive oil, emphasis on the basil. We use a food processor for convenience but follow the tradition of processing ingredients separately to ensure we preserve the appropriate texture of each.** Good quality cheese is essential for a rich, full-flavored pesto. Seek out true Italian Parmesan cheese, as well as pecorino Sardo, a sheep's milk cheese from Sardinia. If you can't find pecorino Sardo, don't use pecorino Romano, which is too strong. The best substitute is manchego, a Spanish sheep's milk cheese. To store pesto, press a piece of plastic wrap against its surface and refrigerate for up to three days.

1¾ ounces Parmesan cheese (without rind), chopped into rough 1-inch pieces

1 ounce pecorino Sardo cheese (without rind), chopped into rough 1-inch pieces

¼ cup pine nuts

2 medium garlic cloves, smashed and peeled

Kosher salt

⅓ cup extra-virgin olive oil

2½ ounces fresh basil (about 5 cups lightly packed)

12 ounces dried pasta

In a food processor, process both cheeses until broken into rough marble-sized pieces, about 10 seconds, then pulse until they have the texture of coarse sand, 5 to 10 pulses, scraping the bowl as needed. Transfer to a small bowl.

In the food processor, combine the pine nuts, garlic and ¼ teaspoon salt. Process until a smooth, peanut butter–like paste forms, about 1 minute, scraping the bowl as needed. Add the cheeses and about ½ of the oil and process until mostly smooth, 10 to 20 seconds, scraping the bowl as needed; the mixture should hold together when pressed against the bowl with a silicone spatula.

Using a chef's knife, roughly chop the basil, then add to the food processor. Pulse about 10 times, scraping the bowl several times, until the basil is finely chopped and well combined with the cheese mixture. Add the remaining oil and pulse just until incorporated, about 2 pulses. The pesto should be thick, creamy and spreadable.

In a large pot, bring 4 quarts water to a boil. Add the pasta and 1 tablespoon salt, then cook, stirring occasionally, until just shy of al dente. Reserve about ½ cup of the cooking water, then drain the pasta. Transfer the pasta to a large warmed bowl and top with the pesto. Pour in ⅓ cup of the reserved cooking water for long pasta shapes (such as spaghetti and linguine) or ¼ cup cooking water for short pasta shapes (such as penne and fusilli). Toss to combine.

Fresh Egg Pasta

Start to finish: 40 minutes, plus resting
Makes 1 pound pasta

Fresh egg pasta is rich in flavor and has a delicate yet satisfying texture that's both tender and sturdy. Unlike dried pasta, where the sauce is paramount, well-made fresh pasta shines alongside its pairing, as in our elegantly delicate fettuccine Alfredo (recipe p. 230). To make these luxurious, golden-hued noodles, we use a fairly large number of egg yolks plus a whole egg, along with all-purpose flour and just a small amount of water. Determining the right amount of eggs is a balancing act—too many and the dough becomes difficult to roll out, as the fat in the yolks disrupts the formation of gluten. But too few and the dough will lack the desired richness. Given multiple passes through a pasta machine to produce long, thin sheets, the dough can be filled and made into ravioli, tortellini or other stuffed shapes, or it can be cut into fettuccine, tagliatelle or pappardelle as instructed in the directions. If you don't own a pasta machine but are skilled with a rolling pin, the dough can be rolled into sheets by hand.

**1 large whole egg, plus
7 large egg yolks**

**2 cups (260 grams)
all-purpose flour,
plus more for dusting**

Kosher salt, for cooking

In a 2-cup liquid measuring cup or small bowl, beat together the whole egg, egg yolks and 2 tablespoons water.

To make the dough in a food processor: Put the flour in a food processor. With the processor running, slowly stream in the egg mixture. Process until the dough leaves the sides of the bowl in large chunks, 1 to 2 minutes. If the dough feels dry and doesn't hold together when pinched, add water, 1 teaspoon at a time, as needed. If the dough feels sticky, you will have the chance to knead in more flour after turning the dough out onto the counter.

To make the dough by hand: Put the flour in a large bowl and make a well in the center. Add the egg mixture; using a fork, stir the flour into the eggs, working from the outside edges into the center, until all of the flour is incorporated. Form into a rough ball. If the dough feels dry and doesn't hold together when pinched, add water, 1 teaspoon at a time, as needed. If the dough feels sticky, you will have the chance to knead in more flour after turning the dough out onto the counter.

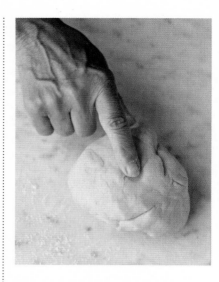

Lightly dust the counter with flour; if the dough feels wet and sticky, apply a heavier layer of flour to the work surface. Turn the dough out onto it and knead until smooth and shiny, 5 to 10 minutes. Press a finger into the surface of the dough; it should bounce back quickly, within 2 seconds. Cover the dough with a kitchen towel or plastic wrap and let rest at room temperature for 1 hour, or wrap tightly in plastic wrap and refrigerate up to 24 hours.

Line a rimmed baking sheet with a kitchen towel and lightly dust with flour. If the dough has been refrigerated, let it stand, still wrapped in plastic, at room temperature for about 15 minutes before proceeding.

Uncover or unwrap the dough and cut it into quarters. Set 3 pieces aside and cover with plastic wrap. Shape the remaining piece into a rough 4-by-6-inch rectangle. Using a pasta machine or a stand mixer fitted with a pasta attachment, roll the dough through several times, gradually reducing the thickness setting on the machine, until it forms a long sheet about 1/16 inch thick. It's important that the dough be of an even thickness. If the pasta sheet is longer than 14 inches, cut in half for slightly shorter lengths.

Dust the surface of the dough with flour, then accordion-fold it into thirds; set it on a cutting board. Using a chef's knife and a decisive cutting motion (do not use a sawing action), cut the dough crosswise into ¼-inch-wide strips for tagliatelle or fettuccine, up to ½ inch wide for pappardelle. Unfold the pasta and transfer to the prepared baking sheet, gently separating the strands, then toss to lightly coat with flour; keep uncovered. Roll and cut the remaining dough in the same way. If not cooking right away, dust with additional flour and keep uncovered at room temperature for up to 1 hour, or cover with a kitchen towel and refrigerate for up to 12 hours.

To cook the noodles, follow the directions in the pasta recipe that you are making, or in a large pot, bring 4 quarts water to a boil. Add 1 tablespoon salt and the pasta, then cook, stirring occasionally, until al dente. Reserve some of the cooking water if directed in your recipe, then drain the pasta.

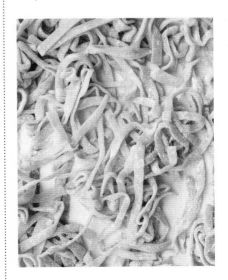

PASTA WITH SPICY TOMATO AND PANCETTA SAUCE

Start to finish: 30 minutes
Servings: 4 to 6

Zuppa forte, also known as zuppa di soffritto, is an old-school Neapolitan dish made by slow-cooking meats with garlic and other aromatics, along with tomatoes and preserved chilies, until reduced and concentrated. The rich, thick, spicy paste-like mixture can be spread on crusty bread, though it's more commonly diluted and used as soup base or pasta sauce. During a visit to Naples we especially loved the wonderfully balanced, intensely flavorful version we tasted at La Cantinetta, a tiny eatery/grocery store/wine shop where octogenarian Maria Notaro does the cooking. Zuppa forte traditionally was made with odds and ends of meats, including offal, but the Neapolitan cooks we consulted said pancetta would be a reasonable stand-in. (For best flavor, it's important to purchase pancetta that contains a decent amount of fat. In our experience, the type sold pre-diced is too lean and cooks up with a tough, leathery

texture.) We then determined a combination of tomato paste, browned to develop flavor, and canned whole tomatoes, blended until smooth, yielded the best taste and consistency, and that simmering the sauce in a skillet was a quick way to concentrate it. The preserved chilies were the most difficult ingredient to approximate. We landed on Korean gochujang, which may seem out of place, but the thick, fermented paste delivers a similar complex spiciness along with welcome notes of umami. If you can source Calabrian chili paste, which is spicy, tangy and salty, it, too, is great. Salvatore Giugliano at Ristorante Mimì alla Ferrovia serves his zuppa forte–dressed pasta with fresh basil and ricotta, garnishes that complement the richness and intensity of the sauce.

14½-ounce can whole peeled tomatoes

**2 tablespoons gochujang (see headnote) or
1 tablespoon Calabrian chili paste**

Kosher salt and ground black pepper

¼ cup extra-virgin olive oil

4 ounces pancetta (see headnote), chopped

4 medium garlic cloves, minced

4 bay leaves

2 tablespoons tomato paste

1 sprig rosemary

1 pound penne, ziti or rigatoni pasta

½ cup lightly packed fresh basil, torn

Whole-milk ricotta cheese, to serve

In a large pot, bring 4 quarts water to a boil. In a blender, puree the tomatoes with juices and gochujang until smooth, 30 to 60 seconds; set aside.

While the water heats, in a 12-inch skillet, combine the oil, pancetta, garlic, bay, tomato paste, rosemary and ½ teaspoon pepper. Cook over medium, stirring often, until the pancetta has rendered some of its fat and the tomato paste darkens and begins to stick to the pan, 6 to 8 minutes. Add the pureed tomato mixture and bring to a simmer, scraping up any browned bits. Simmer, uncovered and stirring often, until very thick and the fat separates, about 10 minutes.

Meanwhile, when the water reaches a boil, add 1 tablespoon salt and the pasta; cook, stirring occasionally, until just shy of al dente. Reserve about 1½ cups of the cooking water, then drain the pasta and return it to the pot. (If the sauce is done ahead of the pasta, remove the skillet from the heat.)

Scrape the sauce into the pot with the pasta and add ¾ cup of the reserved cooking water. Cook over medium, stirring and tossing often, until the sauce clings and the pasta is al dente, 2 to 4 minutes; add more reserved pasta water as needed to loosen the noodles if the mixture is very dry and sticky.

Off heat, remove and discard the bay and rosemary. Taste and season with salt and pepper, then stir in the basil. Serve topped with dollops of ricotta.

PASTA CON FAGIOLI

Start to finish: 35 minutes
Servings: 6

We thought this rustic pasta and bean dish from Sicily would feel heavy, but the starches are lightened by tomatoes, rosemary and lemon. We were taught how to make it by Piera Ferruzza, winery cook at Cantina della Val di Suro, and Maria Enza Arena, shopkeeper in the hilltop town of Castelbuono. In Italy, dried borlotti beans (often called cranberry beans in the U.S.) are used. For weeknight ease, we opted for canned beans. Some producers label canned borlotti beans as "Roman beans." If you cannot find them, use pink or kidney beans, which have a similar creaminess and mildly sweet flavor. Don't use cannellini beans, which are too tender. The pasta is boiled only until very slightly softened, then drained and rinsed to stop the cooking. It finishes cooking when combined with the beans and vegetables.

8 ounces campanelle or other short pasta

Kosher salt and ground black pepper

5 tablespoons extra-virgin olive oil, divided, plus more to serve

2 pints grape or cherry tomatoes

1 large red onion, chopped

1 large fennel bulb, halved, cored and thinly sliced

4 medium garlic cloves, minced

1 tablespoon minced fresh rosemary

1 teaspoon fennel seeds

¾ teaspoon red pepper flakes

Two 15½-ounce cans Roman beans (see headnote), drained but not rinsed

2 cups low-sodium chicken broth

2 teaspoons grated lemon zest, plus 2 tablespoons lemon juice

2 ounces pecorino Romano cheese, grated (1 cup)

In a large Dutch oven over medium-high, bring 2 quarts water to a boil. Add the pasta and 1½ teaspoons salt. Cook, stirring occasionally, until just shy of al dente. Reserve 2 cups of cooking water, then drain and rinse with cold water until cool; set aside.

In the same pot, over medium-high, heat 3 tablespoons of oil until barely smoking. Add the tomatoes, then cover, reduce to medium and cook, stirring occasionally, until lightly charred, about 5 minutes. Add the onion, sliced fennel and ¼ teaspoon salt, then cook on medium-high, stirring occasionally, until the vegetables begin to soften, about 5 minutes.

Add the garlic, rosemary, fennel seeds and pepper flakes, then cook, stirring, until fragrant, about 30 seconds. Stir in the beans, broth and ½ cup of the reserved cooking water. Bring to a simmer over medium-high. Cover, reduce to medium and cook, stirring once or twice, until the vegetables are tender, about 10 minutes.

239

Add the pasta and cook, stirring frequently, until the pasta is al dente and the sauce is creamy, 3 to 5 minutes. If needed, add the remaining reserved cooking water 1 tablespoon at a time to reach the proper consistency. Off heat, stir in the lemon zest and juice and the remaining 2 tablespoons oil. Taste and season with salt and pepper. Serve with the cheese and additional oil for drizzling.

SPAGHETTI WITH SHRIMP, TOMATOES AND WHITE WINE

Start to finish: 45 minutes
Servings: 4 to 6

In Venice, Italy, cookbook author Marika Contaldo Seguso taught us to make a regional classic, scampi alla busara. Large, sweet, shell-on prawns are bathed in a sauce made with fresh tomatoes and flavored with a splash of white wine, smashed garlic cloves and a sprinkling of pepper flakes. She paired her scampi alla busara with al dente pasta, a terrifically delicious, though not strictly traditional, combination. We adapted Seguso's recipe using shelled shrimp in place of the prawns; to build flavor into our sauce, we briefly simmer the shrimp tails in the wine reduction, then remove them before the tomatoes are added.

1 pound spaghetti

Kosher salt and ground black pepper

4 tablespoons extra-virgin olive oil, divided, plus more to serve

4 medium garlic cloves, smashed and peeled

1½ pounds extra-large shrimp (21/25 per pound), peeled (tails removed and reserved) and deveined

⅓ cup dry white wine

2 pounds ripe plum tomatoes, cored and chopped

1 cup lightly packed fresh basil, torn

2 teaspoons white sugar

½ teaspoon red pepper flakes

In a large pot, bring 3 quarts water to a boil. Add the spaghetti and 2 teaspoons salt; cook, stirring occasionally, until just shy of al dente. Reserve about 1 cup of the cooking water, then drain the pasta and return it to the pot; set aside.

In a 12-inch skillet over medium, heat 2 tablespoons of the oil until shimmering. Add the garlic and shrimp tails, then cook, stirring occasionally, until the garlic begins to brown, 3 to 4 minutes. Add the wine, bring to a simmer and cook, stirring, until it has reduced by about half, 2 to 3 minutes. Using tongs or a slotted spoon, remove and discard the garlic and shrimp tails.

Into the wine reduction, stir the tomatoes, half of the basil, the sugar, pepper flakes and ½ teaspoon each salt and black pepper. Bring to a simmer over medium-high, then reduce to medium and simmer, stirring occasionally, until the tomatoes are softened and jammy and the juices have fully evaporated, 12 to 15 minutes.

Add the shrimp and cook, stirring occasionally, until they begin to turn pink, about 2 minutes. Pour the mixture over the spaghetti in the pot, then add the remaining 2 tablespoons oil and ½ cup of the pasta water. Cook over medium, tossing with tongs, until the sauce clings to the spaghetti and the shrimp are cooked through, 3 to 4 minutes; add more cooking water 1 tablespoon at a time if the mixture looks dry.

Off heat, taste and season with salt and pepper, then stir in the remaining basil. Serve drizzled with additional oil.

PASTA ALL'AMATRICIANA

Start to finish: 30 minutes
Servings: 4

Amatriciana is a minimalist equation of pasta, tomatoes, guanciale and pecorino Romano cheese, and in Rome it's served with barely any sauce, as we learned from Mario Ive, retired artillery colonel in the Italian army and cookbook author. The cooking method—using as little liquid as possible when cooking the sauce—concentrates flavors in the sauce, which coats the pasta nicely. We apply that principle for the pasta in this recipe, as well, cooking spaghetti in half the amount of water (2 quarts) we usually use. To that we add a chunk of pecorino Romano, which infuses the noodles with rich, savory flavor. We also under-cook the pasta, allowing it to finish cooking in the sauce. One 14½-ounce can of whole tomatoes, drained and cooked down, is plenty to dress four servings. Likewise, just 3 ounces of pancetta—more widely available than guanciale—provides ample flavor. Be sure to purchase thinly sliced pancetta and chop it finely to ensure the pieces crisp well.

3 tablespoons extra-virgin olive oil, divided

3 ounces thinly sliced pancetta, finely chopped

10 medium garlic cloves, thinly sliced

½ teaspoon red pepper flakes

¾ cup dry white wine

14½-ounce can whole peeled tomatoes, drained, juices reserved, tomatoes crushed by hand into small pieces

1-ounce chunk pecorino Romano cheese, plus more finely grated, to serve

Kosher salt and ground black pepper

12 ounces spaghetti

Pasta Boiling 101

How much water and salt do you need when boiling pasta? It varies.

Classic
For cooking **1 pound of pasta,** our default is to boil it in **4 quarts of water** with **1 tablespoon kosher salt.** This amount of water is ample enough that it recovers heat quickly after the pasta is added and gives the noodles room to circulate so they don't stick together, even with minimal stirring. This volume also creates suitably starchy cooking water that can be reserved (save it before you drain it) then added to sauces to help them thicken and cling to the noodles.

Super Starched
When we want particularly starchy water for sauces, we cook **1 pound of pasta** in **3 or even just 2 quarts of water.** This creates extra-starchy liquid that serves as an important ingredient in the sauce, giving it volume as well as a clingy, lightly thickened consistency. Use **2 teaspoons kosher salt for 3 quarts** and **1½ teaspoons for 2 quarts.** Note that boiling pasta in a reduced amount of water requires more frequent stirring to ensure the noodles don't stick together or to the bottom of the pot.

No Water
Some recipes are tailored to cook pasta directly in the sauce, eliminating the need for a separate pot of boiling water. For this technique, the sauce is usually very loose and watery, but the consistency thickens as the noodles hydrate and release some starch. Cooked this way, pasta also absorbs flavorings and is seasoned from outside to inside. In sauce-simmered pasta recipes, make sure to stir often, especially along the bottom of the pot or pan, to prevent sticking and scorching. Also, don't salt the mixture as generously as if boiling the pasta in water.

In a 12-inch skillet over medium, heat 1 tablespoon of the oil until shimmering. Add the pancetta and cook, stirring, until well-browned and crisp, 5 to 7 minutes. Using a slotted spoon, transfer to a paper towel-lined plate and set aside.

Return the skillet to medium and add the garlic; cook, stirring, until light golden brown, about 2 minutes. Stir in the pepper flakes and cook until fragrant, about 30 seconds. Add the wine, increase to medium-high and cook, stirring, until most of the liquid has evaporated, 5 to 7 minutes. Add the drained tomatoes and cook, stirring, until heated, about 2 minutes. Stir in 3 tablespoons of the reserved tomato juice, then remove from the heat.

Meanwhile, in a large pot, bring 2 quarts of water and the pecorino chunk to a boil, stirring occasionally to prevent the cheese from sticking to the pot. Stir in the pasta and 1 teaspoon salt. Cook, stirring often, until the pasta is just shy of al dente. Remove and discard the pecorino, then drain the pasta in a colander set in a large heat-safe bowl; reserve the cooking water.

Set the skillet over medium-high, stir in 1½ cups of the reserved pasta water and bring to a simmer. Add the drained pasta, tossing with tongs. Cook, stirring occasionally, until most of the liquid has been absorbed, 3 to 6 minutes.

Off heat, stir in the remaining 2 tablespoons oil, the pancetta and 2 teaspoons black pepper. Transfer to a serving bowl and serve with grated pecorino on the side.

....

CREAMY FOUR-CHEESE PASTA

Start to finish: 45 minutes

Servings: 6 to 8

Rich and creamy pasta ai quattro formaggi—or pasta with four cheeses—is the Italian equivalent of American mac and cheese. The cheeses can vary, though funky Gorgonzola and nutty Parmesan are typical. We use those along with creamy mascarpone and fontina, an Italian semi-soft cow's milk cheese that melts well. A short pasta with contours or crevices for catching the creamy sauce works best—we especially like campanelle, with its frilly edges and hollow centers. We use only 3 quarts of water to boil the pasta so the liquid is extra starchy, then use some of the cooking water to help to thicken and bind the sauce. To finish, a few minutes under the broiler lightly crisps and browns the surface.

1 tablespoon salted butter, room temperature

1 pound campanelle, gemelli or penne pasta

Kosher salt and ground black pepper

1 cup whole milk

4 ounces fontina cheese, shredded (1 cup)

½ cup mascarpone cheese

2 ounces Gorgonzola cheese, crumbled (½ cup)

2 ounces Parmesan cheese, finely grated (1 cup)

½ teaspoon grated nutmeg

¼ cup finely chopped fresh flat-leaf parsley, basil or chives

Heat the broiler with a rack positioned about 6 inches from the element. Coat a broiler-safe 9-by-13-inch baking dish with the butter. In a large pot, bring 3 quarts water to a boil. Add the pasta and 2 teaspoons salt, then cook, stirring occasionally, until al dente. Reserve 1 cup of the cooking water, then drain; set the pasta aside.

In the same pot over medium, bring the reserved cooking water and the milk to a simmer. Add the fontina, mascarpone and Gorgonzola; whisk until mostly melted, about 1 minute. Stir in half of the Parmesan, the nutmeg, ¼ teaspoon salt and 1 teaspoon pepper; it's fine if the mixture is not perfectly smooth. Add the pasta and parsley; cook, stirring constantly, until the sauce begins to cling to the pasta, 1 to 2 minutes. Remove from the heat and let stand uncovered for 5 minutes, stirring occasionally, to allow the

Spaghetti with Clams

Start to finish: 35 minutes
Servings: 4

At Perduto, a canal-side restaurant in Venice, Italy, chef Gianpiero Turdo taught us how to make a regional pasta classic: bigoli con vongole (bigoli with clams). **When boiling the pasta, we drain it when it is not quite al dente. The noodles will finish cooking in the reduced clam juices, a technique that infuses the spaghetti with the sweet, briny notes of the clams.** Bigoli is a long, thick, round extruded noodle, sometimes made with whole-wheat flour, sometimes with eggs. Spaghetti or bucatini are good substitutes. Scrub the clams well to remove as much grit as possible.

12 ounces spaghetti or bucatini

Kosher salt and ground black pepper

**3 tablespoons extra-virgin olive oil,
 plus more to serve**

4 medium garlic cloves, smashed and peeled

¼ teaspoon red pepper flakes

1 cup dry white wine

3 pounds littleneck or Manila clams, scrubbed

½ cup finely chopped fresh flat-leaf parsley

Lemon wedges, to serve

In a large pot, bring 2 quarts water to a boil. Stir in the pasta and 1½ teaspoons salt, then cook, stirring occasionally, until just shy of al dente. Reserve about 2 cups of the cooking water, then drain; set aside.

In a large Dutch oven over medium-high, combine the oil and garlic; cook, stirring until the garlic is lightly browned, about 2 minutes. Add the pepper flakes and cook, stirring, until fragrant, about 30 seconds. Remove and discard the garlic. Stir in the wine, bring to a simmer and cook until reduced to about ¼ cup, 6 to 8 minutes.

Stir in the clams, cover and cook, stirring occasionally; as the clams open, transfer them to a large bowl. When all clams have opened, simmer the juices in the pot until reduced by half.

Add the pasta and any accumulated clam juices (but not the clams themselves) in the bowl to the pot. Cook, constantly stirring and tossing, until the pasta is al dente, 2 to 3 minutes, adding reserved pasta water as needed so the noodles are lightly sauced.

Off heat, stir in the parsley, then taste and season with salt and pepper. Return the clams and any remaining juices to the pot; toss to combine. Serve drizzled with additional oil and with lemon wedges on the side.

243

mixture to thicken slightly. Taste and season with salt and pepper.

Transfer the pasta to the prepared baking dish in an even layer. Sprinkle with the remaining Parmesan. Broil until the top is browned in spots, 5 to 6 minutes. Cool for about 10 minutes before serving.

POTATO GNOCCHI WITH PANCETTA AND GARLIC

Start to finish: 30 minutes
Servings: 4 to 6

Gnocchi, the pillowy Italian dumplings, take well to a host of sauces. Here, we serve them simply, tossed with pancetta, garlic, Parmesan and red pepper flakes for a little heat, a combination inspired by a recipe we learned from Antonio Cioffi, chef at La Vecchia Cantina in Ravello, a hilltop town along the Amalfi coast. This dish is delicious with homemade potato gnocchi (recipe p. 246) but for a quick weeknight dinner, feel free to use store-bought gnocchi instead. Whatever type you use, follow the instructions for cooking your gnocchi first, as they are simply reheated in a skillet with a handful of ingredients for a few minutes before serving.

2 pounds gnocchi, homemade or store-bought (see headnote)

4 ounces pancetta, finely chopped

3 tablespoons extra-virgin olive oil, divided

6 medium garlic cloves, thinly sliced

¼ to ½ teaspoon red pepper flakes

2 tablespoons lemon juice

¼ cup finely chopped fresh flat-leaf parsley or basil

1 ounce Parmesan cheese, finely grated (½ cup)

Cook and drain the gnocchi according to your recipe or the package instructions, reserving about 1½ cups of the cooking water; set aside.

In a 12-inch nonstick skillet over medium, cook the pancetta, stirring often, until browned and crisped, 5 to 7 minutes. Using a slotted spoon, transfer to a small bowl; set aside. Pour off and discard all but 1 tablespoon of the fat from the pan.

Return the skillet to medium and add 1 tablespoon of the oil and the garlic. Cook, stirring often, until the garlic is light golden brown, about 2 minutes. Using the slotted spoon, transfer to the bowl with the pancetta.

Return the skillet to medium and add the gnocchi, pepper flakes and ½ cup of the reserved cooking water. Cook, stirring and tossing often, until the gnocchi are heated through, 3 to 5 minutes; add up to ½ cup more reserved water as needed to form a silky sauce. Add the pancetta and garlic; cook, stirring, until heated through, about 1 minute.

Off heat, stir in the remaining 2 tablespoons oil, the lemon juice and parsley. Taste and season with salt and black pepper. Serve sprinkled with the Parmesan.

RIGATONI WITH ROMAN BROCCOLI SAUCE

Start to finish: 35 minutes
Servings: 4

This is an adaptation of a pasta we had in Rome. There, cooks use the leaves that grow around heads of broccoli to make a flavorful sauce for pasta. In the U.S., most of the leaves are stripped off before broccoli is sold. Our recipe instead uses the stems, which are equally flavorful and produce a silky sauce. Baby spinach retains the color of the original recipe.

1 pound broccoli, stems and florets separated

Kosher salt and ground black pepper

1½ cups packed baby spinach

2 medium garlic cloves, chopped

4 tablespoons (½ stick) salted butter, cut into 4 pieces

1 tablespoon drained capers

½ teaspoon red pepper flakes

2 tablespoons finely grated lemon zest, divided

12 ounces rigatoni pasta

1 ounce pecorino Romano or Parmesan cheese, finely grated (½ cup), plus more to serve

In a large pot, bring 4 quarts water and 1 tablespoon salt to a boil. Peel the broccoli stems, reserving any leaves, and cut crosswise into ½-inch rounds. Add the stems and leaves to the boiling water and cook until fully tender, about 10 minutes. Stir in the spinach and cook until wilted, about 20 seconds. Using a slotted spoon, transfer the vegetables to

a blender; reserve ½ cup of the cooking water. Keep the water at a boil.

Cut the broccoli florets into 1- to 1½-inch pieces. Add the florets to the boiling water and cook until crisp-tender, about 3 minutes. Using the slotted spoon, transfer to a colander and rinse under cold water until cooled. Again keep the water at a boil.

To the blender, add the garlic, butter, capers, pepper flakes, ¼ teaspoon salt, 1 tablespoon of the lemon zest and the reserved broccoli cooking water. Puree until smooth and bright green, about 30 seconds. Taste and season with salt and pepper.

Stir the rigatoni into the boiling water and cook until al dente. Reserve ½ cup of the cooking water, then drain. Return the pasta to the pot and add the broccoli florets, the broccoli puree, ¼ cup of the reserved cooking water, the remaining 1 tablespoon lemon zest and the cheese.

Cook over medium, stirring constantly, until the sauce thickens slightly and the pasta is well coated, 1 to 2 minutes. Remove from the heat. Taste and season with salt and pepper.

CHANGE THE WAY YOU COOK

Throw Away Your Garlic

It will sound strange to red sauce-loving Americans, but Italian cooks sometimes throw their garlic away.

When they want a more subtle approach to this seasoning, Italians start by sautéing a handful of peeled and lightly crushed cloves in olive oil. After a few minutes — and before the garlic browns and turns acrid — they spoon it out and throw it away.

At that point, the garlic has done its job, infusing the oil with gentle flavor and aroma that more evenly permeates the noodles and sauce without overpowering the nuances of the dish. And without leaving unpleasant pungent chunks of garlic floating in your sauce. We do this with our spaghetti with clams (recipe p. 243).

There is, of course, a time and place for the bracing flavor of copious garlic, Italian-American garlic bread, for example. But often, we prefer the more subtle approach of using it to season the oil, rather than saturate the sauce.

Potato Gnocchi

Start to finish: 1¾ hours,
plus cooling
Makes about 2 pounds,
serving 4 to 6

Our take on classic potato gnocchi was informed by a hands-on cooking lesson from Australian chef Peter Orr when he was proprietor of Robert, his former restaurant in Paris' 11th arrondissement. **Weighing potatoes on a kitchen scale after cooking and draining is the best way to ensure the right quantity is used to create the perfectly balanced gnocchi dough.** And for processing the cooked potatoes, a ricer or food mill delivers the fine, smooth texture needed for perfectly light, fluffy gnocchi. A potato masher works, too, but the dumplings will be slightly denser (but still delicious). The gnocchi can be cooked, cooled completely on the wire rack, then transferred to a baking sheet that has been lined with parchment and misted with cooking spray; cover with plastic wrap and refrigerate for up to 24 hours. For longer storage, after covering with plastic, freeze until solid, about two hours, then transfer to a zip-close bag and freeze for up to a month. To thaw, spread the dumplings in an even layer on a lightly oiled baking sheet and let stand at room temperature until soft to the touch, about one hour. Heat the chilled or thawed gnocchi by adding them to sauce that is already hot, tossing with a silicone spatula until warmed.

2 pounds russet potatoes, peeled and cut into 1-inch chunks

Kosher salt

1 cup plus 2 tablespoons all-purpose flour, plus more for shaping

½ teaspoon baking powder

1 large egg, lightly beaten

In a large pot, combine the potatoes and 4 quarts water. Bring to a boil over high, then stir in 1 tablespoon salt. Reduce to medium-high and cook, stirring occasionally, until the potatoes break apart when pierced with a knife, 15 to 20 minutes. Meanwhile, set a wire rack in a rimmed baking sheet and line another baking sheet with kitchen parchment.

Drain the potatoes in a colander, shaking the colander to remove excess water. Transfer the potatoes to the prepared rack in an even layer, then cool to room temperature. Meanwhile, in a small bowl, whisk together the flour, baking powder and 1 teaspoon salt.

Weigh out 1¼ pounds (about 4 cups) of the cooled cooked potatoes into a large bowl; save the remainder for another use. Reserve the rack and the baking sheet for cooling the cooked gnocchi. Pass the potatoes through a ricer or a food mill fitted with the fine disk back into the bowl, or mash them with a potato masher until smooth.

Sprinkle the flour mixture evenly over the mashed potatoes. Using your hands, lightly toss the potatoes to

distribute the flour mixture. Add the egg and gently mix with your hands until incorporated. Turn the dough out onto a lightly floured counter and gently knead just until smooth; do not over knead.

Using a bench scraper, divide the dough into 4 pieces and cover with a kitchen towel. Using your hands, roll one piece of dough against the counter into a rope about 18 inches long and about ¾ inch in diameter. Cut the rope

into ½-inch pieces and lightly dust the pieces with flour. Dip the back of the tines of a fork into flour, then gently press into each piece to create a ridged surface. Transfer the gnocchi to the parchment-lined baking sheet; try to not allow them to touch. Shape the remaining pieces of dough in the same way.

In a large pot, bring 4 quarts water to a boil. Add 1 tablespoon salt followed by about a third of the gnocchi. Return to a boil, stirring once or twice, and cook for 2 minutes (the gnocchi will float to the surface even before they are cooked through). Using a slotted spoon and allowing excess water to fall back into the pot, transfer the gnocchi to the prepared rack; spread them out so they don't touch. The gnocchi will be very soft at this point, but will firm up as they cool. Return the water to a boil, then cook and drain the remaining gnocchi in the same way, in two more batches.

After the final batch of gnocchi has been transferred to the rack, reserve cooking water as needed for saucing; discard the remainder. Let the gnocchi cool for at least 10 minutes or up to 1 hour to allow them to firm up.

247

PASTA WITH PECORINO-ZUCCHINI SAUCE AND BASIL

Start to finish: 40 minutes

Servings: 4 to 6

From Italy's Amalfi Coast, pasta alla nerano features long, thin pasta tossed with a velvety sauce made with pureed zucchini. It's an elegant yet easy dish that's luxurious but not heavy. We use a minimal amount of water to cook the pasta, then blend some of the starchy liquid with tender, sautéed zucchini to create creamy consistency without cream. If you own an immersion blender, it works well for making the zucchini-garlic puree; simply transfer the ingredients to be blended to a medium bowl. When smooth, return the mixture to the pot.

1½ pounds medium zucchini

1 pound spaghetti OR bucatini

Kosher salt and ground black pepper

3 tablespoons extra-virgin olive oil, plus more to serve

3 medium garlic cloves, smashed and peeled

2 tablespoons salted butter, cut into 2 pieces

2 ounces pecorino Romano cheese, finely grated (1 cup), plus more to serve

½ cup lightly packed fresh basil, chopped

Thinly slice the zucchini on the diagonal. Stack several slices and cut lengthwise into matchsticks. Repeat with the remaining slices; set the zucchini aside.

In a large pot, bring 3 quarts water to a boil. Add the spaghetti and 2 teaspoons salt, then cook, stirring occasionally, until al dente. Reserve about 1½ cups of the cooking water, then drain; set aside.

In the same pot, combine the oil and garlic. Cook over medium, stirring, until the garlic is golden brown, 1 to 2 minutes. Transfer the garlic to a small plate, then add the zucchini to the pot. Cook, stirring occasionally, until the zucchini is lightly browned and soft enough to mash with a fork, 10 to 12 minutes. Remove the pot from the heat. Add half of the zucchini to a blender along with the garlic and ½ cup reserved pasta water. Puree until the mixture is smooth, about 30 seconds.

To the zucchini in the pot add the puree, drained pasta, butter, pecorino, basil and another ½ cup reserved pasta water. Cook over medium, tossing, until heated through and the mixture is creamy and the pasta is lightly sauced, 2 to 3 minutes; add more reserved pasta water as needed if the mixture looks thick and dry. Off heat, taste and season with salt and pepper. Serve drizzled with additional oil and sprinkled with additional cheese.

SHRIMP AND COUSCOUS WITH TOMATOES AND TOASTED ALMONDS

Start to finish: 40 minutes

Servings: 4

Trapani, Sicily, is closer to North Africa than it is to mainland Italy, so it's no surprise that Trapanese cuisine is strongly influenced by Moorish flavors and ingredients. Couscous alla Trapanese combines the couscous and spices of the Maghreb with seafood harvested from the waters off Trapani. Our simple one-pot rendition of the dish cooks shrimp and couscous at the same time, but does so gently, using the residual heat trapped in a covered pot. Flat-leaf parsley adds both grassy herbal flavor and bright color. You'll need a full bunch to obtain the 1 cup finely chopped stems and leaves that's sautéed with the aromatics and the ¼ cup roughly chopped leaves for garnish.

5 tablespoons extra-virgin olive oil, divided

½ cup sliced almonds

1 medium yellow onion, chopped

4 medium garlic cloves, chopped

¼ teaspoon ground cinnamon

1 cup finely chopped fresh flat-leaf parsley leaves and stems, plus ¼ cup roughly chopped leaves (see headnote)

Kosher salt and ground black pepper

28-ounce can diced fire-roasted tomatoes

¾ cup couscous

1½ pounds extra-large (21/25 per pound) shrimp, peeled, tails removed and deveined

In a large pot over medium, heat 3 tablespoons of oil until shimmering. Add the almonds and cook, stirring, until golden, about 2 minutes. Using a slotted spoon, transfer to a small bowl; set aside.

To the oil remaining in the pot, add the onion, garlic, cinnamon, finely chopped parsley leaves and stems, ¾ teaspoon salt and 1 teaspoon pepper. Cook over medium, stirring often, until the onion has softened, about 6 minutes. Stir in the tomatoes with juices and 1½ cups water, then bring to a boil over medium-high. Stir in the couscous and shrimp. Return to a boil, then cover, remove from the heat and let stand until the couscous is tender and the shrimp are opaque throughout, about 10 minutes. Stir to combine and fluff the couscous, then taste and season with salt and pepper.

Transfer the couscous and shrimp to a serving dish. Sprinkle with the roughly chopped parsley and almonds, then drizzle with the remaining 2 tablespoons oil.

SPICED COUSCOUS WITH BUTTERNUT SQUASH AND PISTACHIOS

Start to finish: 30 minutes

Servings: 4 to 6

More often than not, couscous is simply prepared and served as a side dish. But inspired by the rich, fragrant spicing and savory-sweet profile of many types of Moroccan tagines, we created this recipe for a skillet full of colorful couscous that's hearty enough to stand on its own. (But it's also a terrific accompaniment to roasted and grilled meats, as well as fish and kebabs.) We like the deeper flavor that chicken broth gives the dish, but if you're cooking for vegetarians, feel free to use vegetable broth instead.

3 tablespoons extra-virgin olive oil, divided, plus more to serve

1 pound butternut squash, peeled, seeded and cut into ½-inch cubes (about 4 cups)

1 medium red onion, chopped

1 teaspoon ground cumin

½ teaspoon ground ginger

½ teaspoon ground cinnamon

Kosher salt and ground black pepper

1 pint cherry or grape tomatoes, halved

2 cups low-sodium chicken broth or vegetable broth

1½ cups couscous

½ cup roasted pistachios, chopped

½ cup lightly packed fresh mint, chopped

249

In a 12-inch nonstick skillet over medium, heat 2 tablespoons oil until shimmering. Add the squash and cook, stirring occasionally, until browned on all sides and beginning to soften, 6 to 8 minutes. Using a slotted spoon, transfer to a medium bowl.

To the skillet, add the remaining 1 tablespoon oil and the onion. Cook over medium, stirring occasionally, until beginning to brown, 3 to 4 minutes. Add the cumin, ginger, cinnamon and ½ teaspoon each salt and pepper. Cook, stirring, until fragrant, about 30 seconds. Stir in the tomatoes and squash, followed by the broth. Bring to a simmer over medium-high, then stir in the couscous. Cover, remove from the heat and let stand for 10 minutes.

Using a fork, fluff the mixture, then taste and season with salt and pepper. Transfer to a serving dish. Sprinkle with the pistachios and mint, then drizzle with additional oil.

In a 12-inch skillet over medium-high, melt 3 tablespoons of the butter. Add the onion and ½ teaspoon each salt and pepper, then cook, stirring, until it begins to soften, 3 to 5 minutes. Add the garlic and cook, stirring, until fragrant. Add the couscous and cook, stirring often, until it begins to brown.

Pour in the wine and cook, stirring, until the pan is almost dry, about 1 minute. Add 3 cups water and ½ teaspoon salt, then cook, stirring occasionally, for 5 minutes. Stir in the asparagus stalks and cook, stirring, for 3 minutes, then stir in the asparagus tips. Continue to cook, stirring, until almost all the liquid has been absorbed and the asparagus is tender, about another 2 minutes.

Off heat, add the Parmesan, parsley and remaining 1 tablespoon butter, then stir until the butter melts. Taste and season with salt and pepper. Serve sprinkled with additional Parmesan and parsley.

PEARL COUSCOUS "RISOTTO" WITH ASPARAGUS

Start to finish: 30 minutes

Servings: 4

Classic risotto is made with starchy medium-grain Italian rice, such as Arborio or carnaroli. This "risotto" uses pearl couscous (which actually is a pasta) and a simplified risotto cooking method to produce "grains" with a rich, creamy consistency. The wheaty flavor of pearl couscous (sometimes called Israeli couscous or ptitim) is a perfect match for grassy, subtly sweet asparagus and the salty, nutty flavor of Parmesan cheese.

4 tablespoons (½ stick) salted butter, cut into 1-tablespoon pieces

1 medium yellow onion, chopped

Kosher salt and ground black pepper

3 medium garlic cloves, thinly sliced

1 cup pearl couscous

⅓ cup dry white wine

1 pound asparagus, trimmed and cut on the diagonal into ½-inch pieces; reserve the stalks and tips separately

1 ounce Parmesan cheese, finely grated (½ cup), plus more to serve

½ cup lightly packed fresh flat-leaf parsley, finely chopped, plus more to serve

TOASTED PEARL COUSCOUS WITH CHICKEN AND CHICKPEAS

Start to finish: 30 minutes

Servings: 4

Palestinian maftool, a pasta similar to pearl couscous, and chickpeas inspired this quick and easy one-pot meal. Before cooking the couscous pilaf-style, we toast the seed-sized bits to deepen their wheaty flavor and aroma. A sauté of browned garlic, onion, cumin and allspice creates a heady base for simultaneously poaching boneless chicken thighs and steaming the toasted couscous; the chicken gets a 5-minute head start before the couscous is added so everything finishes at the same same time. A spoonful of tangy-sweet pomegranate molasses brightens the flavors while balancing the warm, earthy spices.

3 tablespoons extra-virgin olive oil, divided

1 cup pearl couscous

4 medium garlic cloves, chopped

1 medium yellow onion, chopped

3 large carrots, peeled, quartered lengthwise and cut into ½-inch pieces

Kosher salt and ground black pepper

1 tablespoon ground cumin

½ teaspoon ground allspice

1 pound boneless, skinless chicken thighs, trimmed and halved

2 bay leaves

15½-ounce can chickpeas, rinsed and drained

1 teaspoon pomegranate molasses, plus more to serve

1 cup lightly packed fresh flat-leaf parsley, roughly chopped

In a large Dutch oven over medium-high, heat 1 tablespoon of the oil until shimmering. Add the couscous and cook, stirring, until golden brown, about 3 minutes. Transfer to a small bowl. In the same pot over medium-high, heat the remaining 2 tablespoons oil until shimmering. Add the garlic and cook, stirring, until beginning to brown, about 30 seconds. Add the onion, carrots, 1 teaspoon each salt and pepper, then cook, stirring occasionally, until browned bits have developed on the bottom of the pan, 3 to 5 minutes. Add the cumin and allspice, and cook, stirring, until fragrant, about 30 seconds.

Stir in the chicken, bay, ½ teaspoon salt and 2 cups water. Bring to a boil, then cover, reduce to medium-low and simmer for 5 minutes. Stir in the couscous, cover and simmer until the chicken is opaque when cut into and the couscous is tender but not mushy, about 8 minutes.

Off heat, stir in the chickpeas, pomegranate molasses and half the parsley. Remove and discard the bay, then taste and season with salt and pepper. Transfer to a serving bowl and sprinkle with the remaining parsley. Serve with additional pomegranate molasses for drizzling.

ORECCHIETTE WITH BROCCOLINI

Start to finish: 40 minutes

Servings: 4

Orecchiette with broccoli rabe (orecchiette con cime di rapa) is a signature pasta dish from the Puglia region of southern Italy. We were taught how to make it by Nunzia da Scalo, a cook in Bari, Italy. The bitterness of rabe is challenging for some palates, so we use sweeter, milder Broccolini. However, if you like the assertiveness of rabe, it can easily be used in place of the Broccolini, though rabe will cook a little more quickly. We boil the pasta in a minimal amount of water, then the starchy liquid that remains becomes the base for the sauce that marries the orecchiette and Broccolini. A finishing sprinkle of toasted seasoned breadcrumbs adds a crisp texture.

6 tablespoons extra-virgin olive oil, divided

8 medium garlic cloves, 4 minced, 4 thinly sliced

8 oil-packed anchovy fillets, minced

¾ cup panko breadcrumbs

1½ pounds Broccolini, trimmed and cut crosswise into ¼-inch pieces

½ to 1 teaspoon red pepper flakes

Kosher salt and ground black pepper

12 ounces orecchiette pasta

In a large Dutch oven over medium-high, heat 2 tablespoons of oil until shimmering. Add the minced garlic and half the anchovies, then cook, stirring, until fragrant, about 45 seconds. Add the panko and cook, stirring, until golden brown, about 3 minutes. Transfer to a bowl and set aside; wipe out the pot.

In the same pot over medium-high, heat 2 tablespoons of the remaining oil until shimmering. Add the Broccolini, pepper flakes, sliced garlic, ¾ teaspoon salt and ½ teaspoon black pepper. Cook, stirring occasionally, until the Broccolini is crisp-tender and the garlic is golden brown, 6 to 7 minutes. Add ½ cup water and continue to cook, stirring, until most of the moisture has evaporated and the Broccolini is fully tender, about 2 minutes. Transfer to a medium bowl and set aside.

In the same pot over medium-high, boil 5 cups water. Add 1 teaspoon salt and the pasta, then cook, stirring occasionally, until the pasta is al dente. Stir in the Broccolini mixture, the remaining 2 tablespoons oil and the remaining anchovies. Continue to cook over medium-high, stirring constantly, until the liquid has thickened enough to cling lightly to the pasta and Broccolini, about 1 minute. Remove from the heat, then taste and season with salt and pepper. Transfer to a serving bowl and sprinkle with the breadcrumbs.

MISO-WALNUT SOBA WITH BOK CHOY

Start to finish: 20 minutes
Servings: 4

Nutty, wholesome Japanese buckwheat noodles and bok choy are sauced with a puree of toasted walnuts and miso that delivers a double hit of umami. The starchy water that results from cooking soba is called soba yu; we use a little of it to help the sauce blend smoothly and also cling to the noodles. You can use either sweeter, milder white miso, or saltier, earthier red miso—or even a blend if you happen to have both types. To add a little citrusy heat and hints of sesame, pass shichimi togarashi, a Japanese spice blend, at the table for sprinkling to taste.

10 ounces dried soba noodles

1 pound baby bok choy, trimmed and thinly sliced crosswise

⅓ cup walnuts, toasted, plus chopped toasted walnuts, to serve

3 tablespoons white miso or red miso

2 tablespoons grapeseed or other neutral oil

2 medium garlic cloves, smashed and peeled

Kosher salt and ground black pepper

Lemon wedges, to serve

Bring a large pot of water to a boil. Add the soba and cook, stirring occasionally, until al dente. Reserve ¾ cup cooking water, then add the bok choy to the pot and cook until the soba is tender and the bok choy is crisp-tender, about 1 minute. Drain in a colander, rinse and drain again; return to the pot.

In a blender, combine 3 tablespoons of the reserved cooking water, the walnuts, miso, oil and garlic; puree until smooth. Add the walnut-miso mixture to the soba mixture, then toss, adding more reserved water as needed until the noodles are lightly sauced. Taste and season with salt and pepper. Serve sprinkled with chopped toasted walnuts and with lemon wedges.

BUTTERY UDON WITH SHIITAKE MUSHROOMS

Start to finish: 30 minutes
Servings: 4

They may seem an unlikely pairing, but sweet, creamy butter and bold, salty soy sauce are a fantastic flavor match. In this recipe, the duo adds richness and umami to Japanese udon, wheat noodles that cook up with a satisfying chewiness. Fresh shiitake mushrooms sautéed in butter bring a meatiness to the vegetarian dish and make it feel more complete. If you like, top each serving with a runny-yolked fried egg.

12 ounces dried udon noodles

4 tablespoons salted butter, cut into 1-tablespoon pieces, divided

8 ounces shiitake mushrooms, stemmed, caps sliced about ¼ inch thick

2 medium garlic cloves, finely grated OR 2 teaspoons finely grated fresh ginger OR both

¼ cup soy sauce, plus more if needed

Toasted sesame seeds, to serve

In a large pot, bring 3 quarts water to a boil. Add the noodles and cook, stirring occasionally, until just shy of al dente. Reserve ¼ cup of the cooking water, then drain the noodles in a colander. Rinse under cold water until cool to the touch, then drain again; set aside.

In the same pot over medium-high, melt 2 tablespoons butter. Add the mushrooms and cook, stirring occasionally, until beginning to brown, about 3 minutes. Reduce to medium and add the garlic; cook, stirring, until fragrant, about 30 seconds. Add the noodles, followed by the soy sauce; cook over medium-high, stirring and tossing, until heated, about 1 minute.

Add the reserved cooking water and the remaining 2 tablespoons butter; cook, tossing, until the noodles are slick, glossy and tender, about 2 minutes. Off heat, taste and season with additional soy sauce. Serve sprinkled with sesame seeds

Optional garnish: Thinly sliced scallions OR shichimi togarashi OR both

Japanese Noodles 101

Japanese noodles come in a variety of thicknesses, lengths and textures, and some cook more quickly than Italian pastas. Chewy varieties such as ramen are great in soups and stir-fries, while stretchy, delicate somen noodles make great salads. (In fact, they're a better choice than Italian pasta, which can turn mealy when cold.) In general, Japanese noodles should be cooked in a generous amount of water until tender—not al dente. Tasting for doneness is the best way to know when your noodles are ready. Some require rinsing after cooking to remove excess starch, and all are cooked without salt. Here are the varieties we reach for most often and how we like to cook them.

RAMEN

Chewy and stretchy, ramen noodles are made of wheat flour and an alkaline solution, which gives them their yellow hue. Most famously consumed in a brothy soup, but also great stir-fried or served as a noodle salad. Most commonly sold in the U.S. in instant form, but also available fresh and dried. We typically use dried, non-instant ramen, which typically come in straight bundles that cook in about 4 minutes. Drain and rinse in cold water, or drain and immediately add to soup.

Stir-Fried Ramen with Cabbage and Bean Sprouts

In a 12-inch nonstick skillet, toss **6 ounces dried ramen** (cooked and drained) with **1 tablespoon sake, 1 tablespoon grapeseed or other neutral oil** and **½ teaspoon soy sauce.** Set over medium-high and cook, without stirring, until the noodles begin to brown on the bottom, about 2 minutes. Add **2 cups mung bean sprouts, 2 cups thinly sliced green cabbage, 2 tablespoons sake** and **2 tablespoons water.** Cover and cook until the vegetables are crisp-tender, 3 to 4 minutes. Uncover and stir in **2½ tablespoons oyster sauce, 4 teaspoons soy sauce, 1 tablespoon oil, ¼ teaspoon white sugar** and **¼ teaspoon ground black pepper.** If desired, top with **2 fried eggs.**

UDON

Chewy and well-kneaded, udon noodles are made from wheat flour, water and salt and are available in a variety of thicknesses. Usually served hot in soup, stir-fried or chilled with dipping sauce. Sold dried, frozen and fresh (refrigerated and shelf-stable). We prefer the firm, springy texture of frozen udon, but dried is more widely available. Cooking times vary, depending on the brand and the noodles' thickness; check the cooking instructions on the package, but check for doneness a few minutes early. Drain and rinse with water to stop the cooking.

254

Udon Noodle Soup with Pork and Spinach

In a medium bowl, whisk together **1 tablespoon each white miso** and **soy sauce**. Cut one **1-pound pork tenderloin** (trimmed of silver skin) in half lengthwise, then slice each half crosswise about ¼ inch thick. Add the pork to the bowl and stir. In a large pot, bring **4 quarts of water** to a boil. Add **4 ounces dried udon noodles** and cook until tender. Drain, rinse under lukewarm water, drain again, then divide among 4 serving bowls. In the same pot, bring **1½ quarts low-sodium chicken broth** to a boil over medium-high. In a small bowl, whisk **3 tablespoons white miso** with 2 tablespoons of the broth. Add the mixture to the pot along with **1 tablespoon soy sauce** and **1 tablespoon finely grated fresh ginger**. Reduce to medium and simmer gently for 10 minutes, then bring to a boil over medium-high. Add the pork and cook, stirring, until for 2 minutes. Off heat, stir in **8 ounces baby spinach** and **3 tablespoons unseasoned rice vinegar**. Ladle the soup over the noodles, then sprinkle with **6 scallions** (thinly sliced).

SOBA

Gray-brown and nutty, soba noodles are made from a blend of buckwheat and wheat flours or all buckwheat. Often served chilled with a dashi-soy dipping sauce or hot in a dashi-based broth, though we also like them in noodle salads. Sold dried and frozen fresh. Pale green cha soba are flavored with matcha tea. We prefer the clean, nutty flavor of dried, 100 percent buckwheat soba. Cook for 7 to 8 minutes, or until tender. Drain and rinse with cold water until cold to the touch.

Dipping Sauce for Cold Soba

In a small saucepan over medium, simmer **1 cup low-sodium chicken broth, ½ cup soy sauce, ½ cup mirin** and **¼ cup sake** for 3 minutes. Transfer to a bowl and refrigerate until cold. Divide the sauce between four bowls. Serve with cold cooked, drained and rinsed soba noodles, along with thinly sliced scallions, toasted sesame seeds and wasabi paste for stirring into the dipping sauce.

SHIRATAKI

Bouncy, gelatinous and glassy, shirataki noodles have little flavor. Made from yam starch, water and pickling lime, they often are added to hot pots like sukiyaki, but also are used in stir-fries and noodle salads. Most commonly sold refrigerated and packed in liquid. Though they are pre-cooked, we prefer to drain and rinse the noodles, then blanch them in boiling water for about 3 minutes to improve the taste and texture. Drain and rinse with cold water.

Shirataki Noodles with Peanut Sauce

In a medium bowl, whisk together **5 tablespoons creamy peanut butter, 3 tablespoons soy sauce, 2 tablespoons white sugar, 1 tablespoon unseasoned rice vinegar, 1 small garlic clove** (finely grated) and **1 teaspoon finely grated fresh ginger**. Add two **7-ounce packages shirataki** (blanched, drained and rinsed) and toss until evenly coated with the sauce. Serve topped with **4 scallions** (thinly sliced) and pickled ginger.

SOMEN

Delicate, pale and thin, somen noodles are made from wheat flour dough that is oiled, then stretched several times. Usually served chilled in summer months with a soy dipping sauce. Sold dried, packaged in bundles. Add to boiling water and cook until tender, 2 or 3 minutes, stirring gently to prevent sticking, then drain and rinse with cold water until cool to the touch.

Somen Noodle Salad

In a small bowl, combine **⅓ cup soy sauce, ¼ cup unseasoned rice vinegar, 3 tablespoons white sugar, 1 tablespoon grapeseed** or **other neutral oil** and **2 teaspoons toasted sesame oil,** then whisk until the sugar dissolves. Top cooked and drained somen noodles with **shredded lettuce, cucumber matchsticks, thinly sliced radishes, thinly sliced scallions and toasted sesame seeds.** Serve with the dressing on the side.

Chinese Hot Oil Noodles with Bok Choy

Start to finish: 30 minutes
Servings: 4

A basic bowl of noodles gets a quick blast of flavor when it's topped with garlic, scallions and cilantro and then finished with a few tablespoons of sizzling oil that bloom the aromatics. Flat, moderately wide noodles are ideal in our take on northern China's you po mian; dried udon, fettuccine or pappardelle are great shelf-stable options. Malty, subtly sweet and a touch smoky, Chinese black vinegar is worth seeking out; if not available, balsamic vinegar makes a solid replacement. Make sure to use heat-proof bowls that can withstand the temperature of smoking-hot oil.

¼ cup soy sauce

1 tablespoon Chinese black vinegar or balsamic vinegar

12 ounces baby bok choy, trimmed and separated into individual leaves

12 ounces fettuccine, pappardelle or dried udon

¼ cup lightly packed fresh cilantro, chopped

2 scallions, thinly sliced

¾ to 1 teaspoon red pepper flakes

4 medium garlic cloves, finely grated, divided

½ cup grapeseed or other neutral oil

Kosher salt

In a small bowl, stir together the soy sauce and vinegar; set aside. Bring a large pot of water to a boil. Add the bok choy and cook, stirring occasionally, until the stems are tender-crisp, 2 to 3 minutes. Using a slotted spoon, transfer to a colander; keep the water at a boil. Shake the colander to remove any water, then divide the bok choy among 4 heat-proof serving bowls.

To the boiling water, add the noodles and cook, stirring occasionally, until just shy of tender. Drain, shaking the colander to remove as much water as possible. If using dried udon, rinse under cold water and drain again. Divide the noodles among the bowls.

Divide the soy sauce-vinegar mixture among the serving bowls, pouring a generous tablespoon over each. Toss the contents of each bowl to combine. Top each with cilantro, scallions, pepper flakes and garlic; do not stir.

In a small saucepan over medium-high, heat the oil until barely smoking. Working quickly, pour 2 tablespoons oil over each bowl; you should hear a sizzle as the oil "sears" the aromatics. Toss, then serve immediately, with salt on the side for sprinkling to taste.

KOREAN SPICY CHILLED NOODLES

Start to finish: 30 minutes
Servings: 4

This classic Korean dish is a pasta salad of sorts, with bold contrasting flavors and textures. Somen is the Japanese name for the type of dried wheat noodle to use here; in Korean they are called somyeon. The noodles are slender and creamy white; look for them, often packaged in bundles, in the Asian section of the grocery store or in Asian markets. Gochujang is a Korean fermented red pepper paste—it's an essential ingredient in this dish. Made with ¼ cup gochujang, the noodles are assertively spicy. To turn down the heat, reduce the amount to 3 tablespoons. If you like, add a halved or quartered hard- or soft-cooked egg on top of each portion.

3 to 4 tablespoons gochujang

2½ tablespoons unseasoned rice vinegar, plus more as needed

2 tablespoons soy sauce

1½ tablespoons white sugar

1½ tablespoons toasted sesame oil

2 tablespoons sesame seeds, toasted, divided

1 cup drained cabbage kimchi, thinly sliced, plus 2 tablespoons kimchi juice

½ English cucumber

8 ounces somen noodles (see headnote)

Ice

Kosher salt

4 scallions, thinly sliced on the diagonal

Bring a large pot of water to a boil. Meanwhile, in a large bowl, whisk together the gochujang, vinegar, soy sauce, sugar, sesame oil, 1 tablespoon of the sesame seeds and the kimchi juice. Set aside.

Thinly slice the cucumber on the diagonal. Stack several slices and cut lengthwise into matchsticks. Repeat with the remaining slices. Set aside.

Add the noodles to the boiling water and cook, stirring frequently, until tender, about 2 minutes. Drain in a colander, then add 1 cup ice cubes on top. Rinse the noodles under cold running water, tossing constantly, until com-

pletely cool to the touch. Remove any unmelted ice cubes, then drain well.

Add the drained noodles to the gochujang mixture, along with the kimchi. Toss, then taste and season with salt and additional vinegar. Transfer to a shallow serving bowl, then mound the scallions and cucumber on top. Sprinkle with the remaining 1 tablespoon sesame seeds. Toss just before serving.

THAI PORK, GLASS NOODLE AND HERB SALAD

Start to finish: 40 minutes

Servings: 4

The minced-meat salad known as larb is a traditional dish from the Isaan region in northeastern Thailand. The version we make here, known as larb woon sen, features glass noodles (woon sen in Thai) that look almost translucent when cooked. You might find them labeled as bean threads, bean vermicelli or cellophane noodles. Toasted rice powder, or khao kua, is a key ingredient in larb—it contributes unique flavor, absorbs a small amount of the liquid, and brings a bit of crunch and nuttiness to the dish. Larb typically includes Thai ground roasted chilies; to mimic that taste, we toast red pepper flakes. The dish is finished with lots of fresh mint and cilantro. Both the noodles and the ground pork soak up all the contrasting flavors—salty, sour, spicy and herbal.

4 ounces glass noodles (see headnote)

Boiling water, to soak the noodles

2 tablespoons jasmine rice

1 to 2 teaspoons red pepper flakes

3 tablespoons fish sauce

3 tablespoons lime juice, plus lime wedges to serve

2 teaspoons white sugar

1 large shallot, halved and thinly sliced

1 teaspoon grapeseed or other neutral oil

8 ounces ground pork

Kosher salt and ground black pepper

1 cup lightly packed fresh mint

1 cup lightly packed fresh cilantro

2 scallions, thinly sliced

Place the noodles in a medium heatproof bowl and add boiling water to cover. Let stand until the noodles are tender, about 15 minutes. Drain in a colander and rinse under cold water. Using kitchen shears, snip the noodles in several places to cut them into shorter lengths.

While the noodles soak, in a 10-inch skillet over medium, toast the rice, stirring often, until golden brown, 6 to 8

minutes. Transfer to a small bowl and cool for about 10 minutes.

While the rice cools, in the same skillet over medium, toast the pepper flakes, stirring, until fragrant, 30 to 60 seconds. Transfer to a large bowl, then add the fish sauce, lime juice, sugar and shallot; whisk to combine. Set the dressing aside and reserve the skillet.

Using a spice grinder or mortar and pestle, pulverize the toasted rice to a coarse powder. Return the powder to the small bowl; set aside.

In the same skillet over medium-high, heat the oil until shimmering. Add the pork and cook, breaking the meat into fine bits so there are no clumps, until no longer pink, 4 to 5 minutes. Immediately add the pork and any juices to the dressing, along with the noodles, ¼ teaspoon salt, ½ teaspoon black pepper and half of the rice powder; toss well. Let stand for 10 to 15 minutes, tossing occasionally.

Add the mint, cilantro and scallions; toss. Taste and season with salt and black pepper, then transfer to a serving dish and sprinkle with the remaining rice powder. Serve with lime wedges.

SCALLION NOODLES WITH GROUND PORK

Start to finish: 35 minutes
Servings: 4

The Shanghainese dish called cong you ban mian combines wheat noodles with fried scallions, the flavorful oil that results from frying them and salty, savory soy sauce. A lot of deep, bold flavor is wrested from a small handful of ingredients. Cutting the scallions into thin strips before cooking requires a little knifework but allows them to crisp evenly and quickly. And once fried, they integrate nicely with the noodles rather than fall to the bottom of the bowl. Ground pork makes our version hearty enough to serve as a main dish. Dried Asian wheat noodles about the size of thin spaghetti work well in this recipe; non-instant dried ramen is a good choice, as are thin lo mein noodles (don't use wide, flat lo mein). A sprinkle of thinly sliced fresh chilies, though not traditional, balances the richness of the dish and adds a welcome kick of heat.

2 bunches scallions

10 ounces dried Asian wheat noodles (see headnote)

⅓ cup grapeseed or other neutral oil

8 ounces ground pork

⅓ cup soy sauce

3 tablespoons white sugar

Kosher salt

1 or 2 Fresno or jalapeño chilies, stemmed and sliced into thin rounds (optional)

In a large pot, bring 4 quarts water to a boil. While the water heats, cut the scallions into 2- to 3-inch lengths, then slice lengthwise into thin strips, reserving the whites and greens separately. To the boiling water, add the noodles, then cook until tender (refer to package instructions for cooking times). Drain in a colander and rinse under cold water until cool to the touch; set aside.

In a large skillet over medium, heat the oil until shimmering. Add the scallion whites and cook, stirring occasionally, until golden brown, 5 to 7 minutes. Add about half of the scallion greens and cook, stirring occasionally, until well-browned and beginning to crisp, another 5 to 8 minutes. Using tongs or a slotted spoon, transfer to a bowl and set aside.

Add the pork to the oil remaining in pan and cook over medium, stirring to break the meat into small pieces, until the meat is well-browned and crisp, 7 to 10 minutes. Stir in the soy sauce and sugar, then bring to a simmer, scraping up any bits stuck to the pan.

Reduce to low and add the noodles and fried scallions. Cook, tossing to combine, until the noodles are heated through, about 1 minute. Remove from the heat, then taste and season with salt. Toss in the remaining scallion greens. Divide among individual bowls and top with fresh chilies (if using).

Garlicky Peanut Noodles

Start to finish: 20 minutes
Servings: 4

This Asian-inspired noodle dish comes together in a flash. **Peanut butter, a classic component of Asian noodle sauces, adds flavor as well as body. Soy sauce (or fish sauce) and miso balance the richness with a double-dose of umami (as well as salty notes), and chili-garlic sauce (or Sriracha) adds a bright hit of heat.** The noodles are delicious warm or at room temperature, topped with garnishes of your choice; see the suggestions below. We especially like a drizzle of chili crisp, an oil-based condiment infused with red pepper flakes and other spices.

**12 ounces linguine OR spaghetti
OR dried lo mein**

¼ cup crunchy OR creamy peanut butter

3 medium garlic cloves, finely grated

2 tablespoons unseasoned rice vinegar

2 tablespoons soy sauce OR fish sauce

**1 to 2 tablespoons chili-garlic sauce
OR Sriracha sauce**

1 tablespoon white miso

**4 scallions, quartered lengthwise,
then cut into 1-inch lengths**

Kosher salt

In a large pot, bring 4 quarts water to a boil. Reserve ½ cup of the hot water; set aside. Add the pasta to the pot, then cook, stirring occasionally, until tender.

Meanwhile, in a small bowl, whisk together the peanut butter, garlic, vinegar, soy sauce, chili-garlic sauce, miso and ¼ cup of the reserved water.

When the pasta is done, drain and return to the pot. Off heat, add the peanut butter mixture and toss until evenly coated. If needed, add more of the reserved water 1 tablespoon at a time to thin the sauce. Stir in the scallions, then taste and season with salt.

Optional garnish: Chopped roasted peanuts **OR** cucumber matchsticks **OR** chili oil **OR** chili crisp

BLACK BEAN NOODLES WITH PORK AND MUSHROOMS

Start to finish: 30 minutes
Serves: 4

This riff on Chinese zha jiang mian—or noodles with pork and fermented bean sauce—substitutes prepared black bean garlic sauce for the traditional and harder-to-find fermented yellow or brown bean paste. On its own, the sauce tastes intense, but its boldness is balanced by the neutral flavor of the noodles and the freshness of the cucumber. You can find it in the Asian aisle of most larger grocery stores. Make sure to thoroughly drain the noodles before portioning them; excess water clinging to them will dilute the sauce.

12 ounces dried wide, thick wheat noodles (such as udon)

2 tablespoons grapeseed or other neutral oil

8 ounces fresh shiitake mushrooms, stemmed and finely chopped

12 ounces ground pork

4 scallions, white and light green parts minced, dark green tops thinly sliced

4 medium garlic cloves, minced

½ teaspoon red pepper flakes

½ cup dry sherry

3 tablespoons black bean garlic sauce

1 tablespoon hoisin sauce

1 tablespoon low-sodium soy sauce

2 tablespoons plus 1 teaspoon unseasoned rice vinegar, divided

½ English cucumber, thinly sliced on the diagonal, then cut into matchsticks

In a large pot, bring 4 quarts of water to a boil. Add the noodles and cook until al dente, 5 to 6 minutes. Reserve 1 cup of the cooking water, then drain the noodles and rinse under cool water until cold. Drain well, then set aside in the colander.

Meanwhile, in a 12-inch skillet over medium-high, heat the oil until shimmering. Add the mushrooms and cook until softened and the bits clinging to the bottom of the pan begin to brown, about 3 minutes. Add the pork and cook until crispy and caramelized, about 6 minutes.

Stir in the minced scallions, garlic and pepper flakes, then cook until fragrant, about 1 minute. Add the sherry and cook, scraping the pan, until evaporated. Stir in the reserved cooking water, black bean sauce, hoisin and soy sauce. Bring to a simmer and cook over medium, stirring occasionally and breaking up any large bits of pork, until the sauce has the consistency of thin gravy, 4 to 5 minutes. Off heat, stir in 2 tablespoons of the vinegar.

While the sauce simmers, season the cucumber with the remaining 1 teaspoon of rice vinegar. Divide the noodles among serving bowls, then spoon the sauce over them. Top with sliced scallion greens and cucumber.

Stir-Fries

STIR-FRIED HOISIN CHICKEN AND BELL PEPPERS

Start to finish: 25 minutes

Servings: 4 to 6

Thick, savory-sweet, umami-rich hoisin sauce drives the flavor in this stir-fry that pairs snappy bell peppers with tender chicken breast. Be sure to slice the chicken crosswise, or against the grain, so the muscle fibers are short rather than stringy. The cooking here goes quickly, so be sure the ingredients are prepped and at the ready before you head to the stove. Serve with steamed rice.

¼ cup hoisin sauce

2 tablespoons dry sherry OR sake

1 tablespoon soy sauce, plus more if needed

3 tablespoons grapeseed or other neutral oil

2 medium green OR red OR orange
OR yellow bell peppers OR a combination,
stemmed, seeded and sliced about ¼ inch thick

2 medium garlic cloves, minced

1 tablespoon finely grated fresh ginger

½ teaspoon red pepper flakes

1½ pounds boneless, skinless
chicken breasts, sliced crosswise ¼ inch thick

In a small bowl, stir together the hoisin, sherry and soy sauce; set aside. In a 12-inch skillet over medium-high, heat the oil until shimmering. Add the bell peppers and cook, stirring occasionally, until softened and beginning to brown, 4 to 5 minutes. Add the garlic, ginger and pepper flakes, then cook, stirring, until fragrant, 30 to 60 seconds.

Add the chicken and cook, stirring occasionally, until lightly browned and opaque throughout, 7 to 8 minutes. Add the hoisin mixture and cook, stirring, until the sauce slightly thickens, 1 to 2 minutes. Off heat, taste and season with additional soy sauce, if needed.

Optional garnish: Thinly sliced scallions

KHMER-STYLE STIR-FRIED CHICKEN AND GINGER

Start to finish: 35 minutes

Servings: 4 to 6

This is our rendition of the Khmer stir-fry known as mouan cha k'nyei (English spellings vary) in which fresh ginger figures as prominently as the chicken. Cut into matchsticks and stir-fried until it begins to brown, the ginger mellows, and its raw, sharp sting gives way to a subtle pepperiness and sweet, floral notes. A combination of fish sauce and oyster sauce lends the dish loads of umami, while a little sugar balances the saltiness. Ginger prep is the most involved aspect of this simple stir-fry; the easiest method is to thinly slice the peeled root crosswise into coins (cutting against the grain this way minimizes the fibrousness), then stack a few slices and cut the pile into matchsticks. Serve with steamed jasmine rice.

3 tablespoons grapeseed or other neutral oil

3 ounces fresh ginger, peeled, thinly sliced crosswise, then cut into matchsticks (about 1 cup)

2 pounds boneless, skinless chicken thighs, trimmed and cut crosswise into 1-inch pieces

1 medium red onion, cut into ¾-inch wedges

1 bunch scallions, white parts thinly sliced, green parts cut into 1-inch pieces, reserved separately

3 medium garlic cloves, finely grated

2 tablespoons fish sauce

1 tablespoon oyster sauce

1 tablespoon white sugar

Kosher salt

In a 12-inch skillet over medium, combine the oil and ginger, then cook, stirring often, until the ginger has softened and is just beginning to brown, 3 to 5 minutes. Add the chicken, onion, scallion whites and garlic; increase to medium-high and cook, stirring occasionally, until the chicken no longer is pink when cut into and the onion has softened, 7 to 9 minutes.

Add the fish sauce, oyster sauce, sugar, scallion greens and 1 tablespoon water; stir until the chicken and vegetables are evenly coated. Off heat, taste and season with salt then transfer to a serving dish.

265

CHANGE THE WAY YOU COOK

Oil for High-Heat Cooking

High-heat cooking—techniques such as searing and stir-frying—results in well-browned steaks and crisp-tender vegetables, but it requires oil with a high smoke point. That's the temperature at which the chemical compounds that make up the oil break apart, releasing smoke and acrid flavors and smells.

But we've found that many published smoke points vary greatly from those we've noted at Milk Street. So we tested eight common home cooking oils for how high we could heat them before they became unfit for use. We limited our testing to highly refined oils—less refined oils have much lower smoke points than oils with few or no impurities. That ruled out extra-virgin olive oil and unrefined coconut oil, among others.

We tested by heating 2 tablespoons of each oil in a stainless-steel skillet over medium-high. When each was barely smoking, we took its temperature using two different infrared thermometers. We repeated this process three times with each oil.

Type of oil	Average smoke point
Grapeseed Oil	494
Safflower Oil	470
Peanut Oil	467
Canola Oil	453
Olive Oil	449
Extra Light Olive Oil	446
Refined Coconut Oil	423
Avocado Oil	412

Our favorite for high-heat cooking—and the one that consistently had the highest smoke point—was grapeseed oil, which is made from grape seeds, a byproduct of wine-making. Safflower oil—made by extracting oil from the seeds of the safflower, a cousin of the sunflower—was the second most durable oil. And the biggest surprise: olive oil. Though extra-virgin olive oil is ill-suited for high-heat cooking, we were impressed by how hot we could get refined olive oil.

THAI CASHEW CHICKEN

Start to finish: 35 minutes
Servings: 4

The Thai stir-fried cashew chicken, or gai pad med mamuang himmaphan, that home cook and food blogger Rawadee Yenchujit taught us in her Bangkok kitchen was a revelation. Deliciously filled with contrasting tastes and textures and with balanced savoriness, sweetness and spice plus loads of umami, it bore little resemblance to the goopy, sugary dish Thai restaurants tend to serve in the U.S. We tried to do without Thai chili paste, or chili "jam"—nam prik pao, in Thai—but we discovered it's an important element in the stir-fry. The mixture is thick, dark red and rather oily. Made by blending fried shallots, garlic, dried chilies, shrimp paste, tamarind and other ingredients, the paste is intensely and inimitably flavorful. Thai Kitchen roasted chili paste is sold in small jars in the international aisle of most supermarkets. Whole árbol chilies bring spiciness and aroma that supplements the red pepper flakes, but they're optional, so feel free to leave them out. Steamed jasmine rice is the perfect accompaniment.

3 tablespoons soy sauce, divided

2 tablespoons all-purpose flour

Kosher salt and ground black pepper

1½ pounds boneless, skinless chicken thighs, trimmed and cut into ¾- to 1-inch pieces

1½ tablespoons Thai chili paste (see headnote)

1½ tablespoons white sugar

1 tablespoon oyster sauce

5 tablespoons grapeseed or other neutral oil, divided

1 cup roasted cashews

6 dried árbol chilies (optional)

6 medium garlic cloves, minced

¾ to 1¼ teaspoons red pepper flakes

1 medium red onion, cut into 1-inch pieces

1 bunch scallions, cut into 1-inch lengths

In a medium bowl, combine 1 tablespoon of the soy sauce, the flour, 2 tablespoons water, ¼ teaspoon salt and 1 teaspoon black pepper; whisk until smooth. Add the chicken and toss to coat; set aside.

to brown, 1 to 2 minutes. Stir in the chicken and accumulated juices, then pour the sauce mixture down the sides of the pan. Cook, stirring and scraping, until the sauce thickens slightly and lightly coats the chicken and onion, 1 to 2 minutes. Stir in the scallions and cashews with árbol chilies (if used); cook, stirring, until the scallions are just wilted, about 30 seconds. Remove from the heat. Taste and season with salt and black pepper.

STIR-FRIED LEMON GRASS CHICKEN

Start to finish: 40 minutes
Servings: 4

Vietnamese stir-fried lemon grass chicken, called gà xào sả ớt, is a quick, flavor-packed dish that comes together quickly. To create our recipe, we looked to two of our favorite Vietnamese cooks, Andrea Nguyen and Charles Phan, borrowing elements from each of their versions to create our own. Like Nguyen, we briefly marinate pieces of boneless chicken thighs before cooking. And like Phan, we add sliced red onion to the mix. The spicy heat in the stir-fry comes from two sources: sambal oelek, an Indonesian-style chili paste with a bright, sharp flavor (Asian garlic-chili sauce works, too) and jalapeños sliced into thin rings. Serve with steamed jasmine rice.

2 pounds boneless, skinless chicken thighs, trimmed and cut into 1½-inch pieces

4 medium garlic cloves, minced

3 stalks lemon grass, trimmed to the lower 6 inches, dry outer layers discarded, bruised

1 tablespoon fish sauce

1 tablespoon sambal oelek or Asian chili-garlic sauce

2 teaspoons white sugar

Kosher salt and ground black pepper

3 tablespoons grapeseed or other neutral oil

1 medium shallot, halved and thinly sliced

1 medium red onion, halved and sliced about ½ inch thick

2 jalapeño chilies, stemmed and sliced into thin rings

In a small bowl, combine the remaining 2 tablespoons soy sauce, chili paste, sugar, oyster sauce and 3 tablespoons water, then whisk until the sugar dissolves; set the sauce aside.

In a 12- to 14-inch wok or 12-inch skillet over medium-high, heat 1 tablespoon of the oil until shimmering. Add the cashews and árbol chilies (if using); cook, stirring, until the nuts are fragrant and browned, 1 to 2 minutes. Transfer to a small bowl and set aside. Wipe out the pan.

Set the pan over high and heat 1 tablespoon of the remaining oil until barely smoking, swirling to coat. Add half of the chicken mixture; cook, stirring intermittently and scraping up any browned bits, until well browned, 2 to 3 minutes, then transfer to another medium bowl. Using 1 tablespoon of the remaining oil, cook the remaining chicken mixture in the same way and transfer to the bowl with the first batch.

Return the pan to medium-high and add the remaining 2 tablespoons oil, garlic and pepper flakes; cook, stirring, until the garlic is golden brown, about 30 seconds. Add the onion and cook, stirring and scraping, until just beginning

267

In a **medium bowl,** toss the chicken with the garlic, lemon grass, fish sauce, sambal, sugar, ½ teaspoon salt and ¾ teaspoon pepper. Set aside at room temperature for about 15 minutes.

In a **12-inch skillet** over medium-high, heat the oil until barely smoking. Add the chicken and cook without stirring until browned on the bottom, 3 to 5 minutes. Add the shallot and cook, stirring occasionally, until the chicken is browned all over, 4 to 6 minutes.

Stir in the onion, jalapeños and ½ cup water, scraping up any browned bits. Cook, stirring often, until the chicken is lightly glazed and no longer pink when cut into, 3 to 5 minutes. Remove and discard the lemon grass, then taste and season with salt and pepper.

THREE-CUP CHICKEN WITH BASIL

Start to finish: 35 minutes (15 minutes active)
Servings: 4

Taiwanese three-cup chicken is named for the formula once used to prepare the dish: one cup each of sesame oil, soy sauce and rice wine. Not surprisingly, recipes no longer adhere to that ratio, but the name has stuck. Bone-in chicken legs that have been hacked into pieces are customarily used in this one-pan dish; we opted for boneless, skinless chicken thighs for easier prep and eating. Serve with rice and steamed or stir-fried vegetables.

2 tablespoons toasted sesame oil

8 medium garlic cloves, minced

¼ cup minced fresh ginger

1 bunch scallions, cut into 1-inch lengths

1 tablespoon grapeseed or other neutral oil

2 pounds boneless, skinless chicken thighs, trimmed and cut into 1-inch-wide strips

¾ cup sake

3 tablespoons soy sauce

2 tablespoons packed brown sugar

1 teaspoon cornstarch

3 cups lightly packed fresh basil leaves, torn if large

In a 12-inch nonstick skillet over medium, combine the sesame oil, garlic, ginger and scallions. Cook, stirring, until the garlic begins to brown, about 5 minutes. Transfer to a small bowl and set aside.

In the same skillet over medium-high, heat the grapeseed oil until just smoking. Add the chicken in an even layer and cook without stirring until browned, about 5 minutes. Transfer to a medium bowl and set aside.

In the same skillet over medium-high, bring the sake, soy sauce and sugar to a simmer and cook, stirring, until syrupy, about 4 minutes. Return the chicken and accumulated juices to the skillet and stir. Bring to a simmer, then reduce heat to medium-low and cook, stirring occasionally, until the chicken is cooked through, about 6 minutes.

In a small bowl, stir together the cornstarch and 1 tablespoon water. While stirring the chicken mixture, pour in the cornstarch mixture. Bring to a simmer and cook, stirring constantly, until the sauce is thickened, about 1 minute. Off heat, add the basil and sesame oil mixture and stir until the basil begins to wilt, about 30 seconds.

STIR-FRIED GOCHUJANG CHICKEN

Start to finish: 30 minutes
Servings: 4

Flavor-packed, spicy-sweet gochujang elevates a couldn't-be-simpler chicken stir-fry. The complexly flavored Korean refrigerator staple is balanced by the pepperiness and pungency of ginger and garlic, plus a splash of salty soy sauce and a spoonful of sugar rounding everything out. We get deeply flavorful browning on the chicken by cooking it on each side without stirring. Serve with steamed rice and a chilled beer.

¼ cup gochujang

3 tablespoons soy sauce

1 tablespoon white sugar

3 tablespoons neutral oil

1½ pounds boneless, skinless chicken thighs, trimmed and cut crosswise into thirds

3 medium garlic cloves, finely chopped

3 tablespoons finely chopped fresh ginger

In a small bowl, whisk together the gochujang, soy sauce and sugar; set aside.

In a 12-inch skillet over medium-high, heat the oil until shimmering. Add the chicken in an even layer and cook without stirring until browned on the bottom, about 5 minutes. Reduce to medium, then flip the chicken and cook without stirring until browned on the second sides, 3 to 4 minutes.

Add the garlic and ginger; cook, stirring, until fragrant, about 30 seconds. Add the gochujang mixture and cook, scraping up any browned bits and occasionally turning the chicken, until the sauce has thickened lightly and coats the chicken, 2 to 3 minutes.

Optional garnish: Toasted sesame seeds OR sliced scallions OR both

Mastering Wok Hei at Home

Wok hei refers to the distinctive flavor imparted to food during high-heat cooking in a wok. Chinese American cookbook author Grace Young defines it as "breath of a wok," though "wok energy" is a more literal translation. Descriptions of wok hei flavor range from smoky or caramelized to grilled and charred.

It's a style of cooking rooted in Cantonese cuisine, though it is found across Southeast Asia and—thanks to immigration during the 1800s—many American Chinese restaurants. A host of factors contribute to wok hei, but two are particularly notable: the carbon steel woks and the high-octane gas burners found in most restaurants.

Those burners, which can reach more than 150,000 BTUs, generate intense heat quickly. The carbon steel woks, like cast-iron skillets, are seasoned with a coating of polymerized oils, creating a naturally nonstick surface. The interaction of the heat and oil-coated pan produces smoke and speedy caramelization that coat food as it cooks.

But many home cooks struggle to reproduce this effect, even in China. Home stovetop gas burners often max out at 18,000 BTUs, and few cooks have well-seasoned carbon steel woks. Hacks to replicate this abound, but many are cumbersome.

Curious whether wok hei is a goal worth pursuing, we sought out Gigg Kamol, Thailand's Iron Chef and owner of several Bangkok restaurants, including Phed Mark, which is famous for its pad kra pao, a spicy basil and pork stir-fry in which wok hei is a key ingredient unto itself.

He prepared side-by-side versions of his signature dish—one traditionally, the other over lower heat to mimic home cooking conditions. The low-and-slow version was undeniably delicious, but the wok hei sample—which began with billowing smoke rising from the wok—was rich with savory, smoky flavor that edged toward char, but never tasted of burnt, just depth.

Kamol has spent years trying to replicate wok hei with home cooking equipment. But even letting the pan sit for prolonged periods over high heat wasn't enough. The empty pan would smoke, but as soon as ingredients were added, the pan cooled and never was able to recover to a sufficient temperature.

The problem was in trying to replicate restaurant equipment conditions. Success came when Kamol instead worked to duplicate not the conditions, but the flavors. This meant adding ingredients in ways that maximize caramelization.

He calls it saucing the wok, not the food. Pouring sauce over food reduces its contact with the wok, limiting its contact with heat. But when he pushed the food to one side and drizzled the sauce directly on the surface of the pan, it sizzled, caramelized and developed deeper, richer flavor.

To further enhance this effect, he also cooks proteins first to give them time to release and cook off any water, which would dilute the other flavors.

We used his technique for our pad Thai (recipe p. 291) and loved the results. But the same approach works for all manner of stir-fry where the smoky richness of wok hei is desired.

270

In a medium bowl, mix the sugar and soy sauce. Add the chicken and toss, then let stand for 10 minutes.

Drain the marinade into a small bowl and reserve. In a 12-inch skillet over medium-high, heat the oil until barely smoking. Add the chicken and cook, stirring occasionally, until no almost no pink remains, about 3 minutes. Add the garlic and the reserved marinade; cook, stirring, until the chicken is opaque throughout, about 2 minutes. Remove the pan from the heat. Add the butter and half the chilies; stir until the butter melts. Taste and season with salt and pepper. Serve sprinkled with the remaining chilies and with scallions.

SPICY BUTTER-SOY CHICKEN

Start to finish: 20 minutes (10 minutes active)
Servings: 4

This simple stir-fry was inspired by Filipino salpicao, a dish that dresses tender cubes of beef with a garlicky soy-butter sauce. Lean, mild-tasting chicken breasts get a big savory-sweet flavor boost from just a few high-impact ingredients. We like the mild burn that results when the seeds are left in the serranos, but you can remove the seeds for less heat. Serve with rice to soak up the sauce.

3½ teaspoons packed light brown OR dark brown sugar

3 tablespoons soy sauce

1½ pounds boneless, skinless chicken breasts, cut into ½- to ¾-inch chunks

1 tablespoon neutral oil

2 medium garlic cloves, minced

5 tablespoons salted butter, cut into 5 pieces

2 serrano chilies, stemmed and sliced into thin rings (see headnote)

Kosher salt and ground black pepper

Scallions, thinly sliced on the diagonal, to serve

VIETNAMESE-STYLE STIR-FRIED BEEF WITH TOMATOES

Start to finish: 30 minutes
Servings: 4 to 6

Vietnamese thịt bò xào khoai tây combines beef with Western vegetables, namely potatoes (khoai tây in Vietnamese) that typically are deep-fried until crisp. This recipe is a potato-free riff on that dish, and it derives loads of depth, savoriness and umami from garlic, fish sauce, soy sauce and tomatoes. We leave the seeds in the chilies for noticeable but not scorching heat; feel free to remove them to tone down the spiciness. If you wish to stay true to the inspiration stir-fry, serve this atop french fries. Otherwise, steamed jasmine rice is a fine accompaniment.

1½ pounds beef sirloin tips or flank steak, trimmed, cut into 3-inch pieces with the grain, then thinly sliced against the grain

1 medium red onion, halved and thinly sliced

2 tablespoons fish sauce

1 tablespoon soy sauce, plus more as needed

2 teaspoons cornstarch

1 teaspoon white sugar

3 tablespoons grapeseed or other neutral oil, divided

2 medium garlic cloves, minced

2 serrano or jalapeño chilies, stemmed and thinly sliced on the diagonal

4 plum tomatoes, cored and cut into 6 wedges each

3 scallions, thinly sliced on the diagonal

STIR-FRIES

271

In a medium bowl, combine the sirloin tips, onion, fish sauce, soy sauce, cornstarch and sugar; toss to combine. In a 12-inch nonstick skillet over medium-high, heat 1 tablespoon oil until barely smoking. Add half of the beef mixture in an even layer and cook without stirring until well browned on the bottom, 4 to 5 minutes. Stir, redistribute in an even layer and cook until no longer pink, 3 to 4 minutes; transfer to a small bowl. Using 1 tablespoon of the remaining oil, cook the remaining beef mixture in the same way, then transfer to the bowl with the first batch.

In the same skillet over medium-high, combine the remaining 1 tablespoon oil, the garlic and chilies; cook, stirring, until lightly browned, 1 to 2 minutes. Add the tomatoes and cook, stirring occasionally, until they just begin to soften, about 4 minutes.

Stir in the beef mixture and accumulated juices, then remove the pan from the heat. Taste and season with additional soy sauce. Transfer to a serving dish and sprinkle with the scallions.

LOMO SALTADO

Start to finish: 35 minutes
Servings: 4

Peru's lomo saltado, a quick stir-fry of soy-marinated beef, tomatoes and onions, is part of chifa cuisine—Asian-influenced dishes created by indentured Chinese workers in the late 19th century. For our take, we developed deeper flavor by mixing ground cumin into the soy sauce marinade. Tenderloin is often used here, but we preferred sirloin tips (also called flap meat) for their meatier flavor as well as lower price. And we seared the meat instead of stir-frying. Readily available jalapeño peppers made a good substitute for the traditional yellow ají peppers. If you prefer little to no spiciness, halve and seed the jalapeño before slicing it into half rings. Classic lomo saltado is frequently served over french fries; your favorite, frozen or otherwise, would be a good choice here. Steamed rice is an equally good accompaniment.

1½ pounds sirloin tips, trimmed, cut into 3-inch pieces and sliced ½ inch thick against the grain

1½ teaspoons ground cumin

Kosher salt and ground black pepper

5 tablespoons soy sauce, divided

3 tablespoons grapeseed or other neutral oil, divided

1 large red onion, halved and cut into ½-inch half rings

¼ cup red wine vinegar

2 medium garlic cloves, minced

1 jalapeño chili, stemmed and sliced into thin rounds

1½ cups grape tomatoes, halved

In a medium bowl, combine the beef, cumin, ½ teaspoon salt, 1 teaspoon pepper, and 2 tablespoons of the soy sauce. Marinate at room temperature for 10 minutes. Pat the meat dry and set aside.

In a 12-inch skillet over high, heat 1 tablespoon of oil until barely smoking. Add half of the meat in a single layer and cook, turning once, until well browned on both sides, 2 to 3 minutes total. Transfer to a plate. Repeat with 1 tablespoon of the remaining oil and the remaining meat.

In the same pan over medium-high, heat the remaining 1 tablespoon oil until shimmering. Add the onion and cook, stirring, until just starting to soften, about 2 minutes.

Stir in the vinegar and remaining soy sauce, scraping the bottom of the pan to remove any browned bits. Cook for about 1 minute, or until the sauce thickens slightly. Stir in the garlic and jalapeño and cook until the garlic is fragrant, about 30 seconds. Add the tomatoes and the meat along with any accumulated juices. Cook until the meat is just warmed through, about 30 seconds. Taste and season with salt and pepper.

STIR-FRIED BLACK PEPPER BEEF

Start to finish: 20 minutes
Servings: 4

This stir-fry is an homage to pepper steak, the Chinese-American takeout staple. A combination of powerhouse ingredients like savory-sweet oyster sauce, spicy black peppercorns and umami-rich soy sauce yields a punchy yet well-rounded dish. For maximum heat, use the full 2 tablespoons peppercorns. Cooking the crushed peppercorns for a couple minutes with the onion and bell pepper blooms their fragrance and flavors.

3 tablespoons neutral oil, divided

1 medium red OR yellow onion, halved and sliced ½ inch thick

1 medium red bell pepper, stemmed, seeded and cut into ½-inch strips OR 3 medium celery stalks, thinly sliced on the diagonal

1½ to 2 tablespoons black peppercorns, coarsely cracked

1 pound flank steak, cut with the grain into 2- to 3-inch pieces, then thinly sliced against the grain

2 tablespoons oyster sauce

2 tablespoons soy sauce

In a 12-inch skillet over high, heat 2 tablespoons oil until barely smoking. Add the onion and bell pepper; cook, stirring often, until the onion begins to wilt, about 2 minutes. Add the peppercorns and cook, stirring, until the mixture is fragrant and the onion begins to brown at the edges, 1 to 2 minutes. Transfer to a plate and set aside.

In the same skillet over high, heat the remaining 1 tablespoon oil until barely smoking. Add the beef in an even layer and cook, without stirring, until well browned on the bottom and the pieces release easily from the skillet, 2 to 3 minutes. Stir in the vegetable-peppercorn mixture. Add the oyster and soy sauces; cook, stirring, until the beef is tender and the sauce clings to the meat, 1½ to 3 minutes.

Optional garnish: Chopped cilantro **OR** lime wedges **OR** a combination

STIR-FRIED CHILI-GARLIC BEEF

Start to finish: 30 minutes
Servings: 4

For this stir-fry, we like to use either beef sirloin tips (also called sirloin flap meat) or flat iron steak. No matter which cut you choose, it's important to thinly slice the beef against the grain. This helps make the meat more tender because the muscle fibers are shortened instead of long and stringy. Use an electric spice grinder to pulverize the Sichuan peppercorns to a powder. Serve the stir-fry with plenty of steamed rice.

1 pound beef sirloin tips or flat iron steak, trimmed

4 tablespoons low-sodium soy sauce, divided

1 teaspoon Sichuan peppercorns, ground

6 tablespoons grapeseed or other neutral oil, divided

3 tablespoons chili-garlic sauce

5 medium garlic cloves, finely grated

4 teaspoons unseasoned rice vinegar

2 teaspoons toasted sesame oil

1 teaspoon white sugar

1 medium red onion, halved and thinly sliced

1 large red or yellow bell pepper, stemmed, seeded and thinly sliced

Roughly chopped fresh cilantro, to serve

Cut the beef with the grain into 2-inch pieces, then thinly slice each piece against the grain. In a medium bowl, stir together the beef, 1 tablespoon of soy sauce and the Sichuan pepper. In a small bowl, stir together the remaining 3 table-spoons soy sauce, 4 tablespoons of neutral oil, chili-garlic sauce, garlic, vinegar, sesame oil and sugar.

In a 12-inch nonstick skillet over medium-high, heat 1 tablespoon of the remaining neutral oil until barely smoking. Add half the beef in an even layer and cook without stirring until well browned, 1 to 2 minutes. Stir, scraping the pan, and cook, stirring, until no pink remains, 1 to 1½ minutes; transfer to a plate. Using the fat remaining in the pan, repeat with the remaining beef.

In the empty skillet over medium-high, heat the remaining 1 tablespoon neutral oil until barely smoking. Add the onion and bell pepper, then cook, stirring occasionally, until the vegetables begin to soften, about 3 minutes. Stir in the soy sauce mixture and any beef juices. Cook, stirring, until the liquid has thickened, about 1 minute. Remove from the heat and stir in the beef. Transfer to a serving dish and sprinkle with cilantro.

SPICY DRY-FRIED BEEF AND CELERY

Start to finish: 40 minutes
Servings: 4

In Chinese cooking, dry-frying, or gan bian, is a technique in which a protein or vegetable first is browned, then is stir-fried with aromatics and seasonings that cling to the browned surfaces. Dry-fried dishes aren't saucy like typical stir-fries, but the flavors are intense and concentrated. Beef and celery is a classic dry-fried combination. For this version, we use a tender, meaty strip steak, cut it into matchsticks, and brown it in a hot skillet before introducing the other ingredients. Salty, savory fermented chili-bean paste called toban djan provides loads of umami (chili-garlic sauce is a good alternative) and Sichuan peppercorns bring their unique tongue-tingling spice. Serve with steamed jasmine rice.

6 or 7 medium celery stalks, thinly sliced on the diagonal (about 4 cups), plus celery leaves (optional), to serve

Kosher salt

¼ cup grapeseed or other neutral oil

1 pound strip steak, trimmed of fat and silver skin, thinly sliced crosswise, slices stacked and cut against the grain into matchsticks

2-inch piece fresh ginger, peeled and cut into matchsticks

2 to 3 teaspoons Sichuan peppercorns, finely ground

2 tablespoons chili-bean sauce (toban djan) or chili-garlic sauce

2 tablespoons low-sodium soy sauce

2 teaspoons Chinese black vinegar or unseasoned rice vinegar

Chili oil, to serve (optional)

In a colander set over a bowl or sink, toss the sliced celery with ¼ teaspoon salt; let stand for about 10 minutes. Using your hands, squeeze the celery to remove excess moisture; set aside.

In a 12-inch skillet over medium-high, heat the oil until barely smoking. Add the beef in an even layer and cook, stirring occasionally, until all the liquid from the beef has cooked off and the meat is well browned, 6 to 9 minutes. Add the celery and ginger; cook, stirring often, until the celery is tender-crisp, about 3 minutes. Add the Sichuan pepper, chili-bean sauce, soy sauce and vinegar, then cook, stirring, until fragrant, about 1 minute.

Off heat, taste and season with salt. Transfer to a serving dish and sprinkle with celery leaves (if using) and drizzle with chili oil.

STIR-FRIED BEEF WITH FRESH HERBS

Start to finish: 20 minutes

Servings: 4

This quick and simple stir-fry is our adaptation of a recipe from "Cooking South of the Clouds" by Georgia Freedman. The dish is from southern Yunnan province in China, an area along the border with Myanmar and Laos. Freedman calls for fiery Thai chiles, but we opt for milder Fresnos or jalapeños. Serve with rice or spoon it into lettuce cups.

2 tablespoons soy sauce

1½ teaspoons finely grated fresh ginger

1 teaspoon cornstarch

¼ teaspoon white sugar

2 teaspoons grapeseed or other neutral oil

1 pound 80 to 85 percent lean ground beef

3 Fresno or jalapeño chilies, stemmed, seeded and finely chopped

1½ cups lightly packed fresh mint, roughly chopped

¾ cup lightly packed cilantro leaves, roughly chopped

In a small bowl, whisk together the soy sauce, ginger, cornstarch and sugar. Set aside. In a 12-inch nonstick skillet over medium, heat the oil until shimmering. Add the beef and cook, stirring and breaking up the meat, until mostly browned but some pink still remains, 3 to 4 minutes.

Add the chilies and soy sauce mixture, then cook until no pink remains, 1 to 2 minutes. Remove from the heat and stir in the mint and cilantro.

275

Soy Sauce Primer

Soy sauce has been around for a millennium. Originally used as a preservative, it was mostly homebrewed until the 16th century. It's traditionally made with a cultured blend of soybeans, roasted wheat and saltwater. After a lengthy fermentation (typically between four months and a year), the mixture is filtered and pasteurized. Synthetic soy sauces—made from hydrolyzed vegetable protein, hydrochloric acid, corn syrup and caramel color—can be produced in days or weeks.

Perhaps the best way to subdivide soy sauce is by country of origin. Though the condiment is produced in Vietnam, Korea, Indonesia and beyond, most varieties are from Japan and China. Japanese soy sauce (shoyu) tends to be lighter in viscosity and less salty than Chinese soy sauce (jiangyou). Japanese brands are also typically made with more wheat, which gives them a sweeter, tangier taste than their Chinese counterparts.

Soy sauce is as multifarious as oil and vinegar. Whatever variety you buy, check the label. Look for the phrase "naturally brewed" or "fermented." Soybeans, wheat, salt and water should take the lead in the ingredient list. This guide to some of the most common soy sauces should help.

Chinese light soy sauce (sheng chou) is made from the first pressing of the soybean mixture. It has lighter color and body than its dark counterpart, so won't discolor food. Sheng chou is the most commonly used soy sauce in Chinese cuisine and sometimes is labeled "superior" or "thin soy sauce." Light soy sauce is not to be mistaken with "lite" or low-sodium soy sauce.

Chinese dark soy sauce (lao chou), the product of later pressings, is denser, sweeter and—obviously—darker than sheng chou. Lao chou is used in braising to give color to dishes. This technique is sometimes called red-cooking. Light and dark soy sauces are often combined in Chinese cooking for balanced flavor and color.

Japanese dark soy sauce (koikuchi shoyu) has a deeper color, more balanced flavor and fuller body than its light variant. It is made with soy, wheat, salt and water, and is used in generous amounts as a seasoning and in dipping sauces, as well as for basting, marinating and simmering. This is the default in Japanese cooking; if a Japanese brand doesn't specify which type of soy sauce it is, it's koikuchi.

Japanese light soy sauce (usukuchi shoyu) is saltier than koikuchi, but it's lighter in color and thinner in body. It is usually used as seasoning in dishes where the dark color of regular soy sauce is not desirable

Tamari is made with little to no wheat and, as a result, has a strong soy flavor. The Japanese product—some would argue it's not a soy sauce at all—is more viscous and darker than koikuchi. It's often used in dipping sauces and for basting. If you are avoiding gluten, make sure the tamari's label reads "gluten-free" and check the ingredient list.

Sweet soy sauce (kecap manis) is dark, syrupy, sweet and Indonesian in origin. Flavored with palm sugar, garlic and spices (star anise, galangal and ginger), it is used liberally in Indonesia for marinating, in noodle dishes and stir-fries, as well as for the base for dipping sauces.

STIR-FRIED MASALA-SPICED PORK WITH PEAS

Start to finish: 40 minutes

Servings: 4

This stir-fry was inspired by a dish called pork ularthiyathu from the state of Kerala in southwestern India. Traditional recipes slowly braise the meat, then "dry-fry" it with aromatics until dark, rich and intensely flavored. We make a weeknight-friendly version by stir-frying chunks of boneless pork loin chops with sliced onion and select spices. Peas add pops of color and sweetness. For balance and contrast in texture, we make a tangy onion and fresh chili salad and pile it onto the stir-fry just before serving. Serve steamed basmati rice alongside.

1 large yellow onion, halved and thinly sliced

2 serrano chilies, stemmed and sliced into thin rings

2 tablespoons white vinegar

Kosher salt and ground black pepper

4 tablespoons grapeseed or other neutral oil, divided

1 tablespoon yellow mustard seeds

4 medium garlic cloves, finely grated

1 tablespoon finely grated fresh ginger

2 teaspoons garam masala

1½ pounds boneless pork loin chops, cut into ½- to ¾-inch chunks

½ cup frozen peas

¼ cup lightly packed fresh cilantro

In a small bowl, stir together a quarter of the onion, half of the chilies, the vinegar and ⅛ teaspoon salt. In a 12-inch skillet over medium-high, heat 3 tablespoons oil until shimmering. Add the remaining onion, the mustard seeds and ¼ teaspoon salt; cook, stirring, until lightly browned, 4 to 5 minutes. Add the remaining chili, the garlic, ginger and garam masala; cook, stirring, until fragrant, about 1 minute.

Push the mixture to the perimeter of the pan; add the remaining 1 tablespoon oil to the clearing. Add the pork in an even layer and sprinkle with ½ teaspoon each salt and pepper. Cook without stirring until browned on the bottom,

about 3 minutes. Stir to combine with the onion; cook, scraping up any browned bits, until the pork is browned all over, 4 to 5 minutes. Add the peas and ¼ cup water; cook, stirring, until the pork is lightly glazed, about 1 minute. Taste and season with salt and pepper. Transfer to a serving dish and top with the reserved onion mixture and cilantro.

SWEET-AND-SOUR STIR-FRIED PORK WITH PINEAPPLE

Start to finish: 30 minutes

Servings: 4

Sweet-and-sour pork with pineapple is a Cantonese classic called gu lao rou. The American takeout version of the dish typically is a greasy, gloppy affair that downplays the pork, pineapple and vegetables in favor of a cloying, candy-like sauce. Our riff skips the deep-frying of the meat, moderates the sugariness and ratchets up the flavor of fresh ginger and chilies. The result is a stir-fry that's lighter, brighter and fresher but maintains that irresistible sweet-sour profile. Serve with steamed jasmine rice.

In a 12-inch nonstick skillet over medium-high, heat the oil until shimmering. Add the pork in an even layer and cook, stirring only once or twice, until the pork is lightly browned, 4 to 5 minutes. Add the bell pepper and cook, stirring occasionally, until the pepper is lightly browned, 4 to 5 minutes. Add the pineapple, chilies and ginger, then cook, stirring occasionally, until the pineapple begins to brown, 2 to 3 minutes.

Stir in the vinegar, remaining 2 tablespoons soy sauce and remaining 1 tablespoon sugar. Cook, stirring often, until the meat and vegetables are lightly coated with the sauce, 1 to 2 minutes.

Off heat, taste and season with additional soy sauce and vinegar. Transfer to a serving dish and sprinkle with the scallions.

1½ pounds boneless pork shoulder, trimmed, cut into 2-inch-wide strips and thinly sliced

3 tablespoons soy sauce, divided, plus more if needed

½ teaspoon plus 1 tablespoon white sugar, divided

1 tablespoon cornstarch

3 tablespoons grapeseed or other neutral oil

1 medium red bell pepper, stemmed, seeded and chopped

1 cup chopped fresh pineapple (½-inch chunks)

2 or 3 serrano chilies, stemmed, seeded and thinly sliced on the diagonal

1-inch piece fresh ginger, peeled and cut into matchsticks (about 3 tablespoons)

⅓ cup unseasoned rice vinegar, plus more if needed

3 scallions, thinly sliced on the diagonal

In a medium bowl, combine the pork, 1 tablespoon of the soy sauce, ½ teaspoon of the sugar and the cornstarch; stir until the pork is evenly coated.

SESAME STIR-FRIED KIMCHI PORK

Start to finish: 30 minutes

Servings: 6

Pork tenderloin and kimchi headline this stir-fry, but fresh shiitake mushrooms and a full bunch of scallions add to its umami-rich appeal. For a meatless alternative, substitute a 14-ounce container of extra-firm tofu, drained and cut into 1-inch cubes.

1-pound pork tenderloin, trimmed of silver skin

2½ cups well-drained napa cabbage kimchi, roughly chopped, plus 2 tablespoons kimchi juice, divided

2½ tablespoons soy sauce, divided

Kosher salt and ground black pepper

3 tablespoons grapeseed or other neutral oil, divided

8 ounces shiitake mushrooms, stems discarded, caps sliced ¼ inch thick

3 medium garlic cloves, thinly sliced

3 tablespoons mirin

1 tablespoon toasted sesame oil

2 tablespoons sesame seeds, toasted, divided

1 bunch scallions, thinly sliced, divided

Cut the tenderloin in half lengthwise, then slice each half crosswise about ¼ inch thick. In a medium bowl, toss the pork with 1 tablespoon of the kimchi juice, 1 tablespoon of the soy sauce and ½ teaspoon pepper.

In a 12-inch skillet over high, heat 1 tablespoon of the grapeseed oil until barely smoking. Swirl to coat the pan, then add the pork and cook, stirring, until no longer pink, about 4 minutes. Transfer to a clean bowl.

In the same pan over medium-high, heat 1 tablespoon of the remaining oil until barely smoking. Add the mushrooms and ½ teaspoon of salt. Cook, stirring occasionally, until the liquid released by the mushrooms has mostly evaporated, about 5 minutes.

Stir in the remaining 1 tablespoon oil and the garlic and cook until fragrant, about 1 minute. Return the pork to the pan with any accumulated juices and cook until the juices evaporate, 30 to 60 seconds.

Add the kimchi, mirin, the remaining 1 tablespoon kimchi juice and the remaining 1½ tablespoons soy sauce. Reduce to medium and cook, stirring and scraping up any browned bits, until the kimchi is heated through, about 3 minutes. Stir in the sesame oil, half of the sesame seeds and half of the scallions. Transfer to a platter and sprinkle with the remaining scallions and sesame seeds.

STIR-FRIED PORK AND SWEET PEPPERS WITH PEANUTS

Start to finish: 45 minutes

Servings: 4 to 6

The flavors in this colorful stir-fry are a fantastic combination of savory, sweet, tangy, garlicky, spicy and nutty. Briefly marinating the sliced tenderloin means the meat browns beautifully in the skillet and also adds flavor and moisture to an otherwise lean and mild cut. Balsamic vinegar may seem like an odd ingredient in a stir-fry, but it mimics the subtle sweetness, moderate acidity and maltiness of Chinese black vinegar and probably already is in your pantry. Serve with steamed white rice.

1¼-pound pork tenderloin, trimmed of silver skin and sliced crosswise ⅛ to ¼ inch thick

3 tablespoons grapeseed or other neutral oil, divided

3 tablespoons dry sherry, divided

2 tablespoons soy sauce, divided

3 garlic cloves, 1 minced, 2 thinly sliced

1 tablespoon cornstarch

2 to 3 tablespoons chili-garlic sauce

1½ tablespoons balsamic vinegar

2 medium red, yellow or orange bell peppers, stemmed, seeded and cut into 1- to 1½-inch pieces

1 bunch scallions, whites thinly sliced, greens cut into 1½-inch lengths, reserved separately

½ cup roasted peanuts, roughly chopped

In a medium bowl, stir together the pork, 1 tablespoon of the oil, 1 tablespoon of the sherry, 1 tablespoon of the soy sauce, the minced garlic and the cornstarch. Let stand for about 15 minutes. Meanwhile, in a small bowl, stir together the remaining 2 tablespoons sherry, remaining 1 tablespoon soy sauce, chili-garlic sauce and vinegar.

In a 12-inch nonstick skillet over medium-high, heat another 1 tablespoon oil until barely smoking. Add the pork in an even layer and cook, stirring once or twice, until well browned, 4 to 5 minutes; transfer to a plate. Add the remaining 1 tablespoon oil to the skillet and heat until shimmering. Add the bell peppers and cook, stirring occasionally, until tender-crisp, 6 to 7 minutes. Add the scallion whites and sliced garlic; cook, stirring, until

fragrant, 30 to 60 seconds. Add the pork and accumulated juices, sauce mixture and scallion greens; cook, stirring, until the sauce is lightly thickened, 30 to 60 seconds. Off heat, stir in half the peanuts. Transfer to a serving dish and sprinkle with the remaining peanuts.

THAI STIR-FRIED PORK WITH BASIL, CHILIES AND GARLIC

Start to finish: 30 minutes

Servings: 4

Pad kraprao, meaning "fried holy basil," is a fragrant, flavor-packed Thai staple. We enjoyed a handful of iterations in Bangkok, where Thai cooks taught us to balance the recipe's medley of bold, punchy ingredients. Despite the dish's name, the basil isn't actually fried, but wilted into the mix at the very end of cooking. What is stir-fried is a zingy chili-garlic paste, followed by finely chopped or ground meat, and the finisher is a salty-sweet, slightly funky mixture of oyster, soy and fish sauces. Tiny yet assertively spicy Thai bird chilies are traditionally used, but we found easier-to-source Fresnos offered adequate heat and bright, fruity notes. In Thailand, the dish often is incendiary. For our version, we suggest seeding the chilies to start, but if you love a fiery kick, keep the seeds in a few or all of them. Holy basil, with leaves that are vaguely heart-shaped, has a peppery, menthol-like bite and is more savory than sweet Italian basil. If you don't have access to it, either Thai or Italian basil works wonderfully, but you'll need to use 50 percent more. A fried egg tops it all off, the runny yolk adding creaminess while the crisp edges provide crunch. Serve with steamed jasmine rice, perfect for soaking up the delicious garlicky sauce.

7 medium garlic cloves, smashed and peeled

4 or 5 Fresno chilies, stemmed, seeded and roughly chopped (see headnote)

1 tablespoon oyster sauce

1 tablespoon soy sauce

1 tablespoon fish sauce

1 tablespoon packed light brown sugar

6 tablespoons grapeseed or other neutral oil, divided

4 large eggs

1 pound ground pork

2 cups (1 ounce) lightly packed fresh holy basil or 3 cups (1½ ounces) lightly packed Thai or Italian basil, torn (see headnote)

Steamed jasmine rice, to serve

In a food processor, combine the garlic and chilies. Pulse until finely chopped, with some slightly larger pieces remaining, 8 to 10 pulses. In a small bowl, whisk together the oyster sauce, soy sauce, fish sauce, sugar and ½ cup water. Set both the garlic-chili mixture and the sauce mixture near the stove.

In a 12- to 14-inch wok over medium-high, heat 2 tablespoons of the oil until barely smoking. Reduce to medium, then crack 2 eggs into the center of the wok, each in a different spot. Use a silicone spatula to gently push the edges of the egg whites toward the yolks to try to keep the eggs separate (it's fine if the whites touch in spots). Cook, occasionally spooning some of the hot oil over them, until the whites are fully set and the edges are crisp and browned, 3 to 4 minutes. Using a thin metal spatula, transfer the eggs to a paper towel-lined plate. Using 2 tablespoons of the remaining oil, cook the remaining eggs the same way; set the eggs aside. Wipe out the wok.

Return the wok to medium-high and heat the remaining 2 tablespoons oil until barely smoking. Add the garlic-chili mixture and cook, stirring, until fragrant and lightly

browned, 1 to 2 minutes. Add the pork and cook, stirring, until the meat is broken up into mostly small bits, 1 to 2 minutes. Add the sauce mixture and cook, stirring, until the pork is no longer pink and the liquid thickens slightly but remains saucy, about 3 minutes. Off heat, add the basil and stir until just wilted.

Divide the rice and the stir-fry among serving plates and top each portion with an egg.

TO MAKE IN A SKILLET:

Follow the recipe to process the garlic and chilies and combine the sauce mixture. In a 12-inch skillet over medium-high, heat 4 tablespoons of the oil until barely smoking. One at a time, crack the eggs into the skillet, each in a different spot, then use a silicone spatula to gently push the edges of the egg whites toward the yolks to try to keep the eggs separate (it's fine if the whites touch in spots). Cook, occasionally spooning some of the hot oil over, until the whites are fully set and the edges are crisp and browned, 3 to 4 minutes. Using a thin metal spatula, transfer the eggs to a paper towel-lined plate; set aside. Wipe out the skillet, return it to medium-high and heat the remaining 2 tablespoons oil until shimmering. Add the garlic-chili mixture and cook, stirring, until fragrant and lightly browned, 45 to 60 seconds. Add the pork and cook, stirring, until broken up into mostly small bits, 1 to 2 minutes. Add the sauce mixture and cook, stirring, until the pork is no longer pink and the liquid thickens slightly but remains saucy, about 3 minutes. Off heat, add the basil and stir until just wilted. Serve as directed.

Buying and Caring for Your Wok

A wok's thin metal composition, gently curved sides and broad surface area make it ideal for rapid heating and quick searing; foods won't stew in their own juices. Here are our top tips for buying and caring for one.

When shopping for a wok, look for a flat-bottomed model, which will sit flat on a conventional burner and heat evenly (round-bottomed woks, designed for a different style of burner, require a stabilizing ring to use on Western stoves and will never heat quite as well). We prefer the quick heating and light weight of carbon-steel pans.

A roughly 14-inch diameter is ideal because it is large enough to stir-fry up to four servings at once, but won't require a ton of storage space. Look for a wok with a heat-safe handle and a helper handle on the opposite side; a full wok can be unwieldy without it.

While you're shopping for a wok, be sure to pick up a wok spatula (or wok shovel), which is designed to fit the wok's curvature. If you don't have one, try a flexible fish spatula and tongs.

We like carbon-steel woks because they're inexpensive, rugged and can develop a natural nonstick coating without the worrying chemicals of typical nonstick surfaces. To get that surface, carbon-steel woks must be seasoned before use.

INITIAL SEASONING

Scrub the wok or skillet with hot soapy water to remove any protective layer of oil or wax coating the surface, then dry and set over medium heat. Use a paper towel held with tongs to spread 1 tablespoon vegetable oil evenly over the interior of the pan. Leave on the heat until it smokes, then hold it at that stage for 1 minute. Use a new paper towel held with tongs to wipe the pan clean. Repeat the process until the pan develops a golden-brown patina, three to five repetitions. The pan may look blotchy, but will even out with use.

DAILY USE

Set the pan over medium heat and add 1 teaspoon of vegetable oil. Use a paper towel held with tongs to wipe the oil evenly over the pan. When the oil smokes, hold it at that stage for 1 minute, then wipe clean with a new paper towel held with tongs. Allow the pan to cool for 3 to 5 minutes, then

add the oil or butter for cooking. Don't skip the cooling step or the pan will be too hot and burn the cooking fat.

DAILY CARE

Treat your seasoned pan well. Never plunge a hot carbon-steel pan into cold water; the thermal shock can crack the pan. And avoid soap; it will dissolve the seasoning. After cooking, clean the pan with a wet sponge (and a little coarse salt mixed with oil if needed to scrub away stubborn bits), dry it well and wipe lightly with oil before storing.

STIR-FRIED CHILI SHRIMP

Start to finish: 30 minutes

Servings: 4

Singaporean chili crab inspired this fast, pantry-friendly shrimp stir-fry. Aside from deveining the shrimp and peeling the ginger, the only knifework needed is slicing the onion (and the scallion or cilantro, if you're using them). You can substitute shrimp that are slightly smaller or larger, but be sure to adjust the cooking time accordingly. Serve with steamed jasmine rice.

¼ cup plus 2 tablespoons ketchup

¼ cup plus 2 tablespoons unseasoned rice vinegar

1½ tablespoons soy sauce OR fish sauce

1½ tablespoons chili-garlic sauce OR Sriracha

1 teaspoon white sugar

1½ pounds extra-large shrimp (21/25 per pound), peeled, deveined and patted dry

Kosher salt and ground black pepper

3 tablespoons grapeseed or other neutral oil, divided

½ medium red onion, thinly sliced
OR 2 large shallots, halved and thinly sliced

2 tablespoons finely grated fresh ginger
OR 4 garlic cloves, thinly sliced

In a small bowl, stir together the ketchup, vinegar, soy sauce, chili-garlic sauce and sugar; set aside. In a large bowl, toss the shrimp with ½ teaspoon salt and ¼ teaspoon pepper.

In a 12-inch nonstick skillet over medium-high, heat 1 tablespoon oil until barely smoking. Add half the shrimp in an even layer and cook without stirring until deep golden brown on the bottoms, about 2 minutes. Stir and cook until opaque on both sides, another 20 to 30 seconds. Transfer to a plate. Using 1 tablespoon of the remaining oil, cook the remaining shrimp in the same way.

To the now-empty skillet over medium-high, add the remaining 1 tablespoon oil, the onion and ginger; stir to combine. Cover and cook, stirring occasionally, until the onion begins to brown, about 1 minute. Add the ketchup mixture and cook, scraping up any browned bits, until the mixture is slightly thickened, about 30 seconds. Add ½ cup water and cook, stirring often, until a spatula drawn through the sauce leaves a trail, about 2 minutes.

Add the shrimp and accumulated juices to the skillet; stir to combine. Cover, remove from the heat and let stand until the shrimp are heated through, 1 to 2 minutes.

Optional garnish: Lime wedges **OR** sliced scallions **OR** chopped fresh cilantro **OR** a combination

TRINIDAD PEPPER SHRIMP

Start to finish: 30 minutes

Servings: 4

Trinidad pepper shrimp, a stir-fry that pairs fruity habanero chili with ginger and soy sauce, is a result of the Chinese influence on the local cuisine. Chinese immigrants began to arrive in Trinidad in the early 19th century. Ketchup may be an unexpected ingredient, but it is traditional and gives the sauce a welcome sweetness and glaze-like consistency. If you like, serve with lime wedges and steamed rice.

1½ pounds extra-large (21/25 per pound) shrimp, peeled, deveined and patted dry

Kosher salt and ground black pepper

3 tablespoons grapeseed or other neutral oil, divided

1 tablespoon finely grated fresh ginger

2 teaspoons soy sauce, divided

1 medium carrot, peeled and thinly sliced on the diagonal

½ medium red onion, sliced ½ inch thick

1 poblano chili, stemmed, seeded and chopped into ½-inch pieces

8 medium garlic cloves, minced

1 habanero chili, stemmed, seeded and minced

⅓ cup ketchup

Chopped fresh cilantro or sliced scallions, to serve

Season the shrimp with salt and pepper. In a 12-inch nonstick skillet over medium-high, heat 1 tablespoon of oil until barely smoking. Add half the shrimp in a single layer and cook, without stirring, until golden brown, about 45 seconds. Stir and cook until pink and opaque on all sides, another 20 to 30 seconds. Transfer to a bowl. Repeat with 1 tablespoon of the remaining oil and the remaining shrimp. Add the ginger and 1 teaspoon soy sauce to the shrimp in the bowl; toss to combine.

In the same skillet, heat the remaining 1 tablespoon oil over medium-high until barely smoking. Add the carrot and onion and cook, stirring once or twice, until lightly charred, 2 to 3 minutes. Add the poblano, garlic and habanero, then cook, stirring constantly, until fragrant, about 30 seconds. Add ½ cup water, the remaining 1 teaspoon soy sauce and the ketchup. Cook over medium-high, stirring occasionally, until the sauce is thick enough that a spoon leaves a trail when drawn through it, 2 to 4 minutes.

Remove the skillet from the heat. Stir in the shrimp and any accumulated juices, cover and let stand until the shrimp are opaque throughout, 2 to 4 minutes. Taste and season with salt and pepper. Serve sprinkled with cilantro.

THAI-STYLE VEGETABLE STIR-FRY WITH GARLIC AND BLACK PEPPER

Start to finish: 30 minutes
Servings: 4

In the Thai kitchen, kratiem prik Thai is an aromatic, flavor-packed paste of garlic, black pepper and cilantro root. It often is used to season meat and seafood, but in this recipe we combine the ingredients (we substitute cilantro stems for hard-to-find roots) to add punch to a simple vegetable stir-fry. Napa cabbage and mushrooms provide meaty flavor, while snow peas (or bell peppers) offer color, sweetness and crunch. If you don't have fish sauce or want to make the dish vegetarian, use an equal amount of low-sodium soy sauce.

1½ tablespoons fish sauce

2 teaspoons packed light brown sugar

Kosher salt and ground black pepper

3 tablespoons grapeseed or other neutral oil

4 medium garlic cloves, minced

2 tablespoons minced cilantro stems, plus ¼ cup lightly packed leaves, roughly chopped

14-ounce head napa cabbage, halved lengthwise, bottom 1 inch trimmed, cut crosswise into ½-inch-wide pieces (about 7 cups)

4 ounces shiitake mushrooms, stemmed and thinly sliced OR cremini mushrooms, thinly sliced

4 ounces snow peas, trimmed OR 1 red bell pepper, stemmed, seeded and thinly sliced

In a small bowl, stir together the fish sauce, sugar and 1 teaspoon pepper. Whisk until the sugar dissolves, then set aside. In a 12-inch nonstick skillet over medium-high, cook the oil, garlic and cilantro stems, stirring occasionally, until golden brown, 2 to 4 minutes. Add the cabbage, mushrooms and peas, then cook, stirring occasionally, until the vegetables begin to char and soften, 4 to 6 minutes.

Working quickly, add the fish sauce mixture. Immediately cover the pan, reduce to medium and cook, occasionally shaking the pan without lifting the lid, for 2 minutes. Uncover and cook, stirring often, until the skillet is dry, about 2 minutes. Taste and season with salt and pepper. Transfer to a serving dish and sprinkle with the cilantro leaves.

Optional garnish: Scallions thinly sliced on the diagonal OR Sriracha sauce OR both

GLAZED SPICY-SWEET STIR-FRIED VEGETABLES

Start to finish: 40 minutes
Servings: 4

This stir-fry of mixed vegetables, all coated in a spicy-sweet gochujang glaze, takes inspiration from Eric Kim, author of "Korean American." We take a cue from Kim and salt the zucchini before cooking to expel excess liquid, resulting in well-seasoned squash with a firm, meaty bite. We've added carrots for sweetness and crunch and shiitake mushrooms for their umami-richness, as well as baby bok choy, which

brings fresh, mildly bitter notes. The resulting vegetable melange, filled with color and texture, is cooked in mellow, garlic-infused oil, then finished with a sticky sauce of bold gochujang balanced by tart vinegar, salty soy sauce and brown sugar—a delicious, weeknight-easy dinner, completed simply by a bowl of rice.

1 medium (8-ounce) zucchini, halved lengthwise and cut on the diagonal into 1½-inch pieces

Kosher salt and ground black pepper

2 tablespoons gochujang

2 tablespoons soy sauce

4 teaspoons lightly packed light or dark brown sugar

1 tablespoon unseasoned rice vinegar

¼ cup grapeseed or other neutral oil

3 medium garlic cloves, smashed and peeled

4 ounces shiitake mushrooms, stemmed, caps halved

4 ounces baby bok choy, trimmed, halved and sliced lengthwise about ½ inch thick

1 medium carrot, peeled, halved lengthwise and thinly sliced on the diagonal

2 teaspoons sesame seeds, toasted

In a medium bowl, rub the zucchini with 1 teaspoon salt; let stand for 15 minutes. Squeeze the zucchini to remove excess liquid, then pat dry with a kitchen towel.

Meanwhile, in a small bowl, whisk together the gochujang, soy sauce, sugar, vinegar and ¼ teaspoon pepper.

In a 12-inch skillet, combine the oil and garlic. Cook over medium-high, stirring and flipping the garlic, until golden, 2 to 3 minutes. Remove and reserve the garlic; heat the oil until barely smoking. Add the zucchini in an even layer and cook, stirring once or twice, until well browned, 5 to 7 minutes. Add the mushrooms, bok choy, carrot and toasted garlic. Cook, stirring often, until wilted, about 3 minutes. Add the gochujang mixture; cook, stirring, until the vegetables are tender-crisp and glazed, 1 to 2 minutes. Off heat, taste and season with salt and pepper. Serve sprinkled with the sesame seeds.

SICHUAN DRY-FRIED CAULIFLOWER

Start to finish: 25 minutes
Servings: 4

The Mandarin term for dry-frying, sometimes called dry-searing, is gan bian. It's essentially a two-stage cooking technique. A protein or vegetable first is parcooked in oil until the surfaces are browned and any moisture on the exterior has evaporated. The food then is stir-fried with aromatics and seasonings that reduce and cling to the browned surfaces. The resulting dish is more or less sauce-free. Green beans are the vegetable most often cooked in this manner, but in our version we use cauliflower. Sichuan peppercorns provide their resinous, tongue-tingling heat, while optional árbol chilies add a more direct spiciness. Serve with white or brown rice.

2-pound head cauliflower, trimmed

¼ cup grapeseed or other neutral oil

1 tablespoon Sichuan peppercorns

6 medium garlic cloves, smashed and peeled

3 dried árbol chilies, broken in half (optional)

2 tablespoons soy sauce

1 tablespoon dry sherry

1 teaspoon white sugar

4 scallions, cut into 1-inch lengths

1 tablespoon finely grated fresh ginger

Chili oil, to serve

Using a chef's knife, cut the cauliflower in half top to bottom. Set each half flat side down and cut parallel with the stem into rough ¼-inch slices; the florets will break up a bit as you cut, especially at the ends.

In a 12-inch skillet over medium, heat the oil until shimmering. Add the cauliflower in an even layer and cook without stirring until browned, about 6 minutes. Sprinkle in the Sichuan peppercorns and cook, stirring about every minute or so, until the cauliflower is spotty brown all over, 5 to 7 minutes.

Add the garlic and árbol chilies (if using), then cook, stirring often, until fragrant, about 1 minute. Stir in the soy sauce, sherry and sugar. Cook until the skillet is mostly dry, about 1 minute. Stir in the scallions and ginger, then continue to cook until the scallions are slightly wilted, about another 1 minute. Transfer to a serving dish and serve with chili oil for drizzling.

STIR-FRIED BROCCOLI WITH SICHUAN PEPPERCORNS

Start to finish: 30 minutes
Servings: 4

Restaurants and even some homes in China use super-charged wok burners to get the high heat that quickly renders raw vegetables tender on the outside, crisp on the inside. We mix oil and water for a skillet-friendly method. The water begins the cooking as it steams off, leaving the oil behind to finish—and lightly brown—the broccoli. We season the dish with Sichuan peppercorns, which don't provide heat so much as a pleasant resinous flavor and an intriguing tingling sensation on your lips and tongue. To enhance their flavor and aroma, we toasted the peppercorns over medium heat for about 2 minutes, let them cool, then ground them to a fine powder in a spice grinder.

3 tablespoons unseasoned rice vinegar, divided

1½ tablespoons soy sauce

1 teaspoon white sugar

Kosher salt

3 medium garlic cloves, finely grated

1½ teaspoons finely grated fresh ginger

¼ to ½ teaspoon red pepper flakes

2 scallions, white parts minced, green parts thinly sliced on the diagonal, reserved separately

1¼ pounds broccoli, florets cut into 1-inch pieces, stems peeled and sliced ¼ inch thick

3 tablespoons peanut oil, divided

2 teaspoons toasted sesame oil

½ to 1 teaspoon Sichuan peppercorns, toasted and finely ground

In a small bowl, stir together ⅓ cup water, 2 tablespoons vinegar, the soy sauce and sugar. In another small bowl, combine the garlic, ginger, pepper flakes and minced scallions. Set both bowls aside.

In a 12-inch skillet, combine 2 tablespoons water and ¼ teaspoon salt; stir until the salt dissolves. Add the peanut oil and broccoli, then cover, set the pan over medium-high and cook for 1 minute; the water should reach a simmer. Uncover and cook, stirring occasionally, until the broccoli is tender-crisp and browned in spots, 8 to 10 minutes. Transfer to a large plate.

287

Return the skillet to medium-high, add the remaining 1 tablespoon peanut oil and the garlic-ginger mixture. Cook, stirring, until fragrant, 10 to 15 seconds. Add the soy sauce mixture and simmer, stirring and scraping up any browned bits, until slightly reduced, 2 to 3 minutes. Return the broccoli to the skillet and stir to coat.

Off heat, stir in the sesame oil, remaining 1 tablespoon vinegar and ½ teaspoon ground Sichuan pepper. Taste and season with more Sichuan pepper, if desired. Serve sprinkled with the sliced scallion greens.

HOT-AND-SOUR STIR-FRIED POTATOES

Start to finish: 30 minutes
Servings: 4

We don't often think to stir-fry potatoes, but that's how they're cooked in the classic Sichuan dish called tudou si. Cut into matchsticks, the potatoes are soaked to remove some of their starch, then are stir-fried until tender but with just a hint of crispness at the core, not until totally yielding in texture. We flavor the potatoes with finely ground, tongue-tingling Sichuan peppercorns (pulverize them in an electric spice grinder), dried chilies for supplemental

heat and Chinese black vinegar (also known as Chinkiang vinegar; balsamic vinegar is a reasonably good substitute) to add tanginess. The potatoes should be cut into ⅛-inch matchsticks, though the length of the sticks isn't so important. We suggest using the julienne blade on a mandoline or, if you're up for some knife work, do the prep by hand with a chef's knife. Another option is to get a slicing assist from the mandoline or a food processor fitted with the ⅛-inch slicing disk, then cut the slices, stacked a few high, into matchsticks with a knife.

1 pound medium (2 to 2½ inches in diameter) red OR Yukon Gold potatoes, unpeeled, cut into matchsticks (see headnote)

2 tablespoons soy sauce

1 tablespoon toasted sesame oil

1 tablespoon Chinese black vinegar OR balsamic vinegar

½ teaspoon white sugar

2 tablespoons grapeseed or other neutral oil

2 medium garlic cloves, minced

1 to 2 teaspoons Sichuan peppercorns, finely ground

4 dried árbol chiles, broken in half OR ½ teaspoon red pepper flakes

2 scallions, thinly sliced on the diagonal

In a large bowl, cover the potatoes with 6 cups water. Swish them around and let the potatoes soak for 10 to 15 minutes to remove excess starch. Meanwhile, in a small bowl, stir together the soy sauce, sesame oil, vinegar and sugar; set aside.

Drain the potatoes in a colander and rinse well under running cold water. Working in batches if needed, transfer to a clean kitchen towel and thoroughly wring dry.

In a 12-inch nonstick skillet over medium-high, heat the neutral oil until shimmering. Add the potatoes and cook, stirring occasionally, until lightly browned and tender-crisp, 5 to 6 minutes. Add the garlic, Sichuan pepper and chilies, then cook, stirring, until fragrant, 30 to 60 seconds. Add the soy sauce mixture and cook, tossing, until the liquid reduces to a light glaze and the potatoes are tender with just a little crispness at the center, 1 to 1½ minutes. Transfer to a serving dish and sprinkle with the scallions.

STIR-FRIED CUMIN TOFU

Start to finish: 30 minutes, plus marinating
Servings: 4

Xinjiang cumin lamb, a classic stir-fry that originated in the Xinjiang region of northwestern China, pairs lamb or sometimes beef with whole cumin seeds and chilies. We swap the meat for protein-rich tofu, marinating it with soy sauce and vinegar before searing it in a hot pan. Chinese black vinegar makes a great addition to the marinade, though easier-to-find balsamic makes a good substitute, as it mimics the sweet-tart, lightly syrupy character of Chinese black vinegar.

3 tablespoons soy sauce, divided

2 tablespoons balsamic vinegar, divided

Kosher salt and ground black pepper

14-ounce container firm OR extra-firm tofu, drained, patted dry, halved lengthwise, then cut crosswise into ½-inch-thick planks

¼ cup cornstarch

3 tablespoons grapeseed or other neutral oil, divided

1 medium yellow onion, halved and thinly sliced

4 teaspoons cumin seeds, lightly crushed OR 2 teaspoons ground cumin

4 medium garlic cloves, minced

½ teaspoon red pepper flakes

In a pie plate or shallow bowl, stir together 1 tablespoon of the soy sauce, 1 tablespoon of the vinegar and ½ teaspoon each salt and black pepper. Add the tofu and toss to coat. Let stand at room temperature for at least 15 minutes or up to 1 hour. Pat the tofu dry in the pie plate. Sprinkle with the cornstarch and toss to coat, gently pressing to adhere.

In a 12-inch nonstick skillet over medium-high, heat 2 tablespoons of the oil until shimmering. Add the tofu, distributing it in an even layer, and cook until golden brown and crisp on the bottom, 3 to 4 minutes. Flip the tofu and cook until golden brown on the second sides, another 3 to 4 minutes. Transfer to a paper towel-lined plate; set aside. Wipe out the skillet.

In the same skillet over medium-high, heat the remaining 1 tablespoon oil until barely smoking. Add the onion and cumin; cook, stirring occasionally, until the onion is charred in spots and slightly softened, 3 to 5 minutes. Add the garlic and pepper flakes, then cook, stirring, until fragrant, 30 to 60 seconds. Add the tofu, remaining 2 tablespoons soy sauce, remaining 1 tablespoon vinegar and 2 tablespoons water. Cook, stirring often, until the liquid has evaporated, about 1 minute. Off heat, taste and season with salt and black pepper.

Optional garnish: Scallions, thinly sliced on the diagonal **OR** chili oil **OR** both

CHANGE THE WAY YOU COOK

Three Korean Jangs

Three fermented soy-based sauces known as jangs form the pungent flavor base of Korean cooking. "That is the holy trinity of mother sauces of Korean food," says Hooni Kim, author of "My Korea." "Almost 99 percent of Korean dishes have one or two, or sometimes all three."

Doenjang is a pungent, fermented soybean paste similar to Japanese miso, but stronger and less smooth and sweet. To make it, cooked soybeans are formed into blocks called meju and fermented for up to three months. The meju is combined with a salt solution and again aged in large clay pots called onggi. The solids that sink to the bottom is the doenjang, while the dark, flavorful liquid at the top is **ganjang,** similar to soy sauce.

The third sauce, **gochujang,** is a red paste with a texture and savoriness similar to doenjang but with a spicy chili kick. Meju is mixed with ganjang, sticky rice, salt, malt and chili powder and fermented in the onggi, which are left outside in the sun for at least six months or up to five years. The onggi are porous, which helps foster even more fermentation for deeper flavor.

STIR-FRIED TOFU AND MUSHROOMS WITH LEMON GRASS

Start to finish: 35 minutes

Servings: 4

In this Southeast Asian-inspired stir-fry, we toss mild tofu with two powerhouse ingredients, fish sauce and Sriracha, then brown the cubes in hot oil. When the tofu is out of the pan, we stir-fry meaty mushrooms and add citrusy lemon grass and savory scallions, building layers of contrasting flavors, and finish by tossing everything together. Be sure to pat the tofu dry after cubing it. Wicking away excess moisture means the tofu will better absorb seasonings for bigger, bolder flavor and brown better. Serve the stir-fry with steamed jasmine rice.

3 tablespoons fish sauce

3 teaspoons Sriracha OR chili-garlic sauce, divided

Kosher salt and ground white pepper OR black pepper

14-ounce container extra-firm OR firm tofu, drained, cut into ¾-inch cubes and patted dry

4 tablespoons neutral oil, divided

12 ounces cremini mushrooms, thinly sliced OR shiitake mushrooms (stemmed), thinly sliced OR a combination

2 stalks fresh lemon grass, trimmed to the bottom 6 inches, dry outer layers discarded, minced

1 bunch scallions, thinly sliced, whites and greens reserved separately

In a medium bowl, stir together the fish sauce, 1 teaspoon Sriracha and ½ teaspoon pepper. Add the tofu and toss to coat. In a 12-inch nonstick skillet over medium-high, heat 2 tablespoons oil until barely smoking. Add the tofu, distributing it in an even layer. Cook, stirring, until golden brown on most sides, 3 to 4 minutes. Transfer to a paper towel-lined plate; set aside.

In the same skillet over medium-high, heat the remaining 2 tablespoons oil until barely smoking. Add the mushrooms and cook, stirring occasionally, until tender and lightly browned, about 3 minutes. Add the lemon grass, scallion whites and the remaining 2 teaspoons Sriracha; cook, stirring, until fragrant, about 1 minute. Add the tofu and cook, stirring occasionally, until heated through, about 2 minutes.

Off heat, stir in half of the reserved scallion greens. Taste and season with salt and pepper. Serve sprinkled with the remaining scallion greens.

Optional garnish: Lime wedges OR chopped roasted peanuts OR chopped fresh cilantro OR a combination

PAD THAI WITH SHRIMP

Start to finish: 1 hour

Servings: 4

Across Bangkok, we tasted more than a dozen versions of pad Thai to understand the iconic noodle stir-fry and find a way to adapt the dish to American home kitchens. Suwan Pimtatong, cook at Hot Shoppe Restaurant, showed us how to build umami richness without dried shrimp, a common pad Thai ingredient that isn't easy to find in U.S. supermarkets. Additionally, we were able to achieve nuances of wok hei, the difficult to attain (on a home cooktop) hints of smokiness that come from stir-frying in a wok over a raging-hot fire (see p. 270). The key is to add ingredients in batches to prevent the wok temperature from dropping precipitously. A few pointers for success: A 12- to 14-inch wok is essential, ideally one made of carbon steel that is well seasoned and conducts heat quickly. Use a neutral oil with a high smoke point; grapeseed or safflower is a good choice. Each time oil is heated in the empty wok, be sure it is smoking-hot before adding any ingredients. Use the cooking times as guidelines, don't take them as scripture, as burner output and heat-conduction properties of woks can differ

greatly. Finally, be sure to have all ingredients and equipment, including a serving dish, ready before you head to the stovetop. Once cooking begins, it demands your full attention and is done in minutes.

10 ounces ¼-inch-wide rice noodle sticks

2 tablespoons tamarind pulp

⅓ cup boiling water

2½ tablespoons packed light brown sugar or grated palm sugar

2 tablespoons oyster sauce

2 tablespoons soy sauce

1½ tablespoons fish sauce

1 cup bean sprouts

1 cup lightly packed fresh chives or slender scallions, cut into 1-inch lengths

½ cup roasted peanuts, chopped

4 tablespoons grapeseed or safflower oil (see headnote), divided

12 ounces medium (41/50 per pound) shrimp, peeled (tails removed) and deveined

1 medium shallot, halved and thinly sliced

3 medium garlic cloves, minced

½ to ¾ teaspoon red pepper flakes

2 large eggs, beaten

Lime wedges, to serve

Fresh chilies in vinegar, to serve (optional, recipe p. 293)

Place the noodles in a large bowl and add hot water to cover (the water should feel hot to the touch, but should not be scalding). Let stand, stirring once or twice to separate any strands that are sticking together, for about 30 minutes; the noodles will become pliable but will not fully soften.

Meanwhile, in a small bowl, combine the tamarind pulp and boiling water; stir with a fork to break up the pulp. Cover and let stand for about 30 minutes. Strain the mixture through a fine-mesh sieve set over another small bowl; press on the solids and be sure to scrape the underside of the sieve to collect the pulp that clings; you should have about ¼ cup. Wipe out the small bowl used to hydrate the tamarind, then measure 3 tablespoons of the strained tamarind into it (reserve the remainder for another use). Add the sugar, oyster sauce, soy sauce and fish sauce. Stir until the sugar dissolves; place near the stove.

Drain the noodles in a colander. Shake the colander to remove excess water and set near the stove. In a medium bowl, toss together the bean sprouts, chives and peanuts; also set near the stove.

In a 12- to 14-inch wok over high, heat 1 tablespoon of the oil until smoking, swirling to coat. Add the shrimp and cook, stirring, until just beginning to curl and turn pink, 1 to 2 minutes; the shrimp will not be fully cooked. Transfer to a large plate; set aside. Wipe out the wok.

Return the wok to high and heat 2 tablespoons of the remaining oil until smoking, swirling to coat. Add the shallot, garlic and pepper flakes; cook, stirring, until fragrant and lightly browned, 20 to 30 seconds. Add the eggs (they will immediately puff up) and cook, stirring from the edges inward, until the curds are barely set and shiny, 20 to 30 seconds.

Add half of the noodles. Cook, stirring, tossing and moving the noodles in a circular motion against the sides of the wok while also breaking up the eggs, until the noodles are dry, sizzling and no longer stark white in color, 1 to 1½ minutes. Drizzle the remaining 1 tablespoon of oil down the sides of the wok and add the remaining noodles; cook in the same way until the mixture is once again dry and sizzling.

Pour half of the sauce mixture down the sides of the wok; it should bubble immediately and begin to thicken. Cook, tossing and moving the noodles in a circular motion against the sides of the wok, until the liquid is absorbed, about 30 seconds. Add the remaining sauce mixture and cook in the same way.

Add the shrimp (discard any accumulated juices) and half of the bean sprout mixture. Cook, stirring, until the shrimp are opaque throughout and the sprouts are just wilted, 1 to 2 minutes. Taste the noodles; if they are still too firm, drizzle in water 2 tablespoons at a time and cook, stirring, until the noodles are tender. Toss in the remaining sprout mixture. Transfer to a platter and serve with lime wedges and chilies in vinegar (if using).

PAD THAI WITH TOFU

Cut 8 ounces firm or extra-firm tofu into ½- to ¾-inch cubes. Place in a single layer on a plate lined with a double thickness of paper towels. Cover with additional paper towels, place another plate on top, then set a few cans or jars on top as weights; let stand while you soak the noodles, prepare the tamarind and mix the sauce ingredients. Follow the recipe, substituting the tofu for the shrimp and stir-frying until the tofu is golden brown on all sides, about 3 minutes, setting it aside, then returning it to the wok as with the shrimp.

PAD THAI WITH GROUND PORK

Follow the recipe, omitting the shrimp. When the shallot, garlic and pepper flakes are fragrant and lightly browned, add 8 ounces ground pork; cook, stirring and breaking the pork into small bits, until the meat is lightly browned, 2 to 3 minutes. Make a clearing in the center of the mixture and add the eggs to the clearing, then continue with the recipe.

FRESH CHILIES IN VINEGAR

Start to finish: 10 minutes

Makes about ¼ cup

In a small bowl or glass container, stir together **¼ cup unseasoned rice vinegar, 1 Fresno or serrano chili** (stemmed and sliced into thin rounds) and **a pinch kosher salt.** Cover and set aside until ready to use or refrigerate for up to 3 days.

YAKIUDON WITH PICKLED GINGER

Start to finish: 45 minutes
Servings: 4

This Japanese stir-fried noodle dish is largely about the chew, which comes from hearty wheat udon noodles. We got the dense chewiness we wanted by using the Italian technique of cooking noodles until al dente—still quite firm. Japanese noodles often are rinsed after cooking, and chilling helps prevent them from turning soggy. We streamlined the process by adding ice to the strainer as we rinsed the udon under cold running water. Fresh udon is sold frozen, refrigerated and in shelf-stable packages, but for this recipe we used dried noodles, which are more widely available. The sharp bite of pickled ginger complements the salty, savory noodles. If you're not up to making your own, look for jars of it in the grocery store's Asian section. Also in that section, look for shichimi togarashi, a Japanese spice blend for sprinkling on at the table to add a little heat.

12 ounces dried udon noodles

2 tablespoons plus 2 teaspoons grapeseed or other neutral oil, divided

¼ cup soy sauce

2 tablespoons mirin

1 teaspoon white sugar

3 small dried shiitake mushrooms, broken in half

8 ounces fresh shiitake mushrooms, stemmed, halved if large, thinly sliced

1 small yellow onion, halved and thinly sliced

2 medium garlic cloves, minced

12 ounces baby bok choy, trimmed and sliced crosswise ½-inch thick

2 scallions, thinly sliced on bias

1 tablespoon sesame seeds, toasted

Shichimi togarashi, to serve (optional)

Pickled ginger, to serve (see sidebar)

In a large pot, bring 4 quarts of water to a boil. Add the udon, stir well and cook until al dente. Drain the noodles, then add 2 cups of ice to the strainer. Run under cool water, tossing, until the noodles are chilled. Drain well, then transfer to a large bowl. Toss with 2 teaspoons of oil, then set aside.

In a small saucepan over medium, combine the soy sauce, ¼ cup water, the mirin and sugar. Bring to a simmer, stirring, then add the dried mushrooms, pushing them into the liquid. Remove from the heat, cover and set aside until the mushrooms have softened and cooled, 20 to 30 minutes.

Remove the mushrooms from the soy sauce mixture, squeezing them to allow any liquid to drip back into the pan. Remove and discard the stems, then finely chop. Transfer to a medium bowl and set aside.

In a large nonstick skillet over medium-high, heat 1 tablespoon of the remaining oil. Add the fresh mushrooms and cook, stirring occasionally, until lightly browned and slightly shrunken, about 3 minutes. Add the onion, drizzle with the remaining 1 tablespoon oil and cook, stirring occasionally, until the onion is softened, about 3 minutes. Stir in the garlic and cook until fragrant, about 30 seconds. Add the bok choy and cook, stirring, until the leaves are wilted and the stem pieces are crisp-tender, about 2 minutes. Add to the chopped dried shiitakes.

Set the now-empty skillet over medium and add the udon, gently tossing them with tongs. Add the vegetable mixture, gently toss a few times, then add the soy sauce mixture and ½ teaspoon ground white pepper. Cook, tossing constantly, until the noodles are heated and have absorbed most of the liquid, about 2 minutes. Transfer to serving bowls and sprinkle with scallions and sesame seeds. Serve with shichimi togarashi and pickled ginger.

PICKLED GINGER

Start to finish: 45 minutes (15 minutes active)
Makes 1⅓ cups

Look for large, plump, chunky pieces of fresh ginger without many nubs; they will be easier to peel and slice. A mandoline works well for slicing, but a Y-style peeler works, too.

¾ cup unseasoned rice vinegar

¼ cup water

2 tablespoons white sugar

½ teaspoon kosher salt

4 ounces fresh ginger, peeled and sliced paper thin

In a small bowl, stir together the vinegar, water, sugar and salt. Stir in the ginger. Cover and refrigerate for 30 minutes. Keeps for up to 1 week.

STIR-FRIED NOODLES WITH KIMCHI AND PORK

Start to finish: 30 minutes
Servings: 4 to 6

This is an umami-packed, noodle-based version of another weeknight favorite, kimchi fried rice. Butter may seem out of place, but its richness smooths the edges and adds a welcome velvetiness. If you like, sprinkle some furikake or crumble some crisp toasted nori onto the noodles just before serving.

10 ounces dried udon noodles

2 teaspoons plus 2 tablespoons grapeseed or other neutral oil

2 to 3 tablespoons gochujang

2 tablespoons soy sauce

4 teaspoons white sugar

1 tablespoon kimchi juice, plus 1½ cups drained kimchi, roughly chopped

2 teaspoons toasted sesame oil

8 ounces ground pork

1 bunch scallions, sliced on the diagonal, whites and greens reserved separately

2 tablespoons salted butter, cut into 4 pieces

Kosher salt and ground black pepper

3 tablespoons sesame seeds, toasted

In a large pot, bring 4 quarts water to a boil. Add the noodles and cook, stirring occasionally, until tender. Drain in a colander and rinse under cold water until cool to the touch. Drain again and toss with the 2 teaspoons neutral oil, then set aside.

In a small bowl, whisk together the gochujang, soy sauce, sugar, kimchi juice, sesame oil and ¼ cup water; set aside.

In a 12-inch nonstick skillet over medium-high, heat the remaining 2 tablespoons neutral oil until shimmering. Add the pork and scallion whites; cook, breaking the meat into small bits, just until no longer pink, about 3 minutes.

Increase to high and add the butter, kimchi and ½ teaspoon pepper. Cook, stirring often, until browned, about 2 minutes.

Add the noodles and toss, then add the gochujang mixture. Cook, stirring and tossing, until the noodles are heated through and the sauce clings, 2 to 3 minutes. Off heat, toss in the scallion greens and sesame seeds. Taste and season with salt and pepper.

SINGAPORE CURRY NOODLES

Start to finish: 30 minutes

Servings: 4

This dish did not originate in Singapore, so how it came to be named is something of a mystery. But the thin, fragrant, sunny-colored noodles tangled with egg, tender-crisp vegetables, shrimp and char siu (Cantonese roasted pork) have become a popular menu item in many Chinese-American restaurants. Our simplified version has no pork; the eggs and shrimp provide plenty of substance. The correct noodle to use here is thin, wiry rice vermicelli or rice sticks, sometimes labeled maifun.

4 ounces rice vermicelli (see headnote)

Boiling water, for soaking the noodles

2 tablespoons Shaoxing wine or dry sherry

1 tablespoon soy sauce

1 tablespoon curry powder

½ teaspoon packed brown sugar

Kosher salt and ground black or white pepper

2 large eggs

3 tablespoons grapeseed or other neutral oil, divided

8 ounces large shrimp (26/30 per pound), peeled, deveined (tails removed) and halved lengthwise

3 medium garlic cloves, minced

1 medium carrot, peeled and cut into matchsticks

4 ounces sugar snap peas, trimmed, strings removed (if present) and halved on the diagonal

Place the noodles in a medium heatproof bowl and add enough boiling water to cover. Let stand until fully tender, about 3 minutes. Drain in a colander, rinse under cold running water until completely cooled, then drain again. Using kitchen shears, snip the noodles in several places to cut them into shorter lengths.

Meanwhile, in a small bowl, whisk together the Shaoxing wine, soy sauce, curry powder, sugar, ½ teaspoon pepper and 3 tablespoons water. In another small bowl, whisk the eggs.

In a 12-inch nonstick skillet over medium-high, heat 1 tablespoon oil until barely smoking. Add the eggs and immediately swirl the pan to spread them into a thin layer.

Cook, swirling the pan and spreading the eggs with a spatula as needed, until just set but still shiny, about 30 seconds. Transfer to a cutting board; reserve the skillet. Chop the eggs into small pieces; set aside.

Season the shrimp with salt and pepper. In the same skillet over medium-high, heat 1 tablespoon of the remaining oil until shimmering. Add the shrimp in an even layer and cook without stirring until lightly browned on the bottom, 1½ to 2 minutes. Transfer to a plate; set aside.

Return the skillet to medium-high and add the remaining 1 tablespoon oil and the garlic. Cook, stirring, until fragrant and lightly browned, about 1 minute. Add the carrots, snap peas and ¼ teaspoon salt; cook, stirring often, until the vegetables are tender-crisp, 2 to 4 minutes. Add the Shaoxing mixture followed by the noodles, tossing until the noodles are uniformly colored, about 1 minute. Return the shrimp and eggs to the skillet; cook, tossing, until the shrimp are opaque throughout and the mixture is dry, 2 to 3 minutes. Off heat, taste and season with salt and pepper.

PERUVIAN STIR-FRIED CHICKEN AND NOODLES

Start to finish: 40 minutes
Servings: 4

This salty-sweet chicken and noodle stir-fry is our take on tallarín saltado, a chifa staple. Born of Chinese migration to Peru in the late 19th century, chifa cuisine combines South American and East Asian flavors and ingredients. In this recipe, garlicky chicken and peppers are coated in a soy- and oyster sauce-based glaze, then tossed with thin, chewy noodles. Though traditionally made with wine vinegar, we love the fruity yet mellow acidity added by balsamic. A Fresno or jalapeño chili—our stand-in for Peru's floral-hot ají amarillos—provides a touch of bright heat. Fragrant cilantro and tart lime complete the approachable dish, which tastes at once familiar and totally unique.

8 ounces spaghetti

Kosher salt and ground black pepper

3 tablespoons oyster sauce

2 tablespoons soy sauce

2 tablespoons balsamic vinegar

3 tablespoons grapeseed oil or other neutral oil

1 pound boneless, skinless chicken thighs, trimmed and cut into ¾-inch strips

1 medium red onion, halved and sliced into ½-inch wedges

3 medium garlic cloves, thinly sliced

1 medium red, yellow or orange bell pepper, stemmed, seeded and thinly sliced

1 Fresno or jalapeño chili, stemmed, halved and thinly sliced

2 tablespoons lime juice, plus wedges to serve

¼ cup lightly packed fresh cilantro

In a large saucepan, bring 2 quarts water to a boil. Add the pasta and 1 tablespoon salt, then cook, stirring occasionally, until just shy of al dente. Reserve about ½ cup of the cooking water, then drain. In a small bowl, stir together the oyster sauce, soy sauce and vinegar; set aside.

In a 12-inch skillet over medium-high, heat the oil until barely smoking. Add the chicken, onion and garlic, distributing the ingredients evenly, then sprinkle with ¼ teaspoon

each salt and pepper. Cook, without stirring, until the chicken is well browned on the bottom and releases easily from the pan, about 4 minutes. Add the oyster sauce mixture and cook, stirring and scraping up any browned bits, until the sauce is syrupy, 3 to 4 minutes. Add the bell pepper and chili; cook, stirring occasionally, until the vegetables begin to soften, about 2 minutes.

Add the pasta and stir to combine. Add the reserved pasta water and cook, tossing constantly, until the noodles are al dente, 2 to 3 minutes. Off heat, stir in the lime juice. Taste and season with salt and pepper. Sprinkle the finished stir-fry with cilantro and serve with lime wedges on the side.

Oven Bakes

CHANGE THE WAY YOU COOK

For Better Roasting, Ditch the Roasting Pan

For perfectly golden brown, crispy roasted meats and vegetables, start by skipping the roasting pan.

That's because a baking sheet can deliver better oven browning than a roasting pan. The higher walls of roasting pans actually shield ingredients from the heat, preventing efficient browning. But the shorter sides of baking sheets allow for greater air circulation—and thus evaporation—around the ingredients.

For best results, it's also important to group ingredients by cooking time. Combining slower- and faster-cooking ingredients can result in over- or undercooked food. Use two baking sheets if possible. But if two pans aren't an option, longer-cooking items—such as hardy root vegetables—should be given a head start, while more delicate items can be added to the pan later. And avoid crowding the pan or including items that release a lot of liquid, which undermines the browning process.

Especially for items that cook quickly, such as seafood and delicate vegetables, we like to heat the pan in the oven before adding the ingredients. This jump-starts the roasting process, immediately searing foods for extra browning.

Heavyweight baking sheets are essential; thin pans can warp at the high heat of most roasting recipes. And avoid nonstick pans, as the coating can't withstand higher temperatures and scratches easily. Finally, be sure to use a rimmed pan (sometimes called a sheet pan) rather than a cookie sheet, which has no sides.

CHICKEN TRAYBAKE WITH POBLANO CHILIES, TOMATOES AND ONIONS

Start to finish: 45 minutes (20 minutes active)
Servings: 4 to 6

Family-friendly chicken fajitas inspired this easy dinner on a baking sheet. We add the ingredients in stages to ensure each cooks perfectly. First, we cook earthy poblano chilies and onions until tender. Then sweet-tart tomatoes join the mix, followed by boneless chicken parts, which need only a quick-roast to cook through. Tangy tomatillos can be substituted for tomatoes, bringing more bright acidity. For a low-effort taco night, serve with warm tortillas and an array of condiments.

3 tablespoons extra-virgin olive oil

2 medium garlic cloves, finely grated

1 tablespoon chili powder OR 2 teaspoons ground cumin plus ¼ teaspoon cayenne

Kosher salt and ground black pepper

1½ pounds boneless, skinless chicken breasts OR thighs, trimmed

2 medium red OR white onions, peeled and cut into 1-inch wedges

2 poblano chilies, stemmed, seeded and cut into 1- to 1½-inch strips

1 pint grape OR cherry tomatoes OR 4 medium tomatillos (about 8 ounces), husked, cored and halved

Heat the oven to 500°F with a rack in the middle position. In a medium bowl, stir together the oil, garlic, chili powder, 1¼ teaspoons salt and ½ teaspoon pepper. Measure 2 tablespoons of the oil-spice mixture into a wide, shallow dish; add the chicken and turn to coat, rubbing in the seasonings; set aside.

To the remaining oil-spice mixture, add the onions and chilies. Toss, then distribute evenly on a rimmed baking sheet. Roast until the vegetables begin to brown and soften, 8 to 10 minutes. Remove the baking sheet from the oven, stir in the tomatoes and place the chicken on top. Roast until the thickest part of the breasts (if using) reaches 160°F and the thickest part of the largest thigh (if using) reaches 175°F, another 15 to 20 minutes.

Transfer the chicken to a cutting board and let rest for 5 minutes. Meanwhile, transfer the vegetables and any accumulated juices to a platter. Thinly slice the chicken, then taste and season with salt and pepper and transfer to the platter.

Optional garnish: Mexican crema **OR** sour cream **OR** hot sauce **OR** lime wedges **OR** a combination

---

TANDOORI-INSPIRED CHICKEN AND CAULIFLOWER TRAYBAKE

Start to finish: 55 minutes (20 minutes active)
Servings: 4

Indian tandoori chicken inspired this six-ingredient meal on a baking sheet. We cut slashes into bone-in chicken parts to allow the seasonings to really work their way into the meat. Yogurt not only tenderizes the chicken, it gets the seasonings to stick and assists with browning. Garam masala is warm and sweet, whereas curry powder is savory and earthy; use whichever you prefer or have. Serve with basmati rice and/or warm naan.

1 cup plain whole-milk yogurt, divided

4 tablespoons neutral oil, divided

1 tablespoon finely grated fresh ginger OR 4 medium garlic cloves, finely grated OR both

2 tablespoons sweet paprika

1½ tablespoons garam masala OR curry powder

Kosher salt and ground black pepper

3 pounds bone-in, skin-on chicken thighs OR chicken leg quarters, trimmed and patted dry

2-pound head cauliflower, trimmed and cut into 1-inch florets

In a large bowl, whisk together ½ cup yogurt, 2 tablespoons oil, the ginger, paprika, garam masala, 2½ teaspoons salt and ¼ teaspoon pepper. Measure 2 tablespoons of the mixture into a small bowl and stir in the remaining ½ cup yogurt; cover and refrigerate until ready to serve.

Using a sharp knife, cut parallel slashes, spaced about 1 inch apart, in the skin side of each piece of chicken, cutting all the way to the bone. Add the chicken to the yogurt mixture in the large bowl and turn to coat, rubbing the yogurt into the slashes. Transfer the chicken skin-side up to the center of a rimmed baking sheet, arranging the pieces in a single layer; let stand at room temperature for about 30 minutes; wipe out the bowl.

In the same bowl, toss the cauliflower with the remaining 2 tablespoons oil, ½ teaspoon salt and ¼ teaspoon pepper. Transfer to the baking sheet in an even layer around the chicken. Let stand at room temperature while the oven heats.

Heat the oven to 475°F with a rack in the middle position. Roast until the thickest part of the largest thigh or leg quarter reaches 175°F, 30 to 35 minutes. Transfer the chicken and cauliflower to a platter and serve with the yogurt sauce.

Optional garnish: Chopped fresh cilantro **OR** lemon wedges **OR** both

Greek Chicken and Potato Traybake

Start to finish: 45 minutes
Servings: 4

The Greek dish known as kotopoulo skorthato typically is called "Greek garlic-lemon chicken" in English, but the ensemble also includes potatoes, making it a delicious complete meal. For our take on the classic, we use our trusty traybake technique—**we roast the ingredients on a rimmed baking sheet in a hot oven to ensure the quickest cooking possible and to develop caramelization.** At the end, we also toss in black olives, dill and capers to ratchet up the flavors. If using chicken breasts, try to purchase pieces that are close in size so they cook at the same rate.

1 teaspoon dried oregano

¼ to ½ teaspoon red pepper flakes

Kosher salt and ground black pepper

Four 12-ounce bone-in, skin-on chicken breasts or 3 pounds bone-in, skin-on chicken thighs, trimmed and patted dry

2 tablespoons extra-virgin olive oil

1½ pounds medium Yukon Gold potatoes, unpeeled, cut into 1-inch-thick wedges

2 lemons, halved crosswise

8 medium garlic cloves, peeled

½ cup pitted Kalamata olives, roughly chopped

2 tablespoons drained capers

3 tablespoons roughly chopped fresh dill, divided

Heat the oven to 475°F with a rack in the middle position. In a large bowl, stir together the oregano, pepper flakes, 1½ teaspoons salt and ½ teaspoon black pepper. Sprinkle 2 teaspoons of the mix onto all sides of the chicken. To the remaining seasoning mix in the bowl, add the oil, potatoes, lemon halves and garlic, then toss to coat.

Place the garlic in the center of a rimmed baking sheet, then arrange the chicken, skin up, around the garlic; this place-ment helps prevent the garlic from scorching during roasting. Arrange the lemons, cut sides up, and the potatoes in an even

layer around the chicken. Roast until the thickest part of the breasts (if using) reaches 160°F and the thickest part of the largest thigh (if using) reaches 175°F, about 30 minutes.

Using tongs, transfer the chicken and lemon halves to a serving platter. Push the potatoes to the edge of the baking sheet, leaving the garlic in the center. Using a fork, mash the garlic to a rough paste. Add the olives, capers and 2 table-spoons of the dill to the baking sheet, then, using a wide metal spatula, stir and toss the ingredients, scraping up any browned bits.

Transfer the potato mixture to the platter, placing it around the chicken. Sprinkle with the remaining 1 tablespoon dill.

HOISIN BROCCOLI AND TOFU TRAYBAKE

Start to finish: 40 minutes
Servings: 4 to 6

This simple vegetarian traybake combines several pantry staples—hoisin, soy sauce and garlic—with broccoli and tofu and yields a hearty, satisfying main. A 475°F oven develops the right amount of flavorful char on the broccoli and cooks the florets to a pleasing tender-crisp texture. Serve with steamed rice.

¾ cup hoisin sauce

3 tablespoons soy sauce

3 medium garlic cloves, finely chopped

1 tablespoon toasted sesame oil

1 pound broccoli crowns, cut into 1½-inch florets

14-ounce container firm OR extra-firm tofu, drained, halved lengthwise, cut crosswise into ½-inch-thick slices and pressed dry

Toasted sesame seeds, to serve

Heat the oven to 475°F with a rack in the middle position. Line a rimmed baking sheet with foil and mist with cooking spray.

In a small bowl, stir together the hoisin, soy sauce, garlic and sesame oil. In a medium bowl, toss the broccoli with half of the hoisin mixture until evenly coated. Distribute in an even layer on the prepared baking sheet. Transfer the remaining hoisin mixture to the now-empty bowl, add the tofu and gently toss to coat. Place the tofu on the baking sheet, arranging it in a single layer, being sure that all the slices lay flat against the baking sheet.

Roast the broccoli and tofu without stirring until the broccoli is charred and tender-crisp, about 25 minutes. Using a wide metal spatula, transfer to a platter. Sprinkle with sesame seeds.

Optional garnish: Chopped fresh cilantro

CHANGE THE WAY YOU COOK

Roast Your Citrus

For mellow, tangy flavor we often broil or bake our lemons, which makes the fruit extra-juicy while taming its acidity just a bit. It takes almost no effort; we simply cut the lemons in half and cook them with the protein. Note: if the recipe also calls for lemon zest be sure to zest before cutting the lemons; it's easier to zest them whole. When the meat or fish is done, we squeeze the lemon halves (waiting until they cool off or using tongs) and use the juice in sauces or as a finishing drizzle.

We use this technique for all types of dishes, including a chicken traybake inspired by Greek kotopoulo skorthato (recipe p. 302). Lemon halves get broiled for our lemon-garlic salmon (recipe p. 395), and the warm juices go into a sauce based on Italian salmoriglio. For our roasted chicken (recipe p. 406), the lemon is tucked into the cavity of the chicken at the start of cooking. When the chicken's done, the juices are ready to be squeezed into a simple sauce for brightness without harshness.

303

WHITE BEANS AND CARROTS WITH ROASTED ORANGE VINAIGRETTE

Start to finish: 50 minutes

Servings: 4 to 6

This meatless traybake starts by roasting sturdy root vegetables and licorice-y fennel. Once the vegetables are tender, we toss in cannellini beans (canned, for convenience) that are marinated in a vinaigrette spiked with orange zest and thyme, then give the mix a few more minutes in the oven to warm through. Orange halves roasted with the vegetables turn succulent and their acidity mellows with cooking; we squeeze the juice and add it to the dressing that's tossed with the still-warm vegetable-bean mixture. A sprinkle of chopped nuts completes the dish, adding toastiness and crunch. Rainbow carrots make the traybake especially colorful, or if you're a fan of parsnips, use them in place of or in combination with the carrots. This is hearty enough to be a vegetarian main, but also makes a terrific holiday side.

2 oranges

1 pound (4 or 5) medium carrots, peeled, quartered lengthwise and cut into 4-inch sections

8 ounces (3 medium) golden beets, peeled and cut into ½-inch wedges

1 large red onion, halved and sliced ½ inch thick

1 medium fennel bulb, trimmed, halved lengthwise, cored and cut in ½-inch wedges

5 tablespoons extra-virgin olive oil, divided, plus more to serve

2 tablespoons chopped fresh thyme, divided

Kosher salt and ground black pepper

3 tablespoons white balsamic vinegar

15½-ounce can cannellini beans, rinsed and drained

½ cup hazelnuts OR whole almonds, toasted and roughly chopped

Heat the oven to 425°F with a rack in the middle position. Grate 1 tablespoon zest from the oranges, then halve them crosswise. In a large bowl, toss the carrots, beets, onion, fennel, 2 tablespoons oil, half of the thyme, 1 teaspoon salt and ½ teaspoon pepper. Distribute in an even layer on a rimmed baking sheet, along with the orange halves; reserve the bowl.

Roast until the carrots and beets are just tender, 35 to 40 minutes, stirring once halfway through. Meanwhile, in the reserved bowl, whisk together the remaining 3 tablespoons oil, the orange zest, the remaining thyme, vinegar and ½ teaspoon each salt and pepper. Add the beans and toss to coat.

Remove the baking sheet from the oven. Using a slotted spoon, transfer the beans to the baking sheet, stirring them in; reserve the dressing in the bowl. Roast until the edges of some of the vegetables begin to brown, 5 to 10 minutes.

Remove the baking sheet from the oven. Using tongs, squeeze the juice from the orange halves into the reserved dressing in the bowl; discard the halves. Whisk the dressing, then transfer the warm vegetable-bean mixture to the bowl and toss to coat. Taste and season with salt and pepper. Transfer to a platter, sprinkle with the hazelnuts and drizzle with additional oil.

HONEY-MISO SALMON AND BROCCOLINI TRAYBAKE

Start to finish: 30 minutes
Servings: 4

Miso, soy sauce and honey make a savory-sweet, umami-rich marinade for meaty, fat-rich salmon. Some of the mixture is set aside and combined with orange juice and zest, creating a savory-sweet sauce for drizzling over the finished dish. While the fish marinates, the Broccolini gets a head start on roasting. Then once the quick-cooking salmon is added, the traybake is nearly done. Serve with steamed rice, and perhaps a leafy green salad alongside.

2 tablespoons white OR red miso

2 tablespoons soy sauce

2 tablespoons honey

3 tablespoons neutral oil, divided

Four 6-ounce center-cut salmon fillets (1 to 1¼ inches thick), patted dry

1 tablespoon grated orange zest, plus 2 tablespoons orange juice

1 pound Broccolini, trimmed OR broccoli crowns, cut into 1-inch florets

Kosher salt and ground black pepper

Heat the oven to 425°F with a rack in the middle position. In a small bowl, whisk together the miso, soy sauce, honey and 1 tablespoon oil. Transfer half of the mixture to a wide, shallow dish; add the salmon skin-side up and set aside. Stir the orange zest and juice into the mixture remaining in the bowl; set aside.

On a rimmed baking sheet, toss the Broccolini with the remaining 2 tablespoons oil and ½ teaspoon each salt and pepper. Distribute in an even layer, then roast until beginning to brown at the edges, about 15 minutes.

Remove the baking sheet from the oven. Using a wide metal spatula, scrape up and flip the Broccolini, pushing it to the edges. Add the salmon, skin-side down, to the center of the baking sheet. Roast until the fish flakes easily and the Broccolini is lightly charred and tender-crisp, 7 to 10 minutes. Transfer to a platter and drizzle with the miso-orange sauce.

Optional garnish: Toasted sesame oil **OR** toasted sesame seeds **OR** sliced scallions **OR** red pepper flakes **OR** a combination

CRISPED CHICKPEA AND CAULIFLOWER TRAYBAKE WITH LEMON-GARLIC YOGURT

Start to finish: 35 minutes
Servings: 4

Contrasting flavors and textures make an easy traybake special. Cauliflower takes on light charring and becomes supple and tender while chickpeas roast alongside, turning toasty and crisp. A lemony, garlicky yogurt sauce ties everything together, and a spice blend does double duty, seasoning the cauliflower-chickpea mixture as well as the sauce. Curry powder lends a golden hue and an earthy spiciness; baharat, a Middle Eastern seasoning mix, leans toward warm, nutty, smoky-sweet notes. Serve as a side to meaty fish, like salmon or swordfish, or roasted chicken or lamb, or make it a light vegetarian main.

305

¼ cup plus 1 tablespoon extra-virgin olive oil, divided

3 teaspoons curry powder OR baharat, divided

Kosher salt and ground black pepper

2½- to 3-pound head cauliflower, trimmed
and cut into 1-inch florets

15½-ounce can chickpeas, rinsed and drained

⅓ cup plain whole-milk yogurt

1 tablespoon grated lemon zest, plus 2 tablespoons
lemon juice, plus lemon wedges, to serve

1 medium garlic clove, finely grated

Heat the oven to 425°F with a rack in the middle position.
In a large bowl, stir together ¼ cup oil, 2 teaspoons curry
powder, 1 teaspoon salt and ½ teaspoon pepper. Add the
cauliflower and chickpeas; toss to coat, rubbing the seasonings in. Transfer to a rimmed baking sheet in an even layer.
Roast until the cauliflower is fully tender and lightly charred
and the chickpeas have crisped, 50 to 60 minutes, stirring
after 20 and 40 minutes.

Meanwhile, in a small bowl, stir together the yogurt, lemon
zest and juice, garlic, the remaining 1 tablespoon oil, the
remaining 1 teaspoon curry powder and ¼ teaspoon of salt.

Transfer the cauliflower-chickpea mixture to a serving dish,
then taste and season with salt and pepper. Spoon on the
yogurt sauce or serve the sauce on the side, along with
lemon wedges.

Optional garnish: Pomegranate molasses **OR** thinly sliced
fresh mint **OR** chopped fresh cilantro **OR** Aleppo pepper
OR a combination

CHOW MEIN TRAYBAKE WITH BROCCOLI AND BELL PEPPERS

Start to finish: 40 minutes

Servings: 4

Inspired by a recipe in Hetty McKinnon's cookbook "To
Asia, With Love," we created this oven-only noodle dish,
but we took some liberties, swapping instant ramen for
the thin Chinese egg noodles customarily used to make
chow mein. The ramen doesn't require actual cooking—
it needs only to hydrate in boiling water for a few minutes.
We skip the splatter and stirring of stovetop cooking by
using a baking sheet and a hot oven to oven-fry noodles
alongside broccoli and sweet bell peppers. To finish,
we toss everything with a simple blend of oyster sauce,
hoisin sauce and garlic (or ginger), which brings delicious
umami, saltiness and sweetness.

3 tablespoons soy sauce

2 teaspoons oyster sauce

2 medium garlic cloves, finely grated
OR 2 teaspoons finely grated fresh ginger OR both

Kosher salt and ground black pepper

Three 3-ounce packages instant ramen
noodles, seasoning packets discarded

3 cups boiling water

5 tablespoons neutral oil, divided

12 ounces broccoli crowns, cut into
1½-inch florets

2 medium red bell peppers, stemmed,
seeded and sliced into ¼-inch strips

Heat the oven to 500°F with a rack in the middle position.
In a small bowl, stir together the soy sauce, oyster sauce,
garlic, ¾ teaspoon pepper and 3 tablespoons water; set
aside.

Place the noodles in a large heatproof bowl, pour in the
boiling water and stir. Let stand, stirring once or twice,
until the noodles are pliable, about 6 minutes, then drain.
Toss with 3 tablespoons oil, then set aside.

Meanwhile, generously mist a rimmed baking sheet
with cooking spray. On the baking sheet, toss the broccoli
with 1 tablespoon of the remaining oil, then distribute
in an even layer. Roast until just starting to soften, about
4 minutes.

Using a spatula, push the broccoli to one end of the baking sheet. Pile the bell peppers onto the center, drizzle with the remaining 1 tablespoon oil and toss. Push the peppers to the opposite end of the baking sheet. Add the noodles to the center in an even layer. Roast until the broccoli is lightly charred, the peppers are tender and the noodles begin to crisp, 10 to 12 minutes.

Remove from the oven and drizzle the noodles and vegetables with the soy sauce mixture. Using tongs, toss well. Taste and season with salt and pepper.

Optional garnish: Thinly sliced scallions **OR** chili-garlic sauce **OR** toasted sesame seeds **OR** a combination

Know Your Oven Temperatures

Some people are more successful at kitchen improv than others. But cooking well without recipes isn't so much about innate talent as it is understanding key equipment. And mastering the oven is at the top of the list. Winging it in the kitchen is easier once you familiarize yourself with oven temperature zones.

Once you understand the five basic temperature ranges—and the foods that cook best in them—it's easier to simply toss a chicken in to roast, bake up a quick bread, crank out some roasted carrots or whip up a pizza for dinner.

And since not all of this is intuitive—for example, a low oven is best for delicate custards, but also for braised meats—we've broken down the most common oven recipes into the temperatures ranges where they do best.

Low (275°F to 325°F)
Baked custards; dried beans; tough, long-cooking roasts; stews and other braises

Moderate (325°F to 350°F)
Most baked goods (cakes, cookies, muffins, quick breads, etc.)

Medium-High (375°F to 400°F)
Blind-baked pastry, pork loin, well-marbled beef roasts, whole chickens

Hot (425°F to 450°F)
Biscuits and scones, chicken parts, potatoes for roasting, puff pastry

Extra-Hot (475°F to 500°F)
Fish fillets, high-moisture yeasted doughs (pizza, flatbreads, etc.), most vegetables for roasting

OVEN BAKES

307

ROASTED BUTTERNUT SQUASH WITH CHICKPEAS, HERBS AND TAHINI

Start to finish: 45 minutes

Servings: 4

This colorful vegetarian dish, inspired by a recipe in "The Lebanese Kitchen" by Salma Hage, matches the sweetness of roasted butternut squash and shallots with a tangy, nutty lemon-tahini dressing. We toss the squash and shallots with tahini and oil before roasting—this helps the vegetables caramelize while deepening the sesame flavor of the tahini. A handful of toasted pumpkin seeds adds color and crunch.

4 tablespoons tahini, divided

3 tablespoons extra-virgin olive oil, divided

Kosher salt and ground black pepper

2-pound butternut squash, peeled, halved lengthwise, seeded and cut crosswise into 1-inch-thick half moons

4 medium shallots, quartered lengthwise

15½-ounce can chickpeas, rinsed and drained

4 tablespoons lemon juice, divided

1 tablespoon ground coriander

½ teaspoon red pepper flakes

1 medium garlic clove, finely grated

½ cup lightly packed fresh mint, roughly chopped

½ cup lightly packed fresh flat-leaf parsley, roughly chopped

Heat the oven to 450°F with a rack in the middle position. In a small bowl, whisk together 2 tablespoons of tahini, 2 tablespoons of oil and ½ teaspoon each salt and black pepper. On a rimmed baking sheet, combine the squash and shallots, then drizzle with the tahini mixture and toss; reserve the bowl. Distribute the vegetables in an even layer, cover with foil and roast for 15 minutes.

Meanwhile, in a medium bowl, stir together the chickpeas, 2 tablespoons of lemon juice, 1 tablespoon of oil, the coriander, red pepper flakes and ¼ teaspoon salt; set aside. After the squash and shallots have roasted for 15 minutes, uncover and add the chickpeas, distributing them evenly. Roast, uncovered, until the vegetables are well browned

and a skewer inserted into the thickest squash pieces meets no resistance, another 15 minutes.

Meanwhile, in the reserved bowl, whisk the remaining 2 tablespoons tahini, the remaining 2 tablespoons lemon juice, the garlic, ¼ teaspoon salt and 1 teaspoon water; the mixture should be have the consistency of thin yogurt (if too thick, whisk in additional water 1 teaspoon at a time to thin).

When the squash and shallots are done, remove the baking sheet from the oven. Add the mint and parsley, then toss. Transfer to a serving platter and drizzle with the tahini-lemon mixture.

GOCHUJANG-GLAZED TOFU AND BOK CHOY TRAYBAKE

Start to finish: 45 minutes (25 minutes active)
Servings: 4

This salty-sweet and subtly spicy traybake takes inspiration from the Korean gochujang-glazed tofu dish, dubu gang-jeong. To start, we bake cornstarch-coated tofu in a ripping-hot oven to give it a crisp crust and flavorful browning. We then brush it with a gochujang-honey glaze, which concentrates and caramelizes. Leafy green baby bok choy joins the tofu midway through, its tender-crisp stems and lightly charred leaves offering lots of textural and flavor contrast to the tofu. Steaming-hot rice is a perfect match for this well-seasoned traybake.

2 tablespoons neutral oil

2 tablespoons gochujang

2 tablespoons honey

2 tablespoons toasted sesame oil, divided, plus more to serve

Kosher salt and ground black pepper

¼ cup cornstarch

14-ounce container firm OR extra-firm tofu, drained, patted dry and cut into ½-inch planks

12 ounces baby bok choy, halved lengthwise and patted dry OR green beans, trimmed

Heat the oven to 475°F with a rack in the upper-middle position. Brush a rimmed baking sheet with the neutral oil. In a small bowl, whisk together the gochujang, honey, 1 tablespoon sesame oil, ½ teaspoon salt and ¼ teaspoon pepper; set aside.

Put the cornstarch in a wide, shallow dish; add the tofu and turn to coat. Place the tofu in the center of the prepared baking sheet, shaking off the excess starch and spacing the planks about ½ inch apart. Bake until the tofu is lightly browned and releases easily from the baking sheet, 15 to 18 minutes. Meanwhile, in a medium bowl, toss the bok choy with the remaining 1 tablespoon sesame oil and ¼ teaspoon each salt and pepper.

Remove the baking sheet from the oven and lightly brush the tops and sides of the tofu with some of the gochujang mixture. Using a thin metal spatula, flip the tofu, then

lightly brush with gochujang mixture. Arrange the bok choy around the tofu. Bake until the tofu and bok choy are lightly browned, about 10 minutes.

Flip the tofu and bok choy, then once again lightly brush the tofu with gochujang mixture. Bake until the tofu is well browned, about 5 minutes. Remove from the oven and brush the tofu with any remaining gochujang mixture. Transfer to a platter and drizzle with additional sesame oil.

Optional garnish: Thinly sliced chives OR scallions OR toasted sesame seeds OR furikake OR crumbled nori snacks

CHICKEN AND CREMINI MUSHROOM TRAYBAKE WITH ROASTED RED PEPPER SAUCE

Start to finish: 50 minutes / Servings: 4

We use bone-in, skin-on chicken parts for this traybake. If the quicker-cooking breasts reach 160°F before the thighs and drumsticks hit 175°F, simply remove them and continue cooking the dark meat. We look to the flavors of Provence, pairing mushrooms and roasted red peppers with the delicate, anise-like flavor of ground fennel. The peppers — we save time and start with the jarred variety — cook a bit more in the pan, then go into a subtly sweet scallion-accented pan sauce. If you can't find ground fennel seed at the supermarket, grind your own by processing a generous 1 tablespoon whole fennel seeds in a spice grinder until fine.

1 tablespoon ground fennel seeds

1 tablespoon granulated garlic

Kosher salt and ground black pepper

1½ pounds cremini mushrooms, trimmed, kept whole

2 roasted red peppers, kept whole

¼ cup extra-virgin olive oil

3 pounds bone-in, skin-on chicken parts, trimmed and patted dry

1 tablespoon firmly packed light or dark brown sugar

1 tablespoon dried oregano

10 medium garlic cloves, peeled

2 teaspoons unseasoned rice vinegar

4 scallions, thinly sliced

Heat the oven to 450°F with a rack in the middle position. In a small bowl, stir together the fennel, granulated garlic and 1 teaspoon salt. In a medium bowl, toss the mushrooms and red peppers with 1 tablespoon of the spice mixture and the oil; set aside. Into the remaining spice mixture, stir the brown sugar, oregano, ½ teaspoon salt and 2 teaspoons pepper.

On a rimmed baking sheet, evenly season both sides of the chicken parts with the spice mixture. Place the garlic cloves in the center of the baking sheet, then arrange the chicken parts, skin up, around the garlic; this prevents the garlic from scorching during roasting. Place the roasted peppers around the chicken, then scatter the mushrooms in an even layer over them.

Roast until the thickest part of the breast (if using) reaches about 160°F and the thickest part of the largest thigh/leg (if using) reaches about 175°F, 30 to 40 minutes.

Using tongs, transfer the chicken and mushrooms to a platter and transfer the roasted peppers to a cutting board; leave the garlic on the baking sheet. Carefully pour ¼ cup water onto the baking sheet, then use a wooden spoon to scrape up any browned bits. Pour the liquid, along with the garlic cloves, into a medium bowl. Roughly chop the roasted peppers and add to the bowl, then use a fork or potato masher to mash the mixture until almost smooth. Stir in the vinegar and half the scallions, then spoon the sauce over the chicken. Sprinkle with the remaining scallions.

PORK TENDERLOIN AND ACORN SQUASH TRAYBAKE WITH PAPRIKA AND CARAWAY

Start to finish: 1 hour
Servings: 4 to 6

Quick-cooking, mild pork tenderloin pairs well with a variety of ingredients. This dinner-on-a-baking-sheet is seasoned with caraway seeds (grind them in a spice grinder or with a mortar and pestle) and sweet paprika, plus brown sugar to aid with caramelization. Acorn squash and red onions go in the oven; the tenderloins are added halfway through. The browned bits left after the pork and vegetables are removed from the baking sheet add depth of flavor to a simple sauce.

1½- to 2-pound acorn squash, halved lengthwise, seeded and cut into 2-inch wedges

2 medium red onions, root end intact, each cut into 8 wedges

4 tablespoons extra-virgin olive oil, divided

Kosher salt and ground black pepper

2 tablespoons caraway seeds, ground

2 tablespoons sweet paprika

2 tablespoons packed brown sugar

Two 1¼-pound pork tenderloins, trimmed of silver skin

¼ cup apple cider

1 tablespoon cider vinegar

1 tablespoon Dijon mustard

3 tablespoons salted butter, cut into 3 pieces

2 tablespoons finely chopped fresh chives

Heat the oven to 475°F with a rack in the upper-middle position. Mist a rimmed baking sheet with cooking spray. Place the squash and onions on the baking sheet, then drizzle with 2 tablespoons oil and sprinkle with ½ teaspoon each salt and pepper; toss, then distribute in an even layer. Roast for 20 minutes. Meanwhile, in a small bowl, stir together the caraway, paprika, sugar and ½ teaspoon each salt and pepper. Coat each tenderloin with 1 tablespoon oil, then sprinkle both on all sides with the spice mixture, pressing so the seasonings adhere.

Remove the baking sheet from the oven. Using a wide metal spatula, flip the vegetables and push them to the perimeter of the baking sheet. Place the tenderloins in the center, evenly spacing them. Return to the oven and roast until the centers of the tenderloins reach 135°F and a skewer inserted into the squash meets no resistance, 18 to 20 minutes.

Transfer the tenderloins to a cutting board; transfer the squash and onions to a platter. Add the cider, vinegar and mustard to the baking sheet, then scrape up any browned bits. Add the butter and chives; whisk until the butter is melted. Taste and season with salt and pepper.

Slice the tenderloins and transfer them to the platter. Pour the sauce and any accumulated juices on the cutting board over the pork and vegetables.

How to Make a Traybake Pan Sauce

We love the ease of roasting on a baking sheet, which gives us better air circulation, quicker cooking and better browning. But the benefits don't stop there. The fond created in the bottom of the pan can be an excellent starting point for a simple and flavorful pan sauce.

We pick a simple blend of herbs and spices to start—say coriander and ginger for chicken—then add aromatics such as garlic or scallions to the baking sheet, surrounding the vegetables with the meat so they don't overcook. As the meat roasts, the aromatics caramelize and soften, ready to be chopped into a sauce and mixed into the deglazed pan drippings.

For a Greek-inspired chicken traybake we toss the chicken parts with oregano and pepper flakes. Then we add lemon halves and garlic cloves. Once the cooking's done, we mash the cloves into a paste on the pan and mix in olives, capers and dill for a delicious and virtually no-effort flavor boost.

The method can be switched up with different herbs and spices and finished with a dash of citrus or something stronger. For a sausage traybake, for instance, we roast sweet apples and onions alongside kielbasa and then use hard apple cider or beer to deglaze the baking sheet.

OVEN BAKES

311

Fish Baked with Tomatoes, Capers and White Wine

Start to finish: 50 minutes
Servings: 4

This simple fish bake delivers tons of flavor but requires minimal prep. You'll need a good amount of capers—¼ to ½ cup—along with some caper brine, which brings saltiness and tang to balance the sweetness of the vegetables. The onion and tomatoes get a head start on baking. **Once the vegetables are soft and jammy we place the fish fillets on top, that way they stay moist while cooking and have a chance to absorb the aromatic flavors.** If your fillets are thicker or thinner than about 1 inch, adjust the baking time up or down to ensure the fish doesn't wind up dry and overcooked. Serve with warm, crusty bread or a rice or orzo pilaf.

¼ cup extra-virgin olive oil

2 medium garlic cloves, minced

**2 tablespoons caper brine, plus
¼ to ½ cup drained capers**

1 teaspoon dried thyme

**Four 6-ounce cod OR sea bass fillets
(each about 1 inch thick)**

Kosher salt and ground black pepper

**1 pint cherry or grape tomatoes
OR 12 ounces ripe plum tomatoes, cored
and cut in 1-inch chunks**

1 medium red onion, halved and thinly sliced

¼ cup dry white wine

Heat the oven to 400°F with a rack in the middle position. In a small bowl, whisk together the oil, garlic, caper brine and thyme. Season the fish on both sides with salt and pepper, then place skinned (or skin) side down in a pie plate or other wide, shallow dish. Spoon 2 tablespoons of the oil mixture onto the fillets, dividing it evenly; refrigerate until ready to use.

In a 9-by-13-inch baking dish, toss together the remaining oil mixture, the capers, tomatoes, onion, wine and ½ teaspoon each salt and pepper. Bake, uncovered, until the onion has

softened and the tomatoes have broken down and released their juices, 30 to 35 minutes; stir once about halfway through.

Remove the baking dish from the oven and stir the vegetables. Place the fillets on top, spacing them evenly, and bake until the fish flakes easily, 8 to 10 minutes. Using a wide metal spatula, transfer the fish to a platter or individual plates, then spoon the tomato mixture on top.

Optional garnish: Chopped fresh flat-leaf parsley **OR** dill

SMOKY CHICKEN AND
SWEET POTATO TRAYBAKE

Start to finish: 45 minutes
Servings: 4

A mix of honey, smoked paprika and orange zest deliver high-impact flavor in this ultra-easy chicken traybake. Even the knife work here is minimal—you'll only need to trim the chicken, quarter an orange and cut the vegetables into wedges. After transferring the roasted chicken and vegetables to a platter, we combine the drippings that remain on the baking sheet with softened butter and the juice squeezed from the roasted orange. The ingredients come together into a glossy, savory-sweet sauce that will make dinner taste far more labor-intensive than it actually was.

¼ cup honey

2 tablespoons extra-virgin olive oil

Grated zest of 1 orange, orange cut into quarters

1 tablespoon smoked paprika

½ to ¾ teaspoon cayenne pepper (optional)

Kosher salt and ground black pepper

3 pounds bone-in, skin-on chicken thighs, trimmed and patted dry

2 medium sweet potatoes (1 pound total), cut lengthwise into ¾-inch wedges

1 small red onion, peeled and cut into 1-inch wedges, with root end intact

2 tablespoons salted butter, cut into 2 pieces, room temperature

Heat the oven to 475°F with a rack in the middle position. In a small bowl, whisk together the honey, oil, orange zest, paprika, cayenne (if using), 1½ teaspoons salt and 1 teaspoon pepper.

On a rimmed baking sheet, combine the chicken, sweet potatoes and onion. Drizzle on the honey mixture and rub it into the chicken and vegetables. Arrange the chicken skin up in a single layer in the center, then arrange the vegetables in an even layer around the chicken. Place an orange quarter, cut side up, in each corner of the baking sheet. Roast until spotty brown and the thickest part of the thighs reach 175°F, 30 to 35 minutes.

Using tongs, transfer the chicken and vegetables to a platter; tent with foil. With the tongs, squeeze the juice from the orange quarters onto the baking sheet; discard the quarters. Add the butter and whisk, scraping up any browned bits, until melted and combined with the pan juices. Taste and season with salt and pepper. Pour half of the sauce over the chicken and vegetables; serve the remainder on the side.

SAUSAGE TRAYBAKE WITH
APPLES AND ONIONS

Start to finish: 40 minutes (15 minutes active)
Servings: 4 to 6

We pair savory sausages with sweet apples and onions, which get a flavor boost from spicy mustard; a glug of hard apple cider or beer is used to deglaze the baking sheet. We love the double dose of apple flavor from cider, though a crisp lager or malty amber beer also is delicious; if you prefer, use low-sodium chicken broth instead. Select apples with a firm texture yet thin skin that stays tender during roasting. Honeycrisp and Gala are good options.

2 medium red OR yellow onions, halved and sliced about ½ inch thick

1 tablespoon torn fresh sage OR 2 teaspoons fresh thyme, plus chopped sage or thyme to serve

2 tablespoons extra-virgin olive oil

Kosher salt and ground black pepper

1¼ pounds firm apples, quartered lengthwise and cored (see headnote)

1½ pounds kielbasa OR bratwurst OR sweet or hot Italian sausages, poked in several places with a paring knife

¼ cup hard apple cider OR beer OR broth (see headnote)

2 tablespoons whole-grain mustard OR Dijon mustard, plus more to serve

Heat the oven to 450°F with a rack in the middle position. On a rimmed baking sheet, toss together the onions, torn sage, oil and ½ teaspoon each salt and pepper; distribute in an even layer. Roast until the onions begin to soften and brown, about 10 minutes.

Remove from the oven and stir the onions. Add the apples and arrange the sausages on top. Roast until the centers of the sausages reach 160°F and the onions and apples are tender and lightly browned, 15 to 20 minutes.

Transfer the sausages and apples to a platter, leaving the onions in the pan. Pour the cider over the onions and stir, scraping up any browned bits. Stir in the mustard, then taste and season with salt and pepper. Transfer the onion mixture to the platter, spooning it around the sausages and apples. Sprinkle with chopped sage and serve with additional mustard.

Optional garnish: Chopped fresh dill OR pickled peppers OR both

KIMCHI AND BROCCOLI OVEN-FRIED RICE

Start to finish: 50 minutes (30 minutes active)
Servings: 4 to 6

This unique method of making fried rice comes from Hetty McKinnon, Sydney native turned Brooklynite, cookbook author and creator of Peddler Journal. It's a terrific way to use up a jar of cabbage kimchi, but it's also a delicious reason to buy kimchi if you don't already have some on hand. Cooked rice that's fully chilled is best for making fried rice because the grains won't turn mushy when heated. Steam, cool and refrigerate some in advance if you can; otherwise store-bought already cooked rice is an option. We particularly like the stickiness and chew of short- or medium-grain rice, but regular long-grain is fine, too (don't use jasmine or basmati—the grains are too delicate).

4 cups cold cooked white rice (see headnote)

1 pound broccoli florets cut into bite-size pieces (about 4 cups)

1 medium carrot, peeled and thinly sliced on the diagonal

1 bunch scallions, thinly sliced, white and green parts reserved separately

3 tablespoons grapeseed or other neutral oil

2 cups drained napa cabbage kimchi, roughly chopped, plus 2 tablespoons kimchi juice

3 tablespoons soy sauce, plus more to serve

1 tablespoon toasted sesame oil

6 large eggs

Kosher salt and ground black pepper

Sesame seeds, toasted, to serve

Heat the oven to 475°F with a rack in the upper-middle position. Mist a rimmed baking sheet with cooking spray. In a large bowl, combine the rice, broccoli, carrot, scallion whites and neutral oil. Mix, breaking up any clumps of rice, until evenly coated with the oil. Distribute in an even layer on the prepared baking sheet and bake until the vegetables begin to brown, about 20 minutes.

Meanwhile, in a medium bowl, stir together the kimchi and juice, soy sauce and sesame oil.

Remove the baking sheet from the oven (close the oven door). Pour the kimchi mixture evenly over the rice mixture, then use a spatula to scrape and stir until well combined. With the bottom of a ½-cup dry measuring cup, make 6 evenly spaced wells in the rice mixture. Crack an egg into each well, mist the eggs with cooking spray and sprinkle with salt and pepper.

Return the baking sheet to the oven and cook until the egg whites are set but the yolks wobble when the baking sheet is jiggled, 6 to 8 minutes. Cool for a couple minutes, then sprinkle with the scallion greens and sesame seeds. Serve with soy sauce for drizzling.

BAKED MEATBALLS WITH SPICY TOMATO SAUCE

Start to finish: 1 hour (20 minutes active)
Servings: 4

A go-to pantry flavor solution does double duty when we add it to both meatballs and sauce. Depending on your mood and what you have on hand, give the dish a Mexican flair with smoky-spicy chipotle chilies in adobo, or use the spice paste harissa for a taste of North Africa. We roast cherry tomatoes until they burst—their juices mingle with the seasonings to form a luscious sauce. Then we nestle in the meatballs and roast everything in the same pan. Serve with crusty bread for dipping in the sauce. Refrigerate the meatballs before cooking; this firms them up so they'll hold their shape as they roast.

2 pints cherry OR grape tomatoes

6 medium garlic cloves, 4 cloves smashed and peeled, 2 cloves finely grated, reserved separately

¼ cup extra-virgin olive oil

2 medium chipotle chilies in adobo sauce, chopped, plus 2 teaspoons adobo sauce, divided OR 1 tablespoon plus 2 teaspoons harissa paste, divided

Kosher salt and ground black pepper

⅓ cup panko breadcrumbs

1 pound 90 percent lean ground beef OR ground lamb

Chopped fresh cilantro OR flat-leaf parsley, to serve

Heat the oven to 425°F with a rack in the middle position. In a 9-by-13-inch baking dish, toss together the tomatoes, smashed garlic, oil, chipotle chilies **OR** 1 tablespoon harissa, ¼ teaspoon each salt and pepper and ¼ cup water. Bake, uncovered, until the tomatoes have broken down, 30 to 35 minutes; stir once about halfway through.

Meanwhile, in a medium bowl, combine the panko and ½ cup water. Let stand until the panko softens, about 5 minutes, then use your hands to mash to a smooth paste. Add the beef, grated garlic, adobo sauce **OR** 2 teaspoons harissa and ½ teaspoon each salt and pepper; mix thoroughly with your hands. Divide into 12 portions, rolling them into smooth balls. Place on a large plate and refrigerate until ready to use.

Remove the baking dish from the oven and nestle the meatballs in the tomato sauce. Bake, uncovered, until the meatballs are browned and the centers reach 160°F, about 15 minutes. Taste and season the sauce with salt and pepper. Sprinkle with cilantro.

Optional garnish: Crumbled cotija **OR** feta cheese

LEBANESE BAKED KAFTA WITH POTATOES AND TOMATOES

Start to finish: 1½ hours (1 hour active), plus cooling
Servings: 4 to 6

It's easy to see why kafta bil sanieh, a casserole, if you will, of sliced potatoes, rounds of tomatoes and flavorful kafta (seasoned meatballs or meat patties), is Lebanese comfort food. The ingredients are shingled into a baking dish and baked until the flavors meld and the textures become deliciously succulent and tender. Our rendition, based on a recipe from "The Palestinian Table" by Reem Kassis, starts with a simple no-cook tomato sauce in the bottom of the baking dish, where juices collect during baking and form a delicious sauce. To ensure the potatoes cook evenly and thoroughly, we precook them by roasting them for about 10 minutes, enough time to begin making the kafta. We especially like the flavor of ground lamb kafta, but if you prefer, use 80 percent lean ground beef instead. Serve with rice pilaf.

1 pound Yukon Gold potatoes, unpeeled, sliced into ¼-inch rounds

2 tablespoons plus ¼ cup extra-virgin olive oil, divided

Kosher salt and ground black pepper

1 pound ground lamb or 80 percent lean ground beef

1 medium yellow onion, halved and grated on the large holes of a box grater

½ cup finely chopped fresh flat-leaf parsley

½ teaspoon ground allspice

½ teaspoon ground cinnamon

14½-ounce can crushed tomatoes

2 medium garlic cloves, minced

1 pound plum tomatoes, cored and sliced into ¼-inch rounds

1 small green bell pepper or Anaheim chili, stemmed, seeded and sliced into thin rings

Heat the oven to 450°F with a rack in the middle position. On a rimmed baking sheet, toss the potatoes with 1 tablespoon of oil and ¼ teaspoon salt. Distribute in a single layer and roast without stirring just until a skewer inserted into the potatoes meets no resistance, 10 to 13 minutes. Remove from the oven and set aside to cool slightly. Leave the oven on.

While the potatoes cook, line a second baking sheet with kitchen parchment. In a medium bowl, combine the lamb, onion, parsley, allspice, cinnamon, ¾ teaspoon salt and ¼ teaspoon pepper. Using your hands, mix gently until just combined; do not overmix. Divide the mixture into about 20 golf ball-size portions (1½ to 1¾ inches in diameter) and place on the prepared baking sheet. Flatten each ball into a patty about 2½ inches wide and ¼ inch thick (it's fine if the patties are not perfectly round); set aside until ready to assemble.

In a 9-by-13-inch baking dish, combine the crushed tomatoes, garlic, the ¼ cup oil, ½ teaspoon salt and ¼ teaspoon pepper. Stir well, then distribute in an even layer. Shingle the potatoes, tomato slices, green pepper rings and meat patties in 3 or 4 rows down the length of the baking dish, alternating the ingredients. Drizzle with the remaining 1 tablespoon oil and sprinkle with pepper.

Bake, uncovered, until the kafta and potatoes are browned and the juices are bubbling, 25 to 35 minutes. Cool for about 10 minutes before serving.

IRAQI-INSPIRED BROILED SALMON WITH TOMATOES AND ONION

Start to finish: 35 minutes
Servings: 4

This recipe was inspired by the Iraqi dish known as masgouf—fish grilled over an open fire and smothered with cooked onions and tomatoes. We cook salmon fillets under the broiler, so you don't need to fire up the grill and the dish comes together easily even on weeknights. Sliced onion and cherry tomatoes are roasted at a high temperature to caramelize them and concentrate their sweet flavors. Curry-seasoned salmon then is nestled into the sauce and quickly broiled, so make sure your baking dish is broiler-safe.

1 teaspoon curry powder

Kosher salt and ground black pepper

**Four 6-ounce center-cut salmon fillets
(each 1 to 1¼ inches thick), patted dry**

1 medium red OR yellow onion, halved and thinly sliced

1 pint cherry OR grape tomatoes

4 tablespoons extra-virgin olive oil, divided

2 tablespoons tomato paste

2 tablespoons lemon OR orange juice, divided, plus 1 tablespoon grated lemon OR orange zest

1 teaspoon ground coriander OR ½ teaspoon ground ginger OR both

½ cup lightly packed fresh flat-leaf parsley, finely chopped

Heat the oven to 475°F with a rack in the upper-middle position. In a small bowl, stir together the curry powder, ½ teaspoon salt and ¼ teaspoon pepper. Season the salmon all over with the mixture; set aside.

In a broiler-safe 9-by-13-inch baking dish, stir together the onion, tomatoes, 2 tablespoons oil and ¼ teaspoon each salt and pepper. Distribute in an even layer and roast until the tomatoes are beginning to burst, about 15 minutes.

Meanwhile, in a small bowl, whisk together the tomato paste, 1 tablespoon lemon juice, the coriander and ½ cup water. In another small bowl, stir together the parsley, the remaining 2 tablespoons oil, remaining 1 tablespoon lemon juice, lemon zest and ¼ teaspoon pepper; set aside for serving.

Remove the baking dish from the oven and turn the oven to broil. Stir the tomato paste mixture into the onion and tomatoes. Nestle the salmon skin (or skinned) side down into the mixture, then spoon some of the onion and tomatoes over the top. Broil until both the salmon and tomato-onion mixture are spotty brown and the fish flakes easily, 4 to 6 minutes.

Cool for about 5 minutes, then spoon the parsley mixture over the top.

Optional garnish: Toasted and roughly chopped pine nuts

SHRIMP AND FETA BAKE

Start to finish: 1 hour 10 minutes (30 minutes active)

Servings: 4

This is an oven-baked version of garides saganaki, a classic Greek dish that combines sweet shrimp with tangy tomatoes and briny feta cheese. The tomato mixture spends about 45 minutes in the oven to soften the vegetables and concentrate their flavors before the shrimp—which are done in a flash—are stirred in. Serve directly from the baking dish, with plenty of warm, crusty bread to sop up all of the juices.

1 tablespoon plus 1 teaspoon extra-virgin olive oil, divided, plus more to serve

2 teaspoons dried oregano, divided

2 pounds ripe tomatoes, cored and roughly chopped

1 medium fennel bulb, trimmed, halved, cored and thinly sliced against the grain

1 medium red onion, halved and sliced about ½ inch thick

Kosher salt and ground black pepper

1½ pounds extra-large shrimp (21/25 per pound), peeled, deveined and patted dry

4 ounces feta cheese, crumbled (1 cup)

3 tablespoons finely chopped fresh flat-leaf parsley

Heat the oven to 425°F with a rack in the middle position. In a 9-by-13-inch baking dish, toss together the 1 tablespoon oil, 1 teaspoon oregano, the tomatoes, fennel, onion and ¼ teaspoon each salt and pepper. Distribute in an even layer, then cover with foil and bake for 15 minutes. Meanwhile, in a medium bowl, toss together the shrimp, the

remaining 1 teaspoon oregano, the remaining 1 teaspoon oil and ½ teaspoon each salt and pepper; set aside.

Uncover the baking dish and stir the tomato mixture. Continue baking, uncovered, until the vegetables fully soften, about another 30 minutes. Remove from the oven; leave the oven on.

Using a silicone spatula, lightly mash the tomato mixture, then stir in the shrimp, distributing in an even layer. Bake, uncovered, until the shrimp are beginning to turn opaque, about 3 minutes. Stir, flipping the shrimp, then bake until the shrimp are just opaque throughout, about another 2 minutes.

Remove from the oven, stir in half of the feta and let stand for about 5 minutes. Sprinkle with the remaining feta and the parsley, then drizzle with additional oil. Serve from the baking dish.

HARISSA-ROASTED SALMON WITH LEMON, OLIVE AND PARSLEY RELISH

Start to finish: 50 minutes (15 minutes active)

Servings: 4

Harissa, the North African spice paste we consider a pantry staple, adds flavor to salmon fillets along with garlic and lemon juice. After roasting, we serve the fillets with a simple three-ingredient relish made by combining parsley, lemon zest and chopped green (or black) olives. We use the bold, zingy intensity of the herbal garnish to balance the fattiness of the salmon. Serve with couscous, and perhaps a cucumber or tomato salad.

3 tablespoons harissa paste

2 tablespoons extra-virgin olive oil, divided

3 medium garlic cloves, finely grated

1 tablespoon grated lemon zest, plus 2 teaspoons lemon juice, plus lemon wedges to serve

Kosher salt

Four 6-ounce center-cut skin-on salmon fillets (each 1 to 1¼ inches thick), patted dry

½ cup lightly packed fresh flat-leaf parsley OR cilantro, roughly chopped

½ cup pitted green OR black olives, roughly chopped

Set a wire rack in a rimmed baking sheet and mist it with cooking spray. In a small bowl, stir together the harissa, 1 tablespoon oil, garlic, the lemon juice and 1 teaspoon salt. Place the salmon skin side down on the rack. Rub the harissa mixture onto the top and sides of the fillets. Let stand at room temperature while the oven heats.

Heat the oven to 450°F with a rack in the middle position. Meanwhile, in a small bowl, stir together the parsley, olives, the remaining 1 tablespoon oil, the lemon zest and ¼ teaspoon salt.

Roast the salmon until the flesh flakes easily and the harissa mixture has deepened in color, 12 to 14 minutes. Serve the fillets with the parsley-olive mixture and lemon wedges.

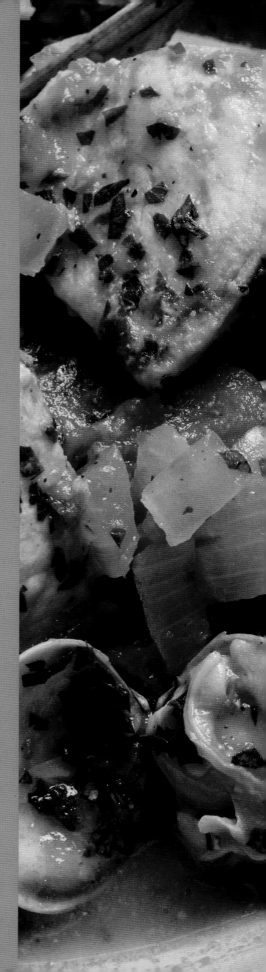

Braises & Stews

Spanish Summer Vegetable Stew

Start to finish: 50 minutes
Servings: 4 to 6

Pisto manchego is the Spanish equivalent of French rata-touille. The hearty, colorful vegetarian stew can be served as a tapa (small plate), as a side dish or topped with a fried egg as a meal in itself. **To achieve just the right texture and flavor we add the vegetables to the pot in stages so each cooks for just the right amount of time and retains its character in the finished dish.** This pisto is without eggplant, a common addition in many versions, and for flavor and color balance, we like to use one green bell pepper and one red, but if you like, replace the green with a yellow or orange pepper. Serve with crusty bread to soak up the juices.

⅓ cup extra-virgin olive oil, plus more to serve

2 medium yellow onions, chopped

Kosher salt and ground black pepper

1 medium zucchini OR yellow summer squash (about 8 ounces), quartered lengthwise and cut crosswise into ½-inch pieces

4 medium garlic cloves, thinly sliced

1 medium green bell pepper, stemmed, seeded and cut into ½-inch pieces

1 medium red bell pepper, stemmed, seeded and cut into ½-inch pieces

1 pound ripe tomatoes, cored and finely chopped

In a large pot over medium, heat the oil until shimmering. Add the onions and ¼ teaspoon salt, then cover and cook, stirring occasionally, until softened but not browned, 8 to 10 minutes. Add the zucchini and garlic. Increase to medium-high and cook, uncovered and stirring occasionally, until the zucchini is beginning to soften, about 7 minutes.

Stir in both bell peppers and cook, stirring occasionally, until the peppers are softened, about 7 minutes. Add the tomatoes, ½ teaspoon each salt and pepper, then cook, stirring occasionally, until the tomatoes have softened and the mixture is stewy, about 5 minutes. Taste and season with salt and pepper. Serve drizzled with additional oil.

In a large Dutch oven over medium, heat the coconut oil until shimmering. Add the onion, 1 teaspoon salt and ½ teaspoon pepper, then cook, stirring, until light golden brown and softened, 7 to 10 minutes.

Stir in the garlic and chilies, then cook until fragrant, about 30 seconds. Add the black-eyed peas, bay leaves and 5 cups water. Bring to a simmer over medium-high, then reduce to medium and cook, uncovered, stirring occasionally, until the flavors meld, about 15 minutes.

Stir in the sweet potatoes and 1 teaspoon salt. Cover, reduce to medium-low and cook until the potatoes are tender, 10 to 15 minutes. Off heat, stir in the tomatoes, parsley and lemon juice. Taste and season with salt and pepper. Serve with lemon wedges.

BLACK-EYED PEA AND SWEET POTATO STEW

Start to finish: 40 minutes
Servings: 6

Both sweet potatoes and black-eyed peas are staples of West African cooking. In this recipe for Senegalese ndambe (pronounced NAM-bay), they're simmered together to make a hearty vegetarian stew. Our version is based on a recipe from Pierre Thiam's "Yolele!" cookbook. Canned black-eyed peas keep this dish fast and simple.

2 tablespoons unrefined coconut oil

1 large yellow onion, finely chopped

Kosher salt and ground black pepper

8 medium garlic cloves, minced

2 Fresno chilies, stemmed and sliced into thin rings

Three 14½-ounce cans black-eyed peas, rinsed and drained

2 bay leaves

1 pound sweet potatoes, peeled and cut into ½-inch cubes

1 pound plum tomatoes, cored and chopped

1 cup finely chopped fresh flat-leaf parsley leaves

2 tablespoons lemon juice, plus lemon wedges, to serve

BARLEY, BEAN AND BUTTERNUT STEW

Start to finish: 1 hour 10 minutes (30 minutes active
Servings: 4 to 6

To create this hearty stew, we took inspiration from cholent, a long-simmered Jewish dish traditionally made for the Sabbath. It usually includes beef along with barley and vegetables, but we opted for a lighter, fresher meat-free version with chunks of earthy-sweet butternut squash. Be sure to use pearled barley, which has been polished, or "pearled," to remove the outer husk and bran layers; this shortens the cooking time. To enhance the barley's nutty flavor, we toast the grains for a few minutes before simmering them.

1 cup pearled barley

2 tablespoons extra-virgin olive oil

1 medium yellow onion, halved and sliced about ½ inch thick

Kosher salt and ground black pepper

3 tablespoons tomato paste

1 tablespoon sweet paprika

1 quart low-sodium vegetable broth OR chicken broth

1 pound butternut squash, peeled, seeded and cut into 1½-inch chunks (about 4 cups)

15½-ounce can kidney beans OR cannellini beans OR pinto beans, rinsed and drained

½ cup finely chopped fresh flat-leaf parsley OR dill

In a large pot over medium-high, toast the barley, stirring occasionally, until lightly browned, 4 to 5 minutes. Transfer to a small bowl; set aside.

In the same pot over medium, heat the oil until shimmering. Add the onion and ½ teaspoon salt, then cook, stirring occasionally, until the onion starts to soften and brown, 4 to 5 minutes. Add the tomato paste and cook over medium-high, stirring, until the paste browns and slightly sticks to the pot, about 2 minutes. Stir in the paprika and 1 teaspoon pepper.

Add the broth and 2 cups water and scrape up the browned bits. Stir in the barley, squash and beans. Bring to a boil, then reduce to medium-low, cover and simmer, stirring occasionally, until the barley and squash are tender, 40 to 45 minutes. Off heat, stir in the parsley. Taste and season with salt and pepper.

Optional garnish: Prepared horseradish **OR** sliced radishes

CHANGE THE WAY YOU COOK

Ingredient Swaps

Bold, simple cooking sometimes hinges on having just the right high-flavor ingredient. Unfortunately, our inspiration and cravings don't always match what's in our pantry. Maybe we've run out, or we might be reluctant to invest in something we've never tried before.

For those times when the right ingredient isn't handy, it's good to know some simple substitutions that draw on kitchen staples. With that in mind, we experimented to find similar-tasting alternatives for some of Milk Street's favorite—albeit less common—flavorings.

To make sure our substitutions passed the taste test, we did side-by-side comparisons of recipes that prominently feature the original ingredient. Some of our substitutions came together fairly intuitively, such as our formula for hot paprika. Others were more challenging.

For example, while we found that there's no faking the distinctive, complex tang that comes from fermentation in ingredients such as red miso and gochujang, we found that easier-to-find white miso could serve as the backbone for creating taste-alike substitutes.

Ingredient (1 T)	Substitution
Aleppo Pepper	1 T sweet paprika + ¾ t cayenne
Gochujang	1 T white miso + 1 t Sriracha + ½ t molasses
Harissa	2 t Sriracha + 1 t extra-virgin olive oil + ½ t red pepper flakes +½ t chili powder
Hot Paprika	1 T sweet paprika + ¼ t cayenne
Pomegranate Molasses	2¼ t aged balsamic vinegar + ½ t honey + ¼ t molasses
Red Miso	2½ t white miso + ½ t soy sauce + ⅛ t cocoa powder
Sumac	2 t finely grated lemon zest, 1 t fresh lemon juice + 1 t minced dried cranberry
White Balsamic	1 T unseasoned rice vinegar + ½ t honey
Za'atar	1½ t dried thyme + 1 t finely grated lemon zest + ¾ t sesame seeds + ⅛ t salt

T=tablespoon   t=teaspoon

PERSIAN RED LENTIL AND POTATO STEW WITH TOMATOES AND LIME

Start to finish: 25 minutes
Servings: 4

Dal adas is a vegetarian red lentil stew from southern Iran. The starting point for our recipe comes from "From a Persian Kitchen" by Atoosa Sepehr. To simplify the spicing, we use curry powder and supplement with a little ground cinnamon. And for bright flavor, we add chopped tomatoes that have been lightly cooked with the aromatics and spices. In non-summer months, opt for a pint of cherry or grape tomatoes; they don't need to be cored, but do chop them. Serve this thick, hearty stew with basmati rice or warmed flatbread.

¾ cup red lentils, rinsed and drained

1 medium Yukon Gold potato, peeled and cut into ¼-inch cubes

Kosher salt and ground black pepper

3 tablespoons neutral oil or ghee

1 medium yellow onion, finely chopped

2 medium garlic cloves, minced

1 serrano or Fresno chili, stemmed, seeded and minced or ½ teaspoon cayenne pepper

1½ teaspoons curry powder

¼ teaspoon ground cinnamon

12 ounces ripe tomatoes, cored and chopped

1 tablespoon lime juice

2 scallions, thinly sliced

In a large saucepan, combine the lentils, potato, 2¾ cups water and ½ teaspoon each salt and pepper. Bring to a simmer over medium-high, then reduce to medium and simmer, uncovered and stirring occasionally, until the lentils and potatoes are tender but still hold their shape, 12 to 16 minutes.

Meanwhile, in a 10-inch skillet over medium-high, heat the oil until shimmering. Add the onion, garlic and ½ teaspoon salt; cook, stirring occasionally, until lightly browned, 3 to 5 minutes. Add the chili, curry powder and cinnamon, then cook, stirring, until fragrant, about 30 seconds. Add the tomatoes and cook, scraping up any browned bits, until they

soften, about 2 minutes. Remove the pan from the heat. Stir the lime juice and half of the scallions; set aside.

When the lentils are done, stir in the tomato mixture. Taste and season with salt and pepper. Serve sprinkled with the remaining scallions.

SPANISH SHRIMP AND CHICKPEA STEW

Start to finish: 35 minutes
Servings: 4

At Palacio Carvajal Girón, in the Extremadura region of Spain, we tasted a delicious shellfish and chickpea stew. Requiring a ham- and langoustine-infused broth and made with dried chickpeas, the dish was a time- and labor-intensive preparation. Our much-simplified version captures the essence of the stew in a fraction of the time. A combination of Spanish smoked paprika and standard sweet paprika give the stew deep color and earthy complexity without overwhelming the shrimp.

bowl. Cook without stirring until browned on the bottom, about 2 minutes. Using a slotted spoon, return the shrimp to the bowl.

In the same pot over medium, melt the butter. Add the leek and cook, stirring occasionally, until softened, 4 to 5 minutes. Add the garlic and the reserved paprika mixture, then cook, stirring, until fragrant, about 1 minute. Stir in the chickpeas, the reserved chickpea liquid and the clam juice. Bring to a simmer, then reduce to low, cover and cook for 10 minutes, stirring once or twice. Meanwhile, remove and discard the tails from the shrimp and cut each shrimp in half crosswise.

Remove the pot from the heat and stir in the shrimp along with accumulated juices. Cover and let stand until the shrimp are opaque throughout, 2 to 3 minutes. Taste and season with salt and pepper. Serve sprinkled with parsley and drizzled with additional oil.

SPICY KOREAN-STYLE BRAISED COD

Start to finish: 30 minutes

Servings: 4

This skillet braise is a simplified version of daegu jorim, or Korean braised cod. We build an umami-rich braising liquid by combining sake, mirin, soy sauce and gochujang (Korean fermented chili paste), plus garlic, ginger and chilies. In the Korean kitchen, steaks of fatty fish, such as black cod or mackerel, are commonly used in daegu jorim, but we opt for easy-to-source Atlantic cod fillets. Earthy, subtly sweet daikon radish is a standard ingredient in the braise but Yukon Gold potatoes work nicely, too. We also add bok choy for color and to round out the braise. If you like, sprinkle sliced scallions or toasted sesame seeds as a garnish, and/or drizzle some sesame oil. Be sure to serve steamed short-grain rice alongside, and kimchi would be a great accompaniment, too.

1½ cups sake

⅓ cup mirin

¼ cup soy sauce

3 tablespoons gochujang

4 medium garlic cloves, minced

2 tablespoons minced fresh ginger

2 tablespoons smoked paprika

1 tablespoon sweet paprika

Kosher salt and ground black pepper

1 pound extra-large (21/25 per pound) shrimp, peeled (tails left on), deveined and patted dry

2 tablespoons extra-virgin olive oil, plus more to serve

2 tablespoons salted butter

1 medium leek, white and light green parts halved lengthwise, thinly sliced, rinsed and dried

4 medium garlic cloves, minced

15½-ounce can chickpeas, ½ cup liquid reserved, drained

8-ounce bottle clam juice

Chopped fresh flat-leaf parsley, to serve

In a medium bowl, stir together both paprikas and ¾ teaspoon pepper; measure 2 tablespoons into a small bowl and set aside. Add the shrimp to the paprika mixture in the medium bowl and toss to coat; set aside.

In a large Dutch oven over medium-high, heat the oil until shimmering. Add the shrimp in an even layer; reserve the

1 or 2 Fresno or jalapeño chilies, stemmed and sliced into thin rounds

12 ounces daikon radish, peeled, quartered lengthwise and cut crosswise into ½-inch pieces or 12 ounces medium Yukon Gold potatoes, peeled and sliced into ½-inch rounds

Four 6-ounce skinless cod fillets, each about 1 inch thick

8 ounces baby bok choy, trimmed and cut crosswise into 1-inch pieces

Kosher salt and ground black pepper

In a 12-inch skillet, stir together the sake, mirin, soy sauce, gochujang, garlic, ginger and chilies; bring to a boil over medium-high, stirring occasionally. Add the daikon, then cover, reduce to medium, and cook, flipping and stirring the radish every 5 minutes or so, until a skewer inserted into the pieces meets no resistance, 10 to 15 minutes.

Slide the cod fillets into the skillet and scatter the bok choy over the top. Cover partially and cook over medium, turning the fish and stirring the vegetables just once or twice, until the cod flakes easily and the sauce is slightly thickened, 5 to 8 minutes. Taste and season with salt and pepper.

CURRY-COCONUT BRAISED FISH

Start to finish: 20 minutes
Servings: 4

Comfortingly creamy with a little hit of heat, this easy weeknight dish was inspired by chef Edward Lee, author of "Smoke & Pickles," which explores his philosophy of finding innovative ways to blend Southern cuisine and Asian flavors. The coconut milk curry evokes traditional Thai flavors as well as fish amok, the Cambodian classic fish curry often served steamed in a banana leaf. And assembly couldn't be simpler—dump everything but the fish into a pot for about 10 minutes, then add the fish to gently cook for another 10. Any thick, firm whitefish, such as cod, hake or Chilean sea bass, will work. Avoid a thin fillet such as sole or tilapia, which will break down in the braising liquid. Using full-fat coconut milk was important, as it will not break as the vegetables cook. Low-sodium chicken broth gave us better control over the dish's final seasoning.

14-ounce can full-fat coconut milk

2 medium carrots, peeled, halved lengthwise and cut into ½-inch pieces

1 medium yellow onion, halved and thinly sliced

6 garlic cloves, finely grated

2 teaspoons turmeric

2 teaspoons curry powder

½ teaspoon red pepper flakes

1 cup low-sodium chicken broth

1½ pounds firm white fish, cut into 2-inch chunks

Kosher salt and ground white pepper

Steamed white rice, to serve

Lime wedges, to serve

In a large Dutch oven over medium-high, combine the coconut milk, carrots, onion, garlic, turmeric, curry powder and pepper flakes. Cook over medium heat, uncovered and stirring occasionally, until thickened and the vegetables are softened, about 10 minutes.

Stir in the broth and bring to a simmer. Season the fish with salt and white pepper, then stir into the pot. Cover and cook over low until the fish flakes easily when poked with a fork but remains intact, 7 to 10 minutes. Taste and season with salt and pepper. Serve over steamed white rice with lime wedges.

ITALIAN SEAFOOD STEW WITH TOMATOES AND WHITE WINE

Start to finish: 30 minutes
Servings: 4

The Italian fishermen's stew called brodetto comes from the Adriatic coast. Some traditional regional versions are elaborate, made with myriad types of seafood, others feature just a single variety of fish. But all are meant to use the daily catch from the local waters. For our simple weeknight stew, we use firm white fish along with mussels or clams, which release flavorful liquid into the fragrant tomato-based broth. Swordfish is firm and retains its meatiness, while cod tends to flake apart. Other types of fish that work well are monkfish and halibut. If you opt for

clams instead of mussels, look for ones about 1½ inches in diameter so they cook in the times indicated in the recipe. Serve with crusty bread for dipping.

28-ounce can whole peeled tomatoes

1 pound boneless, skinless firm white fish, such as swordfish steaks or cod fillets, cut into 2-inch pieces

3 medium garlic cloves, finely grated

1 teaspoon grated lemon zest, plus 1 teaspoon lemon juice

1 cup lightly packed fresh flat-leaf parsley, finely chopped, divided

3 tablespoons extra-virgin olive oil, divided

Kosher salt and ground black pepper

1 medium yellow onion, chopped

1 tablespoon tomato paste

½ cup dry white wine

4 bay leaves

2 pounds mussels or small hardshell clams (about 1½ inches in diameter), scrubbed

Reserve ½ **cup juice** from the tomatoes, then drain the tomatoes; discard the remaining juice. Using your hands, crush the tomatoes; set the reserved juice and tomatoes aside separately. In a medium bowl, toss the fish with the garlic, lemon zest, 2 tablespoons of parsley, 1 tablespoon of oil and ¼ teaspoon salt; set aside.

In a large Dutch oven over medium, heat the remaining 2 tablespoons oil until shimmering. Add the onion and ½ teaspoon salt, then cover and cook, stirring occasionally, until translucent, 3 to 5 minutes. Add the tomatoes and the tomato paste. Cook, stirring, until heated through, about 2 minutes. Add the wine, bay, 1 teaspoon pepper and the reserved tomato juice, then bring to a simmer over medium-high.

Add the fish and return to a simmer, then scatter the mussels over the top. Immediately cover, reduce to medium and cook for 4 minutes; the mussels should just begin to open when agitated. Gently stir, turning the fish so the pieces cook evenly. Re-cover and cook until the fish flakes easily and the mussels have opened, another 3 to 5 minutes.

Discard any mussels that have not opened. Remove and discard the bay, then taste and season with salt and pepper. Stir in the lemon juice and the remaining parsley.

JAMAICAN-STYLE FISH STEW

Start to finish: 40 minutes
Servings: 4 to 6

This simple skillet stew is rich with Caribbean flavors. It's inspired by a dish called Jamaican run-down, which simmers mackerel in coconut milk, along with tomatoes, thyme and aromatics. The cooking liquid reduces to a luxurious sauce with spiciness and fruity notes from the habanero chili, tropical flavor from the coconut and brightness from the lime juice. Instead of mackerel, which can be difficult to source and also has an assertiveness that's polarizing, we use mild, firm sea bass fillets. Serve with fried plantains or rice and beans.

2 tablespoons grapeseed or other neutral oil

1 medium yellow onion, halved and thinly sliced

2 medium garlic cloves, minced

1 habanero chili, stemmed and sliced into thin rings

¼ teaspoon ground allspice

12 ounces ripe tomatoes, cored and chopped

¾ cup coconut milk

2 large thyme sprigs

Kosher salt and ground black pepper

1½ pounds skinless sea bass or snapper fillets, about 1 inch thick, cut into 1½-inch chunks

2 tablespoons lime juice, plus lime wedges to serve

3 scallions, thinly sliced

In a 12-inch skillet over medium-high, heat the oil until shimmering. Add the onion and cook, stirring occasionally, until softened and beginning to brown, 4 to 5 minutes. Add the garlic, habanero and allspice; cook, stirring, until fragrant, 30 to 60 seconds. Stir in the tomatoes and cook, stirring occasionally, until they begin to break down and release their liquid, 3 to 4 minutes.

Add the coconut milk and ¾ cup water; scrape up any browned bits. Add the thyme, ½ teaspoon salt and ¼ teaspoon pepper, then bring to a simmer. Cover and simmer, stirring occasionally, until the tomatoes have fully broken down and the sauce is slightly thickened, about 10 minutes.

Nestle the fish into the sauce. Bring to a gentle simmer and cook, stirring gently and occasionally, until the fish is opaque throughout, 4 to 5 minutes. Off heat, remove and discard the thyme, then stir in the lime juice. Taste and season with salt and pepper. Serve with lime wedges.

COD AND HARISSA TAGINE

Start to finish: 50 minutes (20 minutes active)

Servings: 4

Moroccan tagines prepared with whole fish inspired this simple skillet dinner. With fresh fennel, garlic, a few choice seasonings and spicy harissa, the cooking liquid is infused with a bold flavor and fragrance. Mild and flaky cod fillets work beautifully, but any firm-textured white fish will do. Just make sure to adjust the cooking time as needed—for every 1 inch of thickness, simmer gently for about 8 minutes. A starchy side, such as couscous, steamed potatoes or warmed bread, is the perfect accompaniment.

5 tablespoons extra-virgin olive oil, divided

3 tablespoons harissa, divided

2 medium fennel bulbs, trimmed and thinly sliced (about 4 cups)

4 medium garlic cloves, thinly sliced

1 teaspoon coriander seeds

Kosher salt and ground white pepper

1 teaspoon ground turmeric

Four 6-ounce skinless cod fillets

**2 teaspoons grated lemon zest, plus
2 tablespoons lemon juice**

¼ cup pimento-stuffed green olives, chopped

¼ cup sliced almonds, toasted

In a 12-inch skillet over medium, stir together 3 tablespoons of oil, 2 tablespoons of harissa, the fennel, garlic, coriander, ¾ teaspoon salt and ¼ teaspoon white pepper. Cover and cook, stirring occasionally, until the fennel has softened, 15 to 20 minutes.

Meanwhile, in a medium bowl, stir together the remaining 2 tablespoons oil, the remaining 1 tablespoon harissa, the turmeric, ¼ teaspoon salt and ¼ teaspoon white pepper. Add the fish and turn to coat on all sides; set aside.

To the skillet, add ¼ cup water and bring to a simmer. Nestle the fish into the fennel, cover and cook over medium-low until the fish is opaque and flakes easily with a fork, 8 to 10 minutes. Stir in the lemon juice. Taste and season with salt and pepper. Remove from the heat.

In a small bowl, stir together the lemon zest, olives and almonds. Sprinkle evenly over the fish; bring the skillet to the table for serving.

Greek Braised Chicken with Tomatoes and Cinnamon

Start to finish: 1¼ hours (35 minutes active)
Servings: 4

The rustic, homey Greek dish called kota kapama stews chicken with fragrant cinnamon, sweet-tart tomatoes and, more often than not, white or red wine. **For this recipe, we use bone-in, skin-on chicken thighs and braise them in a minimal amount of liquid. This way, the chicken cooks mostly in the juices it releases. Without other ingredients to dilute the flavor, the resulting sauce is wonderfully rich and full-bodied.** Kota kapama traditionally is served with orzo or other noodles, but any starchy side—from crusty bread to mashed potatoes—works well.

1 teaspoon ground cinnamon

½ teaspoon ground allspice

Kosher salt and ground black pepper

3 pounds bone-in, skin-on chicken thighs, trimmed and patted dry

1 tablespoon extra-virgin olive oil

1 medium red onion, thinly sliced

4 medium garlic cloves, thinly sliced

2 tablespoons tomato paste

½ cup dry white wine

8 ounces plum tomatoes, cored and chopped

½ cup lightly packed fresh mint, chopped

In a small bowl, stir together the cinnamon, allspice and 1 teaspoon each salt and pepper. Use the mixture to season the chicken all over, gently rubbing it in.

In a large Dutch oven over medium, heat the oil until shimmering. Place the chicken skin side down and cook without stirring until well browned and the pieces release easily from the pot, 10 to 12 minutes. Transfer the chicken skin side up to a plate and set aside. Pour off and discard all but 1 tablespoon of fat from the pot.

Set the pot over medium and add the onion, garlic and tomato paste. Cook, stirring occasionally, until the mixture is lightly browned, about 2 minutes. Add the wine and cook,

scraping up any browned bits, until almost fully evaporated, about 1 minute. Stir in the tomatoes and bring to a simmer. Return the chicken to the pot, placing the pieces skin side up, then add the accumulated juices. Cover, reduce to medium-low and cook until a skewer inserted into the chicken meets no resistance, 35 to 45 minutes.

Transfer the chicken to a serving platter. Taste the sauce and season with salt and pepper, then spoon it over the chicken. Sprinkle with the chopped mint.

CHICKEN VINDALOO

Start to finish: 1 hour 20 minutes
Servings: 4

Vindaloo, an Indian dish of Portuguese influence, typically is associated with the state of Goa on India's southwestern coast, but the curry is popular the world over. It is made with pork, lamb or chicken, and is notable for its vinegary tang, a generous dose of garlic and the spiciness of dried chilies. The Kashmiri chili powder used in India is vibrantly colored with moderate heat; we found a mixture of sweet paprika and cayenne to be a good substitute. If you purchase Kashmiri chili powder, substitute 4 teaspoons for the paprika and cayenne. Serve with basmati rice.

¼ cup plus 2 tablespoons white vinegar, divided

12 medium garlic cloves, smashed and peeled

1-inch piece fresh ginger, peeled and roughly chopped

2 tablespoons sweet paprika

2 tablespoons packed brown sugar

4 whole cloves or ⅛ teaspoon ground cloves

2½ teaspoons ground turmeric

2 teaspoons cumin seeds

½ to 1 teaspoon cayenne pepper

¼ teaspoon ground cinnamon

Kosher salt and ground black pepper

2 pounds boneless, skinless chicken thighs, trimmed and halved

2 tablespoons neutral oil

Fresno or jalapeño chilies, stemmed and sliced into thin rings, to serve

Fresh cilantro leaves, to serve

In a blender, combine ¼ cup vinegar, garlic, ginger, paprika, sugar, cloves, turmeric, cumin, cayenne, cinnamon, ¾ teaspoon salt, 1¼ teaspoons pepper, and 3 tablespoons water. Puree until smooth, scraping the blender as needed. Pour into a medium bowl, add the chicken and toss to coat. Let stand at room temperature for 15 minutes.

In a large Dutch oven over medium, heat the oil until shimmering. Add the chicken and marinade in an even layer. Cook without stirring until the marinade has browned and the chicken releases easily from the pot, 5 to 9 minutes. Stir, then add ⅓ cup water and bring to a simmer. Cover, reduce to medium-low and cook, stirring occasionally, until a skewer inserted into the chicken meets no resistance, 35 to 45 minutes.

Stir in the remaining 2 tablespoons vinegar, increase to medium and cook, stirring often, until the sauce is thick enough that a spoon drawn through leaves a trail, about 8 minutes. Taste and season with salt and pepper. Transfer to a serving dish and sprinkle with sliced chilies and cilantro.

NORTH AFRICAN CHICKEN COUSCOUS

Start to finish: 1¼ hours (40 minutes active)
Servings: 6

We got an education in couscous in Tunisia, including a lesson from Amel Cherif, a home cook who showed us, in her apartment kitchen on the outskirts of Tunis, the basics of making light, flavorful couscous. For our version, we use an 8-quart pot fitted with a stackable steamer insert that sits on top. If you don't own one, a large pot and a folding steamer basket worked well, too. Whisking the liquid from the stew into the steamed couscous is a key step, deeply flavoring the grain-like pasta and helping it stay fluffy and distinct. Harissa is a North African chili and spice paste that brings heat, complex flavor and a red hue to any dish to which it's added. If you can find DEA brand, sold in a tube and cans, it's our preferred harissa. We start the recipe using ¼ cup harissa to flavor the stew, then finish by mixing another ¼ cup into the stew liquid just before whisking it with the steamed couscous. If your harissa is particularly spicy or you prefer less heat, reduce the second addition of harissa.

2 cups couscous

4 tablespoons extra-virgin olive oil, divided, plus more to serve

Kosher salt and ground black pepper

1½ tablespoons ground turmeric

2 pounds boneless, skinless chicken thighs, trimmed and halved crosswise

1 pound Yukon Gold potatoes, cut into 1½-inch chunks

6 medium carrots, peeled, halved lengthwise and cut into 2-inch pieces

1 large red onion, root end intact, peeled and cut into 8 wedges

2 jalapeño chilies, stemmed and thinly sliced

6 medium garlic cloves, minced

2 tablespoons tomato paste

½ cup harissa paste (more or less, to taste), divided

Lemon wedges, to serve

In a medium bowl, combine the couscous and 2 tablespoons oil, rubbing with your fingers until coated. Stir in 1¼ cups water and ¼ teaspoon salt; let stand for 15 minutes.

Meanwhile, in a medium bowl, stir together the turmeric, ½ teaspoon salt and 1 teaspoon pepper. Add the chicken and toss to coat; set aside for 15 minutes. In a large bowl, combine the potatoes, carrots, onion, 1 tablespoon of the remaining oil, ½ teaspoon salt and 1 teaspoon pepper. Toss to coat, then set aside.

Stir the couscous to separate the granules, then mound it in a steamer insert or basket that fits into an 8-quart pot; set aside. Set the 8-quart pot over medium-high and heat the remaining 1 tablespoon oil until barely smoking. Add the jalapeños and cook, stirring occasionally, until slightly softened, about 1 minute. Add the garlic, tomato paste and ¼ cup harissa; cook, stirring, until the mixture begins to brown, 1 to 2 minutes.

Add 2 cups water and bring to a simmer. Place the chicken in the pot, then top with the vegetables and any liquid in the bowl; do not stir. Bring to a simmer, then set the steamer insert or basket with the couscous on the pot; if using a folding steamer basket, set it directly on the vegetables. Cover, reduce to low and cook, maintaining a gentle simmer, until the chicken and vegetables are tender, about 45 minutes; do not stir the couscous or the stew.

Remove the steamer basket and transfer the couscous to a large bowl; cover with foil to keep warm. Stir the vegetables into the chicken, cover and let stand for 5 minutes.

Using a slotted spoon, transfer the chicken and vegetables to a large bowl; taste and season with salt and pepper. Measure out 2 cups of the cooking liquid in the pot. Stir the remaining ¼ cup harissa into it.

Whisk the couscous until no clumps remain, then whisk in the cooking liquid-harissa mixture. Taste and season with salt and pepper. Transfer the couscous to a large, deep platter and make a well at the center. Spoon the chicken and vegetables into the well. Drizzle with additional oil and serve with lemon wedges.

CHICKEN PAPRIKASH

our 40 minutes (25 minutes active)
Servings: 4 to 6

paprikás csirke, or chicken paprikash, blends techniques from restaurant chefs and home cooks who taught us their recipes during our visit to Budapest, Hungary. We learned that in addition to a generous amount of onion, sautéed until sweet and softened to create a flavor base, there are a couple other keys to achieving fullness and complexity in the iconic dish. Paprika (both sweet and hot) is, of course, a defining ingredient in the dish—one that adds a touch of heat, a rusty hue and thickening power to boot— but multiple forms of capsicums, or peppers, are essential for depth and range of flavor. To that end, we include jarred roasted red peppers, blended to a smooth puree, to bring a silky sweetness, plus a fresh banana (or wax) pepper, finely chopped, for tangy, fruity notes. Additionally, the freshness of the paprika is important. If yours has been in the pantry for a while and has lost its verve (it should be bright red, not dull brown, and full of fragrance), it won't deliver. Seek out fresh, quality paprika, and in particular look for brands produced in Hungary. With a lush, velvety sauce, paprikash traditionally is served with homemade dumplings called nokedli and a tangy-creamy cucumber salad called uborka saláta that brings brightness and texture (see sidebars).

½ cup drained jarred roasted red peppers

2 tablespoons lemon juice, divided

4 teaspoons hot paprika, divided

1 teaspoon white sugar

Kosher salt and ground black pepper

1 tablespoon extra-virgin olive oil

1 large yellow onion, finely chopped

1 ripe medium tomato, cored and chopped

2 banana peppers or wax peppers, 1 stemmed, seeded and finely chopped, 1 stemmed, seeded and thinly sliced, reserved separately

¼ cup sweet paprika

2 cups low-sodium chicken broth

3 pounds boneless, skinless chicken thighs, trimmed

¾ cup sour cream

Hungarian dumplings (see sidebar), to serve

Cucumber salad with sour cream (see sidebar), to serve

In a blender, combine the roasted peppers, 1 tablespoon of the lemon juice, 1 teaspoon of the hot paprika, the sugar and ½ teaspoon salt. Puree, scraping the jar as needed, until smooth, about 30 seconds. Set aside.

In a large Dutch oven over medium-high, heat the oil until barely smoking. Stir in the onion, tomato and finely chopped banana pepper. Cover, reduce to medium and cook, stirring often, until the tomato has broken down and the onion is softened and light golden brown, about 10 minutes.

Stir in the sweet paprika, remaining 3 teaspoons hot paprika, broth and half of the pepper puree. Bring to a simmer, then cover, reduce to low and cook, stirring occasionally, for 30 minutes.

Add the chicken and stir until well coated. Bring to a boil over medium-high, then cover, reduce to medium-low and simmer, stirring occasionally, until a skewer inserted into the chicken meets no resistance, about 40 minutes.

Off heat, stir in the remaining 1 tablespoon lemon juice. Push the chicken to the side; add the remaining pepper puree and the sour cream to the liquid. Whisk to incorporate, then stir to combine the sauce and chicken. Taste and season with salt and black pepper. Serve garnished with the sliced banana pepper and with the dumplings and cucumber salad.

HUNGARIAN DUMPLINGS (NOKEDLI)

Start to finish: 1 hour (30 minutes active)
Servings: 4 to 6

The rustic, freeform Hungarian dumplings that are served alongside paprikash are called nokedli. They're similar to German Spätzle, and, in fact, often are made with a Spätzle maker. But not to worry if you don't own one. Many Hungarian cooks use a more rustic way of forming them by ladling the batter onto a small, smooth-surfaced cheese board or cutting board and scraping small bits of it into the boiling water. For the tenderest dumplings, be sure to let the batter rest for 30 minutes before use. Or, if convenient, refrigerate the batter for up to 24 hours, but bring to room temperature before making the nokedli. While the paprikash simmers is a good time to cook the dumplings.

2 cups all-purpose flour

½ teaspoon grated fresh nutmeg

Kosher salt and ground black pepper

2 large eggs

In a large bowl, whisk together the flour, nutmeg, 1 teaspoon salt and ½ teaspoon pepper. In a small bowl or liquid measuring cup, whisk the eggs and 1 cup water. Add the egg mixture to the flour mixture; whisk until the ingredients form a smooth batter. Cover and let stand at room temperature for 30 minutes. Meanwhile, line a rimmed baking sheet with kitchen parchment and mist with cooking spray.

In a large pot, bring 4 quarts water to a boil. Stir in 1 tablespoon salt. Holding a small, smooth-surfaced wooden cutting board or cheese board above the water, ladle about 1 cup batter on the board (reduce the amount of batter if your board is very small). Using an offset spatula or butter knife, quickly scrape small bits of the batter, in narrow, ribbon-like sections, off the board into the boiling water. When all of the batter onto the board has been scraped into the water, set the board aside. Return the water to a boil and cook for 1 minute, stirring once or twice; the dumplings will float to the surface after about 30 seconds, before they are cooked through.

Using a slotted spoon, scoop the dumplings out of the water, let excess water fall back into the pot, then distribute in an even layer on the prepared baking sheet. Cover with foil to keep warm, then cook the remaining batter in the same way.

CUCUMBER SALAD WITH SOUR CREAM

Start to finish: 1 hour
Servings: 4 to 6

This creamy yet refreshing cucumber salad, called uborka saláta, is a traditional accompaniment to paprikash. The skin on an English cucumber is thin, but we prefer to remove it anyway. Salting the sliced cucumber for an hour prior to dressing removes excess moisture that otherwise would turn the salad watery. Be sure to drain the slices after salting and pat them dry with paper towels.

1 English cucumber, peeled, halved lengthwise and thinly sliced

Kosher salt and ground black pepper

¼ cup white vinegar

2 teaspoons white sugar

½ cup sour cream

In a medium bowl, toss the cucumber with 1 teaspoon salt. Cover and let stand at room temperature for about 1 hour to remove excess moisture. Drain in a colander, then pat dry with paper towels; wipe out the bowl.

In the same bowl, combine the vinegar and sugar; whisk until the sugar dissolves, then whisk in the sour cream. Add the cucumber and toss. Taste and season with salt and pepper. Serve at room temperature.

SENEGALESE BRAISED CHICKEN WITH ONIONS AND LIME

Start to finish: 1¼ hours, plus marinating

Servings: 4

With just a few ingredients, yassa ginaar delivers multiple layers of flavor—savory yet sweet with lightly caramelized onions, citrusy with lime zest and juice, meaty from the deeply browned chicken, and spicy from the heat of a habanero chili. Our version is based on a recipe in "Yolele!" by Pierre Thiam, who marinates then sears the chicken, then uses the marinade as a base for the flavorful sauce. Bouillon concentrate adds to the savoriness of the dish; our preferred brand is Better than Bouillon. Serve with steamed rice.

4 tablespoons peanut oil, divided

3 tablespoons grated lime zest, plus 6 tablespoons lime juice

1 habanero chili, seeded and minced

Kosher salt and ground black pepper

2 teaspoons chicken bouillon concentrate (see headnote)

2 pounds bone-in, skin-on chicken breasts, thighs or drumsticks, trimmed

3 medium yellow onions, halved and thinly sliced

Finely chopped fresh chives, to serve

In a large bowl, stir together 3 tablespoons of oil, the lime zest, habanero, 1½ teaspoons salt and 1 teaspoon pepper. Transfer 2 teaspoons of the mixture to a small bowl and set aside. To the remaining oil-zest mixture, whisk in the lime juice, bouillon and ¼ cup water. Add the chicken and onions and toss. Cover and let marinate at room temperature for 1 hour or refrigerate up to 2 hours, stirring once.

Remove the chicken from the marinade and pat dry with paper towels. Set a colander over a large bowl and strain the onions, reserving both the marinade and the onions.

In a large Dutch oven over medium-high, heat the remaining 1 tablespoon oil until barely smoking. Add the chicken, skin side down, and cook until well browned, about 4 minutes. Transfer to a plate and pour off and discard all but 1 tablespoon of the fat. Set the pot over medium heat and stir in the onions and ¼ cup water, scraping up any browned bits. Cover and cook, stirring frequently, until the onions are softened and lightly browned, 15 to 20 minutes.

Stir the reserved marinade into the onions. Return the chicken, skin side up, to the pot, nestling the pieces in the sauce, then pour in any accumulated juices. Reduce to medium-low, cover and cook, stirring occasionally, until a skewer inserted into the thickest part of the meat meets no resistance, about 25 minutes.

Using a slotted spoon, transfer the chicken to a serving platter or shallow bowl. Off heat, stir the reserved oil-zest mixture into the onions, then taste and season with salt and pepper. Spoon the onions and sauce around the chicken and sprinkle with chives.

SMOTHERED CHICKEN WITH BOURBON AND MISO

Start to finish: 50 minutes (25 minutes active)

Servings: 4

This is our adaptation of a recipe from "Smoke and Pickles" by Edward Lee. It's a fantastic East Asian-inflected spin on an all-American favorite: smothered pork chops. A combina-

tion of umami-rich ingredients, woodsy bourbon and sweet-tangy orange juice produces a silky, deeply flavored mushroom sauce for smothering tender bone-in chicken legs. Steamed Asian rice or light, fluffy biscuits are good accompaniments.

2 tablespoons soy sauce

1 tablespoon miso, preferably red miso

½ cup orange juice

4 bone-in, skin-on chicken leg quarters (about 3 pounds total), patted dry

Kosher salt and ground black pepper

2 tablespoons grapeseed or other neutral oil

2 medium yellow onions, chopped

12 ounces shiitake mushrooms, stemmed and thinly sliced

4 medium garlic cloves, smashed and peeled

⅓ cup bourbon

In a small bowl, whisk together the soy sauce and miso until smooth. Whisk in the orange juice and set aside. Season the chicken on both sides with salt and pepper. In a large Dutch

Make Your Own Berbere

Vibrant in both color and taste, berbere (bear-ba-ree) is a bold spice blend that is the backbone of numerous Ethiopian dishes. Its primary ingredient is dried red chilies—also called berbere—which are finely ground with numerous dried herbs and spices. Though blends vary, most include coriander, garlic, black cumin, ginger, basil, ajwain, nigella, fenugreek and Ethiopian cardamom (which resembles dried figs). Though berbere is available at well-stocked supermarkets and online spice shops, it's easy to make a simpler homemade version using readily available spices. In a small bowl, stir together **¼ cup smoked sweet paprika, 2 tablespoons sweet paprika, 2 teaspoons cayenne pepper, 2 teaspoons ground ginger, 2 teaspoons onion powder, 2 teaspoons ground coriander, 1½ teaspoons granulated garlic or garlic powder, 1¼ teaspoons ground cardamom, 1 teaspoon dried basil** (ground or crushed to a powder in a spice mill or mortar and pestle) and **½ teaspoon ground cumin.** Keep in an airtight container in a cool, dry spot for up to two months.

oven over medium-high, heat the oil until shimmering. Add the chicken skin down and cook undisturbed until well browned, about 5 minutes. Flip and cook until the second sides are also well browned, another 5 minutes. Transfer to a large plate, then pour off and discard all but 2 tablespoons fat from the pot.

Return the pot to medium-high. Add the onions, mushrooms and garlic, then cook, stirring occasionally, until the vegetables are softened and beginning to brown, about 5 minutes. Add the bourbon and cook, scraping up the browned bits, until most of the liquid has evaporated, about 30 seconds. Pour in the miso mixture and 2 cups water, then bring to a simmer. Return the chicken skin up to the pot and pour in the accumulated juices. Cover, reduce to medium-low and cook, adjusting the heat as needed to maintain a gentle simmer, until the thickest parts of the legs reach 175°F, 20 to 25 minutes.

Using tongs, transfer the chicken to a serving dish. Bring the sauce to a boil over high and cook, uncovered and stirring occasionally, until the sauce has thickened to a gravy consistency, 7 to 9 minutes. Taste and season with salt and pepper, then spoon over the chicken.

ETHIOPIAN CHICKEN STEW

Start to finish: 1 hour 10 minutes (30 minutes active)
Servings: 4 to 6

Doro wat, a succulent chicken stew fragrant with spices and savory-sweet with a preponderance of onions, is the national dish of Ethiopia. We were taught how to make it by home cook Tigist Chane in Addis Ababa. A generous measure of berbere, Ethiopia's signature spice blend, gives the dish its deep reddish-brown hue. Berbere is sold in spice shops and most well-stocked supermarkets; because its chili heat varies from brand to brand, we call for a range in the amount. Alternatively, you can easily mix your own berbere (recipe p. 337). If you wish to hone your knife skills, feel free to chop the 2 pounds of onions by hand, but a food processor gets the job done quickly. Trim, peel and quarter the onions, then pulse about 10 times until finely chopped; it's fine if the pieces are a bit uneven. As a cooking fat, we use Indian ghee to mimic the flavor of Ethiopian fermented butter. Look for ghee in the dairy case next to the butter or in the grocery aisle near the coconut oil. If it's not available, butter is a fine substitute. Whole hard-cooked eggs are traditionally simmered into doro wat at the end, but we prefer sliced hard-cooked eggs as an optional garnish, along with chopped fresh chilies. Injera, a spongy, slightly sour Ethiopian flatbread, is the typical accompaniment, but rice or warmed naan are good, too.

5 tablespoons ghee, divided

2 pounds (3 large) red onions, finely chopped (see headnote)

Kosher salt and ground black pepper

⅓ to ½ cup berbere (see headnote)

10 medium garlic cloves, minced

2 pounds boneless, skinless chicken thighs, trimmed and halved

3 scallions, thinly sliced on the diagonal

1 jalapeño or Fresno chili, stemmed, seeded (if desired) and finely chopped (optional)

2 or 3 hard-cooked eggs, peeled and sliced (optional)

Lemon wedges, to serve

338

In a large Dutch oven over medium-high, heat 2 tablespoons of the ghee until shimmering. Add the onions and ½ teaspoon salt, then cook, stirring occasionally and reducing the heat if the onions begin to brown before they soften, until lightly browned and completely softened, 10 to 15 minutes.

Stir in the remaining 3 tablespoons ghee, the berbere and ¾ cup water. Stir in the garlic, followed by the chicken. Reduce to medium-low, cover and cook at a simmer, stirring occasionally, until a skewer inserted into the chicken meets no resistance, about 30 minutes.

Uncover, increase to medium-high and cook, stirring and scraping along the bottom of the pot, until the stew is thickened and a wooden spoon leaves a brief trail when drawn through the sauce, 5 to 8 minutes. Taste and season with salt and pepper. Serve topped with the scallions, chilies (if using) and sliced eggs (if using); serve with lemon wedges on the side.

CHICKEN TAGINE WITH ARTICHOKES, OLIVES AND LEMON

Start to finish: 50 minutes
Servings: 4 to 6

A unique piece of cookware that has come to symbolize Moroccan cuisine, a tagine is a shallow earthenware pot with a cone-shaped lid. The word also refers to stewy dishes, like this rendition of a Moroccan classic, that are cooked in the tagine. Fresh artichokes are highly seasonal and require time and patience to prep, so instead we use frozen artichoke hearts so this braise comes together easily. Saffron lends a golden hue and its inimitable flavor to the braise, complemented by the warmth of coriander and ground ginger. To be efficient, prep the artichokes, cilantro, olives and lemon juice while the chicken simmers.

2 tablespoons extra-virgin olive oil

1 large leek, white and light green parts quartered lengthwise, thinly sliced crosswise, rinsed and drained

Kosher salt and ground black pepper

2 medium garlic cloves, finely grated

1 teaspoon ground coriander

1 teaspoon ground ginger

¼ teaspoon saffron threads

2½ pounds bone-in, skin-on chicken thighs, skin removed and discarded

½ cup pitted green olives, roughly chopped

6 ounces frozen artichoke hearts, thawed, quartered if whole and patted dry (about 1½ cups)

½ cup lightly packed fresh cilantro, chopped

2 tablespoons lemon juice

In a 12-inch skillet over medium-high, heat the oil until shimmering. Add the leek and ¼ teaspoon each salt and pepper; cook, stirring occasionally, until softened and beginning to brown, 5 to 7 minutes. Add the garlic, coriander and ginger, then cook, stirring, until fragrant, 30 to 60 seconds. Add ¾ cup water and the saffron and bring to a simmer, scraping up any browned bits. Add the chicken and turn to coat. Cover, reduce to medium and simmer, stirring occasionally, until a skewer inserted into the largest thigh meets no resistance, 20 to 25 minutes.

Add the olives, artichokes and half of the cilantro; cook, uncovered and stirring occasionally, until the sauce is slightly thickened, 6 to 8 minutes. Off heat, stir in the lemon juice, then taste and season with salt and pepper. Transfer to a serving dish and sprinkle with the remaining cilantro.

VIETNAMESE BRAISED LEMON GRASS CHICKEN

Start to finish: 1 hour (30 minutes active)
Servings: 4

In Ho Chi Minh City, Vietnam, home cook Phạm Thị Thanh Tâm taught us to make her version of braised chicken with lemon grass. Seasoned with turmeric, garlic, chilies and fish sauce—staple ingredients in the Vietnamese kitchen—the dish was remarkably simple, yet wonderfully aromatic and full of flavor. Instead of mincing fresh lemon grass, which requires a good amount of time and effort, we simply bruise the stalks so they split open and release their essential oils into the braising liquid; we remove and discard the stalks when cooking is complete. The soy sauce in the recipe is our own addition, a stand-in for the MSG and pork bouillon that Pham used, and we opt to thicken the braising liquid with a little cornstarch to give the sauce just a little body. Serve the chicken with steamed jasmine rice.

1 tablespoon grapeseed or other neutral oil

6 medium garlic cloves, minced

2 Fresno or jalapeño chilies, stemmed, seeded and thinly sliced

1 tablespoon ground turmeric

3 stalks fresh lemon grass, trimmed to the bottom 6 inches, dry outer layers discarded, bruised

1 cup low-sodium chicken broth

2 tablespoons soy sauce

2 tablespoons packed brown sugar

2½ pounds bone-in, skin-on chicken thighs, skin removed and discarded, patted dry

1 teaspoon cornstarch

2 tablespoons lime juice

1 tablespoon fish sauce

Ground black pepper

Cilantro or sliced scallions, to serve

In a large Dutch oven over medium, heat the oil until shimmering. Add the garlic, chilies and turmeric, then cook, stirring, until fragrant, about 30 seconds. Add the lemon grass, broth, soy sauce, sugar and 1 cup water, then bring to a simmer. Add the chicken skinned side down in an even layer and return to a simmer. Cover, reduce to medium-low

and cook until a skewer inserted into the chicken meets no resistance, 30 to 40 minutes.

Using tongs, transfer the chicken skinned side up to a serving bowl. Cook the braising liquid over medium until reduced by about half, about 12 minutes. Remove and discard the lemon grass. In a small bowl, stir together the cornstarch and 1 tablespoon water. Whisk the mixture into the braising liquid, return to a simmer and cook, stirring constantly, until lightly thickened, about 1 minute.

Off heat, stir the lime juice and fish sauce into the braising liquid, then taste and season with pepper. Return the chicken and any accumulated juices to the pot, cover and let stand until heated through, about 5 minutes. Return the braise to the serving bowl and sprinkle with cilantro.

GEORGIAN-STYLE BRAISED CHICKEN WITH TOMATOES AND HERBS

Start to finish: 50 minutes
Servings: 4

The traditional Georgian stew called chakhokbili, which in the past was made with pheasant but now is more common with chicken, inspired this skillet braise. To build a solid flavor base, we sear bone-in chicken thighs (for ease, just the skin side) on the stovetop, but the braising takes place in a hot oven, where the heat is steady and all-encompassing, so you will need an oven-safe skillet. To be efficient and to keep the herbs bright and fresh, wash, dry and chop the mint and cilantro (and/or parsley) while the chicken cooks.

3 teaspoons ground coriander, divided

Kosher salt and ground black pepper

3 pounds bone-in chicken thighs, trimmed and patted dry

2 tablespoons extra-virgin olive oil

1 large red onion, halved and thinly sliced

3 medium garlic cloves, minced

½ teaspoon red pepper flakes

3 pounds ripe tomatoes, cored, seeded and roughly chopped

½ cup lightly packed fresh mint, roughly chopped

¼ cup finely chopped fresh cilantro, fresh flat-leaf parsley or a combination

Heat the oven to 450°F with a rack in the middle position. In a small bowl, stir together 2 teaspoons of coriander,

1 teaspoon salt and ½ teaspoon black pepper, then sprinkle onto both sides of the chicken.

In a 12-inch oven-safe skillet over medium, heat the oil until shimmering. Add the chicken, skin side down, and cook until well browned, 5 to 7 minutes. Transfer the chicken to a plate, pour off and discard all but 2 tablespoons of oil from the skillet and return to medium.

Add the onion and cook, stirring occasionally, until beginning to soften, 3 to 5 minutes. Add the remaining 1 teaspoon coriander, the garlic, pepper flakes and ½ teaspoon salt; cook, stirring, until fragrant, about 30 seconds. Add the tomatoes and cook, scraping up any browned bits, until they begin to release their juices, 3 to 5 minutes.

Return the chicken, skin side up, to the pan, nestling but not submerging the pieces in the tomato mixture, then add any accumulated juices. Transfer to the oven and cook until the thickest part of the thighs not touching bone reaches 175°F, 20 to 25 minutes. Remove from the oven (the handle will be hot) and serve sprinkled with the herbs.

KOREAN CHICKEN AND VEGETABLE STEW

Start to finish: 45 minutes
Servings: 4 to 6

This spicy, umami-filled stew is called dakdoritang in Korean. The flavor backbone comes from soy sauce and gochujang, a Korean fermented chili paste. Look for gochujang, packed in red plastic containers or bottles, in the international aisle of supermarkets or in Asian grocery stores. If you like, drizzle with sesame oil or sprinkle with toasted sesame seeds before serving. Steamed white rice is the perfect accompaniment.

1 tablespoon grapeseed or other neutral oil

1 medium yellow onion, chopped

3 medium carrots, peeled and sliced into ½-inch rounds

2 medium garlic cloves, finely chopped

2 tablespoons finely grated fresh ginger

3 tablespoons gochujang

3 tablespoons soy sauce, plus more as needed

1 tablespoon honey

3 pounds bone-in, skin-on chicken thighs, drumsticks or a combination, trimmed and patted dry

1½ pounds Yukon gold potatoes, unpeeled, cut into 1-inch chunks

4 scallions, thinly sliced on the diagonal

In a large Dutch oven over medium-high, heat the oil until shimmering. Add the onion and carrots, then cook, stirring occasionally, until the onion softens and begins to brown, 5 to 7 minutes.

Add the garlic and ginger; cook, stirring, until fragrant, 30 to 60 seconds. Add 5 cups water and stir in the gochujang, soy sauce and honey. Add the chicken and potatoes, then bring to a simmer. Simmer, uncovered, until the potatoes are tender and a skewer inserted into the chicken meets no resistance, 25 to 30 minutes.

Off heat, taste and season with additional soy sauce. Serve sprinkled with the scallions.

COLOMBIAN COCONUT BRAISED CHICKEN

Start to finish: 40 minutes
Serves: 4

Traditionally, pollo con leche de coco is made with fresh coconut milk. We found that canned coconut milk—regular and light—was so rich and heavy it eclipsed the other ingredients in the braise. We opted instead to make our own coconut milk with unsweetened shredded coconut and hot water. The process took only a few minutes and yielded a light, flavorful coconut milk that worked wonderfully. If you require a shortcut, 1½ cups coconut water is an acceptable option, but the flavor will be less complex. We liked this paired with coconut rice, but plain rice is good, too.

1½ cups unsweetened shredded coconut

2 tablespoons grapeseed or other neutral oil

1 teaspoon ground turmeric

1 medium yellow onion, finely chopped

8 medium garlic cloves, minced

1 tablespoon tomato paste

1½ teaspoons ground allspice

1 tablespoon soy sauce

Kosher salt

2 pounds boneless, skinless chicken thighs, trimmed

1 tablespoon lime juice, plus lime wedges to serve

1 pint cherry or grape tomatoes, quartered

In a blender, combine the coconut and 2 cups warm water. Let stand until the coconut begins to soften, about 1 minute. Blend on high until creamy, 1 to 2 minutes. Strain through a fine-mesh strainer set over a large measuring cup or medium bowl, pressing on the solids; you should have 1½ cups strained coconut milk. Discard the solids; set the coconut milk aside.

In a large Dutch oven over medium, heat the oil until shimmering. Stir in the turmeric and cook until fragrant and the oil has turned yellow, about 30 seconds. Add the onion, and garlic and cook, stirring occasionally, until the onion is softened, about 3 minutes. Stir in the tomato paste and allspice until well combined, then stir in the coconut milk, soy sauce and ½ teaspoon salt. Bring to a simmer, nestle the chicken in an even layer in the liquid, then cover and reduce to medium-low. Cook until the chicken is no longer pink when cut, 18 to 22 minutes, flipping the pieces halfway through.

Using tongs, transfer the chicken to a bowl. Bring the liquid to a simmer over medium and cook, stirring frequently, until thickened and reduced by about half, about 12 minutes. Pour in any accumulated chicken juices and simmer another minute. Off heat, stir in the lime juice and tomatoes. Taste and season with salt, then return the chicken to the pot, turning to coat. Cook until heated through, 2 to 3 minutes. Transfer to a serving bowl and serve with lime wedges.

Homemade Coconut Milk

Start to finish: 5 minutes
Makes 14 ounces

In side-by-side tastings of homemade and canned coconut milks, we favored the homemade, which was light and smooth compared to canned, which had a thick, viscous body. We wondered if ingredients could account for the difference, but the can listed the same two we'd used—coconut and water. Turns out, it's the processing method that matters. Canned milk is made from finely ground coconut meat that's extracted via a screw press—the same type used to separate wood pulp and water for making paper. The extract is recombined with water to produce a milk of uniform consistency and fat—usually between 19 and 21 percent. Our homemade milk uses shredded coconut that has 30 percent fat, but even with blending and pressing on the solids, only some of the fat emulsifies with the water, producing a milk that is lighter in both flavor and body.

1¾ cups unsweetened shredded coconut

2⅓ cups warm water

In a blender, combine the coconut and water. Let stand until the coconut begins to soften, about 1 minute. Blend on high until creamy, 1 to 2 minutes. Pour into a fine-mesh strainer set over a large measuring cup or medium bowl, pressing on the solids. Discard the solids. You should have 1¾ cups milk, or about 1 can.

BRAISES & STEWS

343

HUNGARIAN PEPPER STEW WITH TOMATOES AND SAUSAGE

Start to finish: 50 minutes

Servings: 4 to 6

We tasted many versions of lecsó—a rustic, hearty pepper stew—throughout Hungary. Our recipe is a blend of those taught to us by cookbook author Zsófia Mautner and Tibor Rosenstein, owner and chef of Restaurant Rosenstein in Budapest. Rosenstein's version incorporates sausage, adding depth and heft to the vegetables. To emulate robustly smoky and savory Hungarian sausage, we call on two grocery store staples: bacon for rich smokiness and kielbasa for texture and spice. Sweet and subtly hot, Hungarian wax peppers are the traditional go-to, though hard to find in the U.S. In their place, we opted for an easier-to-source blend of yellow bell peppers and mildly spicy banana, cubanelle or Anaheim peppers. Like other classic Hungarian dishes, such as paprikash, lecsó is seasoned with a healthy dose of paprika. Its earthy-sweet notes complement both the peppers and sausage, while giving the stew an especially luscious consistency. We love serving this with crusty bread, but it also is delicious spooned over rice, mashed potatoes or nokedli, Spätzle-like Hungarian dumplings (recipe p. 335).

8 ounces kielbasa or other smoked sausage, halved lengthwise and sliced into ¼-inch half-moons

1 tablespoon grapeseed or other neutral oil

2 ounces bacon, chopped

1 medium yellow onion, halved and thinly sliced

Kosher salt

2 medium yellow bell peppers (about 1 pound total), stemmed, seeded and cut into ¾-inch pieces

4 banana peppers or 3 cubanelle or Anaheim peppers (about 1 pound total), stemmed, seeded and cut into ¾-inch pieces

2 medium garlic cloves, minced

4 teaspoons sweet paprika, divided

¾ teaspoon hot paprika or ¾ teaspoon sweet paprika plus ¼ teaspoon cayenne pepper

1 pound ripe tomatoes, cored and chopped

In a large Dutch oven over medium-high, combine the sausage and oil. Cook, stirring occasionally, until lightly browned, about 5 minutes. Using a slotted spoon, transfer the sausage to a plate; set aside.

Reduce to medium, add the bacon and cook, stirring occasionally, until lightly browned, 3 to 4 minutes. Add the onion and ¼ teaspoon salt; cook, stirring often, until lightly browned, about 5 minutes. Add both types of peppers, the garlic, 1 teaspoon of the sweet paprika, the hot paprika and ½ cup water. Scrape up any browned bits, then cook, uncovered and stirring occasionally, until the peppers begin to soften, about 3 minutes. Stir in 1½ cups water, cover partially, and bring to a simmer. Cook, stirring occasionally, until the peppers are fully softened, 12 to 15 minutes.

Stir in the tomatoes, sausage and remaining 1 tablespoon sweet paprika. Cook, partially covered, until the tomatoes release their juices but have not broken down, 3 to 5 minutes. Taste and season with salt.

GONZALO GUZMÁN'S POZOLE ROJO

Start to finish: 2¼ hours (50 minutes active)
Servings: 6

Chef Gonzalo Guzmán's pozole rojo (pork, red chili and hominy stew), from his book "Nopalito," is boldly flavored with ancho chilies, herbs, cumin and aromatics. He blends some of the hominy (dried corn kernels treated with alkali, then cooked until tender) with some of the braising liquid, then adds the puree back to the soup to give the broth body. Guzmán says garnishes are a key component of pozole and encourages piling them high onto individual servings. A long list is included here, but you can offer as many or as few as you like. The pozole can be made a few days in advance, then reheated for serving.

4 large ancho chilies, stemmed and seeded

Boiling water

2 medium garlic cloves, divided

½ large white onion, roughly chopped

¾ teaspoon dried Mexican oregano

½ teaspoon cumin seeds

Kosher salt

¼ medium yellow onion

4 cilantro stems

1 bay leaf

2 pounds boneless pork shoulder, trimmed and cut into 1-inch cubes

4 cups rinsed and drained store-bought canned hominy (from two 29-ounce cans)

FOR SERVING:

Shredded green cabbage

Thinly sliced radishes

Thinly sliced red onion

Chili powder

Cilantro leaves

Tortilla chips

Lime halves

Place the chilies in a medium heatproof bowl and add boiling water to cover. Let stand until the chilies are softened, about 20 minutes. Remove the chilies from the water and transfer to a blender; reserve the water. Add

1 garlic clove, the white onion, oregano, cumin and a generous pinch of salt to the blender, then puree until smooth, about 2 minutes, scraping down the jar as needed and adding just enough of the soaking water to form a thick, smooth paste.

In a piece of cheesecloth, wrap the remaining garlic clove, yellow onion, cilantro stems and bay; secure with kitchen twine to form a small bundle. Set aside.

Season the pork with salt. In a large pot, combine the pork, chili puree and cheesecloth bundle, then stir in 3 quarts water. Season generously with salt and bring to a boil. Reduce to a simmer and cook, uncovered, until a skewer inserted into the pork meets no resistance, about 1 hour. Remove from the heat.

In the blender, puree ½ cup of hominy with about ½ cup of the braising liquid from the pork until smooth, about 20 seconds. Stir the puree and the remaining 3½ cups hominy into the pot and bring to a simmer over medium-high. Remove from the heat and let stand for 5 minutes. Using a wide, shallow spoon, skim off and discard the fat on the surface.

Bring the pozole back to a simmer over medium-high. Taste and adjust the seasoning with salt. Ladle into bowls and serve with cabbage, radishes, red onion, oregano, chili powder, cilantro, tortilla chips and limes.

MEXICAN WEDDING STEW
WITH PORK

Start to finish: 4 hours (45 minutes active)
Servings: 6 to 8

This is our version of the traditional chili-rich Mexican stew prepared for special occasions. The ingredients vary by region, but to keep things simple we opted to use widely available ancho and guajillo chilies and cocoa powder instead of Mexican chocolate. With warm spices and a touch of fruitiness from raisins, the flavor profile falls somewhere between a mole negro and a basic asado de puerco. The corn tortillas that are toasted and pureed with the softened chilies give the sauce a velvety consistency that clings to the fork-tender chunks of pork. Serve with rice or warmed tortillas.

3 ounces (5 medium) ancho chilies, stemmed, seeded and torn into pieces

3 ounces (10 medium) guajillo chilies, stemmed, seeded and torn into pieces

4 cups boiling water

3 corn tortillas

1 quart low-sodium chicken broth

¾ cup raisins

2 tablespoons extra-virgin olive oil

1 large white onion, chopped

10 medium garlic cloves, chopped

2 teaspoons dried oregano, preferably Mexican oregano

2 teaspoons ground cumin

1 teaspoon ground cinnamon

28-ounce can diced fire-roasted tomatoes, drained

1 tablespoon cocoa powder

Kosher salt and ground black pepper

5 pounds boneless pork butt, trimmed and cut into 2-inch cubes

Heat the oven to 325°F with a rack in the lower-middle position. In a 12-inch skillet over medium-high, toast the chilies, pressing with a wide metal spatula and flipping halfway through, until fragrant, about 30 seconds. Transfer to a medium bowl and add the boiling water; reserve the skillet. Let stand until the chilies are softened, about 20 minutes, then drain.

While the chilies soak, in the same skillet over medium-high, toast the tortillas, turning frequently, until lightly charred, 2 to 4 minutes. Transfer to a plate and let cool slightly, then tear into pieces.

In a blender, combine half the broth, half the chilies, half the tortillas and half the raisins. Puree until smooth, about 1 minute, scraping down the blender as needed. Transfer to a bowl, then repeat with the remaining broth, chilies, tortillas and raisins; stir into the first batch. Measure ½ cup of the puree into a small bowl, cover and refrigerate until needed.

In a large Dutch oven over medium-high, combine the oil and onion. Cook, stirring occasionally, until the onion is lightly browned, about 5 minutes. Stir in the garlic, oregano, cumin and cinnamon, then cook, stirring, until fragrant, about 30 seconds. Add the tomatoes and cook, stirring occasionally, until most of the moisture has evaporated, about 5 minutes. Stir in the chili puree, the cocoa and pork, then bring to a simmer. Cover, transfer to the oven and cook for 2 hours.

Remove the pot from the oven. Uncover and stir, then return to the oven uncovered. Cook until a skewer inserted into the pork meets no resistance, about 1 hour.

Remove the pot from the oven. Tilt to pool the liquid to one side, then use a wide spoon to skim off and discard as much fat as possible. Stir the reserved chili puree into the stew, then cook on the stovetop over medium until heated through, about 5 minutes. Taste and season with salt and pepper.

THAI BRAISED PORK AND EGGS WITH STAR ANISE AND CINNAMON

Start to finish: 1 hour 40 minutes (30 minutes active)
Servings: 6

Moo palo is a classic Thai braise that combines the richness of pork belly and eggs in savory-sweet broth flavored with Chinese five-spice powder. For our version, we opted for easier-to-source pork shoulder; it's a leaner cut but it cooks up equally flavorful. Traditionally, hard-cooked eggs are simmered with the pork and take on a brown hue from the braising liquid, along with a firm texture from long cooking. We opted instead to simply garnish the bowlfuls with hard-cooked eggs so their color is brighter and texture more tender. And rather than use five-spice powder, which can give the braise a muddled, overspiced flavor, we preferred the cleaner, purer notes of whole cloves, star anise and cinnamon sticks. Serve the pork and eggs with steamed jasmine rice. As with most braises, this dish tastes even better the next day.

1 bunch cilantro, stems chopped, leaves roughly chopped, reserved separately

8 medium garlic cloves, smashed and peeled

1 tablespoon whole white peppercorns

3 whole cloves

6 tablespoons low-sodium soy sauce, plus more as needed

⅓ cup fish sauce

⅓ cup packed dark brown sugar, plus more as needed

5 star anise pods

Three 3-inch cinnamon sticks

4 pounds boneless pork shoulder, trimmed and cut into 1½-inch chunks

6 cold large eggs in their shells

In a blender, combine the cilantro stems, garlic, peppercorns, cloves, soy sauce, fish sauce and 6 tablespoons water. Puree until almost smooth, about 20 seconds. Set aside.

In a large Dutch oven over medium-high, stir together the sugar and 1 tablespoon water. Bring to a simmer and cook, stirring often, until the sugar turns foamy, then dry and begins to smoke lightly, 3 to 4 minutes. Stir in the cilantro stem–garlic mixture, then add 7 cups water to the blender, swirl to rinse it, then add the water to the pot. Stir, scraping up any caramelized sugar.

Add the star anise, cinnamon sticks and pork, distributing the meat in an even layer. Bring to a boil, then cover and reduce to medium-low and cook, adjusting the heat as needed to maintain a gentle simmer, for 50 minutes.

Meanwhile, fill a large saucepan with 3 inches of water; bring to a boil. Using a slotted spoon, lower the eggs into the water. Cook, maintaining a vigorous simmer but not a hard boil, for 12½ to 13 minutes. While the eggs cook, fill a large bowl with about 4 cups ice and 2 cups water. When the eggs are done, quickly transfer them to the ice bath; cool for 3 minutes, then remove. Gently tap each egg against the counter, turning it so the shell cracks all around. Peel away the shell and thin membrane, then set the eggs aside.

After the pork has simmered for 50 minutes, uncover, increase heat to medium and cook until a skewer inserted into the pork meets no resistance, 20 to 30 minutes. Remove and discard the star anise and cinnamon sticks, then let stand for about 5 minutes. Tilt the pot to pool the liquid to one side, then use a wide spoon to skim off and discard as much fat as possible from the surface of the liquid. Taste and season with additional soy sauce, then return to a simmer over medium.

Spoon the pork and broth into bowls. Cut the eggs lengthwise in halves or quarters and place 2 or 4 pieces in each bowl, then top with cilantro leaves.

SPICY PORK WITH LEEKS AND ROASTED RED PEPPERS

Start to finish: 45 minutes
Servings: 4

Tigania is the Greek cook's simple—and flavorful—solution to leftovers. It means "from the frying pan" and is a catchall term for a braised dish traditionally made with scraps of pork and whatever vegetables are on hand. They are seared, then simmered, though what happens next depends on where you are. The dish might come swimming in lemon juice and olive oil in Crete or flavored with honey and thyme in the Peloponnese. Our version was inspired by Diane Kochilas' take in "The Glorious Foods of Greece," which uses white wine and leeks, the way tigania is done in the northern region of Macedonia. Kochilas seasons pork shoulder with paprika before simmering; we found boneless country-style pork ribs cooked more quickly and stood up well to the bold Mediterranean ingredients. We use six large leeks, which seems like a lot, but they reduce to a creamy, rustic sauce that pairs well with the tender meat. Serve with pita bread, rice or simple roasted potatoes.

¾ teaspoon red pepper flakes

Kosher salt and ground black pepper

2¾ teaspoons dried oregano, divided

2 pounds boneless country-style pork spareribs, trimmed and cut into 1½-inch chunks

1 tablespoon grapeseed or other neutral oil

2 tablespoons extra-virgin olive oil

6 large leeks, white and light green parts sliced ½-inch thick, rinsed and dried

4 medium garlic cloves, coarsely chopped

1 cup dry white wine

7-ounce jar roasted red peppers, drained and diced (about 1 cup)

½ cup pitted green olives, chopped

2 tablespoons fresh oregano, minced

Lemon wedges, to serve

In a large bowl, stir together the pepper flakes, ½ teaspoon salt and 1 teaspoon pepper, and ¾ teaspoon of the dried oregano. Add the pork and toss.

In a 12-inch skillet over medium-high, heat the grapeseed oil until barely smoking. Add the pork in a single layer and cook without disturbing until dark golden brown on the bottom, about 5 minutes. Stir and cook until no longer pink, about another 2 minutes. Using a slotted spoon, transfer to a large plate.

Pour off and discard the fat from the pan, then return to medium-high. Add the olive oil, leeks, garlic, the remaining 2 teaspoons dried oregano and ¼ teaspoon salt. Cook, stirring and scraping up any browned bits, until the leeks begin to soften, 3 to 4 minutes. Stir in the pork, then the wine. Bring to a simmer and cover, then reduce to low and cook until the pork is tender, about 30 minutes.

Stir in the roasted red peppers and olives. Taste and season with salt and pepper. Transfer to a serving plate and sprinkle with fresh oregano. Serve with lemon wedges.

PORK AND CHORIZO STEW WITH PEPPERS

Start to finish: 1 hour (35 minutes active)
Servings: 4

Carcamusa, a Spanish tapas dish, traditionally calls for three different types of pork—fresh pork, cured ham and chorizo—all simmered with seasonal vegetables in tomato sauce. To simplify our weeknight version, we skipped the ham and opted for jarred roasted red peppers. If you can find jarred piquillo peppers from Spain, use an equal amount in place of the roasted peppers; their flavor is slighter deeper, sweeter and more intense. Serve the dish with slices of grilled rustic bread.

6 ounces Spanish chorizo, casing removed, halved lengthwise and thinly sliced

8 medium garlic cloves, peeled

2½ teaspoons dried oregano

2½ teaspoons ground cumin

Kosher salt and ground black pepper

28-ounce can whole peeled tomatoes, drained, juices reserved

1¼-pound pork tenderloin, trimmed of silver skin and cut into ½-inch pieces

3 tablespoons grapeseed or other neutral oil, divided

1 large yellow onion, finely chopped

½ cup dry sherry

10.4-ounce jar piquillo peppers (see headnote), drained and cut into ½-inch pieces (1 cup)

1 cup roughly chopped flat-leaf parsley

In a food processor, combine half of the chorizo, the garlic, oregano, cumin, 1 teaspoon pepper and 3 tablespoons of the tomato juices. Process until smooth, about 2 minutes, scraping the sides of the bowl as needed. Transfer 3 tablespoons of the chorizo paste to a medium bowl and stir in ½ teaspoon salt and another 1 tablespoon of the tomato juices. Add the pork and toss, then marinate at room temperature for 15 minutes. Meanwhile, add the drained tomatoes to the chorizo paste in the processor and process until smooth, about 1 minute; set aside.

In a 12-inch skillet over medium-high, heat 1 tablespoon of the oil until barely smoking. Add the pork in a single layer and cook without stirring until well-browned, 4 to 6 minutes. Return the pork to the bowl. Add the remaining 2 tablespoons oil to the skillet and heat over medium until shimmering. Add the onion, cover and cook, stirring occasionally, until softened, about 8 minutes.

Add the sherry and cook, scraping up any browned bits, until most of the liquid evaporates, 2 to 4 minutes. Stir in the tomato-chorizo mixture and remaining tomato juice. Bring to a simmer, then reduce to medium-low. Cover and cook until the flavors meld, about 10 minutes.

Uncover and continue to cook, stirring occasionally, until slightly thickened, another 5 minutes. Return the pork and any accumulated juices to the skillet and add the remaining chorizo and piquillo peppers. Cook, stirring occasionally, until the pork is heated through, about 5 minutes. Stir in the parsley, then taste and season with salt and pepper.

BRAZILIAN BLACK BEAN STEW WITH PORK AND BEEF

Start to finish: 4¼ hours (40 minutes active)
Servings: 8 to 10

During a visit to São Paulo, we learned that there are as many versions of Brazilian feijoada as there are cooks who make it, but one thing is constant: It is hearty, soulful fare. Feijoada can be an elaborate celebratory meal made with a dozen or more cuts of pork and beef, each removed from the pot and served individually, buffet-style, along with the stewed beans. It also can be a basic, workaday stew simply ladled into bowls. Ours is more like the latter: a streamlined serve-from-the-pot version, but with rich, slow-cooked flavor. We do, however, skip the hard-to-source meats, such as Brazilian beef jerky and smoked pork ribs, that are included in traditional feijoada. Instead, we use cuts that are easy to find at the supermarket, including bone-in beef short ribs and smoked ham hock, collagen-rich cuts that lend the broth flavor and body. The addition of cachaça, a Brazilian spirit distilled from sugar cane, is a unique touch from Francisco Gameleira, chef at A Figueira Rubaiyat restaurant in São Paulo. We also borrowed his idea to include a little

orange juice; these liquids help lift the heftiness with a bit of bright sweetness. Feijoada is commonly served with orange slices or wedges along with "vinagrete," a salsa-like mixture of chopped tomatoes, onion and herb—both bring welcome color and freshness. Serve the stew with rice and, for a typical Brazilian meal, with sautéed collard greens and farofa, or toasted cassava flour.

12 ounces thick-cut bacon, chopped

3 medium celery stalks, chopped

2 medium yellow onions, chopped, divided

8 medium garlic cloves, chopped

1 bunch cilantro, stems minced, leaves roughly chopped, reserved separately

3 bay leaves

1 teaspoon ground cumin

Kosher salt and ground black pepper

¼ cup cachaça (see headnote) or white rum

¼ cup orange juice, plus wedges to serve

1 pound dried black beans, rinsed

1¼ pounds bone-in beef short ribs

1 pound smoked ham hock

1 pound linguiça or chorizo sausage links

1 pound ripe tomatoes, cored and chopped

In a large Dutch oven over medium-high, cook the bacon, stirring occasionally, until lightly browned, 5 to 8 minutes. Add the celery, 1 onion, the garlic, cilantro stems, bay, cumin and ½ teaspoon pepper. Reduce to medium and cook, stirring often, until the vegetables are translucent, 10 to 15 minutes.

Add the cachaça and orange juice; scrape up any browned bits. Stir in the beans and 3½ quarts water, then bring to a boil over high. Add the short ribs and ham hock; stir to combine. Reduce to medium-low and simmer, stirring occasionally, for 2 hours; skim off and discard any scum that rises to the surface during simmering.

Add the linguiça and cook, uncovered and stirring occasionally, until the beans are fully tender and the meat from the short ribs and ham hock is falling off the bones, about 1½ hours.

Meanwhile, in a medium bowl, stir together the tomatoes, the remaining 1 onion, the cilantro leaves and ½ teaspoon each salt and pepper. Cover and refrigerate until ready to use.

No-Sear Lamb or Beef and Chickpea Stew

Start to finish: 2¼ hours (40 minutes active)
Servings: 4

We skip the sear but keep the flavor by adding layers of seasonings in this no-stock stew based on the Yemeni dish known as maraq. We start with a dry seasoning mix—paprika, cumin, cardamom, cinnamon, salt and pepper. It does double duty, with half the mixture rubbed onto the meat and the rest briefly cooked in the pot with onion, butter and tomato paste. Cooking the seasonings with the fat and tomato paste blooms their flavors and lightly browns the tomato paste. For the savory sweetness of roasted whole garlic cloves without the trouble of roasting a head separately, we slice off the top of the head, then add it whole to the stew to cook alongside the meat. We like the flavor and texture of lamb shoulder. Boneless beef chuck works, too, but needs an extra 1 cup of water and must cook for 1½ hours before the carrots are added.

1 tablespoon sweet paprika

2 teaspoons ground cumin

1 teaspoon ground cardamom

¼ teaspoon ground cinnamon

Kosher salt and ground black pepper

1¼ pounds boneless lamb shoulder or boneless beef chuck roast, trimmed and cut into ¾-inch chunks

1 head garlic

2 tablespoons salted butter

1 large yellow onion, chopped

2 tablespoons tomato paste

3 medium carrots, peeled, halved lengthwise and cut crosswise into ½-inch pieces

15½-ounce can chickpeas, rinsed and drained

3 ounces baby spinach (about 3 cups)

1 cup chopped fresh cilantro, plus more to serve

3 tablespoons lemon juice

Whole-milk yogurt, to serve (optional)

In a medium bowl, stir together the paprika, cumin, cardamom, cinnamon, 1½ teaspoons salt and ½ teaspoon pepper. Reserve half of the spice mixture in a small bowl, then add the meat to the remaining spice mixture and toss until evenly coated; set aside. Cut off and discard the top third of the garlic head, but leave the head intact; set aside.

In a large Dutch oven over medium-high, melt the butter. Add the onion and cook, stirring occasionally, until softened and beginning to brown, 5 to 8 minutes. Add the tomato paste and the reserved spice mixture, then cook, stirring constantly, for about 1 minute. Add 6 cups water if using lamb or 7 cups water if using beef, then bring to a boil over high. Add the meat and the garlic head, cut side down, then return to a boil. Cover partially, reduce to low and cook for 1 hour if using lamb or 1½ hours if using beef, stirring occasionally and adjusting the heat as needed to maintain a gentle simmer.

Add the carrots and continue to cook, partially covered and stirring occasionally, until the carrots and meat are tender, about another 30 minutes. Using tongs, remove the garlic head and, holding the head cut side down, squeeze the cloves into the stew. Stir in the chickpeas and spinach, then cook, stirring occasionally, until the chickpeas are heated through and the spinach is wilted, about 5 minutes.

Off heat, stir in the cilantro and lemon juice, then taste and season with salt and pepper. Serve topped with yogurt and sprinkled with additional cilantro.

Stop Searing Stew Meat

For years, we accepted the Western European notion that the best stews start by searing the meat. Now we know better.

The theory goes that the Maillard reaction—the high heat-triggered response between proteins and simple sugars that produces the flavors and aromas we associate with seared and roasted meats—is essential to developing deeply flavored stews. Trouble is, it's a time-consuming and messy nuisance. It also isn't the only way to develop flavor.

To create deep, complex flavor without browning, cooks around the world work in layers, adding seasonings at different times to maximize their impact. Indian cooks, for example, add the same spice at multiple stages of cooking. Cumin added with fat and alliums at the start of cooking will season differently than cumin added at the end.

In our no-sear lamb stew (recipe p. 351), we use a simple spice mix two ways, rubbing half directly onto the meat, while cooking the other half with onion, butter and tomato paste. The fat blooms the seasonings and the browned tomato paste, adds the sort of savory notes we usually get from browning the meat, and provides a base layer of flavor.

Herbs are another way to effortlessly add layers of flavor. We typically save our herbs for the end, keeping flavors fresh and vibrant. And we use them not by the pinch or spoonful, but often by the cupful. See our recipe for Moroccan harira, p. 364.

When the beans and meats are done, remove the pot from the heat. Using tongs, transfer the short ribs, ham hock and sausages to a large plate; let cool slightly. Remove and discard the bay. Cut the sausages into pieces of the desired size and return them to the pot. Using your fingers, shred the meat from the ribs and hock into bite-size pieces, discarding the skin, bone and gristle; stir the meat into the pot. Taste and season with salt and pepper.

Serve the feijoada with the tomato salsa and orange wedges alongside.

COLOMBIAN BRAISED BEEF

Start to finish: 4 hours (30 minutes active)
Servings: 4

Named for its dark, sweet sauce, posta negra is a classic Colombian dish made by braising beef in a flavorful liquid seasoned with panela sugar and spices. For our version, we call for a 5-pound beef chuck roast; it's a fat-rich cut, so trim it well before tying the roast. In the end, the meat will be superbly tender and succulent. In Colombia, the dish might be served with fried plantains, yucca fritters and a simple salad; we liked this rich beef with an easy pico de gallo (recipe p. 562) and/or mashed potatoes.

5-pound boneless beef chuck roast, trimmed and patted dry

Kosher salt and ground black pepper

2 tablespoons grapeseed or other neutral oil

1 large yellow onion, chopped

10 medium garlic cloves, peeled

2 tablespoons tomato paste

½ cup packed dark brown sugar

2 cinnamon sticks

1 tablespoon whole allspice

2 teaspoons black peppercorns

1 teaspoon whole cloves

1 cup dry red wine

¼ cup Worcestershire sauce

1 cup pitted prunes, coarsely chopped

1 tablespoon cornstarch

3 tablespoons red wine vinegar

Heat the oven to 300°F with a rack in the lower-middle position. Using kitchen twine, tie the roast at 2-inch intervals. Season on all sides with salt and pepper.

In a large Dutch oven over medium-high, heat the oil until shimmering. Add the onion and ¼ teaspoon salt, then cook, stirring, until the onion is well browned, 5 to 7 minutes. Stir in the garlic and cook until fragrant, about 30 seconds. Add the tomato paste and cook, stirring constantly, until it begins to brown, about 2 minutes. Stir in the brown sugar, cinnamon, allspice, peppercorns and cloves. Pour in the wine, bring to a simmer and cook until thick and syrupy, 3 to 5 minutes. Stir in the Worcestershire sauce and prunes.

Place the roast in the pot, then turn to coat with the liquid. Cover and bake until a paring knife inserted into the thickest part meets no resistance, 3½ hours. Transfer the roast to a shallow baking dish and loosely tent with foil. Let rest for 30 minutes.

Meanwhile, set a fine-mesh strainer over a medium bowl. Pour the contents of the pot into the strainer and press on the solids with a silicone spatula to extract as much liquid and pulp as possible; scrape the underside of the strainer to collect the pulp. Discard the solids. Let the liquid and pulp settle for about 5 minutes (you should have about 1½ cups), then skim off the fat. Return the defatted liquid and pulp to the Dutch oven and bring to a simmer over medium.

In a small bowl, stir together 3 tablespoons water and the cornstarch. Whisk into the simmering liquid and cook, stirring constantly, until lightly thickened, about 2 minutes. Stir in the vinegar. Taste and season with salt and pepper.

Transfer the roast to a cutting board. Remove and discard the twine. Cut the meat against the grain into ½-inch slices and transfer to a platter. Pour about 1 cup of the sauce over the meat. Serve with the remaining sauce on the side.

ROMAN BRAISED BEEF WITH TOMATO AND CLOVES

Start to finish: 4 hours (30 minutes active)
Servings: 6

In Rome, cloves are used to flavor the pot roast-like dish known as garofolato di manzo alla Romana. Cloves, known as chiodi di garofano, give the dish its name. The earthy, subtly smoky and slightly bitter flavor of cloves complements the natural sweetness of the onion, fennel and tomatoes used to flavor this dish. The beef typically is cooked as a large roast, similar to a pot roast. We prefer cutting a chuck roast into chunks and simmering the meat as a stew. This ensures that the pieces are succulent and flavorful throughout, while also slightly reducing the cooking time. For cool contrast, we make a salad of fresh fennel, tomatoes and parsley to serve with the stew. Polenta or crusty bread is an excellent accompaniment for absorbing the flavorful sauce.

6 to 7 pounds boneless beef chuck roast, trimmed and cut into 2-inch chunks

¾ teaspoon ground cloves

Kosher salt and ground black pepper

4 ounces pancetta, roughly chopped

6 medium garlic cloves, smashed and peeled

1 medium yellow onion, halved and thinly sliced

1 medium fennel bulb, trimmed, halved, cored and thinly sliced

28-ounce can whole peeled tomatoes, crushed

2 teaspoons fresh thyme, minced

Heat the oven to 325°F with a rack in the lower-middle position. Place the beef in a large bowl and season with the cloves, 1½ teaspoons salt and 2 teaspoons pepper.

In a large Dutch oven over low, cook the pancetta, stirring occasionally, until sizzling and the fat has begun to render, about 5 minutes. Increase the heat to medium-low and continue to cook, stirring occasionally, until the pieces begin to brown, another 7 minutes. Add the garlic, onion and fennel, then increase to medium. Cook, stirring occasionally, until the vegetables are softened and translucent, about 6 minutes. Stir in the tomatoes and bring to a simmer. Stir in the beef, then cover, transfer to the oven and cook for 2 hours.

Remove the pot from the oven. Stir, then return to the oven uncovered. Cook until a skewer inserted into a piece of beef meets no resistance, another 1 to 1½ hours. Using a slotted spoon, transfer the meat to a medium bowl. With a wide spoon, skim off and discard the fat from the surface of the cooking liquid, then bring to a boil over medium-high, scraping up any browned bits. Cook until the liquid has thickened to the consistency of heavy cream, 10 to 12 minutes.

Stir in the thyme, then return the beef to the pot. Reduce to medium and cook, stirring occasionally, until the meat is heated through, about 5 minutes. Taste and season with salt and pepper.

SLAVONIAN-STYLE SHEPHERD'S STEW

Start to finish: 3 hours (50 minutes active)
Servings: 6

From the Slavonia region of Croatia, čobanac is a meat-centric stew rich with paprika and thickened in part by shredded root vegetables that break down during a long, slow simmer. Though referred to as shepherd's stew (čoban translates as shepherd), the dish traditionally is made with not only lamb but also beef, pork and wild game. To simplify, we opted to use only beef; chuck roast is our cut of choice for its meaty flavor, nice marbling and ample collagen that helps make a full-bodied broth. To achieve just the right amount of earthy flavor and an undercurrent of spicy heat, we use both sweet and hot paprika; if you aren't able to find hot paprika, 2 teaspoons sweet paprika plus ½ to 1 teaspoon cayenne pepper is a fine substitution. Simple dumplings are a classic—and delicious—addition to this stew, but they are not essential. If you'd like to include them, see the recipe that follows; the dough is made and added to the pot at the end of cooking. If you skip the dumplings, mashed potatoes or warm, crusty bread are excellent accompaniments.

2½ pounds beef chuck roast, trimmed and cut into 1-inch cubes

Kosher salt and ground black pepper

3 tablespoons extra-virgin olive oil

2 medium yellow onions, chopped

2 large carrots, peeled and shredded on the large holes of a box grater

2 medium parsnips, peeled and shredded on the large holes of a box grater

3 medium garlic cloves, smashed and peeled

1 bunch flat-leaf parsley, stems minced and leaves chopped, reserved separately

4 tablespoons tomato paste, divided

¼ cup plus 2 tablespoons sweet paprika, divided

1 tablespoon hot paprika (see headnote)

3 bay leaves

1 cup dry red wine

2 tablespoons brown mustard

1 bunch fresh dill, finely chopped

In a medium bowl, toss the beef with ¾ teaspoon salt and 1 teaspoon pepper; set aside. In a large Dutch oven over medium, combine the oil, onions and ¼ teaspoon salt. Cook, stirring occasionally, until softened but not browned, about 5 minutes. Add the carrots, parsnips, garlic and parsley stems, then cook, stirring occasionally, until lightly browned, 8 to 10 minutes.

Stir in 2 tablespoons of the tomato paste and cook, stirring often, until it begins to brown and stick to the bottom of the pot, 2 to 4 minutes. Add the ¼ cup sweet paprika, the hot paprika and bay. Cook, stirring, until fragrant, about 30 seconds. Whisk in the wine and 6 cups water, then bring to a simmer over medium-high, stirring often. Stir in the beef and return to a simmer. Reduce to low, cover and cook until a skewer inserted into the beef meets no resistance, about 2 hours, stirring occasionally.

Remove the pot from the heat. Tilt the pot to pool the cooking liquid to one side, then use a wide spoon to skim off and discard as much fat as possible. Remove and discard the bay.

In a medium bowl, stir together the remaining 2 tablespoons tomato paste, the remaining 2 tablespoons sweet paprika and the mustard. Whisk about 1 cup of the cooking liquid into the tomato paste mixture, then stir it into the pot. Return to a simmer over medium-high, then stir in the parsley leaves and half the dill. Taste and season with salt and pepper. Serve sprinkled with the remaining dill.

DUMPLINGS

After stirring the tomato paste–paprika mixture into the stew, set the pot aside and make the dumpling dough. In a medium bowl, whisk together **½ cup all-purpose flour, ¼ teaspoon baking powder** and **¼ teaspoon kosher salt.** Add **2 large eggs** (beaten) and **2 tablespoons finely chopped fresh dill,** then stir until a smooth dough forms. Return the stew to a simmer over medium-high, stir in the parsley leaves and half the dill, then taste and season with salt and pepper. Using 2 small spoons, drop the dough in 1-teaspoon portions into different areas of the pot. Return to a simmer and cook, uncovered and without stirring, until the dumplings are puffed and cooked through, about 10 minutes. Serve sprinkled with the remaining dill.

HUNGARIAN GOULASH

Start to finish: 2¾ hours (1 hour active)
Servings: 4 to 6

Hungary's national dish, goulash—or gulyás in Hungarian—has countless variations. Some are soupy; others thick and meaty. Our version takes inspiration from Tibor Rosenstein, chef/owner at Rosenstein restaurant in Budapest, whose unique method makes for a deeply flavorful stew. He incorporates the cooking liquid and spices in stages, allowing them to reduce between additions and concentrate into a complex, velvety sauce. Root vegetables are a must; their sweet notes balance all the beefy richness. We opted for celery root—also known as celeriac—which has a parsnip-like texture and earthy, celery-like flavor. As is the case with many Hungarian dishes, paprika—both hot and sweet—is a key seasoning; be sure the paprika you use for this is fresh, fragrant and vibrant in color. Hungarian red pepper paste, usually made with sweet and spicy peppers, plus acetic acid, also is essential. We approximate this by pureeing a few easy-to-source ingredients.

½ cup drained jarred roasted red peppers

1 tablespoon lemon juice

1 teaspoon white sugar

¾ teaspoon hot paprika

Kosher salt and ground black pepper

2 tablespoons salted butter

1 tablespoon grapeseed or other neutral oil

2 medium yellow onions, finely chopped

8 ounces banana peppers or wax peppers (about 5), stemmed, seeded and finely chopped

4 ounces celery root, peeled and shredded on the large holes of a box grater (1 cup)

3 medium garlic cloves, minced

3 pounds boneless beef chuck roast, trimmed and cut into ¾- to 1-inch chunks

4 tablespoons plus 2 teaspoons sweet paprika, divided

1 pound Yukon Gold potatoes, peeled and cut into ½-inch cubes

Chopped fresh flat-leaf parsley, to serve

In a blender, combine the roasted peppers, lemon juice, sugar, hot paprika and ½ teaspoon salt. Puree, scraping the blender jar as needed, until smooth, about 30 seconds; set aside.

In a large Dutch oven over medium-high, heat the butter and oil until the butter is melted. Add the onions and banana peppers; cook, stirring occasionally, until the onions are translucent, about 6 minutes. Add the celery root, garlic, 1½ teaspoons salt and ¾ teaspoon pepper. Cook, stirring occasionally, until the vegetables are lightly browned, 5 to 7 minutes.

Stir in the pepper puree, followed by the beef. Add 2½ cups water, then bring to a simmer. Cook, uncovered and stirring occasionally, until a spoon drawn through the mixture leaves a brief trail, about 45 minutes.

Stir in 2 tablespoons of the sweet paprika and another 2 cups water. Simmer, uncovered and stirring occasionally, until a spoon drawn through the mixture once again leaves a brief trail, about 30 minutes. Add 2 tablespoons of the remaining sweet paprika and another 2 cups water; cook in the same way until a skewer inserted into the beef meets just a little resistance, about another 30 minutes.

Stir in 3 cups water and return to a simmer, then stir in the potatoes and remaining 2 teaspoons sweet paprika. Simmer until a skewer inserted into the beef and potatoes meets no resistance and the sauce is smooth and emulsified, about 25 minutes. Off heat, taste and season with salt and pepper. Serve sprinkled with parsley.

357

SPANISH BEEF STEW
WITH MUSHROOMS AND SHERRY

Start to finish: 2½ hours (40 minutes active)
Servings: 4 to 6

A corner of the Andalusia region in southern Spain is home to sherry, the unique fortified wine that is produced in an area known as the Sherry Triangle. The city of Jerez de la Frontera—commonly shortened to Jerez—is one of the points of that triangle, and also the location of Mantúa restaurant, where chef Israel Ramos taught us his recipe for guiso de ternera, or beef stew. With tender, succulent pieces of beef, silky, supple mushrooms and a braising liquid rich with both sherry wine and sherry vinegar, the stew was familiar and comforting, yet deliciously different thanks to

the wine's tangy, nutty notes and the aged woodsiness and mellow acidity of the vinegar. We adapted Ramos' recipe, adding turnip along with the carrots and cinnamon to complement the wine. There are many varieties of sherry, each with unique characteristics, but for this recipe simply seek a fino or manzanilla sherry—both are dry, bright and light, and therefore excellent counterpoints for the richness of the beef and mushrooms. If you wish to make a stew with deeper, weightier flavors, try amontillado or palo cortado, darker and more full-bodied types of sherry. As for the sherry vinegar, if you can spare the expense, opt for gran reserva which is aged for at least 10 years and has a smooth, complex flavor, balanced acidity and mahogany hue. If that's not an option, reserva or any aged sherry vinegar, though less nuanced than gran reserva, will work perfectly well.

2 tablespoons extra-virgin olive oil

2 pounds boneless beef chuck roast, trimmed of excess fat and cut into 1- to 1½-inch pieces

4 medium garlic cloves, peeled

1 medium yellow onion, halved and thinly sliced

Kosher salt and ground black pepper

2 medium carrots, peeled and sliced ½ inch thick

1 small white turnip, peeled and cut into ½-inch cubes

2 bay leaves

1 cinnamon stick

4 teaspoons sweet paprika

½ teaspoon grated nutmeg

1 cup fino or manzanilla sherry (see headnote)

1 quart low-sodium beef broth

2 tablespoons good-quality aged sherry vinegar (see headnote), plus more to taste

4 ounces oyster or cremini mushrooms, trimmed and thinly sliced

In a large Dutch oven over medium-high, heat the oil until shimmering. Add the beef and garlic, then cook, stirring occasionally, until lightly browned, about 5 minutes. Using a slotted spoon, transfer to a medium bowl and set aside; reserve the fat in the pot.

To the same pot, add the onion and 1 teaspoon salt; cook over medium, stirring often, until golden brown, 8 to 10 minutes. Add the carrots, turnip, bay, cinnamon, paprika and nutmeg; cook, stirring, until fragrant, about 30 seconds. Add the sherry and bring to a simmer over medium-high, scraping up any browned bits; cook, stirring occasionally, until reduced by about half, 3 to 5 minutes.

Stir in the broth, vinegar and ¼ teaspoon pepper. Return the beef and garlic, along with the accumulated juices, to the pot. Bring to a simmer, then cover partially. Reduce to medium-low and cook, stirring occasionally, until a skewer inserted into the beef meets just a little resistance, about 1½ hours.

Stir in the mushrooms and cover completely. Reduce to low and cook, stirring once or twice, until the mushrooms are tender, 10 to 15 minutes. Off heat, remove and discard the cinnamon and bay. Taste and season with salt, pepper and additional vinegar, if needed.

Less Liquid, More Flavor

For juicier braised meat, just add more liquid, right? Wrong. For better braises, we aim low on the liquid.

Braising meats in minimal liquid, such as water or broth, in a covered pot allows the meat to simmer gently in its own juices. In some cases, we don't add any liquid at all and instead rely on the juices that the protein itself releases as it cooks, or on the moisture exuded by the vegetables that also are in the pot. This method produces concentrated braising liquids that are easily transformed into richly flavored sauces.

If using wine in a low-liquid braise, it's best to add it two-thirds of the way through simmering or near the end. If added at the get-go, the wine's acidity and tannins can leave the braise tasting too tangy or astringent. If added at a later point, however, the wine will not reduce to the same degree, so its flavors are more vibrant.

The low- to no-liquid method works best when braising in the oven, as a consistently gentle simmer is easier to maintain in the steady, even heat of the oven. No babysitting or burner adjustments needed to prevent over-reducing or scorching.

BEEF, ORANGE AND OLIVE STEW

Start to finish: 4½ hours (1 hour active)
Servings: 6 to 8

Our version of this hearty stew from the south of France uses well-marbled chuck roast. The dish gets robust flavor from Provençal ingredients—red wine, olives, anchovies and garlic. Wine is key; we wait until the beef is cooked before we add it, retaining more of the flavors. A bold, full-bodied dry red wine such as Côtes du Rhône or syrah is ideal, as it holds its own against the other big flavors.

6 to 7 pounds boneless beef chuck roast, well trimmed and cut into 2-inch cubes

Kosher salt and ground black pepper

4 medium carrots, peeled and cut crosswise into ½-inch rounds, divided

3 anchovy fillets, patted dry

2 tablespoons extra-virgin olive oil

2 medium garlic cloves, thinly sliced

1 medium yellow onion, chopped

1 cup pitted Kalamata olives, rinsed, patted dry and chopped, divided

2½ cups dry red wine

1 medium red bell pepper, stemmed, seeded and cut into 1-inch pieces

1 tablespoon grated orange zest, plus ⅓ cup orange juice

2 teaspoons red wine vinegar

1 cup lightly packed fresh flat-leaf parsley, roughly chopped

Heat the oven to 325°F with a rack in the lower-middle position. In a large Dutch oven, toss the beef with 1 tablespoon salt and 2 teaspoons pepper. Add ½ the carrots, the anchovies, oil, garlic and onion, then toss. Cover, transfer to the oven and cook for 2 hours.

Remove the pot from the oven and stir in ½ cup of the olives. Return to the oven uncovered and cook until a knife inserted into a piece of beef meets no resistance, 1 to 1½ hours.

Using a slotted spoon, transfer the meat to a large bowl, leaving the vegetables in the pot. Set a fine-mesh strainer over a fat separator or medium bowl. Pour the meat juices into the strainer, pressing on the solids to extract as much liquid as possible; discard the solids. You should have about 2½ cups liquid; if needed, add with water.

Pour the wine into the now-empty pot and bring to a boil over medium-high, scraping up any browned bits. Reduce to medium and simmer, stirring occasionally, until the wine is reduced by half, about 8 minutes. Meanwhile, if you strained the meat juices into a bowl, use a spoon to skim off and discard the fat from the surface.

Pour the defatted cooking liquid into the pot and add the remaining carrots and the bell pepper. Return to a simmer and cook, uncovered and stirring occasionally, until the vegetables are tender and the sauce is slightly thickened, 10 to 15 minutes. Stir in the orange juice and beef. Continue to cook, stirring occasionally, until the sauce begins to cling to the meat, 3 to 6 minutes.

Off heat, stir in the remaining ½ cup olives, the orange zest, vinegar and half of the parsley. Taste and season with salt and pepper. Sprinkle with the remaining parsley.

SICHUAN RED-BRAISED BEEF

Start to finish: 3 hours (45 minutes active)
Servings: 4 to 6

Fuchsia Dunlop taught us to make spicy Sichuan red-braised beef during a visit to her home in London. She explained that red-braising is a common Chinese cooking technique, but in the Sichuan kitchen, instead of soy, toban djan is the ingredient that lends both flavor and color. Dunlop demonstrated her recipe for hongshao niurou from her book "The Food of Sichuan"; this adaptation is our simplified version. Toban djan, a fermented paste made with salted chilies and beans and sometimes other seasonings, supplies deep savoriness and loads of umami. Look for it in jars in the international aisle of supermarkets or in Asian grocery stores. If you can't find it, ¼ cup red miso mixed with 3 tablespoons chili-garlic sauce is a decent substitute. If you'll be shopping at an Asian market, also look for black cardamom pods. With smoky notes and hints of menthol, the spice has a flavor that's markedly different from more widely available green cardamom and white cardamom, so do not substitute with these varieties. If black cardamom is not an option, simply omit it—the stew will still be delicious. Serve with steamed rice, or, Dunlop says, even mashed potatoes.

2 tablespoons grapeseed or other neutral oil

⅓ cup chili-bean sauce (toban djan; see headnote), plus more if needed

2-inch piece fresh ginger, cut into 3 pieces and bruised

2 star anise pods

2 black cardamom pods (optional)

2 teaspoons Sichuan peppercorns, finely ground

⅓ cup Shaoxing wine or dry sherry

3 pounds boneless beef chuck roast, trimmed and cut into 1½-inch chunks

1 tablespoon soy sauce

4 scallions, thinly sliced, white and green parts reserved separately

1 pound medium carrots

Kosher salt and ground black pepper

Cilantro sprigs, to serve

Chili oil, to serve

Heat the oven to 350°F with a rack in the lower-middle position. In a large Dutch oven over medium, heat the oil until shimmering. Add the chili-bean sauce, ginger, star anise, black cardamom (if using) and Sichuan pepper; cook, stirring, until the oil turns red and the mixture is fragrant, 1½ to 2 minutes. Add the wine and cook, scraping up any browned bits, until most of the liquid has evaporated, about 1 minute. Stir in the beef, soy sauce, scallion whites and 5 cups water. Bring to a simmer over medium-high, then cover, transfer to the oven and cook for 1½ hours.

Meanwhile, peel the carrots, then roll-cut them: Set a carrot on a cutting board and, with a chef's knife held at a 45 degree angle to the carrot, trim off and discard the tip. Roll the carrot one-quarter turn and, with the knife still at the same angle, make another cut. Continue rolling and cutting until you reach the end of the carrot; discard the top. Repeat with the remaining carrots; set aside.

Remove the pot from the oven. Stir, then return to the oven uncovered. Cook until a skewer inserted into the beef meets no resistance and the meat is lightly browned, about 30 minutes. Stir in the carrots and cook in the oven, uncovered, until the carrots are tender, about 20 minutes.

361

Remove the pot from the oven, then remove and discard the ginger, star anise and cardamom pods (if used). Taste and season with salt and black pepper, and, if desired, stir in additional chili-bean sauce. Serve sprinkled with the scallion greens and cilantro sprigs. Offer chili oil for drizzling to taste.

BAROLO-BRAISED BEEF SHORT RIBS

Start to finish: 5 hours (50 minutes active)
Servings: 4 to 6

Brasato al barolo, or beef braised in Barolo wine, is a classic dish from Piedmont in northern Italy. Customarily, the beef is a roast that is slow-cooked, then sliced and served like a pot roast. The cooking liquid, rich with the essence of wine, beef and aromatics, becomes a resplendent sauce. For a more elegant take on the dish we opted for bone-in beef short ribs. They start out tough but are well marbled; slow, gentle braising renders them succulent and tender. Seek out meaty ribs—English cut (not flanken-style), if ordering from a butcher—that ideally are 4 to 5 inches in length so each rib is a single serving. The braise is named for the wine used in its making—Barolo, a deep, complex Piedmontese wine. But it isn't cheap, so you might consider Barbaresco or Nebbiolo d'Alba, though any decent dry red works. The beef requires a few hours of braising, so instead of stovetop simmering, which demands a watchful eye and burner adjustments, we rely on the steady, even heat of the oven. The ribs won't fit comfortably in a Dutch oven, so you will need a roasting pan that measures about 13-by-16 inches, plus heavy-duty, extra-wide foil to cover it. Polenta is a traditional accompaniment, but mashed potatoes would be equally delicious.

½ ounce dried porcini mushrooms

¾ cup boiling water

4 ounces pancetta, chopped

2 tablespoons extra-virgin olive oil

8 ounces cremini mushrooms, trimmed and chopped

2 large yellow onions, halved and thinly sliced

2 medium carrots, peeled and chopped

2 medium celery stalks, chopped

4 medium garlic cloves, smashed and peeled

2 tablespoons tomato paste

750-ml bottle Barolo wine (see headnote)

2 cups low-sodium beef broth

3 bay leaves

3 thyme sprigs

1 large rosemary sprig

6 pounds bone-in beef short ribs, trimmed, each 4 to 5 inches long (see headnote)

Kosher salt and ground black pepper

¼ cup all-purpose flour

3 tablespoons salted butter, room temperature

3 tablespoons finely chopped fresh flat-leaf parsley

Heat the oven to 475°F with a rack in the lower-middle position. In a small bowl, combine the porcini mushroom and boiling water; set aside. Meanwhile, in a large roasting pan, combine the pancetta, oil, cremini mushrooms, onions, carrots, celery, garlic and tomato paste. Using your hands, rub the paste into the other ingredients. Roast, without stirring, until deeply browned, about 40 minutes.

While the aromatics are roasting, in a large saucepan over medium, bring the wine to a bare simmer, then reduce to medium-low to maintain a bare simmer (it should steam, with only a few bubbles occasionally breaking the surface), until reduced to about 1½ cups, about 30 minutes. Remove from the heat and add the broth, bay, thyme and rosemary. Using a fork, transfer the porcini from their soaking liquid to the wine mixture, then pour the mushroom soaking liquid through a fine-mesh strainer into the wine mixture.

When the aromatics are deeply browned, remove the roasting pan from the oven; reduce the oven temperature to 325°F. Bring the wine mixture to a simmer over medium-high. Nestle the short ribs meaty side down in the aromatics in the roasting pan, then add the wine mixture. Cover tightly with extra-wide, heavy-duty foil; if the pan has fixed raised handles, be sure to get a good seal around the base of the handles. Transfer to the oven and cook for 3½ hours.

Remove the roasting pan from the oven and carefully remove the foil, allowing the steam to vent away from you; reserve the foil. Using tongs, flip each rib meaty side up. Return the pan, uncovered, to the oven and cook until a skewer inserted into the ribs meets no resistance,

45 minutes to 1 hour. Using tongs, transfer the ribs to a platter and tent with the reserved foil. Let rest for 20 minutes.

While the ribs rest, set a fine-mesh strainer over a large saucepan. Scrape the contents of the roasting pan into the sieve; press on the solids to extract as much liquid as possible, then discard the solids. Tilt the pan to pool the liquid to one side, then use a wide spoon to skim off and discard as much fat as possible; you should have about 3 cups defatted liquid. Bring to a simmer over medium-high, then reduce to medium and cook until reduced to about 2½ cups, about 5 minutes. Meanwhile, in a small bowl, mix the flour and butter until homogeneous.

With the liquid simmering over medium-low, whisk in the butter-flour mixture a spoonful at a time. Return to a simmer and cook, whisking often, until the sauce no longer tastes starchy and is thick enough to coat the back of a spoon, about 5 minutes. Off heat, taste and season with salt and pepper.

Uncover the short ribs and pour on about half of the sauce. Sprinkle with the parsley. Transfer the remaining sauce to a serving bowl and serve on the side.

MAKE-AHEAD INSTRUCTIONS

Follow the recipe to braise the short ribs. When the ribs are fully tender, after removing the roasting pan from the oven, flip each piece meaty side down, then let cool completely. Re-cover the pan with the foil and refrigerate for up to 48 hours. To finish, use a spoon to remove and discard the solidified fat on the surface of the braising liquid and bring to room temperature. Put the pan, covered with foil, in a 350°F oven until the ribs are heated through, 20 to 30 minutes. Continue with the recipe to strain the cooking liquid (you will not need to skim the fat off the liquid after straining) and make the sauce.

MOROCCAN BEEF, TOMATO AND CHICKPEA STEW

Start to finish: 2½ hours (45 minutes active)
Servings: 4 to 6

Harira is a Moroccan stew—or a thick, hearty soup—served during Ramadan as a way to break the fast. Made with meat, tomatoes, spices and chickpeas, it's not surprising the deeply satisfying meal is served year-round. We sampled several versions on a trip to Morocco, but most loved the one taught to us in Fes by home cook Houda Mehdi. We based our recipe on hers, opting for stovetop simmering instead of pressure cooking, swapping beef for lamb and using canned chickpeas for convenience. Though harira typically is thickened with flour, Mehdi prefers to use pureed cooked vegetables (potatoes and carrots), because she says—and we agree—that the stew tastes cleaner and brighter. We follow her lead and mash the vegetables that have simmered until tender to a coarse puree. The harissa, a North African spice paste, is our own addition; we like the heat and complexity it lends the stew.

2 tablespoons extra-virgin olive oil

1 large red onion, chopped

2 medium carrots, peeled and chopped

2 medium celery stalks, chopped

1 bunch cilantro, chopped, stems and leaves reserved separately

Kosher salt and ground black pepper

3 tablespoons tomato paste

2 tablespoons harissa paste, plus more to serve

2 teaspoons ground turmeric

1½ pounds ripe tomatoes, halved, pulp grated on the large holes of a box grater and skins discarded

1½ pounds Yukon Gold potatoes, peeled and cut into ½-inch cubes

1 quart low-sodium beef broth

1½ pounds boneless beef short ribs, trimmed and cut into 3-inch chunks

Two 15½-ounce cans chickpeas, drained but not rinsed

2 tablespoons lemon juice, plus lemon wedges to serve

In a large Dutch oven over medium, heat the oil until shimmering. Add the onion, carrots, celery, cilantro stems and ½ teaspoon salt. Cover and cook, stirring occasionally, until the vegetables begin to brown, 6 to 8 minutes. Add the tomato paste and cook, stirring, until the paste begins to brown and stick to the pot, about 1 minute. Stir in the harissa and turmeric, followed by the tomatoes. Bring to a simmer over medium-high and cook, stirring occasionally, until the mixture begins to thicken, about 5 minutes.

Stir in the potatoes and broth, then bring to a simmer. Add the beef, stir to combine and return to a simmer. Cover, reduce to medium-low and cook, stirring occasionally and adjusting the heat as needed to maintain a simmer, until a skewer inserted into the beef meets no resistance, about 1½ hours.

Remove the pot from the heat. Transfer the beef to a cutting board and cut it into bite-size pieces. Using a potato masher, mash the vegetables in the pot to a coarse puree. (Alternatively, use an immersion blender to process the vegetables and cooking liquid.) Return the beef to the pot.

Stir in the chickpeas. Bring to a simmer over medium and cook, uncovered and stirring occasionally, until the chickpeas are heated through and tender, about 15 minutes, adding water, if needed, to thin the soup to the desired consistency. Off heat, stir in the lemon juice and cilantro leaves. Taste and season with salt and pepper. Serve with additional harissa on the side.

365

Seafood

SNAP PEA AND RADISH SALAD WITH OLIVE OIL–TUNA

Start to finish: 30 minutes

Servings: 6

Italian tonnato is a silky sauce made with olive oil–packed tuna. It traditionally is served with chilled slices of veal, but we use it as a sauce for a crisp, colorful salad of blanched sugar snap peas and peppery red radishes. It's important to use tuna packed in olive oil for this recipe. Its texture and taste are richer than tuna in water or vegetable oil, and you will use some of the oil as a flavor-boosting ingredient. Some varieties of snap peas are stringless; if yours are, you need only to trim the stem ends.

Kosher salt and ground black pepper

1 pound sugar snap peas, trimmed, strings removed if present

1-pound bunch red radishes, trimmed and thinly sliced

2 tablespoons poppy seeds OR toasted sliced almonds

5 tablespoons extra-virgin olive oil, divided

Two 5-ounce cans olive oil–packed tuna, drained, oil reserved, flaked into bite-size pieces

2 tablespoons grated lemon zest, plus 2 tablespoons lemon juice

¼ cup mayonnaise

Fill a large bowl with ice water. In a large saucepan, bring 2 quarts water to a boil. Stir in 1 tablespoon salt and the snap peas, then cook until the peas are bright green and tender-crisp, about 2 minutes. Drain in a colander, transfer to the ice water. Let stand until completely cooled, about 2 minutes. Drain again, reserving the bowl, then pat the peas dry.

In the same bowl, toss together the peas, radishes, poppy seeds, 2 tablespoons of oil and ¼ teaspoon each salt and pepper. In a medium bowl, toss the tuna with 3 tablespoons of the reserved tuna oil, the lemon zest and juice, and ¼ teaspoon each salt and pepper.

In a blender, combine half of the tuna mixture, the mayonnaise and 1 tablespoon water. Puree, drizzling in the remaining 3 tablespoons oil, until the mixture is smooth. Taste and season with salt and pepper. Spread the puree on a serving platter. Spoon the vegetables on top, then scatter on the remaining tuna mixture.

PAN-FRIED TUNA CAKES WITH YOGURT-CAPER SAUCE

Start to finish: 45 minutes

Servings: 4

This recipe was inspired by Israeli seasoned fish cakes known as ktzitzot dagim. Traditional versions usually are prepared with fresh fish and might be fried, baked or cooked directly in a sauce. We've opted for canned tuna, making this an easy recipe for weeknight dinners. We use yogurt two ways: to add tanginess to the fish cakes and as a creamy dipping sauce served alongside. Choose good-quality, water-packed tuna, as its flavor is purer and lighter than the oil-packed variety. Be sure to drain the tuna, then give it a light squeeze before adding it to the mixture; this prevents the patties from becoming soggy.

¾ cup plain whole-milk yogurt, divided

2 tablespoons drained capers, chopped

Kosher salt and ground black pepper

4 tablespoons grapeseed or other neutral oil, divided

2 medium shallots OR ½ medium yellow onion, finely chopped

Two 5-ounce cans water-packed tuna, drained, flaked and lightly squeezed to remove excess water

1 large egg, beaten

½ cup panko breadcrumbs

2 teaspoons grated lemon zest, plus lemon wedges to serve

1 teaspoon ground cumin

In a small bowl, stir together ½ cup of the yogurt, the capers and ¼ teaspoon pepper; set aside. In a 12-inch nonstick skillet over medium, heat 1 tablespoon oil until shimmering. Add the shallots and ½ teaspoon salt, then cook, stirring occasionally, until softened, 6 to 8 minutes. Transfer to a medium bowl; reserve the skillet.

To the bowl with the shallots, add the tuna, egg, panko, lemon zest, cumin, ¼ teaspoon pepper and the remaining ¼ cup yogurt. Stir until well combined. Form into 8 balls and place on a baking sheet. Using your hands, press each ball into a 2½-inch patty.

In the same skillet over medium-high, heat the remaining 3 tablespoons oil until shimmering. Add the patties, reduce to medium and cook until golden brown on the bottoms, 2 to 3 minutes. Using a wide spatula, flip the patties and cook until golden brown on the second sides, about another 3 minutes. Transfer to a paper towel–lined plate and sprinkle lightly with salt.

Transfer the tuna cakes to a serving platter and serve with the yogurt sauce and lemon wedges.

Optional garnishes: Hot sauce **OR** finely chopped fresh cilantro **OR** both

---

CHANGE THE WAY YOU COOK

Sizing Up Shrimp

Shrimp sizing can be confusing. They're generally sold by count per pound but the names attached to the counts aren't regulated and can vary.

Below is our sizing protocol.

Size	Count per Pound
Small	51/60
Medium	41/50
Large	26/30
Extra-Large	21/25
Jumbo	16/20

Shrimp typically can be purchased frozen from the freezer case or "fresh" at the seafood counter (the shrimp at the seafood counter were in all likelihood frozen but thawed for sale). Seek shrimp that have not been treated with sodium tripolyphosphate (STPP), a chemical that forces the crustaceans to absorb water, which results in diluted flavor as well as a translucent appearance and an oddly firm, rubbery texture when cooked. If you're buying frozen shrimp, check the ingredients label on the package, as STPP must be listed if it was used in processing; if you're shopping at the seafood counter, your best bet is to ask.

To devein shrimp that aren't already cleaned, use a paring knife to make a shallow cut along the outer curvature of the shrimp, then pluck out and discard the thin, dark vein, if present, that runs down its length.

GINGER-SCALLION SKILLET SHRIMP WITH NAPA CABBAGE

Start to finish: 30 minutes

Servings: 4

This light, flavor-packed dish is simple to prepare. In less than 15 minutes, large briny-sweet shrimp—coated in bold seasonings including ginger, soy, mirin, sesame oil and lime—are steamed to perfection. Fragrant scallion greens and tender napa cabbage leaves layered over the shrimp add vibrant pops of color as well as supple crunch. During cooking, the combined moisture of the shrimp, marinade and vegetables creates a zingy, savory-sweet sauce that's especially delicious spooned over rice.

4 scallions, white parts minced, green parts cut into 2-inch pieces, reserved separately

½ bunch cilantro, stems minced, leaves roughly chopped, reserved separately

¼ cup mirin

2 tablespoons soy sauce

1 tablespoon finely grated fresh ginger

1 tablespoon toasted sesame oil

1 teaspoon grated lime zest, plus 2 tablespoons lime juice

Kosher salt and ground black pepper

1½ pounds extra-large shrimp (21/25 per pound), peeled (tails removed), deveined and patted dry

4 ounces napa cabbage, cut lengthwise into 2-inch strips, then crosswise into 2-inch pieces (about 2 cups)

In a 12-inch skillet off heat, stir together the scallion whites, cilantro stems, mirin, soy sauce, ginger, sesame oil, lime zest and ¼ teaspoon salt. Add the shrimp and toss to coat, then distribute in an even layer. Scatter the scallion greens and cabbage over the top.

Set the pan over medium, cover and cook undisturbed until the shrimp are pink at the edges and beginning to curl, 6 to 9 minutes, stirring once about halfway through. Remove from the heat and let stand, covered, until the shrimp are opaque throughout, 2 to 3 minutes.

Stir in the lime juice and half the cilantro leaves, then taste and season with salt and pepper. Serve sprinkled with the remaining cilantro leaves.

BROILED SHRIMP WITH GARLIC, LEMON AND HERBS

Start to finish: 30 minutes

Servings: 4

In this recipe, an easy puree of fresh herbs, garlic and olive oil is used two ways: Some of it coats the uncooked shrimp as a quick marinade, then a splash of lemon juice is stirred into the rest to create a bright sauce for serving. Be sure to pat the shrimp thoroughly dry so they'll brown and char nicely under the broiler. A touch of sugar in the marinade also promotes browning. We call for extra-large shrimp here; use slightly larger or smaller ones if you like, but adjust the cooking time accordingly.

1 cup lightly packed fresh flat-leaf parsley OR cilantro OR basil OR a combination

4 scallions, roughly chopped

2 medium garlic cloves, smashed and peeled

1½ teaspoons grated lemon zest, plus 1 tablespoon lemon juice

piercing through 2 points. Place on the prepared rack, slathering the top of the shrimp with any remaining puree from the bowl. Let stand at room temperature while you heat the broiler.

Heat the broiler with a rack about 4 inches from the element. Broil until the shrimp are pink with light brown spots, about 3 minutes. Remove the baking sheet from the oven, flip the skewers and continue to broil until the shrimp are just opaque and lightly charred, 2 to 4 minutes.

Transfer the skewers to a serving platter. Stir the lemon juice into the reserved herb puree and drizzle over the shrimp.

¼ to ½ teaspoon red pepper flakes (optional)

Kosher salt and ground black pepper

½ cup extra-virgin olive oil

1½ pounds extra-large (21/25 per pound) shrimp, peeled, deveined and patted dry (see headnote)

½ teaspoon white sugar

Line a broiler-safe rimmed baking sheet with foil, set a wire rack in the baking sheet and mist it with cooking spray. In a food processor, combine the parsley, scallions, garlic, lemon zest, pepper flakes (if using), ¼ teaspoon salt and ½ teaspoon black pepper. Pulse until finely chopped, about 8 pulses. Scrape the sides of the bowl, then add the oil and process until bright green and almost smooth, about 30 seconds. Transfer ¼ cup of the puree to a small bowl; set aside for serving.

In a medium bowl, toss together the shrimp, the remaining herb puree, sugar and ¼ teaspoon each salt and black pepper. Thread the shrimp onto 4 to 6 metal skewers, dividing them evenly; skewer each shrimp in a C shape,

TUSCAN-STYLE SHRIMP WITH WHITE BEANS

Start to finish: 25 minutes
Servings: 4

With its miles of coastline and reputation as the home of mangiafagioli—or bean eaters—it's no surprise that shrimp and white beans are a classic pairing in the cuisine of Tuscany, Italy. In this quick, easy recipe, the two are the stars, but with so few supporting ingredients, it's important to use a dry white wine that's good enough to drink on its own. Serve warm or at room temperature with a leafy salad and crusty bread to round out the meal.

3 tablespoons extra-virgin olive oil, plus more to serve

1 medium yellow onion, finely chopped

1 sprig fresh rosemary OR ½ teaspoon dried rosemary

½ teaspoon red pepper flakes

Kosher salt and ground black pepper

Two 15½-ounce cans butter beans OR cannellini beans, rinsed and drained

¾ cup dry white wine

1 pound extra-large (21/25 per pound) shrimp, peeled and deveined

1 cup lightly packed fresh flat-leaf parsley OR fresh basil, roughly chopped

In a 12-inch skillet over medium-high, heat the oil until shimmering. Add the onion, rosemary, pepper flakes and ½ teaspoon salt; cook, stirring occasionally, until the onion is translucent, 4 to 6 minutes. Stir in the beans, then add the wine and cook, uncovered and stirring occasionally, until the pan is dry, 5 to 7 minutes.

Stir in the shrimp. Cover, reduce to medium-low and cook until the shrimp are opaque throughout, 4 to 5 minutes; stir once about halfway through.

Off heat, taste and season with salt and black pepper. Remove and discard the rosemary sprig (if used). Stir in the parsley and serve drizzled with additional oil.

SHRIMP WITH MANGO, COCONUT AND MUSTARD SEEDS

Start to finish: 30 minutes
Servings: 4

Savory, sweet, subtly spicy and with a tropical fruitiness, this dish is a dryish curry, with a flavorful, well-balanced sauce that cloaks the plump, tender shrimp. A ripe fresh mango yields the brightest, freshest flavor, but if convenience is a priority, use frozen mango chunks. Serve basmati rice alongside. And if you happen to have some cilantro, add some just before serving as a garnish.

1½ pounds extra-large (21/25 per pound) shrimp, peeled and deveined

1 teaspoon ground turmeric

Kosher salt and ground black pepper

2 tablespoons grapeseed or other neutral oil

1 small red onion, halved and thinly sliced

1 tablespoon brown mustard seeds

1 tablespoon finely grated fresh ginger

4 medium garlic cloves, finely grated

1 Fresno or jalapeño chili, stemmed, seeded and minced

½ cup unsweetened shredded coconut

1 large ripe mango, peeled, pitted and cut into rough ½-inch cubes, or 12 ounces (3 cups) frozen mango chunks, thawed

1 teaspoon grated lime zest, plus

1 tablespoon lime juice

In a medium bowl, toss the shrimp, turmeric and ½ teaspoon salt; set aside. In a 12-inch skillet over medium, heat the oil until shimmering. Add the onion and cook, stirring occasionally, until beginning to brown, 5 to 6 minutes. Add the mustard seeds, ginger, garlic and half of the chili; cook, stirring, until fragrant, about 1 minute.

Stir in the coconut, mango and 1 cup water, then bring to a simmer. Reduce to medium-low and cook, uncovered and stirring occasionally, until the mango is soft and most of the water has evaporated, 6 to 8 minutes.

Using a fork, mash the mango until mostly smooth but with some chunks, then stir in the shrimp. Cook, uncovered, over medium, stirring only once or twice, until the shrimp are opaque throughout, 5 to 6 minutes. Off heat, stir in the remaining chili and the lime zest and juice. Taste and season with salt and pepper.

MOROCCAN HARISSA-GARLIC SHRIMP

Start to finish: 30 minutes
Servings: 4 to 6

This stewy, spicy Moroccan shrimp dish is deeply rich and flavorful but astoundingly simple to make. The recipe is based on the version of crevettes pil pil that home cook Houda Mehdi demonstrated for us in her kitchen in Fes, Morocco. All of the elements—the warm spices, sweet-tart tomatoes, citrusy lemon and herbal cilantro—together are a delicious match for briny-sweet shrimp. The amount of olive oil—½ cup—may seem excessive, but that much is needed to gently oil-poach the shrimp, leaving them plump, tender and full of flavor. We find that salting the shrimp and letting them stand for about 15 minutes allows the seasoning to penetrate, so don't bypass this step. Serve with warm flatbread for soaking up the sauce.

1½ pounds extra-large shrimp (21/25 per pound), peeled (tails removed), deveined and patted dry

Kosher salt and ground black pepper

½ cup extra-virgin olive oil

6 medium garlic cloves, finely grated

2 tablespoons harissa paste

1 tablespoon sweet paprika

1 tablespoon ground cumin

2 teaspoons ground coriander

½ teaspoon ground turmeric

8 ounces (2 medium) ripe tomatoes, cored, seeded and chopped

3 tablespoons chopped fresh cilantro

2 tablespoons lemon juice, plus 1 lemon, thinly sliced

In a medium bowl, toss the shrimp with ½ teaspoon salt. Let stand at room temperature for about 15 minutes.

In a 12-inch nonstick skillet over medium, heat the oil until shimmering. Add the garlic and harissa; cook, stirring, until fragrant, about 30 seconds. Add the paprika, cumin, coriander and turmeric, then cook, stirring, until the mixture is darkened and fragrant, 1 to 2 minutes.

Reduce to low and stir in the tomatoes and shrimp. Distribute the mixture in an even layer, cover and cook, stirring occasionally, until the shrimp begin to curl and turn opaque on the exteriors, 2 to 4 minutes. Remove the pan from the heat and let stand, covered, until the shrimp are opaque throughout, about 2 minutes.

Stir in the cilantro and lemon juice, then taste and season with salt and pepper. Line a wide, shallow serving bowl with the lemon slices and pour in the shrimp and sauce.

DRUNKEN SHRIMP WITH TEQUILA

Start to finish: 35 minutes
Servings: 4 to 6

These camarones borrachos—or "drunken shrimp"—are food writer and recipe developer Paola Briseño-González's version of a dish served up by Sergio Peñuelas at 106 Seafood Underground, a casual outdoor eatery located, literally, in the backyard of a residence in Inglewood, California. Peñuelas uses head-on shelled shrimp, which are amazingly flavorful but difficult to source. For this recipe, you can peel and devein the shrimp so they're easy to eat or you can leave the shells on, as they contain loads of flavor and do an excellent job of trapping the garlicky, spicy sauce. Use a tequila that's labeled as "blanco," "plata," "white" or "silver"—it should be clear and lack color—rather than a variety that's rested (reposado) or aged (añejo). If you like, serve with rice on the side, as Peñuelas does, and with lots of napkins if you've left the shells on the shrimp.

salt and ¼ teaspoon black pepper. Bring to a simmer over medium-high and simmer, stirring occasionally, until the mixture is reduced to about ⅔ cup and turns red, 6 to 9 minutes.

Reduce to medium, add the shrimp and cook, stirring and turning occasionally, until pink and opaque throughout, about 3 minutes for shelled shrimp or about 5 minutes for shell-on shrimp.

Off heat, stir in the cilantro, then taste and season with salt and black pepper. Transfer to a shallow serving bowl and garnish with the cucumber and onion. Serve with lime wedges.

2 pounds extra-large (21/25 per pound) shrimp, peeled and deveined (if desired; see headnote)

2 teaspoons lime juice, plus lime wedges to serve

Kosher salt and ground black pepper

½ cup tequila (see headnote)

3 tablespoons extra-virgin olive oil

3 tablespoons salted butter, cut into 3 pieces

6 medium garlic cloves, minced

2 to 3 teaspoons red pepper flakes

¼ cup lightly packed fresh cilantro, roughly chopped

½ cucumber, peeled and thinly sliced

½ small red onion, thinly sliced

In a large bowl, stir together the shrimp, lime juice and ½ teaspoon salt; set aside. In a liquid measuring cup or small bowl, combine the tequila and 1 cup water.

In a 12-inch skillet over medium, heat the oil and butter until the butter foams. Add the garlic and cook, stirring often, until fragrant but not browned, 1 to 2 minutes. Add the tequila-water mixture, red pepper flakes, 1 teaspoon

SCALLOPS AL AJILLO

Start to finish: 25 minutes
Servings: 4

Gambas al ajillo, or shrimp with garlic, is a popular Spanish tapa. For a new take on the classic, we swapped sweet, buttery sea scallops for the shrimp and created a portion generous enough to be served as a light main course. Look for U15 sea scallops—the sizing indicates there are fewer than 15 scallops per pound. Slightly larger or smaller ones will work, too. Serve with a simple salad of bitter greens to round out the meal.

1 to 1¼ pounds dry sea scallops (see headnote), side tendons removed

Kosher salt

⅓ cup extra-virgin olive oil

12 medium garlic cloves, smashed and peeled

1 teaspoon smoked paprika

½ teaspoon red pepper flakes or 1 árbol chili, broken in half

2 teaspoons sherry vinegar

½ cup lightly packed fresh flat-leaf parsley, roughly chopped

Crusty bread, to serve

Pat the scallops dry with paper towels, then place them on a paper towel–lined plate. Season them all over with salt; set aside. In a 10-inch skillet, combine the oil and garlic. Set the pan over medium-high and cook, stirring often, until starting to brown at the edges, about 2 minutes. Remove the pan from the heat and, using a slotted spoon, transfer the garlic to a small bowl; set the garlic aside.

Return the skillet to medium-high and heat the oil until shimmering. Quickly pat the scallops dry once again and place in the pan, spacing them evenly apart. Cook without disturbing until they are lightly browned on the bottoms and release easily from the pan, 2 to 4 minutes. Flip, then add the paprika, pepper flakes and reserved garlic, swirling the pan to incorporate.

Quickly spoon some of the hot oil over each scallop to baste, then remove the pan from the heat. Cover and let stand until the scallops are opaque throughout, about 5 minutes. Uncover and bring to a simmer over medium, then stir in the vinegar and parsley. Remove from the heat, then taste and season with salt. Transfer to a serving plate with bread for soaking up the flavorful oil.

How to Shop for Scallops

Sweet, buttery sea scallops are fast cooking, delicious and make a great light main. They often can sub in for shrimp in classic recipes like the Spanish tapa gambas al ajillo, shrimp with garlic.

But buying scallops can be confusing; not everything out there is worth your time or money.

In general look for U15 sea scallops—the sizing indicates there are fewer than 15 scallops per pound (slightly larger or smaller ones, will work, too).

Just as importantly, seek out "dry" sea scallops, ones that have not been treated with sodium tripolyphosphate. If purchasing frozen, check the ingredients label; at the seafood counter, make sure the scallops are not sitting in a pool of liquid, or ask. Another tell is color: dry scallops have a pale coral hue, whereas treated scallops are stark white.

If you're sautéing scallops, don't forget to pat the scallops dry before salting them, as well as just before placing them in the skillet. Wicking away excess moisture ensures nice, quick caramelization in the pan. (Keeping the scallops on a paper towel-lined plate while they wait to be cooked helps, too.) Don't attempt to move the scallops immediately after placing them in the skillet. They will stick at first but then release after they've formed a bottom crust.

SEAFOOD

375

Place the scallops on a paper towel-lined plate. Season lightly on all sides with salt; set aside. In a 12-inch nonstick skillet over medium-high, heat the oil until barely smoking. Quickly pat the scallops dry once again and place in the pan, a flat side down, spacing them evenly apart. Cook without disturbing until golden brown on the bottoms and they release easily from the pan, 2 to 4 minutes. Flip each scallop, then add the butter, capers and scallion whites, swirling the pan to incorporate.

Cook, spooning some of the hot butter over the scallops, until the butter smells nutty and the scallops are opaque throughout, 2 to 3 minutes. Remove the pan from the heat and, using tongs, transfer the scallops to a serving plate. To the skillet, add the lemon zest and juice; stir to combine. Taste and season with salt and pepper, then pour the sauce over the scallops. Sprinkle with the scallion greens.

SEA SCALLOPS WITH BROWNED BUTTER, CAPERS AND LEMON

Start to finish: 25 minutes
Servings: 4

Sea scallops get the piccata treatment in this quick supper. We pair the sweet, briny scallops with nutty browned butter, salty capers and puckery lemon. And we use the lemon juice to deglaze the pan after cooking the scallops to create a sauce that is both rich and bright. When shopping, look for U15 dry sea scallops—the sizing indicates there are fewer than 15 scallops per pound. Serve with crusty bread and a leafy salad dressed with a bright vinaigrette.

1 to 1¼ pounds dry sea scallops (see headnote), side tendons removed and discarded, patted dry

Kosher salt and ground black pepper

2 tablespoons extra-virgin olive oil

4 tablespoons salted butter, cut into 4 pieces

¼ cup drained capers

2 scallions, thinly sliced on the diagonal, whites and greens reserved separately

1 teaspoon grated lemon zest, plus 1 tablespoon lemon juice, plus lemon wedges to serve

STEAMED MUSSELS WITH HARISSA AND HERBS

Start to finish: 35 minutes
Servings: 4

Steamed mussels make a flavorful dinner that can be on the table with little prep and in about half an hour. We cook these with harissa, a North African chili and spice paste, balanced with a bit of honey, then finish them with a generous amount of herbs for bright, fresh flavor and color. Chickpeas make the dish more substantial and satisfying. Be sure to turn off the heat as soon as you see the mussels begin to open, then cover the pot right away and allow the mussels to gently finish cooking in the residual heat. Warm bread, either a crusty loaf or flatbread such as pita, is great for dunking in the sauce.

4 tablespoons salted butter, cut into 1-tablespoon pieces, divided

1 medium yellow onion, halved and thinly sliced

6 medium garlic cloves, peeled and thinly sliced

Kosher salt and ground black pepper

¼ cup harissa paste, plus more to serve

15½-ounce can chickpeas, rinsed and drained

½ cup dry white wine

1 teaspoon honey

3 pounds mussels, scrubbed and debearded,
if needed

½ cup chopped fresh dill

½ cup chopped fresh cilantro

In a large Dutch oven over medium, melt 2 tablespoons
butter. Add the onion, garlic and ½ teaspoon each salt and
pepper. Cook, stirring often, until the onion is golden
brown, 5 to 8 minutes. Add the harissa and cook, stirring,
until the paste begins to brown, about 1 minute.

Stir in the chickpeas, wine, honey and ½ cup water. Bring to
a boil over medium-high, then stir in the mussels and return

to a boil. Cover and cook just until the mussels begin to
open, 2 to 3 minutes. Remove from the heat; let the mussels
steam, covered, until they fully open, 3 to 5 minutes, quickly
stirring once about halfway through.

Using a slotted spoon, transfer the mussels to a serving
bowl, discarding any that did not open. Bring the cooking
liquid to a boil over medium-high, then add the remaining
2 tablespoons butter and stir until melted. Taste and season
with salt and pepper. Off heat, stir in half of the dill and
cilantro, then pour the sauce over the mussels. Sprinkle
with the remaining herbs and serve with additional harissa.

STEAMED CLAMS WITH CORN, FENNEL AND CRÈME FRAÎCHE

Start to finish: 30 minutes
Servings: 4

Think of this as a chowder for eating with your fingers. Finished with a small measure of crème fraîche (or whole-milk yogurt), the briny-sweet liquid released by the clams becomes a subtly creamy broth that's as delicious as the clams themselves. If you can, use corn kernels cut from freshly shucked ears (you'll need two good-sized ears to get the 2 cups kernels called for in the recipe), but frozen corn works in the off-season. Serve with oyster crackers, or with crusty bread for mopping up the broth.

2 tablespoons extra-virgin olive oil

1 medium fennel bulb, trimmed, halved, cored and thinly sliced

1 medium yellow onion, halved and thinly sliced

2 teaspoons fennel seeds

Kosher salt and ground black pepper

2 cups corn kernels (see headnote)

2 pounds hard-shell clams (about 1½ inches diameter), such as littleneck or Manila, scrubbed

¼ cup crème fraîche OR plain whole-milk yogurt

In a large Dutch oven over medium, heat the oil until shimmering. Add the fennel, onion, fennel seeds and a pinch of salt; cook, stirring occasionally, until the vegetables are lightly browned, about 6 minutes.

Stir in the corn and 1 cup water. Bring to a boil, then stir in the clams. Cover and cook, stirring only once or twice, until the clams have opened, about 8 minutes. Stir once more, then remove and discard any clams that did not open. Off heat, stir in the crème fraîche and ½ teaspoon pepper. Taste and season with salt.

Optional garnish: Hot sauce **OR** chopped fresh flat-leaf parsley **OR** lemon wedges **OR** a combination

Pan-Seared Salmon with Red Chili–Walnut Sauce

Start to finish: 25 minutes

Servings: 4

Heating a skillet over medium-high, then lowering the temperature once the salmon is in the pan ensures a nice sear without the risk of scorching, And finishing the cooking off heat, using just the pan's residual heat, ensures the fish stays moist and won't overcook. We paired salmon fillets with a spicy Georgian-style condiment called red adjika, which is made with garlic, chilies, a few spices, tomato and umami-rich walnuts. If you can only find whole fennel seeds, not ground, simply whirl ½ teaspoon whole seeds in a spice grinder to a fine powder. And try to purchase fillets of the same thickness so they cook at the same rate.

1 teaspoon ground coriander

½ teaspoon dry mustard

½ teaspoon ground fennel seeds

Kosher salt

Four 6-ounce center-cut salmon fillets (each 1 to 1¼ inches thick), patted dry

¼ cup walnuts

2 Fresno chilies, stemmed and quartered

2 medium garlic cloves, peeled

1 plum tomato, cored and quartered

¼ cup drained roasted red bell peppers, patted dry

1 tablespoon grapeseed or other neutral oil

In a small bowl, whisk together the coriander, mustard, fennel and 1 teaspoon salt. Season the flesh side of the salmon fillets with 1½ teaspoons of the spice mixture and set aside.

In a food processor, combine the remaining spice mixture, the walnuts, chilies, garlic, tomato and roasted peppers. Pulse until the mixture is finely chopped, 10 to 15 pulses, scraping down the bowl as needed.

In a 12-inch nonstick skillet over medium-high, heat the oil until shimmering. Place the salmon flesh side down in the pan, then immediately reduce to medium. Cook, undisturbed, until golden brown, 4 to 6 minutes. Using a wide metal

spatula, carefully flip the fillets, then cover the pan and remove from the heat. Let stand until the thickest part of the fillets reach 120°F or are nearly opaque when cut into, about another 5 minutes for 1-inch-thick fillets or about 8 minutes if 1¼ inches thick. Transfer the salmon to a platter.

Return the skillet to medium-high and add the walnut-chili puree. Cook, stirring often, until the liquid released by the puree has evaporated and the sauce is thick, 2 to 3 minutes. Spoon about 1 tablespoon of the sauce on top of each fillet, then serve with the remaining sauce on the side.

HOT-AND-SOUR SHRIMP CURRY

Start to finish: 40 minutes
Servings: 4

The coastal state of Goa in southwestern India is home to ambot tik, a prawn curry that's spicy with Kashmiri chilies and tangy with tamarind or kokum (a type of dried fruit used as a souring agent in the cooking of some regions of India). Many versions also include coconut, a rich, cooling counterpoint to the heat of the chilies and the pungency of fresh ginger and garlic. In our adaptation, hot paprika (or sweet paprika plus cayenne pepper) supplies the spiciness and white vinegar adds the acidity—no difficult-to-source ingredients needed. If you like, garnish the dish with fresh cilantro and serve it with basmati rice to soak up the delicious sauce.

1½ pounds extra-large shrimp (21/25 per pound), peeled, deveined and patted dry

1 teaspoon ground turmeric, divided

Kosher salt and ground black pepper

3 tablespoons grapeseed or other neutral oil, divided

1 tablespoon finely grated fresh ginger

CHANGE THE WAY YOU COOK

The One-Sided Seafood Sear

Fish and shellfish can quickly overcook, which can make it a challenge to develop a crisp, flavorful crust before the inside gets tough.

We've been conditioned to think that seafood has to be browned on both sides, but we flip that notion on its head and sometimes sear on just one side.

The fillets or shrimp have a chance to develop a brown and flavorful crispy bottom. After that we can pull the pan off the heat and finish the cooking with gentle, residual heat for food that is beautifully crisp on the outside and still moist and tender on the inside. Another option is to remove the partially cooked fillets or shrimp from the pan, use the empty skillet to make a sauce, and then return the fish or shrimp to the sauce to finish cooking.

2 medium garlic cloves, finely grated

1 teaspoon hot paprika or ¾ teaspoon sweet paprika plus ½ teaspoon cayenne pepper

1 teaspoon ground coriander

1 teaspoon ground cumin

1 pound ripe tomatoes, cored and chopped

½ cup coconut milk

2 tablespoons white vinegar

In a medium bowl, toss the shrimp with ½ teaspoon turmeric and ½ teaspoon each salt and black pepper. In a 12-inch skillet over medium-high, heat 1 tablespoon oil until barely smoking. Add half of the shrimp in a single layer and cook, without stirring, until browned on the bottom, 2 to 3 minutes. Using a slotted spoon, transfer to a plate. Using 1 tablespoon of the remaining oil, brown the remaining shrimp in the same way.

Set the now-empty skillet over medium and add the 1 remaining tablespoon oil, the remaining ½ teaspoon turmeric, the ginger, garlic, paprika, coriander, cumin and ½ teaspoon salt. Cook, stirring, until fragrant, about 15 seconds. Add the tomatoes and ½ cup water; bring to a simmer, scraping up any browned bits. Reduce to medium and simmer, uncovered and stirring occasionally, until the tomatoes have broken down, about 10 minutes.

Off heat, using a potato masher, crush the tomato mixture to a thick puree. Stir in the coconut milk and bring to a simmer over medium. Add the shrimp and accumulated juices; cook, stirring occasionally, until the shrimp are opaque throughout, 1 to 2 minutes. Off heat, stir in the vinegar, then taste and season with salt and black pepper.

SHRIMP ROUGAILLE

Start to finish: 30 minutes

Servings: 4

Rougaille or rougail—the spelling is dependent on geography, Mauritius in the first case, Réunion in the latter—is a Creole tomato sauce that shows the European and Indian influences on the cuisines of those two islands off the east coast of Africa. Spicy with chilies and fragrant with ginger, the sauce is simple to make and pairs wonderfully with a number of ingredients. Salted fish or sausage are common, but we add sweet, subtly briny shrimp. Serve with rice.

½ teaspoon cayenne pepper, divided

Kosher salt and ground black pepper

1½ pounds extra-large shrimp (21/25 per pound) peeled, deveined and patted dry

3 tablespoons extra-virgin olive oil

1 tablespoon finely grated fresh ginger

2 medium garlic cloves, minced

½ teaspoon dried thyme

4 scallions, whites minced, greens sliced on the diagonal, reserved separately

1 bunch cilantro, stems minced, leaves roughly chopped, reserved separately

1 pound ripe tomatoes, cored and chopped

In a small bowl, stir together ¼ teaspoon cayenne and ½ teaspoon salt. Season the shrimp on both sides with the mixture.

In a 12-inch skillet over medium-high, heat the oil until barely smoking. Add half of the shrimp in a single layer and cook without stirring until golden on the bottom, 45 to 60

seconds. Using a slotted spoon, transfer to a plate. Brown the remaining shrimp in the oil remaining in the pan, then transfer to the plate with the first batch.

To the oil remaining in the skillet, add the ginger, garlic, thyme, scallion whites, cilantro stems, the remaining ¼ teaspoon cayenne, ¼ teaspoon salt and ½ teaspoon black pepper. Cook over medium, stirring often, until fragrant, about 1 minute. Add the tomatoes and 1 cup water; bring to a simmer, scraping up any browned bits, then cook, stirring occasionally and adjusting the heat as needed to maintain a steady but gentle simmer, until the sauce is slightly thickened, about 5 minutes.

Add the shrimp and accumulated juices. Cook, stirring, until the shrimp are opaque throughout, 2 to 3 minutes. Remove the pan from the heat and stir in the cilantro leaves. Taste and season with salt and black pepper. Transfer to a serving dish and sprinkle with scallion greens.

VENETIAN-STYLE SHRIMP IN TOMATO–WHITE WINE SAUCE

Start to finish: 35 minutes

Servings: 4

From the coast of Veneto, Italy, gamberi alla busara is a dish of whole shell-on prawns in a garlicky tomato sauce spiked with white wine. For this weeknight version, we use shelled shrimp, but we prefer them extra-large (21 to 25 shrimp per pound) so the dish has heft and substance. Some recipes for gamberi alla busara include breadcrumbs that thicken the sauce. We, however, prefer to toast some panko breadcrumbs and sprinkle them on top to add crisp texture. Serve with warm crusty bread for dipping into the sauce.

5 tablespoons extra-virgin olive oil, divided

½ cup panko breadcrumbs

8 tablespoons finely chopped fresh flat-leaf parsley, divided

Kosher salt and ground black pepper

1½ pounds extra-large tail-on (21/25 per pound) shrimp, peeled and deveined, patted dry

6 medium garlic cloves, thinly sliced

1 medium shallot, finely chopped

½ teaspoon red pepper flakes

½ cup dry white wine

28-ounce can whole peeled tomatoes, crushed by hand

In a 12-inch nonstick skillet over medium-high, heat 2 tablespoons of oil until shimmering. Add the panko and cook, stirring often, until golden brown, about 2 minutes. Transfer to a small bowl and stir in 2 tablespoons of parsley and ¼ teaspoon each salt and black pepper; set aside.

In the same skillet over medium-high, heat 1 tablespoon of the remaining oil until shimmering. Add half the shrimp in an even layer and cook without disturbing until golden brown on the bottoms, 1 to 2 minutes; transfer to a large plate. Repeat with another 1 tablespoon oil and the remaining shrimp; set the shrimp aside.

In the same skillet over medium-high, heat the remaining 1 tablespoon oil until shimmering. Add the garlic, shallot and pepper flakes, then cook, stirring constantly, until the garlic is light golden brown, about 30 seconds. Add the wine

and cook, stirring, until the liquid has almost evaporated, 30 to 60 seconds. Add the tomatoes with juices and ¼ teaspoon salt. Cook, stirring occasionally, until the mixture is slightly thickened, 6 to 7 minutes.

Add the shrimp and accumulated juices to the pan, along with the remaining 6 tablespoons parsley. Cook, stirring, until the shrimp are opaque throughout, 1 to 2 minutes. Transfer to a serving dish and sprinkle with the toasted breadcrumbs.

MEXICAN SHRIMP IN GARLIC SAUCE

Start to finish: 30 minutes

Servings: 4

There are many versions of this coastal Mexican dish, but its defining characteristics are a bold use of garlic and a bright citrus flavor. Though traditional recipes may require roasting or slow-cooking whole heads of garlic, we first mellow the allium's pungency by steeping it in lime juice for a few minutes. We then coax out its sweet, nutty notes by gently pan-frying it in a little oil. A knob of butter—also

from the heat and continue stirring, allowing the pan's residual heat to finish the cooking, until the shrimp are opaque on both sides, another 20 to 30 seconds. Transfer to a medium bowl. Repeat with 1 tablespoon of the remaining oil and the remaining shrimp, adding them to the first batch.

Allow the empty skillet to cool for about 5 minutes, then add the remaining 1 tablespoon oil, the garlic-lime mixture and ¼ teaspoon salt. Set the pan over medium-low and cook, stirring frequently and scraping up any browned bits, until the garlic is softened and golden brown, about 5 minutes.

Add the jalapeño and any accumulated shrimp juices, then cook until the chili is softened, 1 to 2 minutes. Taste and season with salt and pepper. Off heat, add the shrimp, cilantro and butter, then stir until the butter has melted and mixed into the sauce.

traditional—tossed in at the end balances the garlic and lime and creates a silky sauce that clings lightly to the shrimp. Rice is a classic accompaniment, but crusty bread is delicious, too.

1½ pounds extra-large (21/25 per pound) shrimp, peeled (tails left on), deveined and patted dry

Kosher salt and ground black pepper

10 medium garlic cloves, finely chopped

2 tablespoons lime juice

3 tablespoons grapeseed or other neutral oil, divided

1 small jalapeño chili, stemmed, seeded and finely chopped

¼ cup lightly packed fresh cilantro, finely chopped

2 tablespoons salted butter, cut into 2 pieces

Season the shrimp with ¼ teaspoon salt and ½ teaspoon pepper. In a small bowl, stir together the garlic and lime juice; set aside. In a 12-inch nonstick skillet over medium-high, heat 1 tablespoon of oil until barely smoking. Add half the shrimp in an even layer and cook without stirring until deep golden brown, about 2 minutes. Stir, remove the pan

SALMON IN COCONUT-CURRY SAUCE

Start to finish: 30 minutes
Servings: 4

For this simple skillet dinner, we borrowed from "In Bibi's Kitchen" by Hawa Hassan. Instead of mackerel, we use salmon fillets and pair them with a saucy mix of vegetables simmered in coconut milk. A small measure of curry powder, a stand-in for the Somali spice blend called xawaash, flavors the dish and gives the sauce a pale golden hue. Serve with steamed rice.

Four 6-ounce center-cut salmon fillets, patted dry

Kosher salt and ground black pepper

1 tablespoon grapeseed or other neutral oil

4 scallions, thinly sliced, white and green parts reserved separately

4 medium garlic cloves, minced

1 pint cherry or grape tomatoes, halved

2 medium carrots, peeled and shredded on the large holes of a box grater

1 teaspoon curry powder

14-ounce can coconut milk

2 jalapeño chilies, stemmed, seeded and thinly sliced

1 tablespoon lime juice

Season the salmon on both sides with salt and pepper. In a 12-inch nonstick skillet over medium-high, heat the oil until shimmering. Add the salmon flesh side down, then immediately reduce to medium. Cook, undisturbed, until golden brown, 4 to 6 minutes. Using a wide, thin spatula, transfer the salmon browned-side up to a plate.

Return the skillet to medium-high and add the scallion whites and the garlic. Cook, stirring often, until lightly browned, 1 to 2 minutes. Add the tomatoes, carrots, curry powder and ½ teaspoon salt; cook, stirring, until the liquid released by the tomatoes has almost evaporated, about 5 minutes. Stir in the coconut milk, chilies and ¼ cup water, then bring to a simmer. Cover and cook over medium-low, stirring occasionally, until the carrots are softened, 6 to 9 minutes.

Stir in the lime juice and return the salmon, skin side down, to the pan. Cover, reduce to low and cook until the thickest parts of the fillets reach 120°F or are nearly opaque when cut into, 3 to 5 minutes. Off heat, taste the sauce and season with salt and pepper. Serve sprinkled with the scallion greens.

SEARED COD WITH PERUVIAN-STYLE OLIVE SAUCE

Start to finish: 30 minutes
Servings: 4

Peruvian pulpo al olivo, or octopus with olive sauce, served as the inspiration for this quick but elegant dinner. The olive sauce is the standout here, and it comes together with remarkable ease. Black olives, mayonnaise and lime juice are whirred in a blender until smooth, along with a little cayenne to mimic the heat of ají amarillo, a Peruvian yellow chili paste. Cod and snapper are our first choices for this dish, but you could use salmon instead. While the fillets finish cooking with the skillet's residual heat, we throw together a simple, colorful salad to serve on the side.

½ cup mayonnaise

½ cup pitted black olives, drained, plus 1 tablespoon chopped pitted black olives

¼ teaspoon cayenne pepper

1 teaspoon grated lime zest, plus 2 tablespoons plus 1 teaspoon lime juice, divided

Four 6-ounce cod OR snapper OR salmon fillets, patted dry

Kosher salt and ground black pepper

1 tablespoon extra-virgin olive oil

6 cups lightly packed baby arugula OR baby spinach (about 4 ounces)

1 cup cherry OR grape tomatoes, halved

½ medium red onion, thinly sliced

In a blender, combine the mayonnaise, the ½ cup olives, the cayenne and the lime zest and 1 teaspoon lime juice. Blend until smooth, scraping the jar as needed, about 1 minute. Set the sauce aside.

Season the fish all over with salt and black pepper. In a 12-inch nonstick skillet over medium-high, heat the oil until shimmering. Place the fish skin or skinned side up in the pan, then immediately reduce to medium. Cook, undisturbed, until golden brown on the bottoms, 4 to 6 minutes.

Using a wide metal spatula, carefully flip the fillets, then cover the pan and remove from the heat. Let stand until the thickest parts of the fillets are opaque throughout and the flesh flakes easily, about 4 minutes for 1-inch-thick fillets or up to 7 minutes if 1¼ inches thick.

After removing the pan from the heat, in a large bowl, combine the arugula, tomatoes, onion, the remaining 2 tablespoons lime juice and the chopped olives. Toss, then taste and season with salt and black pepper.

Onto individual plates or a serving platter, spread the olive sauce. Place the fillets on top, then arrange the salad around the fish.

SWORDFISH WITH POTATOES, TOMATOES AND CAPERS

Start to finish: 35 minutes
Servings: 4

The southern Italian dish called pesce spada alla ghiotta pairs meaty swordfish with a rustic tomato sauce. To make our version a complete one-pan meal, we add Yukon Gold potatoes. The swordfish steaks are browned in olive oil and finish cooking, along with the potatoes, in a garlicky tomato sauce. Capers and basil infuse the dish with bold Mediterranean flavors.

Four 6-ounce swordfish steaks, patted dry
Kosher salt and ground black pepper

4 tablespoons extra-virgin olive oil, divided, plus more to serve

1 medium red onion, halved and thinly sliced

4 medium garlic cloves, thinly sliced

¼ to ½ teaspoon red pepper flakes

8 ounces Yukon Gold potatoes, unpeeled, cut into ½-inch pieces

14½-ounce can diced tomatoes

3 tablespoons drained capers

2 teaspoons lemon juice

½ cup lightly packed fresh basil, chopped

Season the fish with salt and pepper. In a 12-inch skillet over medium-high, heat 2 tablespoons of oil until shimmering. Add the fish and cook, undisturbed, until well browned, 5 to 7 minutes. Using a thin metal spatula, transfer the steaks to a plate, turning them browned side up.

In the same skillet over medium-low, heat the remaining 2 tablespoons oil until shimmering. Add the onion, garlic, pepper flakes and ¼ teaspoon salt. Cook, stirring occasionally, until the onion is lightly browned, 2 to 3 minutes. Stir in the potatoes, then add the tomatoes with juices, and 2 tablespoons water. Bring to a boil over medium-high, then cover, reduce to medium and cook, stirring occasionally and maintaining a simmer, until a skewer inserted into the potatoes meets no resistance, 10 to 14 minutes.

Stir in the capers and lemon juice, then nestle the steaks in the sauce and pour in any accumulated juices. Cover, reduce to low and cook until the fish is opaque throughout, 4 to 6 minutes. Serve sprinkled with the basil and drizzled with additional oil.

CHANGE THE WAY YOU COOK

A Saucy Solution to Seafood

Mild, quick-cooking fish fillets are a great start to a week-night supper, so long as you avoid the twin challenges of overcooking and under-seasoning. We solve both problems in one stroke by cooking the fish in a well-seasoned sauce.

We pair rich, firm salmon with robust ingredients such as chorizo, the smoky Spanish sausage, and harissa, the North African paste that delivers bright flavor with a spicy kick. Lean, mild cod is a great partner to tangy tomato-based sauces and it pairs wonderfully with punchy, briny ingredients such as olives and capers.

Typically, we start with the sauce ingredients. Once the aromatics and other ingredients have softened and/or caramelized, we nestle the fillets in the sauce to poach in the well-seasoned mixture. The gentle, even heat means the interior will cook properly without running the risk of a tough, overdone exterior and the flavors have a chance to mix and meld.

SALMON WITH MATBUCHA

Start to finish: 35 minutes
Servings: 4

Matbucha is a North African cooked "salad" made with olive oil, garlic, tomatoes, sweet peppers and spicy chilies. With a jammy, spoonable consistency, it typically is served as a dip or spread, but we think it makes a delicious sauce that complements the richness of salmon. In our matbucha, we use roasted red peppers, which are sweet and silky straight out of the jar, and we ratchet up the complexity with some harissa paste (and/or cumin) and chopped olives (and/or) capers. Serve with crusty bread or warm flatbread for dipping into the sauce.

4 tablespoons extra-virgin olive oil, divided

**3 teaspoons grated lemon zest, divided, plus
2 tablespoons lemon juice**

3 teaspoons sweet paprika, divided

**2 teaspoons harissa paste OR ground cumin,
divided OR both**

Kosher salt and ground black pepper

**Four 6-ounce center-cut salmon fillets
(each 1 to 1¼ inches thick), patted dry**

**14½-ounce can whole peeled tomatoes,
crushed by hand**

**1 cup roasted red peppers, patted dry
and sliced**

3 medium garlic cloves, thinly sliced

**½ cup pitted black OR green olives,
OR ¼ cup drained capers OR a combination**

In a small bowl, stir together 2 tablespoons oil, 1 teaspoon lemon zest, 1 teaspoon paprika, ½ teaspoon harissa (and/or cumin, if using), ½ teaspoon salt and ¼ teaspoon pepper. Rub this mixture all over the salmon and set aside.

In a 12-inch nonstick skillet over medium-low, combine the remaining 2 tablespoons oil, the tomatoes with juices, roasted peppers, garlic, the remaining 2 teaspoons paprika and the remaining 1½ teaspoons harissa (and/or cumin, if using). Cover and cook, stirring occasionally, until the mixture is thick and jammy, 10 to 15 minutes.

Stir in the remaining 2 teaspoons lemon zest. Nestle the salmon fillets skin side up in the tomato mixture. Re-cover and cook until the thickest parts of the fillets reach 120°F or are translucent at the very center when cut into, 6 to 8 minutes.

Remove the pan from the heat. If desired, carefully peel off and discard the skin from each fillet, then transfer the fillets to individual plates, flipping them skin (or skinned) side down. Return the sauce to simmer over medium. Add the olives and lemon juice, then cook, stirring, until heated through, about 2 minutes. Taste and season with salt and pepper. Spoon the sauce over and around the salmon.

Optional garnish: Chopped fresh cilantro **OR** flat-leaf parsley **OR** thinly sliced jalapeño chili **OR** a combination

SALMON WITH SWEET PEPPERS AND CHORIZO

Start to finish: 40 minutes
Servings: 4

The rich flavor and firm texture of salmon pair perfectly with sweet peppers made into pipérade, a Basque relish-like stew of peppers, tomatoes, onion and garlic. Piment d'esplette is the authentic seasoning for pipérade, but instead we use a combination of sweet paprika and cayenne, both of which are probably already in your pantry. And for smoky, meaty flavor, we sauté slices of Spanish chorizo; the rendered fat helps cook the vegetables and the browned chorizo simmers with peppers for a few minutes at the end. We prefer salmon at medium doneness—that is, cooked until the center is translucent. To cook the fish until opaque

throughout, simmer the fillets for a few minutes longer, or until the center reaches 125°F to 130°F. Serve with warm, crusty bread.

Four 6-ounce center-cut salmon fillets

Kosher salt and ground black pepper

3 tablespoons extra-virgin olive oil, plus more to serve

2 ounces Spanish chorizo, quartered lengthwise and thinly sliced

2 medium red or orange bell peppers (or 1 of each), stemmed, quartered lengthwise, seeded and thinly sliced crosswise

1 medium red onion, halved and thinly sliced

1 teaspoon sweet paprika

¼ teaspoon cayenne pepper

¼ cup dry vermouth or white wine

14½-ounce can diced tomatoes

3 large thyme sprigs

Season the salmon on both sides with salt. In a 12-inch skillet over medium, combine the oil and chorizo and cook, stirring occasionally, until the oil has taken on a reddish hue and the chorizo begins to brown, 3 to 4 minutes. Using

a slotted spoon, transfer the chorizo to a small plate and set aside.

Set the skillet over medium-high and heat the fat until shimmering. Add the bell peppers, onion, paprika, cayenne and ¼ teaspoon salt. Cook, stirring occasionally, until the vegetables are wilted and tender, 5 to 8 minutes. Add the vermouth and cook, scraping up any browned bits, until the wine has evaporated, about 1 minute.

Add the tomatoes with juices along with the thyme, then bring to a simmer. Nestle the salmon fillets, skin-side up, in the mixture. Reduce to medium, cover and simmer, until the thickest parts of the fillets reach 115°F to 120°F, 6 to 8 minutes.

Remove the pan from the heat. Using tongs, carefully peel off and discard the skin from each fillet. Using a wide metal spatula, transfer the salmon to serving plates, flipping each piece so the skinned side faces down. Bring the pepper mixture to a simmer over medium-high, add the chorizo and cook, stirring occasionally, until slightly thickened, 2 to 4 minutes. Taste and season with salt and pepper. Remove and discard the thyme, then spoon the mixture over and around the salmon and drizzle with additional oil.

SLOW-ROASTED FISH WITH LEMON GRASS AND SAMBAL

Start to finish: 40 minutes (10 minutes active)
Servings: 4 to 6

We bake fish fillets at a low temperature to keep them tender and moist in this vibrant and spicy slow-roast. Sambal oelek—a tangy Indonesian chili sauce—forms the base of the marinade, which we enhance with lemon grass, shallot and turmeric. Look for sambal oelek in the international aisle of the supermarket; if not available, chili-garlic sauce is a good stand-in. Be sure to use a skin-on fillet (or fillets): the skin holds the flesh together, ensuring the delicate cooked fish can be easily transferred from baking sheet to platter. Serve over steamed jasmine rice, sprinkled with fresh cilantro leaves.

¼ cup neutral oil

**2 stalks fresh lemon grass, trimmed to the bottom
6 inches, dry outer layers discarded, roughly chopped**

1 medium shallot, roughly chopped

2 tablespoons sambal oelek OR chili-garlic sauce

1 tablespoon packed brown sugar

¾ teaspoon ground turmeric

Kosher salt and ground black pepper

**One 2-pound or two 1-pound skin-on red snapper
OR fluke OR haddock fillet(s)**

Heat the oven to 275°F with a rack in the lower-middle position. In a blender, combine the oil, lemon grass, shallot, sambal oelek, sugar, turmeric, 1 teaspoon salt and ¼ teaspoon pepper. Pulse a few times, then blend on high, scraping the blender jar as needed, until the paste is as smooth as possible, about 1 minute.

Place the fish skin side down on a rimmed baking sheet. Brush the paste evenly onto the flesh side of the fillet(s), then bake until the flesh flakes easily, about 30 minutes.

Remove the baking sheet from the oven. Using a thin metal spatula, transfer the fillet(s) to a serving platter.

Optional garnish: Lime wedges OR fresh cilantro leaves OR both

MISO-GLAZED BROILED SALMON

Start to finish: 30 minutes
Servings: 4

Soy sauce, mirin, white miso and honey combine to create a sweet-savory balance in this super-simple recipe. Some of the glaze mixture is kept aside for serving—drizzle it over the salmon or onto a side of sautéed greens or broccoli.

3 tablespoons white miso

5 teaspoons honey, divided

1 tablespoon soy sauce

2 teaspoons mirin

1½ teaspoons toasted sesame oil

¼ teaspoon cayenne pepper

Four 6-ounce center-cut salmon fillets (each 1 to 1¼ inches thick), patted dry

1 tablespoon sesame seeds, toasted

In a small bowl, whisk together the miso, 4 teaspoons of honey, the soy sauce, mirin, sesame oil and cayenne. Measure out 2 tablespoons and brush onto the top and sides of the salmon fillets. Let stand at room temperature for 20 minutes.

Meanwhile, into the remaining miso mixture, whisk the remaining 1 teaspoon honey and 2 tablespoons water; set aside. Heat the broiler with a rack about 6 inches from the broiler element. Mist a wire rack with cooking spray, then set in a broiler-safe rimmed baking sheet.

Evenly space the fillets, skin down, on the rack. Broil until the thickest parts of the fillets reach 120°F, or are nearly opaque when cut into, 6 to 8 minutes.

Transfer to a serving platter and drizzle with about 2 tablespoons of the miso mixture, then sprinkle with sesame seeds. Serve with the remaining miso mixture.

Optional garnish: Thinly sliced scallions

SLOW-COOKED SNAPPER WITH CHILI AND LIME

Start to finish: 1 hour (25 minutes active)
Servings: 4 to 6

Pescado zarandeado is a grilled fish dish popular on Mexico's Pacific coast, particularly in the states of Sinaloa and Nayarit. We first sampled it in the town of San Vicente at Restaurante Bar Fernando. Traditionally, a fragrant, deep-red paste of dried chilies, tomato and achiote coats the flesh of a butterflied snapper or snook. The fish is cooked slowly over coals until only lightly charred so its finished texture is tender yet meaty. To adapt it for year-round cooking and simplify it for the oven, we opted for skin-on fillets rather than a butterflied whole fish. (We stuck with snapper, though we also loved the texture of fluke and haddock.) To replicate the flavor of the seasoning paste, we rely on a combination of mild, fruity guajillo and smoky, raisin-y ancho, as well as soy sauce—an ingredient commonly used in the region's cuisine. As for the achiote, we like paste form; look for it in the international aisle of well-stocked supermarkets, in Latin American grocery stores or online. If achiote paste is not available, sweet paprika lends a similar red hue but with different flavor nuances. The recipe yields twice as much chili paste as needed, so refrigerate the extra for up to a week. We like to slather it on ears of corn as they cook and use it to baste chops on the grill. We like to serve the fish with lime wedges, warm corn tortillas and thinly sliced cucumber and red onion to add color, crunch and freshness.

1 medium ancho chili, stemmed and seeded

1 medium guajillo chili, stemmed and seeded

Boiling water, for soaking the chilies

2 tablespoons lime juice, plus lime wedges to serve

2 tablespoons soy sauce

2 tablespoons tomato paste

1 tablespoon extra-virgin olive oil

1 teaspoon achiote paste (see headnote) or 1¼ teaspoons sweet paprika

1 teaspoon dried oregano, preferably Mexican oregano

Kosher salt and ground black pepper

One 2-pound or two 1-pound skin-on red snapper,

fluke or haddock fillet(s) (see headnote)

Flaky salt, to serve (optional)

½ cucumber, thinly sliced

½ medium red onion, thinly sliced

Warm corn tortillas, to serve

Place the chilies in a small heatproof bowl and add enough boiling water to cover. Cover and let stand until soft and pliable, about 20 minutes. Meanwhile, heat the oven to 275°F with a rack in the upper-middle position. Set a wire rack in a broiler-safe rimmed baking sheet.

Using a slotted spoon, transfer the chilies and 2 tablespoons of the soaking water to a blender; discard the remaining liquid. To the blender, add the lime juice, soy sauce, tomato paste, oil, achiote, oregano and ¼ teaspoon salt. Blend on high until thick and smooth, scraping the blender jar as needed. Reserve ¼ cup of the paste for brushing onto the fish; save the remainder for another use.

Place the fish skin side down on the prepared rack. Brush the reserved paste evenly onto the flesh side of the fillet(s). Bake until the flesh flakes easily or the thickest part reaches 125°F, about 30 minutes. Remove the baking sheet from the oven; heat the oven to broil.

Return the baking sheet to the oven and broil until the fish is brown and charred in spots, 3 to 5 minutes. Using a thin metal spatula, transfer the fillet(s) to a serving platter. Sprinkle with flaky salt (if using) and serve with the lime wedges, cucumber, onion and tortillas.

SAUTÉED COD FILLETS WITH SPICY CILANTRO SAUCE

Start to finish: 25 minutes
Servings: 4

Zhoug, a spicy pesto-like condiment with a base of cilantro and often parsley, is said to have Yemeni origins, but it is popular throughout the Levant and Middle East. Its zip and pungency comes from fresh chilies, a small handful of spices and fresh garlic. Olive oil supplies fruity richness. We found zhoug just the thing to add bold, bracing flavor to mild-tasting fillets of white fish. Readily available cod works well in this recipe, but snapper and tilapia also are good. Whichever you choose, for quick, even cooking, look for fillets no thicker than about 1 inch. Be sure to dry the fish well by patting it with paper towels, especially if it was previously frozen; removing excess moisture helps ensure they brown well in the pan.

4 cups lightly packed fresh cilantro leaves and tender stems (about 1 large bunch), roughly chopped

2 medium garlic cloves, smashed and peeled

2 serrano chilies, stemmed, halved and seeded

1½ teaspoons ground coriander

½ teaspoon ground cumin

¼ teaspoon ground cardamom

Kosher salt and ground black pepper

¼ cup plus 2 tablespoons extra-virgin olive oil, divided

Four 6-ounce skinless cod, snapper or tilapia fillets, each about 1 inch thick, patted dry

Lemon wedges, to serve

To make the zhoug, in a food processor, combine the cilantro, garlic, chilies, coriander, cumin, cardamom, and ½ teaspoon each salt and pepper. Process until roughly chopped, about 20 seconds. Add ¼ cup of the oil and process until smooth, about another 30 seconds. Transfer ¼ cup of the zhoug to a small bowl; set aside for serving.

Season the fish all over with salt and pepper, then brush the boned sides with half of the remaining zhoug. In a 12-inch nonstick skillet over medium-high, heat the remaining 2 tablespoons oil until shimmering. Add the fillets zhoug side down, brush the tops with the remaining zhoug and cook, undisturbed, until golden brown on the bottoms, 3 to 5 minutes.

Using a wide metal spatula, carefully flip the fillets. Cook until golden brown on the second sides and the fillets are opaque throughout, about 3 minutes. Using the spatula, transfer the fillets to a platter. Serve with the reserved zhoug and lemon wedges.

BARBADOS GRILLED FISH

Start to finish: 1 hour 10 minutes (35 minutes active
Servings: 4

On the island of Barbados, meaty and moderately rich wahoo is the fish of choice for marinating in a fragrant lime-spiked garlic, chive and onion puree. We found mahi mahi fillets to be a great stand-in for hard-to-find wahoo. Or you could use swordfish or halibut, but if the pieces are thicker than 1 inch, they will take slightly longer to cook. If the fish you purchased was previously frozen or seems particularly wet, refrigerate it on a paper towel-lined plate for a few hours before marinating. This will remove excess liquid that otherwise would prevent the fish from browning.

1 small yellow onion, roughly chopped

1 bunch fresh chives, roughly chopped (½ cup)

2 medium garlic cloves, smashed and peeled

1½ tablespoons chopped fresh thyme

1 tablespoon distilled white vinegar

1 tablespoon grated lime zest, plus
2 tablespoons lime juice

1 teaspoon packed light or dark brown sugar

⅛ teaspoon ground allspice

Kosher salt and ground black pepper

Four 6-ounce mahi mahi fillets
(about 1 inch thick), patted dry

Bajan Hot Pepper Sauce (see sidebar),
to serve

In a food processor, combine the onion, chives, garlic, thyme, vinegar, lime zest, sugar, allspice, ¾ teaspoon salt and ½ teaspoon pepper. Process until coarsely chopped, about 5 seconds. Scrape the bowl and add the lime juice, then process to a coarse puree, about another 10 seconds.

Place the fish in a glass or ceramic baking dish. Scrape the marinade on top, then turn to coat both sides. Let stand at room temperature for 30 minutes.

Prepare a charcoal or gas grill. For a charcoal grill, spread a large chimney of hot coals evenly over one side of the grill bed; open the bottom grill vents and the lid vent. Heat the grill, covered, for 5 minutes, then clean and oil the grate. For a gas grill, turn all burners to high and heat, covered, for 15 minutes, then clean and oil the cooking grate; leave the primary burner on high and turn the remaining burner(s) to low.

Place the fish on the grill, allowing the marinade to cling to the fillets. Grill, uncovered, until lightly grill-marked, about 5 minutes. Using a wide metal spatula, flip and cook until lightly grill-marked on the second sides and the center of the thickest pieces reaches 130°F, about 5 minutes. Transfer to a platter. Serve with Bajan pepper sauce.

BROILER METHOD

Follow the recipe to marinate the fish. After marinating for 30 minutes, heat the broiler with a rack about 6 inches from the element. Place the fish on an oiled, broiler-safe rimmed

baking sheet, allowing the marinade to cling to the fillets. Broil until lightly browned around the edges and the center of the thickest pieces reaches 130°F, about 5 minutes, rotating about halfway through. Transfer to a platter. Serve with Bajan pepper sauce.

BAJAN HOT PEPPER SAUCE

Start to finish: 15 minutes
Makes ½ cup

This hot sauce gets its heat from spicy Scotch bonnet chilies. If you can't find those, habanero chilies are a good substitute. To keep your fingers from being coated in spicy capsaicin, use the chilies' stems as a sort of handle while slicing the sides from the center seed pod. A quick blanch in boiling water tames the chilies' spiciness, but won't affect their subtle fruity flavor. Refrigerated in an airtight container, the hot sauce will keep for up to two weeks.

2 Scotch bonnet or habanero chilies

3 medium garlic cloves, peeled

3 scallions, roughly chopped

3 tablespoons white vinegar

1½ teaspoons ground turmeric

1 teaspoon packed light or dark brown sugar

Kosher salt

2 tablespoons yellow mustard

2 teaspoons lime juice

Bring a small saucepan of water to a boil. Holding each chili by its stem, slice the sides away from the seed pod, discard the stems and seed pods. Add the chilies and garlic to the boiling water and blanch for 1 minute. Using a slotted spoon, transfer to a food processor.

Add the scallions, vinegar, turmeric, sugar and ¼ teaspoon salt to the processor. Pulse until chopped, about 10 pulses. Scrape the bowl. Add the mustard and lime juice, then process until not quite completely smooth, about another 10 seconds. Transfer to a small bowl or jar, cover and refrigerate.

MASALA-RUBBED BLACKENED SALMON

Start to finish: 30 minutes
Servings: 4

A mixture of garam masala, curry powder and paprika seasons salmon fillets before they're seared until deeply browned in a hot skillet. This recipe calls for skin-on fillets, but skinless works, too—just make sure to start them skinned side down in the pan. Try to purchase fillets of equal thickness so they cook through at the same rate. A cooling yogurt-mint sauce is the perfect accompaniment to the salmon.

1 tablespoon sweet paprika

3 teaspoons garam masala, divided

3 teaspoons curry powder, divided

Kosher salt and ground black pepper

Four 6-ounce skin-on salmon fillets (about 1 inch thick)

1 cup plain whole-milk yogurt

¼ cup finely chopped fresh mint

1 tablespoon honey

1 tablespoon grated lemon zest, plus 1 tablespoon lemon juice, plus lemon wedges to serve

2 tablespoons grapeseed or other neutral oil

In a small bowl, stir together the paprika, 2 teaspoons of garam masala, 2 teaspoons of curry powder and 1 teaspoon each salt and pepper. Sprinkle evenly over all sides of the fillets, rubbing it in.

In another small bowl, whisk together the yogurt, mint, honey, lemon zest and juice, the remaining 1 teaspoon garam masala and the remaining 1 teaspoon curry powder. Taste and season with salt and pepper; set aside.

In a 12-inch nonstick skillet over medium-high, heat the oil until barely smoking. Add the salmon skin side down, reduce to medium and cook without disturbing until well browned, 2 to 3 minutes. Using tongs or a wide metal spatula, carefully flip each fillet. Continue to cook until well browned on the second sides and the thickest part of each fillet registers 115°F to 120°F, 5 to 8 minutes. Transfer to a platter, flipping the fillets skin side down, and serve with the yogurt sauce and lemon wedges.

BROILED LEMON-GARLIC SALMON WITH ARUGULA

Start to finish: 30 minutes

Servings: 4

Salmoriglio is a simple southern Italian marinade and sauce that marries extra-virgin olive oil, garlic, herbs and lemon. The combination is perfect for rich, meaty salmon. The ingredients do double duty, seasoning the fish before cooking, then creating the sauce that finishes the dish. We broil lemon halves alongside the salmon; this renders the fruit extra-juicy while tempering its acidity. Baby arugula or spinach makes a colorful bed for the fillets and pairs beautifully with the sauce.

1 lemon

1 medium garlic clove, finely grated

**1 teaspoon minced fresh oregano OR
½ teaspoon dried oregano, crumbled**

Kosher salt and ground black pepper

3 tablespoons extra-virgin olive oil, divided

1½ teaspoons honey

Four 6-ounce salmon fillets, each about 1 inch thick

5-ounce container baby arugula OR baby spinach

Heat the broiler with a rack about 6 inches from the element. Mist a broiler-safe wire rack with cooking spray, then set in a broiler-safe rimmed baking sheet.

Mastering the Fish Fillet

Frozen or fresh, fish fillets are a great fast-cooking protein, but they can come in a bewildering array of sizes, from chunky cubes to slender strips, sometimes in the same packet.

The trick here is to go by thickness. If you get a large single fillet, often the case with cod, cut into as many pieces of a similar thickness as you need for even cooking; it may be as many as five or six. If you wind up with very thin fillets, fold them in half or in thirds to approximate the thickness of other solid pieces.

And when cooking the fish, don't feel you have to bring all the pieces to the finish line simultaneously. Check frequently for doneness and remove pieces as they are done.

White fish generally is done when it loses its translucency and can easily be flaked with a fork. For salmon, which can be cooked to medium (still a bit translucent), we sometimes use internal temp. But for fully cooked salmon and most other types of fish, the flesh should flake easily.

Grate 2 teaspoons zest from the lemon; set the lemon aside. In a small bowl, combine the zest, garlic, oregano and ½ teaspoon each salt and pepper. Measure ½ teaspoon of this mixture into a wide, shallow dish. Stir 2 tablespoons oil into the remaining zest mixture in the bowl; set aside.

To the zest mixture in the shallow bowl, stir in the remaining 1 tablespoon oil, honey, ¼ teaspoon salt and ½ teaspoon pepper. Add the salmon and turn to coat, rubbing the seasonings in. Place the fillets skin side down on the prepared rack. Halve the reserved lemon crosswise and trim the ends so the halves sit stably; place cut sides up alongside the salmon. Broil until the edges of the fillets are firm to the touch and the flesh flakes easily, 4 to 6 minutes.

Squeeze the juice from the lemon halves into the reserved zest-oil mixture; whisk to combine, then taste and season with salt and pepper. Place the arugula on a serving platter, creating a bed for the fish. Nestle the fillets into the greens and drizzle with the sauce.

SAUTÉED SNAPPER WITH GREEN BEANS AND TOMATOES

Start to finish: 25 minutes

Servings: 4

In "French Food at Home," Laura Calder shares a recipe for a simple yet elegant one-skillet, six-ingredient (not counting the salt and pepper) sautéed fish supper. Our riff yields a slightly more substantial vegetable accompaniment to serve with the fillets but is equally easy to prepare. We like green beans, but if you prefer, use pencil-thin asparagus instead. Red snapper is a mild, firm-textured white fish that holds up nicely to sautéing. Flounder is a good alternative, as it typically is of the same thickness as snapper. Halibut works nicely, too, but the fillets are thicker and therefore require a few more minutes in the pan.

Four 6-ounce skinless red snapper fillets (½ to 1 inch thick)

Kosher salt and ground black pepper

2 tablespoons extra-virgin olive oil, divided

8 ounces green beans, trimmed and halved

1 pint cherry or grape tomatoes

2 tablespoons salted butter, cut into 2 pieces

2 tablespoons white balsamic vinegar

Season the fish on both sides with salt and pepper. In a 12-inch nonstick skillet over medium-high, heat 1 tablespoon of oil until shimmering. Add the beans and cook,

stirring only once or twice, until spottily browned, 3 to 4 minutes. Add the tomatoes and ½ teaspoon each salt and pepper. Cook, stirring occasionally, until the tomatoes begin to char and burst and the beans are tender-crisp, 3 to 5 minutes. Transfer the vegetables to a serving platter.

In the same skillet over medium-high, heat the remaining 1 tablespoon oil until shimmering. Add the fillets skinned side up and cook, undisturbed, until golden brown, 2 to 3 minutes. Using a wide metal spatula, flip each fillet, then add the butter while swirling the pan. Cook over medium-high, occasionally basting the fish with the fat, until the fillets are opaque throughout, about another 3 minutes. Using the spatula, place the fillets on top of the vegetables.

Set the skillet over medium, add the vinegar and cook, stirring to combine with the fat, just until heated through, 30 to 60 seconds. Pour the mixture over the fish.

COD AND CHICKPEAS IN TOMATO-ROSEMARY SAUCE

Start to finish: 30 minutes

Servings: 4

Cod and chickpeas are a common pairing in the Spanish kitchen. We borrowed that combination for this one-pan dinner. Chickpeas simmer in a garlicky, herb-infused tomato sauce seasoned with paprika, then cod fillets are nestled in and poached until tender and flaky. This recipe requires little knifework, and with everything cooked together in a single skillet, the dish comes together quickly and easily. Hot paprika imparts a bit of heat; if you don't have any on hand, sweet paprika plus a little cayenne makes a fine substitute. Serve with thick slices of toasted crusty bread to sop up the savory sauce.

3 tablespoons extra-virgin olive oil

4 medium garlic cloves, thinly sliced

1 teaspoon hot paprika OR ¾ teaspoon sweet paprika plus ¼ teaspoon cayenne pepper

28-ounce can whole peeled tomatoes, crushed by hand

Two 15½-ounce cans chickpeas, rinsed and drained

2 bay leaves

1 rosemary sprig OR ½ teaspoon dried rosemary

Kosher salt and ground black pepper

Four 6-ounce skinless cod fillets, patted dry

2 teaspoons grated lemon zest, plus
lemon wedges to serve

In a 12-inch skillet over medium, heat the oil and garlic,
stirring often, until the garlic starts to brown, 1 to 2
minutes. Stir in the paprika, then add the tomatoes with
juices, chickpeas, bay, rosemary, 1 teaspoon salt, ½ teaspoon pepper and ½ cup water. Bring to a simmer over
medium-high, then reduce to medium-low and simmer,
uncovered and stirring occasionally, until the tomatoes
have broken down, about 10 minutes.

Nestle the cod skinned side down in the sauce, then spoon
on some of the sauce. Cover and cook until the fish flakes
easily, 6 to 8 minutes, adjusting the heat as needed to
maintain a simmer.

Off heat, remove and discard the bay and rosemary sprig
(if used). Stir in the lemon zest. Taste and season with salt
and pepper. Serve with lemon wedges.

Optional garnish: Chopped fresh flat-leaf parsley

FISH POACHED IN
TOMATO-GARLIC BROTH

Start to finish: 45 minutes
Servings: 4

There are many versions of pesce all'acqua pazza, or "fish in
crazy water," but all involve poaching or simmering fish in a
tomato broth or sauce. For our version, anchovies, black
olives and capers bring bold, punchy flavor to mild-flavored
fillets. Though this recipe calls for cod, any firm, meaty,
white-fleshed fish would work. Be sure to have some crusty
bread for serving—or even better, toast some baguette slices,
then rub them with garlic and brush them with olive oil.

Four 6- to 8-ounce skinless cod fillets

Kosher salt and ground black pepper

3 tablespoons extra-virgin olive oil

1 teaspoon finely chopped anchovy fillets

4 medium garlic cloves, finely chopped

¼ teaspoon red pepper flakes

1 medium yellow onion, finely chopped

½ cup dry white wine

1 pound grape tomatoes, halved

½ cup pitted Kalamata olives, halved

2 tablespoons drained capers

⅓ cup torn fresh basil leaves

Season the cod fillets on both sides with salt and pepper.
In a 12-inch skillet over medium, heat the oil until shimmering. Add the anchovy and cook, stirring and mashing, until
the bits dissolve, about 1 minute. Add the garlic and pepper
flakes and cook, stirring, until the garlic begins to brown,
45 to 60 seconds. Add the onion and ½ teaspoon salt, then
cover and reduce to medium-low. Cook, stirring, until the
onion is softened, 3 to 4 minutes.

Pour in the wine, bring to a simmer over medium-high and
cook, uncovered, until the liquid is almost fully evaporated,
1 to 2 minutes. Add the tomatoes and cook, uncovered and
stirring occasionally, until they begin to break down, about
3 minutes. Stir in 1 cup water, the olives and capers, then
bring to a simmer.

Nestle the fish in a single layer in the sauce and reduce to
medium-low. Cover and cook until the center of the fillets
reach 120°F or the flesh flakes easily when cut, 5 to 8

ula to transfer them to individual

igh and cook the sauce,
tly, 2 to 3 minutes. Taste and
poon around the fish, dividing
the basil and black pepper.

OVEN-FRIED FISH STICKS

Start to finish: 45 minutes

Servings: 4 to 6

This recipe turns mild, firm-fleshed fillets into flavorful fish sticks, but without the hassle of stovetop frying. For a crisp, light coating, we use panko breadcrumbs, but we process them so they're a little finer and a better textural match for the flaky fish, and we mix in a couple tablespoons of cornstarch to help the crumbs adhere. Buttery Ritz crackers are a terrific alternative to panko. We skip the beaten egg typically used to bind the crumbs to the fish and opt instead for mayonnaise flavored with mustard. Use for fish tacos by tucking the fish sticks, along with shredded cabbage and cilantro and chipotle-lime mayonnaise (recipe p. 399) into warm tortillas.

2 cups panko breadcrumbs OR roughly crushed Ritz crackers

2 tablespoons cornstarch

2 teaspoons sweet paprika

Kosher salt and ground black pepper

⅓ cup mayonnaise

2 teaspoons yellow mustard OR Dijon mustard

1½ pounds boneless, skinless cod OR snapper fillets

Lemon wedges, to serve

Heat the oven to 475°F with a rack in the lowest position. Place a wire rack in a rimmed baking sheet and mist the rack with cooking spray.

In a food processor, combine the panko, cornstarch, paprika and ¼ teaspoon each salt and pepper. Pulse to fine crumbs, about 8 pulses. Alternatively, place the ingredients in a gallon-sized zip-close plastic bag and pound with a rolling pin until fine. Transfer to a pie plate or other wide, shallow dish.

In a small bowl, stir together the mayonnaise, mustard and ¼ teaspoon each salt and pepper.

Cut the fish into ¾- to 1-inch-thick by 2- to 3-inch long fingers. Pat dry with paper towels. Brush the fish on all sides with the mayonnaise mixture. Working a few at a time, coat the pieces on all sides with the panko mixture, pressing so the crumbs adhere. Place the fish sticks on the prepared rack. When all of the fish has been breaded, mist evenly with cooking spray.

Bake until the fish sticks are golden brown, 10 to 13 minutes; rotate the baking sheet about halfway through. Serve with lemon wedges.

CHIPOTLE-LIME MAYONNAISE

Start to finish: 5 minutes
Makes about ½ cup

In a small bowl, stir together ⅓ **cup mayonnaise, 1 chipotle chili in adobo sauce** (minced), **2 teaspoons lime juice** and **2 tablespoons chopped fresh cilantro**. Taste and season with **kosher salt** and **ground black pepper.**

FENNEL-STEAMED SALMON WITH WARM OLIVE AND CAPER VINAIGRETTE

Start to finish: 30 minutes
Servings: 4

In this riff on a recipe from "Patricia Wells at Home in Provence," high-impact Provençal ingredients are an ideal match for rich, meaty salmon. We steam the fish atop a bed of sliced fennel to add sweet, licorice-like perfume; after cooking, the tender-crisp slices make a delicious accompaniment. We prefer salmon cooked to medium doneness—that is, until only the center is translucent. For well-done fillets, steam the fish for a couple minutes longer than indicated. If you prefer white fish over salmon, thick fillets of striped bass or sea bass work well, but increase the steaming time to about 10 minutes. No matter the type of fish you choose, try to select fillets of equal thickness so they cook at the same rate.

2 small fennel bulbs (about 1 pound total), halved, cored and thinly sliced (about 4 cups)

1 teaspoon grated lemon zest, plus ¼ cup lemon juice

Kosher salt and ground black pepper

Four 6-ounce salmon fillets, each about 1 inch thick

6 sprigs dill, plus 1 tablespoon chopped fresh dill

1 cup pimento-stuffed green olives, roughly chopped

¼ cup drained capers

¼ cup extra-virgin olive oil

¼ teaspoon red pepper flakes

In a medium bowl, toss the fennel with the lemon zest and ¼ teaspoon each salt and black pepper; set aside. Season the salmon all over with salt and pepper.

Place a folding steamer basket in a large Dutch oven. Add enough water to fill the bottom of the pot without submerging the basket. Remove the basket. Cover the pot and bring to a simmer over medium-high.

Line the basket with the fennel. Place the salmon skin down on the fennel, then lay the dill sprigs on the fillets. Turn off the heat under the pot, then set the basket in it. Cover and return to a simmer over medium. Steam until the thickest parts of the fillets reach 115°F to 120°F (for medium doneness), 7 to 9 minutes; the fennel should be tender but not completely soft.

Meanwhile, in a small saucepan over medium, combine the olives, capers, oil and pepper flakes. Cook, stirring, just until sizzling gently, about 2 minutes. Add the lemon juice and cook, stirring, just until warm, another 1 to 2 minutes. Cover and set aside.

When the salmon is done, remove and discard the dill sprigs. Using a metal spatula, transfer the fennel and fillets, skin down, to a serving platter. Sprinkle with the chopped dill, then spoon on the warm sauce.

GINGER-SCALLION STEAMED COD

Start to finish: 45 minutes

Servings: 4

In southern China, cooks have a worry-free method for cooking delicate, flaky white fish to perfection: steaming the fish whole with aromatics-spiked water. The mild heat slowly firms the protein, allowing it to stay moist. We adapted the technique, using skinless cod fillets for convenience and lining our steamer basket with cabbage leaves to mimic the skin of the whole fish. Rubbing the fillets with a seasoning paste of ginger, cilantro, scallions and soy sauce produced deep flavor in the mild-tasting fish. We drew on another classic Chinese technique for a flavorful finish—topping the fillets with raw chopped scallions and serrano chilies, then pouring sizzling-hot oil over them to bring out the flavors and aromas. Though this recipe calls for cod, haddock and halibut—or any firm, thick white fish fillets—also work. Because fillets vary in thickness, a general guide is to steam them for about 8 minutes per 1-inch thickness.

3 tablespoons chopped fresh cilantro leaves, plus ¼ cup whole leaves, divided

6 scallions, 3 minced and 3 thinly sliced on the diagonal, divided

2 tablespoons finely grated fresh ginger

6 tablespoons soy sauce, divided

3 tablespoons grapeseed or other neutral oil, divided

Four 6-ounce skinless cod, haddock or halibut fillets

6 large green cabbage leaves, plus 2 cups thinly sliced green cabbage

2 tablespoons unseasoned rice vinegar

2 teaspoons white sugar

1 teaspoon ground white pepper

1 serrano chili, stemmed and sliced into thin rings

1 tablespoon toasted sesame oil

In a wide, shallow bowl, stir together the chopped cilantro, the minced scallions, ginger, 2 tablespoons of soy sauce and 1 tablespoon of grapeseed oil. Add the fish and coat on all sides. Let stand at room temperature for 10 minutes.

Place a steamer basket in a large pot. Add enough water to fill without reaching the basket. Remove the basket. Cover the pot and bring to a simmer over medium-high. Line the basket with 4 of the cabbage leaves. Place the fish fillets on the leaves, then cover with the remaining 2 leaves. Turn off the heat under the pot, then set the basket in the pot. Cover and return to a simmer over medium. Steam until the fish flakes easily, 8 to 12 minutes.

Meanwhile, in a small bowl, whisk the remaining 4 tablespoons soy sauce, the rice vinegar, sugar and white pepper. Transfer 3 tablespoons to a medium bowl, add the sliced cabbage and toss. Arrange on a serving platter. Reserve the remaining dressing.

When the fish is ready, discard the cabbage leaves covering it. Use a spatula to transfer the fillets to the platter, placing them on the sliced cabbage. Sprinkle with the sliced scallions and the serrano.

In a small skillet over medium-high, heat the remaining 2 tablespoons grapeseed oil until barely smoking. Carefully pour the oil over the fillets. Drizzle with the sesame oil and sprinkle with the cilantro leaves. Serve with the reserved dressing on the side.

SEARED ZA'ATAR SWORDFISH WITH CUCUMBER SALAD

Start to finish: 30 minutes
Servings: 4

Swordfish has a sturdy, firm texture that withstands searing in a hot skillet until well browned and nicely crusted. For this recipe, we cut swordfish steaks into large chunks and season them with salt, pepper and za'atar (a Middle Eastern dried herb and spice blend) before placing them in a hot pan. A simple cucumber salad, served as a bed under the fish, counters the swordfish's meatiness with fresh flavor and crisp texture.

1 English cucumber, thinly sliced

1 large shallot, halved and thinly sliced

⅓ cup lightly packed fresh flat-leaf parsley

1 tablespoon red wine vinegar

4 tablespoons extra-virgin olive oil, divided

5 teaspoons za'atar, divided, plus more to serve

Kosher salt and ground black pepper

1½ pounds swordfish steaks, cut into 1½-inch chunks

In a large bowl, toss together the cucumber, shallot, parsley, vinegar, 3 tablespoons oil, 3 teaspoons za'atar and salt and pepper to taste. Transfer to a platter.

Season the swordfish on all sides with salt and pepper and the remaining 2 teaspoons za'atar. In a 12-inch nonstick skillet over medium-high heat, heat the remaining 1 tablespoon oil until shimmering. Add the fish in an even layer and cook, turning once, until golden on the top and bottom, 3 to 4 minutes per side. Place on top of the salad, then sprinkle with additional za'atar and drizzle with additional oil.

BAKED SALTED SALMON
WITH DILL

Start to finish: 1¾ hours (15 minutes active)
Servings: 4 to 6

We were taught how to make this salmon by chef Nikolas Paulsson of the Lanternen restaurant on the Oslo fjord in Norway. For our take, we use a 2-pound skin-on center-cut side of salmon and salt it for about an hour before baking in a moderate oven. When shopping, look for a salmon side about 1 inch thick at its thickest part; pieces that are thicker or thinner will require timing adjustments when baking. The salmon will be slightly underdone when removed from the oven; a tented 5- to 10-minute rest will finish the cooking and bring the internal temperature up to 120°F at the thickest part. At this temperature, the fish should be just opaque, not translucent.

3 tablespoons finely chopped fresh dill, plus more to serve

Kosher salt and ground black pepper

2-pound skin-on center-cut side of salmon (see headnote), pin bones removed

2 tablespoons grapeseed or other neutral oil

Lemon wedges, to serve

Quick-pickled cucumbers (see following recipe), to serve

Line a rimmed baking sheet with kitchen parchment. In a small bowl, combine the dill and 1 tablespoon salt, then rub the mixture with your fingers to break down the dill. Place the salmon flesh side up on the prepared baking sheet. Rub the dill-salt mixture into the surface and sides. Refrigerate, uncovered, for 45 to 60 minutes.

Heat the oven to 350°F with a rack in the middle position. Line a second rimmed baking sheet with kitchen parchment, then mist with cooking spray. Rinse the salmon under cold water, rubbing to remove the salt. Pat completely dry with paper towels, then place flesh side up on the second baking sheet. Coat the surface of the fish with the oil and season with pepper. Bake until the edges are opaque and firm to the touch and the center of the thickest part reaches 112°F to 115°F, 12 to 15 minutes.

Remove the baking sheet from the oven and tent the salmon with foil; let rest 5 to 10 minutes (the temperature of the fish will climb to about 120°F). Using 2 large spatulas, carefully transfer to a serving platter. Sprinkle with chopped dill and serve with lemon wedges and pickled cucumbers.

QUICK-PICKLED CUCUMBERS

Start to finish: 15 minutes, plus chilling
Makes about 2 cups

½ cup white vinegar

¼ cup white sugar

Kosher salt

1 tablespoon finely chopped fresh dill

1 English cucumber, trimmed, quartered lengthwise and thinly sliced on the diagonal

In a large bowl, stir together 1 cup water, the vinegar, sugar, 1 teaspoon salt and dill. Stir in the cucumber, then cover and refrigerate for at least 1 hour or up to 24 hours.

chicken

Roasted Chicken with White Wine Jus

Start to finish: 2 hours (20 minutes active)
Servings: 4

This is a simple and straightforward roasted chicken that makes a buttery, yet bright sauce from the juices. The fresh herbs and lemon halves that are tucked in the cavity don't season the chicken per se, but they do contribute flavor and aroma to the juices that are the base of the sauce. And the acidity of the lemon mellows slightly with cooking, so the juice that's squeezed into the sauce at the end doesn't over-whelm with tanginess. Roasting on a flat wire rack in a rimmed baking sheet allows for improved heat circulation, resulting in better browning and more even cooking; a broiler pan with a slotted top works nicely, too.

4-pound whole chicken, patted dry, fat near the cavity removed and discarded

4 to 6 sprigs fresh tarragon OR rosemary OR thyme OR flat-leaf parsley, plus 1 tablespoon chopped

1 lemon, halved crosswise

1 tablespoon extra-virgin olive oil

Kosher salt and ground black pepper

¾ cup dry white wine

4 tablespoons salted butter, cut into 4 pieces

Heat the oven to 425°F with a rack in the middle position. Set a wire rack in a rimmed baking sheet. Set the chicken breast side up on the rack. Place the tarragon and lemon halves in the cavity of the chicken. Tie the legs together with kitchen twine and tuck the wing tips back. Brush the bird all over with the oil and season with salt and pepper. Roast until the thighs reach 175°F, about 1¼ hours.

Using tongs, tilt the chicken so the juices run out of the cavity, then transfer the chicken to a cutting board; let rest for about 15 minutes. Meanwhile, remove the rack from the baking sheet; pour about half the wine onto the baking sheet or broiler pan. Scrape up any browned bits, then carefully pour the mixture into a medium saucepan; add the remaining wine. Bring to a simmer over medium and cook until reduced by about half, 8 to 10 minutes. Remove from the heat.

Untie the chicken, then remove and reserve the lemon halves from the cavity. Carve the chicken and transfer to a platter. Return the sauce mixture to a simmer over medium, then remove from the heat and whisk in the butter until melted. Add the chopped tarragon to the sauce, then squeeze in 2 tablespoons juice from the lemon halves. Taste the sauce and season with salt and pepper. Pour any accumulated juices on the cutting board onto the chicken. Serve with the sauce.

SPICE-RUBBED ROASTED CHICKEN WITH GREEN-HERB CHUTNEY

Start to finish: 2 hours / Servings: 6

Our starting point for this recipe was Nik Sharma's Hot Green Chutney–Roasted Chicken from his book, "Season." We loved the idea of an Indian-inflected spin on roasted chicken, but we aimed to simplify by serving the green chutney—a simple puree of herbs and aromatics—on the side instead of applying it under the chicken skin before roasting. Like Sharma, we use a large bird (5½ to 6 pounds) so the dish serves six or yields ample leftovers. If you prefer, use a 4-pound chicken and season it with only half of the spice rub (the remainder can be reserved for another use); reduce the roasting time to 60 to 70 minutes.

3 tablespoons ground coriander, divided

2 tablespoons ground cumin, divided

1 tablespoon sweet paprika

1 tablespoon garam masala

¼ teaspoon cayenne pepper

Kosher salt and ground black pepper

5½- to 6-pound whole chicken, patted dry

4 cups lightly packed baby arugula
(3 ounces)

1 cup lightly packed fresh cilantro

1 medium garlic clove, smashed and peeled

2 serrano chilies, stemmed and halved

½ cup extra-virgin olive oil

1 tablespoon lime juice, plus lime wedges
to serve

Heat the oven to 425°F with a rack in the lower-middle position. Place a V-rack inside a large roasting pan. In a small bowl, stir together 2 tablespoons of coriander, 1 tablespoon of cumin, the paprika, garam masala, cayenne and 1 teaspoon salt. Working over a large plate, rub all of the spice mixture evenly over the chicken, using all of the rub and any that has fallen onto the plate, then tie the legs together with kitchen twine. Transfer the chicken breast side up to the rack in the roasting pan. Roast until well browned, the thickest part of the breast reaches 160°F and the thickest part of the thigh reaches 175°F, 70 to 80 minutes.

While the chicken cooks, in a food processor, combine the arugula, cilantro, garlic, serranos, the remaining 1 tablespoon coriander, the remaining 1 tablespoon cumin and ½ teaspoon salt. Process until coarsely chopped, about 30 seconds. With the machine running, pour the oil through the feed tube, then process until finely chopped, another 30 seconds. Transfer to a small bowl, then stir in the lime juice. Cover and refrigerate.

When the chicken is done, transfer it to a cutting board and let rest for 30 minutes. Remove the rack from the roasting pan. While the chicken rests, add ½ cup water to the roasting pan and stir, scraping up any browned bits. Pour the liquid into a medium bowl, then let settle for 5 minutes. Skim off and discard any fat from the surface. Stir 3 tablespoons of the defatted liquid into the arugula-cilantro mixture, then taste and season with salt and pepper; discard the remaining liquid.

Carve the chicken and arrange on a platter. Drizzle with about 3 tablespoons of the chutney, then serve with lime wedges and the remaining chutney on the side.

407

Heat the oven to 450°F with a rack in the middle position. In a 12-inch oven-safe skillet, combine the potatoes, lemon halves, oregano sprigs, ½ teaspoon salt and ¼ teaspoon pepper. Drizzle with the oil and toss, then turn the lemon halves cut sides up. Season the chicken on all sides with salt and pepper, then set it on top of the potato mixture. Roast until the thighs reach 175°F, 1¼ to 1½ hours.

Remove the skillet from the oven (the handle will be hot). Using tongs, tilt the chicken so the juices run out of the cavity and into the skillet, then transfer the bird to a cutting board. Let rest for about 10 minutes.

Meanwhile, set the pan on the stovetop over medium; cook the drippings and potatoes, stirring, until most of the liquid evaporates and the mixture begins to sizzle, 3 to 4 minutes. Off heat, squeeze the juice from the lemon halves into the potato mixture, then stir in the tapenade and chopped oregano. Taste and season with salt and pepper. Carve the chicken and serve with the potatoes.

ROASTED CHICKEN AND POTATOES WITH OLIVES AND OREGANO

Start to finish: 1¾ hours (15 minutes active)
Servings: 4

An oven-safe skillet offers two advantages for roasting a whole chicken. First, the low sides mean better heat circulation around the bird, which results in good browning. Second, when the chicken is done, the pan can go directly onto the stovetop so that the drippings are easily reduced. We also add fingerling potatoes to the skillet, so the main dish and side cook together. Keep in mind that the skillet's handle will be hot when the pan is removed from the oven.

2 pounds fingerling potatoes

1 lemon, halved

4 oregano sprigs, plus 2 tablespoons chopped fresh oregano

Kosher salt and ground black pepper

2 tablespoons extra-virgin olive oil

4-pound whole chicken, patted dry, legs tied and wing tips tucked to the back

2 tablespoons black olive tapenade OR ½ cup chopped pitted Kalamata olives

CHICKEN ROASTED WITH GARLIC-HERB CRÈME FRAÎCHE

Start to finish: 1¾ hours (45 minutes active), plus refrigeration and standing time
Servings: 4

In "Summer Kitchens," Ukraine-born Londoner and cookbook author Olia Hercules writes, "Chicken smothered and baked in cultured cream is an old classic, but sometimes I like to go one step further." So she packs bold flavor into crème fraîche by mixing it with fresh herbs and garlic before slathering it onto a whole bird. In our adaptation of her simple yet succulent pot-roasted chicken, we coat the bird inside and out with garlicky, herby crème fraîche and refrigerate it for at least two hours or up to 24 hours before roasting. The crème fraîche not only adheres the garlic and herbs to the bird, its high fat content helps with browning and adds flavor. (Sour cream, which is much leaner, is not a suitable substitute.) Hercules shreds the meat off the bones after cooking, but we like to serve the chicken carved, its richly browned skin adding to the flavor and overall allure. We also make a simple sauce to serve alongside.

1 bunch dill, leaves and stems, roughly chopped (about 2 cups)

1 bunch flat-leaf parsley or cilantro, leaves and stems, roughly chopped (about 2 cups)

6 medium garlic cloves, smashed and peeled

Kosher salt and ground black pepper

1 cup crème fraîche

3½- to 4-pound whole chicken, patted dry inside and out

2 tablespoons lemon juice

In a food processor, combine the dill, parsley or cilantro, garlic and 1 teaspoon each salt and pepper. Process until the herbs are finely chopped, about 1 minute. Add the crème fraîche and process just until combined, 20 to 30 seconds, scraping the bowl as needed; do not overprocess. Transfer ½ cup of the mixture to a small bowl, cover and refrigerate for making the sauce. Scrape the remainder into another small bowl and refrigerate until chilled and slightly thicker, about 30 minutes; this portion will be used directly on the chicken.

Place the chicken in a metal 9-by-13-inch baking pan. Using a spoon, spread ¼ cup of the crème fraîche mixture for the chicken in the cavity of the bird. Tie the legs together with kitchen twine. Slather the remaining crème fraîche mixture all over the exterior of the chicken (it's fine if some of it falls into the pan). Cover loosely with plastic wrap and refrigerate for at least 2 hours or up to 24 hours.

About 1 hour before roasting, remove the chicken from the refrigerator and let stand, still covered, at room temperature. Heat the oven to 425°F with a rack in the lower-middle position.

After the chicken has stood for about 1 hour, remove the plastic wrap and tent the pan with a large sheet of extra-wide foil; try to keep the foil from touching the chicken. Roast for 40 minutes. Remove the crème fraîche mixture for the sauce from the refrigerator and let stand at room temperature.

Working quickly, remove the foil from the chicken, pour ¾ cup water into the pan and continue to roast, uncovered, until the thickest part of the breast registers 160°F and the thighs reach 175°F, another 20 to 30 minutes; if at any point the pan is close to dry, add water to prevent scorching.

Carefully tip the juices from the cavity of the bird into the pan, then transfer the chicken to a cutting board. Let rest while you make the sauce.

Scrape up any browned bits in the bottom of the pan, then pour the liquid into a fine-mesh strainer set over a liquid measuring cup. Let the liquid settle for a few minutes, then use a spoon to skim off and discard the fat from the surface. You should have ½ to ¾ cup defatted liquid; if you have more, you will need to reduce it to that amount. Either way, pour the liquid into a small saucepan and bring to a simmer over medium-high; if needed cook, stirring occasionally, until reduced to ½ to ¾ cup. Remove the pan from the heat, whisk in the reserved ½ cup crème fraîche mixture and the lemon juice. Taste and season with salt and pepper.

Carve the chicken and transfer to a platter. Pour about ¼ cup of the sauce over the chicken, then serve with the remaining sauce on the side.

The Spatchcock Speed-Up

One of our favorite roast chicken hacks is, quite literally, a hack.

Spatchcocking, or butterflying, the bird involves cutting out the backbone—a good pair of kitchen shears is all you need— and pressing the bird flat.

That solves the problem of uneven cooking, putting breasts and thighs on the same plane so they cook in about the same time. It also ups the odds for well-seasoned, super-crispy skin. We use seasoned pastes or rubs and slide them under and over the skin for fast, reliable flavor.

1.

2.

1. Set the chicken breast down on a cutting board. Using sturdy kitchen shears, cut along one side of the backbone from top to bottom.

2. Repeat the cut on the other side of the backbone, then remove and discard the backbone.

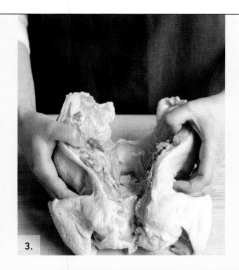

3.

4.

3. Spread the sides of the chicken, opening it like a book and flattening it as much as possible.

4. Flip the chicken breast up, then use your hands to press firmly on the highest point of the breast to flatten the bird. The breast bone may crack.

5. If desired, the skin of the thighs and breasts can be loosened from the edges to allow seasonings to be rubbed under the skin.

5.

POLLO ALLA MATTONE
WITH WILTED KALE

Start to finish: 1 hour (35 minutes active)
Servings: 4

Pollo alla mattone, or "chicken under a brick," is a Tuscan dish in which a chicken (pollo) is spatchcocked, marinated and grilled or roasted under a brick (mattone). The weight presses the chicken down, ensuring the bird makes good contact with the cooking surface, rendering fat and ensuring beautiful browning and crisping. We start the bird breast side down in a skillet on the stovetop, then weight it and slide the skillet into the oven to finish cooking. As a "brick" we use a second heavy skillet or a large, heavy pot (such as a cast-iron Dutch oven). However, if you happen to have a couple clean bricks on hand, you could wrap them in heavy-duty foil for use as weights. We use the flavorful drippings in the skillet after roasting to wilt some lacinato kale to serve as a side (lacinato kale sometimes is sold as dinosaur or Tuscan kale). A halved lemon tucked into the pan alongside the chicken becomes juicy and mellow with roasting and is perfect for squeezing at the table to lift and brighten the flavors.

3 tablespoons extra-virgin olive oil, divided

4 medium garlic cloves, finely grated

1 lemon, zest finely grated, lemon halved crosswise

½ to ¾ teaspoon red pepper flakes

Kosher salt and ground black pepper

3½- to 4-pound whole chicken

1 sage sprig, plus 1 tablespoon finely chopped sage, reserved separately

2 rosemary sprigs

2 tablespoons salted butter, cut into 2 pieces

1 bunch lacinato kale, stemmed and sliced into thin ribbons

In a small bowl, stir together 2 tablespoons oil, the garlic, lemon zest, pepper flakes, 1½ teaspoons salt and ½ teaspoon black pepper. Place the chicken, breast down, on a cutting board. Using sturdy kitchen shears, cut along both sides of the backbone, end to end. Remove and discard the backbone (or save it to make broth). Spread open the chicken, then turn it breast up. Use the heel of your hand

to press down firmly on the thickest part of the breast, until the wishbone snaps. Rub the garlic mixture all over both sides of the chicken and into the skin. Let stand, uncovered, at room temperature while the oven heats. Heat the oven to 450°F with a rack in the lowest position.

In a 12-inch oven-safe skillet over medium-high, heat the remaining 1 tablespoon oil until shimmering. Place the chicken breast down in the skillet and reduce to medium. Place a small sheet of foil over the chicken, followed by a second heavy skillet or pot on top. Cook until the skin is golden brown, rotating the skillet periodically, and removing the weight and foil and checking every 4 to 5 minutes to ensure even browning, 10 to 15 minutes.

Using tongs, carefully transfer the chicken breast side up to a large plate. Pour off and discard the fat in the skillet. Place the sage sprig and the rosemary in the skillet, then slide the chicken, breast up, on top. Place the lemon halves cut side down in the skillet. Transfer to the oven and roast until the thickest part of the breast reaches 160°F, 25 to 35 minutes.

Remove the skillet from the oven (the handle will be hot). Carefully transfer the chicken and lemon halves to a cutting board and let rest while you cook the kale. Remove and discard the herb sprigs from the skillet.

Set the pan over medium-high and bring the pan juices to a simmer. Add the butter and stir until melted, then add the kale, the chopped sage and ¼ teaspoon black pepper. Cook, stirring often, until the kale is just tender and wilted, 4 to 6 minutes. Taste and season with salt and black pepper. Transfer the kale to a serving platter. Carve the chicken and arrange the pieces on the kale. Serve with the lemon halves.

413

SPATCHCOCKED ROASTED CHICKEN WITH GOCHUJANG BUTTER

Start to finish: 1 hour (15 minutes active) / Servings: 4

Our Korean-inspired seasoning paste elevates a simple roast chicken with spicy-sweet flavor. The blend includes softened butter, gochujang and honey, plus fresh ginger and garlic, which mellow and sweeten as they cook. We smear the mixture under the bird's skin, directly on the meat, so it takes on the bold flavors. Gochujang, one of our pantry staples, is a fermented chili paste commonly used in Korean cooking; it is loaded with spiciness, a hint of sweetness and lots of umami. You'll find it in the international section of the supermarket or in Asian grocery stores. Serve with steamed rice.

4 tablespoons salted butter, room temperature

¼ cup gochujang

4 teaspoons finely grated fresh ginger

3 medium garlic cloves, finely grated

1 tablespoon honey

Kosher salt

4-pound whole chicken

Heat the oven to 425°F with a rack in the middle position. Set a wire rack in a rimmed baking sheet. In a small bowl, stir together the butter, gochujang, ginger, garlic, honey and ½ teaspoon salt; set aside.

Place the chicken breast down on a cutting board. Using sturdy kitchen shears, cut along both sides of the backbone, end to end; remove the backbone and discard. Spread open the chicken, then turn it breast up. Using the heel of your

hand, press down firmly on the thickest part of the breast until the wishbone snaps.

Season the underside of the chicken with salt, then place it breast up on the wire rack. With your fingers, carefully loosen the skin from the meat on the breast and thighs. Using a spoon, distribute the butter mixture under the skin in those areas, then massage the skin to evenly spread the mixture and rub it into the flesh. Season the skin side with salt, then tuck the wing tips to the back.

Roast until well browned and the thighs reach 175°F, about 40 minutes. Let the chicken rest for about 10 minutes, then carve.

CHUTNEY-GLAZED SPATCHCOCKED CHICKEN

Start to finish: 1 hour 20 minutes (20 minutes active)
Servings: 4

Spatchcocking a chicken—that is, cutting out its backbone and opening up and flattening the bird—allows for even browning and relatively quick cooking because all of the meat is on the same plane. For this spatchcocked bird, we make a simple glaze with fruity, tangy-sweet mango chutney mixed with butter for richness, ground ginger for warm spiciness and turmeric for savoriness and golden color. If your mango chutney is especially chunky, mash it with a fork or spoon to break up any large pieces of fruit. The glaze mixture does double duty here—a portion is set aside for combining with cilantro and lemon juice just before serving to make a sauce to serve at the table. An herbed grain pilaf or steamed basmati rice is a perfect accompaniment.

4 tablespoons salted butter, cut into 4 pieces

1 teaspoon ground ginger

1 teaspoon ground turmeric

½ cup mango chutney (see headnote)

4-pound whole chicken

Kosher salt and ground black pepper

2 tablespoons finely chopped fresh cilantro

3 tablespoons lemon juice, plus more as needed

Heat the oven to 425°F with the rack in the middle position. Line a rimmed baking sheet with foil, then set a wire rack on top. In a small saucepan over medium, melt the butter. Add the ginger and turmeric and cook, stirring, until the spices are fragrant, 30 to 60 seconds. Remove from the heat and stir in the chutney. Measure 3 tablespoons of the mixture into each of 2 small bowls to use for glazing; set the remaining mixture aside in the saucepan, covered, for making the sauce.

Place the chicken breast down on a cutting board. Using sturdy kitchen shears, cut along both sides of the backbone, end to end; remove and discard the backbone (or save it to make broth). Spread open the chicken, then turn it breast up. Use the heel of your hand to press down firmly on the thickest part of the breast, until the wishbone snaps. Pat the chicken dry with paper towels, then season on all sides with salt and pepper. Place skin side up on the prepared rack and brush evenly with the chutney mixture from one of the small bowls. Roast for 40 minutes. Meanwhile, wash and dry the brush.

Remove the chicken from the oven and, using the clean brush, apply the chutney mixture from the second bowl. Continue to roast until the thighs reach 175°F, another 10 to 15 minutes. Remove from the oven and let rest for 10 minutes.

While the chicken rests, set the saucepan over medium-low and heat, stirring, until just warmed through, 1 to 2 minutes. Off heat, stir in the cilantro and lemon juice. Taste and season with salt, pepper and additional lemon juice, if needed, then transfer to a serving bowl. Carve the chicken and serve with the sauce.

CHANGE THE WAY YOU COOK

Season Under the Skin

Cooking chicken with the skin on protects the meat from direct heat, helping it remain tender and juicy. In some cases, it also produces the bonus of crisp, richly flavorful skin. But the skin is a barrier to seasonings, so simply applying ingredients—no matter how big and bold—to the exterior does little to flavor the meat. Mostly, they slide off or get scorched.

Instead, let the skin work for—not against—developing deeper flavor. Sliding seasonings under the skin keeps them in place, allows them direct contact with the meat and protects them from scorching. Plus, the skin still protects the meat and crisps.

Here are two seasoning blends to try. Smear the mixture under the skin on chicken parts or on a whole bird.

For a spicy, punchy, herbal paste inspired by zhoug, the pesto-like condiment said to have originated in Yemen, in a small bowl, stir together ½ cup lightly packed fresh cilantro **OR** fresh flat-leaf parsley **OR** a combination (finely chopped); ¼ cup extra-virgin olive oil; 3 tablespoons finely chopped pickled jalapeños; 2 teaspoons grated lemon zest; 1 teaspoon ground coriander **OR** ground cardamom **OR** a combination; ½ teaspoon kosher salt; and ¼ teaspoon ground black pepper.

For a seasoning paste that draws on umami-packed ingredients to deliver a big flavor payoff, in a small bowl, stir together 4 tablespoons salted butter (room temperature); 3 tablespoons white **OR** red miso; 2 tablespoons finely grated Parmesan cheese; 3 medium garlic cloves (finely grated); 1 tablespoon tomato paste; and ½ teaspoon ground black pepper.

ZA'ATAR-ROASTED CHICKEN

Start to finish: 50 minutes

Servings: 4

Za'atar is a Middle Eastern blend of herbs and sesame seeds; look for it in well-stocked markets, Middle Eastern grocery stores or online. We mix za'atar with dried oregano to boost its herbal flavor. Use chicken breasts, legs, thighs or a combination.

3 tablespoons za'atar seasoning

2 teaspoons dried oregano

1¼ teaspoons white sugar

Kosher salt and ground black pepper

3 pounds bone-in, skin-on chicken parts, trimmed and patted dry

10 medium garlic cloves, peeled

1 tablespoon finely grated lemon zest, plus ¼ cup lemon juice

2 tablespoons extra-virgin olive oil

2 tablespoons minced fresh oregano

Heat the oven to 450°F with a rack in the middle position. In a small bowl, combine the za'atar, dried oregano, sugar, 1½ teaspoons salt and 2 teaspoons pepper.

Place the chicken parts on a rimmed baking sheet and evenly season both sides with the za'atar mixture. Place the garlic cloves in a single layer down the center of the baking sheet, then arrange the chicken parts, skin up, around the garlic; this prevents the garlic from scorching during roasting.

Roast the chicken until the thickest part of the breast (if using) reaches 160°F and the thickest part of the largest thigh/leg (if using) reaches 175°F, 30 to 40 minutes. The meat should show no pink when cut into. Transfer the chicken to a platter; leave the garlic on the baking sheet.

Using a fork, mash the garlic to a paste on the baking sheet. Carefully pour ⅓ cup water onto the baking sheet and use a wooden spoon to scrape up any browned bits. Pour the mixture into a small bowl and whisk in the lemon zest and juice, oil and fresh oregano. Taste and season with salt and pepper. Serve the sauce with the chicken.

ROASTED CHICKEN BREASTS WITH GRAPES AND SHERRY VINEGAR

Start to finish: 1 hour (20 minutes active)

Servings: 4

Melissa Clark understands that pairing contrasting flavors—as in the French bistro classic of roasted chicken and red grapes—easily elevates everyday meals. We were inspired by her version for this weeknight riff using chicken breasts. Try to purchase breasts of similar size so they cook at the same rate. We preferred 12-ounce breasts which take 30 to 35 minutes in the oven. Breasts weighing about 1 pound each will require 40 to 50 minutes. If you can find ground fennel seed, use 2 teaspoons in place of grinding your own. We liked the flavor and texture of grainy mustard, but regular Dijon worked, too.

4 teaspoons fennel seeds, finely ground

Kosher salt and ground black pepper

Four 12-ounce bone-in, skin-on chicken breasts, patted dry

2 tablespoons extra-virgin olive oil, divided

small bowl, stir together the grapes, 2 tablespoons vinegar, the sugar and ¼ teaspoon each salt and pepper.

Transfer the chicken and onions to a platter; let rest for about 10 minutes. Meanwhile, add the grapes and their juices to the now-empty baking sheet, scrape up any browned bits and return to the oven. Cook until the grapes just begin to soften and most of the liquid has evaporated, 8 to 10 minutes.

Remove the baking sheet from the oven. Add the remaining 2 tablespoons vinegar, the butter, tarragon and mustard; stir until the butter is melted and the mixture is well combined. Taste and season with salt and pepper. Spoon the mixture over the chicken and onions.

ROASTED CHICKEN WITH HERBS AND TOMATOES

Start to finish: 1 hour 10 minutes / Servings: 4

Our spin on Diane Kochilas' recipe for a roasted quartered chicken uses only thighs, and we cook them in the oven in a 12-inch skillet so that when they're done, it's a simple matter to reduce the juices to a flavorful sauce on the stovetop. You will, however, need an oven-safe 12-inch skillet to prepare this recipe; it will be quite full once all the ingredients are placed in it, but with cooking the volume will reduce. When saucing the chicken, pour the liquid around and between the pieces so they don't lose their beautifully crisped skin.

1 medium red onion, halved and thinly sliced

1 pint grape or cherry tomatoes

6 medium garlic cloves, smashed and peeled

4 oregano sprigs, plus 2 tablespoons finely chopped fresh oregano

2 rosemary sprigs

2 bay leaves

4 tablespoons extra-virgin olive oil, divided

Kosher salt and ground black pepper

½ cup dry white wine

½ cup low-sodium chicken broth

2½ pounds bone-in chicken thighs, trimmed and patted dry

2 tablespoons lemon juice, plus lemon wedges to serve

2 medium red onions, root ends intact, peeled, each cut into 8 wedges

12 ounces (2 cups) seedless red grapes, halved

4 tablespoons sherry vinegar, divided

2 teaspoons white sugar

2 tablespoons salted butter, cut into 2 pieces

⅓ cup finely chopped fresh tarragon

1 tablespoon whole-grain mustard

Heat the oven to 475°F with a rack in the middle position. In a small bowl, stir together the fennel seed, ½ teaspoon salt and ½ teaspoon pepper. Brush the skin side of the chicken breasts with 1 tablespoon oil, then season on all sides with the fennel seed mixture; reserve the bowl. Place the chicken in the center of a rimmed baking sheet, spaced evenly apart.

In a medium bowl, toss the onion wedges with the remaining 1 tablespoon oil and ¼ teaspoon each salt and pepper. Arrange the wedges around the perimeter of the baking sheet. Roast until the thickest part of the largest breast reaches 160°F, 30 to 35 minutes. Meanwhile, in the reserved

Heat the oven to 450°F with a rack in the middle position. In an oven-safe 12-inch skillet, toss together the onion, tomatoes, garlic, oregano sprigs, rosemary, bay, 2 tablespoons of oil, ½ teaspoon salt and 1 teaspoon pepper. Push the ingredients to the edges of the pan, clearing the center, then tuck the herbs under the vegetables. Pour the wine and broth over the vegetables.

Season the chicken on all sides with salt and pepper. Place the pieces skin-side up in the center of the skillet, arranging them snugly in a single layer. Roast until the chicken is well browned and the thickest part of the thighs not touching bone reaches 175°F, 40 to 45 minutes.

Carefully set the skillet on the stovetop (the handle will be hot). Using tongs, transfer the chicken to a platter and tent with foil. Remove and discard the herb sprigs and bay. Bring the contents of the skillet to a boil over medium-high and cook, stirring occasionally and adding any accumulated chicken juices, until reduced and a spatula drawn through the mixture leaves a trail, 5 to 8 minutes.

Off heat, stir in the chopped oregano and lemon juice, then whisk in the remaining 2 tablespoons oil. Taste and season with salt and pepper. Spoon the sauce around the chicken.

JERUSALEM-STYLE "MIXED-GRILL" CHICKEN

Start to finish: 35 minutes
Servings: 4 to 6

Jerusalem mixed grill, or meorav yerushalmi, is a popular Israeli street food, one that is said to originate in Jerusalem's Mahane Yehuda market. The term "mixed" refers to the sundry ingredients that go into the dish—chicken meat, hearts, spleen and liver, along with bits of lamb, plus onions and spices. To re-create a simplified mixed grill at home, we borrowed from chef Daniel Alt's version at The Barbary and Omri McNabb's take on it at The Palomar, two London restaurants that serve up modern Levantine and Middle Eastern cuisine. We limited the meat to boneless, skinless chicken thighs and seasoned them assertively with select spices. Our "grill" is a nonstick skillet on the stovetop. Amba, a pickled mango condiment, is commonly served with mixed grill to offset the richness of the meat; we quick-pickle sliced red onion to offer a similar acidity and brightness. Nutty, creamy tahini sauce is, of course, a requirement. Serve with warmed pita.

¼ cup white vinegar

½ teaspoon white sugar

Kosher salt and ground black pepper

1 large red onion, halved and thinly sliced

⅓ cup tahini

4 tablespoons lemon juice, divided

3 tablespoons extra-virgin olive oil, divided

1½ teaspoons ground coriander

1 teaspoon ground allspice

1 teaspoon ground turmeric

¾ teaspoon ground cinnamon

2 pounds boneless, skinless chicken thighs, trimmed and cut into 1½-inch chunks

In a small bowl, stir together the vinegar, sugar and ¼ teaspoon salt until the sugar and salt dissolve. Stir in 1 cup of sliced onion; set aside. In another small bowl, mix together the tahini and 2 tablespoons of lemon juice, then whisk in 6 tablespoons water. Season to taste with salt and pepper; set aside.

SICHUAN-STYLE COLD POACHED CHICKEN WITH DOUBLE SESAME SAUCE

Start to finish: 4 hours (40 minutes active)
Servings: 4 to 6

Fuchsia Dunlop, London-based cookbook author and expert in Chinese cuisine, taught us how to make Sichuan poached chicken, which is served chilled and dressed with various sauces. One of our favorites was bang bang ji, a sauce made of sesame paste, soy, chili oil, tongue-tingling Sichuan peppercorns, plus sugar and Chinese black vinegar. The flavors were perfectly balanced, the ingredients coalescing into a superbly delicious chicken salad. This is our spin on her recipe. Chinese sesame paste is made from toasted sesame seeds; if it proves difficult to source, tahini is a fine stand-in. As a garnish, Dunlop fries raw peanuts until golden brown. But since the raw nuts can be hard to come by, we opt for roasted peanuts and sizzle them in hot oil to enhance their texture and deepen their flavor. If you like, serve on a bed of lettuce leaves or cucumber slices.

4 scallions, whites lightly smashed, greens thinly sliced, reserved separately

2-inch piece fresh ginger, cut into 2 or 3 pieces and bruised

Kosher salt

3½- to 4-pound whole chicken, giblets discarded, left to stand at room temperature for about 30 minutes

1 teaspoon sesame seeds

½ teaspoon Sichuan peppercorns

¼ cup grapeseed or other neutral oil

2 tablespoons salted roasted peanuts

¼ cup chili oil, plus more to serve

2 tablespoons Chinese sesame paste or tahini (see headnote)

2 tablespoons soy sauce

2 teaspoons toasted sesame oil

1½ teaspoons Chinese black vinegar or balsamic vinegar

1½ teaspoons white sugar

In a medium bowl, stir together 2 tablespoons of oil, the coriander, allspice, turmeric, cinnamon and ½ teaspoon each salt and pepper. Add the chicken and the remaining sliced onion, then stir until evenly coated.

In a 12-inch nonstick skillet over medium-high, heat the remaining 1 tablespoon oil until barely smoking. Add the chicken mixture in an even layer and cook, uncovered and stirring only every 2 to 3 minutes, until the chicken is well browned all over and no longer is pink when cut into, 10 to 12 minutes.

Off heat, stir in the remaining 2 tablespoons lemon juice, then taste and season with salt and pepper. Transfer to a serving dish, drizzle lightly with some of the tahini sauce and top with the pickled onion. Serve the remaining tahini sauce on the side.

Poached Chicken

Start to finish: 45 minutes (15 minutes active)
Makes about 3 cups shredded meat

This recipe yields tender, moist shredded breast or thigh meat that can be used for chicken salad, to fill tacos or tostadas, or to add to fried rice or grain-based dishes. Feel free to add other aromatics to the pot, including fresh ginger, lemon grass, celery, carrots or herbs, such as thyme and bay. The poaching liquid, while not as rich and flavorful as classic long-simmered chicken stock or broth, can be reserved for making soups and stews or for cooking grains.

3 pounds bone-in, skin-on chicken breasts or thighs

1 medium yellow onion, root end intact, quartered lengthwise

A few garlic cloves, smashed and peeled

A handful of flat-leaf parsley sprigs (optional)

Kosher salt

In a large pot, combine the chicken, onion, garlic, parsley (if using), 1 teaspoon salt and 9 to 10 cups water (enough to cover the solids by 1 inch). Bring to a simmer over medium-high, then reduce to medium and simmer gently, uncovered and stirring occasionally, until the thickest part of the largest breast (if using) reaches 150°F, or the thickest part of the largest thigh (if using) reaches 165°F, 10 to 15 minutes. Remove from the heat and let the chicken cool in the liquid for 15 minutes.

Using tongs, transfer the chicken to a large plate; set aside to cool. Meanwhile, if you are not reserving the broth for another use, remove about ½ cup for moistening the chicken after shredding, then discard the remainder. If you are reserving the broth, strain it through a fine-mesh sieve set over a medium bowl; discard the solids. (Alternatively, use a slotted spoon to scoop out and discard the solids, then transfer the broth to a container.) Cool the broth, then cover and refrigerate for up to 3 days.

When the chicken is cool enough to handle, shred it, discarding the skin and bones. Add a few tablespoons of the reserved broth to lightly moisten the meat. Can be refrigerated in an airtight container for up to 3 days.

In a large (at least 8-quart) pot, combine 4½ quarts water, the scallion whites, ginger and 1 tablespoon salt; bring to a boil over high. Slowly lower the chicken into the water breast side up, letting the liquid flow into the cavity. If the chicken floats and isn't fully submerged, weigh it down with a heat-proof plate. Return the liquid to a boil, then reduce heat to medium and cook, uncovered and at a bare simmer, for 30 minutes, flipping the chicken breast side down after 15 minutes. Turn off the heat, cover the pot and let stand for 30 minutes.

Transfer the chicken to a large plate and cool for 20 minutes. Reserve 3 tablespoons poaching liquid for finishing the dish; discard the remainder or strain and reserve for another use. Refrigerate the chicken, uncovered, until chilled, 1½ to 2 hours.

Meanwhile, in a small saucepan over medium, toast the sesame seeds, stirring often, until fragrant and golden brown, about 3 minutes. Transfer to a small plate; set aside. In the same pan over medium, toast the Sichuan peppercorns, stirring, until fragrant, about 1 minute. Transfer to a mortar and pestle or spice grinder, cool slightly, then grind until fine; set aside.

In the same pan, combine the neutral oil and peanuts. Cook over medium, stirring occasionally, until the nuts are golden brown, 4 to 6 minutes. Using a slotted spoon,

transfer to a paper towel-lined plate and cool. Discard the oil. Roughly chop the peanuts; set aside.

In a small bowl, combine the chili oil, sesame paste, soy sauce, sesame oil, vinegar, sugar, Sichuan pepper and 2 tablespoons of the chicken poaching liquid. Whisk until smooth and creamy; set aside.

Shred the chilled chicken, pulling the meat into large bite-size pieces and discarding the skin and bones. Transfer the meat to a platter. Drizzle with the remaining 1 tablespoon reserved poaching liquid and toss. Drizzle the sesame sauce over the chicken, then sprinkle with the peanuts, scallion greens and sesame seeds. If desired, drizzle with additional chili oil.

CIRCASSIAN CHICKEN

Start to finish: 45 minutes

Servings: 6

Circassian chicken, çerkez tavuğu in Turkish, is a popular meze dish and an elevated form of chicken salad. This is our adaptation of a recipe from Emine Nese Daglar, a home cook who resides in Istanbul, and grandmother of chef Cagla Gurses. To stale the bread for making the sauce, simply leave the slices out for a few hours; they should feel dryish on the surface but not brittle. Serve with warm pita bread, and sliced radishes and pickles.

3 pounds bone-in, skin-on chicken breasts or thighs

1 medium yellow onion, root end intact, peeled and quartered lengthwise

5 medium garlic cloves, smashed and peeled

About 10 sprigs flat-leaf parsley, plus ¼ cup roughly chopped fresh flat-leaf parsley

Kosher salt and ground black pepper

3 slices stale white sandwich bread (see headnote), crusts removed (about 4 ounces)

1 cup walnuts, chopped

3 tablespoons lemon juice

1 tablespoon extra-virgin olive oil

1 tablespoon salted butter, cut into 2 pieces

1 tablespoon Aleppo pepper or 2 teaspoons sweet paprika

In a large pot, combine the chicken, onion, garlic, parsley sprigs, 1½ teaspoons salt, ½ teaspoon black pepper and 7 cups water. Bring to a simmer over medium-high, then cover, reduce to low and cook, occasionally turning the chicken, until the thickest part of the largest breast (if using) reaches 160°F, 20 to 25 minutes, or the thickest part of the largest thigh (if using) reaches 175°F, 25 to 30 minutes. Using tongs, transfer the chicken to a large plate; set aside until cool enough to handle.

While the chicken cools, strain the broth through a fine-mesh sieve set over a medium bowl. Transfer the garlic cloves to a blender jar; discard the remaining solids. Using tongs or a slotted spoon, lower each slice of bread into the broth just until fully moistened; using your hands, gently squeeze to remove excess liquid and add the bread to the blender. Measure 3 tablespoons walnuts and set aside for garnish; add the remainder to the blender. Start the blender, then remove the center cap on the blender lid. With the blender running on high, stream in about ¼ cup broth and puree

until the mixture is smooth and has the consistency of pourable yogurt; leave the sauce in the blender and set aside.

Shred the chicken into bite-size pieces, discarding the skin and bones. Add the meat to a large bowl. Measure 1 cup of the sauce and add to the chicken along with the lemon juice; toss. If the mixture is too thick, stir in additional broth a few teaspoons at a time to thin. Taste and season with salt and black pepper.

Onto a serving platter, spoon the remaining sauce and spread in an even layer. Spoon the chicken mixture on top and sprinkle with the chopped parsley and reserved walnuts.

In an 8-inch skillet over medium, heat the oil and butter until the butter melts. Add the Aleppo pepper and cook, swirling the pan, until the mixture is fragrant and the fat takes on a reddish hue, about 1 minute. Drizzle the mixture over the chicken and serve.

VIETNAMESE CHICKEN CURRY

Start to finish: 35 minutes, plus marinating
Servings: 4

The category of complexly spiced dishes we know collectively as "curry" was brought to Vietnam by Indian immigrants who arrived in the country in the 19th century, while both Indochina and the port of Pondicherry, India, were under French rule. Lemon grass, fish sauce and star anise were incorporated as curry ingredients to adapt the flavors to local palates. As a result, Vietnamese curry has a uniquely bright, yet deeply savory taste and aroma. Though many versions of cà ri gà, or chicken curry, call for store-bought curry powder, we prefer to mix our own spices so we can control the seasoning. Serve with steamed jasmine rice.

¼ cup grapeseed or other neutral oil

4 medium garlic cloves, smashed and peeled

3-inch piece fresh ginger, peeled and roughly chopped

1 medium yellow onion, roughly chopped

3 stalks lemon grass, trimmed to the lower 5 or 6 inches, dry outer layers discarded, thinly sliced

2 tablespoons coriander seeds

2 teaspoons ground turmeric

1 teaspoon ground cinnamon

Kosher salt and ground black pepper

2 pounds boneless, skinless chicken thighs, trimmed and cut crosswise into 1- to 1½-inch pieces

5 star anise pods

2 medium carrots, peeled, halved and sliced ¼ inch thick

2 tablespoons fish sauce

¼ cup lime juice

Chopped fresh cilantro, to serve

In a blender, combine the oil, garlic, ginger, onion, lemon grass, coriander, turmeric, cinnamon, ½ cup water, ½ teaspoon salt and 1 teaspoon pepper. Blend until completely smooth, 1 to 2 minutes, scraping the blender jar as needed. Transfer the puree to a medium bowl, add the chicken and stir until evenly coated. Cover and refrigerate for at least 30 minutes or up to 1 hour.

In a 12-inch skillet, combine the chicken and all of the marinade, the star anise and carrots. Bring to a simmer over medium-high and cook, stirring occasionally, until the marinade begins to brown, 6 to 7 minutes. Stir in ⅓ cup water and the fish sauce. Return to a simmer, then cover, reduce to medium-low and cook, stirring occasionally and adjusting the heat as needed to maintain a simmer, until the carrots are crisp-tender, about 5 minutes. Uncover and continue to cook, stirring, until the sauce thickens enough to cling to the chicken, about another 5 minutes.

Remove from the heat and stir in the lime juice. Remove and discard the star anise, then taste and season with salt and pepper. Transfer to a serving dish and sprinkle with cilantro.

423

KADAI CHICKEN CURRY

Start to finish: 1 hour

Servings: 4

At APB Cook Studio cooking school in Mumbai, cooking instructor Shivani Unakar taught us how to make this chicken curry with tomatoes and bell peppers. A kadai is an Indian wok, the cooking vessel traditionally used for cooking this dish, but Unakar used a Dutch oven, so that's what we reached for when re-creating the curry. Two tablespoons of Kashmiri chili powder—which has a stunning red hue, a fine, powdery texture and mild spiciness—lends the curry a rich, burnished red hue. It's sold in spice shops and Indian markets, but if you cannot find it, a fresh jar of sweet paprika is a decent substitute, with a little cayenne to add a touch of heat. Ghee is a type of clarified butter often used in Indian cooking; its flavor is slightly sweet and nutty, and because the milk solids have been removed, it has a higher smoke point than regular butter. Look for ghee sold in jars in the refrigerator case near the butter or in the grocery aisle next to the coconut oil. Serve the curry with basmati rice.

2 pounds boneless, skinless chicken thighs, trimmed and cut crosswise into thirds

2 tablespoons Kashmiri chili powder (see headnote) or 2 tablespoons sweet paprika plus ¼ teaspoon cayenne pepper

1 tablespoon ground coriander

2 teaspoons ground turmeric

Kosher salt and ground black pepper

4 tablespoons ghee, divided

1 medium green bell pepper, stemmed, seeded and chopped

1 medium red bell pepper, stemmed, seeded and chopped

1 large red onion, finely chopped

2 tablespoons tomato paste

2 tablespoons cumin seeds

1 tablespoon finely grated fresh ginger

4 medium garlic cloves, finely grated

14½-ounce can diced tomatoes with juice

2 cups low-sodium chicken broth or water

¼ cup finely chopped fresh cilantro

In a large bowl, mix together the chicken, chili powder, coriander, turmeric and 1 teaspoon each salt and black pepper. Stir in ¼ cup water; let stand at room temperature while you continue with the recipe or cover and refrigerate for up to 1 hour.

In a large Dutch oven over medium-high, heat 1 tablespoon of the ghee until barely smoking. Add the green bell pepper and cook without stirring until lightly charred, about 5 minutes. Transfer to a small bowl; set aside.

To the same pot over medium, add the remaining 3 tablespoons ghee and heat until shimmering. Add the red bell pepper and onion, then cook, stirring often, until softened, 5 to 7 minutes. Add the tomato paste and cook, stirring, until the paste begins to brown and stick to the pot, about 3 minutes. Add the cumin, ginger and garlic, then cook, stirring, until fragrant, about 30 seconds. Stir in the diced tomatoes with juices, scraping up any browned bits. Bring to a simmer and cook, stirring occasionally, until most of the liquid has evaporated, 3 to 5 minutes.

Add the broth and bring to a simmer. Add the chicken and its marinade, then cover partially and simmer until a skewer inserted into the chicken meets just a little resistance, about 35 minutes.

Increase to medium-high and bring the mixture to a vigorous simmer. Cook, stirring often, until the sauce clings heavily to the chicken, about another 5 minutes. Off heat, stir in the green bell pepper and the cilantro, then taste and season with salt and black pepper.

CAPE MALAY CHICKEN CURRY

Start to finish: 1 hour
Servings: 6

Lemony and richly savory, Cape Malay curry is a chicken and vegetable one-pot from South Africa. Its ingredients are similar to those in Indian curries, but the techniques are different, creating a refreshingly light curry. Spices, for instance, aren't ground but are dropped, whole, into the broth and often discarded just before serving. We learned to make it from Cape Malay cooking expert Faldela Tolker at her home in Cape Town's Bo-Kaap neighborhood. Like Tolker, we built the flavor base of our Cape Malay curry on lightly browned onions. We also used whole fennel seed and cumin seed, allowing them to add both texture and flavor. Tolker broke down a whole chicken for her dish, but we liked the ease of boneless, skinless thighs, which stay moist and taste richer than chicken breasts.

1 tablespoon fennel seeds

1 tablespoon cumin seeds

1 teaspoon ground turmeric

Kosher salt and ground black pepper

2 pounds boneless, skinless chicken thighs, trimmed and patted dry

2 tablespoons grapeseed or other neutral oil

2 medium yellow onions, chopped

4-ounce chunk fresh ginger, peeled and cut into 5 or 6 pieces

4 medium garlic cloves, minced

2 serrano chilies, stemmed and halved lengthwise

2 cups low-sodium chicken broth or water

1 pint grape or cherry tomatoes

Two 3-inch cinnamon sticks

2 bay leaves

1 pound Yukon Gold potatoes, unpeeled, cut into 1-inch cubes

2 tablespoons lemon juice, plus lemon wedges, to serve

½ cup lightly packed fresh mint, torn

Cooked basmati or jasmine rice, to serve

In a bowl, mix the fennel, cumin, turmeric and 1 teaspoon each salt and pepper. Season the chicken with 1 tablespoon of the mixture.

In a large Dutch oven over medium-high, heat the oil until barely smoking. Add the onions and cook, stirring occasionally, until lightly browned, 8 to 10 minutes. Stir in the ginger, garlic and chilies, then cook, stirring, until fragrant, about 30 seconds. Stir in the broth, tomatoes, cinnamon, bay and remaining spice mixture, then submerge the chicken thighs.

Bring to a simmer, then cover and cook for 25 minutes, adjusting the heat to maintain a steady but gentle simmer. Stir in the potatoes, cover and return to a simmer. Cook until the chicken and potatoes are tender, another 12 to 15 minutes.

Using tongs, transfer the chicken to a large plate. Remove and discard the ginger, cinnamon, bay and chili halves, then continue to simmer over medium until the liquid is slightly reduced, about 5 minutes.

Meanwhile, using two forks, pull the chicken into bite-size pieces. Return the chicken to the pot and stir to combine, taking care not to break up the potatoes. Stir in the lemon juice, then taste and season with salt and pepper. Transfer to a serving bowl and sprinkle with mint. Serve with rice and lemon wedges.

THAI GREEN CURRY CHICKEN AND VEGETABLES

Start to finish: 45 minutes

Servings: 4

Bright and aromatic, Thai green curry, or gaeng keow waan, is brimming with complexly layered tastes and textures. Our version is an adaptation taught to us by home cook and food blogger Rawadee Yenchujit, who incorporates coconut water as well as coconut milk for superlative flavor. Sweet and creamy, but also spicy and herbal, it calls on a bold home-made curry paste that comes together quickly in a blender and can be made ahead, then stored in an airtight container in the refrigerator for up to 24 hours. In addition to pieces of tender chicken, we've included carrots and peas (or edamame), but the curry is delicious with any vegetable: Yenchujit prepared it with coconut hearts and tiny, marble-sized Thai eggplants. Fresh makrut lime leaves can be purchased in well-stocked supermarkets alongside the fresh herbs and in certain Asian grocery stores. They add a distinctly sharp, citrusy flavor, but if you can't find them, don't worry—the dish is plenty flavorful without. Serve the curry with steamed jasmine rice.

FOR THE CURRY PASTE:

1 lime

1¼ cups lightly packed fresh cilantro stems and leaves, roughly chopped

3 medium garlic cloves, smashed and peeled

2 serrano chilies, stemmed, seeded and roughly chopped

2 makrut lime leaves (optional; see headnote)

1 stalk lemon grass, trimmed to the bottom 6 inches, dry outer layers discarded, roughly chopped

1 medium shallot, roughly chopped

1-inch piece fresh ginger, peeled and roughly chopped

2 tablespoons unsweetened coconut water

1½ tablespoons fish sauce

¼ teaspoon kosher salt

¼ teaspoon ground white pepper

FOR THE CURRY:

14-ounce can coconut milk, divided

1½ pounds boneless, skinless chicken thighs, trimmed and cut into 1-inch pieces

2 tablespoons packed light brown sugar or grated palm sugar

1 tablespoon fish sauce

Kosher salt and ground white pepper

2 cups unsweetened coconut water

2 medium carrots, peeled and sliced about ¼ inch thick on the diagonal

2 serrano or Fresno chilies, stemmed and thinly sliced on the diagonal

½ cup frozen peas or shelled edamame, thawed

2 cups lightly packed fresh Thai or Italian basil, torn if large

To make the curry paste, using a vegetable peeler (preferably a Y-style peeler), remove the zest from the lime in long strips; try to remove only the colored portion of the peel, not the white pith underneath. Squeeze 1 tablespoon juice from the lime and add it to a blender, along with the zest and remaining ingredients. Blend on high, scraping the blender jar as needed, until the paste is as smooth as possible, 2 to 3 minutes; set aside.

To make the curry, in a 12- to 14-inch wok or a Dutch oven over medium-high, bring 1¼ cups coconut milk to a simmer. Stir in the curry paste and cook, stirring occasionally, until slightly thickened and reduced, 2 to 4 minutes. Stir in the chicken, sugar, fish sauce and ½ teaspoon salt, followed by the coconut water. Bring to a simmer and cook, uncovered and stirring occasionally, until the chicken is no longer pink when cut into and the broth is reduced by about a third, about 15 minutes; adjust the heat as needed to maintain even bubbling across the surface.

Stir in the carrot, chilies, peas and half the basil; cook, stirring occasionally, until the carrots are tender-crisp, 3 to 5 minutes. Off the heat, stir in the remaining coconut milk and remaining basil. Taste and season with salt and white pepper.

JAPANESE-STYLE CHICKEN AND VEGETABLE CURRY

Start to finish: 1 hour
Servings: 4

Japanese curry is wildly popular. Some restaurants specialize in the dish, offering dozens of iterations, from basic beef curry to fried cutlets and croquettes with curry, hamburger curry, even curried omelets. At home, Japanese curry typically is made using commercially produced "bricks," which are seasonings mixed with a roux and packaged much like bars of chocolate. Added near the end of cooking, a curry brick, broken into pieces, melts into the mix, seasoning the dish as well as thickening it. Sonoko Sakai, a Los Angeles-based cooking instructor and author of "Japanese Home Cooking," blends her own curry powder, which she uses to create all-natural, additive-free home-made curry bricks. This recipe is our adaptation of Sakai's chicken curry. We simplified her curry powder and skipped the brick-making process in favor of a built-in roux for thickening. Serve with steamed short-grain rice or mixed-grain rice (recipe p. 186) and, if you can find it, fukujinzuke, a crunchy, savory-sweet pickle-like condiment that's commonly offered alongside Japanese curry. Lemon wedges for squeezing are a nice touch, too.

1 pound boneless, skinless chicken thighs, trimmed and cut into 1-inch pieces

Kosher salt and ground black pepper

5 tablespoons salted butter, cut into 1-tablespoon pieces, divided

1 medium yellow onion, halved and thinly sliced

2 medium garlic cloves, finely grated

1½ teaspoons finely grated fresh ginger

3 tablespoons all-purpose flour

1 tablespoon curry powder (recipe follows)

8 ounces Yukon Gold potatoes, peeled and cut into ½-inch chunks

1 medium carrot, peeled and sliced into ½-inch rounds

1 small red bell pepper, stemmed, seeded and cut into ½-inch pieces

2 tablespoons soy sauce

1 tablespoon mirin

427

In a medium bowl, toss the chicken with ½ teaspoon each salt and pepper; set aside. In a large Dutch oven over medium-high, melt 2 tablespoons of the butter. Add the onion and cook, stirring occasionally, until golden brown, about 9 minutes. Push the onion to the edges of the pot, add the chicken to the center and cook, stirring just once or twice, until the chicken is no longer pink on the exterior, 2 to 3 minutes. Reduce to medium, then stir the onion into the chicken. Add the garlic, ginger and remaining 3 tablespoons butter, then cook, stirring, until the butter melts. Add the flour and cook, stirring constantly, until lightly browned, 2 to 3 minutes; some of the flour will stick to the bottom of the pot. Add the curry powder and continue to cook, stirring constantly, until fragrant and toasted, 2 to 3 minutes.

Working in two additions, add 1 cup water while stirring and scraping the bottom of the pot to loosen the browned bits, then cook, stirring, until the mixture is smooth and thick, about 2 minutes. Stir in another 1¼ cups water and bring to a simmer. Add the potatoes, carrot and bell pepper, then cook, uncovered and stirring occasionally and scraping the bottom of the pot, until a skewer inserted into the potatoes and carrots meets no resistance, about 20 minutes; adjust the heat as needed to maintain a simmer.

Stir in the soy sauce, mirin and ½ teaspoon pepper. Cook, stirring often, until the curry is thick enough to lightly coat the chicken and vegetables, 2 to 4 minutes. Remove from the heat, then taste and season with salt and pepper.

JAPANESE-STYLE CURRY POWDER

Start to finish: 15 minutes
Makes about ⅓ cup

In an 8-inch skillet over medium, toast **1 small (1-inch diameter) dried shiitake mushroom** (stemmed and broken in small pieces) and **1½ teaspoons each brown or black mustard seeds, coriander seeds, fennel seeds and cumin seeds**, stirring, until fragrant, 2 to 4 minutes. Transfer to a small bowl and cool for about 5 minutes. In a spice grinder, process the toasted spice mixture to a fine powder, 1 to 2 minutes, periodically shaking the grinder. Return to the bowl and stir in **1½ teaspoons ground ginger; 1 teaspoon ground turmeric; ½ teaspoon each sweet paprika and ground black pepper cloves; and ¼ teaspoon each ground cloves and ground cinnamon.** Store in an airtight container for up to 2 months.

BUTTER CHICKEN

Start to finish: 1 hour 25 minutes (45 minutes active), plus marinating / Servings: 4 to 6

In our take on the butter chicken made for us in Mumbai by home cook Rumya Misquitta, boneless chicken thighs are briefly marinated in yogurt and spices, then broiled until lightly charred. We then make a separate sauce. In many recipes, butter and heavy cream supply richness. But we do as we were taught in India and use cashews pureed with a small amount of water until smooth.

1 cup plain whole-milk yogurt

2 tablespoons honey

1 tablespoon sweet paprika

½ teaspoon cayenne pepper

4 tablespoons garam masala, divided

2 tablespoons ground cumin, divided

2 tablespoons finely grated fresh ginger, divided

Kosher salt and ground black pepper

2½ pounds boneless, skinless chicken thighs, cut crosswise into 3 strips

1 cup roasted salted cashews

4 tablespoons (½ stick) salted butter, divided

1 large yellow onion, finely chopped

6 medium garlic cloves, finely grated

28-ounce can crushed tomatoes

¼ cup finely chopped fresh cilantro

2 tablespoons lime juice

In a large bowl, whisk together the yogurt, honey, paprika, cayenne, 3 tablespoons of the garam masala, 1 tablespoon of the cumin, 1 tablespoon of the ginger and 1 teaspoon salt. Add the chicken and stir until evenly coated. Cover and refrigerate for at least 30 minutes or up to 1 hour.

Heat the broiler with a rack about 6 inches from the broiler element. Line a broiler-safe rimmed baking sheet with foil, set a wire rack in the baking sheet and mist it with cooking spray. In a blender, puree the cashews with ¾ cup water until smooth, about 1 minute; set aside.

In a large Dutch oven over medium, melt 2 tablespoons of the butter. Add the onion and cook, stirring occasionally, until beginning to brown, about 5 minutes. Stir in the remaining 1 tablespoon ginger and the garlic, then cook until fragrant, about 30 seconds. Stir in the remaining 1 tablespoon garam masala and the remaining 1 tablespoon cumin. Add the cashew puree and cook, stirring constantly, until the mixture begins to brown, about 3 minutes. Stir in the tomatoes and 2 cups water, scraping up any browned bits. Add the remaining 2 tablespoons butter and bring to a simmer, stirring to combine. Reduce to medium and cook, stirring often, until the sauce is thick enough to heavily coat a spoon, 12 to 14 minutes. Taste and season with salt and pepper. Remove from the heat and cover to keep warm.

Arrange the chicken with its marinade still clinging to it in an even layer on the prepared rack. Broil until well browned and lightly charred on both sides, 15 to 20 minutes, flipping the pieces once about halfway through. Transfer to the sauce, bring to a simmer over medium and cook, stirring occasionally, until a skewer inserted into the chicken meets no resistance, about 10 minutes. Off heat, stir in the cilantro and lime juice, then let stand for 5 minutes. Taste and season with salt and pepper.

CHANGE THE WAY YOU COOK

Slash and Season for Deeper Flavor

When we cook chicken, we usually skip the marinades. No matter how bold the ingredients, few of the flavor molecules in a marinade are able to penetrate the protein, so the flavor is barely skin deep. Even worse, acidic marinades—anything with vinegar or citrus juices, even yogurt—can turn chicken mushy if soaked too long.

Instead, we use a simple trick to ensure our seasonings get deep into the chicken—we cut slashes into the meat. Those cuts allow flavor to get deep inside and create more surface area for sauces and seasonings to cling to.

It's a technique we learned from Andrea Nguyen, author of "Vietnamese Food Any Day," who uses it to thoroughly season bone-in chicken parts for grilling. And we found it works just as well for chicken oven roasted. In fact, our testing found that this technique not only seasons meat better, it also cuts cooking time, as it exposes more of the flesh to the oven heat.

While we love this method for bone-in chicken thighs and legs, we don't use it for breasts, which already are susceptible to drying out. But for thighs and legs, the method is simple: Cut parallel slashes no more than 1 inch apart, slicing down to the bone. Use your sharpest knife for clean cuts; dull blades will tear the flesh. Then toss the chicken in the sauce or seasonings, rubbing it into the slashes—guaranteeing deeper flavor, faster.

MOROCCAN-INSPIRED ROASTED SPICED CHICKEN

Start to finish: 45 minutes

Servings: 4

This recipe is our weeknight adaptation of djej mechoui, which translates from the Arabic as "grilled chicken." Made the Moroccan way, the bird is seasoned with spices and herbs, along with smen, or fermented butter, before cooking. For our version, we throw together a simple spice-and-herb infused butter and brush it onto chicken leg quarters that then are roasted in a hot oven. The best way to lightly crush the cumin seeds is with a mortar with a pestle, or you can pulse them in a spice grinder. Either way, be careful not to process them to a powder so they retain their texture. Smoked paprika is a Spanish spice, but it lends rich color along with a flavor evocative of outdoor grilling.

5 tablespoons salted butter

4 medium garlic cloves, minced

2 tablespoons cumin seeds, lightly crushed

1 tablespoon smoked paprika

¼ to ½ teaspoon cayenne pepper

Kosher salt and ground black pepper

2 tablespoons finely chopped fresh cilantro, plus whole leaves to serve

2 tablespoons finely chopped fresh flat-leaf parsley, plus whole leaves to serve

2 teaspoons packed light brown sugar

1 teaspoon lemon juice, plus lemon wedges, to serve

3 pounds bone-in, skin-on chicken leg quarters, patted dry

Heat the oven to 450°F with a rack in the middle position. Line a rimmed baking sheet with foil and set a wire rack on top. In a small saucepan over medium, melt the butter. Add the garlic and cumin, then cook, swirling the pan, until the seeds sizzle, 60 to 90 seconds. Stir in the paprika, cayenne and 1 teaspoon black pepper. Cook until the spices are fragrant, 30 to 60 seconds. Remove from heat and whisk in the cilantro, parsley, sugar and lemon juice; set aside.

Using a sharp knife, cut parallel slashes on each chicken leg about 1 inch apart all the way to the bone on both sides of each leg. Season all over with salt, then brush both sides

with about half of the butter mixture. Place the chicken skin up on the prepared rack and roast for 10 minutes.

Brush the remaining butter mixture onto the surface of the chicken. Continue to roast until well browned and the thickest part of the thigh reaches 175°F, about another 15 minutes

Transfer the chicken to a serving platter and let rest for 10 minutes. Sprinkle with cilantro and parsley leaves, then serve with lemon wedges on the side.

MISO-GARLIC SLASHED CHICKEN

Start to finish: 40 minutes (15 minutes active), plus marinating / Servings: 4

This recipe delivers big flavor and a delicious main with minimal work. Umami-packed white miso does the heavy lifting and gets an assist from soy sauce, rice vinegar, sugar, ginger and garlic, each ingredient holding its own. Slashes cut into bone-in chicken parts allows the seasonings to really get into the meat instead of just sitting on the surface. With more of the interior exposed, the chicken cooks a bit more quickly, too.

¼ cup white miso

¼ cup soy sauce

¼ cup unseasoned rice vinegar

2 tablespoons white sugar

1 tablespoon finely grated fresh ginger

4 medium garlic cloves, finely grated

3 pounds bone-in skin-on chicken leg quarters
OR bone-in skin-on chicken thighs, trimmed

In a large bowl, whisk together the miso, soy sauce, vinegar, sugar, ginger and garlic. Using a sharp knife, cut parallel slashes, spaced about 1 inch apart, in the skin side of each piece of chicken, cutting all the way to the bone. Add the chicken to the bowl and, using your hands, rub the marinade onto the chicken and into the slashes. Cover and refrigerate for at least 1 hour or for up to 2 hours.

Heat the oven to 450°F with a rack in the middle position. Line a rimmed baking sheet with foil and set a wire rack in the baking sheet. Mist the rack with cooking spray.

Arrange the chicken skin side up on the prepared rack. Roast until well browned and the thickest part of the thigh registers 175°F, 20 to 25 minutes. Using tongs, transfer the chicken to a platter. Let rest for about 10 minutes before serving.

Optional garnish: Toasted sesame seeds **OR** sliced scallions **OR** both

A Better Way to Skewer

Chunky bits of meat arranged neatly on skewers—often punctuated by shiny round vegetables—look great going on the grill or under the broiler. But the final results can be less than photo-perfect.

The meat may end up burned on the outside while still raw within, seasonings tend to slide off during the cooking process, and the vegetables wind up shriveled.

So, we make our skewers meat-only and opt for strips rather than squares, scrunching the straggly bits onto the skewers. The meat cooks faster and provides plenty of surface area for applying flavorful rubs and sauces. A more flavorful skewer? Looks good to us.

CHICKEN

431

SINGAPORE CHICKEN SATAY

Start to finish: 35 minutes, plus marinating
Servings: 4

In Singapore, satay—thin strips of boldly seasoned and skewered meat—is cooked quickly over long beds of hot coals. The skewers are flipped frequently to ensure even cooking and plenty of delicious charred bits at the edges. It typically is served with a thin vinegar-based sauce that includes a scant amount of peanut butter and chopped peanuts for flavor and texture.

FOR THE CHICKEN:

2 tablespoons grated fresh ginger

6 medium garlic cloves, finely grated

¼ cup white sugar

3 tablespoons toasted peanut oil

2 tablespoons ground turmeric

4 teaspoons ground cumin

Kosher salt

2 pounds boneless, skinless chicken thighs, trimmed and cut lengthwise into 1-inch-wide strips

FOR THE SAUCE:

¼ cup boiling water

1 tablespoon creamy peanut butter

¼ cup soy sauce

¼ cup unseasoned rice vinegar

2 tablespoons white sugar

2 tablespoons toasted peanut oil

2 teaspoons grated fresh ginger

1 medium garlic clove, finely grated

2 teaspoons chili-garlic sauce

½ teaspoon ground turmeric

¼ cup finely chopped salted dry-roasted peanuts

To prepare the chicken, in a large bowl, combine the ginger, garlic, sugar, oil, turmeric, cumin, 1½ teaspoons salt and ½ cup water. Stir until the sugar dissolves, then stir in the chicken. Cover and refrigerate for 2 to 3 hours.

To make the sauce, in a medium bowl, whisk the boiling water and peanut butter until smooth. Whisk in the soy sauce, vinegar and sugar, then set aside. In a small skillet over medium, heat the oil, ginger and garlic. Cook, stirring, until fragrant, about 1 minute. Stir in the chili-garlic sauce and turmeric, then cook until fragrant, about 30 seconds. Whisk the garlic mixture into the soy sauce mixture. Reserve ¼ cup for basting the chicken. Cover and refrigerate the remaining sauce for serving.

About 30 minutes before skewering and cooking the chicken, remove the serving sauce from the refrigerator. Stir in the chopped peanuts. Heat the broiler with a rack about 4 inches from the element. Set a wire rack in a rimmed broiler-safe baking sheet and mist with cooking spray.

Drain the chicken in a colander. Thread 2 or 3 pieces of chicken onto each of eight 8-inch metal skewers, evenly dividing the meat and pushing the pieces together, but not tightly packing them. Evenly space the skewers on the wire rack.

Broil the chicken until beginning to brown, 5 to 7 minutes. Flip the skewers and continue to broil until the second sides begin to brown, another 4 to 6 minutes. Remove from the oven and brush the surface of each skewer with 1 to 2 tablespoons of the reserved sauce. Continue to broil until well-charred, 2 to 4 minutes. Remove from the oven once again, flip the skewers and brush with another 1 to 2 table-spoons of the reserved sauce. Continue to broil until the second sides begin to char and the chicken is cooked through, another 2 to 4 minutes. Serve with the dipping sauce.

TURKISH-STYLE CHICKEN KEBABS

Start to finish: 1 hour, plus marinating
Servings: 4

For this take on chicken kebabs, we draw inspiration from Türkiye, the country that gave shish kebabs their name. Biber salçası, or Turkish red pepper paste, is a traditional ingredient in many versions of tavuk şiş. We use easier to find Fresno chilies, which we puree, along with roasted bell peppers and a touch of tomato paste. Our puree also uses Aleppo pepper; look for it in well-stocked markets and spice shops. If Aleppo pepper is not available, substitute 1 tablespoon sweet paprika plus ¼ teaspoon cayenne pepper or red pepper flakes. We prefer chicken thighs over breasts for their richer flavor. Plus, dark meat is more forgiving when it comes to doneness.

½ cup drained roasted red bell peppers, patted dry

6 medium garlic cloves, smashed and peeled

2 Fresno chilies, stemmed, seeded and roughly chopped

¼ cup extra-virgin olive oil

2 tablespoons dried mint

2 tablespoons Aleppo pepper (see headnote)

1 tablespoon honey

1 tablespoon tomato paste

Kosher salt

1½ tablespoons lemon juice

2 pounds boneless, skinless chicken thighs, trimmed and cut crosswise into 1-inch strips

3 tablespoons chopped fresh mint

In a food processor, combine the roasted red peppers, garlic, chilies, oil, dried mint, Aleppo pepper, honey, tomato paste and 1 teaspoon salt. Process until almost smooth, 45 to 60 seconds, scraping the sides as needed. Measure 3 tablespoons of the puree into a small bowl, then stir in the lemon juice; cover and refrigerate. Transfer the remaining puree to a medium bowl, add the chicken and toss to coat. Cover and refrigerate for at least 1 hour or up to 12 hours.

Prepare a charcoal or gas grill. For a charcoal grill, ignite a large chimney three-quarters full of coals, let burn until lightly ashed over, then distribute evenly over one side of the grill bed; open the bottom grill vents and the lid vent. For a

gas grill, turn all burners to high and heat, covered, for 15 minutes, then clean and oil the grate; turn all burners to medium-high.

While the grill heats, remove the reserved puree from the refrigerator. Thread the chicken onto eight 10- to 12-inch metal skewers, evenly dividing the pieces and scraping off excess marinade. Place the skewers on the hot side of the grill (if using charcoal), and cook, uncovered, turning every 2 to 3 minutes, until evenly charred on all sides and the thickest piece is opaque when cut into, 10 to 12 minutes. Transfer to a serving platter. Stir the fresh mint into the reserved puree and serve with the kebabs.

CHICKEN CUTLETS WITH GARLIC, CHILIES AND PEANUTS

Start to finish: 35 minutes
Servings: 4

This quick sauté of chicken cutlets with an Asian-inflected pan sauce was inspired by a recipe in "Searing Inspiration" by Susan Volland. Garlic, ginger and red pepper flakes season a sherry-based sauce, while butter stirred in at the end rounds out the flavors. Fragrant jasmine rice is the perfect accompaniment.

2 tablespoons soy sauce, divided

Four 5- to 6-ounce chicken breast cutlets, pounded to an even ¼-inch thickness

Ground black pepper

3 tablespoons peanut oil, divided

4 medium garlic cloves, finely grated

1 tablespoon finely grated fresh ginger

½ teaspoon red pepper flakes

4 scallions, thinly sliced, white and green parts reserved separately

½ cup dry sherry

⅓ cup unsalted roasted peanuts, roughly chopped

2 tablespoons salted butter, cut into 2 pieces

In a medium bowl, combine 1 tablespoon soy sauce and the chicken, turning to coat. Let stand for 10 minutes. Pat the cutlets dry with paper towels, then season with pepper.

In a 12-inch nonstick skillet over medium-high, heat 2 tablespoons of oil until shimmering. Add the chicken

in a single layer and cook until well browned on both sides, 4 to 6 minutes total, flipping once halfway through. Transfer to a platter and tent with foil to keep warm.

Allow the pan to cool for a couple minutes, then add the remaining 1 tablespoon oil, the garlic, ginger, pepper flakes and scallion whites. Cook over medium, stirring, until the mixture is fragrant, about 30 seconds. Off heat, add the sherry, the remaining 1 tablespoon soy sauce, half the peanuts and any accumulated juices from the chicken.

Return to medium and cook, scraping up any browned bits, until the sauce is slightly thickened, about 1 minute. Off heat, add the butter and stir until fully incorporated. Pour the sauce over the chicken, then sprinkle with scallion greens and the remaining peanuts.

CRISPY DIJON CHICKEN CUTLETS WITH CUCUMBER-DILL SALAD

Start to finish: 30 minutes
Servings: 4

Whole-grain Dijon mustard mixed into the egg that coats these breaded cutlets gives the chicken a bright, pleasantly sharp flavor. You can use regular Dijon mustard in place of the whole-grain, but add another splash of water when beating the eggs so the mixture has a consistency that lightly but thoroughly coats the cutlets. The freshness and crunch of a cucumber salad dressed simply with lemon and dill is the perfect foil for the pan-fried cutlets.

1 English cucumber, halved lengthwise and thinly sliced

2 tablespoons lemon juice

1 tablespoon chopped fresh dill

Kosher salt and ground black pepper

⅓ cup all-purpose flour

2 tablespoons cornstarch

2 large eggs

2 tablespoons whole-grain Dijon mustard

1¾ cups panko breadcrumbs

Four 5- to 6-ounce chicken breast cutlets, pounded to an even ¼-inch thickness

10 tablespoons grapeseed or other neutral oil, divided

In a small bowl, stir together the cucumber, lemon juice, dill, ½ teaspoon salt and ¼ teaspoon pepper. Set aside. Set a wire rack in each of 2 rimmed baking sheets. In a pie plate or wide, shallow bowl, stir together the flour and cornstarch. In a second similar dish, use a fork to beat the eggs, mustard and 1 tablespoon water until well combined. In a third, stir together the panko and ¼ teaspoon each salt and pepper.

Season each cutlet on both sides with salt and pepper. One at a time, dredge the cutlets through the flour mixture, turning to coat and shaking off any excess, then coat both sides with egg, and finally dredge through the panko,

pressing so the crumbs adhere. Place the cutlets on one of the prepared racks.

In a 12-inch skillet over medium-high, heat 6 tablespoons of oil until shimmering. Add 2 cutlets and cook undisturbed until golden brown, 1 to 2 minutes. Using tongs, flip and cook until the second sides are golden brown, about 1 minute. Remove the skillet from the heat. Transfer the cutlets to the second prepared rack. Repeat with the remaining 4 tablespoons oil and remaining cutlets, adjusting the heat as needed if the cutlets brown too quickly. Serve with the cucumber salad.

Chicken en Cocotte

Start to finish: 1 hour 35 minutes (15 minutes active)
Servings: 4

There is little prep involved in this chicken en cocotte—or chicken in a pot—and most of the cooking is hands-off. Chicken en cocotte is a French classic; a cocotte is simply a covered oven-safe dish or casserole similar to a Dutch oven. The technique produces chicken that is cooked through but still tender and juicy. We found that cooking the chicken breast side down in the pot allows the delicate white meat to gently poach in the wine while the legs cook up above, a technique that helps equalize the cooking of the white meat (done at 160°F) and dark meat (done between 175°F to 180°F).

4- to 4½-pound whole chicken, wings tucked and legs tied

Kosher salt and ground black pepper

5 tablespoons salted butter, divided

1 large yellow onion, cut into 8 wedges

8 medium garlic cloves, peeled and halved

1½ cups dry white wine

10 thyme sprigs

3 tablespoons lemon juice

2 tablespoons Dijon mustard

½ cup finely chopped fresh tarragon leaves

Heat the oven to 400°F with a rack in the lower-middle position. Using paper towels, pat the chicken dry then season with salt and pepper.

In a large Dutch oven (at least 7-quart capacity) over medium, melt 1 tablespoon of the butter. Add the onion and garlic and cook until lightly browned, about 5 minutes. Add the wine and bring to a simmer. Lay the thyme sprigs on the onion mixture. Set the chicken breast side down over the thyme and onions.

Cover and bake until a skewer inserted into the thickest part of the breast meets no resistance or the thickest part of the breast reaches 160°F and the thighs reach 175°F to 180°F, 55 to 65 minutes. Using tongs inserted into the cavity of the chicken, carefully transfer it to a large baking dish, turning it breast side up. Let rest for at least 15 minutes.

Meanwhile, remove and discard the thyme sprigs. Tilt the pot to pool the liquid to one side and use a wide spoon to skim off and discard the fat. Bring to a simmer over medium and cook until thickened and reduced to about 1 cup (with solids), about 5 minutes. Off heat, whisk in the remaining 4 tablespoons butter, the lemon juice and mustard. Taste and season with salt and pepper.

Remove the legs from the chicken by cutting through the hip joints. Remove and discard the skin from the legs, then separate the thighs from the drumsticks. Remove the breast meat from the bone, remove and discard the skin, then cut each crosswise into thin slices. Arrange the chicken on a platter. Transfer the sauce to a bowl, stir in the tarragon and serve with the chicken.

CHICKEN EN COCOTTE WITH MUSHROOMS, LEEKS AND CHIVES

Start to finish: 1¾ hours (30 minutes active)
Servings: 4

This take on chicken en cocotte employs the classic French pairing of mushrooms with leeks and chives. Mushrooms add umami flavor and lemon juice and whole-grain mustard perk up the butter-enriched wine sauce with bright acidity. To be efficient, chop the chives while the chicken cooks. Serve with mashed potatoes, egg noodles or steamed rice.

4- to 4½-pound whole chicken, wings tucked and legs tied

Kosher salt and ground black pepper

5 tablespoons salted butter, divided

1½ pounds cremini mushrooms, quartered

3 large leeks, white and light green parts sliced crosswise, rinsed and dried

8 medium garlic cloves, peeled and halved

1½ cups dry white wine

10 thyme sprigs

3 tablespoons lemon juice

2 tablespoons whole-grain Dijon mustard

6 tablespoons finely chopped fresh chives, plus more to serve

Heat the oven to 400°F with a rack in the lower-middle position. Using paper towels, pat the chicken dry, then season on all sides with salt and pepper. Set aside.

In a large (at least 7-quart) Dutch oven over medium-high, melt 1 tablespoon of butter. Add the mushrooms, leeks and garlic, then cook, stirring occasionally, until the mushrooms have released their liquid and most of it has evaporated, about 12 minutes. Add the wine and bring to a simmer. Lay the thyme sprigs on top, then place the chicken breast down in the pot. Cover and bake until the thickest part of the breast reaches 160°F and the thighs reach 175°F, 55 to 65 minutes. Using tongs inserted into the cavity, carefully transfer to a baking dish, turning it breast side up. Let rest for 15 minutes.

While the chicken rests, remove and discard the thyme sprigs from the pot. Bring the cooking liquid to a simmer over medium and cook until thick enough to lightly coat a

spoon, about 5 minutes. Off heat, add the remaining 4 tablespoons butter, the lemon juice and mustard, then stir until the butter melts. Taste and season with salt and pepper. Stir in the chives.

Transfer the chicken to a cutting board. Remove the legs from the chicken by cutting through the hip joints. Remove and discard the skin from the legs, then separate the thighs from the drumsticks by cutting through the joints. Remove the breast meat from the bone, remove and discard the skin, then cut each breast half crosswise into thin slices. Arrange the chicken in a serving dish. Spoon the sauce and vegetables over and around the chicken. Sprinkle with additional chives.

KOREAN FRIED CHICKEN

Start to finish: 40 minutes, plus marinating
Servings: 4 to 6

In Seoul, we learned that South Korea is home to multiple styles of fried chicken. Of them, we were especially smitten with dakgangjeong—two-bite pieces of crisp, well-seasoned chicken coated with a sticky, garlicky, sweet-salty, umami-rich glaze. Our recipe is based on versions shown to us by chefs Ryan Phillips and Donill Keum. As they taught us, we briefly marinate our chicken in a soy-based mixture to guarantee that each bite is thoroughly seasoned. We then remove the chicken but reserve some of the marinade to combine with flour, cornstarch and water, creating a slurry for coating the pieces before slipping them into the hot oil. The slurry fries into a light, crisp crust. But the real trick to dakgangjeong is double-frying the chicken, with a few minutes of rest between stints in the hot oil. This creates a superlative crispness—one that holds its texture even after saucing—without overcooking the chicken. Finally, we toss the golden-brown, just-fried pieces with a simple no-cook gochujang-honey sauce that clings deliciously and makes this fried chicken all the more enticing.

½ cup plus 2 tablespoons soy sauce, divided, plus more if needed

1 tablespoon finely grated fresh ginger

Ground black pepper

2 pounds boneless, skinless chicken thighs, trimmed and cut crosswise into 2- to 3-inch sections

¼ cup plus 2 tablespoons gochujang

3 tablespoons honey

2 tablespoons white sugar

1 tablespoon unseasoned rice vinegar

2 medium garlic cloves, finely grated

1 cup cornstarch

¾ cup all-purpose flour

2 quarts peanut or canola oil, plus more if needed

4 scallions, thinly sliced

Sesame seeds, toasted, to serve

In a medium bowl, stir together ½ cup of the soy sauce, the ginger and 2 teaspoons pepper. Add the chicken and stir to coat. Cover and refrigerate for 30 to 45 minutes. Meanwhile,

in a large bowl, whisk together the remaining 2 tablespoons soy sauce, gochujang, honey, sugar, vinegar and garlic; set aside. Line a rimmed baking sheet with a double thickness of paper towels.

Using a slotted spoon, transfer the chicken to the prepared baking sheet, letting excess marinade drip back into the bowl. Reserve ¼ cup of the marinade (if the amount comes up short, make up the difference with additional soy sauce); discard the remainder and reserve the bowl. Pat the chicken dry with additional paper towels.

In the reserved bowl, whisk together the reserved marinade, cornstarch, flour and 1¼ cups water; set aside. Set a wire rack in a rimmed baking sheet. Pour enough oil into a large Dutch oven to reach a depth of about 1½ inches. Heat over medium-high to 350°F. Meanwhile, add one-third of the chicken to the slurry and turn to coat.

When the oil has reached 350°F, working quickly and using tongs, one at a time remove the chicken pieces from the slurry, letting excess drip back into the bowl, and carefully add to the oil. Fry the chicken, stirring occasionally, until light golden brown, about 2 minutes. Using tongs, transfer to the prepared rack. Return the oil to 350°F. In 2 additional batches, coat the remaining chicken in the slurry and fry in the same way, allowing the oil to return to temp between batches.

After removing the third batch of chicken from the pot, return the oil to 350°F. Add the first batch of chicken plus half of the second batch to the oil. Cook, stirring occasionally, until crisp and deep golden brown, 2 to 3 minutes; the oil will sizzle at first, but as moisture evaporates, the sizzling will subside. Return the chicken to the rack. Return the oil to 350°F and fry the remaining chicken in the same way.

Transfer the hot chicken to the gochujang mixture in the large bowl. Using a silicone spatula, toss until evenly coated. Transfer to a platter and sprinkle with the scallions and sesame seeds.

HARISSA HOT WINGS

Start to finish: 1 hour 25 minutes (15 minutes active)
Servings: 4 to 6

This riff on buffalo wings features international flavor inspiration. Za'atar is a Middle Eastern herb, spice and seed blend; we use it to season both the wings and sauce. The base for the sauce is North African harissa paste, a fiery, fragrant mixture of red chilies and spices. If you purchase whole chicken wings, you will need to separate them into drumettes and flats (wingettes) and also remove and discard the wing tips; purchase a total of 3 pounds to account for the weight lost with wing tip removal.

2½ pounds chicken drumettes, flats (wingettes) or a combination

¼ cup plus 1 tablespoon za'atar, divided

Kosher salt and ground black pepper

2 cups all-purpose flour

1 tablespoon granulated garlic

3 tablespoons grapeseed or other neutral oil

6 tablespoons salted butter

½ to ¾ cup harissa paste

2 tablespoons cider vinegar

1 tablespoon white sugar

Thinly sliced scallions or chopped fresh cilantro, to serve

In a large bowl, combine the chicken wings, ¼ cup za'atar, 3 tablespoons water and 1 tablespoon salt, then stir until evenly coated. Cover and refrigerate for at least 30 minutes or up to 1 hour. Meanwhile, heat the oven to 450°F with a rack in the middle position. Set a wire rack in a rimmed baking sheet and mist the rack with cooking spray.

In another large bowl, whisk together the flour, garlic, ½ tablespoon salt and 1 tablespoon pepper. Working in 3 batches, transfer the wings to the flour mixture and toss until well coated, pressing so that the flour mixture adheres. Transfer the wings to the prepared rack, shaking off excess flour and arranging them in an even layer with the thick-skinned sides facing up. Bake for 30 minutes.

Remove from the oven and brush the tops of the wings with the oil. Continue to bake until golden, about another 15 minutes. Remove from the oven and cool for about 5 minutes.

While the wings cool, in a small saucepan over medium, melt the butter. Add the 1 tablespoon za'atar and cook, stirring, until fragrant, about 30 seconds. Add the harissa and cook, stirring, until slightly thickened, about 2 minutes. Off heat, whisk in the vinegar and sugar, then taste and season with salt.

Transfer the wings to a large bowl. Add ½ cup of the sauce and toss to coat. Transfer to a platter and sprinkle with scallions. Serve the remaining sauce on the side.

439

JAPANESE-STYLE CHICKEN MEATBALLS

Start to finish: 50 minutes
Servings: 4

Japanese chicken meatballs, called tsukune, are a standard offering in izakayas (pub-like gathering places) and restaurants specializing in yakitori. Sometimes shaped into cigars rather than orbs, the meatballs are grilled on skewers and finished with tare (pronounced tah-reh), a savory-sweet soy-based seasoning sauce. Vigorously mixing the meat mixture with either your hands or a silicone spatula helps create structure and a characteristic "bounciness," so don't feel the need to be gentle when combining, as if making meatloaf or burgers. Instead of skewering and grilling the tsukune, we shape the mixture into small, thick meatballs, skip the skewers and do all the cooking in a nonstick skillet on the stovetop. To add a little spice to the tsukune, offer shichimi togarashi (Japanese seven spice blend) or yuzu kosho (Japanese chili and citrus paste) at the table.

½ cup sake

½ cup mirin

¼ cup soy sauce

2 medium garlic cloves, 1 smashed and peeled,
1 finely grated

2-inch piece fresh ginger, 2 teaspoons finely grated,
the remainder thinly sliced and bruised

1 pound ground chicken, preferably dark meat

4 scallions, minced, divided

⅓ cup panko breadcrumbs

1 large egg white

1 tablespoon toasted sesame oil

Ground black or white pepper

2 tablespoons grapeseed or other neutral oil,
plus more for oiling your hands

Line a rimmed baking sheet with kitchen parchment and mist with cooking spray; set aside. In a 12-inch nonstick skillet over medium-high, combine the sake, mirin, soy sauce, smashed garlic and bruised ginger. Bring to a boil and cook, stirring often, until reduced to ⅓ cup, 6 to 8 minutes. Remove and discard the garlic and ginger; transfer the mixture to a small bowl. Rinse out and dry the skillet.

In a large bowl, combine the chicken, grated garlic, grated ginger, ¼ cup of the scallions, panko, egg white, sesame oil and ¼ teaspoon pepper. Using your hands or a silicone spatula, vigorously stir and knead the mixture until well combined and sticky. Using lightly oiled hands, divide the mixture into 16 portions (about 2 tablespoons each), form each into a ball and place on the prepared baking sheet. Lightly press each ball to slightly flatten it into a 1- to 1¼-inch round.

In the same skillet over medium-high, heat the neutral oil until shimmering. Place the meatballs in the skillet, reduce to medium and cook until lightly browned on the bottoms, about 4 minutes. Flip each meatball and add the sake-soy mixture; continue to cook, occasionally turning the meatballs and basting them with the sauce, until the centers reach 160°F and the exteriors are glazed, 5 to 7 minutes; reduce the heat if the soy mixture is reducing too quickly.

If desired, transfer the meatballs and glaze to a serving dish. Sprinkle with the remaining scallions.

CHICKEN TINGA

Start to finish: 1 hour 10 minutes (40 minutes active)
Servings: 4

Tinga poblana de pollo is a stewy dish of shredded chicken in a light, fresh tomato sauce that's spicy and smoky with chipotle chilies. It's an excellent filling for tacos or topping for tostadas. For our version, based on the recipe we learned in Mexico, we poach chicken breasts, shred the meat into bite-size pieces, then add the chicken to the tomato-chipotle sauce that has been simmered separately. Mexican oregano, which has earthy, citrus notes, is more closely related to verbena than to Mediterranean oregano, which is in the mint family. If you can't find it, substitute an equal amount of dried marjoram.

1½ pounds bone-in, skin-on chicken breasts

1 large white onion, halved and thinly sliced, divided

6 medium garlic cloves, minced, divided

2 medium carrots, peeled and thinly sliced

2 bay leaves

Kosher salt and ground black pepper

2 tablespoons neutral oil

1 teaspoon dried Mexican oregano (see headnote)

½ teaspoon ground cumin

1 bunch cilantro, chopped, stems and leaves reserved separately

2 chipotle chilies in adobo sauce, chopped, plus 2 teaspoons adobo sauce

1 pound ripe tomatoes, cored and roughly chopped

½ teaspoon packed light brown sugar

In a large saucepan, combine 7 cups water, the chicken, a quarter of the onion, half the garlic, the carrots, bay and 1½ teaspoons salt. Bring to a simmer over medium-high, then reduce to low, cover and cook at a bare simmer. Cook until the chicken is opaque throughout and the thickest part registers 160°F, 20 to 30 minutes; flip the breasts once about halfway through.

Using tongs, transfer the chicken to a large plate and set aside to cool. Strain enough of the cooking liquid through a fine-mesh strainer to yield 1 cup; discard the remainder. Using 2 forks or your hands, shred the chicken into bite-size pieces, discarding the skin and bones.

In a 12-inch skillet over medium, heat the oil until shimmering. Add the remaining onion, remaining garlic and 1 teaspoon salt. Cook, stirring, until the onion has wilted, 2 to 4 minutes. Add the oregano, cumin and cilantro stems, then cook, stirring, until fragrant, about 30 seconds. Stir in the chipotle chilies and adobo sauce, tomatoes and sugar. Increase to medium-high and cook, stirring often, until the tomatoes begin to release their liquid, 2 to 3 minutes. Add the reserved cooking liquid, scraping up any browned bits. Bring to a boil and cook, stirring often, until the sauce is slightly thickened and clings to the skillet, 5 to 8 minutes.

Stir in the shredded chicken, reduce to medium-low and cook, stirring occasionally, until the sauce clings to the meat, about 2 minutes. Taste and season with salt and pepper, then stir in the cilantro leaves.

Pork

PORK TENDERLOINS WITH FIG-OLIVE RELISH

Start to finish: 35 minutes

Servings: 6

Quick-cooking, tender and mild pork tenderloin makes a standout supper when we pair it with bold seasonings. To create a savory-sweet flavor profile that pairs well with lean, mild-tasting pork tenderloin, we were inspired by briny and umami-packed Provençal tapenade. We use fig jam as a base and stir into it some of the ingredients that give tapenade its bold character: olives, capers, olive oil and thyme. Herbes de Provence seasons both the pork and relish—it's a one-stroke way to infuse a dish with the flavor and fragrance of several types of Mediterranean herbs. For best flavor, look for brine-packed black olives sold in jars; the canned variety is too bland. And if you have relish left over after serving, use it as a spread for crostini, paired with pungent blue cheese or creamy ricotta. You will need an oven-safe 12-inch skillet for this recipe.

1 tablespoon plus 1 teaspoon herbes de Provence, divided

Kosher salt and ground black pepper

Two 1¼-pound pork tenderloins, trimmed of silver skin, halved crosswise

2 tablespoons grapeseed or other neutral oil

½ cup fig jam

2 tablespoons extra-virgin olive oil

1 cup pitted black olives, finely chopped

2 tablespoons drained capers, minced

1 teaspoon grated orange zest

2 medium garlic cloves, finely grated

1 tablespoon red wine vinegar

1 tablespoon minced fresh thyme

Heat the oven to 450°F with a rack in the middle position. In a small bowl, stir together 1 tablespoon herbes de Provence, ½ teaspoon salt and 1 teaspoon pepper. Use to season the pork on all sides, rubbing the seasonings into the meat.

In an oven-safe 12-inch skillet over medium-high, heat the neutral oil until shimmering. Add the pork and cook, turning occasionally, until lightly browned on all sides, about 4 minutes. Transfer the skillet to the oven and roast until the center of the thickest piece reaches 135°F or is just slightly pink when cut into, 9 to 12 minutes. Remove from the oven; the handle will be hot. Using tongs, transfer the pork to a platter and let rest while you make the relish.

In a medium bowl, stir together the fig jam, olive oil, the olives, capers, orange zest, garlic, vinegar, thyme and the remaining 1 teaspoon herbes de Provence. Taste and season with salt and pepper. Cut the pork into medallions 2 to 3 inches thick and return to the platter. Serve with the tapenade.

PAN-ROASTED PORK TENDERLOIN WITH CARAWAY, CELERY AND APPLE

Start to finish: 35 minutes

Servings: 6

This skillet dinner with a fantastic combination of flavors and textures was inspired by a recipe from "Kachka," by Bonnie Frumkin Morales, chef at the acclaimed Kachka restaurant in Portland, Oregon. Be sure to use hard cider, not fresh, or the sauce will be too sweet. The pork is browned on the stovetop and finishes cooking in the oven, so you will need a 12-inch skillet that is oven-safe.

1 tablespoon caraway seeds, coarsely ground, divided

Kosher salt and ground black pepper

Two 1 to 1¼-pound pork tenderloins, trimmed of silver skin and halved crosswise

2 tablespoons extra-virgin olive oil

4 medium celery stalks, thinly sliced on the diagonal

12-ounce bottle hard (alcoholic) cider

1 tablespoon honey

1 sweet, crisp apple (such as Gala or Honeycrisp), quartered lengthwise, cored and thinly sliced crosswise

2 tablespoons salted butter, cut into 2 pieces

1 tablespoon whole-grain mustard

1 tablespoon cider vinegar

¼ cup lightly packed fresh dill, chopped

Heat the oven to 450°F with a rack in the middle position. In a small bowl, mix half of the caraway, 1 teaspoon salt and ½ teaspoon pepper. Sprinkle the mixture all over the pork, rubbing it in so the seasonings adhere.

In an oven-safe 12-inch skillet over medium-high, heat the oil until barely smoking. Add the pork and cook, turning occasionally, until lightly browned on all sides, about 4 minutes total. Scatter the celery around the pork, then transfer the skillet to the oven. Roast until the center of the thickest part of the pork reaches 135°F or is just slightly pink when cut into, 9 to 12 minutes.

Remove the skillet from the oven (the handle will be hot), transfer the pork to a platter and tent with foil. To the skillet, add the remaining caraway, the cider and honey.

Bring to a simmer over medium and cook, stirring, until reduced by half, 5 to 6 minutes. Add the apple and cook, stirring occasionally, until tender, 3 to 4 minutes.

Off heat, whisk in the butter and mustard. Stir in the vinegar, dill and any accumulated pork juices, then taste and season with salt and pepper. Transfer the pork to a cutting board. Using a slotted spoon, transfer the celery-apple mixture to the now-empty platter. Thinly slice the pork, arrange on the platter and pour on the sauce.

CARAMELIZED PORK WITH ORANGE AND SAGE

Start to finish: 25 minutes

Servings: 6

Looking for a way to add flavor to pork tenderloin, we drew inspiration from Francis Mallmann, the Argentine chef known for using live fire to char vegetables, meat and fruit. Mallmann tops pork tenderloin with brown sugar, thyme and a fruity orange confit tinged by bay leaves and black peppercorns. The flavorful coating is seared onto the surface in a cast-iron griddle until the orange and thyme are crispy and charred. To simplify, we streamlined the orange confit: Orange zest and fresh sage, coarsely chopped, gave a similar texture and fragrance. Gently pounding the tenderloin ensured a flat surface for a sugar mixture to adhere. We broiled the pork instead of searing and used coarse turbinado sugar; it kept its shape and crunch better under the broiler. If the sugar gets too dark before the meat comes to temperature, turn off the oven; the pork will finish cooking in the residual heat.

center and the sugar mixture is golden brown, 5 to 7 minutes, rotating the pan halfway through. Transfer to a carving board and let rest.

Meanwhile, return the skillet to medium-high heat on the stovetop. Add the orange juice and remaining 1 tablespoon of sage and cook, scraping up any browned bits, until the sauce is syrupy, 2 to 3 minutes. Stir in the vinegar. Taste and season with salt and pepper. Serve the pork over the sauce.

2 pounds pork tenderloin, trimmed, cut into 6 pieces

Kosher salt and ground black pepper

99 grams (½ cup) turbinado sugar

3 strips orange zest, chopped (1 tablespoon), plus ½ cup orange juice (1 to 2 oranges)

2 tablespoons chopped fresh sage, divided

¼ teaspoon cayenne pepper

2 tablespoons olive oil

2 tablespoons cider vinegar

Heat the broiler to high with a rack 6 inches from the element. Pat the pork dry, then use a meat mallet or a small heavy skillet to gently flatten the pieces to an even 1-inch thickness. Season with salt and pepper. In a small bowl, use your fingers to rub together the sugar, orange zest, 1 tablespoon of the sage and the cayenne. Set aside.

In a 12-inch broiler-safe skillet over medium-high, heat the oil until just beginning to smoke. Add the pork and cook until deep golden brown on one side, about 3 minutes. Transfer the pork browned side up to a large plate; reserve the skillet. Press the sugar mixture onto the tops of the pork pieces in an even layer. Return to the skillet, sugar side up. Set under the broiler until the meat registers 135°F at the

JAPANESE GINGER PORK

Start to finish: 45 minutes
Servings: 4

Shoga means "ginger" in Japanese, and yaki translates as "grilled," though the term sometimes is applied to foods that are fried or griddled. In the popular dish known as shogayaki, thinly sliced pork is cooked with a lightly sweetened, very gingery soy-based sauce. We use pork tenderloin cut into quarters and pounded into thin cutlets. A quick soak in a marinade that later becomes the sauce ensures the cutlets are thoroughly flavored. Shredded green cabbage and steamed rice are classic accompaniments.

¼ cup soy sauce

3 tablespoons mirin

2 tablespoons sake

1 tablespoon white miso

1½ tablespoons finely grated fresh ginger

1¼-pound pork tenderloin, trimmed
of silver skin

2 tablespoons grapeseed or
other neutral oil

2 teaspoons white sugar

1 bunch scallions, cut into 1-inch pieces

½ small head green cabbage, cored and
finely shredded (about 3 cups)

Cooked Japanese-style short-grain rice,
to serve

In a wide, shallow bowl, whisk together the soy sauce, mirin, sake, miso and ginger. Cut the pork tenderloin in half crosswise, making the tail-end half slightly larger, then cut each piece in half lengthwise. Place 2 pieces of pork between 2 large sheets of plastic wrap. Using a meat pounder, gently pound each piece to an even ¼-inch thickness. Repeat with the 2 remaining pieces. Add the cutlets to the soy mixture and turn to coat, then let marinate at room temperature for 15 minutes.

Remove the cutlets from the marinade, letting the excess drain back into the bowl; reserve the marinade. Pat the cutlets dry with paper towels. In a 12-inch skillet over medium-high, heat 1 tablespoon of oil until shimmering. Add 2 cutlets in a single layer and cook undisturbed until well browned, 2 to 3 minutes. Using tongs, flip each piece and continue to cook until the second sides are well browned, about another 2 minutes. Transfer to a large plate, then wipe out the skillet with paper towels. Repeat with the remaining oil and cutlets.

Return the skillet to medium-high and add the reserved marinade, sugar and ¼ cup water. Bring to a simmer and cook, scraping up any browned bits, until the mixture thickens and a spoon drawn through it leaves a 1- to 2-second trail, about 3 minutes. Stir in the scallions, then add the pork and any accumulated juices. Cook, stirring gently, until the scallions are wilted and the pork is heated through, about 1 minute. Serve with the shredded cabbage and rice.

GERMAN PORK SCHNITZEL

Start to finish: 40 minutes
Servings: 4

During a visit to Berlin, we learned that the coating for authentic German pork Schnitzel, or Schweineschnitzel, is dry breadcrumbs made from kaiser rolls, which are extremely fine-textured. For ease, we developed this recipe using store-bought plain dry breadcrumbs, but if you'd like to make kaiser crumbs, which are a touch sweeter, wheatier and fresher tasting than prepared breadcrumbs, see following recipe. Indian ghee (clarified butter) is a counter-intuitive ingredient for Schnitzel, but adding just a small amount to the frying oil adds richer, fuller flavor; look for ghee in the refrigerator case near the butter or in the grocery aisle alongside the coconut oil. If you cannot find it, the Schnitzel still is tasty without. To fry the cutlets, we use a large Dutch oven instead of a skillet; the pot's high walls safely contain the hot oil and reduce splatter on the stovetop. To test if the oil is at the correct temperature, an instant or deep-fry thermometer is best. Lingonberry preserves and lemon wedges are classic Schnitzel accompaniments.

1 cup all-purpose flour

2 large eggs

1 tablespoon plus 2 cups grapeseed
or other neutral oil

1 cup plain dry breadcrumbs (see headnote)

1¼-pound pork tenderloin, trimmed
of silver skin

Kosher salt and ground black pepper

2 tablespoons ghee (optional)

Lingonberry preserves, to serve (optional)

Lemon wedges, to serve

Set a wire rack in a rimmed baking sheet and place in the oven on the middle rack; heat the oven to 200°F. Put the flour in a wide, shallow bowl. In a second wide, shallow bowl, beat the eggs with the 1 tablespoon oil. Put the breadcrumbs in a third wide, shallow bowl.

Cut the pork tenderloin in 2 pieces crosswise, making the thinner end slightly larger, then cut each piece in half again. Place 2 pieces between 2 large sheets of plastic wrap. Using a meat pounder, gently pound each piece to an even ⅛-inch thickness. Repeat with the 2 remaining pieces. Season each cutlet on both sides with salt and pepper.

One at a time, coat the cutlets on both sides with flour, shaking off the excess, then dip into the eggs, turning to coat and allowing excess to drip off, then coat both sides with breadcrumbs, pressing to adhere. Place the cutlets on a large plate, stacking them if needed.

In a large Dutch oven over medium-high, heat the 2 cups oil and ghee (if using) to 360°F. Carefully place 1 or 2 cutlets in the oil—add only as many as will fit without overlapping—and cook, gently jostling the pot so oil flows over the cutlets, until light golden brown on both sides, 2 to 3 minutes total; use tongs to flip the cutlet(s) once about halfway through. Transfer to the prepared rack in the oven to keep warm.

Return the oil to 350°F and cook the remaining cutlets in the same way. Serve with lingonberry preserves (if using) and lemon wedges.

HOW TO MAKE KAISER ROLL BREADCRUMBS

Heat the oven to 300°F with a rack in the middle position. Tear 6 to 8 plain kaiser rolls (about 1 pound) into 1-inch pieces, then distribute in an even layer on a rimmed baking sheet. Toast until completely dry but not browned, about 45 minutes, stirring every 15 minutes or so. Cool completely, then transfer to a food processor and process to fine, even crumbs, about 2 minutes. Makes about 1 cup

PORK CHOPS WITH KIMCHI, SCALLIONS AND BROWNED BUTTER

Start to finish: 40 minutes

Servings: 4

Tart, spicy kimchi complements and contrasts sweet, juicy pork in this single-skillet meal. We begin by searing the pork chops until caramelized, then use the remaining fat to build a bright, kimchi-based pan sauce, balanced by rice vinegar and mirin (sake is a good, and slightly more savory, substitute). Browned butter contributes rich, nutty notes, bringing everything together. The chops finish cooking in the sauce, so don't worry if they're underdone after their initial sear. Serve with steamed rice, greens or both.

Four 1-inch-thick bone-in, center-cut
pork loin chops (about 8 ounces each),
patted dry

Kosher salt and ground black pepper

2 tablespoons neutral oil

2 cups chopped cabbage kimchi,
plus 3 tablespoons kimchi juice

3 tablespoons salted butter,
cut into 3 pieces

¼ cup mirin OR sake

1 tablespoon unseasoned rice vinegar

1 bunch scallions, thinly sliced
on the diagonal

Season the pork chops on both sides with salt and pepper. In a 12-inch skillet over medium-high, heat the oil until barely smoking. Add the chops, reduce to medium and cook until browned on the bottoms, about 6 minutes. Flip and cook until lightly browned on the second sides

(they will not be fully cooked), about 2 minutes. Transfer to a plate, then pour off and discard all but 1 tablespoon fat from the skillet.

Set the skillet over medium and heat the fat until shimmering. Add the kimchi and cook, stirring once or twice, until lightly browned in spots, about 4 minutes. Push the kimchi to the edges of the pan and add the butter to the center. Cook, without stirring, until the butter is browned and smells nutty, about 3 minutes. Stir the kimchi into the butter, then add the mirin and scrape up any browned bits. Add ½ cup water and bring to a simmer over medium-high. Nestle the chops, keeping the more deeply browned sides

up, in the kimchi mixture, then add the accumulated juices. Cook, uncovered, until the thickest parts not touching bone reach 135°F, about 6 minutes.

Remove the pan from the heat. Transfer the chops to a platter or individual plates. Into the kimchi mixture, stir the kimchi juice, vinegar and about three-fourths of the scallions, then taste and season with salt and pepper. Spoon the mixture over the chops and sprinkle with the remaining scallions.

Optional garnish: Toasted sesame seeds **OR** toasted sesame oil

449

Italian Sweet-and-Sour Pork Chops

Start to finish: 40 minutes
Servings: 4

Pork chops easily dry out during cooking, so we use residual heat to hit the perfect doneness without overcooking the meat. Italian agrodolce is a sweet-and-sour combination commonly used with vegetables, but here we pair the flavor profile with pork chops. After being seared in a skillet, the chops need to rest so the juices redistribute throughout the meat. This is the perfect time to make a quick pan sauce. Use bone-in chops that are about 1-inch thick—they're more flavorful than boneless and are thin enough to cook through on the stovetop. We chose red wine vinegar for its bright acidity; we found balsamic vinegar to be too sweet for this.

Four 8-ounce bone-in center-cut pork chops, each about 1 inch thick, patted dry

Kosher salt and ground black pepper

2 tablespoons grapeseed or other neutral oil, divided

3 medium shallots, chopped

2 tablespoons honey

⅔ cup red wine vinegar

3 tablespoons salted butter, cut into 6 pieces

1 cup lightly packed fresh flat-leaf parsley, chopped, divided

Using a paring knife, make a couple vertical cuts in the silver skin that encircles the meat on each chop; try to cut through the silver skin without cutting into the meat. Season the chops on both sides with salt and pepper.

In a 12-inch skillet over medium, heat 1 tablespoon of oil until barely smoking. Add the chops and cook until well browned on the bottom, 3 to 5 minutes. Flip and cook until the centers reach 135°F, another 3 to 4 minutes. Transfer to a large plate and tent with foil.

Return the empty pan to medium, add the shallots and cook, stirring, until browned and slightly softened, 2 to 3 minutes. Add the honey and cook, stirring, until slightly darkened, about 30 seconds. Add the vinegar and simmer over medium-high until reduced to ½ cup, about 2 minutes. Whisk in the

butter 1 piece at a time, making sure it's almost fully incorporated before adding another. If the sauce breaks, add a few drops of water while swirling the pan until the sauce is once again shiny and emulsified.

Off heat, stir in half the parsley. Return the chops and any accumulated juices to the skillet and turn to coat. Season to taste, then sprinkle with the remaining parsley.

PORK CHOPS IN CHIPOTLE SAUCE

Start to finish: 30 minutes

Serves: 4

For this recipe, we brown only one side of ½-inch-thick bone-in pork chops, which allows us to then simmer them in a chipotle-tomato sauce without overcooking the meat. Slightly thicker pork chops also work: If using ¾- to 1-inch chops, brown the chops on both sides (about 6 minutes total) before removing them from the pan. Partially cover the skillet during simmering and increase the simmering time to 7 to 9 minutes. If you like, add more adobo sauce after simmering to up the spiciness. Serve with warmed tortillas or roasted potatoes.

1 pound ripe plum tomatoes, cored and cut into chunks

1 medium white onion, cut into chunks

4 medium garlic cloves, peeled

4 chipotle chilies in adobo and the sauce clinging to them, plus adobo as needed

1 teaspoon ground cumin

Kosher salt and ground black pepper

4 center-cut bone-in pork chops, about 8 ounces each and about ½-inch thick, patted dry

1 tablespoon grapeseed or other neutral oil

¾ teaspoon dried oregano

1½ ounces cotija cheese, crumbled

Fresh cilantro leaves, roughly torn, to serve

In a blender, combine the tomatoes, onion, garlic, chilies, cumin and ½ teaspoon salt. Blend on high until smooth, about 1 minute. Using a paring knife, make a couple vertical cuts in the silver skin that encircles each chop; evenly space the cuts and try to cut through the silver skin without cutting into the meat. Season the chops on both sides with salt and pepper.

In a 12-inch skillet over medium-high, heat the oil until beginning to smoke. Add 2 of the chops in a single layer and cook until well browned, about 3 minutes. Transfer to a large plate, turning the chops browned side up. Repeat with the remaining 2 chops. Let the empty skillet cool for 2 to 3 minutes.

Add the tomato puree and oregano to the skillet. Cook over medium, stirring and scraping up any browned bits, until slightly thickened, 10 to 15 minutes; adjust the heat as needed to maintain a simmer. Return the chops and any accumulated juices to the pan, nestling the chops into the sauce. Spoon sauce over the chops to submerge. Cook, uncovered, until the meat near the bone reaches 160°F or is just barely pink when cut, 4 to 5 minutes.

Transfer the chops to a platter. Taste the sauce and season with salt and pepper; for added spiciness, stir in additional adobo to taste. Spoon the sauce over and around the chops, then sprinkle with the cotija and cilantro.

SALT-AND-PEPPER PORK CHOPS WITH SPICY SCALLIONS

Start to finish: 45 minutes

Servings: 4

The salt-and-pepper treatment is a Cantonese technique applied to meat, seafood and tofu. The protein typically is deep-fried, but here we opt to pan-fry pork that we first dust in cornstarch seasoned generously with Sichuan pepper, black pepper and cayenne. In a classic salt-and-pepper dish, chilies and garlic are quickly fried and tossed with the cooked protein for big, bold, in-your-face flavors. We, however, finish the pork with a fresh, punchy uncooked mix of sliced scallions, chopped cilantro, minced chilies, rice vinegar and grated ginger. The easiest way to grind the tongue-tingling Sichuan peppercorns for this recipe is in an electric spice grinder. Serve with steamed jasmine rice.

1 bunch scallions, thinly sliced

1 cup lightly packed fresh cilantro, roughly chopped

1 Fresno or jalapeño chili, stemmed, seeded and minced

2 tablespoons unseasoned rice vinegar

1 tablespoon finely grated fresh ginger

Kosher salt and ground black pepper

3 tablespoons cornstarch

1 tablespoon Sichuan peppercorns, finely ground

½ to 1 teaspoon cayenne pepper

½ teaspoon Chinese five-spice powder

8 boneless (about 1½ pounds) thin-cut pork loin chops/cutlets (¼ to ½ inch thick), patted dry

⅓ cup grapeseed or other neutral oil

In a medium bowl, toss together the scallions, cilantro, chili, vinegar, ginger and ¼ teaspoon salt; set aside. In a wide, shallow dish, mix together the cornstarch, Sichuan pepper, cayenne pepper, five-spice, 2 teaspoons black pepper and 1 teaspoon salt. Dredge the cutlets in the cornstarch mixture, turning to coat both sides and pressing so the mixture adheres, then transfer to a large plate, stacking or shingling as needed.

In a 12-inch nonstick skillet over medium-high, heat the oil until barely smoking. Add half of the cutlets and cook until browned on the bottoms, 2 to 3 minutes. Using tongs, flip the cutlets and cook until golden brown on the second sides, about 1 minute. Transfer to a platter and tent with foil. Cook the remaining cutlets in the same way, using the oil remaining in the skillet. Spoon the scallion-cilantro mixture onto the chops and serve.

Pork Primer

Beyond tossing bacon or sausages into a skillet for a quick fry up, pork comes with a learning curve. As a general rule, mild, lean cuts should be cooked via dry heat to 135°F to preserve a juicy, tender texture. Cooked much longer, and the meat toughens and dries out. Rich, marbled cuts require slow-and-low cooking to a virtually fall-apart texture to render the ample stores of fat and soften the tough muscle fiber. Here's a few guidelines for cooking our favorite cuts of pork.

Pork tenderloins have a mild, neutral flavor and tender texture if cooked carefully to 135°F (with 5-degree carry-over cooking, the finished temperature will be around 140°F). A single tenderloin weighs about 1 pound, so is sized to serve two or three. Dry heat, like sautéing, stir frying, roasting or grilling, is the best bet; browning will intensify the mild flavor.

Not to be confused with the tenderloin, **pork loin roasts** are large, lean roasts—boneless or bone-in—with a top layer of fat that helps keep the meat moist as it cooks. It's a mild-flavored cut that's good for feeding a crowd. Pork loin roasts are best roasted at a mid-range temperature or grill-roasted to add smokiness. A cylindrical-shaped muscle, a pork loin can be butterflied and stuffed to enhance its mild flavor.

Pork loin chops, made by cutting the pork loin muscle into single-sized portions, will have slightly different textures and flavors, depending from where they are cut. Rib chops feature loin meat with a rib bone running along one side. Center-cut chops, also known as porterhouse chops, are identifiable by the T-bone that separates the larger loin meat from the smaller, darker portion of tenderloin. As a rule, we prefer bone-in chops because the attached bone helps the meat remain juicy when cooked. And regardless of the type, the thinner the chop, the faster it will cook and vigilance is needed. For chops that can cook through evenly on the stovetop, we favor 1-inch thickness.

Pork shoulder and **pork butt** are rich, well-marbled cuts of pork that typically come in large roast-size pieces. While the two cuts are largely interchangeable, butt (also called "Boston butt") is from high on the leg; thickly marbled shoulder (also called "picnic") is from the lower portion of the leg and typically is more muscular. Both typically are cooked slowly to render the fat, soften the connective tissue and tenderize the tough, working muscles. Simmer these cuts in soups, stews and braises, or roast at an ultra-low temperature.

Pork belly, the cut from which bacon is made, is ultra-rich and flavorful. It typically is braised or cooked via moist heat to tenderize, then cooled and browned to crisp the skin. A little goes a long way.

Pork ribs usually are available in three styles: spareribs, St. Louis-style and baby back. Spareribs are the largest of the trio, including a fair mix of meat, bone and cartilage. St. Louis-style are trimmed spareribs with less bone and cartilage attached. Baby back ribs come from high up on the rib cage—more back than belly—and are the meatiest and most expensive of the bunch, but the racks are smaller in size.

Despite their name, **country-style ribs** are not ribs. Rather, they are thickish slabs of meat, typically boneless, cut from the pork shoulder or the blade (shoulder) end of the loin. The former is fattier, darker in color and comprises a larger number of smaller muscles; the latter is leaner, pinker and displays a good amount of loin muscle. Country-style ribs are suitable for braising, but also can be cooked quickly, like a chop.

PORK

453

COLOMBIAN-STYLE ASADO PORK CHOPS

Start to finish: 1 hour, plus marinating

Servings: 4

At Asadero y Piqueteadero el Pariente in Bogotá, Colombia, we became fans of carne asada, or seasoned meats, poultry and sausages grilled over a eucalyptus fire. When we asked about his seasoning blend, owner Luis Eduardo Beltrán was guarded about the specifics, but did tell us the ingredients. This recipe is our attempt to re-create his asado mix. Instead of a mix of meats, we opted for easy-to-cook, richly flavorful bone-in pork chops. Beltrán includes achiote, a seed that adds vivid red-orange color but mild, earthy notes. We substitute easier-to-source sweet paprika, and cider vinegar is a stand-in for apple wine (a beverage similar to dry hard cider) to bring tart, fruity notes that balance the spices and herbs. A blender makes quick work of the seasoning paste, half of which coats the chops for marinating; the rest is brushed onto the pork midway through cooking. If desired, serve with roasted potatoes and/or fried plantains, as asado is served in Bogotá.

¼ cup sweet paprika

2 scallions, roughly chopped

2 bay leaves

1½ teaspoons ground cumin

1 teaspoon dried thyme

1 teaspoon ground allspice

2 medium garlic cloves, smashed and peeled

3 tablespoons cider vinegar

2 tablespoons packed brown sugar

2 tablespoons grapeseed or other neutral oil

Kosher salt and ground black pepper

Four 10- to 12-ounce bone-in pork loin chops, each ¾- to 1-inch thick, patted dry

Lime wedges, to serve (optional)

In a blender, combine the paprika, scallions, bay, cumin, thyme, allspice, garlic, vinegar, sugar, oil, ¼ cup plus 2 tablespoons water, 2 teaspoons salt and 1 teaspoon pepper. Blend, scraping the jar as needed, until smooth, about 30 seconds. Measure ⅓ cup of the paste into a small bowl, then stir in 2 tablespoons water; cover and set aside or cover and

refrigerate if you will be marinating the chops for more than 2 hours.

Coat the chops on all sides with the remaining seasoning paste, rubbing it into the meat. Set on a large plate or baking dish, cover and refrigerate for at least 1 hour or up to 24 hours.

When you are ready to cook the chops, remove from the refrigerator (along with the reserved seasoning paste, if refrigerated) and let stand at room temperature while you prepare a charcoal or gas grill.

For a charcoal grill, ignite a large chimney of coals, let burn until lightly ashed over, then distribute evenly over one side of the grill bed; open the bottom grill vents. For a gas grill, turn all burners to high. Heat the grill, covered, for 5 to 10 minutes, then clean and oil the grate.

Without scraping off the seasoning paste, place the chops on the grill (on the hot side, if using charcoal). Cook, uncovered, until nicely charred on the bottoms, 5 to 7 minutes. Brush the chops with about half of the reserved seasoning paste, then flip the chops and brush with the remaining reserved seasoning paste. Cook, uncovered, until the second sides are well charred and the centers near the bone reach 135°F or are just barely pink when cut into, another 5 to 7 minutes. Flip the chops once again and cook for about 1 minute to heat the newly applied seasoning paste. Transfer to a platter and tent with foil; let rest for 10 minutes. Serve with lime wedges (if using).

To cook under a broiler: Follow the recipe to make and divide the seasoning paste and marinate the chops. When you are ready to cook, remove the chops from the refrigerator (along with the reserved seasoning paste, if refrigerated) and let stand at room temperature for 20 to 30 minutes. Heat the broiler with a rack positioned about 4 inches from the element. Set a wire rack in a rimmed baking sheet and mist the rack with cooking spray. Without scraping off the seasoning paste, place the chops on the rack, evenly spacing them. Broil until well browned on the surface, 6 to 8 minutes. Brush the chops with about half of the reserved seasoning paste, then flip the chops and brush with the remaining reserved paste. Broil until the second sides are well browned and the centers near the bone reach 135°F or are just barely pink when when cut into, another 6 to 8 minutes. Transfer to a platter and tent with foil; let rest for 10 minutes. Serve with lime wedges (if using).

PORK IN VERACRUZ SAUCE

Start to finish: 50 minutes
Servings: 4

Adriana Luna, who runs La Cocina de Mi Mamá in Mexico City, showed us how to make puntas a la Veracruzana, a dish of sliced pork in garlicky tomato sauce that, to us, tasted both new and familiar. The term "puntas," which translates from the Spanish as "tips," refers to small pieces of meat; "a la Veracruzana" means in the style of Veracruz—that is, prepared with tomato, garlic, olives and capers. The sauce reflects the culinary influence of the Spanish, who arrived in 1519 in what is now the coastal state of Veracruz, on Mexican cuisine. Whereas "a la Veracruzana" typically is applied to fish, Luna used thin slices of pork loin to a delicious result—the mild, lean meat finds a perfect partner in the punchy, tangy-sweet sauce. We adapted her recipe, making it a simpler one-pan affair, but in the spirit of her dish, we use chopped fresh tomatoes, a healthy amount of garlic and finish the puntas with a good dose of parsley.

Serve with charred tortillas or with rice and beans, and, if you like, offer pickled jalapeños on the side.

1 pound boneless pork loin chops (about 1 inch thick), sliced no thicker than ¼ inch on the diagonal

Kosher salt and ground black pepper

3 tablespoons grapeseed or other neutral oil

12 medium garlic cloves, peeled and chopped (about ¼ cup)

½ medium white onion, finely chopped

1½ pounds ripe tomatoes, cored and chopped

3 bay leaves

2 jalapeño chilies, stemmed, seeded and chopped

⅓ cup pimento-stuffed green olives, chopped

2 tablespoons drained capers

1 cup lightly packed fresh flat-leaf parsley, finely chopped

Toss the pork with salt and pepper. In a 12-inch skillet over high, heat the oil until barely smoking. Add the pork in an even layer and cook without stirring until well browned on the bottom, about 3 minutes. Using tongs, transfer the pork to a plate and set aside.

To the fat remaining in the skillet, add the garlic and stir off heat. Set the pan over medium and cook, stirring often, until the garlic is lightly browned, 1 to 2 minutes; adjust the heat as needed if the garlic sizzles too vigorously. Add the onion, ¼ teaspoon salt and ½ teaspoon pepper, then cook over medium, stirring occasionally, until the onion is translucent, 5 to 6 minutes. Stir in the tomatoes, bay and jalapeños. Increase to medium-high and bring to a boil, then cover, reduce to medium and cook, stirring occasionally, until the vegetables are fully softened, about 8 minutes.

Uncover, increase to medium-high and cook, stirring occasionally, until most of the moisture has evaporated and the sauce is thick, 3 to 5 minutes. Add the olives and the pork with accumulated juices. Cook, stirring often, until the pork is no longer pink at the center, 1 to 3 minutes.

Off heat, remove and discard the bay, then stir in the capers and parsley. Taste and season with salt and pepper, then transfer to a serving dish.

ROSEMARY-BALSAMIC SHREDDED PORK

Start to finish: 3¾ hours (30 minutes active)
Servings: 6 to 8 (Makes about 8 cups)

Think of this as a pulled-pork version of Italian porchetta. Fresh rosemary and fennel seeds lend fragrance and flavor, and tangy-sweet balsamic vinegar helps balance the richness of the meat. Piled onto crusty rolls and topped with baby arugula, the pork makes delicious sandwiches. It also is great as a filling for panini or spooned over soft polenta.

3 to 4 pounds boneless pork shoulder, trimmed and cut into 1½-inch chunks

3 tablespoons balsamic vinegar

2 tablespoons packed brown sugar

2 tablespoons chopped fresh rosemary

1 tablespoon fennel seeds

Kosher salt and ground black pepper

1 medium yellow onion, halved and thinly sliced

Chopped fresh flat-leaf parsley, to serve (optional)

Lemon wedges, to serve (optional)

Heat the oven to 325°F with a rack in the lower-middle position. In a large Dutch oven, stir together the pork, vinegar, sugar, rosemary, fennel seeds, ½ cup water and 2 teaspoons each salt and pepper. Distribute the onion over the pork. Cover and cook for 2 hours.

Remove the pot from the oven. Uncover but do not stir. Return the pot to the oven and cook, stirring only once or twice after the pork has been back in the oven for at least 20 minutes, until a skewer inserted into the largest piece meets no resistance and the liquid in the pot has thickened, another 1 to 1½ hours.

Remove the pot from the oven. Tilt the pot to pool the cooking liquid to one side and use a wide spoon to skim off and discard as much fat as possible. Using 2 forks, shred the pork directly in the pot or mash it with a large spoon until the pieces break apart. If desired, serve sprinkled with parsley and with lemon wedges on the side.

Miso-Gochujang Shredded Pork

Start to finish: 3¾ hours (30 minutes active)
Makes about 8 cups (6 to 8 servings)

Cut into chunks, tossed into a Dutch oven with seasonings and cooked slowly for several hours in a 325°F oven, tough and chewy pork shoulder becomes succulent and tender enough to shred. The technique involves little hands-on work, and once the pot is in the oven it requires almost no attention. In this Asian-inflected take on pulled pork, a trio of high-powered ingredients—gochujang (Korean red pepper paste), hoisin and white miso—adds loads of umami-rich, savory-sweet flavor. We like the pork piled onto soft buns with pickled jalapeños. Or pile it onto rice bowls with crisp cabbage slaw.

½ cup gochujang

2 tablespoons hoisin

3 to 4 pounds boneless pork shoulder, trimmed and cut into 1½-inch chunks

2 medium yellow onions, halved and thinly sliced

3 tablespoons white miso

Kosher salt and ground black pepper

Thinly sliced scallions, to serve (optional)

Sesame seeds, toasted, to serve (optional)

Heat the oven to 325°F with a rack in the lower-middle position. In a large Dutch oven, stir together the gochujang, hoisin, pork and ¾ cup water. In a medium bowl, mix the onion and miso, then distribute over the pork. Cover and cook for 2 hours.

Remove the pot from the oven. Uncover but do not stir. Return the pot to the oven and cook, stirring only once or twice after the pork has been back in the oven for at least 20 minutes, until a skewer inserted into the largest piece meets no resistance and the liquid in the pot has thickened, another 1 to 1½ hours.

PORK

Remove the pot from the oven. Tilt the pot to pool the cooking liquid to one side and use a wide spoon to skim off and discard as much fat as possible. Using 2 forks, shred the pork directly in the pot or mash it with a large spoon until the pieces break apart. Taste and season with salt and pepper. If desired, serve sprinkled with sliced scallions and sesame seeds.

PUERTO RICAN SLOW-ROASTED PORK

Start to finish: 7 hours (45 minutes active), plus refrigeration / Servings: 8

Puerto Rico native and now resident of Miami, Teryluz Andreu had fond memories of her mother's pérnil al caldero, a classic Puerto Rican dish of pork roast seasoned with adobo—a garlicky, vinegary, oregano-spiced marinade—that's slow-cooked on the stovetop until succulent and fall-apart tender. She had her mother's recipe for adobo but no method for cooking the roast, and she hadn't had success in recreating the dish. We assisted her with that and, in doing so, learned of pérnil al horno, a similar preparation that cooks in the oven. This recipe melds Andreu's mother's adobo with a simple, hands-off oven-roasting method. The pork slow-cooks at 350°F for hours, then finishes for a few minutes at 500°F to get the golden, crackling-crisp skin that's characteristic of the dish. The cut to use for this is a bone-in, skin-on pork butt roast; you may need to order it from the butcher in advance. For this recipe, you will need a large roasting pan, one that measures about 13 by 16 inches, as well as extra-wide heavy-duty foil. The adobo provides tart, herbal notes that nicely balance the richness of the meat, but if you'd also like a burst of tangy citrus, serve lime wedges alongside.

2 tablespoons extra-virgin olive oil

15 medium garlic cloves, peeled, divided

1 bunch cilantro, chopped, stems and leaves reserved separately

3 tablespoons white vinegar, divided, plus more to taste

2 tablespoons dried oregano, divided

Kosher salt and ground black pepper

5- to 7-pound bone-in, skin-on pork butt roast (see headnote)

5 bay leaves

In a food processor, combine the oil, 10 of the garlic cloves, the cilantro stems, 1 tablespoon of the vinegar, 1 tablespoon oregano, 4 teaspoons salt and 2 teaspoons pepper. Process until a smooth paste forms, scraping the bowl as needed, about 30 seconds.

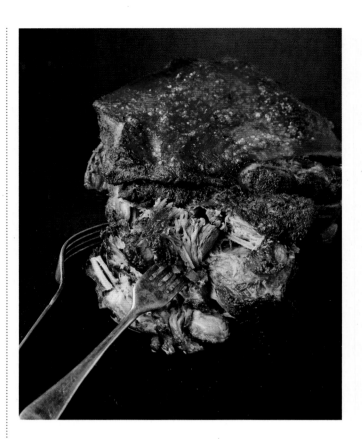

Using your hands, rub the garlic-herb paste all over the roast. Wrap tightly with plastic wrap and set on a large plate. Refrigerate at least 4 hours but preferably longer (up to 24 hours).

Adjust an oven rack to the lower-middle position and heat the oven to 350°F. In a large roasting pan, combine 8 cups water, the remaining 5 garlic cloves, remaining 1 tablespoon oregano and the bay. Unwrap the pork and pat dry with paper towels. Set it skin side down in the pan. Cover tightly with extra-wide, heavy-duty foil; if the pan has fixed raised handles, be sure to get a good seal around the base of the handles. Transfer to the oven and cook for 5 hours.

Remove the roasting pan from the oven and carefully remove the foil, allowing the steam to vent away from you. Using 2 pairs of tongs or tongs and a meat fork, flip the pork skin side up. Pat the skin dry with paper towels and return the roast, uncovered, to the oven. Cook until the thickest part of the pork reaches 210°F to 215°F, or a skewer inserted into the meat meets no resistance, another 1½ to 2 hours.

Remove the roasting pan from the oven. Increase the oven to 500°F. Place a wire rack in a rimmed baking sheet and transfer the roast to the rack; reserve the roasting pan with the juices from the pork. Using paper towels, pat the skin as dry as possible.

When the oven comes up to temperature, return the pork to the oven and cook until the skin is deeply browned and crisped, 8 to 12 minutes. Remove from the oven and let rest for about 30 minutes.

Meanwhile, remove and discard the bay from the juices in the roasting pan, then pour the liquid into a 1-quart liquid measuring cup or a medium bowl. Let settle for a few minutes. Using a large spoon, skim off and discard the fat from the surface of the liquid, then stir in the remaining 2 tablespoons vinegar and the cilantro leaves. Taste and season with salt and pepper, adding more vinegar, if desired.

Using a sharp, slender knife, cut the skin free from the roast and place it fatty side up on a cutting board. With a soup spoon, carefully scrape off and discard as much fat as possible. Flip the skin browned side up and set aside.

Remove and discard the bone from the pork. Slice the pork or cut it into chunks. Arrange on a platter and pour some of the juices over the pork. Using kitchen shears, snip the crisped skin into pieces and scatter over the pork. Serve with the remaining juices on the side.

VIETNAMESE CARAMEL PORK

Start to finish: 50 minutes
Servings: 4

The Vietnamese technique of braising meat or fish in dark, smoky caramel combined with a few aromatics and fish sauce yields intensely savory-sweet, umami-rich flavors. It traditionally is cooked in a clay pot, but we use a skillet. Pork belly is the typical cut, but it's extremely fatty and not always easy to find in grocery stores. Instead, we use shoulder, which is leaner but still well-marbled and rich in pork flavor. The meat, however, must be thinly sliced to achieve the correct tender-chewy texture with just 10 to 14 minutes of cooking. For easiest slicing, after cutting the pork into planks, freeze the pieces uncovered on a plate until partially frozen, about 20 minutes, then use a sharp knife to slice them on the diagonal no thicker than ¼ inch. To round out the meal, serve the pork with jasmine rice and a simple steamed or stir-fried vegetable.

¼ cup white sugar

4 tablespoons coconut water or water, divided

3 tablespoons fish sauce

2 Fresno or serrano chilies, stemmed, seeded (if desired) and sliced into thin rings

2 shallots, halved and thinly sliced

1 stalk lemon grass, trimmed to the bottom 6 inches, dry outer layers discarded, bruised

2 teaspoons finely chopped fresh ginger

Ground black pepper

1½ pounds boneless pork shoulder, cut into 1½- to 2-inch-thick planks, then sliced no thicker than ¼ inch on the diagonal (see headnote)

2 scallions, thinly sliced on the diagonal

Lime wedges, to serve

In a 12-inch skillet, combine the sugar and 2 tablespoons coconut water. Cook over medium-high, occasionally swirling the pan to help the sugar dissolve and to encourage even browning, until the caramel is mahogany in color and smokes lightly, 4 to 6 minutes. Remove the pan from the heat and add the fish sauce along with the remaining 2 tablespoons coconut water; the mixture will bubble vigorously and the caramel will harden in spots.

459

Bring to a simmer over medium and cook, stirring, until the hardened bits have dissolved. Add the chilies, shallots, lemon grass, ginger and 1 teaspoon pepper; cook, stirring, until fragrant, about 30 seconds. Increase to medium-high and stir in the pork. Bring to a simmer and cook, uncovered and stirring occasionally, until the sauce reduces and clings to the pork, 10 to 14 minutes.

Off heat, remove and discard the lemon grass. Transfer to a serving dish and sprinkle with the scallions. Serve with lime wedges.

LACQUERED PORK RIBS WITH HOISIN, HONEY AND FIVE-SPICE

Start to finish: 2¼ hours (30 minutes active), plus resting
Servings: 4

These addictive, salty-sweet pork ribs were inspired by char siu, a popular style of Cantonese barbecued meat often made with long, thin strips of pork shoulder. To season racks of baby back ribs, we combine hoisin, honey, soy sauce, fresh ginger and five-spice powder. Part of the mix goes onto the ribs before they go into the oven; the rest is reserved for glazing during cooking. Brushing ribs with a glazing mixture at 30-minute intervals builds layers of caramelization, resulting in a lacquered finish.

½ cup hoisin sauce

¼ cup honey

1 tablespoon soy sauce

1 tablespoon finely grated fresh ginger
OR 3 medium garlic cloves, finely grated OR both

1½ teaspoons Chinese five-spice powder

Kosher salt and ground black pepper

Two 3- to 3½-pound racks baby back pork ribs

Heat the oven to 325°F with a rack in the middle position. Set a wire rack in a rimmed baking sheet. In a small bowl, whisk together the hoisin, honey, soy sauce, ginger, five-spice, 1 teaspoon salt and ¾ teaspoon pepper. Measure ⅓ cup of the mixture into another small bowl and set aside for glazing. Pour the remainder onto the ribs, rubbing to coat both sides.

Place the ribs meaty side up on the prepared rack. Bake, brushing the surface of the rib racks with about 1 tablespoon of the glaze mixture about every 30 minutes, until well browned and a skewer inserted between the bones meets no resistance, 2 to 2½ hours. Transfer the rib racks to a cutting board and let rest for about 20 minutes. Cut the ribs between the bones and transfer to a platter.

Optional garnish: Toasted sesame seeds **OR** thinly sliced scallions **OR** both

ROSEMARY AND FENNEL PORK RIBS

Start to finish: 3½ hours (15 minutes active)
Servings: 4

In Tuscany, rosticciana is often cooked on a grill and served with other meats, such as steak and sausage. We chose to focus on just the ribs and brought the recipe indoors so we could use the ease of the oven to create just the right moist environment for yielding tender and perfectly browned ribs. The seasonings are simple, so for the fullest, richest flavor, it's best to pulverize your own fennel seeds in a spice grinder. If convenience is key—and you can find ground fennel seed at the grocery store—use the same amount as called for (1 tablespoon). The start-to-finish time for this

recipe may be long, but the hands-on cooking is minimal. These ribs are delicious as is, or drizzle with lemon juice and fruity olive oil, if desired.

Kosher salt and ground black pepper

2 tablespoons packed light brown sugar

4 teaspoons minced fresh rosemary

1 tablespoon fennel seeds, ground

1 teaspoon red pepper flakes

1 teaspoon granulated garlic

Two 2½- to 3-pound racks St. Louis–style pork spareribs

Heat the oven to 325°F with a rack in the middle position. Set a wire rack in a rimmed baking sheet. In a small bowl, combine 1 tablespoon each salt and black pepper, the sugar, rosemary, ground fennel, pepper flakes and garlic. Rub the mixture between your fingertips until well combined and the rosemary is fragrant. Sprinkle evenly over both sides of the racks of ribs, then thoroughly rub it in.

Place the ribs meaty side up on the prepared baking sheet. Transfer to the oven, then pour 3 cups water into the baking sheet. Bake until well browned and a skewer inserted between the bones meets no resistance, 2 to 2½ hours. Transfer the rib racks to a cutting board and let rest for 20 minutes. Cut the ribs between the bones and transfer to a platter.

CHANGE THE WAY YOU COOK

For Easier, Thinner Slicing, Chill Your Meat

Tough cuts of meat, such as pork shoulder, boneless beef short ribs and flank steak, can be made more tender by thinly slicing them against the grain, shortening the otherwise chewy muscle fibers. This is a technique we often employ with stir-fries, sautés, skewers and quick-simmers.

The supple, yielding texture of uncooked meat can make it difficult to cut thin slices. To make slicing easier, we first put the meat in the freezer to firm it up, which allows a knife to glide through it.

Unwrap the meat, place it on a plate and slide it into the freezer. How long to freeze depends on the size of the cut as well as the temperature of your freezer. Smaller pieces might require just 20 minutes or so; larger ones may take twice that. You'll know the meat is ready when it's partially frozen—the exterior should be firm but the center should still have some give. Do not allow the meat to freeze solid or it'll be impossible to slice.

Place the partially frozen meat on a cutting board and, using a chef's knife, slice it against the grain into pieces of the desired thickness. If your recipe says to slice on the bias or on the diagonal, hold the knife so the blade is at about a 45-degree angle to the cutting board. This yields slices with greater surface area.

461

CILANTRO, GARLIC AND LIME MARINATED PORK SKEWERS

Start to finish: 1 hour 20 minutes

Servings: 4 to 6

Cilantro leaves are delicate and tender, but the sturdier stems are even more flavor-packed and are a great way to bring fresh, herbal notes to a dish. For this salty-sweet Southeast Asian-inspired marinade, we employ the stems' bright, grassy flavor, in combination with the leaves, tangy lime juice, brown sugar, garlic and umami-rich fish sauce. Thinly slicing the pork allows it to absorb seasonings, tenderize and cook quickly, but cutting raw meat into small pieces can be tricky. To remedy this, we place it in the freezer for 30 minutes beforehand, firming up the pork for easy knife-work.

2 pounds boneless pork shoulder, trimmed of surface fat and halved lengthwise

1 bunch cilantro, leaves and stems roughly chopped (about 2 cups)

⅓ cup lime juice, plus lime wedges to serve

3 tablespoons fish sauce

3 tablespoons packed light OR dark brown sugar

6 medium garlic cloves, smashed and peeled

1 tablespoon neutral oil

Kosher salt and ground black pepper

Set the pork on a large plate and freeze until the meat is firm and partially frozen, 30 to 60 minutes. Meanwhile, in a blender, combine the cilantro, lime juice, fish sauce, sugar, garlic, oil, ¼ teaspoon salt and 2 teaspoons pepper. Puree until smooth, about 1 minute, scraping the blender jar as needed.

Using a sharp chef's knife, slice the partially frozen pork crosswise into pieces about ⅛ inch thick. The slices will be irregularly shaped; cut them into strips 1 to 1¼ inches wide (it's fine if the strips are not uniform). In a large bowl, combine the pork and cilantro puree; and mix with your hands until evenly coated. Cover and refrigerate for about 30 minutes.

Heat the broiler with a rack about 6 inches from the element. Set a wire rack in a rimmed broiler-safe baking sheet and mist the rack with cooking spray. Thread the pork onto ten 10- to 12-inch metal skewers, scraping off excess marinade, scrunching it together and packing it quite tightly. If some pieces are too wide, too wispy or awkwardly shaped, fold the meat or tuck in the edges as you skewer. Place the skewers on the prepared rack.

Broil until lightly charred on top, 6 to 8 minutes. Remove from the oven, flip the skewers and broil until the second sides are charred, another 6 to 8 minutes. Serve with lime wedges.

Optional garnish: Thai sweet chili sauce **OR** thinly sliced fresh mint **OR** sliced Fresno or jalapeño chilies

SOUVLAKI-INSPIRED PORK SKEWERS

Start to finish: 30 minutes

Servings: 4

In Greece, skewers of garlicky grilled meat called souvlaki are sold on street corners, in restaurants and at the beach. Inspired by the ubiquitous snack, our broiler-cooked iteration incorporates sweet-tart tomatoes, which blister and char in the oven. Zucchini cut into chunks works nicely, too—or even a combination. A yogurt marinade isn't traditional for pork souvlaki, but we like the tenderizing effect it has on the meat. It also makes a creamy, tangy sauce. Serve with rice, orzo pilaf or warmed pita bread.

¾ cup plain whole-milk Greek yogurt

2 tablespoons red wine vinegar

2 tablespoons extra-virgin olive oil

1 tablespoon chopped fresh oregano

3 medium garlic cloves, finely grated

Kosher salt and ground black pepper

1¼-pound pork tenderloin, trimmed of silver skin, halved lengthwise and cut into 1-inch chunks

8 Campari or cocktail tomatoes (about 1½ inches) OR 1 medium zucchini, halved lengthwise and cut into ½-inch pieces OR a combination

Set a wire rack in a broiler-safe rimmed baking sheet and mist it with cooking spray. In a medium bowl, stir together the yogurt, vinegar, oil, oregano, garlic and 1 teaspoon each salt and pepper. Measure ¼ cup of the mixture into a small bowl and stir in 1 tablespoon water; set aside for serving.

Add the pork to the medium bowl and mix until evenly coated. Thread the pork, alternating with the tomatoes, onto four 8- to 10-inch metal skewers. Place the skewers on the prepared rack, spacing them evenly apart. Let stand at room temperature while the broiler heats.

Heat the broiler with a rack about 4 inches from the element. Broil the skewers until lightly charred, 4 to 6 minutes. Remove from the oven, flip and broil until charred on the second sides, another 4 to 6 minutes. Serve with the yogurt sauce.

Optional garnish: Lemon wedges

The Lowdown on Lard

Though it's a four-letter word for many, we think lard has a place in modern cooking. It tastes great stirred into a pot of beans or used to add flakiness to savory or sweet baked goods.

Lard typically is made from pork fat that's been separated from meat, usually by rendering, a slow cooking method that allows the fat to melt. Among many other uses, it's traditionally used to make carnitas, though in our recipe (recipe p. 464) we simmer cubes of pork shoulder until tender, then break the meat into pieces and fry it in a hot skillet with some of the rendered pork fat, a homemade approach to lard. We use conventional lard in our Oaxacan-style refried beans (recipe p. 134) to add rich flavor, and in our flour tortillas (recipe p. 578) for soft, supple chewiness.

Most supermarkets sell Armour brand lard, which is hydrogenated (in some stores, it will be easier to find Armour labeled in Spanish as "manteca"). High-quality lard has become more widely available; look for it in jars. Hydrogenated lard has the lightest—i.e. least—flavor. Leaf lard has some depth and subtle notes of meatiness. Lard keeps indefinitely in the refrigerator or freezer, but will absorb other flavors, so wrap it well or keep the jar tightly sealed. Keep in mind that lard has a lower smoke point than most types of refined neutral cooking oils, so it's not well suited to searing steaks in cast-iron or for deep-frying.

CARNITAS

Start to finish: 4 hours (45 minutes active)
Servings: 4 to 6

Authentic Mexican carnitas involve slow-cooking pork in lard until fall-apart tender, then increasing the heat so the meat fries and crisps. The fried pork then is broken into smaller pieces for eating. In the U.S., however, carnitas usually is made by simmering pork in liquid, then shredding the meat. The result is moist and tender, but lacks intense porkiness as well the crisping traditional to carnitas. Our method melds the two techniques. We cook cubes of pork shoulder in 1 cup each of neutral oil and water, along with spices and aromatics, until the meat is fork-tender. We then break the pork into smaller pieces, moisten it with its own juices, and fry it in a hot skillet. The pork gets to keep its flavor and develop crisp bits. If you have a fat separator, it makes quick work of removing the fat from the cooking liquid: pour the liquid into it after removing the pork from the pot, then return the defatted cooking liquid to the pot, but remember to reserve the fat. You can cook, shred and moisten the pork with the reduced cooking liquid up to three days in advance; fry the pork just before serving so it's hot and crisp. And if you like your carnitas extra-crisp, after browning the first side, use the spatula to flip the pork and cook until the second side is well-browned and crisp, another 5 to 7 minutes. You can serve carnitas simply with rice and beans or make tacos with warmed corn tortillas. Either way, pickled red onions (recipe follows) are a must—their sharp acidity perfectly balances the richness of the pork. Also offer sliced radishes and salsa.

5 to 6 pounds boneless pork butt, not trimmed, cut into 2-inch cubes

1 large yellow onion, halved and thinly sliced

10 medium garlic cloves, smashed and peeled

2 tablespoons ground cumin

2 tablespoons ground coriander

2 teaspoons dried oregano

1 teaspoon red pepper flakes

½ teaspoon dried thyme

Kosher salt and ground black pepper

1 cup grapeseed or other neutral oil

Heat the oven to 325°F with a rack in the lower-middle position. In a large (at least 7-quart) Dutch oven, stir together the pork, onion, garlic, cumin, coriander, oregano, pepper flakes, thyme and 1 teaspoon salt. Stir in the oil and 1 cup water. Cover, transfer to the oven and cook for 3 hours.

Remove the pot from the oven. Stir the pork and return the pot, uncovered, to the oven. Cook until a skewer inserted into the meat meets no resistance, another 30 minutes. Using a slotted spoon, transfer the meat to a rimmed baking sheet in an even layer to cool. Tilt the pot to pool the cooking liquid to one side, then use a wide spoon to skim off as much fat as possible; reserve the fat. Bring the defatted cooking liquid to a simmer over medium-high and cook, stirring occasionally, until reduced to about ⅓ cup, about 5 minutes. Set aside.

When the meat is cool enough to handle, break the chunks into ¾- to 1-inch pieces, discarding any large pieces of fat. Add the pork back to the pot and stir until evenly moistened with the reduced cooking liquid.

In a 12-inch nonstick skillet over medium-high, heat 1 teaspoon of the reserved fat until barely smoking. Add the pork in an even layer and cook without stirring, pressing the meat against the skillet with a spatula, until the bottom begins to brown and the pork is heated through, 3 to 5 minutes. Taste and season with salt and pepper.

PICKLED RED ONIONS

Start to finish: 10 minutes, plus chilling
Makes about 2 cups

1 cup white vinegar

2 teaspoons white sugar

Kosher salt

**2 medium red onions, halved and
thinly sliced**

**1 jalapeño chili, stemmed, halved
lengthwise and seeded**

In a medium bowl, combine the vinegar, sugar and 1 teaspoon salt, then stir until the salt and sugar dissolve. Stir in the onions and jalapeño. Cover and refrigerate for at least 1 hour or up to 24 hours.

SAUSAGES AND LENTILS WITH PARSLEY-CAPER RELISH

Start to finish: 55 minutes (20 minutes active)
Servings: 4

The classic combination of sausages and lentils make a satisfying meal on a cold winter day. There are many ways to prepare the dish; we use a skillet, start to finish. Dark-green French lentils du Puy, which hold their shape beautifully when fully cooked, take their time to soften compared to other types of lentils, so they need to simmer for 20 minutes before the browned sausages are added to the pan. A quick lemon, caper and parsley relish served alongside adds a welcome pop of tangy, herbal and citrusy flavors.

4 tablespoons extra-virgin olive oil, divided

1 pound sweet OR hot Italian sausages

2 medium carrots, peeled and chopped

1 small red OR yellow onion, chopped

Kosher salt and ground black pepper

4 medium garlic cloves, minced

1 cup lentils du Puy, rinsed and drained

**1 teaspoon grated lemon zest, plus
1 tablespoon lemon juice**

**2 cups lightly packed fresh flat-leaf parsley,
finely chopped**

1 tablespoon drained capers, chopped

In a 12-inch skillet over medium-high, heat 1 tablespoon oil until shimmering. Add the sausages and cook, turning occasionally, until browned on all sides, 4 to 6 minutes. Transfer to a plate.

To the fat in the skillet, add the carrots, onion, and ½ teaspoon each salt and pepper. Reduce to medium and cook, stirring occasionally, until the vegetables begin to soften, 5 to 7 minutes. Stir in the garlic, lentils and 2 cups water, then bring to a simmer over medium-high. Cover, reduce to medium-low and simmer, stirring occasionally, for 20 minutes (the lentils will be only partially cooked).

Place the sausages on the lentils, re-cover and cook until the lentils are tender and the sausages reach 160°F, 23 to 25 minutes.

Meanwhile, in a small bowl, whisk together the lemon zest and juice and the remaining 3 tablespoons oil. Stir in the parsley and capers; set aside until ready to serve.

When the lentils and sausages are done, remove the pan from the heat. Transfer the sausages to a cutting board and cut them on the diagonal into pieces of the desired size. Taste the lentils and season with salt and pepper, then transfer to a serving dish. Place the sausages on top. Serve with the parsley-caper relish on the side.

VIETNAMESE-STYLE MEATBALL LETTUCE WRAPS

Start to finish: 35 minutes
Servings: 4

Vietnamese meatballs are often skewered and grilled, but for a quick weeknight meal, a skillet does a fine job. You could serve these over steamed rice or rice vermicelli, but we liked them with herbs and lettuce leaves for wrapping, along with a lime juice and fish sauce mixture for drizzling. They're also a great filling for Vietnamese báhn mì sandwiches.

3 teaspoons grapeseed or other neutral oil, divided

1 pound ground pork

⅓ cup chopped fresh cilantro, plus cilantro sprigs, to serve

Ground black pepper

6 scallions, white and light green parts minced, dark green parts thinly sliced, reserved separately

5 tablespoons fish sauce, divided

2 tablespoons plus 2 teaspoons white sugar, divided

½ cup lime juice

1 or 2 serrano chilies, stemmed, seeded and thinly sliced

2 medium carrots, peeled and shredded

Lettuce leaves, to serve

Coat a large plate with 1 teaspoon of the oil; set aside. In a medium bowl, combine the pork, 3 tablespoons water, cilantro, ½ teaspoon pepper, minced scallions, 2 tablespoons of the fish sauce and the 2 teaspoons sugar. Mix vigorously with a silicone spatula until thoroughly combined, 20 to 30 seconds. The mixture will be soft and sticky. With lightly moistened hands, form into 20 balls and place on the prepared plate. Cover with plastic wrap and refrigerate for 15 minutes.

Meanwhile, in a small bowl, stir together the lime juice, the 3 remaining tablespoons fish sauce, the remaining

2 tablespoons sugar and the chilies until the sugar dissolves. Set aside.

Line another plate with paper towels. In a 12-inch nonstick skillet over medium-high, heat the remaining 2 teaspoons oil until barely smoking. Add the meatballs and cook undisturbed until the bottoms are golden brown, 1 to 2 minutes. Using a spatula, turn each meatball and continue to cook, adjusting the heat as needed and occasionally turning the meatballs, until golden brown all over, 4 to 5 minutes. Transfer to the prepared plate, tent with foil and let rest 5 minutes.

In a small bowl, toss the carrots with 2 tablespoons of the lime juice sauce. Serve the meatballs with the carrots, cilantro sprigs, sliced scallions and lettuce leaves for wrapping. The remaining sauce can be spooned onto the wraps.

TAIWANESE FIVE-SPICE PORK WITH RICE

Start to finish: 40 minutes

Servings: 6

This Taiwanese dish, called lu rou fan, is a one-bowl meal consisting of richly flavored, soy-simmered pork served over steamed rice. Pork belly is traditional. but we found ground pork faster and just as delicious. Hard-cooked eggs are common, but we preferred soft-cooked eggs for their runny yolks. We liked steamed or stir-fried bok choy or broccoli alongside, a balance to the richness of the pork.

1½ pounds ground pork

1 cup low-sodium soy sauce, divided, plus more, as needed

¼ cup grapeseed or other neutral oil

12 ounces shallots, halved and thinly sliced

10 medium garlic cloves, minced

1¼ cups dry sherry

⅓ cup packed dark brown sugar

2 tablespoons five-spice powder

1 tablespoon unseasoned rice vinegar

Steamed rice, to serve

3 scallions, thinly sliced on the diagonal

In a medium bowl, mix the pork with ¼ cup of the soy sauce. Cover and refrigerate until needed.

In a large Dutch oven over medium, heat the oil until shimmering. Add the shallots and cook, stirring, until deeply browned, 15 to 20 minutes. Add the garlic and cook, stirring constantly, until the garlic is fragrant and just beginning to brown, about 1 minute.

Add the sherry, sugar, five-spice and remaining ¾ cup soy sauce. Stir until the sugar has dissolved, then increase to high and bring to a boil. Cook, stirring, until reduced and syrupy and a spoon leaves a clear trail, about 5 minutes.

Reduce to low and allow the simmering to subside. Add the pork, breaking it into small pieces. Cook, stirring, until the meat is no longer pink, 5 to 7 minutes. Stir in the vinegar, then taste and add soy sauce, if needed. Spoon steamed rice into individual bowls and top with the pork. If using eggs, halve them and place on top, then sprinkle with scallions.

467

Beef

Neapolitan Meatballs with Ragù

Start to finish: 50 minutes
Servings: 6 to 8

In Naples, Rosa Vittozzi, part of the family-run Trattoria La Tavernetta, showed us **how to make meatballs Neapolitan style— generously sized and ultra-tender from a high ratio of bread to meat. For our version, we used Japanese panko breadcrumbs. Panko, which has a neutral flavor and a light and fluffy but coarse texture, greatly streamlines the meatball-making process, eliminating the need to remove the crusts from fresh bread, cut and measure, soak in water, then squeeze out excess moisture**. Panko needs only to be moistened with water. Neapolitans serve their meatballs with a basic tomato sauce they refer to as "ragù."

4 tablespoons extra-virgin olive oil, divided, plus more to serve

1 large yellow onion, finely chopped

Kosher salt and ground black pepper

6 medium garlic cloves, finely grated

1½ teaspoons red pepper flakes, divided

6½ ounces (2½ cups) panko breadcrumbs

3 ounces pecorino Romano cheese, 2 ounces finely grated (1 cup), 1 ounce as a chunk, plus more grated, to serve

1 large egg, plus 1 large egg yolk, beaten together

1½ pounds 90 percent lean ground beef

Two 28-ounce cans whole peeled tomatoes

6 to 8 large basil leaves

Heat the oven to 475°F with a rack in the middle position. Line a rimmed baking sheet with kitchen parchment and mist with cooking spray. In a large Dutch oven over medium-high, heat 2 tablespoons of the oil until shimmering. Add the onion and ¼ teaspoon salt, then cook, stirring occasionally, until softened, about 5 minutes. Add the garlic and 1 teaspoon of the pepper flakes; cook, stirring, until fragrant, about 30 seconds. Remove from the heat, then transfer half of the onion mixture to a large bowl.

In a medium bowl, combine the panko and 1¼ cups water; press the panko into the water and let stand until fully

softened, about 5 minutes. Mash with your hands to a smooth paste, then add to the bowl with the onion mixture. Using a fork, mix until well combined and smooth. Stir in the grated cheese, beaten eggs, remaining 2 tablespoons oil, ¾ teaspoon salt and 2 teaspoons black pepper. Add the meat and mix with your hands until completely homogeneous.

Using a ½-cup dry measuring cup, divide the mixture into 8 portions. Using your hands, shape each into a compact ball and place on the prepared baking sheet, spacing them evenly apart. Refrigerate uncovered for 15 to 20 minutes. Re-shape the meatballs if they have flattened slightly, then bake until lightly browned, about 20 minutes. Let cool on the baking sheet set on a wire rack for about 10 minutes.

While the meatballs cook, in a food processor or blender, puree the tomatoes with their juices one can at a time, until smooth, about 30 seconds, transferring the puree to a large bowl. Return the Dutch oven to medium and heat the remaining onion mixture, stirring, until warmed through, about 2 minutes. Stir in the tomatoes, remaining ½ teaspoon pepper flakes, the basil and the chunk of cheese. Bring to a simmer over medium-high and cook until slightly thickened, about 15 minutes. Taste and season with salt and pepper.

Using a large spoon, transfer the meatballs to the sauce, then, using 2 spoons, turn each to coat. Bring to a simmer, then reduce to medium-low, cover and cook for 5 minutes. Remove the pot from the heat and let stand, covered, for 5 minutes to allow the meatballs to firm. Remove and discard the pecorino chunk. Serve with additional grated cheese.

MEATBALLS IN CHIPOTLE SAUCE

Start to finish: 50 minutes (15 minutes active)
Servings: 4

These Mexican meatballs are served in a tomato sauce laced with spicy, smoky chipotle chilies. Canned fire-roasted tomatoes are an easy way to give the sauce flavor that accentuates the smokiness of the chipotles. Instead of browning the meatballs on the stovetop, we roast them in the oven, minimizing splatter and freeing up the skillet for the sauce. Crumbled queso fresco offers a nice color and flavor contrast. Serve with crusty bread, Mexican rice or warmed tortillas.

2 tablespoons grapeseed or other neutral oil

1 medium white onion, finely chopped

Kosher salt and ground black pepper

4 medium garlic cloves, minced

1½ teaspoons dried oregano

1½ teaspoons ground cumin

⅓ cup panko breadcrumbs

1 pound 90 percent lean ground beef

¾ cup chopped fresh cilantro, divided

14½-ounce can diced fire-roasted tomatoes

1 or 2 chipotle chilies in adobo and the sauce clinging to them, chopped

Crumbled queso fresco, to serve (optional)

In a 12-inch skillet over medium-high, heat the oil until shimmering. Add the onion, ½ teaspoon salt and ¼ teaspoon pepper, then cook, stirring occasionally, until browned, about 5 minutes. Add the garlic, oregano and cumin, then cook, stirring, until fragrant, about 30 seconds. Remove from the heat, then transfer ½ cup of the mixture to a large bowl; set aside the skillet with the remaining mixture. Line a rimmed baking sheet with kitchen parchment.

Into the bowl with the onion mixture, stir in the panko and ½ cup water. Let stand until the panko softens, about 5 minutes. Using a silicone spatula or your hands, mash the mixture to a paste, then add the beef, ½ cup of cilantro, ½ teaspoon salt and 1 teaspoon pepper. Mix well, then divide into sixteen 2-tablespoon portions, rolling each into a ball and placing on the prepared baking sheet. Cover and refrigerate for 15 to 30 minutes. Meanwhile, heat the oven to 450°F with a rack in the middle position.

Uncover the meatballs and roast until browned and the centers reach 160°F, 12 to 16 minutes, stirring once about halfway through. Remove from the oven and set aside.

To the skillet with the remaining onion mixture, stir in the tomatoes and ½ cup water. Bring to a simmer over medium-high, then add the chipotle chilies and cook, stirring occasionally, until a spatula drawn through the sauce leaves a trail, about 3 minutes. Taste and season with salt and pepper. Add the meatballs and stir gently to coat with the sauce, then stir in the remaining ¼ cup cilantro and sprinkle with queso fresco (if using).

Secrets to Great Meatballs

The perfect meatball is moist, flavorful, tender and not greasy. And just about every cuisine has its own take, from Turkish köfte to Swedish köttbullar. But we've found a few tactics that help us ensure success with almost any style of meatball.

First, we add a panade—a mixture of bread and a liquid, such as water or milk—to the meat. This produces tender meatballs because the bread not only acts as a sponge for retaining moisture, it also prevents the meat from fully binding to itself, which can produce a tougher texture. The amount of panade varies by recipe, but some traditions—such as classic Neapolitan meatballs—call for as much as a 1:4 ratio.

Second, we often chill meatballs before cooking, especially if the meat mixture is soft. This firms them up so they better hold their shape during cooking. Simply put the shaped meatballs on a plate or baking sheet and slide it into the refrigerator, uncovered, for at least 10 minutes.

Finally, we often favor cooking in the oven rather than the stovetop. Roasting meatballs saves time and effort, especially when making a larger recipe. Roast for about 10 to 15 minutes in a 450° F oven. That said, for the perfect sear, it's hard to beat pan-frying. It takes less time, about 5 to 7 minutes, thanks to the direct heat of the pan.

GREEK MEATBALLS WITH TOMATO SAUCE

Start to finish: 1 hour 20 minutes
Servings: 4 to 6

Known as soutzoukakia, these cigar-shaped meatballs are seasoned with cumin and garlic, then simmered in tomato sauce. The dish has origins in Smyrna, a former Greek settlement and now the Turkish city of Izmir on the Aegean coast. Our recipe is based on the soutzoukakia we learned from Alexandra Manousakis and Afshin Molavi of Manousakis Winery on the Greek island of Crete. Made with a combination of ground lamb and beef, the meatballs have a deep, rich flavor perfectly matched by the tangy-sweet tomato sauce. If you prefer, you can use 1 pound of either type of meat. An instant thermometer is the best way to check the meatballs for doneness; alternatively, cut one open—when done, the center should not be pink. The meatballs are browned on the stovetop, then finish cooking in the same pan in the oven, so you will need a 12-inch oven-safe skillet for this recipe. Soutzoukakia typically are offered as part of a meze spread, but served with rice, they're a terrific main.

2 medium yellow onions, peeled

3 tablespoons panko breadcrumbs

Kosher salt and ground black pepper

1½ pounds ripe tomatoes, halved

8 ounces 80 percent lean ground beef (see headnote)

8 ounces ground lamb

4 medium garlic cloves, finely grated

4 tablespoons finely chopped fresh flat-leaf parsley, divided

4 tablespoons finely chopped fresh mint, divided

3 teaspoons dried oregano, divided

1 teaspoon ground cumin

1 teaspoon sweet paprika

1 large egg, beaten

4 tablespoons extra-virgin olive oil, divided

2 tablespoons tomato paste

Set a box grater in a medium bowl. Grate the onions on the large holes down to the root ends; reserve the box grater. Transfer half of the grated onion to a small bowl and set aside for the sauce. To the grated onion in the medium bowl, add the panko and ½ teaspoon salt; stir, then let stand until the panko is softened, about 10 minutes.

Meanwhile, grate the tomato halves (start with the cut sides against the grater) into another medium bowl; stop when you reach the skin and discard it. Cover and set aside for making the sauce.

To the onion-panko mixture, add the beef, lamb, half of the garlic, 2 tablespoons each of parsley and mint, 2 teaspoons of the oregano, the cumin, paprika, egg and ½ teaspoon pepper. Mix with your hands until well combined. Cover and refrigerate for at least 15 minutes or up to 1 hour.

Heat the oven to 375°F with a rack in the middle position. Divide the chilled meat mixture into 12 evenly sized balls

(a scant ¼ cup each). With wet hands, shape each one into an oblong about 3 inches long.

In a 12-inch oven-safe skillet over medium, heat 3 table-spoons of the oil until shimmering. Add the meatballs and cook, using a thin metal spatula or 2 spoons to gently and occasionally turn them, until lightly browned all over, 6 to 8 minutes. Transfer to a large plate and set aside. Pour off and discard the fat in the skillet.

In the same skillet over medium-high, combine the remaining 1 tablespoon oil, reserved grated onion, remaining garlic, ½ teaspoon salt and ¼ teaspoon pepper. Cook, scraping up any browned bits, until the moisture from the onion has evaporated and the onion and drippings are well browned, about 5 minutes; reduce the heat as needed if browning goes too quickly. Stir in the tomato paste and remaining 1 teaspoon oregano, then add the grated tomatoes; scrape up any browned bits. Bring to a simmer over medium-high and cook, stirring often, until the mixture is slightly thickened, 4 to 5 minutes.

Off heat, nestle the meatballs in the sauce and add the accumulated juices. Transfer the skillet to the oven and cook until the center of the meatballs registers 160°F and the sauce is brown at the edges, 13 to 18 minutes.

Remove the skillet from the oven (the handle will be hot). Serve sprinkled with the remaining 2 tablespoons each parsley and mint.

MOROCCAN MEATBALL TAGINE

Start to finish: 1 hour
Servings: 4

To make this tagine of tender, warmly spiced meatballs simmered in a thick tomato sauce—a much-simplified version of a dish we tasted in Marrakech—we use a 12-inch skillet with a lid and we bring the pan directly to the table for serving. Ras el hanout is a fragrant Moroccan spice blend that may include more than a dozen different ingredients; it's an easy way to add complex North African flavors to your cooking. Look for ras el hanout in well-stocked supermarkets, Middle Eastern grocery stores or spice shops. If it's not available, use 1 tablespoon ground cumin, 1½ teaspoons ground coriander and ½ teaspoon ground cinnamon to achieve a similar warm, savory spiciness.

473

¼ cup extra-virgin olive oil

1 medium yellow onion, finely chopped

Kosher salt and ground black pepper

6 medium garlic cloves, minced

5 teaspoons ras el hanout (see headnote)

1 bunch cilantro, stems minced, leaves roughly chopped, reserved separately

⅓ cup panko breadcrumbs

28-ounce can crushed tomatoes

1 pound 90 percent lean ground beef

⅓ cup pimento-stuffed green olives, roughly chopped

1 tablespoon grated lemon zest

In a 12-inch skillet over medium, heat the oil until shimmering. Add the onion and ½ teaspoon salt, then cook, stirring, until softened, about 5 minutes. Add the garlic, ras el hanout and cilantro stems; cook, stirring, until fragrant, about 30 seconds. Remove the pan from the heat.

Measure ½ cup of the onion mixture into a medium bowl. Add the panko and ¼ cup water; stir to combine, then let

stand until the panko hydrates and softens, about 5 minutes. Meanwhile, return the skillet to medium, add the tomatoes and bring to a simmer, scraping up any browned bits. Cover and set aside off heat while you form the meatballs.

Using your hands, mash the panko mixture to a smooth paste. Add the beef, ¾ teaspoon salt and ½ teaspoon pepper; mix thoroughly with your hands. Divide the mixture into 12 portions and form each into a ball.

Return the sauce to a simmer over medium. Add the meatballs and turn to coat with sauce. Cover and cook at a gentle simmer, stirring and turning the meatballs about every 5 minutes, until the centers of the meatballs reach 160°F and the sauce is lightly thickened, 10 to 12 minutes.

Off heat, taste and season with salt and pepper. Sprinkle with the olives, lemon zest and cilantro leaves and serve directly from the skillet.

BEEF AND RICE MEATBALLS WITH LEMON–OLIVE OIL SAUCE

Start to finish: 40 minutes
Servings: 4

In the Greek dish called youvarlakia avgolemono, beef and rice meatballs dot a lemony soup that's rich and velvety with egg yolks. To simplify, we pair the meatballs with a quick pan sauce inspired by Greek ladolemono, a simple sauce of lemon, olive oil and sometimes herbs. A generous amount of chopped dill lends the dish fresh herbal notes. Serve with warmed pita bread or a rice or orzo pilaf.

1 cup cooked long-grain white rice, room temperature

2 slices hearty white sandwich bread, torn into small pieces

1 cup low-sodium beef broth, divided

4 tablespoons finely chopped fresh dill, divided

Kosher salt and ground black pepper

1 pound 85 percent lean ground beef

1 large egg yolk

3 medium garlic cloves, finely grated

2 teaspoons dried oregano, divided

5 tablespoons extra-virgin olive oil, divided

2 tablespoons lemon juice

In a large bowl, mash the rice with a fork until smooth and pasty. Add the bread, ¼ cup of broth, 2 tablespoons of dill, 1½ teaspoons salt and 1 teaspoon pepper. Using your hands, mix and mash the ingredients to a paste. Add the beef, egg yolk, half of the garlic and 1 teaspoon of oregano, then mix with your hands until the mixture is homogeneous. Divide into 12 portions, form into smooth balls and place on a plate. Refrigerate, uncovered, for about 10 minutes.

In a 12-inch nonstick skillet over medium-high, heat 2 tablespoons of oil until shimmering. Add the meatballs and cook without disturbing until lightly browned on the bottoms, about 3 minutes. Carefully turn the meatballs and cook until browned on the second sides, about another 3 minutes. Add the remaining garlic and the remaining 1 teaspoon oregano and cook, stirring, until fragrant, about 30 seconds. Add the remaining ¾ cup broth, then scrape up any browned bits. Bring to a simmer, then cover, reduce to medium-low and cook, gently stirring once or twice, until the centers reach 160°F, 5 to 7 minutes.

Using tongs, transfer the meatballs to a serving dish and tent with foil. Bring the liquid in the pan to a boil over medium-high and cook, stirring occasionally, until thick enough that a spatula drawn through it leaves a trail, 2 to 3 minutes. Off heat, whisk in the remaining 3 tablespoons olive oil and the lemon juice. Taste and season with salt and pepper. Pour the sauce over the meatballs and sprinkle with the remaining 2 tablespoons dill.

TURKISH SKILLET KEBAB WITH CHARRED PEPPERS AND TOMATOES

Start to finish: 40 minutes (20 minutes active)
Servings: 4

We tried the regional Turkish speciality called tepsi kebabi ("tray kebab" is the English translation) in Antakya. Richly spiced ground meat is combined with onion, garlic, sweet peppers and tomato, then pressed into a tray and baked until browned and bubbling. We use a skillet and add potato wedges. You will need a broiler-safe 12-inch skillet, as the cooking starts in a high-heat oven and finishes under the broiler. Aleppo pepper is mildly spicy with a touch of fruitiness and smoke. You can substitute 4 teaspoons sweet paprika plus ½ teaspoon cayenne pepper. Serve straight from the skillet, with yogurt and warm flatbread for dipping in the flavorful juices.

1 pound medium (about 2-inch) Yukon Gold potatoes, unpeeled, each cut into 6 wedges

2 tablespoons extra-virgin olive oil, divided

Kosher salt and ground black pepper

½ medium red onion, finely chopped

1 medium red bell pepper, stemmed, seeded and finely chopped

2 medium garlic cloves, finely grated

4 teaspoons Aleppo pepper (see headnote)

1 tablespoon ground cumin

2 teaspoons dried thyme

2 teaspoons dried mint

¾ cup lightly packed fresh flat-leaf parsley, chopped

1 pound 90 percent lean ground beef

1 pound ground lamb

¼ cup tomato paste

2 banana or cubanelle peppers, stemmed, seeded and halved lengthwise

4 Campari or cocktail tomatoes, halved

Warm flatbread, to serve

Plain whole-milk yogurt, to serve

Heat the oven to 450°F with racks in the upper- and lower-middle positions. In a medium microwave-safe bowl, toss the potatoes with 1 tablespoon of the oil and ¼ teaspoon each salt and black pepper. Cover and microwave on high until a skewer inserted into the potatoes meets just a little resistance, about 6 minutes. Uncover and set aside.

In a medium bowl, combine the onion, bell pepper, garlic, Aleppo pepper, cumin, thyme, mint, parsley, beef, lamb and 1½ teaspoons salt, then mix with your hands until well combined.

Spread the tomato paste to a broiler-safe 12-inch skillet to cover the bottom. Add the meat mixture and, using your hands, press it into an even layer, all the way to the edges of the skillet. In the same bowl, toss together the banana peppers, tomatoes, remaining 1 tablespoon oil and ¼ teaspoon each salt and black pepper.

Place the potato wedges skin side up on the meat mixture, placing them around the perimeter and gently pressing them in. Inside the ring of potatoes, arrange the banana peppers, cut side down, overlapping them as needed to fit. Arrange the tomato halves, cut side down, inside the ring

of peppers. Bake on the lower rack until the meat reaches 125°F at the center, about 15 minutes. Remove the skillet from the oven (the handle will be hot).

Heat the oven to broil. When it reaches temperature, slide the skillet onto the top rack. Broil until the vegetables are charred and the meat reaches 160°F at the center, 5 to 7 minutes. Transfer to a wire rack and let rest for 5 minutes. Serve from the skillet with warm flatbread and yogurt on the side.

....

BAKED KEFTA WITH TAHINI

Start to finish: 1½ hours (30 minutes active)
Servings: 4 to 6

During a visit to Jordan, we learned the term "kefta" refers to a ground meat mixture flavored with onion and spices that may take a number of different forms. For example, it might be molded around metal skewers and grilled, or it can be pressed into other shapes and cooked in the oven. Tagreed Muhtaseb, a home cook who lives in Amman, taught us how to make her excellent kefta bi tahini (kefta with tahini) in which oblong "meatballs" are baked with potatoes, onion and a rich, lemony tahini-yogurt sauce. In the oven's heat, the flavors meld and fuse deliciously while the surface develops flavorful browning. We adapted Muhtaseb's recipe, precooking the potatoes and onion so they fully and evenly tenderize. We also brush tahini sauce rather sparingly onto the partially cooked kefta instead of saucing them heavily to keep the flavors bright and clean (we do love the sauce, though, so we serve some on the side). Baharat is an all-purpose Middle Eastern spice blend. Look for it in well-stocked supermarkets, spice shops and Middle Eastern markets. Or make your own, following the recipe on p. 126. Serve kefta bi tahini with warm pita bread.

½ cup tahini

¼ cup boiling water

¼ cup plain whole-milk yogurt

¼ cup lemon juice, plus lemon wedges to serve

Kosher salt and ground black pepper

1 pound medium Yukon Gold potatoes, unpeeled, sliced ¼ inch thick

1 tablespoon extra-virgin olive oil

1 large yellow onion, ½ thinly sliced,
½ roughly chopped, reserved separately

2 medium garlic cloves, smashed and peeled

½ cup lightly packed fresh flat-leaf parsley, plus
chopped fresh flat-leaf parsley to serve

1 jalapeño chili, stemmed and seeded

1 tablespoon ghee or salted butter, room temperature

1 pound 80 percent lean ground beef

2 teaspoons baharat (see headnote)

Warm pita bread, to serve

Heat the oven to 450°F with a rack in the middle position.
Put the tahini into a small bowl. Gradually whisk in the
boiling water, followed by the yogurt, lemon juice and
½ teaspoon salt. Measure 2 tablespoons of the tahini sauce
into another small bowl to use for brushing; reserve the
remainder for serving.

In a 9-inch deep-dish pie plate, toss the potatoes with the
oil and ½ teaspoon salt. Shingle the slices in the pie plate
in concentric circles. Scatter on the sliced onion and pour in
¼ cup water. Cover tightly with foil and bake for 30 minutes.

Remove the foil and bake until a skewer inserted into the
potatoes meets no resistance, about another 10 minutes.
Remove from the oven; leave the oven on.

In a food processor, combine the chopped onion, the garlic,
parsley and jalapeño. Process until finely chopped, scraping
the bowl once or twice, about 1 minute. Add the ghee and
pulse until combined, 8 to 10 pulses. Transfer to a medium
bowl and add the beef, baharat, 1½ teaspoons salt and
1 teaspoon pepper. Using your hands, mix until well
combined. Lightly moisten your hands to prevent sticking,
then shape the mixture into nine 3-inch cigars (about ¼ cup
each) and place them, evenly spaced, on top of the potato-
onion mixture.

Bake until the kefta begin to brown and release some juices,
10 to 12 minutes. Remove the pie plate from the oven and
brush the kefta with the 2 tablespoons reserved tahini
sauce. Return to the oven and bake until the kefta are nicely
browned and the centers reach 160°F, another 10 to 12
minutes.

Sprinkle with chopped parsley. Serve with the tahini sauce,
lemon wedges and pita.

CAMBODIAN BEEF SALAD

Start to finish: 35 minutes

Servings: 4

This substantial Khmer-style beef salad combines lots of contrasting tastes and textures. We preferred the meatiness and rich flavor of boneless short ribs, but if they're not available, use flat iron steak instead. Rather than sear the beef and slice it after cooking, we slice it first, then cook it in a flavorful liquid that later becomes the salad dressing. So that the beef is easier to cut into evenly thin slices, freeze it uncovered for about 20 minutes, until partially frozen.

1½ pounds boneless beef short ribs, trimmed and sliced about ⅛ inch thick (see headnote)

Kosher salt and ground black pepper

¼ cup fish sauce

¼ cup lime juice, plus lime wedges to serve

3 tablespoons packed brown sugar

2 tablespoons peanut oil, preferably toasted, plus more to serve

½ small head red cabbage, finely shredded (about 4 cups)

½ English cucumber, halved lengthwise, seeded and thinly sliced on the diagonal

1 jalapeño chili, stemmed and sliced into thin rings

4 scallions, thinly sliced on the diagonal

¼ cup roasted peanuts, chopped

In a medium bowl, toss the beef with ¼ teaspoon salt and 1 teaspoon pepper. In a large saucepan, stir together the fish sauce, lime juice, sugar, oil and ¼ cup water. Bring to a simmer over high, then add the beef and cook, stirring constantly, until the meat is no longer pink, 2 to 3 minutes; the beef will release liquid as it cooks. Remove the pan from the heat and let stand for 10 minutes.

Meanwhile, in a large bowl, combine the cabbage, cucumber ¼ teaspoon salt and ¾ teaspoon pepper. Toss the vegetables with your hands, rubbing in the salt, until they just begin to wilt. Using a slotted spoon, transfer the beef to the bowl with the vegetables, then add the chili and scallions. Add ¼ cup of the beef cooking liquid and toss to combine. Taste and, if desired, toss in additional cooking liquid 1 tablespoon at a time until the salad is dressed to your liking. Transfer to a serving bowl, then top with the peanuts and drizzle with additional oil. Serve with lime wedges.

THAI STEAK AND HERB SALAD WITH SPICY LIME SAUCE

Start to finish: 40 minutes (20 minutes active)

Servings: 4

This salad from the Isaan region of Thailand is a fantastic combination of meaty, tangy, herbal, spicy and allium flavors, with fish sauce adding loads of umami. The Thai name for this dish is nam tok neua, which translates as "waterfall beef." There is conjecture, but no definitive answer on how the salad got its poetic name. Toasted rice powder, called khao kua, is a key ingredient, one that adds texture and a unique, slightly nutty flavor. The powder is made by toasting uncooked rice in a pan until golden brown, then grinding the grains to a coarse powder. Sweet (also called glutinous) rice is the type used to make traditional khao kua, but we opt to use easier-to-source jasmine rice. In our take on nam tok neua, we sear the steak on the

steak, reduce to medium and cook until well browned, 4 to 6 minutes. Flip and cook until the center reaches 120°F for medium-rare, about another 4 minutes. Transfer to a plate, tent with foil and let rest for 10 minutes. Toss the shallots in the dressing. Thinly slice the steak, then add it and its juices to the shallots, along with the herbs, chili (if using) and half of the rice powder; gently toss. Transfer to a platter and sprinkle with the remaining rice powder.

stovetop, slice it thinly, then toss it with sliced shallots that were steeped in the lime and fish sauce dressing. Serve with steamed rice.

2 tablespoons jasmine rice

¼ cup fish sauce

¼ cup lime juice

1 teaspoon white sugar

¼ to ½ teaspoon red pepper flakes

Ground white pepper

1 pound strip steak, about 1-inch thick, trimmed and patted dry

1 tablespoon grapeseed or other neutral oil

3 medium shallots, sliced into thin rings

1 cup lightly packed fresh cilantro

1 cup lightly packed fresh mint

1 Fresno or serrano chili, stemmed and sliced into thin rings (optional)

In a 10-inch skillet over medium, toast the rice until golden brown. Transfer to a small bowl and let cool. Using a spice grinder, pulverize the rice to a coarse powder. Return the powder to the bowl. In a large bowl, whisk the fish sauce, lime juice, sugar, pepper flakes and ½ teaspoon white pepper.

Season the steak with pepper. In the same skillet over medium-high, heat the oil until barely smoking. Add the

SKIRT STEAK SALAD WITH ARUGULA AND PEPPADEWS

Start to finish: 30 minutes
Servings: 4

Italian tagliata inspired our steak salad, which uses economical skirt steak seasoned with a dry rub of salt, pepper and ground fennel. Flank, flat iron and bavette steaks also work well. If the steak comes as a long piece, cut the meat in half to fit the pan. Tangy, sweet Peppadew peppers can be found near the olive bar in most grocers; they come in mild or hot varieties. A Y-style peeler is best for shaving the Parmesan.

2 teaspoons ground fennel

Kosher salt and ground black pepper

1 pound skirt steak, trimmed

7 tablespoons extra-virgin olive oil, divided

3 tablespoons lemon juice

½ cup drained and chopped Peppadew peppers

1 medium garlic clove, thinly sliced

8 ounces baby arugula (about 12 cups lightly packed)

1½ ounce Parmesan cheese, shaved (¾ cup)

In a small bowl, combine the fennel, ½ teaspoon salt and 2 teaspoons pepper. Coat the steak with the seasoning, then let sit for 15 minutes. Meanwhile, in a liquid measuring cup, whisk together 6 tablespoons of the oil, the lemon juice, ¼ teaspoon salt and ½ teaspoon pepper. Set aside.

In a 12-inch skillet over medium-high, heat the remaining tablespoon of oil until barely smoking. Add the steak and sear without moving, until well browned, about 3 minutes. Flip and brown on the second side, about another 2 minutes for rare to medium-rare.

479

Transfer to a plate and let rest for 10 minutes.

Return the skillet to medium-high. Add the Peppadews and garlic, then cook for 30 seconds. Stir the dressing, then add half to the skillet, scraping the pan to deglaze.

In a large bowl, toss the arugula with the remaining dressing and half of the Parmesan, then divide among serving plates. Thinly slice the steak against the grain, then arrange slices over the arugula. Spoon some warm pan sauce over each serving. Top with the remaining Parmesan.

STEAK SALAD WITH WALNUTS, POMEGRANATE MOLASSES AND BLUE CHEESE

Start to finish: 30 minutes

Servings: 4

We use pomegranate molasses to add sweet tang to the dressing for this main-course salad. Its fruity, bright and sweet flavor pairs well with the savory meat and peppery watercress. Crumbled blue cheese (or fresh goat cheese) brings a creamy, salty element that's a delicious complement to the other flavors and textures. Take the time to finely

chop the toasted walnuts; broken down into small pieces, the nuts better cling to the greens, rather than fall to the bottom of the bowl. Serve with warm, crusty bread.

⅓ cup walnuts

1-pound beef strip or rib-eye sirloin steak (about 1 inch thick), trimmed and patted dry

Kosher salt and ground black pepper

5 tablespoons extra-virgin olive oil, divided

2 teaspoons ground coriander

3 tablespoons pomegranate molasses

4-ounce package baby watercress OR 5-ounce container baby arugula

2 ounces gorgonzola OR fresh goat cheese (chèvre), crumbled (½ cup)

In a 12-inch skillet over medium, toast the walnuts, stirring often, until fragrant and lightly browned, 3 to 4 minutes. Transfer to a cutting board and let cool; wipe out the skillet.

Season the steak on both sides with salt and pepper. In a 12-inch skillet over medium-high, heat 1 tablespoon oil until barely smoking. Add the steak and cook until well browned on both sides and the center reaches 125°F (for medium-rare), 8 to 12 minutes, flipping once about halfway through. Transfer to a large platter and let rest 10 minutes. Meanwhile, finely chop the walnuts. In a large bowl, whisk together the remaining 4 tablespoons oil, coriander, pomegranate molasses and ¼ teaspoon each salt and pepper.

Thinly slice the steak and return to the platter. Whisk the accumulated juices from the steak and 2 tablespoons water into the dressing. Add the watercress and walnuts; toss to combine. Top the steak with the salad and sprinkle with the cheese.

RIB-EYE STEAKS WITH ROSEMARY AND POMEGRANATE MOLASSES

Start to finish: 40 minutes, plus marinating, grill prep and resting / Servings: 4

At Manzara Restaurant in Söğüt, in southeastern Türkiye, we tasted a superb grilled rib-eye steak prepared by chef Naci Isik. We thought the fruity, tangy-sweet flavor of pomegranate molasses, the savoriness of onion and the resinous notes of fresh rosemary in the marinade worked together as a delicious complement for the richness and smoky char of the beef. Our adaptation hews closely to Isik's recipe, with a few modifications for cooking in a home kitchen and using ingredients available in the U.S. We recommend seeking out pomegranate molasses that does not contain added sugar; its flavor is purer and more intense than types made with sweetener. This recipe cooks the steaks outdoors on a charcoal or gas grill; see additional instructions to cook the steaks on the stovetop in a cast-iron grill pan (if cooking indoors, be sure to turn on your hood or open a window to vent any smoke).

1 medium white onion, peeled and cut lengthwise into quarters

¼ cup pomegranate molasses, plus more to serve

1 teaspoon Aleppo pepper or ¾ teaspoon sweet paprika plus ¼ teaspoon cayenne pepper

3 teaspoons minced fresh rosemary, divided

Kosher salt and ground black pepper

Two 12- to 14-ounce boneless rib-eye steaks (about 1 inch thick), patted dry

Grapeseed or other neutral oil, for brushing

2 tablespoons salted butter, cut into 4 pieces

Set a box grater in a 9-by-13-inch baking dish. Grate the onion quarters on the large holes, allowing the pulp and juice to fall into the baking dish. To the grated onion, stir in the pomegranate molasses, Aleppo pepper, 1 teaspoon

of rosemary, 1 teaspoon salt and ½ teaspoon black pepper. Add the steaks and turn to coat. Cover and refrigerate for at least 30 minutes or up to 24 hours; flip the steaks once or twice during marination. If refrigerated for longer than 1 hour, remove the steaks from the refrigerator about 30 minutes before grilling.

Prepare a charcoal or gas grill. For a charcoal grill, ignite three-fourths of a large chimney of coals, let burn until lightly ashed over, then distribute the coals evenly over one side of the grill bed; open the bottom grill vents. Heat the grill, covered, for 5 minutes, then clean and oil the grill grate. For a gas grill, turn all burners to high and heat the grill, covered, for 10 to 15 minutes, then clean and oil the cooking grate.

Scrape any excess marinade off the steaks and pat dry with paper towels. Brush one side of the steaks with oil, then place oiled-side down on the grill (on the hot side if using charcoal). Cover and cook until nicely charred on the bottom, about 4 minutes. Brush the side facing up with oil, then flip the steaks. Cover and cook until the second sides are nicely charred and the centers reach 120°F (for medium-rare), another 3 to 4 minutes. Transfer the steaks to a

serving platter, sprinkle each with the remaining rosemary and top each with 2 pieces of butter. Tent with foil and let rest for about 10 minutes.

Transfer the steaks to a cutting board and cut into thin slices on the diagonal. Return to the platter and pour over the juices from the cutting board. Sprinkle with salt and black pepper and, if desired, drizzle with additional pomegranate molasses.

TO COOK IN A STOVETOP GRILL PAN

Follow the recipe to marinate the steaks; if refrigerated for longer than 1 hour, remove the steaks from the refrigerator about 30 minutes before cooking. Brush a 12-inch cast-iron grill pan with 2 teaspoons oil and heat over medium-high until barely smoking. Meanwhile, scrape any excess marinade off the steaks and pat dry with paper towels. Add the steaks to the pan and cook without disturbing until well browned on the bottom, 5 to 7 minutes. Flip the steaks and cook until the second sides are well browned and the centers reach 120°F (for medium-rare), 6 to 8 minutes. Transfer to a serving platter and continue with the recipe to finish and slice.

STRIP STEAKS WITH SPICY TOMATO-BASIL SAUCE

Start to finish: 45 minutes

Servings: 4 to 6

As its name suggests, the Italian classic bistecca alla pizzaiola pairs a meaty steak with the sort of tomato sauce that might typically be used on pizza. There are many ways to prepare the dish, but we keep ours simple and perfect for a weeknight meal. We make a sauce with canned tomatoes, add some punchiness with garlic and pepper flakes, and kick up the umami quotient with a few anchovy fillets (don't worry, the sauce won't taste fishy). We then sear a couple strip steaks, slice and sauce them, then finish the dish with torn fresh basil and fruity olive oil. Serve with thick slices of warm, crusty bread to dip in the sauce.

1 tablespoon extra-virgin olive oil, plus more to serve

2 medium garlic cloves, thinly sliced

2 or 3 oil-packed anchovy fillets, chopped

½ to ¾ teaspoon red pepper flakes

28-ounce can whole peeled tomatoes, crushed by hand

⅓ cup lightly packed fresh basil

Kosher salt and ground black pepper

Two 1-pound beef strip steaks, each about 1 inch thick, trimmed and patted dry

1 tablespoon grapeseed or other neutral oil

In a 12-inch skillet over medium-high, heat the olive oil until shimmering. Add the garlic and cook, stirring, until beginning to turn golden, 30 to 60 seconds. Add the anchovies and pepper flakes; cook, stirring, until fragrant, 30 to 60 seconds. Stir in the tomatoes with juices, a few basil leaves and ¼ teaspoon salt. Bring to a simmer, then simmer, stirring occasionally, until a spatula drawn through the sauce leaves a trail, 12 to 14 minutes. Transfer to a small bowl, cover and set aside; wipe out the skillet.

Season the steaks on both sides with salt and black pepper. In the same skillet over medium-high, heat the neutral oil until barely smoking. Add the steaks, reduce to medium and cook until well browned on the bottoms, 5 to 7 minutes. Using tongs, flip the steaks and cook until the second sides are well browned and the centers register 120°F for medium-rare, another 5 to 7 minutes. Transfer to a platter, tent with foil and let rest for about 10 minutes.

Transfer the steaks to a cutting board and slice them on the diagonal ¼ to ½ inch thick. Return to the platter and spoon on some of the sauce. Tear the remaining basil and sprinkle it over the top, then drizzle with additional olive oil. Serve the remaining sauce on the side.

Cast Iron–Seared Thick-Cut Porterhouse

Start to finish: 30 minutes
Servings: 4

A cast-iron skillet is ideal for searing steaks because it distributes heat evenly and retains it well, which translates to deep, flavorful browning. In this recipe, we cook a porterhouse that's large enough to serve four, then carve the meat off the bone for serving. Because the steak is very thick, it's important for even cooking that it be at room temperature before it hits the skillet. This means taking the steak out of the refrigerator at least 30 minutes before you're ready to cook it. The fat will smoke during cooking—it's unavoidable—but you can turn down the burner a bit to reduce the smoking; it's also a good idea to turn on the hood or open a window. A digital thermometer is the best way to test for doneness, however be sure to temp the center of the loin side—the larger, longer muscle on the steak—without touching the bone. A simple no-cook sauce allows the porterhouse to be the star of the meal. We offer a tangy, bright parsley sauce below.

2-pound bone-in porterhouse steak (about 2½ inches thick), patted dry, room temperature

Kosher salt and ground black pepper

1 tablespoon grapeseed or other neutral oil

Flaky sea salt (optional)

Season the steak all over with salt and pepper. In a 12-inch cast-iron skillet over medium-high, heat the oil until barely smoking. Place the steak in the skillet and press it down to ensure the bottom makes contact with the pan. Cook, undisturbed, until well browned on the bottom, 7 to 10 minutes; reduce the heat slightly if the oil is smoking rapidly.

Using tongs, flip the steak and continue to cook until the second side is well browned and the center of the loin side reaches 120°F for medium-rare, another 6 to 8 minutes. Transfer the steak to a cutting board. Tent with foil and let rest for 10 minutes.

Cut the meat from the bone and thinly slice it. Place on a platter, with the bone (if desired), and drizzle on the juices. Sprinkle with salt (flaky sea salt, if using) and pepper.

Parsley Sauce

Start to finish: 15 minutes
Makes about 1¼ cups

In a small bowl, stir together **½ cup extra-virgin olive oil, 1 cup lightly packed fresh flat-leaf parsley** (finely chopped), **¼ medium red onion** (minced), **2 tablespoons red wine vinegar, ½ teaspoon red pepper flakes** and **¼ teaspoon kosher salt.** Taste and season with additional vinegar and salt, if needed. Use immediately or refrigerate in an airtight container for up to 3 days.

BEEF

483

VIETNAMESE SHAKING BEEF

Start to finish: 30 minutes

Servings: 4

The name of this Vietnamese dish refers to the way cooks shake the pan while the beef cooks. We preferred to minimize the movement, searing the beef to build flavor. Sirloin tips (also called flap meat) or tri-tip are excellent cuts for this recipe—both are meaty, tender and reasonably priced (many recipes for shaking beef call for pricier beef tenderloin). If you can find baby watercress, use a 4-ounce container in place of the regular watercress; baby cress has a particularly peppery bite that pairs well with the beef. Serve with steamed jasmine rice.

1½ pounds beef sirloin tips or tri-tip, trimmed, patted dry, cut into 1½-inch pieces

3 tablespoons soy sauce, divided

Kosher salt and ground black pepper

5 tablespoons lime juice, divided, plus lime wedges, to serve

3 tablespoons fish sauce

2 tablespoons white sugar

2 tablespoons grapeseed or other neutral oil, divided

8 medium garlic cloves, finely chopped

1 small red onion, sliced ¼ inch thick

1 bunch watercress, stemmed

In a medium bowl, toss the beef with 2 tablespoons of the soy sauce and ½ teaspoon pepper. In a small bowl, stir together 4 tablespoons of the lime juice, the fish sauce, sugar and remaining 1 tablespoon soy sauce.

In a 12-inch skillet over medium-high, heat 1 tablespoon of the oil until barely smoking. Swirl to coat the pan, then add the beef in a single layer. Cook without stirring until well browned, about 1½ minutes. Flip and cook until browned on the other side, 1½ minutes. Transfer to a medium bowl.

To the same skillet, add the remaining 1 tablespoon oil, the garlic and 1 teaspoon pepper. Cook over low, stirring constantly, until fragrant and the garlic is no longer raw, about 30 seconds. Pour in the lime juice mixture and any accumulated meat juices (don't add the meat), increase to medium-high and cook, stirring constantly, until the spoon leaves a trail when dragged across the skillet, 2 to 4 minutes.

Add the beef and cook, stirring and scraping up any browned bits, until the sauce clings lightly to the meat, about 2 minutes. Add the onion and stir until slightly softened, about 1 minute. Remove from the heat.

In a bowl, toss the watercress with the remaining 1 table-spoon lime juice and ¼ teaspoon salt. Make a bed of the watercress on a serving platter. Top with the beef mixture and its juices. Serve with lime wedges.

STEAK WITH SMOKY TOMATO BUTTER, SHALLOTS AND WILTED FRISÉE

Start to finish: 45 minutes

Servings: 4

This easy but delicious steak dinner is an adaptation of a recipe in "Gjelina" by Travis Lett, and it gets an impressive meal on the table in well under an hour. Softened butter mixed with smoked paprika, garlic and minced sun-dried tomatoes melts onto simple pan-seared flat iron steaks as they rest. Meanwhile, we sauté shallots, deglaze the pan and quickly wilt in some frisée (or watercress). Warm crusty bread is all you need on the side.

2 tablespoons salted butter, room temperature

¾ teaspoon smoked paprika

3 oil-packed sun-dried tomatoes, patted dry and finely chopped

1 medium garlic clove, finely grated

1 teaspoon sherry vinegar

1½ pounds flat iron steak, cut crosswise into 3 pieces

Kosher salt and ground black pepper

2 tablespoons grapeseed or other neutral oil, divided

4 medium shallots, sliced into ¼-inch rings

¼ cup Madeira or dry sherry

1 small head frisée, cored and torn into bite-size pieces or 1 bunch watercress, trimmed of tough stems

Lemon wedges, to serve

In a small bowl, mash together the butter, paprika, tomatoes, garlic and vinegar; set aside. Season the steaks with salt and pepper.

In a 12-inch skillet over medium-high, heat 1 tablespoon of oil until barely smoking. Add the steak and cook until well browned on both sides and the centers reach 125°F (for medium-rare), 8 to 12 minutes, flipping the pieces once about halfway through. Transfer to a large plate; reserve the skillet. Dollop the butter mixture onto the steak, tent with foil and let rest for 5 minutes.

In the same skillet over medium-high, heat the remaining 1 tablespoon oil until shimmering. Add the shallots and cook, stirring often, until lightly browned, 1 to 3 minutes. Add the wine and ¼ cup water; cook, scraping up the browned bits, until the liquid is syrupy, about 2 minutes. Off heat, add the frisée and quickly turn to coat (do not allow the greens to fully wilt), then taste and season with salt and pepper. Transfer to a platter.

Thinly slice the steak against the grain, then arrange on top of the frisée. Pour on the accumulated juices. Serve with lemon wedges.

....

CHILEAN BEEF, TOMATO AND CORN SAUTÉ

Start to finish: 35 minutes
Serves: 4 to 6

The Chilean comfort food called tomaticán matches sweet, summery tomatoes and corn with savory beef and onions. Though it sometimes is referred to as a stew, it's actually a quick-cooking skillet dish perfect for a weeknight dinner. The recipe from "The Chilean Kitchen" by Pilar Hernandez and Eileen Smith, who aptly describe tomaticán as a "juicy sauté," inspired our version. Serve with rice or potatoes on the side.

1 tablespoon ground cumin

Kosher salt and ground black pepper

1½ pounds beef sirloin steak tips or flat iron steak, cut against the grain on the diagonal into ⅛-inch-thick strips

3 tablespoons extra-virgin olive oil, divided

1 medium yellow onion, halved and thinly sliced

3 ripe medium tomatoes (about 1 pound), cored and cut into ½-inch wedges

1 cup frozen corn kernels, thawed

1 cup lightly packed fresh flat-leaf parsley or cilantro, chopped

1 ripe avocado, halved, pitted, peeled and chopped

Lime wedges, to serve

In a large bowl, stir together the cumin and 1 teaspoon each salt and pepper. Measure 2 teaspoons into a small bowl; set aside. Add the beef to the remaining seasoning mixture and toss to coat.

In a 12-inch skillet over medium-high, heat 2 tablespoons of oil until barely smoking. Add half of the beef in an even layer and cook, without stirring, until browned on the bottom, 1 to 2 minutes. Using tongs, transfer to a plate, leaving the fat in the pan. Cook the remaining beef in the same way, then transfer to the plate.

To the skillet over medium-high, add the remaining 1 tablespoon oil, the onion and a pinch of salt. Cook, scraping up any browned bits, until the onion begins brown, 2 to 3 minutes. Add the tomatoes, corn and the reserved seasoning mix, then cook, stirring occasionally, until the tomatoes begin to soften, about 3 minutes. Add the beef and accumulated juices along with the parsley and cook, stirring, just until heated through, about 1 minute. Taste and season with salt and pepper. Transfer to a serving dish, top with the avocado and serve with lime wedges.

Oven-Perfect Strip Steak with Chimichurri

Start to finish: 1¼ hours (15 minutes active),
plus refrigeration / Servings: 4 to 6

This recipe uses the gentle, controlled heat of the oven to replicate the "reverse sear" technique Argentinians use when grilling beef. Rather than start the steak over high heat to brown, then finish over low heat, the steaks start in a cool oven, then finish with a quick sear in either a blistering-hot cast-iron skillet or on a grill. The result is steak with a deep, flavorful crust that's evenly cooked throughout, not overdone at the surface and just-right at only the core. We call for strip steaks (also called strip loin or New York strip), but bone-in or boneless ribeyes work well, too, as long as they're 1½ to 2 inches thick. We learned to season cuts of beef with nutmeg at La Carbrera in Buenos Aires; the spice doesn't leave a distinct flavor of its own but rather enhances the steaks' meatiness and smoky notes.

Kosher salt and ground black pepper

**1 tablespoon freshly grated nutmeg
(from 2 whole nutmegs)**

2 teaspoons white sugar

**Two 20-ounce strip steaks
(each about 2 inches thick), patted dry**

2 tablespoons grapeseed or other neutral oil

Red Chimichurri (recipe follows)

Set a wire rack in a rimmed baking sheet. In a small bowl, stir together 1 tablespoon each salt and pepper, the nutmeg and sugar. Measure out and reserve 2 teaspoons of the seasoning mixture, then rub the remainder onto all sides of the steaks, pressing it into the meat. Place the steaks on the prepared rack and refrigerate uncovered for at least 1 hour or up to 24 hours.

Heat the oven to 250°F with a rack in the middle position.

Place the baking sheet with the steaks in the oven and cook until the centers reach 110°F, 45 to 55 minutes. Remove from the oven and let stand for up to 30 minutes.

In a 10- or 12-inch cast-iron skillet over medium-high, heat the oil until barely smoking. Place the steaks in the skillet and cook, without moving them, until well browned, about

3 minutes. Using tongs, flip the steaks and cook until the second sides are well browned and the centers reach 120°F (for medium-rare), 2 to 3 minutes. Alternatively, the steaks can be seared for the same time over direct heat on a very hot charcoal or gas grill with a well-oiled grate.

Transfer the steaks to a carving board and let rest for 10 minutes, then cut into thin slices. Place on a platter, pour on the accumulated juices and sprinkle with the reserved seasoning mixture. Drizzle with a few spoonfuls of chimichurri and serve with additional chimichurri on the side.

Chimichurri

In a small saucepan over low, combine **¾ cup neutral oil**, **¼ cup sweet paprika**, **¼ cup red pepper flakes** and **¼ cup dried oregano**. Cook, stirring occasionally, until the mixture begins to bubble, 5 to 7 minutes. Off heat, stir in **2 medium garlic cloves** (finely grated). Cool to room temperature. In a medium bowl, stir together **½ cup balsamic vinegar** and **½ teaspoon salt** until the salt dissolves. Whisk in the cooled oil mixture.

SOMALI-STYLE BEEF AND VEGETABLES

Start to finish: 40 minutes
Servings: 4 to 6

Suqaar is a simple, homey Somali dish of meat and vegetables cooked together in the same pan. Lamb typically is the meat of choice, but in our take we opt for beef. And instead of bell pepper, a common ingredient in suqaar, we add kale, a vegetable not often used in the dish; we like the way the leaves wilt and pull together the other elements while also adding substance and savoriness. A mix of bold, fragrant spices is added in two stages for layered flavor—it seasons the beef before it's seared and also is added to the vegetables as they cook. Serve with rice or a baguette, with lime wedges alongside.

1 tablespoon ground cumin

2 teaspoons ground turmeric

1 teaspoon ground coriander

½ teaspoon ground cinnamon

Kosher salt and ground black pepper

1 pound beef sirloin tips or flank steak, cut with the grain into sections about 4 inches wide, then sliced against the grain about ¼ inch thick

2 tablespoons grapeseed or other neutral oil

1 medium yellow onion, halved and thinly sliced

3 plum tomatoes, cored and chopped

2 medium carrots, peeled and sliced about ¼ thick

1 bunch lacinato kale, stemmed and chopped

½ cup lightly packed fresh cilantro

In a medium bowl, stir together the cumin, turmeric, coriander, cinnamon and ½ teaspoon each salt and pepper. Measure 1 tablespoon into a small bowl and set aside. To the remaining spice mix, add the beef and toss to combine.

In a 12-inch skillet over medium-high, heat the oil until shimmering. Add the beef in an even layer and cook without stirring until browned on the bottom, about 1 minute. Stir, redistribute in an even layer and cook until no longer pink, about 1 minute, then transfer to a large plate.

Set the skillet over medium and add the onion and tomatoes. Cook, scraping up any browned bits and stirring occasionally, until the onion begins to soften, about

5 minutes. Stir in the reserved spice mix, followed by the carrots and ¼ cup water. Bring to a simmer, then cover and cook, stirring occasionally, until the carrots are tender-crisp, about 5 minutes.

Pile on the kale, then cover and cook until the leaves begin to wilt, about 1 minute. Uncover and cook, turning the mixture with tongs, until the kale is tender, about another 1 minute. Add the beef and any accumulated juices, then cook, stirring, until the beef is heated through, 1 to 2 minutes. Off heat, taste and season with salt and pepper, then stir in the cilantro.

ROPA VIEJA

Start to finish: 4 hours (30 minutes active)
Servings: 8

Ropa vieja, considered by many to be the national dish of Cuba, is a stewy mixture of shredded beef with tomatoes, onions and bell peppers, often accented with briny olives. The name translates as "old clothes," a reference to the tattered look of the slow-simmered and shredded meat.

We preferred flank steak for its rich, meaty flavor and unique muscle structure—the fibers shred easily after braising. Look for an extra-large flank steak, which should weigh about 3 pounds, or multiple steaks if you can't find one that large. We like ropa vieja served with rice and beans, along with fresh, crunchy red and white slaw (see below).

3 pounds flank steak, halved lengthwise with the grain, then halved crosswise across the grain

Kosher salt and ground black pepper

3 tablespoons cumin seeds

3 tablespoons coriander seeds

2 tablespoons extra-virgin olive oil

2 medium white onions, halved and thinly sliced lengthwise

2 red bell peppers, stemmed, seeded and sliced ½ inch thick

2 jalapeño chilies, stemmed and sliced into thin rounds

10 medium garlic cloves, peeled

28-ounce can whole peeled tomatoes, crushed

1 cup low-sodium beef broth or water

1 cup pimento-stuffed green olives, roughly chopped

3 tablespoons lime juice, plus lime wedges to serve

Heat the oven to 350°F with a rack in the lower-middle position. Season the meat on both sides with salt and pepper; set aside. In a large Dutch oven over medium, toast the cumin and coriander seeds until fragrant, 1 to 3 minutes. Transfer to a spice grinder and let cool slightly, then pulse until coarsely ground, about 10 pulses; set aside.

In the same pot over medium-high, stir together the oil, onions, bell peppers, jalapeños, garlic, spice mixture and ¾ teaspoon salt. Cover and cook, stirring occasionally, until the vegetables are softened and beginning to brown, 8 to 10 minutes. Stir in the tomatoes and cook, stirring occasionally, until most of the liquid has evaporated, 5 to 7 minutes. Nestle the meat into the vegetables so the pieces are partially submerged. Add the broth, then cover and bake for 2 hours.

Uncover the pot and continue to cook until a paring knife inserted into the meat meets no resistance, about another 1 hour. Remove from the oven and let rest for 20 to 30 minutes.

Using kitchen shears, snip the meat, still in the pot, across the grain into rough 1-inch lengths. Stir in the olives and lime juice, gently breaking up the meat, then taste and season with salt and pepper. Serve with lime wedges.

RED AND WHITE SLAW

Start to finish: 45 minutes (15 minutes active)
Makes about 2 cups

This simple, colorful slaw is great served with ropa vieja . The flavors and textures are best the day the slaw is made.

¼ small head (8 ounces) red cabbage, cored and shredded

¼ small head (8 ounces) green cabbage, cored and shredded

1 jalapeño chili, stemmed and minced

Kosher salt and ground black pepper

¼ cup lime juice

1 tablespoon grapeseed or other neutral oil

¼ cup finely chopped fresh cilantro

3 scallions, thinly sliced

In a medium bowl, toss both cabbages with the jalapeño and 1 teaspoon salt. Cover and refrigerate for at least 30 minutes or up to 1 hour. Stir in the lime juice, oil, cilantro and scallions. Taste and season with salt and pepper.

BEEF BULGOGI

Start to finish: 1¼ hours (35 minutes active),
plus marinating / Servings: 4

Salty, sweet and garlicky, with rich meatiness and an ultra-tender texture, beef bulgogi is a Korean standard. The name translates as "fire meat," and though bulgogi sometimes is charred over flames or cooked on a dome-shaped tabletop grill, when prepared at home it is simply sautéed or stir-fried on the stovetop. Ryan Phillips, a Korean-American chef living in Seoul, taught us his recipe for home-style bulgogi. The soy-based marinade comes together easily and quickly in a blender. It includes Asian pear, which adds subtle sweetness and fruitiness as well as enzymes that help tenderize the meat. Asian pears are seasonal and can sometimes be pricey; if you prefer, a regular ripe pear of any variety is a good stand-in. As for the meat, we tried various cuts and favored rib-eye and strip steak; top sirloin also is a good, more economical cut. Whichever you use, the beef needs to be thinly sliced on the bias to help make the meat more tender. Serve with steamed rice and tangy, spicy kimchi.

1½ pounds rib-eye, strip or top sirloin steak, preferably about 1 inch thick, trimmed of exterior fat and silver skin

8 ounces Asian pear (see headnote), peeled, cored and roughly chopped

5 medium garlic cloves, smashed and peeled

1-inch piece fresh ginger, peeled and cut into 4 or 5 pieces

¼ cup soy sauce

3 tablespoons honey

2 tablespoons mirin

2 tablespoons toasted sesame oil

2 scallions, white and green parts separated but left whole

Kosher salt and ground black pepper

2 teaspoons sesame seeds, toasted

2 tablespoons grapeseed or other neutral oil

Place the beef on a plate and freeze, uncovered, until the surface is firm, about 20 minutes. In a blender, combine the pear, garlic, ginger, soy sauce, honey, mirin, sesame oil, scallion whites, ½ teaspoon salt and ¾ teaspoon pepper. Blend, scraping the jar as needed, until smooth, about 1 minute. Pour into a medium bowl.

Transfer the partially frozen meat to a cutting board. Using a sharp knife, slice the beef diagonally as thinly as possible. Add the meat to the marinade and mix until evenly coated. Cover and refrigerate for at least 2 hours, stirring once or twice, or up to 24 hours, stirring a few times.

About 30 minutes before cooking, remove the beef from the refrigerator and let stand at room temperature; this makes the marinade more fluid so more will drain off. When ready to cook, set a colander in a medium bowl. Drain the beef mixture in the colander, tossing so as much marinade as possible drains off; reserve the marinade. Thinly slice the scallion greens on the diagonal; set aside.

In a 12-inch skillet over medium-high, heat the neutral oil until barely smoking. Add the beef in an even layer, then immediately increase to high. Cook without stirring until the areas at the edges of the pan are well caramelized, 1 to 2 minutes. Stir and cook, stirring only once or twice, until the meat is spottily browned and only 1 to 2 tablespoons liquid remains in the pan, another 4 to 6 minutes.

Add the reserved marinade and cook, stirring, until the marinade has reduced and coats the beef, 1 to 2 minutes. Remove from the heat, then taste and season with salt and pepper. Transfer to a serving dish. Sprinkle with the scallion greens and sesame seeds.

BEEF SUYA

Start to finish: 45 minutes (30 minutes active)
Servings: 4

Eaten on the spot or carried away wrapped in newspaper, the street snack known as suya is popular throughout Nigeria. Suya usually is made with thin strips of beef, but it's the spice rub that sets it apart—typically a blend of ground peanuts, red pepper and other seasonings. For our version of suya, we like flat iron steak, which is easily cut into long, ½-inch-thick strips; look for a single 1½-pound piece. Blade steaks, also known as top blade, are a similar cut and are sometimes labeled flat iron; they are sold in smaller portions and a line of gristle runs down the center of each piece. If you opt for blade steaks, choose the thickest you can find and remove the gristle (which means cutting each steak into two pieces) before slicing the meat into strips. The best way to check the meat for doneness is to cut into a piece at the center of a skewer; it should be medium-rare. We liked serving the suya with cucumber, tomato, cabbage and onion—cooling counterparts to the spicy beef.

½ cup unsalted dry-roasted peanuts

1 tablespoon sweet paprika

1 tablespoon ground ginger

1 tablespoon garlic powder

1 tablespoon onion powder

2 teaspoons packed light brown sugar

1 teaspoon cayenne pepper

Kosher salt and ground black pepper

3 tablespoons grapeseed or other neutral oil

1½ pounds flat iron steak, sliced against the grain into ½-inch-thick strips

1 tablespoon lime juice, plus lime wedges, to serve

In a food processor, combine the peanuts, paprika, ginger, garlic powder, onion powder, sugar, cayenne, ½ teaspoon salt and 1 teaspoon black pepper. Process until finely ground, about 20 seconds. Reserve ⅓ cup of the spice mix, then transfer the rest to a medium bowl; add the oil and stir to form a paste.

In a large bowl, combine the beef with ½ teaspoon of salt. Toss and massage until evenly coated. Add the paste to the

beef, tossing and massaging into the meat. Thread the beef tightly onto four 12-inch metal skewers, fitting multiple pieces of meat on each skewer; they should be tightly packed.

Place the skewers on a wire rack set in a foil-lined rimmed baking sheet. Heat the broiler with a rack set about 4 inches from the element. Broil until well-browned, about 5 minutes, flipping halfway through. Transfer to a plate and let rest for 5 minutes.

Brush the lime juice on both sides of the skewers, then sprinkle with the reserved spice mix. Serve with lime wedges.

ESPETADA-STYLE GRILLED GARLIC AND BAY BEEF SKEWERS

Start to finish: 1 hour 50 minutes (45 minutes active
Servings: 4 to 6

On the Portuguese island of Madeira, espetada refers to beef skewers redolent with garlic and fresh bay. The meat is threaded not onto metal or bamboo but onto fresh-cut branches of bay (also known as laurel) and cooked over the embers of a fire. The bay infuses the meat with its unique menthol notes while also releasing a heady aroma. To re-create espetada at home, we pulverize dried bay leaves in a spice grinder to make a seasoned salt, mix in garlic and olive oil and allow the meat to marinate before threading it onto metal skewers and grilling over charcoal or gas. Flat iron steak or beef sirloin tips offer the best combination of tender texture and rich flavor, but if you're up for a splurge, beef tenderloin also is excellent. Though a bit unconventional, we make a simple Madeira reduction to finish the dish. Seasoned with garlic and some of the bay salt, the glaze-like sauce bolsters the flavors of the beef. Traditionally, espetada is served with a sweet-potato bread called bolo de caco; soft rolls are a good stand-in.

10 dried bay leaves, crumbled

Kosher salt and ground black pepper

**6 medium garlic cloves, finely grated
(about 1½ tablespoons)**

**1 tablespoon plus 2 teaspoons
extra-virgin olive oil, divided**

**2 pounds beef sirloin tips or flat iron steak,
cut into 1½-inch cubes**

½ cup Madeira

**2 tablespoons salted butter, cut into
2 pieces and chilled**

In a spice grinder, combine the bay, 1½ teaspoons salt and 1 teaspoon pepper, then pulverize to a fine powder. In a medium bowl, combine 2 teaspoons of the bay salt, 1 tablespoon of the garlic and 1 tablespoon oil, then use a fork to mash until well combined. Add the beef and toss, rubbing the seasonings into the meat. Thread the beef onto four 10- to 12-inch metal skewers. Place in a large baking dish or on a rimmed baking sheet. Cover and refrigerate for 1 hour or up to 1 day.

Meanwhile, in a small saucepan over medium, heat the remaining 2 teaspoons oil and the remaining bay salt, stirring, until fragrant and sizzling, about 3 minutes. Add the remaining ½ tablespoon garlic and cook, stirring, until fragrant and sizzling, about 10 seconds. Add the Madeira and bring to a simmer, then reduce to low and cook, stirring, until reduced to 2 tablespoons. Cover and set aside off heat.

Prepare a charcoal or gas grill. For a charcoal grill, ignite a large chimney of coals, let burn until lightly ashed over, then distribute evenly over one side of the grill bed; open the bottom grill vents. Heat the grill, covered, for 5 to 10 minutes, then clean and oil the grate. For a gas grill, turn all burners to high and heat, covered, for 15 minutes, then clean and oil the grate.

Place the skewers on the hot side of the grill (if using charcoal). Cook uncovered until the beef is lightly charred on both sides and the center of the thickest piece reaches 125°F for medium-rare, 8 to 12 minutes total, flipping once about halfway through. Transfer to a platter, tent with foil and let rest while you finish the sauce.

Set the pan containing the Madeira reduction over medium and heat uncovered just until steaming. Remove from the heat, add the butter and swirl the pan until the butter is melted and the sauce is emulsified. Remove the meat from the skewers and drizzle with the sauce.

SPICY CHINESE BEEF SKEWERS

Start to finish: 45 minutes
Servings: 4

Street vendors in China sell sizzling skewers of meat hot off the grill, rich with cumin and chilies. Some of the heady spice mixture goes onto the beef just before cooking; the rest is sprinkled on at the end. To make lamb skewers instead of beef, called yang rou chuan, substitute boneless lamb shoulder or leg; make sure to slice the meat against the grain. Though these are typically enjoyed as a snack, if served with some steamed rice and stir-fried vegetables, the skewers make a satisfying dinner.

1½ pounds beef flat iron steak, sliced against the grain into ¼-inch-thick strips

1 tablespoon dry sherry or Shaoxing wine

1 tablespoon soy sauce

2 tablespoons grapeseed or other neutral oil, plus more for grill grate

2½ tablespoons cumin seeds

2½ teaspoons fennel seeds

1½ teaspoons Sichuan peppercorns

2 teaspoons red pepper flakes

Kosher salt

Chili oil, to serve (optional)

In a medium bowl, combine the beef, sherry, soy sauce and oil. Let stand at room temperature while preparing the spice mix and the grill.

In a small skillet over medium-low, toast the cumin, fennel and Sichuan peppercorns until fragrant, about 2 minutes. Transfer to a spice grinder and add the pepper flakes. Process until coarsely ground, about 10 seconds. Transfer to a small bowl and stir in 1 teaspoon salt. Measure out 1 tablespoon of the mix and set aside to use as garnish.

Prepare a charcoal or gas grill for direct, high-heat cooking. For a charcoal grill, ignite a large chimney of coals and let burn until lightly ashed over, then distribute the coals evenly over one side of the grill bed; open the bottom grill vents and the lid vent. For a gas grill, turn all burners to high. Heat the grill, covered, for 10 to 15 minutes, then clean and oil the cooking grate.

While the grill heats, thread the beef onto ten 8- to 10-inch metal skewers, evenly dividing the meat and pushing the pieces together. Sprinkle the spice mixture evenly over both sides of the meat, patting gently to adhere.

Grill until lightly charred, 2 to 3 minutes, then flip and grill until the second sides are lightly charred, another 2 minutes. Transfer to a serving platter, sprinkle both sides of the skewers with the reserved spice mix, then drizzle with chili oil (if using).

OVEN-COOKING METHOD

Follow the recipe through making and portioning the spice mix. Heat the broiler with a rack about 4 inches from the element. Line a rimmed baking sheet with foil, then set a wire rack in the baking sheet. While the broiler heats, thread the beef onto ten 8- to 10-inch metal skewers, evenly dividing the meat. Sprinkle the spice mix evenly over both sides of the meat, patting gently to adhere. Evenly space the skewers on the rack and broil until well browned, 2 to 3 minutes, then flip each skewer and grill until the second sides are well browned, another 2 to 3 minutes. Transfer to a serving platter, sprinkle both sides of the skewers with the reserved spice mix, then drizzle with chili oil, if using.

BEEF AND POTATO CURRY WITH LEMON GRASS AND COCONUT

Start to finish: 45 minutes
Servings: 4

Southeast Asian curries combine Indian influences with regional ingredients such as lemon grass and star anise. For this one, we took inspiration from a recipe in "Best of Malaysian Cooking" by Betty Saw, but instead of calling for a long list of spices, we use Indian curry powder as an easy flavor base; sambal oelek, an Indonesian-style chili paste, adds bright heat to the dish. Look for sambal in well-stocked supermarkets and Asian grocery stores; if it's not available, chili-garlic paste is a good substitute. Serve the curry with lime wedges and jasmine rice.

1½ pounds boneless beef short ribs, trimmed and sliced ⅛ inch thick against the grain

Kosher salt and ground black pepper

2 tablespoons grapeseed or other neutral oil

1 medium red onion, halved thinly sliced

3 medium garlic cloves, smashed and peeled

1½ tablespoons finely grated fresh ginger

2 stalks fresh lemon grass, trimmed to the bottom 6 inches, dry outer layers discarded, bruised

2 tablespoons curry powder

2 star anise pods

1 pound small Yukon Gold potatoes (about 1½ inches in diameter), unpeeled, halved

14-ounce can coconut milk

1 tablespoon sambal oelek or chili-garlic paste, plus more as needed

Season the beef with salt and pepper; set aside. In a large Dutch oven over medium-high, heat the oil until shimmering. Add the onion, garlic, ginger, lemon grass, curry powder, star anise and ½ teaspoon salt. Cook, stirring often, until the onion begins to soften and the mixture is fragrant, about 3 minutes.

Add the beef, potatoes, coconut milk and sambal, then bring to a simmer, scraping the bottom of the pot. Reduce to medium-low, cover and cook, stirring occasionally, until a skewer inserted into the largest potatoes meets no resistance, about 30 minutes.

Off heat, taste and season with salt, pepper and additional sambal. Remove and discard the star anise and lemon grass.

KOREAN GRILLED MARINATED SHORT RIBS

Start to finish: 4 hours (45 minutes active), plus grill prep / Servings: 6

Yangneom galbi, commonly referred to as just "galbi," which translates from the Korean as "rib"—is what comes to mind when most people think of Korean barbecue. Thin-cut beef short ribs marinated in a garlicky soy mixture and cooked quickly on a hot grill are sweet, salty, meaty, fatty, charred, chewy-tender and utterly delicious. This recipe, from Hooni Kim's "My Korea," uses thin flanken-style short ribs. This cut of short rib includes three sections of crosscut bone to which a strip of meat is attached. Flanken-style ribs are sold in some supermarkets, but typically are too thick for galbi, so shop carefully. The ribs to purchase should be no thicker than ¼ inch. Finding them may require a trip to the butcher or to a Korean market, if you have one nearby. If you cannot find thin flanken-style short ribs, use about 2½ pounds skirt steak; cut the steak into 6- to 8-inch sections and marinate for no more than about four hours. Asian pear, an ingredient in the marinade, is seasonal and is easiest to find in the fall and winter. If not available, Kim recommends using a green apple in its place. Galbi is commonly served with lettuce leaves for wrapping pieces of meat and ssamjang, a pungent, salty, umami-rich condiment for spreading onto the lettuce. But feel free to skip these flourishes, as the ribs are great with only steamed rice and kimchi.

1 Asian pear (see headnote), peeled, cored and cut into rough 1-inch chunks

10 medium garlic cloves, smashed and peeled

2-inch piece fresh ginger, peeled and roughly chopped

½ cup sake

½ cup soy sauce

⅓ cup white sugar

¼ cup mirin

Ground black pepper

3 pounds thin (⅛- to ¼-inch-thick) bone-in, flanken-cut beef short ribs (see headnote)

Lettuce leaves, to serve

Ssamjang, to serve (optional)

In a blender, combine the pear, garlic, ginger, sake, soy sauce, sugar, mirin and ½ teaspoon pepper. Blend until smooth, 15 to 20 seconds. Pour the mixture into a 9-by-13-inch baking dish. Add the short ribs, turning them to coat with the marinade, and arrange in an even layer; the ribs should be mostly submerged. Cover and refrigerate for at least 2 hours or up to 24 hours, turning them once or twice to ensure they marinate evenly.

Prepare a charcoal or gas grill. For a charcoal grill, ignite a large chimney of coals, let burn until lightly ashed over, then distribute evenly over one side of the grill bed; open the bottom grill vents. Heat the grill, covered, for 5 minutes, then clean and oil the grate. For a gas grill, turn all burners to high and heat, covered, for 15 minutes, then clean and oil the grate.

Transfer the short ribs from the marinade to a large plate, allowing excess marinade to drip off. Place as many ribs as will comfortably fit on the grill grate (on the hot side if using charcoal). Cook, uncovered, until nicely charred on the bottom, 2 to 3 minutes. Using tongs, flip the ribs and grill until the second sides are nicely charred, about 2 minutes, then transfer to a platter. If not all ribs fit onto the grill, cook the remainder in the same way.

Serve the ribs with lettuce leaves and ssamjang (if using). To eat, smear a little ssamjang on a piece of lettuce, cut a piece of meat from the bone and wrap it in the lettuce.

JAPANESE-STYLE BEEF CURRY

Start to finish: 1 hour (20 minutes active)
Servings: 4 to 6

Curry likely arrived in Japan in the late 19th century with the British who occupied India at the time. The dish was adapted to suit local palates, and Japanese curry, as we now know it, is a much-loved food the world over. It is essentially a thick, savory-sweet, spiced sauce—sometimes ingredients are cooked in it, sometimes the sauce is spooned onto fried cutlets or even plain rice. Most home cooks use store-bought curry "bricks" to make Japanese curry, but we use a mixture of curry powder and garam masala to approximate the flavor. Serve this with steamed short-grain rice and, if you can find it, fukujinzuke, a crunchy, sweet-salty Japanese relish that almost always accompanies curry.

1½ pounds boneless beef short ribs, trimmed and cut into ½-inch chunks

¼ cup all-purpose flour

3 tablespoons neutral oil

1 medium yellow onion, finely chopped

2 tablespoons finely grated fresh ginger

1 tablespoon curry powder

1 tablespoon garam masala

3 cups low-sodium chicken broth

3 tablespoons soy sauce, plus more if needed

2 tablespoons mirin

2 large carrots, peeled, halved lengthwise and sliced ¼ inch thick

½ cup thinly sliced scallions, for garnish

In a medium bowl, toss the beef with the flour until well coated and no flour remains. In a large pot over medium-high, heat the oil until shimmering. Add the beef, reduce to medium and cook, stirring, until lightly browned, about 3 minutes.

Add the onion and ginger. Cook, stirring, until the onion has softened, 2 to 3 minutes. Sprinkle in the curry and garam masala, then cook, stirring, until fragrant, about 30 seconds. Add the broth, soy sauce and mirin, scraping up any browned bits. Bring to a boil, then reduce to medium-low and simmer, uncovered and stirring occasionally, until a skewer inserted into the beef meets no resistance, about 25 minutes.

Add the carrots and cook until tender, 7 to 9 minutes. Remove from the heat, then taste and season with additional soy sauce, if needed. Top with the scallions.

GROUND BEEF AND CHICKPEA CURRY

Start to finish: 40 minutes
Servings: 4

Keema means minced meat; chole translates as chickpeas. Put the two together and you get this easy-to-make but flavorful and satisfying main. We season the curry with garlic, ginger and select spices, and a small can of tomatoes helps form a rich, lightly tangy sauce. If you like, use ground lamb in place of the beef. Prep the cilantro during the simmer time and dinner can be on the table in under 45 minutes. We like this keema chole garnished with sliced jalapeños and plain yogurt, and with lemon wedges and warm flatbread on the side.

2 tablespoons grapeseed or other neutral oil

1 medium yellow onion, chopped

Kosher salt and ground black pepper

3 medium garlic cloves, minced

2 tablespoons minced fresh ginger

2 teaspoons ground cumin

2 teaspoons ground coriander

1 teaspoon ground turmeric

1 pound 90 percent lean ground beef or ground lamb

15½-ounce can chickpeas, drained

14½-ounce can whole peeled tomatoes, crushed by hand

½ cup lightly packed fresh cilantro, chopped

In a 12-inch skillet over medium, heat the oil until shimmering. Add the onion and ½ teaspoon salt, then cook, stirring occasionally, until beginning to brown, 6 to 7 minutes. Add the garlic, ginger, cumin, coriander, turmeric and ½ teaspoon each salt and pepper; cook, stirring, until fragrant, about 30 seconds. Add the beef and cook, stirring occasionally and breaking the meat into small pieces with a wooden spoon, until no longer pink, 4 to 5 minutes.

Stir in the chickpeas and tomatoes with juices. Bring to a simmer over medium-high, then reduce to medium and simmer, uncovered and stirring occasionally until the tomatoes have broken down and the curry is lightly saucy, 12 to 15 minutes. Off heat, taste and season with salt and pepper. Stir in the cilantro.

BEEF CHILI COLORADO TACOS

Start to finish: 3¾ hours (45 minutes active)
Servings: 6 to 8

Carne en chile colorado is a Mexican classic, and one of the delicious offerings that appear on the rotating menu at Walter Soto's El Ruso taqueria trucks that operate in a couple locations in and around Los Angeles. "Colorado" translates from the Spanish as "red-colored," an apt name for the succulent dish of meat, sometimes shredded, sometimes not, in a sauce of pureed dried red chilies. Pork is commonly used to make chili colorado, but this version is Paola Briseño-González's ode to El Ruso's rich, robust beef in red chili sauce. The cut of choice is a boneless chuck roast, which boasts plenty of fat and connective tissue so that long, slow cooking yields rich, tender, full-flavored meat. Either guajillo or New Mexico chilies work here; you can even use a combination. Both are a deep red color, have bright, fruity notes with subdued earthiness, and contain only mild chili heat. El Ruso also is well known for its flour tortillas, so that's the type to serve with the chili colorado for making tacos.

12 medium (about 2½ ounces) guajillo
or New Mexico chilies, stemmed, seeded
and roughly torn

4 medium garlic cloves, smashed and peeled

1 teaspoon dried Mexican oregano

¼ teaspoon ground cumin

Kosher salt and ground black pepper

3 tablespoons all-purpose flour

2½ pounds boneless beef chuck roast,
trimmed and cut into 3-inch chunks

2 tablespoons grapeseed or other neutral oil

1 medium yellow onion, ½ roughly chopped,
½ finely chopped, reserved separately

2 bay leaves

Warm flour tortillas, to serve

½ cup lightly packed fresh cilantro,
chopped

In a medium saucepan, combine the chilies and enough water to cover by about 1 inch. Bring to a boil over medium-high, pressing on the chilies to submerge them. Remove

from the heat, cover and let stand until the chilies are fully softened, 15 to 20 minutes.

Drain the chilies, discarding the water, and put them in a blender along with the garlic, oregano, cumin, 4 cups water and 1½ teaspoons salt. Blend until smooth, about 2 minutes; set aside.

Spread the flour in a pie plate or other wide, shallow dish. Add the beef, turning to coat all sides. In a large Dutch oven over medium-high, heat the oil until shimmering. Add the beef, shaking off the excess flour, and cook, turning occasionally, until well browned on all sides, about 10 minutes; transfer to a large plate.

Pour off and discard any fat in the pot. Add the chili puree and bring to a simmer over medium, scraping up any browned bits. Stir in the roughly chopped onion and bay, then add the beef and any accumulated juices. Return to a simmer, then cover, reduce to medium-low and cook, stirring occasionally and increasing the heat as needed to maintain a vigorous simmer, for 1 hour. If at this point the braising liquid no longer covers the beef, stir in ½ cup water and return to a simmer. Cook, covered, until a skewer inserted into the largest piece of beef meets no resistance and the sauce has the consistency of heavy cream, about another 1 hour. Remove from the heat and let stand, covered, for about 30 minutes. Remove and discard the bay. Using 2 forks, shred the beef. Return to a simmer over medium, stirring occasionally. Taste and season with salt and pepper. Serve with flour tortillas and with the finely chopped onion and cilantro for making tacos.

PRUNE, PEPPERCORN AND FRESH HERB-RUBBED ROAST BEEF

Start to finish: 2¾ hours, plus 48 hours to marinate

Servings: 10

A prune-based marinade helped us transform an economical eye round into a tender and juicy roast. The sugars in the prunes and ketchup create a nicely caramelized crust, while the salt and soy sauce provide seasoning that flavors the meat throughout. The anchovies may be unexpected, but they add rich umami notes. To boost the marinade's effect, we trim the silver skin and poke the meat repeatedly with a fork. The roast beef tasted best after marinating for 48 hours, but 24 will work, too. Serve thinly sliced with fresh horseradish sauce for a clean, contrasting bite.

8 ounces pitted prunes (about 1½ cups)

½ cup soy sauce

¼ cup ketchup

2 tablespoons black peppercorns

2 tablespoons roughly chopped fresh rosemary

2 tablespoons fresh thyme

3 oil-packed anchovy fillets

Kosher salt

5- to 6-pound beef eye round roast, trimmed of silver skin

Fresh horseradish sauce, to serve (optional)

In a food processor, blend the prunes, soy sauce, ketchup, peppercorns, rosemary, thyme, anchovies and 4 teaspoons salt until smooth, about 1 minute. Transfer to a 2-gallon zip-close bag. Poke the roast all over with a fork, then place in the bag. Turn to coat, then seal the bag and refrigerate for 48 hours.

Heat the oven to 275°F with a rack in the middle position. Set a wire rack in a rimmed baking sheet. Remove the roast from the bag and transfer to the rack. Discard the marinade in the bag and brush any marinade clinging to the roast's surface into an even coating. Roast until the center of the meat registers 125°F, 1¾ hours to 2 hours.

Transfer the roast to a carving board, tent with foil and let rest for 30 minutes. Thinly slice and serve with the horseradish sauce, if desired.

FRESH HORSERADISH SAUCE

Start to finish: 5 minutes
Makes about 1½ cups

We prefer the brightness and intensity of fresh horseradish in this sauce, but prepared horseradish works well, too. If you use bottled, reduce the vinegar to 1 tablespoon. Look for fresh horseradish root in the produce section, often near the fresh ginger. Peel and finely grate the root with a wand-style grater. If you have extra horseradish, try grating it into mashed potatoes, or over a warm steak or pork chop.

1 cup sour cream

½ cup freshly grated horseradish root (3-inch piece)

2 tablespoons white wine vinegar

2 teaspoons minced fresh rosemary

Kosher salt

In a small bowl, stir together the sour cream, horseradish, vinegar, rosemary, ½ teaspoon salt and 1 tablespoon water. Use right away or cover and refrigerate for up to 2 days.

Peppercorns

The most widely used spice in the world, peppercorns are grown throughout the tropics. Their distinctive heat comes not from capsaicin, as with chilies, but from piperine, a similarly warm flavor compound. When and how they are harvested determines their flavor and color. Black, red and white all come from the same plant. Pink and Sichuan peppercorns, though often grouped with other peppercorns, are not from the same species. For best flavor, freshly grind or crack peppercorns just before using.

Black

Black peppercorns are picked unripe, briefly fermented, then dried in the sun, where they shrivel and darken. As with wine, terroir affects flavor—the taste of black peppercorns can vary widely, depending on where they're grown. They generally have a robust burst of heat that doesn't linger. Taste varieties to pick what you like, or blend for the best elements of each. Black peppercorns offer the best flavor and texture when coarsely ground, as in stir-fried black pepper chicken with green beans. Or take advantage of their aromatic qualities by mixing whole peppercorns and bay leaves into white rice before steaming,

White

White peppercorns are ripened longer than black before being fermented, dried and hulled. Since the hulls contain much of a peppercorn's flavor, the variety has a milder taste and aroma. In Europe, it's used in many white sauces; in China, it's a defining flavor of hot-and-sour soup; in Southeast Asia, it's matched with fermented fish products, citrus and sweeteners like palm sugar. Mix with black pepper for an everyday seasoning with complexity; add to gingerbread, or pair with fish sauce, lime and brown sugar for marinades.

Green

Green peppercorns are unripened peppercorns that are consumed fresh, dried or brined. They have a mild, peppery bite and subtly herbaceous finish. They are a particularly popular ingredient in French cooking, as in steak au poivre. In Southeast Asian cooking, sprigs of fresh green peppercorns often are tossed into stir-fries and curries. They pair well with red meat, oily fish and vegetables such as cauliflower. Sprinkle whole brined peppercorns into potato or egg salads and use as a garnish for creamy pastas.

Pink

Pink peppercorns are not true peppercorns, but rather the dried berries of two different species of South American trees. They grow in clusters and turn red when ripe. Dried pink peppercorns are mildly spicy, with a delicate, fruity flavor. Pink peppercorns work well in both sweet and savory applications. Crush them lightly and mix with coarse sea salt or melted butter for a finishing sprinkle or drizzle for fish and sautéed vegetables. Coarsely grind, then fold them into shortbread cookie dough, or pair them with sliced strawberries and honey.

Long Pepper

Belonging to the same botanical family as black, white and green peppercorns, long pepper has a subtler flavor with hints of warm spice. It can be used interchangeably with black pepper, though it may not be effectively ground in a pepper mill; use a spice grinder instead. Long pepper is used broadly in Indian, Pakistani, Indonesian and Malaysian cooking, as its warm heat pairs nicely with fish sauce and palm sugar. The warm flavors work particularly well with legumes and in curries.

Sichuan

Sichuan peppercorns are the dried fruit rinds of the prickly ash, a tree native to China. The red varieties are stronger and earthier, and the green are brighter and pinier. When eaten, the peppercorns produce a tingly sensation on the tongue thanks to a compound that creates the perception of touch rather than heat. Sichuan peppercorns usually are toasted, then ground and sifted before use. In Sichuan cooking, the peppercorns are typically paired with fiery chili peppers. The combination is added to stir-fried meats and vegetables, simmered in stews and braises, including the beef noodle soup that is Taiwan's national dish (recipe p. 117). Grind and blend with equal parts kosher salt and sugar to garnish fried chicken and roasted or grilled meats and fish.

PORCINI-RUBBED BEEF TENDERLOIN WITH ROASTED PORTOBELLO MUSHROOMS

Start to finish: 2 hours (1 hour active)
Servings: 8 to 10

A whole beef tenderloin not only is quick and easy to roast, it also is dependably tender despite its leanness. But because its flavor is quite mild, we use a trio of bold ingredients—mushrooms, rosemary and black pepper—to bring depth and savoriness. We create a seasoning rub by finely grinding umami-packed dried porcini mushrooms (shiitakes work, too), rosemary and pepper, and we roast the meat over a layer of fresh portobello mushrooms and sliced onion. The mushroom-onion mixture becomes a rich, flavorful accompaniment to the meat. You will need a large roasting pan—one that measures about 12-by-15 inches—along with a V-style roasting rack.

¼ ounce dried porcini mushrooms or dried shiitake mushroom caps (about 8 small caps), broken into pieces

2 tablespoons fresh rosemary

1 tablespoon black peppercorns

4- to 5-pound beef tenderloin roast, trimmed of fat and silver skin

Kosher salt and ground black pepper

6 tablespoons extra-virgin olive oil, divided

1½ pounds portobello mushroom caps, gills scraped off with a spoon, halved and sliced ¼ inch thick

1 medium sweet onion or yellow onion, halved and sliced ¼ inch thick

1 tablespoon sherry vinegar

1 cup lightly packed fresh flat-leaf parsley, roughly chopped

Flaky salt, to serve (optional)

Working in batches, use a spice grinder to pulverize the porcini to a fine powder, transferring it to a small bowl. Repeat with the rosemary and 2½ teaspoons salt, pulverizing until finely ground and adding it to the mushroom powder. Repeat with the peppercorns. Stir the seasonings, then measure 1 tablespoon into another small bowl and set aside. Sprinkle the remaining mix all over the tenderloin, rubbing it in.

Tuck the tapered end of the tenderloin under itself so the roast is of an even thickness. Using kitchen twine, tie the tenderloin at 1-inch intervals, making sure the tucked portion is secured with the twine. Brush the roast all over with 3 tablespoons oil, place on a V-style roasting rack and set aside at room temperature until ready to roast.

Heat the oven to 450°F with a rack in the middle position. In a large (about 12-by-15 inches) roasting pan, toss the portobello mushrooms, onion, remaining 3 tablespoons oil and ½ teaspoon each salt and ground pepper. Roast for 15 minutes. Remove the pan from the oven, stir the mushroom mixture and set the rack with the tenderloin in the pan. Roast until the thickest part registers 120°F for rare or 125°F for medium-rare, 35 to 45 minutes.

Transfer the roast to a large platter and remove the rack from the pan. Tent the roast with foil and let rest for 30 minutes. If there is liquid in the pan, before proceeding to the next step, stir the mushroom mixture, return the pan to the oven and cook until the liquid has evaporated.

To the mushroom mixture, stir in half of the reserved seasoning mix, the vinegar and parsley. Transfer the rested tenderloin to a cutting board. Remove the twine and carve into ½-inch slices. Pour any juices on the platter and cutting board into the mushroom mixture, then taste the mushrooms and season with salt and pepper. Transfer the mushrooms to the platter, then arrange the sliced tenderloin on top. Sprinkle with the remaining seasoning mix, along with flaky salt (if using).

Pizzas &
Flatbreads

Five Secrets to World-Class Pizza

Homemade pizza dough can be finicky. Getting crusts that develop a crispy exterior but remain chewy at the center is a challenge for most home cooks, never mind the struggle of stretching dough that keeps snapping back. But there is an easy way to tilt the odds in your favor. And it's all about temperature. But we don't mean in the oven. Rather, we focus on the temperature of the dough itself.

The ideal temperature for pizza dough prior to baking is 75°F. That's because the yeast is sufficiently active at this temperature, and the dough has less gluten formation, making it easier to shape and prime for that perfectly chewy texture when it comes out of the oven.

To ensure your pizza dough is at the correct temperature before baking, an hour before you're ready to cook, remove the dough from the refrigerator and set it in a bowl covered with plastic wrap. Set the bowl in a larger bowl filled with 100°F water for 30 minutes, or until the dough reaches 75°F. Change the water as needed.

Four More Tips for Perfect Pizza

Flour Power: We found King Arthur all-purpose flour is best because its higher protein content produces crusts with good flavor and crispy edges while maintaining a good chew.

Stay Out of Hot Water: Using cold water to mix the dough prolongs the fermentation process, which leads to better flavor.

Be Patient: About that fermentation—24 hours builds the best flavor. No shortcuts.

Steel True: A baking steel is preferable to a baking stone. In our tests, the former reached 550°F, while the latter only hit 525°F. If you do use a pizza stone, you may need to increase baking time by 2 to 3 minutes.

WHITE PIZZA WITH ARUGULA

Start to finish: 35 minutes
Makes two 10-inch pizzas

A whipped cream–fontina mixture makes the "sauce" for these pies. During baking, it melts to a creamy consistency, so be sure to crimp the edge of the dough to create a slight retaining wall for the sauce. Lightly dressed arugula is the perfect finishing touch.

¾ cup cold heavy cream

2 ounces shredded fontina cheese, shredded (½ cup)

1½ ounces Parmesan cheese, finely grated (¾ cup)

Kosher salt and ground black pepper

1 tablespoon extra-virgin olive oil

1 teaspoon grated lemon zest, plus 2 teaspoons lemon juice

Semolina flour, for dusting the pizza peel

Two 8-ounce portions homemade or store-bought pizza dough, shaped into 10-inch rounds (see instructions p. 507)

4 cups lightly packed baby arugula

At least 1 hour before baking, heat the oven to 550°F (or 500°F if that's your oven's maximum temperature), with a baking steel or stone on the upper-middle rack.

Using an electric mixer, whip the cream until it holds stiff peaks. Fold in the fontina, Parmesan, a pinch of salt and ½ teaspoon pepper. In a large bowl, whisk together the oil, lemon zest and juice and a pinch of salt; set aside.

Dust a baking peel, inverted baking sheet or rimless cookie sheet with semolina. Transfer the first dough round to the peel and, if needed, reshape into a 10-inch circle. Using the back of a spoon, spread half of the cream mixture on the dough, leaving a 1-inch border around the edge. Using your fingers, crimp the outer ½ inch of the dough to form a raised edge to contain the sauce and cheese. Slide the pizza onto the baking steel and bake until well browned and the cream mixture is bubbling, 7 to 10 minutes (9 to 12 minutes in a 500°F oven).

Using the peel, transfer the pizza to a wire rack. Repeat with the second dough round. After the second pizza has cooled for a few minutes, toss the arugula with the oil mixture. Top the pizzas with the arugula, dividing it evenly.

....

FIG, BLUE CHEESE AND PROSCIUTTO PIZZA

Start to finish: 25 minutes
Makes two 10-inch pizzas

This pizza is defined by a balance of sweet, savory and salty—provided by a classic combination of fresh figs, prosciutto and blue cheese. The prosciutto becomes crisp and adds a welcome textural contrast. If possible, use a good, aged balsamic vinegar, one that is dark and syrupy.

Semolina flour, for dusting the pizza peel

Two 8-ounce portions homemade or store-bought pizza dough, shaped into 10-inch rounds (see instructions p. 507)

2 tablespoons extra-virgin olive oil, divided

6 ounces fresh figs, stemmed and sliced into ¼-inch rounds

3 ounces blue cheese, crumbled (¾ cup)

2 ounces prosciutto (about 4 slices), cut into 2-inch ribbons

1 teaspoon balsamic syrup or aged balsamic vinegar

2 scallions, thinly sliced on the diagonal

Ground black pepper

At least 1 hour before baking, heat the oven to 550°F (or 500°F if that's your oven's maximum temperature), with a baking steel or stone on the upper-middle rack.

Dust a baking peel, inverted baking sheet or rimless cookie sheet with semolina. Transfer the first dough round to the peel and, if needed, reshape into a 10-inch circle. Brush the round with 1 tablespoon oil. Arrange half the fig slices on the dough, then sprinkle with half the blue cheese. Arrange half of the prosciutto between the figs. Bake until the crust is browned and the prosciutto is crisp, 7 to 10 minutes (9 to 12 minutes in a 500°F oven).

Using the peel, transfer the pizza to a wire rack. Let cool for a couple of minutes, then sprinkle with ½ teaspoon of the balsamic syrup, half of the scallions and black pepper. Repeat with the second dough round.

505

Pizza Dough

Start to finish: 1½ days (20 minutes active)
Makes four 8-ounce portions of dough

Though any brand of bread flour will work in this recipe, we liked King Arthur Flour best. It has a higher protein content, producing crusts with good flavor, nicely crisped surfaces, and a satisfying chew. **Making the dough with cool or cold water helps prolong the fermentation process, which develops better flavor. Quart-size zip-close plastic bags coated on the inside with cooking spray are easiest for fermenting the dough, but well-oiled 1-pint bowls or plastic containers with lids work well, too.** Following the overnight fermentation, the dough can be frozen for longer storage; to use, allow to thaw overnight in the refrigerator, then proceed with the recipe.

548 grams (4 cups) bread flour, plus more for dusting

1 tablespoon white sugar

¾ teaspoon instant yeast

1½ cups cool (65°F) water

1 teaspoon table salt

In a stand mixer fitted with the dough hook, combine the flour, sugar and yeast. Mix on low to combine, about 15 seconds. With the mixer running, slowly add the water, then mix on low until a slightly bumpy dough forms and the dough clears the sides of the bowl, about 5 minutes. Cover the bowl with plastic wrap and let rest for 20 minutes.

Uncover the bowl, sprinkle the salt over the dough and mix on low until smooth and elastic, 5 to 7 minutes. If the dough climbs up the hook, stop the mixer, push it down and continue kneading.

Scrape the dough onto a well-floured counter and divide it into 4 pieces. With floured hands, form each into a taut ball and dust with flour. Mist 4 quart-size plastic bags with cooking spray, then add 1 ball to each. Seal and refrigerate for 24 to 72 hours.

About 1 hour before making pizza, lightly oil 4 small bowls. Remove the dough from the bags and set each in a bowl. Cover with plastic wrap, then set each bowl into a larger bowl of 100°F water for 30 minutes, or until the dough reaches 75°F, changing the water as needed. Shape according to directions (see p. 507).

How to Shape Pizza Dough

Store-bought fresh pizza dough or homemade dough made in advance makes pizza doable as a weeknight dinner. Store-bought dough sometimes is half-hearted in flavor, but the right toppings and baking method can make up for many shortcomings.

Shaping Pizza Dough

At least 1 hour before baking, heat the oven to 550°F (or 500°F if that's your oven's maximum temperature), with a baking steel or stone on the upper-middle rack.

Warming the dough to 75°F before shaping it makes it easier to work with. For two 10-inch pizzas, we recommend dividing 1 pound of dough into two 8-ounce balls, putting the dough balls into oiled bowls, covering them with plastic wrap, then setting the bowls into a larger bowl containing 100°F water. Check the temperature of the dough with an instant thermometer after about 30 minutes and change the water as needed. Make sure you have all of your toppings ready before you begin shaping the dough.

For two 10-inch pizzas, turn one portion of dough out onto a counter dusted with all-purpose flour. Flour your hands and, using your fingers and starting at the center and working out to the edges, press the dough into a 10-inch round, turning the dough over once, leaving the perimeter slightly thicker than the center. If the dough stretches but shrinks back, let it rest for 5 minutes to relax the gluten, then try again. Set the first round aside on the counter and cover it with a clean kitchen towel. Shape the second portion of dough in the same way. Top and bake according to the recipe.

THREE-CHEESE PIZZA

Start to finish: 40 minutes
Makes two 10-inch pizzas

This is a simple and classic cheese pizza. We use a quick, no-cook tomato sauce and a mixture of three cheeses for full flavor. Make sure to drain the tomatoes well before processing them, as excess moisture will result in soggy crusts.

14½-ounce can diced tomatoes, drained

½ teaspoon dried oregano

1 small garlic clove, smashed and peeled

¼ teaspoon red pepper flakes

1 tablespoon extra-virgin olive oil

Kosher salt

4 ounces whole-milk mozzarella cheese, shredded (1 cup)

1½ ounces fontina cheese, shredded (½ cup)

1 ounce Parmesan cheese, finely grated (½ cup)

Semolina flour, for dusting the pizza peel

Two 8-ounce portions homemade or store-bought pizza dough, shaped into 10-inch rounds (see instructions left column)

At least 1 hour before baking, heat the oven to 550°F (or 500°F if that's your oven's maximum temperature), with a baking steel or stone on the upper-middle rack.

In a food processor, process the tomatoes, oregano, garlic, pepper flakes, oil and ½ teaspoon kosher salt until smooth, about 30 seconds.

Dust a baking peel, inverted baking sheet or rimless cookie sheet with semolina. Transfer the first dough round to the peel and, if needed, reshape into a 10-inch circle. Using the back of a spoon, spread half of the tomato mixture over the dough, leaving a ½-inch border at the edge. Sprinkle with half each of the mozzarella, fontina and Parmesan. Slide the pizza onto the baking steel and bake until well browned and the cheese is bubbling and spotted brown, 7 to 10 minutes (9 to 12 minutes in a 500°F oven).

Transfer the pizza to a wire rack; let cool. Repeat with the second dough.

BRAZILIAN-STYLE PIZZA DOUGH AND TOMATO SAUCE

Start to finish: 30 hours (30 minutes active)
Makes enough for two 12-inch pizzas

In São Paulo, Brazil, where reportedly half the population of more than 12 million is of Italian descent, pizza reigns supreme. An estimated 1 million pies are served up each day at the 6,000 or so pizzerias across the South American metropolis. But whereas Neapolitan pizza is defined by restraint and exacting standards, we learned that Brazilian pizza is made with an anything-goes attitude. The crust of the typical São Paulo pizza is thicker than that of Neapolitan pizza so it provides good support for generous toppings. And though crisp on the bottom, it tends to be rather soft and tender. The sauce is almost always made from fresh tomatoes, uncooked and seasoned sparingly. To re-create São Paulo-style pizza crust back on home turf, we found that unbleached all-purpose flour yielded the best results (in particular, Gold Medal brand, which has a protein content of about 10.5 percent). And to develop flavor as well as achieve the texture we sought, we allow the dough to rise at room temperature for a couple hours, then refrigerate it for 24 to 72 hours.

FOR THE DOUGH:

520 grams (4 cups) all-purpose flour, plus more as needed and for dusting

2 teaspoons white sugar

1½ teaspoons table salt

1 teaspoon instant yeast

1 tablespoon extra-virgin olive oil, plus more for the bowl and baking sheet

1¼ cups warm water (100°F to 110°F)

Semolina flour, for dusting the peel

FOR THE SAUCE:

1 pint grape tomatoes

1 tablespoon extra-virgin olive oil

½ teaspoon dried oregano

⅛ to ¼ teaspoon red pepper flakes

Kosher salt and ground black pepper

To make the dough, in a stand mixer with the dough hook, mix the all-purpose flour, sugar, salt and yeast on medium until well combined, about 15 seconds. With the mixer on low, drizzle in the oil followed by the water. Knead on low until the mixture forms a smooth, elastic dough that clears the sides of the bowl, 8 to 10 minutes; if the dough sticks to the bowl, knead in additional flour, 1 tablespoon at a time. The finished dough should be soft but not stick to your hands. Lightly oil a large bowl and transfer the dough to it. Cover with plastic wrap and let rise at room temperature until doubled, 1½ to 2 hours.

Mist the insides of two 1-quart zip-close plastic bags with cooking spray. Generously dust the counter with flour, scrape the dough out onto it and divide it in half. With floured hands, form each portion into a taut ball and dust with flour. Place 1 dough ball in each prepared bag, seal and refrigerate for at least 24 or up to 72 hours.

About 4 hours before making pizza, remove the dough from the refrigerator. Brush a rimmed baking sheet with oil. Remove the dough from the bags and place on the baking sheet, spacing them apart. Cover loosely with plastic wrap and let stand at room temperature until the dough has completely lost its chill, about 4 hours; after about 3 hours, heat the oven to 500°F with a baking steel or stone on the upper-middle rack.

After turning on the oven, make the sauce. In a food processor, pulse the tomatoes until chopped into rough ¼-inch bits, about 13 pulses. Transfer to a fine-mesh sieve set over a medium bowl and let drain at room temperature for at least 30 minutes or until ready to use; occasionally shake the sieve to encourage the liquid to drain off and make sure the bottom of the sieve is not touching the liquid that has collected in the bowl.

When you are ready to shape the dough, blot the tomatoes dry with paper towels and transfer them to a small bowl; discard the juices in the bowl. Stir in the oil, oregano and pepper flakes, then season to taste with salt and black pepper.

Dust the counter with flour and transfer 1 portion of dough to the counter. Flour your hands and, using your fingers, press the dough, starting at the center and working out to the edges, into a 13-inch round, flipping the dough once. The round should be thin at the center, with slightly thicker edges.

Lightly dust a baking peel, inverted rimmed baking sheet or rimless cookie sheet with semolina. Transfer the dough to the peel and, if needed, reshape into a 13-inch round. Using the back of a spoon, evenly spread half of the tomato sauce (about ½ cup), leaving a ½-inch border around the edge. Top and bake the pizza as directed in the recipe you're making. After removing the pizza from the oven, shape, sauce, top and bake the second pizza in the same way.

CHANGE THE WAY YOU COOK

Three Ways to Do the Dough Slide

A baking peel obviously is the ideal tool for getting flatbreads, pizzas and similar breads in and out of the oven. When shopping for a peel, look for one with a thin front edge. The edges of some wood peels are quite thick, which can be challenging for maneuvering the bread on and off. Metal peels are thin enough to allow for a smooth transfer. If you opt for wood, be sure the front tapers to a relatively thin edge. Handle lengths can vary, too. Very long handles are for actual pizza ovens, but a home cook only needs one that's about 12" long.

No peel? Here are some other options:

Rimless cookie sheet—This is the next best thing if a peel isn't available. The lack of rim means that the edge of the cookie sheet can be placed directly on the baking stone, so the dough can slide more smoothly off the sheet and directly onto the stone. However, it doesn't have the handle of a peel, so it will take some practice to slide it deep into the oven.

Inverted baking sheet—The rim of a baking sheet makes it hard to slide doughs onto the baking surface. But flipping one upside down works in a pinch. It will take a little practice; due to the rim adding height, you will need to slide the dough over the sharp step down from baking sheet to baking stone. If you generously sprinkle the inverted sheet with semolina flour, move quickly and with confidence, you will be fine.

BRAZILIAN-STYLE PIZZA WITH RICOTTA, ZA'ATAR AND ARUGULA

Start to finish: 30 hours (45 minutes active)
Makes two 12-inch pizzas

This pizza was inspired by the "Napoli in Beirut" pie we tasted at Veridiana Pizzaria in São Paulo. Be sure to dress only half the arugula at a time and only just before adding it to the baked pie, otherwise the greens will wilt.

FOR THE DOUGH:

520 grams (4 cups) all-purpose flour, plus more as needed and for dusting

2 teaspoons white sugar

1½ teaspoons table salt

1 teaspoon instant yeast

1 tablespoon extra-virgin olive oil, plus more for the bowl and baking sheet

1¼ cups warm water (100°F to 110°F)

Semolina flour, for dusting the peel

FOR THE SAUCE AND TOPPINGS:

1 pint grape tomatoes

1 cup whole-milk ricotta cheese

8 tablespoons extra-virgin olive oil, divided

2½ teaspoons dried oregano, divided

2 teaspoons za'atar

1 teaspoon ground sumac

Kosher salt and ground black pepper

1 medium red onion, halved and thinly sliced

⅛ to ¼ teaspoon red pepper flakes

4 cups lightly packed baby arugula

2 tablespoons lemon juice or red wine vinegar, divided

To make the dough, in a stand mixer with the dough hook, mix the all-purpose flour, sugar, salt and yeast on medium until well combined, about 15 seconds. With the mixer on low, drizzle in the oil followed by the water. Knead on low until the mixture forms a smooth, elastic dough that clears the sides of the bowl, 8 to 10 minutes; if the dough sticks to the bowl, knead in additional flour, 1 tablespoon at a time. The finished dough should be soft but not stick to your hands. Lightly oil a large bowl and transfer the dough to it.

Cover with plastic wrap and let rise at room temperature until doubled, 1½ to 2 hours.

Mist the insides of two 1-quart zip-close plastic bags with cooking spray. Generously dust the counter with flour, scrape the dough out onto it and divide it in half. With floured hands, form each portion into a taut ball and dust with flour. Place 1 dough ball in each prepared bag, seal and refrigerate for at least 24 or up to 72 hours.

About 4 hours before making pizza, remove the dough from the refrigerator. Brush a rimmed baking sheet with oil. Remove the dough from the bags and place on the baking sheet, spacing them apart. Cover loosely with plastic wrap and let stand at room temperature until the dough has completely lost its chill, about 4 hours; after about 3 hours, heat the oven to 500°F with a baking steel or stone on the upper-middle rack.

After turning on the oven, make the sauce and prepare the toppings. In a food processor, pulse the tomatoes until chopped into rough ¼-inch bits, about 13 pulses. Transfer to a fine-mesh sieve set over a medium bowl and let drain at room temperature for at least 30 minutes or until ready to

use; occasionally shake the sieve to encourage the liquid to drain off and make sure the bottom of the sieve is not touching the liquid that has collected in the bowl.

While the tomatoes are draining, in a small bowl, stir together the ricotta, 4 tablespoons of the oil, 2 teaspoons of the oregano, the za'atar, sumac and ½ teaspoon each salt and black pepper. In another small bowl, toss together the onion and 1 tablespoon of the remaining oil. Set both the ricotta mixture and the onion aside.

When you are ready to shape the dough, blot the tomatoes dry with paper towels and transfer them to another small bowl; discard the juices in the bowl. Stir in 1 tablespoon of the remaining oil, the remaining ½ teaspoon oregano and the pepper flakes, then season to taste with salt and black pepper.

Dust the counter with flour and transfer 1 portion of dough to the counter. Flour your hands and, using your fingers, press the dough, starting at the center and working out to the edges, into a 13-inch round, flipping the dough once. The round should be thin at the center, with slightly thicker edges.

Lightly dust a baking peel, inverted rimmed baking sheet or rimless cookie sheet with semolina. Transfer the dough to the peel and, if needed, reshape into a 13-inch round. Using the back of a spoon, evenly spread half of the tomato sauce (about ½ cup), leaving a ½-inch border around the edge.

Top the shaped and sauced dough with half of the oil-tossed onion. Slide the pizza into the 500°F oven onto the hot baking steel or stone and bake until the crust is well browned, 8 to 10 minutes. Using the peel, transfer the pizza to a wire rack. Cool for a couple minutes, then dollop on half of the ricotta mixture. Working quickly, in another medium bowl, toss half of the arugula with 1 tablespoon of the remaining oil and 1 tablespoon of the lemon juice, then top the pizza with the arugula.

Shape, sauce, top and bake the second pizza in the same way using the remaining toppings.

511

BRAZILIAN-STYLE PIZZA CARBONARA

Start to finish: 30 hours (1 hour active)
Makes two 12-inch pizzas

This super-savory creation comes from Bráz Pizzaria in São Paulo. They finish their carbonara pizza with raw egg yolk, drizzled on immediately after baking. For ours, we grate the yolks from hard-cooked eggs onto the hot pies as soon as they emerge from the oven.

FOR THE DOUGH:

520 grams (4 cups) all-purpose flour, plus more as needed and for dusting

2 teaspoons white sugar

1½ teaspoons table salt

1 teaspoon instant yeast

1 tablespoon extra-virgin olive oil, plus more for the bowl and baking sheet

1¼ cups warm water (100°F to 110°F)

Semolina flour, for dusting the peel

FOR THE SAUCE AND TOPPINGS:

1 pint grape tomatoes

4 ounces pancetta, finely chopped

1 tablespoon extra-virgin olive oil

½ teaspoon dried oregano

⅛ to ¼ teaspoon red pepper flakes

Kosher salt and ground black pepper

4 ounces whole-milk mozzarella cheese, shredded (2 cups)

2 ounces pecorino Romano cheese, finely grated (1 cup)

Yolks from 4 hard-cooked large eggs, divided

To make the dough, in a stand mixer with the dough hook, mix the all-purpose flour, sugar, salt and yeast on medium until well combined, about 15 seconds. With the mixer on low, drizzle in the oil followed by the water. Knead on low until the mixture forms a smooth, elastic dough that clears the sides of the bowl, 8 to 10 minutes; if the dough sticks to the bowl, knead in additional flour, 1 tablespoon at a time. The finished dough should be soft but not stick to your hands. Lightly oil a large bowl and transfer the dough to it. Cover with plastic wrap and let rise at room temperature until doubled, 1½ to 2 hours.

Mist the insides of two 1-quart zip-close plastic bags with cooking spray. Generously dust the counter with flour, scrape the dough out onto it and divide it in half. With floured hands, form each portion into a taut ball and dust with flour. Place 1 dough ball in each prepared bag, seal and refrigerate for at least 24 or up to 72 hours.

About 4 hours before making pizza, remove the dough from the refrigerator. Brush a rimmed baking sheet with oil. Remove the dough from the bags and place on the baking sheet, spacing them apart. Cover loosely with plastic wrap and let stand at room temperature until the dough has completely lost its chill, about 4 hours; after about 3 hours, heat the oven to 500°F with a baking steel or stone on the upper-middle rack.

After turning on the oven, make the sauce and prepare the toppings. In a food processor, pulse the tomatoes until chopped into rough ¼-inch bits, about 13 pulses. Transfer to a fine-mesh sieve set over a medium bowl and let drain at room temperature for at least 30 minutes or until ready to use; occasionally shake the sieve to encourage the liquid to drain off and make sure the bottom of the sieve is not touching the liquid that has collected in the bowl.

While the tomatoes are draining, in a 10-inch skillet over medium, cook the pancetta, stirring occasionally, until browned and crisp, 8 to 10 minutes. Using a slotted spoon, transfer to a paper towel-lined plate and set aside.

When you are ready to shape the dough, blot the tomatoes dry with paper towels and transfer them to a small bowl; discard the juices in the bowl. Stir in the oil, oregano and pepper flakes, then season to taste with salt and black pepper.

Dust the counter with flour and transfer 1 portion of dough to the counter. Flour your hands and, using your fingers, press the dough, starting at the center and working out to the edges, into a 13-inch round, flipping the dough once. The round should be thin at the center, with slightly thicker edges.

Lightly dust a baking peel, inverted rimmed baking sheet or rimless cookie sheet with semolina. Transfer the dough to the peel and, if needed, reshape into a 13-inch round. Using the back of a spoon, evenly spread half of the tomato sauce (about ½ cup), leaving a ½-inch border around the edge.

Top the shaped and sauced dough with half each of the pancetta, mozzarella and pecorino. Slide the pizza into the 500°F oven onto the hot baking steel or stone and bake until the crust is well browned, 8 to 10 minutes. Using the peel, transfer the pizza to a wire rack. Cool for a couple minutes, then, using the small holes on a box grater, grate 2 of the egg yolks onto the pizza. Sprinkle with black pepper.

Shape, sauce, top and bake the second pizza in the same way using the remaining toppings.

SKILLET PIZZA WITH FENNEL SALAMI AND RED ONION

Start to finish: 50 minutes
Makes two 10- to 12-inch pizzas

If you're wondering what the advantage is of using a skillet to make pizza, know the following: 1) You can skip the hour-long heating of a pizza steel or stone. 2) There's no fumbling with a pizza peel to get the pie into and out of the oven. 3) Your oven will remain free and clear of semolina that must be wiped up lest it later turn to ash. And in terms

of results, a skillet-cooked pizza bakes up with a nicely browned bottom crust with a rich, almost fried crispness. The "baking" starts on the stovetop but finishes in the oven, so you will need a heavy-bottomed skillet, preferably not cast iron (because it's slow to heat), that can withstand 500°F. You can use homemade, store-bought or pizzeria-purchased dough for this recipe. Each pie requires 12 ounces of dough; if you bought refrigerated dough, portion it out, shape each portion into a ball and allow it to come to room temperature, covered with a kitchen towel, on an oiled baking sheet. Finocchiona is a type of salami made with fennel seeds. If you cannot find it, simply use your favorite type of hard salami; pepperoni would work well, too. Or, if you prefer, skip the salami and onion toppings and make simple cheese pizzas.

1 cup canned tomato puree

2 teaspoons plus 4 tablespoons extra-virgin olive oil, divided

¼ teaspoon red pepper flakes

¼ teaspoon dried oregano

1 tablespoon chopped fresh basil, plus 10 large basil leaves

½ medium red onion, thinly sliced

Kosher salt and ground black pepper

1½ pounds pizza dough (see headnote), divided in half and shaped into balls, room temperature

8 ounces whole-milk mozzarella cheese, shredded (2 cups), divided

1 ounce Parmesan cheese, finely grated (½ cup), divided

3 ounces thinly sliced finocchiona salami (see headnote)

Heat the oven to 500°F with a rack in the middle position. In a small bowl, stir together the tomato puree, 1 teaspoon oil, the pepper flakes, oregano and chopped basil; set aside. In another small bowl, stir together the onion, 1 teaspoon of the remaining oil, ¼ teaspoon salt and ¼ teaspoon pepper; set aside.

Brush the entire surface of a heavy-bottomed 12-inch oven-safe skillet with 2 tablespoons of the oil. Set 1 ball of dough on the counter and, using your hands, press and stretch it into a 12-inch round. Transfer the round to the skillet; the dough will climb partway up the sides of the skillet. Spread half of the tomato mixture evenly onto the dough. Sprinkle half of the mozzarella all the way to the

edges of the dough without allowing the cheese to make contact with the skillet, followed by half of the Parmesan. Arrange half of the salami on top, then scatter on half of the onion.

Set the skillet over medium and cook until the oil is bubbling around the perimeter and the crust begins to rise at the edges. Run a silicone spatula around the edge of the pizza, then shake the skillet in a circular motion to make sure the pizza is not sticking. Transfer the skillet to the oven and bake until the crust is well browned and the cheese is bubbling and lightly browned, 9 to 12 minutes.

Remove the skillet from the oven (the handle will be hot) and set it on a wire rack. Using a fork, lift one edge of the pizza, then carefully slide it out of the skillet directly onto the rack, leaving the residual oil in the pan. Pour off and discard the oil; reserve the skillet. Let the pizza cool for about 5 minutes. Tear or roughly chop half of the basil leaves and sprinkle them onto the pizza.

Rinse the skillet (the handle will still be hot) under running water until cool. Wipe it dry, then brush the surface with the remaining 2 tablespoons oil. Shape, top and bake the second piece of dough in the same way.

POUR-IN-THE-PAN PIZZA WITH TOMATOES AND MOZZARELLA

Start to finish: 6 hours (35 minutes active)
Servings: 4 to 6

The crust for this pizza borrows from the Milk Street recipe for a light, open-crumbed focaccia, our re-creation of the focaccia we encountered in Bari, Italy. The pizza dough is unusual in a couple ways: It uses so much water that it verges on a batter and it rises for at least four hours on the counter (be sure to place the bowl in a warm spot). After rising, the dough is poured out onto a greased 13-by-18-inch rimmed baking sheet (also known as a half sheet pan) to rest for 20 minutes before being nudged with oiled fingers to the edges of the pan. Instead of making a single large pizza, you could make two 12-inch pies using low-lipped, disk-shaped pizza pans, like the ones used in American-style pizzerias; see the directions below.

400 grams (2¾ cups plus 2½ tablespoons) bread flour

2 teaspoons white sugar

Two ¼-ounce packets instant yeast (4½ teaspoons)

1½ cups water, 100°F to 110°F

Table salt and ground black pepper

3 tablespoons extra-virgin olive oil, divided, plus more for oiling your hands

1 pound Campari or cherry tomatoes

6 ounces whole-milk mozzarella cheese, shredded (3 cups)

1 teaspoon dried oregano

Kosher or flaky sea salt, for sprinkling (optional)

In a stand mixer with the dough hook, mix the flour, sugar and yeast on medium until combined, about 30 seconds. With the mixer running, add the water and mix on medium until a sticky dough forms, about 5 minutes; scrape the bowl and dough hook once during mixing. Turn off the mixer and let rest 10 minutes. Add 2 teaspoons salt and mix on medium for another 5 minutes. The dough will be shiny, wet and elastic.

Coat a large bowl with 1 tablespoon of the oil. Mist a silicone spatula with cooking spray and use it to scrape the dough into the bowl. Flip the dough with the spatula to oil all sides. Cover tightly with plastic wrap and let rise in a warm spot for 4 to 5 hours.

When the dough is ready, generously mist a 13-by-18-inch rimmed baking sheet with cooking spray, then pour 1 tablespoon of the remaining oil onto the center of the baking sheet. Gently scrape the dough onto the center of the sheet and let rest, uncovered, for 20 minutes.

Meanwhile, heat the oven to 500°F with a rack in the lowest position. If using Campari tomatoes, cut them into quarters; if using cherry tomatoes, cut them in half. Place the tomatoes in a large bowl and mash gently with a potato masher. Transfer to a fine-mesh strainer set over a bowl and set aside to drain until ready to use.

After the dough has rested, oil your hands, and, working from the center, gently push it into an even layer to the edges and into the corners of the baking sheet; be careful not to press out all of the air. It's fine if the dough does not completely fill the pan, but it should come close.

Drizzle the tomatoes with the remaining 1 tablespoon oil, then toss. Scatter over the dough, leaving a narrow border. Let rest for another 30 minutes. Scatter the cheese over the dough, then sprinkle with the oregano, pepper and kosher or flaky salt (if using). Bake until the surface of the pizza is golden brown and the bottom is crisped and well browned, 18 to 20 minutes. Slide the pizza from the pan onto a wire rack and cool for a few minutes before slicing.

HOW TO MAKE TWO 12-INCH ROUND PIZZAS

Follow the recipe to make and rise the dough. When the dough is ready, generously mist two 12-inch round pizza pans with cooking spray, then pour 1 tablespoon oil onto the center of each. Scrape half the dough onto the center of each pan. Continue with the recipe, allowing the dough to rest for 20 minutes before pushing it to the edges of the pans and adding toppings. Bake one at a time, reducing the baking time to 12 to 15 minutes.

TO TOP IT OFF

Because pour-in-the-pan pizza dough is extremely wet, it's important to use toppings that are dry, or the pie will bake up with a soggy surface. The following are some of our favorite toppings; we suggest using no more than two in addition to the tomatoes and mozzarella. Scatter the ingredient(s) onto the tomato-topped dough just before adding the cheese. If you are using high-sodium toppings, such as olives or capers, you may wish to skip the salt that's sprinkled on before baking.

Sliced pepperoni or salami

Black or green olives, pitted and halved

Roasted red peppers, patted dry and cut into strips

Marinated artichoke hearts, patted dry and cut into chunks

Capers, drained and patted dry

INVERTED PIZZA WITH ONIONS, POTATOES AND THYME

Start to finish: 40 minutes

Servings: 4 to 6

In "Tasting Rome," co-authors Katie Parla and Kristina Gill write about pizza made using an innovative method—pizza al contrario—perfected by Gabriele Bonci of Pizzarium in Rome. The "toppings" are put into a pan, covered with dough and baked. Once out of the oven, the pie is inverted, revealing ingredients that have melded with the dough. The browned crust that formed on top during baking becomes a wonderfully crisp bottom. For weeknight ease, we use store-bought refrigerated pizza dough.

2 medium yellow onions, halved and thinly sliced

8 ounces Yukon Gold potatoes, unpeeled, sliced ⅛ to ¼ inch thick

2 tablespoons fresh thyme, roughly chopped

1 tablespoon honey

4 tablespoons extra-virgin olive oil, divided, plus more to serve

Kosher salt and ground black pepper

1½ pounds store-bought refrigerated pizza dough, room temperature

All-purpose flour, for dusting

1 cup whole-milk ricotta cheese

Heat the oven to 500°F with a rack in the lowest position. Mist a rimmed baking sheet with cooking spray. In a large bowl, toss together the onions, potato, thyme, honey, 3 tablespoons of oil and ½ teaspoon each salt and pepper. Distribute the mixture in an even layer on the prepared baking sheet and bake without stirring until the onions begin to brown and the potato is softened but not yet fully cooked, about 15 minutes.

Meanwhile, on a well-floured counter, gently stretch the dough by hand or roll it with a rolling pin into a rough 12-by-16-inch rectangle (the same dimensions as the baking sheet); work from the center outward to help ensure the dough is of an even thickness. If it is resistant or shrinks after stretching or rolling, wait 5 to 10 minutes before trying again; if it is very elastic, you may need to give it 2 or 3 rests.

It's fine if the dough rectangle is a little smaller than the baking sheet.

When the onion-potato mixture is ready, remove the baking sheet from the oven; leave the oven on. Using both hands and being careful not to touch the hot baking sheet, lay the dough over the vegetables, gently stretching and tucking in the edges as needed so the dough fills the baking sheet and covers the vegetables. Brush the surface with the remaining 1 tablespoon oil, then use a fork to poke holes every 2 to 3 inches all the way through the dough. Bake until the surface is well browned, 15 to 17 minutes.

Remove from the oven and immediately invert a wire rack onto the baking sheet. Using potholders or oven mitts, hold the baking sheet and rack together and carefully flip to invert. Lift off the baking sheet. Using a metal spatula, scrape up any onion-potato mixture clinging to the baking sheet and replace it on the pizza. Dollop with the ricotta, cut into pieces and drizzle with additional oil.

INVERTED PIZZA WITH OLIVES, ANCHOVIES AND CARAMELIZED ONIONS

Start to finish: 45 minutes
Servings: 6

Pissaladière is a classic savory tart from the south of France, featuring caramelized onions, savory anchovies and briny black olives—an ideal topping combination for our week-night-simple inverted pizza. Caramelizing thinly sliced onions on a baking sheet makes quick, hands-off work of the task. Once nicely browned, the topping mixture is covered in store-bought pizza dough, then baked until golden. After being inverted upright, the browned crust that formed during baking becomes a wonderfully crisp bottom, no pizza stone required. Fresh thyme and a drizzle of extra-virgin olive oil give the pizza an enticing aroma and shine.

2 medium yellow onions, halved and thinly sliced

3 tablespoons extra-virgin olive oil, divided, plus more to serve

1 tablespoon fresh thyme, chopped

Kosher salt and ground black pepper

2-ounce can oil-packed anchovy fillets (about 10 fillets), drained and roughly chopped

½ cup pitted black olives, roughly chopped

All-purpose flour, for dusting

1½ pounds store-bought refrigerated pizza dough, room temperature

Heat the oven to 450°F with a rack in the lowest position. Line a rimmed baking sheet with kitchen parchment. In a large bowl, toss the onions with 2 tablespoons oil, half of the thyme, ½ teaspoon salt and 1 teaspoon pepper. Spread the onion mixture in an even layer on the prepared baking sheet, then evenly distribute the anchovies and olives over the top. Bake, without stirring, until the onions begin to brown and soften, 20 to 25 minutes.

Meanwhile, on a well-floured counter, use a rolling pin to roll the dough into a 12-by-16-inch rectangle (the same dimensions as the baking sheet); work from the center outward to help ensure the dough is even. If it is resistant or shrinks after rolling, wait 5 to 10 minutes before trying again; if it is very elastic, you may need to give it a few rests.

It's fine if the dough rectangle is slightly smaller than the baking sheet.

When the onion mixture is ready, remove the baking sheet from the oven; leave the oven on. Being careful not to touch the hot baking sheet, lay the dough over the onion mixture, gently stretching and tucking in the edges as needed so the dough fills the baking sheet. Brush with the remaining 1 tablespoon oil, then use a fork to poke holes every 2 to 3 inches all the way through the dough. Bake until the surface is well browned, 15 to 17 minutes.

Remove from the oven and immediately invert a wire rack onto the baking sheet. Using potholders or oven mitts, hold the baking sheet and rack together and carefully invert. Lift off the baking sheet, then slowly peel away the parchment. Using a spatula, scrape off any toppings that cling to the parchment and return them to the pizza. Sprinkle with the remaining thyme and drizzle with additional oil.

Optional garnish: Chopped fresh flat-leaf parsley

517

Yogurt Dough for Pizza and Flatbread

Start to finish: 1½ hours (30 minutes active)
Makes two 12-inch pizzas or flatbreads

This versatile dough is a breeze to make in a food processor and can be used for pizzas with various toppings or Middle Eastern–style flatbreads. The addition of Greek yogurt makes a supple dough that's easy to work with and that bakes up with a chewy-soft crumb and subtle richness. For convenience, the dough can be made a day in advance. After dividing the dough in half and forming each piece into a round, place each portion in a quart-size zip-close bag misted with cooking spray, seal well and refrigerate overnight. Allow the dough to come to room temperature before shaping.

241 grams (1¾ cups) bread flour, plus more for dusting

1½ teaspoons instant yeast

¾ teaspoon table salt

¾ cup plain whole-milk Greek yogurt

1 tablespoon honey

In a food processor, combine the flour, yeast and salt, then process until combined, about 5 seconds. Add the yogurt, honey and ¼ cup water. Process until the mixture forms a ball, about 30 seconds; the dough should be tacky to the touch and should stick slightly to the sides of the bowl. If it feels too dry, add more water, 1 tablespoon at a time, and process until incorporated. Continue to process until the dough is shiny and elastic, about 1 minute.

Transfer the dough to a lightly floured counter. Flour your hands and knead the dough a few times, until it forms a smooth ball. Divide the dough in half and form each half into a taut ball by rolling it against the counter in a circular motion under a cupped hand. Space the balls about 6 inches apart on a lightly floured counter, then cover with plastic wrap. Let rise until doubled in volume, 1 to 1½ hours.

About 1 hour before baking, heat the oven to 500°F with a baking steel or stone on the upper-middle rack. Working one at a time, gently stretch each ball on a lightly floured counter to an oval approximately 6 inches wide and 12 inches long. The dough is now ready to top and bake.

Spinach and Feta Flatbreads

Start to finish: 40 minutes
Makes two 12-inch oval flatbreads

1 pound baby spinach

1 medium shallot, finely chopped

4 tablespoons salted butter, room temperature

3 medium garlic cloves, finely grated

1 tablespoon grated lemon zest

1½ teaspoons sweet paprika

¼ teaspoon red pepper flakes (optional)

Kosher salt and ground black pepper

Semolina flour, for dusting

Yogurt dough for pizza and flatbread, shaped into two 6-by-12-inch ovals

4 ounces feta cheese, crumbled (1 cup)

About 1 hour before baking, heat the oven to 500°F with a baking steel or stone on the upper-middle rack. Put the spinach in a large microwave-safe bowl. Cover and microwave on high until wilted, 2 to 4 minutes. Uncover and let cool slightly, then squeeze the spinach to remove excess moisture; wipe out the bowl. Roughly chop the spinach, then return it to the bowl and add the shallot, butter, garlic, lemon zest, paprika, pepper flakes (if using), 1 teaspoon salt and ½ teaspoon black pepper. Mix with your hands until well combined.

Lightly dust a baking peel, inverted baking sheet or rimless cookie sheet with semolina. Transfer one portion of the shaped dough to the peel and, if needed, reshape into a 6-by-12-inch oval. Spread half of the spinach mixture evenly over the dough, then top with half the feta. Slide the dough onto the baking steel and bake until the edges are golden brown, 9 to 11 minutes.

Using the peel, transfer the flatbread to a wire rack. Top and bake the second portion of dough in the same way, then transfer to the wire rack.

Peperoncini and Cheese Pizzas with Garlic-Herb Oil

Start to finish: 30 minutes
Makes two 12-inch oval pizzas

2 cups lightly packed fresh flat-leaf parsley

½ cup chopped fresh chives

¼ cup lightly packed fresh dill

1 large garlic clove, smashed and peeled

⅔ cup extra-virgin olive oil

Kosher salt and ground black pepper

Semolina flour, for dusting

Yogurt dough for pizza and flatbread, shaped into two 6-by-12-inch ovals

4 ounces fontina cheese, shredded (1 cup)

2 ounces Parmesan cheese, finely grated (1 cup)

1 cup drained peperoncini, stemmed, patted dry and sliced into thin rings

About 1 hour before baking, heat the oven to 500°F with a baking steel or stone on the upper-middle rack. In a food processor, combine the parsley, chives, dill, garlic, oil, 1 teaspoon salt and ½ teaspoon pepper. Process until smooth, about 30 seconds, scraping the bowl as needed. Transfer to a liquid measuring cup and set aside.

Lightly dust a baking peel, inverted baking sheet or rimless cookie sheet with semolina. Transfer one portion of the shaped dough to the peel and, if needed, reshape into a 6-by-12-inch oval. Sprinkle half the mozzarella and half the Parmesan evenly over the dough, then layer on half the peperoncini. Slide the dough onto the baking steel and bake until the edges are golden brown, 9 to 11 minutes.

Using the peel, transfer the pizza to a wire rack. Top and bake the second portion of dough in the same way, then transfer to the wire rack. Stir the herb oil to recombine, then drizzle over the warm pizzas.

CHANGE THE WAY YOU COOK

Flatbread Equipment Tips

Preheated surfaces

Preheating a solid surface to bake on helps concentrate heat on the dough through direct contact, rather than just the indirect heat of the hot air in the oven. For flatbreads specifically, the hot surface helps achieve a good crust. This crust helps set the dough structure that traps the steam that creates puffy pockets of pita and large bubbles in pizza crust.

Beginner—Inverted Baking Sheet

This is a great option for the new baker. Quick to heat and inexpensive, this low-commitment option will produce reliably solid results. If you forget to preheat it along with the oven, it can be added to the hot oven and allowed to heat later.

Intermediate—Baking Stone

Baking stones are heavy and retain heat well, which helps get good texture on an entire batch of flatbreads even with opening and closing the oven door, which cools the oven. The downside of the stone is that it is prone to cracking. It needs to be added to a COLD or COOL oven and preheated as the oven preheats. Adding it to a HOT (500°F) oven can cause it to crack from the temperature shock.

Advanced—Baking Steel

Baking steels are heavy, dense and effective surfaces for baking flatbreads. They are also more expensive than stones and harder to move around due to their heft. Still, nothing beats them at retaining heat and producing bubbled, crispy crusts. They also aren't prone to cracking.

PITA BREAD

Start to finish: 4 hours (40 minutes active)
Servings: Ten 5½ inch pita rounds

Pita bread is a yeast-leavened flatbread from the Mediterranean and Middle East. We make ours with whole-wheat flour and whole-milk yogurt for full flavor and a pleasant chew. Yogurt is common in some flatbreads but is generally not used in pita. We, however, found it helped produce a soft, elastic dough and a tender, but slightly chewy baked bread. To ensure the breads puff nicely and form pockets, they're baked two at a time on a heated baking steel or stone. We preferred a stand mixer for making the dough, but a food processor worked, too. To make the dough in a processor, combine the flours, yeast and sugar in the work bowl and pulse until combined. Add the water, yogurt and 2 tablespoons of oil and process until a smooth, slightly sticky ball forms, about 1 minute. Add additional water, 1½ teaspoons at a time (up to 2 tablespoons total), if the dough feels too dry. Let the dough rest in the processor for 5 minutes, then add the salt and process until smooth and pliable, about 1 minute. Knead by hand on a lightly floured counter for 1 minute, then transfer to an oiled medium bowl and turn to coat. Cover with plastic wrap and let rise in a warm, draft-free spot until not quite doubled in bulk. Continue with the recipe from the third step to shape and bake. It's not unusual if one or two of the rounds don't puff during baking—the bread will still taste great. The ones that do puff will not deflate as they cool. Store leftover pita in a zip-close bag for up to a day. To warm, wrap the pitas in foil and heat for 4 minutes at 300°F.

4 tablespoons grapeseed or other neutral oil, divided

171 grams (1¼ cups) bread flour, plus extra for dusting

175 grams (1¼ cups) whole-wheat flour

2¼ teaspoons instant yeast

2 teaspoons white sugar

¾ cup warm water (100°F to 110°F), plus more if needed

¼ cup plain whole-milk yogurt

1¼ teaspoons table salt

Coat a medium bowl with 1 teaspoon of the oil; set aside. In the bowl of a stand mixer fitted with the dough hook, add both flours, the yeast and sugar. Mix on low until combined, about 5 seconds. Add the water, yogurt and 2 tablespoons of oil. Mix on low until a smooth ball forms, about 3 minutes. Feel the dough; it should be slightly sticky. If not, add water 1½ teaspoons at a time (no more than 2 tablespoons total), mixing after each addition, until slightly sticky. Let rest in the mixer bowl for 5 minutes.

Add the salt and knead on low until smooth and pliable, 10 minutes. Transfer to the prepared bowl, forming it into a ball and turning to coat with oil. Cover with plastic wrap and let rise in a warm, draft-free area until well risen but not quite doubled in volume, 1 to 1½ hours.

Dust a rimmed baking sheet evenly with bread flour. Transfer the dough to the counter. Using a dough scraper or bench knife, divide the dough into 10 pieces (about 2 ounces each). Form each into a tight ball and place on the prepared baking sheet. Brush each ball with ½ teaspoon of the remaining oil, then cover with a damp kitchen towel. Let rise in a warm, draft-free area until well risen but not quite

doubled, 30 to 60 minutes. Meanwhile, heat the oven to 500°F with a baking steel or stone on the upper-middle rack.

Lightly dust two rimmed baking sheets with bread flour and lightly dust the counter. Place a dough ball on the counter; use a lightly floured rolling pin to roll the ball into a round ⅛ inch thick and 5½ inches in diameter. Set on one of the prepared baking sheets. Repeat with the remaining dough balls, placing them in a single layer on the baking sheets. Cover with a damp kitchen towel and let rest for 10 minutes.

Lightly dust a peel with bread flour, then place 2 dough rounds on the peel without flipping them. Working quickly, open the oven and slide the rounds onto the baking steel. Immediately close the door. Bake until the breads have puffed and are light golden brown, about 3 minutes. Using the peel, remove the breads from the oven. Transfer to a wire rack and cover with a dry kitchen towel. Repeat with the remaining dough rounds. Serve warm or room temperature.

YEASTED FLATBREADS WITH ZA'ATAR OIL

Start to finish: 1¼ hours active time
over the course of 1½ to 2½ days
Makes four 6-inch flatbreads

At Magdalena restaurant in Migdal, Israel, chef Yousef "Zuzu" Hanna offers a house-baked flatbread that's a hybrid of Yemeni saluf and Moroccan frena. Soft and chewy, with a puffy, open crumb and golden brown crust, the breads, shaped like slightly flattened mini boules, have a texture somewhere between naan and ciabatta. To re-create it at home, we use a moderately wet yeasted dough and give it multiple rises, including a 24- to 48-hour rise in the refrigerator, so be sure to read the recipe before beginning so you can plan accordingly. Immediately after baking, we brush the surface of the breads with a za'atar-infused oil that also can be served alongside the bread for dipping. Za'atar is a Levantine spice, seed and herb blend; look for it in the spice aisle of the supermarket or in Middle Eastern markets. You will need a baking steel or stone for this recipe, plus a baking peel for sliding the dough onto and off the steel.

521

**548 grams (4 cups) bread flour,
plus more for dusting**

1 tablespoon white sugar

2 teaspoons instant yeast

1½ cups water, cool room temperature (65°F)

3 tablespoons extra-virgin olive oil, divided

1¼ teaspoons table salt

**Semolina flour or fine cornmeal,
for dusting the pizza peel**

Za'atar oil (recipe below)

In a stand mixer with the dough hook, mix the flour, sugar and yeast on low until combined, about 15 seconds. With the mixer running, gradually add the water and 2 table-spoons of oil. Mix on low until the ingredients form a strong dough that clears the sides of the bowl, about 5 minutes. Cover the bowl with plastic wrap and let rest for 20 minutes.

Uncover the bowl, sprinkle the salt over the dough and mix on low until smooth and elastic, 5 to 7 minutes. Meanwhile, coat a large bowl with the remaining 1 tablespoon oil.

Transfer the dough to the prepared bowl. Dip your fingers into the oil pooled at the sides and dab the surface of the dough until completely coated. Using your hands, turn the dough over. Tightly cover the bowl with plastic wrap and let rise at room temperature until the dough is doubled in bulk, about 1 hour. Transfer to the refrigerator and let rise for at least 24 or up to 48 hours.

Line a rimmed baking sheet with kitchen parchment and mist with cooking spray. Lightly flour the counter and turn out the dough. Using a chef's knife or bench scraper, divide the dough into 4 even pieces, each about 8 ounces. Shape each into a taut, smooth ball and place seam side down, evenly spaced, on the prepared baking sheet. Mist the tops of the dough with cooking spray, cover loosely with plastic wrap and refrigerate for 3 hours.

Heat the oven to 500°F with a baking steel or stone on the middle rack. Remove the dough from the refrigerator. Generously flour the counter and set the dough balls on top; reserve the baking sheet. Dust the dough with flour and, using your fingertips, press each into a dimpled disk about 5½ inches wide and ½ inch thick. Return the dough to the baking sheet, evenly spacing the disks. Mist the dough with cooking spray, cover with plastic wrap and let rise at room

temperature until slightly puffy, about 1 hour.

Generously dust a baking peel with semolina. Flour your hands, then gently slide your fingers under one round of dough, lift and transfer to the prepared peel, placing the round near the edge so it will be easier to slide onto the baking steel. Repeat with another round of dough, making sure the two don't touch. Gently shake the peel back and forth to ensure the dough is not sticking, then, working quickly, open the oven and slide the rounds onto the steel.

Bake until the dough is puffed and golden brown, 7 to 10 minutes. Using the peel, transfer the breads to a wire rack. Lightly brush the tops with some of the za'atar oil. Bake the 2 remaining rounds in the same way. Serve the breads warm or at room temperature with the remaining za'atar oil for dipping.

ZA'ATAR OIL

Start to finish: 5 minutes
Makes ½ cup

½ cup extra-virgin olive oil

1 tablespoon za'atar

¼ to ½ teaspoon red pepper flakes

¼ teaspoon kosher salt

In a small saucepan over medium, cook the oil, za'atar and pepper flakes, stirring, until the mixture is fragrant, about 2 minutes. Stir in the salt and let cool. Store at room temperature in an airtight container for up to 1 week.

GREEK YOGURT AND OLIVE OIL FLATBREADS

Start to finish: 1 hour
Makes eight 7-inch flatbreads

These soft, plush flatbreads from chef Marianna Leivaditaki are simple to make. Yogurt and olive oil give them rich flavor and a little semolina flour adds a pleasing texture. The breads are cooked one at a time in a skillet on the stovetop (cast iron works best for browning, but nonstick does a decent job, too) and hot out of the pan, they're brushed with olive oil seasoned with za'atar, sumac and dried oregano. The flatbreads are best fresh, but can be stored in a zip-close bag at room temperature for up to three days; to rewarm, wrap the breads in foil and heat at 350°F for a few minutes.

1 cup warm water (110°F)

¼ cup whole-milk Greek yogurt,
room temperature

½ cup extra-virgin olive oil, divided,
plus more for the bowl

293 grams (2¼ cups) all-purpose flour,
plus more for dusting

85 grams (½ cup) semolina flour

1 tablespoon instant yeast

1 teaspoon table salt, divided

1 teaspoon za'atar

½ teaspoon ground sumac

½ teaspoon dried oregano

In a small bowl, whisk together the water, yogurt and ¼ cup oil. In a large bowl, whisk together both flours, the yeast and ¾ teaspoon salt. Make a well in the center and pour the liquids into the well. Using a silicone spatula, gradually incorporate the dry ingredients into the wet; once combined, the mixture should form a shaggy dough.

Dust the counter with all-purpose flour and turn the dough out onto it; reserve the bowl. Knead the dough until smooth and elastic, about 2 minutes, adding flour as needed to prevent sticking. Lightly coat the same bowl with oil, then return the dough to it. Cover with a clean kitchen towel and let rise at room temperature until the dough has doubled in bulk, 30 to 60 minutes.

Meanwhile, cut eight 9-inch squares of kitchen parchment; set aside. In a small bowl, stir together the remaining

¼ cup oil, the za'atar, sumac, oregano and the remaining ¼ teaspoon salt; set aside.

When the dough is ready, dust the counter with flour, then turn the dough onto the surface. Using a dough scraper or bench knife, divide the dough into 8 pieces, each about 87 grams (3 ounces). Form each portion into a taut ball, keeping the formed balls covered with the kitchen towel as you shape the rest. Set 1 ball on a lightly floured surface and, using a rolling pin, roll it into an 8-inch round about ⅛ inch thick, dusting with flour as needed. Lightly flour a parchment square and set the round on top. Repeat with the remaining dough balls, stacking the rounds on top of each other, with a parchment square between the layers.

Heat a 10- to 12-inch cast-iron skillet over medium until water flicked onto the surface immediately sizzles and evaporates. Pick up a dough round by its parchment liner, invert it into the pan and peel off and discard the parchment. Cook until large bubbles form and the bottom is spottily browned, 1 to 2 minutes. Using tongs, flip the bread and cook until the second side is golden brown, about 1 minute. Transfer to a wire rack and brush the surface with the za'atar oil. Cook the remaining dough rounds in the same way and brush them with za'atar oil. Wipe out the pan if excess flour begins to build up and smoke, and adjust the heat as needed. Serve warm or room temperature.

Flavored Butters

Want a fast-but-flavorful topping for flatbreads?
Try these spicy and savory butters that come together
in a snap.

For garlic-herb butter: Combine 3 tablespoons salted
butter and 1 grated garlic clove in a small saucepan over
medium. Cook, stirring, until the garlic is just beginning to
color, about 30 seconds. Off heat, add 2 tablespoons finely
chopped fresh flat-leaf parsley, 1 tablespoon finely chopped
fresh dill, 1 tablespoon finely chopped fresh cilantro,
tarragon or basil, and a pinch of salt.

For za'atar butter: Combine 3 tablespoons salted butter
and 1 tablespoon za'atar in a small saucepan over
medium. Cook until the butter is bubbling and the seeds
are just beginning to color, about 30 seconds.

For harissa butter: Melt 3 tablespoons salted butter in a
small saucepan over medium. Off heat, stir in 1 tablespoon
harissa.

YOGURT FLATBREADS

Start to finish: 40 minutes
Makes 6 flatbreads

Made throughout the Middle East, non-yeasted flatbreads
are the definition of quick bread, taking relatively little time
to prepare. We added yogurt to a whole wheat- and honey-
enriched dough for both its tangy flavor and tenderizing
qualities. Bread flour gives these flatbreads pleasant chew,
but you can substitute all-purpose flour. If you do use
all-purpose, you will likely have to add a couple extra
tablespoons of flour during kneading because the dough
will be slightly wetter. You'll need a 12-inch cast-iron skillet;
a 10-inch cast-iron skillet will work, too, but there will
be a little less room for maneuvering the rounds when
flipping. We liked serving these with flavored butters,
see preceding recipe.

**206 grams (1½ cups) bread flour, plus
more for dusting**

35 grams (¼ cup) whole-wheat flour

¾ teaspoon table salt

1 teaspoon baking powder

168 grams (¾ cup) plain whole-milk yogurt

2 teaspoons honey

**3 tablespoons salted butter, melted,
or flavored butter (recipe p. 524)**

In a large bowl, stir together both flours, the salt and baking powder. Add the yogurt and honey and stir until a shaggy dough forms. Using your hands, knead in the bowl until the dough forms a cohesive ball, incorporating any dry bits; the dough will be slightly sticky.

Turn the dough out onto a counter dusted with bread flour and continue kneading until the dough is tacky instead of sticky, about 1 minute. The finished dough may appear slightly lumpy; this is fine. Divide into 6 pieces and shape each into a ball. Loosely cover with plastic wrap and let rest for 10 minutes. Meanwhile, heat a 12-inch cast-iron skillet over medium-high.

On a lightly floured counter, roll each ball to an 8-inch circle. Place one dough round in the heated skillet and cook until the bottom is dark spotty brown, 1 to 1½ minutes. Using tongs, flip the round and cook the second side until dark spotty brown, about 1 minute. Transfer to a wire rack, flipping so the first side to cook faces down, then brush with butter. Repeat with the remaining dough rounds. Serve immediately.

TURKISH-STYLE FLAKY FLATBREADS

Start to finish: 1 hour, plus resting and refrigeration
Makes eight 10-inch flatbreads

We tried katmer, a flaky, unleavened flatbread sometimes sweetened with sugar, tahini and/or nuts, in Türkiye. The bread's thin profile, tender texture and golden-brown spots were reminiscent of lavash, but it boasted buttery-rich layers that lighten it considerably and made it especially delicious. A series of rolls and folds, with butter and oil brushed in between, create the dough's signature flakiness. When the katmer hits a hot griddle or skillet, its layers steam apart. The folded dough packets can be made up to 24 hours in advance, then covered and refrigerated; there's no need to let them come to room temperature before the final roll. Serve the finished breads warm or at room temperature with meze or as a part of a meal.

**650 grams (5 cups) all-purpose flour,
plus more if needed and for dusting**

1 teaspoon table salt

**85 grams (6 tablespoons) salted butter,
melted and slightly cooled**

¼ cup plus 2 tablespoons extra-virgin olive oil

In a stand mixer with the dough hook, mix the flour and salt on low to combine, about 5 seconds. With the mixer on low, slowly add 1¾ cups water. Knead until the dough is smooth and clears the sides of the bowl, about 5 minutes. If the dough sticks to the bowl after 5 minutes, knead in up to 2 tablespoons more flour, 1 tablespoon at a time, until it clears the sides.

Lightly flour the counter and turn the dough out onto it. Using a bench knife, divide the dough into 8 even pieces. Form each into a taut ball by rolling it against the counter in a circular motion under a cupped hand. Space the balls about 1 inch apart on a lightly floured surface, then cover with a kitchen towel; let rest for 30 minutes. Meanwhile, in a medium bowl, stir together the butter and oil.

Set 1 dough ball on a lightly floured surface and, using a rolling pin, roll it into a rough 11-inch square of even thickness, dusting with flour as needed. Lightly brush the surface of the dough with about 4 teaspoons of the butter-oil mixture. Fold the top third of the dough down over itself, then fold the bottom third up; press gently to seal. Lightly brush the surface with about 1 teaspoon of the butter-oil mixture. Fold the strip into thirds, forming a small, squar-ish packet; press gently to seal. Dust the surface of the packet with flour, then transfer it to a large plate; repeat with the remaining dough balls, keeping the packets in a single layer. Cover with plastic wrap and refrigerate for at least 30 minutes or up to 24 hours. Meanwhile, cut eight 12-inch squares of kitchen parchment; set aside.

When ready to cook, lightly flour the counter. Set 1 packet on the lightly floured surface and, using a rolling pin, roll it into a 10-inch square of even thickness, dusting with flour as needed. Lightly flour a parchment square and set the dough square on top. Repeat with the remaining dough packets, stacking the dough squares on top of each other, separated by parchment.

Heat a 12-inch cast-iron skillet over medium-high until water flicked onto the surface immediately sizzles. Pick up a dough square by 2 corners, peel it off the parchment and lay it in the skillet, taking care not to let the dough fold over itself. Cook until bubbles form and the bottom is spottily browned, 1 to 2 minutes. Using tongs, flip and cook until the second side is golden brown, 1 to 2 minutes. Cook for about another minute, flipping as needed, until lightly puffed and browned all over. Transfer to a wire rack and cover with a kitchen towel. Cook the remaining dough in the same way. Wipe out the pan if excess flour begins to build up and smoke, and adjust the heat as needed. Serve warm or at room temperature.

CHICKPEA FLOUR FLATBREAD

Start to finish: 30 minutes
Makes four 10-inch crepes

Chickpea flour—rather than wheat flour—creates flatbreads with a crisp. light texture, but just as quick and easy to make. They also are gluten-free and delicious hot from the pan or at room temperature. Chickpea flatbreads are known as socca in France, or as farinata in Italy. Some versions are thicker than others, but all are made with chickpea flour and olive oil. Ours are thin and get great flavor from the rich brown-ing they attain in the skillet. To turn our socca into a light meal, offer an olive and roasted pepper relish.

165 grams (1½ cups) chickpea flour

½ teaspoon table salt

¼ teaspoon ground black pepper

1½ cups warm (100°F) water

¼ cup extra-virgin olive oil, plus more to cook

In a large bowl, whisk together the chickpea flour, salt and pepper. Pour in half of the water and whisk until smooth. While whisking, slowly pour in the remaining water and whisk until combined. Gently whisk in the oil just until incorporated but small beads of oil remain visible.

In a 10-inch nonstick skillet over medium-high, heat 2 teaspoons oil until shimmering. Pour ¼ of the batter (about ½ cup) into the center of the skillet and tilt so the batter completely covers the surface. Cook until the bottom is well browned, 1½ to 2 minutes. Using a metal spatula, carefully flip and cook until the second side is dark spotty brown, about another minute. Transfer to a wire rack. Repeat with remaining batter and 2 teaspoons oil for each flatbread.

Cut each flatbread into 4 wedges and serve with the following topping:

OLIVE AND ROASTED PEPPER RELISH

In a medium bowl, stir together **1 cup chopped pitted green olives, ¼ cup drained and chopped roasted red peppers, ¼ cup chopped fresh flat-leaf parsley, 1 tablespoon drained and rinsed capers, 1 finely grated garlic clove** and **1 teaspoon red wine vinegar.** Let stand for 15 minutes.

MOROCCAN FLATBREADS

Start to finish: 2 hours (20 minutes active), plus cooling
Makes three 7-inch loaves

Khobz is a Moroccan yeasted flatbread that isn't truly flat. It's a low, small, pleasantly dense round loaf present at almost every meal and, being the daily bread, is typically quite plain in flavor. But the bread that home cook Houda Mehdi showed us how to make in her kitchen in Fes, Morocco, was fantastically flavored with sesame, flax and fennel seeds, as well as semolina and wheat bran. Hers was the most delicious khobz we tasted during our time in Fes. We adapted her recipe, adding a small measure of olive oil for a slightly more tender crumb and to lend a little richness, and we baked our breads in a 475°F oven. Leftovers will keep in an airtight container for up to two days; to reheat, wrap the bread in foil and warm in a 400°F oven for about 10 minutes.

618 grams (4¾ cups) all-purpose flour, divided, plus more as needed and for dusting

202 grams (1 cup plus 3 tablespoons) semolina flour

30 grams (½ cup) wheat bran

56 grams (⅓ cup) sesame seeds, toasted

80 grams (½ cup) flax seeds

1 tablespoon fennel seeds, lightly crushed

1 tablespoon instant yeast

1 teaspoon table salt

2½ cups warm water (110°F)

3 tablespoons extra-virgin olive oil, plus more for the baking sheet

In a stand mixer with the dough hook, mix 390 grams (3 cups) of the all-purpose flour, the semolina, wheat bran, sesame seeds, flax seeds, fennel seeds, yeast and salt on low speed until well combined, about 1 minute. With the mixer running, slowly add the water and oil. Mix on low until the dough comes together, about 5 minutes, scraping the bowl once or twice. Cover the bowl and let the dough rest for 20 minutes.

With the mixer running on low, add the remaining 228 grams (1¾ cups) all-purpose flour and knead until the dough is smooth and pulls away from the sides of the bowl, about 7 minutes; if the dough is sticky and clings to the sides of the bowl, knead in additional flour 1 tablespoon at a time until it reaches the proper consistency.

Lightly brush a rimmed baking sheet with oil. Dust the counter with flour and turn the dough out onto it, then divide the dough into 3 pieces. Using your hands cupped around the dough, form each piece into a taut ball on an unfloured area of the counter. Press each ball into a 7-inch round about ¾ inch high, then place on the prepared baking sheet; stagger the rounds to fit. Cover with a kitchen towel and let rise at room temperature until nearly doubled in size, about 1 hour; it's fine if the rounds end up touching each other. Meanwhile, heat the oven to 475°F with a rack in the middle position.

When the breads are properly risen, use a sharp knife to score a slit about 3 inches long into the surface of each round. Bake until the breads are well browned, 18 to 20 minutes. Cool on the baking sheet for about 5 minutes, then transfer the breads to a wire rack and cool completely.

JORDANIAN BEDOUIN FLATBREAD

Start to finish: 2 hours 10 minutes (50 minutes active)
Makes ten 8-inch flatbreads

Shrak is the daily bread on the Bedouin table. The simple, rustic flatbread is as suited to dunking in olive oil and za'atar or serving with hummus and other dips as it is for scooping up stewy or saucy main dishes. We loved the shrak that home cook Fatima Mohammad demonstrated for us during a visit to Petra, Jordan. While seated on the floor, she used her hands, with an assist from gravity, to form a portion dough into a sheet as thin as film and larger than a hubcap, then cooked it swiftly on a saj, or a domed griddle resembling an inverted wok. The bread was soft and supple, with a satisfying chewiness and a subtly nutty yet clean flavor. We wanted to find a way to make shrak at home. The dough, a simple mixture of equal parts (by volume) whole-wheat and all-purpose flours plus salt and water, came together easily in a stand mixer. To shape the dough, we use our hands, plus a rolling pin and an overturned bowl to gently stretch it into a round thin enough to be almost translucent. Without a saj for cooking the bread, we opted for a large cast-iron skillet (a griddle works, too), but because of the skillet's diameter, we make our shrak about the size of a standard flour tortilla. Transferring the ultra-thin dough to the skillet without any folding or wrinkling is a little tricky, so the first attempt may yield an imperfect bread, but shaping and cooking become easier as you get the hang of the technique. Store leftovers in a zip-close bag for up to a day or two; to reheat, sprinkle with a few drops of water, wrap in foil and place in a 400°F oven for about five minutes.

140 grams (1 cup) whole-wheat flour

130 grams (1 cup) all-purpose flour, plus more for dusting

1 teaspoon table salt

In a stand mixer with the dough hook, mix both flours and the salt on medium until well combined, about 30 seconds. With the mixer running on low, slowly add ¾ cup water and mix, scraping the bowl as needed, until the ingredients form a shaggy dough, 4 to 5 minutes. Knead on low until the dough is smooth and elastic and pulls away from the sides of the bowl, about 15 minutes.

Lightly dust the counter and your hands with flour; remove the dough from the mixer and set it on the counter. Shape the dough into a ball, dust lightly with flour and transfer to a large bowl. Cover with plastic wrap and let rest at room temperature for at least 1 hour or up to 2 hours (the dough also can be refrigerated fåor up to 24 hours; bring it to room temperature before shaping).

Lightly flour the counter, turn the dough out onto it and divide it into 10 pieces. Form each piece into a smooth, taut ball. Cover with a kitchen towel and let rest for about 15 minutes.

When you are ready to shape and cook the breads, set an overturned medium bowl with sloping sides and a rounded base about 5 inches in diameter near your work area. Heat a 12-inch cast-iron skillet or griddle over medium-high. Place a wire rack in a rimmed baking sheet and set near the stove. Very lightly flour the counter, place 1 dough ball on top and press it with your hands into a 3-inch disk. Using a rolling pin, roll the disk into a round about 6 inches in diameter. Lift the dough off the counter and, using your fingers and a gentle pulling motion, stretch it into a round about 8 inches. Lightly flour the round, drape it over the overturned bowl and, using your hands, gently and evenly stretch the dough down the sides of the bowl until it is thin enough to be almost translucent; it's fine if a few small tears form. Leave the dough in place on the bowl.

Test if the skillet is properly heated by flicking water onto the surface; it should immediately sizzle and evaporate. If the pan is not yet fully heated, drape a kitchen towel over the bread to prevent drying and allow the pan to heat for another minute or two before testing again.

When the pan is properly heated, use both hands to carefully lift the dough off the bowl and quickly lay the round in the skillet; try to place it flat and without any wrinkles. Cook, using a wide metal spatula to flip the round about every 15 seconds, until lightly blistered on both sides, about 2 minutes; the bread should remain pliable and should not become crisp. Transfer to the prepared rack and cover with a kitchen towel. Shape and cook the remaining portions of dough in the same way, stacking them on the rack.

ITALIAN FLATBREAD

Start to finish: 30 minutes
Makes four 10-inch flatbreads

Flatbread is among the quickest of quick breads. Leavened or not, folded topped or used as a scoop, it appeals with promises of warm, fresh dough. One of our favorite variations originated in Romagna, in northern Italy. There they throw together flour, salt, water or milk, and lard or olive oil to make a quick dough. After a short rest, the flatbread— a piadina—is cooked on a griddle or skillet. The cooked piadine then are stuffed with sweet or savory fillings and folded in half to make a sandwich. We started by finding the right fat for our dough. Butter was wrong. Olive oil gave us a pleasant texture and flavor, but something still was missing. So we gave lard a shot. And what a difference. The piadine were tender with just the right chew. But we wanted yet more suppleness and found our answer in naan, a tender flatbread from India that adds a scoop of yogurt to the dough. Fat hinders gluten development, keeping bread soft. It worked well in our piadine and gave the dough more complex flavor. Though it was not as flavorful, vegetable shortening worked as a substitute for lard. If the dough doesn't ball up in the processor, gather it together and briefly knead it by hand. Roll out the rounds as evenly as possible. Let the dough rest if it resists rolling or snaps back. And if the char on the first piadina is too light, heat the pan several minutes longer. For a simple topping, brush the cooked piadine with our spicy garlic oil or try prosciutto, arugula and ricotta, see following recipes.

½ cup water

¼ cup plain whole-milk yogurt

274 grams (2 cups) bread flour

1 teaspoon table salt

1½ teaspoons baking powder

63 grams (⅓ cup) lard, room temperature

In a liquid measuring cup, whisk together ¼ cup of the water and the yogurt. In a food processor, combine the flour, salt and baking powder. Process for 5 seconds. Add the lard and process until combined, about 10 seconds. With the processor running, add the yogurt mixture. With the processor still running, add the remaining water 1 tablespoon at a time until the dough forms a smooth, moist ball, about 1 minute.

Divide the dough into 4 pieces. Roll each into a ball, then cover with plastic wrap. Let rest for 15 minutes. Meanwhile, prepare toppings.

Roll each dough ball into a 10-inch round. Poke the surfaces all over with a fork. Heat a 12-inch cast-iron skillet over medium until a drop of water sizzles immediately, 4 to 6 minutes. One at a time, place a dough round in the skillet and cook until the bottom is charred in spots, 1 to 2 minutes. Using tongs, flip and cook for 30 seconds. Transfer to a plate and cover loosely with foil.

SPICY GARLIC-AND-HERB OIL

Start to finish: 10 minutes
Makes about 1 cup

Brush this herb-rich oil onto warm piadine to serve alongside soups, stews or salads. Or serve it in a dish as a dip for pieces of torn flatbread. If you like, substitute fresh oregano, marjoram or mint for the dill. The oil works equally well drizzled over pasta, polenta and fried eggs, or as a base for vinaigrettes.

2 cups lightly packed flat-leaf
parsley leaves

10 tablespoons extra-virgin olive oil

½ cup coarsely chopped fresh chives

¼ cup coarsely chopped fresh dill

1 tablespoon red pepper flakes

1 large garlic clove, smashed

½ teaspoon kosher salt

½ teaspoon ground black pepper

In a food processor, combine all ingredients and process until smooth, about 20 seconds, scraping the bowl as needed.

PROSCIUTTO, ARUGULA AND RICOTTA

Start to finish: 10 minutes
Makes 4 piadine

In Romagna, piadine are often served with cured meats, greens and fresh cheeses that soften in the warmth of the freshly cooked bread. If possible, purchase fresh-cut prosciutto, sliced as thinly as possible, and allow it to come to room temperature. The flavor and texture of ricotta cheese varies widely by brand; we like Calabro.

¾ cup whole-milk ricotta cheese

½ teaspoon grated lemon zest,
plus 2 tablespoons lemon juice

Kosher salt and ground black pepper

8 slices prosciutto, room temperature

4 ounces baby arugula (about 4 cups)

3 tablespoons extra-virgin olive oil

In a medium bowl, stir together the ricotta and lemon zest. Taste and season with salt and pepper. Spread the ricotta mixture evenly over half of each piadina, then top with 2 slices of prosciutto. In a medium bowl, toss the arugula with the lemon juice and a pinch of salt. Mound on top of the prosciutto. Drizzle with oil and fold.

TOMATO-OLIVE FOCACCIA

Start to finish: 7¼ hours (40 minutes active), plus cooling
Servings: 12

This recipe recreates the light, open-crumbed focaccia we ate at Panificio Fiore in Bari, Italy. To achieve that texture, the dough must be wet—so wet, in fact, it verges on a thick, yet pourable batter. Resist the temptation to add more flour than is called for. Shaping such a sticky, high-hydration dough by hand is impossible. Instead, the dough is gently poured and scraped into the oiled baking pan; gravity settles it into an even layer. If you have trouble finding Castelvetrano olives, substitute any large, meaty green olive. To slice the baked focaccia for serving, use a serrated knife and a sawing motion to cut through the crust and crumb without compressing it. If desired, serve with extra-virgin olive oil for dipping. For convenience, the dough can be prepared and transferred to the baking pan a day in advance. After it has settled in the pan, cover tightly with plastic wrap and refrigerate. The next day, prepare the toppings. Uncover, top the dough with the olives and tomatoes and let stand at room temperature for 45 minutes, then finish and bake as directed.

531

500 grams (3⅔ cups) bread flour

5 teaspoons instant yeast

1 teaspoon white sugar

2 cups water, cool room temperature

8 tablespoons extra-virgin olive oil, divided

1¾ teaspoons table salt, divided

1 cup cherry tomatoes, halved

1 cup Castelvetrano olives, pitted and halved (see headnote)

1 teaspoon dried oregano

¾ teaspoon ground black pepper

In a stand mixer with the dough hook, mix the flour, yeast and sugar on medium until combined, about 30 seconds. With the mixer on low, drizzle in the water, then increase to medium and mix until the ingredients form a very wet, smooth dough, about 5 minutes. Turn off the mixer, cover the bowl and let stand for 10 minutes. Meanwhile, coat the bottom and sides of a large bowl with 2 tablespoons of oil; set aside.

Sprinkle 1 teaspoon of salt over the dough, then knead on medium until smooth and elastic, about 5 minutes; the dough will be wet enough to cling to the sides of the bowl. Using a silicone spatula, scrape the dough into the oiled bowl. Dip your fingers into the oil pooled at the sides of the bowl and dab the surface of the dough until completely coated with oil. Cover tightly with plastic wrap and let stand at room temperature for 5½ to 6 hours; during this time, the dough will double in volume, deflate, then rise again (but will not double in volume again).

After the dough has risen for about 4½ hours, heat the oven to 500°F with a baking steel or stone on the middle rack. Mist a 9-by-13-inch metal baking pan with cooking spray, then pour 2 tablespoons of the remaining oil in the center of the pan; set aside.

When the dough is ready, gently pour it into the prepared pan, scraping the sides of the bowl with a silicone spatula to loosen; try to retain as much air in the dough as possible. The dough will eventually settle into an even layer in the pan; do not spread the dough with a spatula, as this will cause it to deflate. Set aside while you prepare the tomatoes.

In a medium bowl, use a potato masher to lightly crush the tomatoes. Scatter the olives evenly over the dough, then do the same with the tomatoes, leaving the juice and seeds in the bowl. If the dough has not fully filled the corners of the pan, use your hands to lightly press the toppings to push the dough into the corners. Let stand uncovered at room temperature for 20 minutes.

Drizzle the dough with the remaining 4 tablespoons oil, making sure each tomato is coated. Sprinkle evenly with the oregano, remaining ¾ teaspoon salt and the pepper. Place the pan on the baking steel or stone and bake until golden brown and the sides of the focaccia have pulled away from the pan, 20 to 22 minutes. Cool in the pan on a wire rack for 5 minutes. Using a wide metal spatula, lift the focaccia from the pan and slide it onto the rack. Cool for at least 30 minutes before serving.

CHINESE SESAME-SCALLION BREAD

Start to finish: 2 hours (30 minutes active)

Servings: 4

This bread, known as zhima dabing—which translates as "sesame big pancake"—is similar to Chinese scallion pancakes (cong you bing), but is much larger and thicker and has a lighter, fluffier crumb. The addition of sweet rice flour (also called glutinous) gives the crust a unique crispness and the interior a satisfying chew. If you're unable to find sweet rice flour with the baking ingredients, check the Asian aisle for a white box labeled "mochiko" (the Japanese term for the flour). Chop the scallions by thinly slicing them first, then running the knife over them a few times to further break them down. To make sure the scallions stay fresh, prep them toward the end of the dough's one-hour rising time.

217 grams (1⅔ cups) all-purpose flour, plus more if needed

40 grams (¼ cup) sweet (glutinous) rice flour (see headnote)

1 teaspoon instant yeast

¾ teaspoon table salt, divided

¾ cup warm (100°F) water

1 tablespoon honey

4 teaspoons toasted sesame oil, divided

1 bunch scallions, finely chopped (about 1 cup)

4 tablespoons sesame seeds, divided

2 tablespoons grapeseed or other neutral oil

In a stand mixer fitted with the dough hook, mix both flours, the yeast and ½ teaspoon of salt on low until combined, about 30 seconds. In a liquid measuring cup or small bowl, whisk the water and honey until dissolved. With the mixer on low, slowly pour the honey water into the flour mixture. Continue mixing on low until an evenly moistened dough forms, about 1 minute. Stop the mixer and check the dough; if it feels wet or very sticky, add an additional 1 to 3 tablespoons all-purpose flour. Continue mixing on low until smooth, about 4 minutes. The dough should feel tacky but not stick to your fingers.

Coat a medium bowl with 1 teaspoon of the sesame oil. Place the dough in the bowl and turn to coat. Cover with plastic wrap and let rise in a warm, draft-free spot until the dough has doubled in size, about 1 hour.

Coat a rimmed baking sheet with 1 teaspoon of the remaining sesame oil. Turn the dough out onto the baking sheet and use your hands to press into a 12-by-9-inch rectangle. In a small bowl, toss the scallions with the remaining 2 teaspoons sesame oil, then distribute evenly over the dough. Sprinkle with the remaining ¼ teaspoon salt. Starting from a long side, roll the dough into a cylinder and pinch the seam to seal. Roll the cylinder seam side down, then coil it into a tight spiral and tuck the end under. Using your hands, press the coil to slightly flatten, sprinkle with 2 tablespoons of sesame seeds and press to adhere. Flip the coil and sprinkle the second side with the remaining 2 tablespoons sesame seeds. Press and flatten into an even 10-inch round.

Add the grapeseed oil to a 12-inch nonstick skillet and swirl to evenly coat the bottom. Carefully transfer the dough to the skillet; reshape into a 10-inch round, if needed. Cover with a lid and let rise until about doubled in size, about 30 minutes.

Place the covered skillet over medium and cook until the bottom of the bread is deep golden brown, 5 to 6 minutes. Uncover and, using tongs and a wide metal spatula, carefully flip the bread. Cook until golden on the second side, about 3 minutes. Slide the bread onto a wire rack and let cool for at least 10 minutes. Cut into quarters to serve.

533

RICOTTA SALATA–STUFFED FLATBREAD WITH SHALLOTS

Start to finish: 30 minutes, plus cooling

Servings: 4

Ricotta salata is a firm, dry white cheese with a mild flavor and a distinct saltiness; do not substitute regular (fresh) ricotta cheese, which contains too much moisture and too little salt for this recipe. If you cannot find ricotta salata, queso fresco is a good substitute. The shallot mixture can be made a day ahead and refrigerated for two days; bring to room temperature before using. If you have a favorite pizza dough recipe, feel free to use, but this works fine with store-bought dough. If your oven only goes up to 500°F, add 2 to 4 minutes to the baking time.

3 tablespoons extra-virgin olive oil, divided

2 large shallots, halved lengthwise and thinly sliced (about ½ cup)

2 garlic cloves, thinly sliced

1 teaspoon minced fresh rosemary

Two 8-ounce portions pizza dough, warmed to 75°F

1 cup shredded ricotta salata cheese

¼ cup grated Parmesan cheese

Bread flour, for dusting

Semolina flour, for dusting

Kosher salt and ground black pepper

1 tablespoon flat-leaf parsley leaves

In a small saucepan over medium, combine 2 tablespoons of the oil and the shallots. Cook, stirring occasionally, until softened and lightly golden, 8 to 12 minutes. Add the garlic and rosemary, then cook, stirring, until the garlic just begins to color, about 1 minute. Transfer to a heatproof bowl and let cool to room temperature.

At least 1 hour before baking, heat the oven to 550°F with a baking steel or stone on the upper-middle rack.

On a counter dusted generously with bread flour, use a rolling pin to roll each portion of dough into a 10-inch round. Spoon the shallot mixture evenly over one of the dough rounds, including the oil, leaving a ½-inch border. Sprinkle with the ricotta salata and Parmesan. Gently press the cheese into the dough and season with black pepper.

Lay the second dough round on top, aligning the edges, and press ½ inch from the edge to lightly seal. Using the rolling pin, gently roll the filled dough to a 12-inch round.

Lightly dust a pizza peel, rimless cookie sheet or inverted baking sheet with semolina. Transfer the filled dough to the peel and reshape as needed. Using the tip of a paring knife, cut a few steam vents in the top dough layer, making sure not to cut through to the bottom. Brush the surface with the remaining 1 tablespoon oil and sprinkle with salt. Slide the pie onto the baking steel and bake until well browned, 7 to 8 minutes.

Using the peel, transfer the pie to a wire rack. Let cool for several minutes, then sprinkle with the parsley.

UMBRIAN FLATBREADS WITH SAUSAGE AND BROCCOLI RABE

Start to finish: 50 minutes, plus resting time for the dough
Servings: 4

Torta al testo is a simple Umbrian flatbread that can be an accompaniment to soups or stews, or, as Perugia home cook Silvia Buitoni showed us, the bread can be split and filled to make fantastic sandwiches. Though some versions are leavened with yeast, Buitoni used baking powder for a quick-and-easy dough that can be shaped and skillet-cooked after just a brief rest. We added a small measure of olive oil to her formula to give the bread a little suppleness and richness. The filling for our torta al testo is based on Buitoni's, but instead of the foraged herbs and greens that she steamed then sautéed, we opted for broccoli rabe. To be efficient, prep the filling ingredients while the dough is resting. This recipe calls for a 12-inch cast-iron skillet (the steady heat of cast iron excels at even browning and cooking the flatbreads), but you will need a lid when sautéing the rabe. If your skillet lacks one, use a lid from a similarly sized pot or simply set a baking sheet on top.

FOR THE DOUGH:

260 grams (2 cups) all-purpose flour, plus more for dusting

2 teaspoons baking powder

1 teaspoon table salt

¼ cup extra-virgin olive oil

FOR THE FILLING:

3 tablespoons extra-virgin olive oil, divided, plus more for drizzling

1 pound hot or sweet Italian sausages

1 bunch broccoli rabe, trimmed and halved crosswise

Kosher salt and ground black pepper

2 oil-packed anchovy fillets

2 medium garlic cloves, finely grated

¼ to ½ teaspoon red pepper flakes

For the dough, in a large bowl, whisk together the flour, baking powder and salt. In a 2-cup liquid measuring cup, combine the oil and ½ cup water. While stirring, slowly pour the oil-water mixture into the dry ingredients. Stir until a shaggy dough forms, adding 1 to 3 tablespoons more water as needed if the mixture is too dry. Dust the counter with flour, then turn the dough out onto it. Knead until the dough is smooth and cohesive, about 30 seconds. Divide it in half, shape each piece into a smooth ball and set on a lightly floured surface. Cover with a kitchen towel and let rest for at least 15 minutes or up to 1 hour.

Using your hands, press each dough ball into a 5½-inch round. Heat a 12-inch cast-iron skillet over medium-low until water flicked onto the surface immediately sizzles. Add 1 round to the skillet and cook until well browned in spots, about 4 minutes. Using a wide metal spatula, flip the round and cook until the second side is spotty brown, another 4 minutes. Transfer to a wire rack. Cook the second round in the same way. Let the flatbreads cool while you make the filling.

535

To make the filling, in the same skillet over medium-high, heat 2 tablespoons of the oil until barely smoking. Add the sausages, cover and cook, turning occasionally with tongs, until the centers reach 160°F, about 10 minutes. Transfer to a plate; reserve the skillet.

To the skillet still over medium-high, add the broccoli rabe and ¼ teaspoon salt; stir to coat with the fat in the pan. Cover and cook, stirring, until just shy of tender, 4 to 6 minutes. Push the rabe to one side, then add the remaining 1 tablespoon oil, anchovies, garlic and pepper flakes to the clearing. Cook, stirring and mashing the mixture, until fragrant and the anchovies have broken down, about 1 minute. Stir the mixture into the rabe, then remove from the heat. Taste and season with salt and black pepper; scrape onto another plate.

To assemble, cut each sausage lengthwise into 4 planks of even thickness. Cut each flatbread in half to create 4 half moons. Using a serrated knife, split each piece horizontally. Drizzle the cut sides with oil, then lay the sausage on 4 of the pieces, dividing it evenly. Top the sausage with the rabe. Cover with the untopped sides of the bread and press firmly.

LEBANESE FLATBREADS WITH SPICED BEEF, TOMATOES AND TAHINI

Start to finish: 2 hours
Makes twelve 5-inch pizzas

These delicious savory flatbreads are Middle Eastern in origin, but we learned about them in São Paulo, Brazil, where they're called esfihas (sometimes spelled esfirras). The breads were introduced to Brazil by Arab immigrants, particularly from Lebanon and Syria, in the late 19th century. Esfihas might be formed into dumpling-like buns that fully enclose a filling, but the ones we favored were open-face like pizzas and about the size of a saucer, with a soft, tender, dinner-roll texture. Toppings varied from ground meat seasoned with spice to cheese to hearts of palm. At São Paulo's Restaurante & Rotisserie Halim, Yasmin Sultan showed us how to make pizza-style esfihas. We adapted the recipe, adding some yogurt to the dough for a richer, more tender crumb that's a perfect match for the garlicky, aromatic ground beef and tomato filling spiked with nutty tahini. Za'atar is an herb, seed and spice blend.

It's sold in most well-stocked supermarkets in the spice aisle, or look for it in spice shops or Middle Eastern grocery stores. If you have leftover esfihas, wrap them well and refrigerate for up to two days. Rewarm in a 425°F oven on a wire rack set in a baking sheet for five to eight minutes.

FOR THE DOUGH:

120 grams (½ cup) plain whole-milk yogurt

⅓ cup plus 4 tablespoons extra-virgin olive oil, divided

260 grams (2 cups) all-purpose flour, plus more if needed and for dusting

2 teaspoons instant yeast

1 teaspoon table salt

FOR THE TOPPING:

1 pound ripe tomatoes, cored, seeded and chopped

Kosher salt and ground black pepper

1 pound 85 percent lean ground beef

3 tablespoons za'atar

1 tablespoon ground allspice

2 tablespoons extra-virgin olive oil, plus more for brushing

1 large yellow onion, finely chopped

3 medium garlic cloves, finely grated

½ teaspoon cayenne pepper

¼ cup tahini

Pomegranate molasses, to serve (optional)

To make the dough, in a 2-cup liquid measuring cup or small bowl, whisk together the yogurt, the ⅓ cup of the oil and ⅓ cup water. In a stand mixer with the dough hook, mix the flour, yeast and table salt on medium until well combined, about 15 seconds. With the mixer on low, drizzle in the yogurt mixture. Increase to medium and knead until the mixture forms a smooth, elastic dough that clears the sides of the bowl, 7 to 10 minutes; if the dough sticks to the bowl, knead in additional flour, 1 tablespoon at a time. Meanwhile, coat 2 rimmed baking sheets with 2 tablespoons oil each.

Generously dust the counter with flour and turn the dough out onto it. Divide the dough into 12 portions (about 45 grams/1½ ounces each). Form into smooth balls, then place 6 on each prepared baking sheet, evenly spaced. Cover with

kitchen towels and let rise until doubled in bulk, 45 minutes to 1 hour.

To make the topping, in a colander or fine-mesh sieve set in or over a bowl, toss the tomatoes with 1 teaspoon kosher salt; set aside. In a medium bowl, mix together the beef, za'atar, 3 tablespoons water, allspice and ½ teaspoon each kosher salt and black pepper.

In a 12-inch nonstick skillet over medium, heat the oil until shimmering. Stir in the onion and ½ teaspoon kosher salt, then cover and cook, stirring occasionally, until softened but not browned, 8 to 10 minutes. Add the garlic and cayenne; cook, stirring, until fragrant, about 30 seconds. Stir in the beef mixture, breaking up any clumps. Cover and cook, stirring occasionally, until the meat is no longer pink, about 10 minutes. Transfer to a large bowl, then stir in the tahini; set aside to cool.

To shape, top and bake the pizzas, heat the oven to 500°F with a rack in the middle position. Using your fingers, press each dough ball into a 5-inch round directly on the baking sheet; start at the center of the dough and work outward, leaving the edge slightly thicker. Lightly brush each round with oil.

Shake the colander containing the tomatoes to remove as much moisture as possible. Stir the tomatoes into the meat mixture, then taste and season with kosher salt and pepper. Using a ¼-cup measuring cup, evenly divide the topping among the rounds, then spread in an even layer, leaving a ½-inch edge and firmly pressing it into the dough; it's fine if the rounds end up touching each other. Let rise, uncovered, until the edges of the dough are puffy, 20 to 30 minutes.

Bake the pizzas one baking sheet at a time until the edges are golden brown, 8 to 10 minutes. Cool on the baking sheet on a wire rack, then use a wide metal spatula to transfer the pizzas directly to the wire rack. Cool for a few minutes. Serve warm, drizzled with pomegranate molasses (if using).

TURKISH SPICED-BEEF PIDE

Start to finish: 45 minutes

Servings: 4 to 6

Pide, often referred to as Turkish pizza, is a boat-shaped flatbread topped with ingredients such as ground meat, sausage, cheese and/or vegetables. We use store-bought pizza dough to make these simplified ground-meat kiymali pide, and after baking we finish them with chopped onion and tomato dressed with lemon juice and olive oil, a non-traditional touch that brightens up the colors and flavors. Room-temperature dough is much easier to shape than cold dough, so be sure to allow yours to come to room temperature before use.

1 large red onion, quartered

½ cup chopped roasted red peppers

2 tablespoons tomato paste

2 teaspoons Aleppo pepper or 1½ teaspoons sweet paprika plus ½ teaspoon cayenne pepper

1 tablespoon ground cumin

Kosher salt and ground black pepper

8 ounces 80 percent lean ground beef or ground lamb

1 pound store-bought refrigerated pizza dough, room temperature

2 tablespoons lemon juice

1 tablespoon extra-virgin olive oil, plus more to serve

1 plum tomato, cored, seeded and finely chopped

½ cup lightly packed fresh flat-leaf parsley, roughly chopped

Heat the oven to 500°F with a rack in the upper-middle position. In a food processor, pulse the onion until finely chopped, about 5 pulses. Set aside ¼ cup of the onion. To the processor, add the roasted peppers, tomato paste, Aleppo pepper, cumin, ½ teaspoon salt and 1 teaspoon black pepper. Process until smooth, about 10 seconds, scraping the bowl as needed. Add the beef and pulse just until incorporated, 3 or 4 pulses. Transfer to a small bowl and refrigerate until needed.

Mist a rimmed baking sheet with cooking spray. Divide the dough in half, then gently stretch one piece into an oval about 5 inches wide by 14 inches long; press from the center outward and lift and stretch the edges as needed. If the dough is resistant or shrinks after stretching, wait 5 to 10 minutes before trying again; if it is very elastic, you may need to give it 2 or 3 rests. Place the oval on one side of the prepared baking sheet. Shape the remaining dough in the same way and place it alongside the first.

Spread half the meat mixture on each dough oval, leaving a ½-inch border around the edge. Fold the edge of the dough up over the topping, then gently pinch the fold to create a lip around the perimeter; pinch each end of the ovals to form it into a point, then tuck the tip of the point under itself. Bake until the edges of the crust are well browned, 12 to 14 minutes.

Meanwhile, in a medium bowl, whisk together the lemon juice, oil, and ¼ teaspoon each salt and black pepper. Add the reserved onion, the tomato and parsley, then toss; set aside. Using a wide metal spatula, transfer the pide to a wire rack. Cool for 5 minutes.

Using a slotted spoon, scatter the tomato-onion mixture on top, dividing it evenly and discarding any liquid in the bowl, then drizzle the pide with additional oil.

WEEKNIGHT LAHMAJOUN

Start to finish: 30 minutes

Makes four 8-inch flatbreads

The meat-topped flatbread known as lahmajoun is popular in Türkiye and Armenia. We've created an easy weeknight version by swapping the usual homemade flatbread dough for store-bought pita breads. Simply combine the meat mixture in a food processor and spread onto pita, then bake in a hot oven. When processing the mixture, don't overdo it or the meat may become tough. Pulse a few times, just until combined. If you like, finish the dish with a sprinkling of fresh herbs and a drizzle of cooling yogurt to complement the spiced meat.

Four 8-inch pita breads

1 small red OR yellow onion, roughly chopped

¼ cup roasted red peppers, drained and patted dry

2 tablespoons tomato paste

2 teaspoons smoked paprika

1½ teaspoons ground cumin

¾ teaspoon red pepper flakes

Kosher salt and ground black pepper

8 ounces ground beef OR ground lamb

Heat the oven to 500°F with racks in the upper- and lower-middle positions. Arrange the pita breads on 2 rimmed baking sheets; set aside.

In a food processor, pulse the onion until finely chopped, about 5 pulses. Add the roasted peppers, tomato paste, paprika, cumin, pepper flakes, ½ teaspoon salt and 1 teaspoon black pepper. Process until smooth, about 10 seconds, scraping the bowl as needed. Add the beef and pulse just until incorporated, 3 or 4 pulses.

Divide the beef mixture evenly among the pitas (about a scant ½ cup each) and spread over the rounds, leaving a ½-inch border around the edge. Bake until the pitas are golden brown on the edges and the meat is sizzling, switching and rotating the baking sheets halfway through, 8 to 10 minutes. Cool for a few minutes, then transfer to a cutting board and cut into wedges.

Optional garnish: Chopped fresh flat-leaf parsley OR whole-milk yogurt OR lemon wedges OR fresh mint OR a combination

539

Burgers & Sandwiches

CHANGE THE WAY YOU COOK

For a Better Burger, Chill!

Pre-ground beef generally makes a bad burger. It loses moisture during processing, causing the proteins to become sticky and produce flavorless, dense hamburgers. And if you want to season your burgers, mixing the ground meat can make it even tougher. Luckily, we discovered that briefly freezing the ground beef mitigated all of these problems. It also gave us a chance to thoroughly flavor it without having to overwork the meat.

1. Use two forks to gently and evenly spread the beef over a parchment-lined baking sheet. It doesn't need to cover the entire sheet.

2. Sprinkle the meat with your seasoning mixture, then place in the freezer for 20 minutes, or until starting to firm at the edges.

3. Let the meat stand at room temperature for about 10 minutes, then use spatulas to gently fold the meat and seasonings together. Divide into portions and gently shape into patties.

PITA BURGERS WITH CRISPED CHEESE

Start to finish: 40 minutes
Servings: 4

This burger, inspired by the popular folded cheeseburger served at Miznon, an Israeli restaurant with multiple locations, is seasoned with yellow mustard for spicy tang and dill pickles for brininess. We then fill pita halves with the mixture, forming a thin layer, along with sliced onion and cheese. Cheese hits the skillet when the sandwiches are pan-fried, crisping and developing flavorful caramelization, and creating an irresistible layer that contrasts deliciously with the juicy patties. Be sure to use 90 percent lean ground beef; meat that is higher in fat will shrink and the pitas will be greasy.

1 pound 90 percent lean ground beef

¼ cup chopped drained chopped dill pickles OR sweet pickled peppers OR a combination

2 tablespoons yellow mustard

Kosher salt and ground black pepper

Two 8-inch pita breads, cut into half rounds

½ medium red onion, thinly sliced

8 slices sharp cheddar OR American cheese

1 tablespoon neutral oil

In a medium bowl, combine the beef, pickles, mustard, 1 teaspoon salt and ½ teaspoon pepper; mix thoroughly with your hands. Let stand for about 15 minutes to allow the meat to lose some of its chill.

Open each pita half to form a pocket. Fill each half with a quarter of the meat mixture, spreading it to the edges, then lightly pressing on the outside to flatten. Into each pita pocket, tuck a quarter of the onion, followed by 2 cheese slices; it's fine if the cheese peeks out of the pita and if the bread forms cracks. Brush the pita halves on both sides with the oil.

Heat a 12-inch nonstick skillet over medium until droplets of water flicked onto the surface quickly sizzle. Add 2 of the stuffed pita halves and cook until golden brown on the bottoms, about 4 minutes. Using a wide metal spatula, flip and cook, adjusting the heat as needed, until golden brown on the second sides and the exposed cheese is browned and crisp, about 3 minutes. Transfer to a platter or individual plates. Cook the remaining pita halves in the same way.

GARLIC-ROSEMARY BURGERS WITH TALEGGIO SAUCE

Start to finish: 35 minutes
Servings: 4

These deeply savory burgers were inspired by a recipe by Ignacio Mattos, chef of Estela in New York and author of a book by the same name. Mattos uses fish sauce as a seasoning for steak, but we opted for similarly salty and umami-rich Worcestershire sauce. We combined it with rosemary and garlic to create our basting mixture. These seasonings, combined with a simple taleggio cheese sauce, make these burgers richer and far more flavorful than your average cheeseburger. We recommend brioche buns or Kaiser rolls, as they better resist turning soggy than standard hamburger buns. As for toppings, we liked to keep it simple: sliced tomato or pickled red onions to balance the burgers' richness.

½ cup heavy cream

8 ounces taleggio cheese, rind removed, cut into ½-inch chunks

¼ cup Worcestershire sauce

4 medium garlic cloves, finely grated

2½ tablespoons fresh rosemary, minced

1½ pounds 85 percent lean ground beef

Kosher salt and ground black pepper

1 tablespoon grapeseed or other neutral oil

4 buns, split and toasted

In a small saucepan over medium, heat the cream until just simmering. Stir in the cheese, cover and remove from the heat. Let stand until the cheese is softened and partially melted, about 20 minutes, quickly stirring once halfway through.

Meanwhile, in a small bowl, stir together the Worcestershire sauce, garlic and rosemary. In a medium bowl, combine the beef with 1 tablespoon of the Worcestershire mixture, ¼ teaspoon salt and ½ teaspoon pepper, then mix gently until the seasonings are evenly incorporated. Divide the meat into 4 portions and shape each into a patty about 4½ inches in diameter and about ½ inch thick.

In a 12-inch cast-iron or other heavy skillet over medium-high, heat the oil until lightly smoking. Add the patties and cook for 3 minutes, spooning 1 teaspoon of the Worcestershire mixture over each. Using a wide metal spatula, flip the patties and continue to cook for another 3 minutes, again spooning 1 teaspoon of the sauce onto each. Continue to flip and cook, brushing with the remaining sauce mixture, until the patties are well browned on both sides and the centers reach 125°F for medium-rare or 130°F for medium, another 2 to 4 minutes. Transfer to a plate and let rest for 5 minutes.

Cuban-Spiced Burgers

Start to finish: 1 hour (20 minutes active)
Servings: 4

The southern Florida tradition of the frita, thin beef patties that began as street food in Havana, inspired the spice mixture we used to add flavor to these burgers. **Partially freezing ground beef before mixing in the spices helps prevent the meat from becoming compacted during mixing and shaping, producing a meatier, more tender burger. Even with chilling, it's important to use a light touch when handling the beef.** This recipe can easily be doubled. For a quick and tangy topping, try our 3-minute spicy sauce (see sidebar).

1½ pounds 85 percent lean ground beef

2 teaspoons smoked paprika

2 teaspoons ground cumin

Kosher salt and ground black pepper

1 tablespoon neutral oil

4 burger buns, toasted

Sliced onion, sliced tomato and/or lettuce, for topping

Line a baking sheet with kitchen parchment. Set the beef on the sheet, then use 2 forks to gently spread the meat. In a small bowl, combine the paprika, cumin, ¾ teaspoons salt and ½ teaspoon pepper. Sprinkle over the beef. Freeze until the meat is very cold and beginning to firm up at the edges, about 20 minutes.

Use a silicone spatula to gently fold the spice mixture into the beef without compacting it; it's fine if the spices are not completely blended. If the beef is still partially frozen, let stand 10 to 15 minutes until slightly softened. Divide the beef into 4 even portions. Shape each into a 4-inch patty about ½ inch thick.

In a 12-inch skillet over medium-high, heat the oil until smoking. Add the patties and cook until well browned, about 5 minutes; flip and continue to cook until the center is 125°F for medium-rare, another 4 to 5 minutes. Transfer to a plate and let rest for 5 minutes. Set each burger on a bun and top as desired.

Spicy Sauce

Start to finish: 3 minutes
Makes about 1⅓ cups

1 cup mayonnaise

2 tablespoons hot sauce, plus more as needed

2 tablespoons yellow mustard

¼ teaspoon cayenne pepper

In a medium bowl, whisk all ingredients until smooth. Taste and add more hot sauce, if desired. Cover and refrigerate for up to 1 week.

While the burgers rest, set a fine-mesh strainer over a medium bowl. Stir the cream-cheese mixture thoroughly, then pour it into the strainer and force through with a silicone spatula; the sauce should be smooth and creamy after straining. Stir in ¼ teaspoon pepper.

Spoon about 1 tablespoon of cheese sauce onto the cut sides of both halves of each bun. Place a burger on each bottom bun half, then cover with the tops. Serve the remaining cheese sauce on the side.

CHANGE THE WAY YOU COOK

Simplify Your Cheese Sauce

For the easiest cheese sauce, heat **½ cup heavy cream** over medium. Stir in **8 ounces taleggio, brie, Camembert, Gorgonzola or fresh goat cheese** (rind removed if present and cut in ½-inch chunks), then cover and turn off the heat. After 10 minutes, stir, cover and let stand another 10 minutes. Stir, pass through a strainer, then season with **¼ teaspoon ground black pepper**

SPICED LAMB BURGERS WITH TAHINI-YOGURT SAUCE

Start to finish: 50 minutes (20 minutes active)
Servings: 4

Kibbeh, a popular dish throughout the Levant, is a spiced mixture of bulgur and ground meat. It may be layered with stuffing in a baking dish and baked or shaped into small portions, filled and fried, with the goal of getting a toasty, browned crust that brings out the nuttiness of the bulgur. In this version, we skip the stuffing and form the mixture into patties, then pan-fry them, rather than deep-fry, for ease. Fine bulgur is key for yielding a mixture that holds together. If you can't find fine bulgur, process medium or coarse bulgur in a spice grinder for 10 to 30 seconds. Don't rinse the bulgur before use. If your mixture is very sticky or wet when you attempt to shape it, refrigerate for an additional 10 minutes.

1 medium yellow onion, peeled

½ cup fine bulgur (see headnote)

Kosher salt and ground black pepper

12 ounces ground lamb

1 large egg, beaten

¼ cup pine nuts, toasted and chopped

¾ teaspoon ground allspice

¾ teaspoon ground cardamom

¾ teaspoon ground cinnamon

¼ teaspoon cayenne pepper

6 medium garlic cloves, finely grated

1 cup whole-milk plain yogurt

1 cup lightly packed fresh flat-leaf parsley, chopped

¼ cup tahini

4 tablespoons grapeseed or other neutral oil, divided

Lemon wedges, to serve

Grate the onion on the large holes of a box grater, catching the pulp and liquid in a medium bowl. Stir in the bulgur and 1 teaspoon salt. Set aside for 10 minutes, until the bulgur has absorbed the onion liquid and is slightly softened.

Add the lamb, egg, pine nuts, allspice, cardamom, cinnamon, cayenne, 1 teaspoon black pepper and ⅔ of the grated garlic. Knead with your hands or mix vigorously with a wooden spoon until well combined, then cover and refrigerate for 20 minutes.

Meanwhile, in a small bowl, whisk together the yogurt, parsley, tahini, ¼ teaspoon salt and black pepper and the remaining garlic. Set aside until ready to serve.

Line a rimmed baking sheet with kitchen parchment. Using your hands, form the bulgur-lamb mixture into 12 balls (about 2 heaping tablespoons each) and place on the prepared baking sheet. Using your hands, flatten the balls into ½-inch-thick patties about 2½ inches in diameter.

In a 12-inch skillet over medium, heat 2 tablespoons of oil until barely smoking. Add half the patties and cook undisturbed until browned and crisp on the bottoms, about 4 minutes. Flip and continue to cook until the second sides are browned and crisp, about another 4 minutes, then transfer to a plate. Wipe out the skillet with paper towels and repeat with the remaining oil and patties. Serve with the yogurt-tahini sauce and lemon wedges.

INDIAN-SPICED PORK BURGERS

Start to finish: 35 minutes
Servings: 4

These flavor-packed burgers are a spin on a chouriço-like spiced pork sausage from Goa in southern India. They're especially delicious topped with yogurt, torn fresh mint leaves and thin slices of cucumber or tomato.

⅔ cup panko breadcrumbs

¼ cup plain whole-milk yogurt, plus more to serve

5 teaspoons garam masala

5 teaspoons sweet paprika

1 tablespoon ground cumin

½ teaspoon cayenne pepper

2 large egg yolks

2 medium garlic cloves, finely grated

Kosher salt and ground black pepper

1 pound ground pork

2 tablespoons grapeseed or other neutral oil

4 hamburger buns, toasted

In a large bowl, combine the panko, yogurt, garam masala, paprika, cumin, cayenne, egg yolks, garlic, ¾ teaspoon salt, ½ teaspoon pepper and ¼ cup water. Using a fork, mash the mixture into a smooth paste. Add the pork and mix with your hands until evenly combined. Form into 4 patties, each about 4 inches in diameter, place on a large plate and refrigerate for 15 minutes.

In a 12-inch nonstick skillet over medium, heat the oil until barely smoking. Add the burgers and cook until well browned, 7 to 8 minutes. Flip, reduce to medium-low and continue to cook until the patties are well browned on the second sides and the centers reach 160°F, another 5 to 7 minutes. Transfer to a clean plate, tent with foil and let rest for 5 minutes. Serve on the buns with additional yogurt on the side.

Build a Better Burger

We love a flavorful and nicely crusted burger—beef or otherwise—slathered with toppings and slapped between hunks of bread. A bland, soggy, fall-apart patty? Not so much. So we take a 4-step approach to make sure our patties don't disappoint.

1. **Add robust seasonings** to the patty mix—ground cumin and paprika for our quinoa and bean sandwiches (recipe p. 551); kimchi and gochujang for our salmon burgers (recipe p. 549). And don't overlook whole spices; tender-crunchy spices such as cumin, coriander and coarsely ground black pepper add pops of flavor and texture to burgers of all sorts.

2. **Keep things chill.** Similar to meatballs, we refrigerate the formed patties for 15 minutes. This firms them up so they stay together better in the pan or on the grill.

3. **Give the crust a chance to develop.** Once the patties are cooking, we leave them undisturbed for four minutes or more so the bottoms have a chance to brown. You will know they are ready to flip when they release naturally from the pan or grill grates.

4. **Have the embellishments ready to go.** Most burgers are better when they're hot, so make sure the buns and toppings are prepped so the sandwiches can be assembled as soon as the patties come out of the pan or off the grill.

PARMESAN AND HERB TURKEY BURGERS

Start to finish: 35 minutes
Servings: 4

Mayonnaise and plenty of herbs turn ground turkey into moist and flavorful patties in this take on the classic burger. We preferred the flavor and texture of these burgers when made with ground dark meat turkey, but if you prefer, ground breast meat works, too. Instead of using buns, you also could serve the burgers sandwiched between Bibb or Boston lettuce leaves spread with the herbed mayonnaise.

¾ cup panko breadcrumbs

10 tablespoons mayonnaise, divided

½ cup chopped fresh mint, divided

½ cup chopped fresh cilantro, divided

6 scallions, thinly sliced, white and green parts reserved separately

Kosher salt and ground white pepper

1 pound ground dark meat turkey

¼ cup water

2 ounces Parmesan cheese, finely grated (1 cup)

3 tablespoons lime juice

1 tablespoon grapeseed or other neutral oil

4 hamburger buns, toasted

Line a plate with kitchen parchment and mist with cooking spray. In a food processor, combine the panko, 5 tablespoons of the mayonnaise, ¼ cup each of the mint and cilantro, the scallion whites, ½ teaspoon salt and 1 teaspoon white pepper. Process until smooth, about 1 minute. Transfer to a large bowl, then add the turkey, water and cheese. Mix with your hands. Form into four ½-inch-thick patties, then set on the prepared plate and refrigerate for 15 minutes.

Meanwhile, in a small bowl, stir together the remaining 5 tablespoons mayonnaise, the remaining ¼ cup each mint and cilantro, the scallion greens, the lime juice, ¼ teaspoon salt and ½ teaspoon pepper. Set aside.

In a 12-inch nonstick skillet over medium-high, heat the oil until beginning to smoke. Add the patties, reduce to medium and cook until well browned on the bottoms, about

5 minutes. Flip and cook until the second sides are well browned and the centers reach 165°F. Transfer to a wire rack set in a rimmed baking sheet and let rest for 5 minutes.

Meanwhile, spread the cut sides of each bun with some of the mayonnaise mixture. Sandwich the burgers in the buns and serve with any remaining mayonnaise on the side.

SALMON AND KIMCHI BURGERS

Start to finish: 30 minutes, plus chilling
Servings: 4

In this recipe, salmon burgers get a flavor boost from kimchi and gochujang, two Korean powerhouse ingredients. Achieving tender, nicely textured burgers that hold together can be tricky, but we developed a technique. We process half of the salmon until smooth; this puree helps bind the remaining roughly chopped salmon and the kimchi. If you like, coat the patties with panko breadcrumbs before cooking to create an extra-crispy coating, but the results still are delicious without. Serve the burgers on toasted buns with our quick kimchi-flecked mayonnaise.

¾ cup cabbage kimchi, drained, plus
2 teaspoons kimchi juice

4 scallions, cut into 1-inch pieces OR
1 jalapeño chili, stemmed and quartered OR both

¼ cup plus 2 tablespoons mayonnaise

Kosher salt and ground black pepper

12 ounces boneless, skinless salmon fillets,
pin bones removed, cut into rough 1-inch chunks

1 tablespoon gochujang

2 teaspoons toasted sesame oil

¾ cup panko breadcrumbs (optional)

3 tablespoons grapeseed or other
neutral oil, divided

4 hamburger buns, toasted

In a food processor, combine the kimchi and scallions, then process until finely chopped, 30 to 60 seconds. Transfer ½ cup of the kimchi mixture to a medium bowl. Transfer the remaining mixture to a small bowl, then stir in the mayonnaise, kimchi juice and ¼ teaspoon each salt and pepper; reserve the food processor bowl and blade (no need to clean them). Cover the mayonnaise mixture and refrigerate until ready to serve.

To the food processor, add half of the salmon. Process until smooth, about 1 minute, scraping the bowl as needed. Transfer to the medium bowl with the reserved kimchi mixture and stir to combine. To the processor, add the remaining salmon and pulse until chopped, 3 to 4 pulses. Stir the chopped salmon into the kimchi-salmon mixture. Add the gochujang, sesame oil and ½ teaspoon each salt and pepper; stir until well combined.

With wet hands, divide the kimchi-salmon mixture into 4 even portions. Form each portion into a 3-inch patty and place on a large plate. Refrigerate, uncovered, to firm up the patties, about 15 minutes.

If using panko, put the panko in a pie plate or other wide, shallow dish. One at a time, coat the patties with the panko, gently pressing to adhere and reshaping the patties if needed. Return them to the plate.

In a 12-inch nonstick skillet over medium, heat the grapeseed oil until shimmering. Add the patties and cook until browned on the bottoms, 3 to 4 minutes. Using a wide spatula, flip and cook, adjusting the heat as needed, until browned on the second sides, about another 3 minutes. Transfer to a paper towel–lined plate. Serve on the buns with the kimchi mayonnaise.

Optional garnish: Lettuce leaves **OR** sliced tomatoes **OR** both

CHILEAN-STYLE PORK SANDWICHES

Start to finish: 40 minutes

Servings: 6

Austin, Texas-based culinary consultant and restaurateur Iliana de la Vega was born in Chile, home to lomito, or, as she puts it "the best sandwich in the world." A lomito consists of thin slices of tender, slow-braised pork loin, buttery mashed avocado, juicy tomatoes and ample mayonnaise on a roll. We followed de la Vega's suggestion and used pork tenderloin, cutting cooking time. We thinly slice the pork, pile it on rolls spread with mustard-spiked mayonnaise and top with the traditional avocado and tomatoes.

2½ teaspoons dried oregano, divided

1 teaspoon ground cumin

Kosher salt and ground black pepper

Two 1¼-pound pork tenderloins, trimmed of silver skin and halved crosswise

2 tablespoons grapeseed or other neutral oil

½ cup mayonnaise

1 tablespoon Dijon mustard

1 tablespoon yellow mustard

1 tablespoon lime juice

2 ripe avocados

2 ripe tomatoes, thinly sliced and drained on paper towels

6 crusty but soft-crumbed rolls, split and toasted

In a small bowl, stir together 2 teaspoons oregano, the cumin, 1 teaspoon salt and 2 teaspoons pepper. Using a meat pounder, pound each piece of tenderloin to an even ½-inch thickness. Sprinkle the seasoning mix all over the pork and rub it into the meat.

In a 12-inch skillet over medium-high, heat the oil until barely smoking. Add the pork and cook until well browned on both sides and the centers reach 135°F, 10 to 15 minutes; flip the pieces once about halfway through. Transfer to a platter, tent with foil and let rest for about 10 minutes.

Meanwhile, in a small bowl, whisk together the mayonnaise, both mustards, the lime juice, the remaining ½ teaspoon oregano and ½ teaspoon pepper. Halve and pit the avocados, then scoop the flesh into another small bowl. Roughly mash with a fork, then season to taste with salt and pepper.

Transfer the pork to a cutting board; reserve the accumulated juices on the platter. Thinly slice the meat against the grain, then return to the platter and toss with the juices. Taste and season with salt and pepper.

Spread the mayonnaise mixture on the cut sides of each roll half. Divide the avocado among the bottom halves, then top with pork, dividing it evenly. Top with tomato slices, then the top halves of the rolls.

Quinoa and Black Bean Burgers

Start to finish: 1½ hours (20 minutes active)
Servings: 6

Canned beans, roughly mashed, add meaty, substantial texture to a grain-based burger and help bind the ingredients together so the patty stays firm. Pan-fried until browned and crisp, these vegetarian burgers are terrific sandwiched between buns with your favorite fixings, but also are satisfying on their own with a tossed green salad. White, red or rainbow (tricolor) quinoa all work well, so use whatever you have. If you purchased pre-rinsed quinoa, there's no need to rinse and drain it before cooking.

⅓ cup quinoa (see headnote), rinsed and drained

Kosher salt and ground black pepper

15½-ounce can black beans, drained but not rinsed

1 large egg, lightly beaten

½ cup panko breadcrumbs

2 scallions, finely chopped

½ teaspoon ground cumin

½ teaspoon smoked paprika OR chipotle chili powder

3 tablespoons grapeseed or other neutral oil

In a medium saucepan, stir together the quinoa, a pinch of salt and ⅔ cup water. Bring to a boil over medium-high, then cover, reduce to low and cook without stirring until the quinoa absorbs the liquid, 13 to 15 minutes. Remove the pan from the heat, then drape a kitchen towel across the pan and re-cover. Let stand for 10 minutes. Fluff the quinoa with a fork, transfer to a small plate and cool to room temperature, stirring once or twice, about 30 minutes.

In a large bowl, using a fork or a potato masher, coarsely mash the black beans. Add the quinoa, egg, panko, scallions, cumin, paprika and ½ teaspoon each salt and pepper; stir until well combined. Form into six 3-inch patties and place on a large plate. Refrigerate, uncovered, to firm up the patties, about 15 minutes.

In a 12-inch nonstick skillet over medium-high, heat the oil until barely smoking. Add the patties and cook until browned and crisp on the bottoms, about 5 minutes. Using a wide spatula, flip the patties and cook until browned and crisp on the second sides, about another 2 minutes.

Optional garnish: Sliced cheese **OR** sliced tomato **OR** sliced onion **OR** lettuce leaves **OR** sliced pickles **OR** mayonnaise **OR** a combination

CHORIZO AND CHIMICHURRI SANDWICHES

Start to finish: 30 minutes
Servings: 4

Inspired by Argentinian choripán, this sandwich stars boldly spiced chorizo and chimichurri, Argentina's signature sauce. Tangy with vinegar and grassy with cilantro (or parsley, or both) chimichurri balances the richness and fattiness of sausage. It's essential to use fresh Mexican-style chorizo, which is raw and made with ground pork, as opposed to the Spanish dry-cured or smoked variety; make sure it is link-style chorizo in natural casing. To help the sandwiches remain intact when eaten, we cut a baguette into four sections, then slice through lengthwise on just one side, creating a hinged shape reminiscent of a hot dog bun.

8 tablespoons extra-virgin olive oil, divided

3 tablespoons red wine vinegar

**1½ cups lightly packed fresh cilantro
OR flat-leaf parsley OR a combination,
finely chopped**

1 medium garlic clove, finely grated

½ teaspoon red pepper flakes

Kosher salt and ground black pepper

**1 baguette, cut into 4 sections, split horizontally,
kept hinged on one side**

**4 links Mexican-style chorizo (see headnote),
split horizontally, kept hinged on one side**

To make the chimichurri, in a small bowl, whisk together 4 tablespoons oil, the vinegar, cilantro, garlic, pepper flakes and ¼ teaspoon each salt and black pepper; set aside.

Brush 3 tablespoons of the remaining oil onto the insides of the bread. Heat a 12-inch skillet over medium until droplets of water flicked onto the surface sizzle in a few seconds. Toast one bread section at a time, cut side down, until lightly golden, about 1 minute; remove from the pan and set aside.

In the same skillet over medium, heat the remaining 1 tablespoon oil until shimmering. Cook the sausages, cut sides down, until browned, about 4 minutes. Flip the sausages and cook, turning and flipping as needed, until well browned on both sides and the centers reach 160°F, another 4 to 6 minutes.

Place a sausage on each piece of baguette. Stir the chimichurri to recombine, then spoon it onto the sausages. Close the sandwiches and serve.

Optional garnish: Thinly sliced avocado **OR** sliced tomato **OR** mayonnaise **OR** a combination

GRILLED VIETNAMESE SKIRT STEAK SANDWICHES

Start to finish: 45 minutes
Servings: 4

Bánh mì began with Vietnam's lighter, fluffier take on the baguette—the name roughly translates to "wheat bread"—and are arguably the most prominent example in a history of innovative takes on French cuisine. Crumbs get pulled out to make room for the filling—meat, pickles, mayonnaise, maybe some cilantro—a signature mix of savory, sweet, crunchy and herbal. We take bánh mì to the grill, lightly charring skirt steak for crunch and flavor. Use a supermarket baguette or French rolls with an airy crumb and thin, brittle crust, for this sandwich, not a chewy, rustic bread. You'll need four 7- to 8-inch pieces of bread; cut one or two baguettes into sections or use individual rolls. Pâté

is a classic filling—it adds richness—but the sandwiches are perfectly delicious without it. Other possible additions include thinly sliced cucumber, thin rounds of jalapeño and Sriracha.

½ cup distilled white vinegar

2 tablespoons plus 2 teaspoons
light brown sugar, divided

5 teaspoons fish sauce, divided

Kosher salt and ground black pepper

1 medium carrot, peeled and coarsely shredded (1 cup)

3-inch piece daikon radish, peeled and coarsely
shredded (1 cup)

⅓ cup mayonnaise

2 serrano chilies, stemmed and minced

4 medium garlic cloves, finely grated

1 pound beef skirt steak, trimmed, patted dry
and cut with the grain into 2 pieces

Four 7- to 8-inch pieces of baguette
(see headnote), halved

4 ounces pork pâté (optional)

Cilantro sprigs, to serve

In a medium bowl, whisk the vinegar, 2 tablespoons of sugar, 2 teaspoons of fish sauce and ½ teaspoon salt until the sugar dissolves. Stir in the carrot and daikon; set aside. In a small bowl, stir together the mayonnaise, chilies and ¼ teaspoon each salt and pepper; set aside.

In another medium bowl, stir together the remaining 2 teaspoons sugar, the remaining 3 teaspoons fish sauce, the garlic and 1 teaspoon each salt and pepper. Add the

steak and rub the seasoning mixture into the meat. Let stand at room temperature for 15 minutes.

Prepare a charcoal or gas grill. For a charcoal grill, ignite a large chimney of coals, let burn until lightly ashed over, then distribute evenly over one side of the grill bed; open the bottom grill vents. For a gas grill, turn half of the burners to high. Heat the grill, covered, for 5 to 10 minutes, then clean and oil the cooking grate.

While the grill heats, using your fingers, pull out some of the interior crumb of each piece of bread. The remaining crust and crumb should be about ¾ inch thick.

When the grill is ready, pat the steak dry with paper towels and place on the hot side of the grill. Cook, uncovered, until lightly charred on both sides and the center of the thickest part is pink when cut into, 4 to 6 minutes total, flipping once halfway through. Transfer to a plate and let rest for 10 minutes. Working in batches if needed, place the bread cut sides up on the cool side of the grill and toast until the crust is crisp, 1 to 2 minutes, turning and moving occasionally to avoid scorching.

Cut the steak with the grain into 2-inch wide pieces, then thinly slice each piece against the grain. Stir the accumulated juices from the rested steak into the mayonnaise mixture, then spread onto the cut sides of the top halves of the bread. If using pâté, spread it on the bottom halves of the bread, dividing it evenly. Layer the steak on the pâté, then top with the carrot-radish slaw and cilantro. Cover with the top halves of the bread.

BOCADILLOS WITH FLANK STEAK AND MUSHROOMS

Start to finish: 35 minutes
Servings: 4

A bocadillo is a Spanish sandwich made on baguette-like bread. The fillings for bocadillos run the gamut—from cured meats, to seafood, to egg omelets. This hearty flank steak and mushroom version was inspired by a recipe from "Spain: The Cookbook" written by Simone Ortega and first published in Spain in 1972. Butter lends richness, while lemon juice and fresh parsley lift and brighten the flavors. Also try tucking ribbons of thinly sliced serrano ham or prosciutto into the sandwiches along with the steak.

1 pound beef flank steak, trimmed and cut in half

Kosher salt and ground black pepper

1 tablespoon grapeseed or other neutral oil

1 tablespoon extra-virgin olive oil

8 ounces cremini mushrooms, trimmed and sliced

2 medium shallots, halved and thinly sliced

2 tablespoons salted butter, cut into 2 pieces

4 tablespoons lemon juice, divided

¼ cup finely chopped fresh flat-leaf parsley

Four 7- to 8-inch sections of baguette, split horizontally

Season the steak on both sides with salt and pepper. In a 12-inch skillet over medium-high, heat the neutral oil until barely smoking. Add the steak, reduce to medium and cook until well browned on the bottom, 3 to 4 minutes. Flip and cook until well browned on the second sides and the centers reach 120°F (for medium-rare), 3 to 4 minutes. Transfer to a large plate and tent with foil.

In the same skillet over medium, heat the olive oil until shimmering. Add the mushrooms, shallots and ½ teaspoon pepper, then cook, stirring occasionally, until the moisture released by the mushrooms has almost evaporated, 3 to 5 minutes. Off heat, add the accumulated steak juices, the

butter, 3 tablespoons of lemon juice and the parsley, then stir until the butter melts. Taste and season with salt and pepper.

Cut the steak into thin slices against the grain. Sprinkle with the remaining 1 tablespoon lemon juice, then toss. Taste and season with salt and pepper. Divide the mushroom mixture evenly among the bottom halves of each section of baguette, then top with the steak slices. Cover with the top halves of the baguette.

NIÇOISE-STYLE TUNA SANDWICHES

Start to finish: 25 minutes

Servings: 4

Pan bagnat is a sandwich from Nice in southern France. Made with tuna (or anchovies), olives, hard-cooked eggs, tomatoes and Mediterranean vegetables, it sometimes is described as salade Niçoise between pieces of bread. The classic method for making pan bagnat is to wrap the assembled sandwiches and weight them with a heavy object for a few hours, or even overnight, so the ingredients and flavors meld and the bread soaks up any juices. We press ours for just 15 minutes, but if you're in a rush, you can serve them right away. Thinly sliced fresh fennel and/or baby arugula also are nice tucked into the sandwiches before pressing.

Three 5-ounce cans olive oil-packed tuna, drained, 2 tablespoons oil reserved

¼ cup drained capers

¼ cup pitted black olives, preferably oil-cured, chopped

¼ cup lightly packed fresh tarragon, chopped

1 medium shallot, chopped

1 tablespoon lemon juice

1 tablespoon extra-virgin olive oil

Kosher salt and ground black pepper

Four 8-inch crusty rolls or ciabatta rolls

2 medium ripe tomatoes, cored and sliced about ¼ inch thick

2 hard-cooked eggs, peeled and sliced crosswise

2 medium radishes, thinly sliced

TURKISH-STYLE FISH SANDWICHES

Start to finish: 30 minutes

Servings: 4

Balik ekmek is a Turkish sandwich that tucks grilled mackerel into soft bread, along with fresh tomatoes, onions and leafy herbs or greens that counter the fattiness of the fish. For our version, we broil fillets of firm, meaty white fish that have been seasoned with olive oil, sumac and Aleppo pepper (a mixture of sweet paprika and cayenne is a good stand-in). Those same ingredients, plus lemon juice, season a punchy red onion and parsley salad for topping the fish. Don't use extra-crusty bread or the fillings will be pushed out when you take a bite. Likewise, very soft, squishy buns will turn soggy under the weight of the fillings. The best bet is supermarket French rolls or kaiser rolls.

4 French rolls OR kaiser rolls (see headnote), split horizontally

3 or 4 small to medium ripe tomatoes, cored and sliced into ¼-inch-thick rounds

Kosher salt and ground black pepper

2 teaspoons ground sumac

1 teaspoon Aleppo pepper OR ¾ teaspoon sweet paprika plus ¼ teaspoon cayenne pepper

3 tablespoons plus 1 teaspoon lemon juice, divided

1 small red onion, halved and thinly sliced

⅓ cup mayonnaise

3 tablespoon drained capers, chopped

Four 6-ounce skinless mahi mahi OR haddock fillets (about 1 inch thick), patted dry

5 tablespoons extra-virgin olive oil, divided

1 cup roughly chopped fresh flat-leaf parsley OR mint OR a combination

1 romaine heart, leaves separated

In a medium bowl, stir together the tuna and the reserved oil, the capers, olives, tarragon, shallot, lemon juice, olive oil and ½ teaspoon pepper. Taste and season with salt.

Split each roll horizontally, leaving one side hinged. If the rolls are very thick, pull out and discard some of the crumb so the bread is about ½ inch thick. Divide the tuna mixture evenly among the rolls, distributing it on the bottom halves. Lay the tomato slices on top of the tuna, followed by the eggs and radishes.

Close the sandwiches and press firmly. Set them on a rimmed baking sheet and lay a sheet of foil on top. Place another baking sheet on top, then weight it with a heavy object, such as a large Dutch oven or cast-iron skillet. Let stand for about 15 minutes. To serve, cut each sandwich in half on the diagonal.

Heat the broiler with one rack about 6 inches from the element and another in the lowest position. Mist a broiler-safe wire rack with cooking spray, then set it in a broiler-safe rimmed baking sheet. Separate the roll halves and place them cut sides up on another baking sheet; set aside. Lay the tomato slices in a single layer on a paper towel-lined plate, then sprinkle with salt and black pepper; set aside.

In a small bowl, stir together the sumac, Aleppo pepper, 1 teaspoon salt and ½ teaspoon black pepper. In a medium bowl, stir together 1 tablespoon of the sumac mixture, 3 tablespoons lemon juice and the onion; toss, then set aside. In another small bowl, stir together the mayonnaise, capers, remaining 1 teaspoon lemon juice and ¼ teaspoon each salt and black pepper; set aside.

Place the fillets skinned side down on the prepared rack. Stir 2 tablespoons of the oil into the remaining sumac mixture. Spoon the oil mixture onto the fillets, spreading to cover the surface. Place the fish on the upper oven rack and the rolls on the lower oven rack. Broil until the fish flakes easily and the rolls are lightly toasted, 4 to 5 minutes. Remove both baking sheets from the oven.

To the onion mixture, add the remaining 3 tablespoons oil and the parsley; toss. Spread about 1 tablespoon mayonnaise mixture onto the cut sides of each roll half. Divide the tomato slices among the bottom roll halves, then top with romaine leaves. Using a wide metal spatula, place a fish fillet on each sandwich. Top with the onion-parsley mixture; if desired, drizzle on the liquid remaining in the bowl. Cover with the top halves of the rolls.

CAULIFLOWER KATI ROLLS

Start to finish: 45 minutes
Servings: 4

A kati roll is a popular type of Indian street food. Kebabs wrapped in paratha flatbread once were the norm, but now the rolls may be filled with ingredients of just about any sort, including paneer (a type of fresh cheese), vegetables and eggs. In this recipe, we roast yogurt-coated, garam masala-spiced cauliflower along with red bell pepper and onion in a hot oven until tender and well-browned. Instead of paratha as a wrapper, we use easier-to-find naan and smear the flatbreads with store-bought cilantro chutney before piling on and wrapping up the veggies. Look for cilantro chutney in the international aisle of the supermarket.

1 medium red bell pepper, stemmed, seeded and thinly sliced

1 medium red onion, halved and thinly sliced

1 tablespoon grapeseed or other neutral oil

Kosher salt and ground black pepper

¼ cup plain whole-milk Greek yogurt

2 teaspoons garam masala

⅛ teaspoon cayenne pepper

1-pound head cauliflower, trimmed and cut into ½- to 1-inch florets

4 tablespoons store-bought cilantro chutney, divided

Four 7- to 8-inch naan, warmed

Heat the oven to 500°F with a rack in the middle position. In a medium bowl, toss together the bell pepper, onion, oil, ¼ teaspoon salt and ½ teaspoon black pepper. Transfer to a 9-by-13-inch metal baking pan and distribute in an even layer.

In the same bowl, stir together the yogurt, garam masala, cayenne and ¼ teaspoon each salt and black pepper. Add the cauliflower and toss to coat, then distribute in an even layer on top of the pepper-onion mixture. Roast without stirring until the cauliflower is well browned and a skewer inserted into the largest piece meets no resistance, 20 to 25 minutes.

Remove the vegetables from the oven and stir the cauliflower into the bell pepper-onion mixture. Taste and season with salt and black pepper. Spread 1 tablespoon of chutney onto 1 side of each naan. Spoon the vegetables, dividing them evenly, on top of the chutney in the center of the naan, then roll up each naan around the filling.

CHARRED EGGPLANT PITA SANDWICHES WITH SPICY TAHINI

Start to finish: 30 minutes
Servings: 4

These vegetarian sandwiches were inspired by the Iraqi-Israeli hand food called sabich that stuffs fried eggplant, tomato-cucumber salad, hard-cooked egg, hummus and amba, a pickled mango condiment, into pita bread. For our much-simplified version, broiled slices of za'atar-seasoned eggplant are the "meat," and a harissa-spiked tahini sauce adds spice and richness while quick-pickled onion and tomato liven up the flavors. Other items you may want to tuck into the sandwiches to make them more sabich-like: sliced hard-cooked eggs, hummus, parsley leaves and cucumber pickles.

⅓ cup white vinegar

¾ teaspoon white sugar

Kosher salt and ground black pepper

1 small ripe tomato, cored and chopped

½ small red onion, thinly sliced

1½ pounds eggplant, cut into twelve
½-inch-thick rounds

3 tablespoons extra-virgin olive oil

4 teaspoons za'atar

¼ cup tahini

2 tablespoons lemon juice

2 to 3 tablespoons harissa paste

Two 8-inch pita rounds, each cut into half-rounds

Heat the broiler with a rack about 6 inches from the element. Line a rimmed baking sheet with foil and mist with cooking spray. In a small bowl, stir together the vinegar, sugar and ¼ teaspoon salt until the sugar and salt dissolve. Stir in the tomato and onion; set aside while you prepare the eggplant.

Brush both sides of the eggplant slices with the oil, then sprinkle with the za'atar, along with salt and pepper. Lay the slices on the prepared baking sheet and broil until well charred and a skewer inserted through the center meets no resistance, about 12 minutes, flipping the slices halfway through.

Meanwhile, in another small bowl, whisk together the tahini, lemon juice and ¼ teaspoon each salt and pepper. Whisk in the harissa and 3 tablespoons water; set aside.

When the eggplant is done, set the baking sheet on a wire rack. To fill each sandwich, open a pita half and spread 2 to 3 tablespoons tahini sauce inside. Place 3 eggplant slices in the pita, followed by a quarter of the onion-tomato mixture.

557

CHANGE THE WAY YOU COOK

Next-Level Grilled Cheese

A grilled cheese sandwich is a staple, and for good reason. Crisp, melty, salty, savory—and fast. For times when we want to take our grilled cheese to the next level, we follow these simple steps:

Go beyond cheddar. We use halloumi for our fried sandwiches (recipe p. 559). Halloumi is a Cypriot cheese that has a higher melting point than other cheeses, which means it can be fried or grilled until brown without getting messy. We pair it with peaches for a terrific marriage of salty and sweet.

Spice it up. We add kimchi (and kimchi brine) to our Korean-influenced grilled cheese with ham (recipe p. 561). The crunchy, garlicky kimchi adds texture and a burst of savory flavor. Our molletes, inspired by sandwiches we had in Mexico (recipe p. 561), are paired with fresh pico de gallo enlivened with jalapeño; tailor the heat by adding more or less of the chili seeds.

Smash your sandwich. To maximize toastiness, we follow the lead of Italian paninoteche (sandwich shops) and put a heavy skillet or pot on top of our cheese panini (recipe p. 564). The weight intensifies the bread-pan contact, promoting browning.

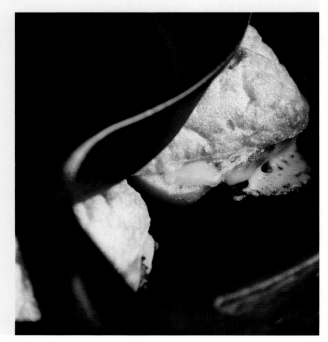

OVEN-BAKED THREE-LAYER CROQUE MONSIEUR SANDWICHES

Start to finish: 35 minutes
Servings: 4

During a trip to Paris and a visit with master fromager Laurent Dubois, we were reminded just how delicious a well-made croque monsieur can be. Dubois' version of the iconic French ham and cheese sandwich inspired us to develop a simple, fuss-free recipe that's doable on a weeknight. A béchamel, or flour-thickened white sauce, is classic, but we take a shortcut and stir together crème fraîche, shredded Gruyère (or Comté) cheese, a couple tablespoons of mustard and a small measure of nutmeg. The mixture mimics the sauciness of a roux-thickened béchamel. And instead of griddling the sandwiches one or two at a time, we cook four at once on a baking sheet in the oven. They're finished with a final slather of "sauce" and a blast of broiler heat for browning. Sliced sandwich bread with a sturdy crumb rather than a soft, cotttony texture is best. We modeled our recipe on Dubois' three-layer creation, so you will need a total of 12 slices for four sandwiches.

½ cup crème fraîche

2 tablespoons Dijon mustard

½ teaspoon grated nutmeg

Kosher salt and ground black pepper

6 ounces Gruyère or Comté cheese, shredded (1½ cups)

12 slices sturdy white sandwich bread

4 tablespoons salted butter, room temperature

6 ounces thinly sliced deli ham

Heat the oven to 400°F with a rack in the middle position. In a small bowl, whisk together the crème fraîche, mustard, nutmeg and ¼ teaspoon each salt and pepper. Stir in the cheese; set aside. Divide the ham into 4 stacks to make portioning easier.

Spread one side of each of 8 slices of bread with the butter, dividing it evenly. Place 4 slices, buttered side down, on a broiler-safe rimmed baking sheet, then spread 1 tablespoon cheese mixture onto each. Top each with half of a ham stack. Place a slice of unbuttered bread on top of each ham layer. Repeat the layering of 1 tablespoon cheese mixture

onto each sandwich, followed by the remaining ham, then top with the remaining buttered bread, with the buttered sides facing up. Bake for 10 minutes.

Using a wide metal spatula, flip each sandwich. Bake until the tops of the sandwiches are lightly browned, 7 to 9 minutes.

Remove the baking sheet from the oven; heat the broiler. Spread each sandwich with the remaining cheese mixture, dividing it evenly. Broil until the surfaces are bubbling and spotty brown, 1 to 1½ minutes. Transfer the sandwiches directly to a cutting board and cool for about 5 minutes. Cut each sandwich in half, then serve.

FRIED HALLOUMI SANDWICHES WITH PEACHES, ARUGULA AND HONEY

Start to finish: 35 minutes

Servings: 4

Halloumi is a semi-firm Cypriot cheese traditionally made from sheep and goat's milk, though these days cow's milk also is used. Its flavor is milky, tangy and briny, but what's unique about halloumi is its high melting point. This means the cheese can be grilled or fried—which it commonly is—to soften its texture and develop rich flavor through browning. We sandwich fried halloumi slices, slivers of juicy, ripe

peaches and peppery arugula between toasted bread brushed with honey infused with thyme and pickled peppers. The combination of salty and sweet is sublime. Aim to purchase about 1 pound of halloumi, but note that packages vary somewhat in weight; a bit more or less will work out fine. If you can't find ciabatta rolls, purchase a whole loaf and cut it into pieces roughly 5 inches square, then split each horizontally.

⅓ **cup honey**

⅓ **cup drained Peppadew peppers or sweet cherry peppers, patted dry and finely chopped**

½ **teaspoon dried thyme**

Ground black pepper

2 ounces baby arugula (about 3 cups lightly packed)

1 tablespoon lemon juice

6 tablespoons extra-virgin olive oil, divided, plus more as needed

4 ciabatta rolls, split

Two 8.8-ounce packages halloumi cheese (see headnote), sliced ¼ to ½ inch thick and patted dry

2 ripe peaches, pitted and thinly sliced

In a small microwave-safe bowl, combine the honey, peppers, thyme and ½ teaspoon black pepper. Microwave, uncovered, on high until fragrant and warm, about 1 minute; set aside. In a medium bowl, toss the arugula with the lemon juice; set aside.

In a 12-inch nonstick skillet over medium-high, combine 2 tablespoons oil and half of the rolls, placing the pieces cut sides down. Cook until golden brown on the bottoms, 2 to 4 minutes, then transfer toasted sides up to a cutting board. Using 2 tablespoons of the remaining oil, toast the remaining bread in the same way.

In the same skillet over medium-high, heat the remaining 2 tablespoons oil until shimmering. Add the halloumi in a single layer and cook, undisturbed for the first couple minutes then occasionally flipping each slice, until browned on both sides, 4 to 6 minutes total; reduce the heat if the cheese is browning too quickly. Remove the pan from the heat.

Brush the toasted sides of the bread with infused honey, dividing it evenly. Lay the peach slices on the bottom halves of rolls, then top with the halloumi, followed by the arugula, evenly dividing the ingredients. Cover with the top halves of the rolls.

8 slices hearty white OR whole-wheat OR rye sandwich bread

4 teaspoons whole-grain mustard OR Dijon mustard

8 slices cheddar OR provolone OR whole-milk mozzarella OR pepper Jack cheese

4 slices cooked bacon (optional)

In a 12-inch nonstick skillet over medium-high, heat the oil until shimmering. Add the onion, ¾ teaspoon salt and ½ teaspoon pepper. Cook, stirring occasionally, until the onion is soft and golden brown, about 10 minutes. Add the kale a large handful at a time, stirring to slightly wilt after each addition. Add ¼ cup water, then reduce to medium, cover and cook, stirring occasionally, until the kale is tender, 10 to 12 minutes. Transfer the kale mixture to a medium bowl; set aside. Wipe out the skillet.

Meanwhile, spread butter over 1 side of each slice of bread, evenly dividing the butter. Flip the slices to be buttered side down, then spread about ½ teaspoon mustard on each slice. Top each of 4 bread slices with 1 slice of cheese, a quarter of the kale mixture and 1 slice of bacon (if using), torn to fit. Top each with a slice of the remaining cheese, then with another slice of bread, buttered side up. Press on the sandwiches to compact the fillings.

Heat the skillet over medium until droplets of water flicked onto the surface quickly sizzle and evaporate. Add 2 of the sandwiches and cook until golden brown on the bottoms,

KALE AND CHEDDAR MELTS WITH CARAMELIZED ONION

Start to finish: 40 minutes
Servings: 4

This recipe gives basic grilled cheese a tasty—and healthful!—update. We combine earthy wilted kale with sweet, caramelized onions and melty cheese, plus a slathering of mustard for tangy contrast. To add a salty-smoky note, tuck crisp bacon slices inside the sandwiches before cooking them. Be sure to use a hearty sandwich bread that's sturdy enough to contain all of the fillings.

2 tablespoons extra-virgin olive oil

1 medium yellow onion, halved and thinly sliced

Kosher salt and ground black pepper

1 large bunch lacinato kale OR curly kale, stemmed and chopped into rough 1-inch pieces (about 12 cups)

2 tablespoons salted butter, room temperature

2 to 3 minutes. Using a wide spatula, flip the sandwiches and cook, pressing down lightly and adjusting the heat as needed, until golden brown on the second sides and the cheese is melted, 2 to 3 minutes. Transfer to a cutting board. Cook the remaining sandwiches in the same way (the second batch may cook faster). Cut each sandwich in half.

KIMCHI GRILLED CHEESE WITH HAM

Start to finish: 30 minutes
Servings: 4

Spicy, garlicky kimchi ups the umami quotient of the classic grilled cheese. The pairing of cheese and kimchi actually isn't new. Budae jjigae, otherwise known as army base stew, originates with the Korean War. It's a hot pot made with American surplus foods, such as hot dogs, baked beans and instant noodles, along with kimchi and American cheese. These sandwiches aren't quite as lavish, but they're indisputably tasty.

⅓ cup mayonnaise

1 tablespoon kimchi juice, plus 1⅓ cups cabbage kimchi, drained and chopped

8 slices hearty white sandwich bread

8 slices cheddar OR pepper Jack OR whole-milk mozzarella cheese

4 slices thinly sliced deli ham OR 4 slices cooked bacon

In a small bowl, stir together the mayonnaise and kimchi brine. Spread evenly over one side of each slice of bread. Flip 4 of the slices to be mayonnaise side down, then top each with 1 slice of cheese, 1 slice of ham (or 1 slice bacon, torn to fit) and a quarter of the kimchi. Top each with a slice of the remaining cheese, then with another slice of bread, mayonnaise side up. Press on the sandwiches to compact the fillings.

Heat a 12-inch nonstick or cast-iron skillet over medium until droplets of water flicked onto the surface quickly sizzle and evaporate. Add 2 of the sandwiches and cook until golden brown on the bottoms, 2 to 3 minutes. Using a wide spatula, flip the sandwiches and cook, pressing down lightly and adjusting the heat as needed, until golden brown on the second sides and the cheese is melted, 2 to 3 minutes. Transfer to a cutting board. Cook the remaining sandwiches in the same way (the second batch may cook faster). Cut each sandwich in half on the diagonal.

MOLLETES WITH PICO DE GALLO

Start to finish: 15 minutes
Servings 4

Mexican molletes are not unlike Italian bruschetti, but the bread is topped with mashed beans and cheese, then toasted until the cheese is melted and browned. They make a great breakfast, light lunch or midday snack. We had molletes in Oaxaca, Mexico, where the bread of choice typically is soft-crumbed, thin-crusted rolls called bolillos that are split open before they're topped. For our version, we opted for ½-inch-thick slices of supermarket bakery bread with a soft crumb; look for a loaf that measures about 10 by 5 inches and weighs about 1 pound. Pico de gallo (fresh tomato salsa) adds color and fresh flavor to the molletes, so we consider it a necessary embellishment; sliced avocado and pickled jalapeños are delicious but optional.

Eight ½-inch-thick slices crusty bread
(see headnote)

¼ cup extra-virgin olive oil

Kosher salt and ground black pepper

2 cups black bean puree (recipe follows)

1 pound whole-milk mozzarella, shredded (4 cups)

½ cup finely chopped fresh cilantro

Pico de gallo (recipe follows), to serve

Sliced avocado, to serve (optional)

Pickled sliced jalapeños, to serve (optional)

Heat the broiler with a rack about 6 inches from the element. Line a broiler-safe rimmed baking sheet with foil and mist with cooking spray. Arrange the bread in a single layer on the baking sheet and brush the tops with the oil. Season with salt and pepper. Broil until the bread is golden brown, 3 to 5 minutes. Flip each slice and broil until the second sides are golden brown, 1 to 2 minutes. Remove from the broiler.

Flip each slice once again. Spread ¼ cup bean puree on each slice, then top each with ½ cup of the cheese. Broil until the cheese is melted and begins to brown, 4 to 6 minutes. Transfer the baking sheet to a wire rack and cool for 5 minutes. Sprinkle with cilantro, then transfer to a platter. Serve with pico de gallo, sliced avocado (if using) and pickled jalapeños (if using).

BLACK BEAN PUREE

Start to finish: 15 minutes
Makes 3 cups

This bean puree is quick and simple to make. It's also versatile: Keep some on hand for use as a filling for tacos, quesadillas or molletes; serve it warm as a side dish to any Mexican-inspired meal; or use it as a dip for tortilla chips. Leftovers can be thinned with water or broth to the desired consistency.

1 tablespoon ground cumin

1 tablespoon ground coriander

Two 15½-ounce cans black beans,
drained (do not rinse), ¼ cup liquid reserved

2 chipotle chilies in adobo sauce,
plus 2 teaspoons adobo sauce

2 tablespoons lime juice

Kosher salt and ground black pepper

½ cup finely chopped fresh cilantro

In a small skillet over medium, toast the cumin and coriander, stirring often, until fragrant, about 1 minute. Transfer to a food processor and add the beans and reserved liquid, chipotle chilies and adobo sauce, lime juice and ½ teaspoon salt. Process until smooth, scraping the bowl as needed. Transfer to a medium bowl. Stir in the cilantro, then taste and season with salt and pepper.

PICO DE GALLO

Start to finish: 30 minutes
Makes about 2 cups

Pico de gallo is a bright, fresh tomato salsa. We use grape or cherry tomatoes because they tend to be dependably sweet and flavorful. For a spicier salsa, leave the seeds in the jalapeño.

1 pint grape or cherry tomatoes,
roughly chopped

¼ small red onion, finely chopped
(about 3 tablespoons)

¼ cup lightly packed fresh cilantro, chopped

½ jalapeño chili, stemmed, seeded and minced

2 teaspoons white vinegar

1½ teaspoons extra-virgin olive oil

Kosher salt

In a medium bowl, stir together the tomatoes, onion, cilantro, chili, vinegar, oil and ½ teaspoon salt. Cover and let stand at room temperature for 15 minutes. Using a slotted spoon, transfer to a serving bowl, letting the liquid drip away. Taste and season with salt.

563

PANINI WITH MORTADELLA, PROVOLONE AND BROCCOLI RABE

Start to finish: 30 minutes
Serves: 4

The grilled sandwiches that we know today as panini are believed to have originated in the mid-20th century in Italy's paninoteche (sandwich shops). Panini offer a tantalizing combination of warm, toasted bread, salty meats and melty cheese. Our panini also include sautéed broccoli rabe, which offers a bitterness to offset the richness of mortadella and provolone while also making these simple sandwiches complete meals. We spread vinegary crushed red peppers on the bread to add piquancy—sometimes labeled as "hoagie spread," it's sold jarred in most supermarkets. Chopped peperoncini or cherry peppers would be a good substitute.

3 tablespoons extra-virgin olive oil, divided

2 medium garlic cloves, peeled and halved

1-pound bunch broccoli rabe, trimmed and chopped into rough ½-inch pieces

Kosher salt

Four 8-inch crusty rolls or ciabatta rolls

4 tablespoons jarred crushed red peppers (see headnote), divided

8 ounces sliced provolone cheese, preferably aged provolone, slices cut in half

8 ounces sliced mortadella

In a 12-inch skillet over medium-high, heat 1 tablespoon of oil until shimmering. Add the garlic and cook, stirring, until the cloves begin to brown, about 30 seconds. Add the broccoli rabe and ½ teaspoon salt, then cook, stirring, until just starting to soften, about 1 minute. Add ¼ cup water, cover and cook, stirring occasionally, until the stem pieces are tender, 4 to 5 minutes. Remove and discard the garlic, then transfer the rabe to a medium bowl; set aside. Wipe out the skillet and set it aside.

Split each roll horizontally, leaving one side hinged. If the rolls are very thick, pull out and discard some of the crumb so the bread is about ½ inch thick. Spread 1 tablespoon of crushed peppers on the inside of the top half of each roll. Top the other side with the broccoli rabe, dividing it evenly. Lay half of the provolone on the rabe, dividing it evenly.

Top the cheese with the mortadella, then finish with the remaining provolone. Close the rolls and press firmly.

In the same skillet over medium, heat 1 tablespoon of the remaining oil until shimmering. Add 2 panini, weight them with a heavy skillet or pot, then cook until the bottoms are nicely toasted, 2 to 3 minutes, adjusting the heat as needed if the bread is browning too quickly. Flip the panini, replace the weight and cook until the second sides are toasted and the cheese begins to melt, 1 to 2 minutes. Transfer to a cutting board. Using the remaining 1 tablespoon oil, toast the remaining 2 panini in the same way. To serve, cut each panini in half on the diagonal.

CHEDDAR, ROASTED ONION AND APPLE TARTINES

Start to finish: 45 minutes (25 minutes active)

Servings: 4

Using a few basic pantry ingredients, we've transformed the classic grilled cheese into delicious open-faced savory-sweet tartines. Thinly sliced apples and onion are roasted in a hot oven to caramelize them and bring out their natural sweetness. They're layered on pieces of baguette with cheddar, Parmesan and a piquant mustard butter, then baked until toasty. Complete the meal with a tossed green salad, if you like.

2 large apples, preferably Granny Smith, peeled, cored and cut into ⅛-inch wedges

1 large red OR yellow onion, halved and thinly sliced

2 tablespoons extra-virgin olive oil

Kosher salt and ground black pepper

4 tablespoons salted butter, room temperature

2 tablespoons Dijon mustard

10- to 12-ounce baguette

2 teaspoons white wine vinegar OR red wine vinegar

6 ounces cheddar cheese, shredded (1½ cups)

1 ounce Parmesan cheese, finely grated (½ cup)

Heat the oven to 425°F with a rack in the middle position. On a rimmed baking sheet, toss together the apples, onion, oil and ½ teaspoon salt, then distribute in an even layer. Roast until the apples are tender and the onion begins to char at the edges, about 15 minutes, stirring once about halfway.

Meanwhile, in a small bowl, stir together the butter and mustard until well combined. Cut the baguette in half crosswise, then each half horizontally to create 4 pieces.

Transfer the apples and onion to a medium bowl, scraping any browned bits into the bowl; wipe off and reserve the baking sheet. Leave the oven on. Stir the vinegar into the apple-onion mixture.

Place the bread cut side up on the baking sheet. Spread the mustard butter on the bread, dividing it evenly. Sprinkle the cheddar evenly onto the bread, then top each with one-fourth of the apple-onion mixture, covering the surfaces. Sprinkle evenly with Parmesan.

Bake until the edges of the bread are toasted and the tops are lightly browned, 8 to 10 minutes. Season each tartine with black pepper.

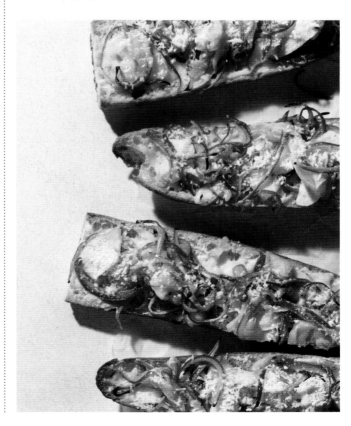

Tortillas

Homemade Corn Tortillas

Start to finish: 1 hour
Makes twelve 6-inch tortillas

In Mexico City we learned that fresh, homemade corn tortillas, warm and perfumed with the lingering sweetness of the corn, are key to a great taco. Making your own corn tortillas using masa harina (flour ground from nixtamalized corn) is not difficult, but it does require a few pieces of equipment. You will need a tortilla press, a 10- or 12-inch nonstick skillet, a 10- to 12-inch cast-iron griddle or skillet, and a spray bottle filled with water. When pressing the tortillas, rounds cut from a clean plastic grocery bag (or a gallon-size zip-close cut into two 8-inch squares) ensure the dough won't stick to the press. For cooking the tortillas, we use a two-stage method. During the second stage, we lightly drag a metal spatula across the tortilla, which often triggers a puffing action. Though a puffed tortilla deflates when removed from the pan, its texture is lighter and airier than one that hasn't risen. But don't worry if your tortillas don't puff—they still will be better than store-bought. If you need more than a dozen tortillas, this recipe can be scaled up.

240 grams (2 cups) masa harina

¼ teaspoon table salt

1½ cups warm water (about 110°F), plus more as needed

In a large bowl, stir together the masa harina and salt. While stirring with a silicone spatula, gradually add the water, then stir until the masa is evenly moistened. Transfer the masa to the counter and knead until smooth and putty-like, about 1 minute. Pinch off a small piece, roll it into a ball and flatten it; if the edges crack, knead in more water, 1 tablespoon at a time, then test again.

Transfer the masa to a large sheet of plastic wrap and wrap it tightly. Let rest at room temperature for at least 15 minutes or up to 1 hour to allow the masa to hydrate. Meanwhile, cut out two 8-inch rounds from a clean plastic grocery bag (alternatively, cut a gallon-size zip-close plastic bag into two 8-inch squares).

Divide the masa into 12 portions (each about 40 grams). Using your hands, roll each into a smooth ball and set on a plate. Lightly spritz with water and cover with a kitchen towel. Set a 10- or 12-inch nonstick skillet over medium-low and a 10- to 12-inch cast-iron skillet or griddle over high. Heat both until the cast-iron pan is very hot, about 10 minutes.

While the pans are heating, line a large plate with another kitchen towel and spritz the towel with water a few times to dampen. Open the tortilla press and lay one of the plastic rounds on the plate. Set 1 masa ball in the center and flatten it slightly with your hand. Cover with the second plastic round. Close the press and press down firmly on the handle. Open the press, rotate the masa in the plastic 180 degrees and press firmly again; the tortilla should be about 6 inches in diameter. If the pans are not yet fully heated, leave the tortilla in the plastic until they are.

Peel off the top plastic round. Using the plastic on the bottom, flip the tortilla onto the palm of your hand and slowly peel away the plastic. Using both hands, carefully place the tortilla in the nonstick skillet and cook until the edges begin to dry and the tortilla releases easily from the pan, about 20 seconds. While the tortilla is cooking, press another ball of masa; set aside.

Using a wide metal spatula, flip the tortilla and cook until it releases easily from the pan, about 30 seconds. Now transfer the tortilla without flipping it to the cast-iron pan. Immediately, quickly and lightly drag the metal spatula across the tortilla 2 or 3 times; the tortilla should begin to puff. Cook until the edges begin to brown on the bottom, 15 to 20 seconds, then flip the tortilla and cook, pressing lightly on the edges, until lightly charred on the second side, about 30 seconds.

Transfer the tortilla to the prepared plate (it will deflate) and enclose in the towel. Cook the second tortilla in the same way and press another; stack the tortillas as they are done and keep them wrapped in the towel (make sure the towel remains lightly moistened with water). Continue until all of the dough has been pressed and cooked. If the masa balls begin to dry out as they sit, lightly spritz them with water. Serve warm.

TACOS AL PASTOR

Start to finish: 1 hour

Servings: 4

We combine tender broiled pork, spicy chilies and the subtle smokiness of charred pineapple in this take on tacos al pastor. The dish is from Mexico but has Levantine roots, stemming from the 19th century when Lebanese immigrants arrived, bringing their tradition of vertical spits for roasting lamb shawarma. Not finding much lamb, cooks switched to pork and instead of sandwiching the meat in flatbread, they used tortillas. Subsequent generations added pineapple and dried chilies. For everyday ease, we use pork tenderloin that has been pounded, briefly marinated and broiled. Chopped pineapple, also broiled, and fresh finely chopped white onion completes the tacos. For some extra color and crunch, offer finely shredded red cabbage for sprinkling. To simplify prep, you can buy fresh pineapple that has already been peeled, cored and sliced.

1 medium pineapple, peeled

¼ cup grapeseed or other neutral oil,
plus more for the baking sheet and pineapple

¼ cup packed dark brown sugar

8 medium garlic cloves, peeled

4 chipotle chilies in adobo, plus
1 tablespoon adobo sauce

4 teaspoons ground cumin

4 teaspoons ancho chili powder

Kosher salt and ground black pepper

2 tablespoons lime juice, divided, plus
lime wedges, to serve

1¼-pound pork tenderloin, trimmed of
silver skin and halved lengthwise

⅓ cup lightly packed fresh cilantro, chopped

8 corn tortillas, warmed

Finely chopped white onion, to serve

Slice the pineapple into seven ½-inch-thick rounds. Quarter 2 rounds, trimming and discarding the core. In a food processor, puree the quartered pineapple slices, oil, brown sugar, garlic, chipotles and adobo, cumin, ancho powder and 2 teaspoons salt until smooth, about 1 minute. Pour ½ cup into a baking dish; pour the rest into a medium bowl and stir in 1 tablespoon of the lime juice. Set both aside.

Place the tenderloin halves between 2 large sheets of plastic wrap. Using a meat mallet, pound the pork to an even ½-inch thickness. Season both sides of each piece with salt and pepper, place in the baking dish and turn to coat with the puree. Let marinate at room temperature for 15 minutes.

Meanwhile, heat the broiler with a rack about 4 inches from the element. Line a broiler-safe rimmed baking sheet with extra-wide foil and mist with cooking spray. Arrange the 5 remaining pineapple slices in a single layer on the prepared baking sheet. Brush the slices with oil and sprinkle with salt and pepper, then broil until charred in spots, 7 to 10 minutes. Transfer the pineapple to a cutting board and set aside; reserve the baking sheet.

Transfer the tenderloin halves to the same baking sheet and broil until charred in spots and the center reaches 140°F or is just barely pink when cut, 7 to 10 minutes. Let rest for 5 minutes.

While the pork rests, chop the pineapple into rough ½-inch cubes, discarding the core. Transfer to a small bowl and stir in the cilantro and the remaining 1 tablespoon lime juice, then taste and season with salt and pepper.

Cut the pork crosswise into thin slices on the diagonal. Transfer to a medium bowl, then stir in any accumulated pork juices along with 3 tablespoons of the reserved pineapple puree. Serve the pork, chopped pineapple and remaining pineapple puree with the tortillas, chopped onion and lime wedges.

STEAK AND BACON TACOS

Start to finish: 40 minutes
Servings: 4

Tacos de alambre, the skillet version of Mexican beef kebabs (alambres), features steak, bacon, peppers, onion, tomato and a blanket of melted cheese. If you like, serve the tacos with additional toppings to add fresh notes to balance the richness. We particularly liked sliced avocado, a squeeze of lime juice, shredded cabbage and fresh cilantro.

1 pound flank steak, cut into thirds with
the grain, then thinly sliced against the grain

1½ teaspoons ground cumin, divided

1½ teaspoons chili powder, divided

Kosher salt and ground black pepper

6 ounces bacon, chopped

1 medium white onion, halved and thinly sliced

4 large jalapeño chilies, stemmed, halved,
seeded and thinly sliced

5 medium garlic cloves, thinly sliced

1 pint cherry or grape tomatoes, halved

4 ounces sliced Jack or Muenster cheese

8 corn tortillas, warmed

In a bowl, season the steak with ½ teaspoon of cumin, ½ teaspoon of chili powder and ½ teaspoon each salt and pepper, tossing to coat. Set aside.

In a 12-inch nonstick skillet over medium, cook the bacon, stirring occasionally, until browned and crisp, 8 to 10 minutes. Using a slotted spoon, transfer to a small bowl. Pour off and discard all but 2 tablespoons of the bacon fat.

Return the skillet to medium-high and heat the fat until shimmering. Add half the steak in an even layer and cook without disturbing until well browned, 1½ to 2 minutes. Stir and continue to cook until no longer pink, 30 seconds. Using tongs, transfer the steak to a bowl. Using the fat remaining in the pan, repeat with the remaining beef.

Return the skillet to medium-high, add the onion and cook without stirring until beginning to brown, about 2 minutes. Stir in the chilies, garlic, the remaining 1 teaspoon cumin, the remaining 1 teaspoon chili powder and ½ teaspoon each salt and pepper, then cook until fragrant, about 30 seconds. Reduce to medium-low and stir in the tomatoes and ¼ cup water.

Continue to cook, stirring occasionally and crushing the tomatoes, until the tomatoes are fully softened, about 7 minutes. Stir in the beef and accumulated juices. Taste and season with salt and pepper. Layer the cheese on top, then sprinkle with the bacon. Cover, reduce to low and cook until the cheese is melted, 2 to 3 minutes. Serve with tortillas for making tacos.

CHILI AND CITRUS–MARINATED FISH TACOS

Start to finish: 1 hour, plus marinating
Servings: 4 to 6

At Casa Jacaranda cooking school in Mexico City, Jorge Fritz and Beto Estúa showed us how to make delicious fish tacos that were not only quick and easy to pull together, but also a feast for the eyes. Snapper, marinated in a blend of citrus juice, guajillo chilies, aromatics and achiote paste, was quickly sautéed before being tucked into tortillas and garnished with a savory-sweet pineapple-based salsa and fresh cilantro, delivering a profusion of flavors in each bite. We adapted their recipe, opting instead to broil the marinated fish, as we found that the intense heat produces delicious charring with minimal fuss and cleanup. For the salsa, we hewed closely to theirs, but added habanero chili for a touch of fruity heat that complements the pineapple (we added habanero to the fish marinade, too). Brick-red annatto paste, made with annatto seeds (also called achiote seeds) plus spices and seasonings, is typically sold in small bricks. Look for it in the international aisle of well-stocked supermarkets, in Latin American grocery stores or online. If you don't have achiote paste, a good substitute can be made by stirring together 1½ tablespoons sweet paprika, ½ teaspoon ground

cumin, ¼ teaspoon granulated garlic, ¼ teaspoon dried oregano, ⅛ teaspoon kosher salt and 1 tablespoon white vinegar to form a stiff paste. Use in place of the paste called for in the recipe.

¾ ounce guajillo chilies (4 medium), stemmed and seeded

1 medium white onion, ½ roughly chopped, ½ finely chopped

2 habanero chilies, stemmed and seeded, 1 left whole, 1 finely chopped

¼ cup orange juice

¼ cup lime juice, plus lime wedges to serve

⅝ ounce achiote paste (2 tablespoons grated on the small holes of a box grater; see headnote)

2 medium garlic cloves, smashed and peeled

1 tablespoon oregano, preferably Mexican oregano

1 teaspoon cumin seeds

Kosher salt and ground black pepper

1½ pounds skinless snapper or mahi mahi fillets

2 tablespoons grapeseed or other neutral oil

1½ cups chopped fresh pineapple (½-inch chunks)

1 medium carrot, peeled and finely chopped

1 large celery stalk, finely chopped

½ cup lightly packed cilantro, chopped

8 to 12 (6-inch) corn tortillas, warmed

In a 12-inch skillet over medium, toast the guajillo chilies, turning occasionally with tongs, until fragrant and just a shade darker in color, 1 to 2 minutes. Transfer to a plate and cool, then break the pods into smaller pieces, discarding any remaining seeds; reserve the skillet.

In a blender, combine the guajillo chilies, the roughly chopped onion, the whole habanero, orange juice, lime juice, achiote paste, garlic, oregano, cumin, ½ teaspoon salt and ¼ teaspoon pepper. Puree until smooth, about 40 seconds, scraping the blender jar as needed.

Place the fish in a 9-inch glass or ceramic pie plate or similar nonreactive dish. Add the puree, then turn the fillets to coat. Cover and refrigerate for at least 1 hour or up to 2 hours.

Meanwhile, in the same skillet over medium-high, heat the oil until shimmering. Add the pineapple and ½ teaspoon salt, then cook, stirring occasionally, until well browned, 5 to 7 minutes. Add the finely chopped onion, the carrot, celery and finely chopped habanero; cook, stirring occasionally, until the vegetables are softened and beginning to brown, 5 to 6 minutes. Transfer to a serving bowl; set aside until ready to serve.

Heat the broiler with a rack about 4 inches from the element. Line a rimmed baking sheet with foil and mist the foil with cooking spray. Place the fish skinned side down on the baking sheet in a single layer, leaving the marinade on the fillets. Broil until the fish is well charred on top and the flesh flakes easily, 5 to 9 minutes.

Using a wide metal spatula, transfer the fish to a cutting board. Cut each fillet crosswise into 1-inch pieces, then transfer to a platter. To serve, put the lime wedges and cilantro in small bowls. Serve the fish with the tortillas, salsa and garnishes for making tacos.

FRIED SHRIMP TACOS WITH SALSA ROJA

Start to finish: 1¼ hours
Makes 8 tacos

At Mariscos Jalisco, Raul Ortega's food truck in the Boyle Heights area of Los Angeles, the tacos de camarón, or shrimp tacos, are the main attraction, and for good reason. Ortega stuffs a perfectly seasoned shrimp filling into tortillas and fries the tacos to golden brown crispness before finishing them with tomato salsa and avocado. His recipe is a closely guarded secret, but in her version of those tacos, food writer and recipe developer Paola Briseño-González attempts to replicate that delicious melding of flavors and textures. The shrimp are chopped in a food processor to make the filling, so though the recipe specifies shrimp of a certain size, just about any size will work.

FOR THE SALSA ROJA:

1 pound ripe plum tomatoes, cored, halved and seeded

¼ large white onion, chopped (about ½ cup)

2 medium garlic cloves, smashed and peeled

1 tablespoon dried Mexican oregano

Kosher salt and ground black pepper

1 cup finely chopped green cabbage

1 cup lightly packed fresh cilantro, chopped

FOR THE TACOS AND SERVING:

8 ounces ripe plum tomatoes, cored, halved and seeded

¾ large white onion, chopped (about 1 heaping cup)

2 medium garlic cloves, smashed and peeled

1 teaspoon dried Mexican oregano

Kosher salt and ground black pepper

8 ounces large (26/30 per pound) shrimp (see headnote), peeled (tails removed) and deveined

3 tablespoons plus 1 cup grapeseed or other neutral oil, divided

3 tablespoons all-purpose flour

Eight 6-inch corn tortillas

1 ripe avocado, halved, pitted, peeled and sliced

Lime wedges, to serve

To make the salsa, in a food processor, combine the tomatoes, onion, garlic, oregano and 1 teaspoon salt. Process until smooth, 1 to 2 minutes. Transfer to a medium bowl; reserve the food processor bowl and blade. Stir the cabbage and cilantro into the puree, then taste and season with salt and pepper. Cover and set aside until ready to serve.

To make the tacos, in the food processor, combine the tomatoes, onion, garlic, oregano, 1 teaspoon salt and ¼ teaspoon pepper. Pulse to a coarse puree, about 10 pulses. Transfer to a small bowl. To the food processor, add the shrimp and pulse until finely chopped, about 4 pulses.

In a 10-inch skillet over medium, heat the 3 tablespoons oil until shimmering. Add the tomato-onion puree and cook, stirring occasionally, until most of the moisture has evaporated, 7 to 9 minutes. Add the flour and cook, stirring, until well incorporated, about 1 minute. Add the shrimp and cook, stirring constantly, until the shrimp turn pink and the mixture has thickened, about 1 minute. Set aside off heat.

Heat a 12-inch skillet over medium until water flicked onto the surface immediately sizzles and evaporates. Add 2 tortillas in a single layer (it's fine if they overlap slightly) and heat, flipping them once, until warm, about 30 seconds per side. Transfer to a kitchen towel and wrap loosely to keep warm and pliable. Repeat with the remaining tortillas, stacking and wrapping them in the towel. Add the remaining 1 cup oil to the skillet; keep warm over low while you fill the tortillas.

Lay 4 of the tortillas on a work surface and divide half of the shrimp mixture evenly among them, placing the filling on one side of the tortilla. Fold the unfilled sides over and press lightly; leave the edges open (do not seal them). Fill the remaining tortillas with the remaining shrimp mixture in the same way.

Return the oil to medium and heat until shimmering (about 350°F). Carefully add 4 of the tacos and cook until golden brown and crisp on the bottoms, about 3 minutes. Using a thin metal spatula, flip each taco and cook until golden brown on the second sides, about 3 minutes, then transfer to a paper towel-lined plate. Fry the remaining tacos in the same way, adjusting the heat as needed.

Transfer the tacos to a serving platter and spoon on some of the salsa. Top with the avocado slices and serve with the remaining salsa and lime wedges on the side.

GREEN ENCHILADAS WITH CHICKEN AND CHEESE

Start to finish: 45 minutes
Servings: 4

To make the filling for these enchiladas, use leftover roasted or grilled chicken or meat from a store-bought rotisserie bird. You also can poach your own chicken. To do so, place 1 pound boneless, skinless chicken breasts in a medium saucepan, cover with chicken broth, bring to a simmer over medium-high, then reduce to low, cover and cook until the thickest part of the meat registers 160°F, about 20 minutes. Let the chicken cool in the liquid until just warm to the touch, then finely chop the meat. Any bottled hot sauce that's not too vinegary (such as Tapatío or Cholula) will work. Chopped white onion and sour cream or Mexican crema are great garnishes.

3 tablespoons extra-virgin olive oil, divided

3 medium poblano chilies (about 12 ounces), stemmed, seeded and chopped

1 pound tomatillos, husked, cored and chopped

1 medium white onion, chopped

6 medium garlic cloves, smashed and peeled

1 tablespoon ground cumin

½ cup low-sodium chicken broth

1 cup lightly packed fresh cilantro

Kosher salt and ground black pepper

1½ cups finely chopped cooked chicken (see headnote)

6 ounces whole-milk mozzarella cheese, shredded (1½ cups)

2 tablespoons hot sauce (see headnote)

Eight 6-inch corn tortillas

Lime wedges, to serve

Heat the oven to 475°F with a rack in the middle position. In a large pot over medium-high, combine 1 tablespoon of the oil, the poblanos, tomatillos, onion and garlic. Cook, stirring occasionally, until the vegetables are well-browned and beginning to soften, 5 to 8 minutes. Stir in the cumin and cook until fragrant, about 30 seconds. Add the broth and cook, stirring occasionally, until the vegetables have softened, about 5 minutes. Remove from the heat and let cool for 5 minutes.

Transfer the mixture to a food processor and process until smooth, about 1 minute. Add the cilantro and continue to process until smooth, about 1 minute. Taste and season with salt and pepper. Spread 1 cup of the sauce in the bottom of a 9-by-13-inch baking dish; set aside.

In a medium bowl, toss together the chicken, cheese, hot sauce, ¾ teaspoon salt and 1 teaspoon pepper; set aside.

Brush both sides of the tortillas with the remaining 2 table-spoons oil, then arrange them on a rimmed baking sheet (it's fine to overlap them slightly). Cover tightly with foil and warm in the oven just until soft and pliable, about 3 minutes.

Uncover the tortillas; reserve the foil. Lay the tortillas out on a large cutting board or clean counter. Divide the chicken mixture evenly among the tortillas (about 3 heaping

tablespoons each), arranging and pressing the filling in a line along the bottom edge of each tortilla.

Working one at a time, roll up the tortillas to enclose the filling and place seam side down in a tight row down the center of the prepared baking dish. Spoon ½ cup of the sauce over the enchiladas. Cover tightly with the reserved foil and bake until the cheese begins to melt out of the ends, about 15 minutes.

Uncover and spread ½ cup of the remaining sauce over the enchiladas. Re-cover and let stand for 5 minutes. Serve with lime wedges and the remaining sauce.

CHANGE THE WAY YOU COOK

Use Tortillas to Thicken Soup

Mexican cooks often use masa, the corn dough used to make tortillas, to thicken soups, stews and sauces. But Oaxaca chef Olga Cabrera Oropeza taught us a pantry-easy shortcut: corn tortillas. The method is simple, soften the tortillas in liquid, blend until smooth, then add the resulting puree to the broth.

We do this with our green mole with chicken (recipe p. 576) taught to us by Oropeza. The tortillas are combined with broth and brought to a boil before going in the blender with a little water. Working on the same principle, we use tortilla chips to thicken our tortilla soup (recipe p. 577). The chips go in with the tomatoes and broth, are brought to a boil and cooked at a simmer until the tomatoes have softened. Then everything goes into the blend to be pureed until smooth.

Keep in mind that the number of tortillas or tortilla chips you'll need depends on how thick you want your soup or sauce. As a rough guide, six or seven 6-inch corn tortillas is a good amount for turning 4 to 5 cups liquid into velvety, lightly clingy braising liquid. For a brothy soup, about 2 cups tortilla chips is a good amount to lend body to about 6 cups of liquid. It's a good idea to err on the side of too little, as you can always blend in more for further thickening.

2 pounds boneless, skinless chicken thighs, trimmed and halved

Kosher salt and ground black pepper

Seven 6-inch corn tortillas

1 quart low-sodium chicken broth

4 medium garlic cloves, peeled

2 medium tomatillos, husked and halved

1 medium poblano chili (about 4 ounces), stemmed, seeded and quartered lengthwise

1 small white onion, root end intact, quartered lengthwise

1 bunch cilantro, leaves and tender stems

1 cup lightly packed fresh flat-leaf parsley

½ cup lightly packed fresh mint

1 teaspoon fennel seeds

1 teaspoon cumin seeds

8 ounces small Yukon Gold potatoes (1 to 1½ inches in diameter), halved

6 ounces green beans, trimmed and cut into 1-inch pieces

1 medium yellow zucchini, cut into 1-inch chunks (about 2 cups)

OAXACAN GREEN MOLE WITH CHICKEN

Start to finish: 1 hour 10 minutes
Servings: 4

When we think of mole, we most often think of mahogany-colored mole negro, flavored with chocolate, dried chilies and nuts. But as we learned from Oaxaca chef Olga Cabrera Oropeza, there is a wide variety of moles, each with a unique character. Mole verde—or green mole—traditionally is made with pork and gets its bright, fresh flavor from a blend of fresh chilies, tomatillos and herbs. For our version, we opted for quicker-cooking but equally tasty chicken thighs, and we sought out supermarket substitutes for hard-to-find epazote and hoja santa, two herbs that are standard ingredients in Mexico (we mimicked their flavors with mint and fennel seeds). Oaxacans thicken this stew-like soup with masa, the corn dough used to make tortillas and tamales. For ease, we opted to use what Oropeza showed us was the second best option: corn tortillas softened in liquid then blended until smooth.

Season the chicken thighs with salt and pepper. In a large pot over medium-high, combine the tortillas and broth, then bring to a boil. Using a slotted spoon, transfer the tortillas (they will have softened) to a blender, add ¼ cup water and blend until smooth, about 1 minute.

Pour the puree into the boiling broth and stir to combine; rinse out the blender and reserve. Add the chicken to the pot, cover and reduce to low. Cook, stirring occasionally and adjusting the heat as needed to maintain a gentle simmer, until a skewer inserted into the chicken meets just a little resistance, 30 to 35 minutes.

Meanwhile, heat the broiler with a rack about 4 inches from the element. Line a rimmed baking sheet with foil. Arrange the garlic, tomatillos, poblano chili and onion in an even layer on the baking sheet. Broil until the vegetables are lightly charred, about 4 minutes, then flip them and continue to broil until the second sides are lightly charred, 3 to 5 minutes. Let cool for about 5 minutes, then transfer to the blender.

Add ½ cup water to the blender, then puree until smooth, about 30 seconds. Add the cilantro, parsley, mint, fennel, cumin, 1 teaspoon salt and ¾ teaspoon pepper. Blend until smooth and bright green, about 2 minutes, scraping the sides as needed. You should have about 2 cups of puree; set aside.

When the chicken is ready, stir the potatoes, green beans and zucchini into the pot. Bring to a simmer over medium and cook, uncovered and stirring occasionally, until the skewer inserted into a potato meets no resistance, about 15 minutes. Stir in the puree, then taste and season with salt and pepper.

TORTILLA SOUP

Start to finish: 40 minutes
Servings: 4 to 6

Our take on sopa de tortilla is a simple, homestyle tortilla soup like the one made for us by home cook Jazmín Martínez in Mexico City. It is pureed for smoothness; contrasting colors, flavors and textures are added with garnishes. For the best results, ripe tomatoes are key—in non-summer months, we find Campari tomatoes to be a good option, as well as cherry or grape tomatoes. The tomatoes need only to be cored before they're tossed into the pot (cherry or grape tomatoes can be used whole). Tortilla chips, called totopos in Mexico, are used in two ways: they're cooked and pureed with the base to thicken the soup, then fresh chips are added to the serving bowls before the soup is ladled in.

2 tablespoons lard or neutral oil

1 large white onion, halved and thinly sliced

6 medium garlic cloves, smashed and peeled

2 jalapeño chilies, stemmed, seeded and sliced

1 teaspoon cumin seeds

1 bunch cilantro, stems roughly chopped, leaves chopped, reserved separately

2 pounds ripe tomatoes (see headnote), cored

2 cups yellow or white tortilla chips, plus more to serve

1½ quarts low-sodium chicken broth

1 teaspoon white sugar

Kosher salt and ground black pepper

Sour cream or crumbled cotija cheese, to serve

Diced avocado, to serve (optional)

In a large pot over medium-high, heat the lard until shimmering. Add the onion and cook, stirring, until softened, about 5 minutes. Add the garlic, jalapeños, cumin and cilantro stems, then cook, stirring, until fragrant, about 30 seconds. Stir in the tomatoes, tortilla chips, broth and sugar. Bring to a boil, then cover, reduce to medium and cook, stirring, at a simmer, until the tomatoes have softened and their skins begin to peel away, about 10 minutes.

Remove the pot from the heat and cool, uncovered, for 5 minutes. Using a blender and working in batches so the jar is never more than half full, puree the mixture until smooth; transfer each batch to a large bowl.

Wipe out the pot, then pour in the puree. Cook over medium, stirring often, until heated, about 5 minutes. Taste and season with salt and pepper, then stir in half of the chopped cilantro leaves. To serve, add tortilla chips to individual bowls, then ladle in soup. Sprinkle with the remaining chopped cilantro leaves and top with sour cream and avocado (if using).

Homemade Flour Tortillas

Start to finish: 1 hour 10 minutes
(40 minutes active)
Makes eight 10-inch tortillas

**Soft, supple and with a satisfying
chew, homemade flour tortillas taste
far better than store-bought brands
and don't take a lot of effort or time to
make.** Lard is traditional in flour
tortillas; many supermarkets sell
non-hydrogenated lard, packed in glass
jars, in the aisle near the coconut and
olive oils. If you prefer, butter also
makes fantastic tortillas. A mixture of
milk and water as the liquid is unconventional; we got the idea from Mexican
chef Enrique Olvera. Milk not only adds
a subtle sweetness, it also helps the
tortillas remain soft and pliable for
longer. If you prefer to skip the milk,
feel free to use only water. A well-seasoned cast-iron skillet or griddle is
essential for cooking the tortillas, as it
heats evenly and holds its temperature.
Its surface also is stick-resistant. The
tortillas are best freshly made, but
leftovers can be cooled, stacked,
wrapped in foil and stored at room
temperature for up to two days. To
reheat, place the foil-wrapped stack in
a 350°F oven for 10 to 15 minutes.

**520 grams (4 cups) all-purpose
flour, plus more for dusting**

½ teaspoon table salt

**113 grams (8 tablespoons) lard, in
1-tablespoon portions, or salted
butter, cut into ½-inch cubes, cool
room temperature**

½ cup whole milk (see headnote)

In a medium bowl, stir together the
flour and salt. Add the lard and, using
your fingertips, rub it into the flour until
the mixture resembles coarse sand.

In a liquid measuring cup, combine
the milk and ¾ cup water. Microwave
on high until the mixture reaches about
110°F, about 30 seconds. Pour into the
flour mixture in 3 or 4 additions,
stirring a few times with a silicone
spatula after each. Once all the liquid
has been incorporated, stir, scraping
the bottom of the bowl, until the
mixture forms a shaggy dough.

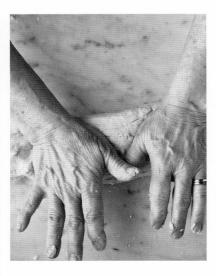

Lightly flour the counter and turn
the dough out onto it. Knead 5 or
6 times to form a smooth ball, then
form into an even 14-inch log. Cut into
8 pieces. Shape each into a taut ball
by rolling it under a cupped hand in a
circular motion against the counter.
Place the balls on a large plate, cover
with a kitchen towel and let rest for
30 minutes.

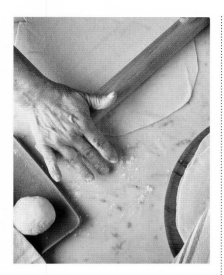  

On a lightly floured counter, use a rolling pin to roll 1 ball into a 10-inch round, then transfer to another large plate or a baking sheet and cover with a kitchen towel. Repeat with the remaining balls, stacking the rounds as they are done; keep the stack covered. Line the plate used to hold the dough balls with the kitchen towel used to cover them; set near the stove.

Heat a 10- or 12-inch cast-iron skillet over medium until water flicked onto the surface sizzles and evaporates within seconds, 4 to 6 minutes. When the skillet is hot, place a dough round in the pan. Cook until bubbles begin to form, then gently shake the pan to ensure the tortilla is not sticking. Cook until the bottom is light spotty brown, 2 to 3 minutes.

Using tongs, flip the tortilla. Cook until the second side is spotty brown, 1 to 2 minutes. Transfer to the prepared plate, then fold the towel over it. Cook the remaining tortillas in the same way, stacking them as they are done. Serve warm.

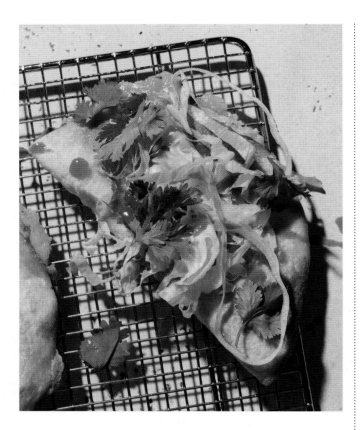

OVEN-FRIED POTATO AND CHEESE TACOS DORADOS

Start to finish: 55 minutes (40 minutes active)
Servings: 4

No need to stand at the stove deep-frying these tacos dorados. They crisp up beautifully in the oven using just a few tablespoons of oil—making them totally doable for weeknight meals. We fill flour tortillas with roughly mashed potatoes and cheese; pickled jalapeños and chipotle chilies in adobo give the filling some kick. Finish the tacos with cool, crisp iceberg lettuce and fresh cilantro, then embellish with more garnishes if you like; see the suggestions below.

5 tablespoons grapeseed or other neutral oil, divided

1½ pounds Yukon Gold potatoes, peeled and cut into ¾-inch cubes

½ cup lightly packed fresh cilantro, chopped, plus cilantro leaves to serve

4 scallions, thinly sliced

1 to 2 tablespoons pickled jalapeños, chopped, plus 1 tablespoon brine

1 chipotle chili in adobo, minced, plus 1 tablespoon adobo sauce

Kosher salt and ground black pepper

Eight 6-inch flour tortillas

8 ounces cheddar OR Monterey Jack cheese, shredded (2 cups)

Shredded iceberg lettuce, to serve

Heat the oven to 475°F with a rack in the middle position. Grease a rimmed baking sheet with 3 tablespoons oil. In a 12-inch nonstick skillet over medium-high, heat the remaining 2 tablespoons oil until shimmering. Add the potatoes, cover and cook, stirring occasionally, until well browned and fully tender, about 12 minutes.

Remove the pan from the heat and lightly mash the potatoes. Stir in the cilantro, scallions, pickled jalapeños and their brine, chipotle and adobo sauce, 1 teaspoon salt and ¼ teaspoon pepper.

Divide the potato filling evenly among the tortillas (about a scant ¼ cup each) and spread it to cover half of each tortilla, then sprinkle with the cheese, dividing it evenly. Fold the unfilled sides over. Arrange the filled tortillas on the prepared baking sheet, then flip each one so both sides are coated with oil.

Bake until the tacos begin to brown and crisp on the bottoms, about 9 minutes. Using a wide metal spatula, flip each taco. Continue to bake until browned on the second sides, about another 3 minutes. Transfer the tacos directly to a wire rack and cool for about 5 minutes. Serve topped with the lettuce and cilantro leaves.

Optional garnish: Diced avocado (or guacamole) **OR** sour cream **OR** salsa **OR** hot sauce **OR** a combination

TOASTED TACOS WITH ADOBO BEANS AND CHEESE

Start to finish: 40 minutes
Servings: 4 to 6

At Restaurante Bar Fernando, a casual eatery in Nayarit on the west coast of Mexico, we tasted simple bean- and cheese-filled tortillas, folded in half and lightly charred. The tacos are a typical side to pescado zarandeado, seasoned fish slow-cooked on an outdoor grill. The beans were so flavorful that we wanted to re-create the tacos at Milk Street. According to Paola Briseño-González, recipe developer and native of the neighboring Mexican state of Jalisco, azufrado is the regional bean variety used in those tacos, and adobo (a blend of earthy, smoky dried chilies plus aromatics and vinegar) is the flavoring. Azufrado beans are difficult to source in the U.S., so we used widely available pintos. Dried chilies, garlic, cumin, oregano and cider vinegar pureed in a blender, then simmered into the beans, mimic the adobo flavors.

2 guajillo, New Mexico or ancho chilies, stemmed, seeded and roughly torn

2 medium garlic cloves, smashed and peeled

¼ teaspoon cumin seeds

2 tablespoons cider vinegar

½ teaspoon dried oregano, preferably Mexican oregano

Kosher salt and ground black pepper

2 tablespoons lard or grapeseed or other neutral oil, plus neutral oil for brushing

Two 15½-ounce cans pinto beans, rinsed and drained

Eight 6-inch corn-flour blend or flour tortillas

4 ounces Monterey Jack or whole-milk mozzarella cheese, shredded (1 cup)

In a 12-inch nonstick skillet over medium-high, toast the chilies, garlic and cumin, stirring, until fragrant and the chilies and garlic are browned in spots, 2 to 3 minutes. Transfer to a blender; reserve the skillet. To the blender, add the vinegar, oregano, ½ cup water, ½ teaspoon salt and ¼ teaspoon pepper. Puree on high until smooth, about 2 minutes; set aside.

In the same skillet over medium-high, heat the lard until shimmering. Add the beans and chili puree; cook, stirring occasionally, until the beans are soft and the pan is dry, about 3 minutes. Working quickly, use a potato masher to mash the beans until relatively smooth. Cook, stirring, until the mixture is thick, about 1 minute. Transfer to a medium bowl, then taste and season with salt and pepper. Wipe out the skillet and set it aside.

Lightly brush both sides of each tortilla with neutral oil. Set the skillet over medium and heat until water flicked onto the surface sizzles and evaporates within seconds. One at a time, warm the tortillas in the skillet, flipping once, until pliable, 20 to 30 seconds per side. As they are done, stack the tortillas on a plate and cover with foil to keep warm. Reserve the skillet.

Lay 2 or 3 warm tortillas on the counter; keep the remaining tortillas covered. Spread 3 tablespoons of the bean mixture over the entire surface, followed by about 2 tablespoons of the cheese. Fold each tortilla in half and press lightly to seal. Using the remaining bean mixture and cheese, fill the remaining tortillas in the same way.

Set the skillet over medium and once again heat until water flicked onto the surface quickly sizzles and evaporates. Place 4 filled tortillas in the pan and cook, occasionally flipping with a metal spatula, until lightly browned on both sides and crisp at the edges, 2 to 3 minutes per side. Transfer to a serving platter. Toast the remaining tortillas in the same way. Serve warm.

581

SHRIMP AND CHEESE TACOS

Start to finish: 40 minutes

Servings: 4

If you think seafood and cheese don't mix, this recipe will change your mind. Tacos gobernador, or "governor's tacos," are a modern Mexican classic said to have originated in the state of Sinaloa. A blend of shrimp and melty cheese is tucked inside tortillas that then are folded and cooked like a quesadilla. The recipe calls for medium shrimp, but since they're chopped, you can use large or extra-large—whatever is most convenient. Swap in corn tortillas for the flour if you like, though you'll need to heat them before adding the filling so they won't break when folded. Just pop them in the hot skillet for a few seconds per side until pliable.

1 pound medium (41/50 per pound) shrimp, peeled, deveined (tails removed), cut into ¾-inch pieces and patted dry (see headnote)

Kosher salt and ground black pepper

3 tablespoons grapeseed or other neutral oil, divided

1 small white OR yellow onion, halved and thinly sliced

1 green bell pepper OR poblano chili, stemmed, seeded and thinly sliced

3 medium garlic cloves, thinly sliced

8 ounces mozzarella cheese, shredded (2 cups)

½ cup chopped fresh cilantro, plus more to serve

3 tablespoons pickled jalapeños, chopped, plus 1 tablespoon brine

Eight 6-inch flour OR corn tortillas (see headnote)

Season the shrimp with ½ teaspoon each salt and pepper; set aside. In a 12-inch nonstick skillet over medium, heat 1 tablespoon oil until shimmering. Add the onion, bell pepper and ½ teaspoon salt; cook, stirring occasionally, until the vegetables begin to brown, 8 to 10 minutes. Add the garlic and shrimp, then cook, stirring occasionally, until the shrimp turn opaque, 2 to 3 minutes.

Transfer the mixture to a large bowl; wipe out and reserve the skillet. Stir the cheese, cilantro and pickled jalapeños and their brine into the shrimp mixture. Taste and season with salt and pepper. Divide the filling evenly among the

tortillas (about ½ cup each) and spread it to cover half of each tortilla. Fold the unfilled sides over and press.

In the same skillet over medium-high, heat 1 tablespoon oil until shimmering. Add 4 of the tacos and cook until golden brown on the bottoms, about 2 minutes. Using a wide spatula, flip the tacos and cook, adjusting the heat as needed, until browned on the second sides, another 2 to 3 minutes. Transfer to a platter.

Cook the remaining tacos in the same way using the remaining 1 tablespoon oil. Serve sprinkled with additional cilantro.

HAM AND CHEESE QUESADILLAS WITH PICKLED JALAPEÑOS

Start to finish: 30 minutes

Servings: 4

In Mexico, these quesadillas are known as sincronizadas, which translates as "synchronized"—an apt description for salty ham and melty cheese sandwiched between toasted tortillas. For assembly, we prefer to toss together shredded cheese and chopped ham, then distribute the mixture among the tortillas. Made this way, the quesadillas hold together better than if the fillings are simply layered on. Feel free to include other add-ins if you like, such as sautéed onions or mushrooms or cooked black beans. Flour tortillas work best, as corn tortillas turn brittle when toasted.

8 ounces cheddar OR Muenster cheese OR a combination, shredded (2 cups)

6 ounces thinly sliced deli ham, chopped

⅓ to ½ cup pickled jalapeños, minced, plus 1 tablespoon brine

2 tablespoons finely chopped fresh cilantro

2 teaspoons ground cumin

Ground black pepper

Four 10-inch flour tortillas

2 tablespoons grapeseed or other neutral oil

In a medium bowl, stir together the cheese, ham, pickled jalapeños and their brine, cilantro, cumin and ½ teaspoon pepper. Spread half the filling evenly over 1 tortilla. Lay another tortilla on top and press together firmly. Repeat with the remaining filling and tortillas.

In a 12-inch nonstick skillet over medium, heat 1 tablespoon oil until shimmering. Add 1 quesadilla and cook,

moving it around a few times to ensure even cooking, until golden brown and crisp on the bottom, 2 to 3 minutes. Using a wide spatula, flip the quesadilla and cook, adjusting the heat as needed, until browned on the second side, about another 2 minutes. Transfer to a cutting board.

Toast the remaining quesadilla in the same way using the remaining 1 tablespoon oil (the second quesadilla probably will cook faster). Cut the quesadillas into wedges and serve.

Optional garnish: Salsa **OR** sour cream **OR** diced avocado **OR** guacamole **OR** hot sauce **OR** a combination

MUSHROOM AND CHEESE QUESADILLAS

Start to finish: 30 minutes
Servings: 4 to 6

You'll find quesadillas of all types in Mexico. In Mexico City, they're often made from fresh masa and without cheese; in other parts of the country, they're made with flour tortillas, with lots of melty Oaxaca cheese. Fillings vary from stewed or griddled meat to squash blossoms to nopales (cactus paddles). In this recipe, we stuff tortillas with a mixture of sautéed mushrooms and cheese, with a little smoky and spicy heat from a chipotle chili. Made with 4- to 5-inch flour tortillas, the quesadillas are perfect for a lunch or snack. If you can't find queso Oaxaca, any mild melting cheese, such as mozzarella or Muenster, will work. Lard is traditional for cooking these quesadillas, but for a vegetarian version, use grapeseed or another neutral oil. For best browning, cook these in a nonstick skillet.

4 tablespoons lard OR neutral oil, divided

1 medium white onion, chopped

1 pound mixed mushrooms, such as cremini, oyster, portobello or shiitakes (stemmed), roughly chopped

Kosher salt and ground black pepper

2 medium garlic cloves, minced

1 chipotle chili in adobo sauce, finely chopped

3 ounces queso Oaxaca OR mozzarella cheese OR Muenster cheese, shredded (¾ cup)

⅓ cup lightly packed fresh cilantro, chopped

Eight 4- to 5-inch flour tortillas

In a 12-inch nonstick skillet over medium-high, heat
2 tablespoons of lard until shimmering. Add the onion and
cook, stirring occasionally, until softened and beginning to
brown, 4 to 5 minutes. Add the mushrooms and ½ teaspoon
each salt and pepper, then cook, stirring occasionally, until
tender and well browned, 7 to 8 minutes. Add the garlic and
chipotle; cook, stirring, until fragrant, 30 to 60 seconds.
Transfer to a medium bowl, then stir in the cheese and
cilantro. Taste and season with salt and pepper. Wipe out
the skillet with paper towels; set aside.

Divide the mushroom mixture evenly among the tortillas,
spreading it over half of each. Fold the unfilled sides over
and press to seal.

In the same skillet over medium-high, heat 1 tablespoon
of the remaining lard until shimmering. Add 4 of the
quesadillas and cook until the tortillas are golden brown
on the bottom, about 2 minutes. Flip and cook, adjusting
the heat as needed, until the second sides are browned,
another 2 to 3 minutes. Transfer to a platter and repeat
with the remaining quesadillas using the remaining
1 tablespoon lard.

CHEESE-CRISPED PINTO BEAN QUESADILLAS

Start to finish: 40 minutes
Servings: 4

These quesadillas boast double the cheese—some is tucked
inside the folded tortillas and the rest is sprinkled on the
outside. As they toast in the oven, the outer layer of cheese
melts and becomes deliciously crisp. Bonus: We cook
quesadillas on a baking sheet to make a big batch all at
once—no need to stand at the stove cooking quesadillas one
by one. To make these vegetarian quesadillas heartier, we
include pinto beans (or black beans), which are microwaved
with chili powder to infuse them with spice; canned red or
green chilies bump up the heat, while lime juice brings an
acidic note.

3 tablespoons neutral oil

Two 15½-ounce cans pinto beans
OR black beans, rinsed and drained

1 tablespoon chili powder

Kosher salt and ground black pepper

2 chipotle chilies in adobo sauce, chopped,
plus 1 teaspoon adobo sauce OR ¼ cup
drained canned green chilies

2 tablespoons lime juice OR cider vinegar

8 ounces pepper Jack OR mozzarella cheese
OR queso Oaxaca, shredded (2 cups)

Eight 6-inch flour tortillas

Heat the oven to 475°F with a rack in the middle position.
Brush the entire surface of a rimmed baking sheet with the oil.

In a large microwave-safe bowl, toss together the beans,
chili powder and ¾ teaspoon salt. Cover and microwave
on high until hot, 3 to 3½ minutes, stirring once halfway
through. Stir in the chipotles with adobo sauce, lime
juice and ½ cup cheese. Using a potato masher, mash the
mixture until relatively smooth. Taste and season with salt
and pepper.

Divide the bean filling evenly among the tortillas and
spread it to cover half of each tortilla. Fold the unfilled sides
over and gently press to seal. Arrange the filled tortillas on
the prepared baking sheet, then flip each one so both sides
are coated with oil. Sprinkle the tops of the tortillas with the
remaining cheese.

Bake until the cheese is melted and the quesadillas begin to brown and crisp on the bottoms, 7 to 9 minutes. Remove the baking sheet from the oven and, using a wide metal spatula, flip each quesadilla. Bake until browned on the second sides, 2 to 4 minutes. Cool on the baking sheet for about 5 minutes. If desired, cut the quesadillas in half, then serve cheese side up.

Optional garnish: Sour cream **OR** salsa **OR** guacamole **OR** pickled jalapeños **OR** a combination

TLAYUDAS

Start to finish: 20 minutes
Servings: 4

Oaxaca, Mexico is home to the antojito (street food) known as the tlayuda, an oversized corn tortilla topped with black beans, cheese, meats and a spate of other ingredients, then toasted on a grill. Since super-fresh, extra-large corn tortillas are difficult to find in U.S., we use flour tortillas instead, and we do as some Oaxacans do and fold them in half to enclose the fillings. For ease, we bake them in a hot oven rather than cook them over a live fire. Fill the tlayudas as you like and cut into wedges just before serving. Pickled red onions are an essential topping.

3 tablespoons grapeseed or other neutral oil

8 ounces fresh Mexican chorizo sausage, casing removed, crumbled

4 large jalapeño chilies, stemmed, seeded and thinly sliced

1 bunch scallions, cut into 1-inch pieces

Four 8-inch flour tortillas

1 cup black bean puree (recipe p. 562)

4 ounces whole-milk mozzarella cheese, shredded (1 cup)

Shredded lettuce, to serve

Pickled red onions (recipe p. 465), to serve

Sliced tomato, to serve

Hot sauce, to serve

Heat the oven to 450°F with a rack in the middle position. In a 12-inch cast-iron or other heavy skillet over medium-high, heat 1 tablespoon of oil until barely smoking. Add the chorizo and cook, stirring occasionally and breaking the meat into small bits, until well browned, about 5 minutes. Using a slotted spoon, transfer the chorizo to a paper towel–lined plate; set aside. Add the jalapeños and scallions to the pan, then cook, stirring occasionally, until the vegetables are lightly charred, 3 to 5 minutes. Transfer to the plate with the chorizo; set aside.

Pour the remaining 2 tablespoons oil onto a rimmed baking sheet and brush to coat the entire surface. Place 2 tortillas on the baking sheet to coat the bottoms with oil, then flip them and coat the second sides. Spread ¼ cup of the bean mixture evenly on half of each tortilla, all the way to the edges. Top the beans on each with ¼ of the cheese, then fold the unfilled half over to cover and press gently to seal. Transfer to a plate. Repeat with the remaining tortillas, beans and cheese.

Place the filled and folded tortillas in a single layer on the baking sheet. Bake until the cheese has melted and the bottoms of the tortillas are golden brown, about 10 minutes. Using a metal spatula, transfer the tlayudas to a wire rack and cool for 5 minutes. Carefully open each and fill as desired with the chorizo-jalapeño-scallion mixture, lettuce, pickled onions, tomato and hot sauce. Re-fold, then cut into wedges. Serve warm.

CHICKEN, SALSA VERDE AND TORTILLA CASSEROLE

Start to finish: 2 hours (1¼ hours active), plus resting
Servings: 8

Though pastel azteca translates from the Spanish as "Aztec cake," the dish often is referred to in English as Mexican lasagna, enchilada casserole or tortilla pie—and understandably so. It is made up of corn tortillas layered with sauce, meat, cheeses, crema (a cultured cream similar to crème fraîche) and vegetables; a stint in the oven brings together all the elements. Our recipe is an adaptation of the pastel azteca taught to us in Mexico City by chef Esmeralda Brinn Bolaños. We swapped chicken thighs for the dark-meat turkey that she used and found readily available substitutes for the locally made Mexican cheeses. We opted for pepper Jack because of its melting qualities and mild spiciness; if you prefer, use regular Jack cheese or even mozzarella. To assemble and bake the casserole, we use a 9-inch springform pan for a presentation that reveals the impressive layers and allows for slicing into wedges for serving.

1 pound poblano chilies

1½ pounds tomatillos, husked and halved

3 medium garlic cloves, smashed and peeled

2 tablespoons white vinegar

1 cup lightly packed fresh cilantro, plus ½ cup chopped fresh cilantro, divided

3 teaspoons ground cumin, divided

Kosher salt and ground black pepper

1 tablespoon grapeseed or other neutral oil

1 pound boneless, skinless chicken thighs

1 large white onion, chopped

1 cup corn kernels, defrosted if frozen

Eight 6-inch corn tortillas

1 cup Mexican crema or one 8-ounce container crème fraîche, room temperature

12 ounces pepper Jack cheese, shredded (3 cups)

4 ounces cotija cheese, grated (1 cup)

2 tablespoons pumpkin seeds, finely chopped (optional)

Heat the broiler with a rack about 6 inches from the element. Place the poblanos on a broiler-safe rimmed baking sheet and broil until charred, about 10 minutes. Flip the chilies and broil until charred on the second sides, 3 to 5 minutes. Transfer to a medium bowl, cover and let steam to loosen the skins while you make the puree and cook the chicken. Turn the oven to 375°F.

In a blender, combine the tomatillos, garlic, vinegar, 1 cup of cilantro, 2 teaspoons of cumin and 1 teaspoon salt. Blend until smooth, about 1 minute, scraping the blender jar as needed.

In a large Dutch oven over medium-high, heat the oil until shimmering. Carefully add the puree (it may splatter) and cook, stirring occasionally, until slightly reduced and a spoon drawn through leaves a brief trail, about 6 minutes. Remove ½ cup of the sauce and set aside. To the remaining salsa in the pot, add the chicken, onion, remaining 1 teaspoon cumin, ¼ teaspoon salt and ½ teaspoon pepper. Bring to a simmer, then cover, reduce to medium-low and cook, stirring occasionally, until a skewer inserted into the chicken meets no resistance, 15 to 20 minutes.

While the chicken cooks, peel the skins off the chilies and remove and discard the stems and seeds. Chop the chilies and set aside. When the chicken is done, remove the pot from the heat. Using 2 forks, shred the chicken; you should have about 3½ cups chicken in salsa. If you have more,

return the pot to medium heat and cook, stirring occasionally, until reduced. Stir in the corn, ¼ cup of the chopped cilantro and the chopped chilies. Taste and season with salt and pepper.

Wrap the exterior of a 9-inch springform pan with a sheet of foil and set on a rimmed baking sheet. Add half of the reserved salsa to the pan and spread in an even layer. Line the bottom of the pan with 2⅔ tortillas, tearing them as needed to fit; it's fine if the tortillas overlap slightly and if a few small spots are uncovered. Spoon in half of the chicken mixture and distribute in an even layer. Dollop with half of the crema, then spread evenly. Sprinkle with a third of the pepper Jack cheese. Repeat the layering using another 2⅔ tortillas, the remaining chicken mixture, the remaining crema and half of the remaining pepper Jack. Layer in the remaining tortillas, then spread evenly with the remaining reserved salsa. Sprinkle on the remaining pepper Jack followed by the cotija. Bake the pastel on the baking sheet until browned on top and bubbling at the edges, about 35 minutes.

Set the baking sheet on a wire rack. Sprinkle the pastel with the remaining ¼ cup chopped cilantro and the pumpkin seeds (if using). Let rest for at least 30 minutes or up to 1 hour.

To serve, run a knife around the inside of the springform pan to loosen. Remove the foil, set the pan on a large, flat platter and remove the sides. Cut into wedges and serve.

How to Make Homemade Tostadas

A tostada is a tortilla that's fried until crisp, then topped with ingredients of any sort. You can purchase tortillas that are already made into tostadas, but homemade tastes much fresher. We use the oven rather than a skillet to make tostadas; this technique requires less oil and allows you to toast more than one at a time.

Heat the oven to 400°F with a rack in the upper-middle position. Brush four 6-inch corn tortillas on both sides with neutral oil, then place them in a single layer on a rimmed baking sheet. Bake until golden brown and crisp, 8 to 10 minutes, flipping them once about halfway through. Let the tostadas cool on the baking sheet. Place the tostadas on individual plates and top as desired.

587

SHRIMP AND AVOCADO TOSTADAS

Start to finish: 30 minutes

Servings: 4

Tostadas make an easy, satisfying meal, and these can be on the table in about 30 minutes. For ease and speed, we use the oven to crisp the tortillas to make the base. We broil the shrimp, then toss them while still warm with mayonnaise and lime juice so they better absorb the seasonings. Garnish the tostadas with chunks of rich, creamy avocado plus quick-pickled red onion for crunch and tang.

½ small red onion, finely chopped

3 tablespoons lime juice, divided, plus lime wedges to serve

Kosher salt and ground black pepper

Four 6-inch corn tortillas

4 tablespoons extra-virgin olive oil, divided

1 pound large (26/30 per pound) OR extra-large (21/25 per pound) shrimp, peeled (tails removed), deveined and patted dry

2 tablespoons mayonnaise

1 ripe avocado, halved, pitted, peeled and cut into ½-inch cubes

Heat the oven to 400°F with a rack in the upper-middle position. In a small bowl, stir together the onion, 2 tablespoons lime juice and a pinch of salt; set aside. Brush the tortillas on both sides with 1 tablespoon oil, then place in a single layer on a broiler-safe rimmed baking sheet. Bake until golden brown and crisp, 8 to 10 minutes, flipping once halfway through. Transfer to individual plates; reserve the baking sheet. Heat the oven to broil with a rack 4 inches from the element.

Place a wire rack in the reserved baking sheet. In a medium bowl, toss together the shrimp, the remaining 3 tablespoons oil and ½ teaspoon salt. Distribute the shrimp in an even layer on the rack. Broil until lightly charred on the surface and just opaque throughout, 4 to 5 minutes.

In another medium bowl, stir together the mayonnaise, the remaining 1 tablespoon lime juice and ¼ teaspoon pepper. Stir in the warm shrimp. Divide the shrimp among the tortillas. Top with the avocado and pickled onion. Serve with lime wedges.

Optional garnish: Chopped fresh cilantro **OR** red pepper flakes **OR** Tajín seasoning **OR** a combination

REFRIED BEAN AND CHEESE TOSTADAS

Start to finish: 35 minutes

Servings: 4

Here's a great way to throw together a quick dinner with lots of flavor and texture using just a handful of basic ingredients. Either canned black beans or pinto beans work for making refried beans, so use whichever you have on hand. Tostadas love garnishes, so see the list below for simple ideas, but feel free to add whatever you like, from fried bacon broken into bits to scrambled eggs.

Four 6-inch corn tortillas

3 tablespoons grapeseed or other neutral oil, divided

1 small yellow OR red onion, chopped

Kosher salt and ground black pepper

1 tablespoon chopped pickled jalapeños, plus more to serve

1 teaspoon chili powder

15½-ounce can black beans OR pinto beans, rinsed and drained

2 ounces Monterey Jack OR cheddar cheese, shredded (1 cup)

Shredded iceberg lettuce OR shredded green cabbage, to serve

Sour cream, to serve

Heat the oven to 400°F with a rack in the upper-middle position. Brush the tortillas on both sides with 1 tablespoon of the oil, then place them in a single layer on a rimmed baking sheet. Bake until golden brown and crisp, 8 to 10 minutes, flipping them once about halfway through. Let the tostadas cool on the baking sheet; leave the oven on.

In a 12-inch nonstick skillet over medium, heat the remaining 2 tablespoons oil until shimmering. Add half of the onion and ½ teaspoon salt; cook, stirring occasionally, until beginning to brown, 3 to 4 minutes. Stir in the pickled jalapeños and chili powder, then add the beans and ⅓ cup water. Bring to a simmer and simmer, uncovered and stirring occasionally, until the liquid is reduced by about half, 3 to 4 minutes. Remove the pan from the heat and mash the mixture to a thick, coarse puree. Taste and season with salt and pepper.

Divide the bean mixture evenly among the tostadas, spreading it to cover. Top each with cheese, dividing it evenly, and bake until the cheese melts, 1 to 2 minutes.

Place the tostadas on individual plates. Sprinkle with the remaining chopped onion, additional pickled jalapeños and lettuce, then spoon on sour cream.

Optional garnish: Lime wedges OR chopped fresh cilantro OR chopped tomato OR sliced or diced avocado OR salsa OR hot sauce OR a combination

Sauces, Salsas & Pickles

CREAMY WHIPPED HUMMUS

Start to finish: 1 hour (15 minutes active), plus soaking
Makes 4 cups

In Israel, hummus is breakfast, not a party dip. Our education began in Tel Aviv at Abu Hassan, the country's premier hummus shop, where customers get wide, shallow bowls of hummus topped with whole chickpeas, a sprinkle of parsley, pops of red paprika and amber cumin. The hummus is light, almost sour cream smooth—and warm. When re-creating the hummus, we found we needed to start with dried chickpeas, not canned, and simmer them with baking soda to ensure they completely softened. Small chickpeas like Whole Foods Market 365 Everyday Value brand worked well. Make sure to soak the chickpeas for at least 12 hours before cooking, and if your chickpeas are on the large side, you'll need to cook them for an additional 10 to 15 minutes, or until starting to break down. And for the smoothest, lightest hummus, process the chickpeas while they're still warm, and give them a full three minutes during the first stage. As for tahini, we liked the Kevala brand, but Soom and Aleppo were good, too. Processing the chickpeas while warm ensures the smoothest, lightest hummus, as will processing

it for a full three minutes in the first stage. Hummus traditionally is served warm and garnished with paprika, cumin, chopped fresh parsley and a drizzle of extra-virgin olive oil. Sometimes a sliced hard-cooked egg is added. Leftover hummus can be refrigerated for up to five days. To reheat, transfer to a microwave-safe bowl, cover and gently heat, adding a few tablespoons of tap water as needed to reach the proper consistency, one to two minutes.

8 ounces (227 grams) dried chickpeas

Kosher salt

½ teaspoon baking soda

¾ cup sesame tahini, room temperature

3½ tablespoons lemon juice

1 to 2 tablespoons extra-virgin olive oil

1 tablespoon chopped fresh parsley

½ teaspoon ground cumin

½ teaspoon paprika

In a large bowl, combine 8 cups of cold water, the chickpeas and 1 tablespoon salt. Let soak at least 12 hours, or overnight.

In a stockpot over high, bring another 10 cups of water and the baking soda to a boil. Drain the soaked chickpeas, discarding soaking water, and add to the pot. Return to a simmer, then reduce to medium and cook until the skins are falling off and the chickpeas are very tender, 45 to 50 minutes.

Set a mesh strainer over a large bowl and drain the chickpeas into it; reserve ¾ cup of the chickpea cooking water. Let sit for 1 minute to let all liquid drain. Set aside about 2 tablespoons of chickpeas, then transfer the rest to the food processor. Add ½ teaspoon of salt, then process for 3 minutes.

Add the tahini. Continue to process until the mixture has lightened and is very smooth, about 1 minute. Use a silicone spatula to scrape the sides and bottom of the processor bowl. With the machine running, add the reserved cooking liquid and the lemon juice. Process until combined. Taste and season with salt.

Transfer the hummus to a shallow serving bowl and use a large spoon to make a swirled well in the center. Drizzle with olive oil, then top with the reserved 2 tablespoons chickpeas, parsley, cumin and paprika.

SPICY FETA DIP

Start to finish: 10 minutes
Makes 3½ cups

Tirokafteri is a Greek cheese-based dip or spread that can be flavored numerous ways. In our version, we build complexity by combining two cheeses with different characteristics: creamy, tangy chèvre (fresh goat cheese) and firm, briny feta. Roasted red peppers give the dip sweetness and color, while the Anaheim chili and hot smoked paprika lend some heat. If you don't have hot smoked paprika, substitute ½ teaspoon sweet smoked paprika plus ¼ teaspoon cayenne pepper.

8 ounces chèvre (fresh goat cheese)

½ cup drained roasted red peppers, patted dry

1 Anaheim chili, stemmed, seeded and chopped

3 tablespoons extra-virgin olive oil, plus more to serve

¾ teaspoon hot smoked paprika

½ teaspoon honey

Kosher salt and ground black pepper

6 ounces feta cheese, crumbled (1½ cups)

½ cup fresh dill, chopped, plus more to serve

In a food processor, combine the goat cheese, roasted peppers, Anaheim chili, oil, paprika, honey and ¼ teaspoon each salt and black pepper. Process until smooth, about 1 minute, scraping the bowl as needed.

Transfer to a medium bowl. Fold in the feta and dill, then taste and season with salt and pepper. Transfer to a serving bowl and top with additional oil, dill and black pepper.

TZATZIKI

Start to finish: 20 minutes
Makes 3½ cups

The cucumber-yogurt dip known as tzatziki is often seasoned with lemon juice in the U.S., but in Greece cooks prefer red wine vinegar because it adds sharp acidity without the citrus notes to compete with the other ingredients. Thick and cooling, tzatziki can be served as a dip or with grilled meats and seafood and fried foods.

2 English cucumbers, halved crosswise

Kosher salt

1¾ cups plain whole-milk or low-fat Greek yogurt

½ cup extra-virgin olive oil

3 medium garlic cloves, finely grated

3 tablespoons chopped fresh mint, plus more to serve

3 tablespoons chopped fresh dill, plus more to serve

4 teaspoons red wine vinegar

Set a colander in a medium bowl, then set a box grater in it. Grate the cucumber halves on the large holes, rotating and grating only down to the seedy core. Discard the cores. Sprinkle the cucumber with 1 teaspoon salt and toss. Set aside to drain for 10 minutes.

Meanwhile, in a medium bowl, whisk the yogurt, oil, garlic, mint, dill and vinegar.

A handful at a time, squeeze the cucumber to remove as much liquid as possible, then set on a cutting board; reserve 2 teaspoons of the cucumber liquid. Finely chop the cucumber, then stir into the yogurt. Stir in the reserved cucumber liquid, taste then season with salt. Transfer to a bowl and sprinkle with mint and dill.

HOMEMADE MAYONNAISE

Start to finish: 10 minutes
Makes about 1¾ cups

For this homemade, handmade mayonnaise, Dijon mustard adds piquancy and helps with emulsification. We found that briefly refrigerating the oil makes it a little easier for the emulsion to come together because the oil is more viscous. However, when beginning to make the mayo, it's still essential to add the oil carefully. Whisking it in drop by drop to start helps ensure the emulsion forms—you will know it has if the mixture begins to thicken and "tighten." The rate at which the oil is added can gradually be increased, but make sure you're whisking continuously as you stream in the oil. If you like, the finished mayo can be flavored with garlic, fresh herbs and/or lemon. Note: The mayonnaise contains raw eggs.

2 large egg yolks

1 tablespoon Dijon mustard

Kosher salt

1⅓ cups sunflower oil, light olive oil or other neutral oil, ideally refrigerated for about 10 minutes

Cold water, as needed

1 tablespoon lemon juice

In a medium bowl set on a non-skid mat or folded damp kitchen towel, whisk together the egg yolks, mustard and ¼ teaspoon salt. While whisking constantly, slowly dribble in oil until the mixture begins to thicken and emulsify. At this point, while whisking constantly, slowly stream in oil until about one-third of it has been added; the mixture will be very thick.

Whisk in 1 tablespoon cold water; the mixture will become pale yellow and looser. Again while whisking, add half of the remaining oil in a thin, fine stream, then whisk in another 1 tablespoon water to loosen. While whisking, stream in the remaining oil.

Whisk in the lemon juice followed by 1 to 2 tablespoons cold water, adding enough so the mayonnaise is glossy pale yellow with a pudding-like consistency. Taste and season with salt. Use right away or cover and refrigerate up to 5 days.

KIMCHI AIOLI

Start to finish: 20 minutes
Makes about 1 cup

Cabbage kimchi plus grated garlic add loads of kick to a mayonnaise base, turning it into a terrific East-meets-West condiment. In addition to finely chopped kimchi, we include kimchi juice for tanginess. How much liquid is in the jar depends on the brand. If yours is relatively dry, use a little more rice vinegar instead to boost the acidity and thin the aioli. Slather this onto a burger, drizzle it onto roasted or fried potatoes, or offer it as a dipping sauce for just about anything.

¾ cup mayonnaise

3 tablespoons finely chopped cabbage kimchi,
plus 1 to 2 tablespoons kimchi juice (see headnote)

1 medium garlic clove, finely grated

1 teaspoon unseasoned rice vinegar,
plus more as needed

Kosher salt and ground black pepper

In a small bowl, stir together the mayonnaise, kimchi and its juice, garlic and vinegar. Taste and season with salt, pepper and additional vinegar. Use immediately or refrigerate in an airtight container for up to 3 days.

HARISSA MAYONNAISE WITH OLIVES AND LEMON

Start to finish: 15 minutes
Makes about 1 cup

This punchy, subtly spicy sauce combines North African flavors. Briny green olives and lemon add texture and bright contrast to spicy harissa. Use it as a spread in sandwiches, as an embellishment for a frittata, as a flourish for roasted vegetables or as a dipping sauce (think whole roasted artichokes). For a tangier sauce with a more cooling quality, use whole-milk Greek yogurt in place of the mayonnaise.

¾ cup mayonnaise OR plain whole-milk
Greek yogurt

⅓ cup finely chopped pitted green
OR black olives OR a combination

1 to 1½ tablespoons harissa paste

1 tablespoon grated lemon zest,
plus 3 tablespoons lemon juice

Kosher salt and ground black pepper

In a small bowl, stir together the mayonnaise, olives, harissa and lemon zest and juice. Taste and season with salt and pepper. Use immediately or refrigerate in an airtight container for up to 3 days.

EGGPLANT AND TAHINI DIP

Start to finish: 50 minutes (20 minutes active)
Servings: 6 to 8

The roasted eggplant and tahini dip called mutabal (also spelled mutabbal or moutabbal) is what many of us in the U.S. think of as baba ghanoush. We found that even in the Middle East, where both dips originate, the names often are used interchangeably, though baba ghanoush typically includes other ingredients, such as tomato and walnuts. Jordanian home cook Ihab Muhtaseb taught us his method for making mutabal, so that's what we're calling this dip. This adaptation of his recipe includes chopped parsley, which adds fresh, grassy notes, and a finishing drizzle of pomegranate molasses for tangy-sweet contrast. If you'd like to further embellish the mutabal, as many restaurants in Jordan do, make the simple tomato-cucumber salad that follows and spoon it on top just before serving. Offer warm flatbread on the side.

2 large or 3 medium eggplants (about 2½ pounds)

2 tablespoons extra-virgin olive oil, plus more to serve

⅓ cup tahini

¼ cup boiling water

3 medium garlic cloves, finely grated

1½ tablespoons lemon juice

1 cup lightly packed fresh flat-leaf parsley, finely chopped

Kosher salt and ground black pepper

2 tablespoons pomegranate seeds

1 tablespoon pomegranate molasses

Heat the oven to 475°F with a rack in the middle position. Line a rimmed baking sheet with foil. Pierce each eggplant several times with the tip of a knife, then coat each all over with 1 tablespoon of the oil. Set the eggplants on the prepared baking sheet and roast until collapsed, wrinkled and blistered all over, 20 to 30 minutes. Remove from the oven and cool on the baking sheet for about 20 minutes.

With the eggplants still on the baking sheet, trim off and discard the stem. Slit each in half lengthwise and open it up. Using a spoon, scoop the flesh from the skin onto a cutting board; discard the skins. Finely chop the eggplant but don't break it down to a puree; it should retain some texture.

In a medium bowl, stir together the tahini and boiling water. Add the eggplant, garlic and lemon juice; stir until well combined, then mix in half of the parsley. Taste and season with salt and pepper. Transfer to a serving bowl and top with the remaining parsley, pomegranate seeds, pomegranate molasses and an additional drizzle of oil.

TOMATO, CUCUMBER AND GREEN CHILI SALAD

Start to finish: 15 minutes
Makes about 1¼ cups

This fresh, bright salad, spooned onto mutabal just before serving adds color, texture and a little heat to the smoky, silky dip. Throw it together while the eggplant is roasting.

1 medium ripe tomato, cored and chopped

1 Persian cucumber, chopped

1 jalapeño chili, stemmed, seeded and minced

1 tablespoon lemon juice

Kosher salt and ground black pepper

In a medium bowl, toss together the tomato, cucumber, jalapeño, lemon juice and ¼ teaspoon each salt and pepper.

MUHAMMARA

Start to finish: 20 minutes
Makes 2 cups

Muhammara is a spicy-tart dip for flatbread made from walnuts and roasted red peppers. The name comes from the Arabic word for reddened, and the dish originated in Syria, where it often is served alongside hummus and baba ganoush. Aleppo pepper is made from ground dried Halaby chilies; it tastes subtly of cumin and fruit, with only mild heat. Look for it in well-stocked markets and spice shops, but if you cannot find it, simply leave it out—the muhammara still will be delicious. Serve with flatbread or vegetables for dipping or use as a sandwich spread.

4 teaspoons ground cumin

7-inch pita bread, torn into rough pieces

1 cup walnuts

Two 12-ounce jars roasted red peppers, drained and patted dry (2 cups)

1 teaspoon Aleppo pepper (optional; see headnote)

½ teaspoon red pepper flakes

Kosher salt and ground black pepper

3 tablespoons pomegranate molasses, plus more to serve

2 tablespoons lemon juice

6 tablespoons extra-virgin olive oil, plus more to serve

Chopped fresh flat-leaf parsley, to serve

In a small skillet over medium, toast the cumin, stirring, until fragrant, about 30 seconds. Remove from the heat and set aside.

In a food processor, process the pita bread and walnuts until finely ground, about 45 seconds. Add the cumin, roasted peppers, Aleppo pepper (if using), pepper flakes and 1 teaspoon each salt and black pepper. Process until smooth, about 45 seconds, scraping the bowl as needed.

Add the pomegranate molasses and lemon juice and process until combined, about 10 seconds. With the machine running, drizzle in the oil. Taste and season with salt and pepper, then transfer to a serving bowl. Drizzle with additional pomegranate molasses and oil, then sprinkle with parsley.

TOMATO AND CHARRED ONION SALSA WITH CHIPOTLE

Start to finish: 1 hour (20 minutes active)
Makes about 2 cups

Guatemalan chirmol is a smoky yet bright mix of charred tomatoes and onions with plenty of fresh herbs. We wanted to create an easy broiler version, but found broiled tomatoes too juicy. We char jalapeños and red onion wedges under the broiler to mellow their flavors and leave the tomatoes raw so they remain plump and firm. The result is a colorful tangy-sweet salsa, delicious with grilled or roasted meats. We also love it spooned over toast, layered in a pita sandwich, tucked into shrimp tacos or scooped up with tortilla chips.

597

1 medium red onion, root end intact, cut into 8 wedges

2 jalapeño chilies, stemmed, halved and seeded

2 tablespoons extra-virgin olive oil, divided

Kosher salt and ground black pepper

1 pint grape OR cherry tomatoes, chopped

2 cups lightly packed fresh cilantro OR mint
OR a combination, finely chopped

1 chipotle chili in adobo sauce, finely chopped

3 tablespoons lime juice

Heat the broiler to high with a rack 4 inches from the
element. On a broiler-safe rimmed baking sheet, mound
together the onion wedges and jalapeños. Drizzle with
1 tablespoon oil and sprinkle with ½ teaspoon salt; toss to
coat. Arrange in an even layer and broil until charred and
tender, 10 to 15 minutes, flipping once halfway through.
Set aside to cool.

When cool enough to handle, chop the jalapeños; add them
to a medium bowl. Trim and discard the root ends from the
onion wedges, then chop and add them to the bowl. Stir in
the tomatoes, cilantro and chipotle chili, then let stand at
room temperature for 30 minutes. Stir in the lime juice
and remaining 1 tablespoon oil. Taste and season with salt
and pepper. Serve right away or refrigerate in an airtight
container for up to 3 days; bring to room temperature
before serving.

FRESH TOMATILLO
AND SERRANO CHILI SALSA

Start to finish: 10 minutes
Makes about 1½ cups

Bright, tangy and moderately spicy, this salsa cruda,
or uncooked salsa, requires little knifework and comes
together quickly in a blender. We make it with only three
ingredients, plus salt, as taught to us by Jorge Fritz and
Beto Estúa of Casa Jacaranda cooking school in Mexico
City. The fresh, acidic flavor of this salsa makes it an ideal
condiment for rich, fatty dishes, but we think it's great on
just about anything, including simple rice and beans, and
even as a dip for tortilla chips.

5 medium tomatillos (9 ounces),
husked and quartered

¼ medium white onion, roughly chopped

3 serrano chilies, stemmed, seeded
and roughly chopped

Kosher salt

In a blender, combine the tomatillos, onion, chilies and
¼ teaspoon salt. Process until smooth, scraping down the
blender jar as needed, about 1 minute. Taste and season
with salt. If serving right away, transfer to a small bowl; if
storing, transfer to an airtight container and refrigerate
up to 2 days.

In a 10-inch skillet over medium, toast all of the chilies, turning occasionally with tongs, until fragrant and just a shade darker in color, about 2 minutes. Transfer to a blender and cool for about 5 minutes.

Blend the chilies until finely chopped, 30 to 60 seconds. Transfer to a small saucepan and add the oil, peanuts, sesame seeds, garlic and ½ teaspoon salt. Cook over medium, stirring often, until fragrant and lightly toasted, 3 to 5 minutes.

Off heat, stir in the vinegar. If serving right away, transfer to a small bowl and let cool; if storing, transfer to an airtight container, cool and refrigerate for up to 2 months (bring to room temperature before serving).

SALSA MACHA

Start to finish: 15 minutes, plus cooling
Makes about 1 cup

Dark, rich salsa macha is oil-based and derives its deep, earthy, smoky flavor from toasted dried chilies, garlic and a combination of nuts and seeds. Some versions are well blended to fully integrate the ingredients, but this one is chunky with chopped peanuts and whole sesame seeds. (We found that a blender does a better job than a food processor at breaking down the toasted chilies.) Salsa macha keeps well in the refrigerator, but bring to room temperature before serving.

¾ ounce guajillo chilies (4 medium),
stemmed and seeded

½ ounce ancho chilies (1 or 2 medium),
stemmed and seeded

1 or 2 chipotle or morita chilies,
stemmed and seeded

½ cup extra-virgin olive oil

⅓ cup salted roasted peanuts, chopped

1½ tablespoons sesame seeds

1 medium garlic clove, finely grated

Kosher salt

2½ teaspoons coconut vinegar
or cider vinegar

COLOMBIAN AVOCADO SALSA

Start to finish: 15 minutes
Makes 3½ cups

Colombian food does not tend to be spicy, so we seeded the chilies for this salsa. The Anaheims gives the sauce deep pepper flavor, while the habanero adds fruitiness and heat.

4 scallions, cut into 1-inch lengths

2 Anaheim chilies, stemmed, seeded
and cut into rough 1-inch pieces

1 habanero chili, stemmed and seeded

1¼ cups lightly packed fresh cilantro

2 tablespoons white vinegar

Kosher salt

3 ripe avocados,
halved and pitted

3 hard-cooked large eggs, peeled
and chopped

2 tablespoons lime juice

1 plum tomato, cored and finely chopped

In a food processor, process the scallions and all 3 chilies until finely chopped, about 20 seconds. Add the cilantro, vinegar and ¾ teaspoon salt. Process until the cilantro is finely chopped, about 10 seconds, scraping the sides as needed.

In a medium bowl, mash the flesh from 2 avocado halves and ⅓ of the chopped eggs with a fork until mostly smooth but with some lumps. Roughly chop the remaining 4 avocado halves and transfer to the bowl. Add the lime juice and fold with a silicone spatula to combine.

Reserve 2 tablespoons of the chopped tomato and 2 tablespoons of the remaining chopped eggs for garnish. Mix the remaining tomato and eggs into the avocado mixture, then gently fold in the chili-cilantro mixture. Taste and season with salt.

Transfer the salsa to a serving bowl and top with reserved tomato and chopped eggs.

SPICY CILANTRO-YOGURT SAUCE

Start to finish: 1 hour (5 minutes active)
Makes 1 cup

This simple yogurt-based Somali hot sauce packs a spicy, herbal punch. It's delicious on just about anything, from fried eggs to grilled chicken. If you're a fan of chili heat, leave the seeds in some—or all—of the serranos.

½ cup whole-milk Greek yogurt

½ cup packed fresh cilantro leaves

¼ cup unseasoned rice vinegar

3 serrano chilies, stemmed and seeded

1 garlic clove, smashed and peeled

¼ teaspoon kosher salt

In a blender, puree all ingredients until smooth and bright green, about 1 minute. Refrigerate, covered, for at least 1 hour or up to 3 days.

PEPPER-LIME DIPPING SAUCE

Start to finish: 10 minutes
Makes about ⅓ cup

In Cambodia, the tangy, salty, peppery dipping sauce called tuk meric typically is paired with the stir-fry called loc lac, but we find that it goes equally well with simply seasoned and grilled shrimp, chicken, beef or vegetables. Toasting the peppercorns in a dry skillet until lightly smoking brings out their pleasantly sharp flavor, enhances their spicy aroma and slightly crisps their texture.

¼ cup black peppercorns, coarsely cracked

¼ cup lime juice

Kosher salt

Light brown sugar

In a small skillet over medium, toast the peppercorns, stirring often, until fragrant and lightly smoking, 2 to 4 minutes. Transfer to a small bowl. Add the lime juice, 1 teaspoon salt and 2 teaspoons packed sugar, then whisk until the sugar and salt dissolve.

RICH AND SAVORY MEAT-FREE GRAVY

Start to finish: 1¼ hours
Makes 2½ cups

This all-purpose vegetarian gravy is rich and full-flavored. We build deep savoriness into it by browning the ingredients and deglazing the flavorful drippings. Plus, we use both miso and tomato paste to lend umami notes; soy sauce also adds depth of flavor and color. If you have dried shiitake mushrooms, simmering one or two (broken into pieces) into the mix adds an extra layer of meaty flavor, but the gravy is delicious without them. If you're serving a crowd, the recipe can be doubled, but use a Dutch oven instead of a saucepan. The gravy can be made up to three days in advance; store in an airtight container in the refrigerator and rewarm gently over medium just before serving.

6 tablespoons (¾ stick) salted butter

8 ounces cremini mushrooms, chopped

Kosher salt and ground black pepper

1 medium yellow onion, chopped

1 medium celery stalk, chopped

1 medium carrot, peeled and thinly sliced

1 tablespoon white or red miso

1 tablespoon tomato paste

⅓ cup all-purpose flour

½ cup dry white wine

1½ tablespoons soy sauce

1 tablespoon black peppercorns

2 bay leaves

½ teaspoon dried thyme

1 or 2 dried shiitake mushrooms, broken into pieces (optional)

In a large saucepan over medium-high, melt the butter. Add the cremini mushrooms and ¼ teaspoon salt, then cook, stirring, until the liquid released by the creminis has evaporated and the mushrooms are well browned, 10 to 12 minutes.

Stir in the onion, cover and cook, stirring occasionally, until it is well browned at the edges, about 5 minutes. Add ¼ cup water, scraping up the browned bits. Stir in the celery and carrot, then cook, stirring, until slightly softened, 3 to 5 minutes.

Stir in the miso and tomato paste, then cook, stirring constantly, until well-browned, 2 to 3 minutes. Stir in ¼ cup water, scraping up the browned bits. Add the flour and cook, stirring constantly, until the mixture is thick and pasty. While stirring, add the wine, followed by 4¼ cups water. Add the soy sauce, peppercorns, bay, thyme and dried shiitakes (if using). Bring to a simmer over medium-high, then reduce to medium-low and cook, uncovered and stirring occasionally, for 30 minutes.

Set a fine-mesh sieve over a large bowl, then strain the gravy, pressing on the solids with a spatula to extract as much liquid as possible; discard the solids. You should have about 2½ cups; if you have more, return the gravy to the saucepan, bring to a simmer over medium and cook, stirring often, until reduced to 2½ cups. Taste and season with salt and pepper.

TAMARIND DIPPING SAUCE

Start to finish: 20 minutes
Makes about 2 cups

This sauce is great with grilled meats, poultry and fish, especially salmon. It's also good with sticky Asian spareribs, stirred into Asian soups, as a base for steaming mussels, or tossed with sliced cucumber and torn mint leaves for a quick salad. Tamarind is a brown pod containing seeds and a sticky, sour pulp. Tamarind pulp is most commonly available as blocks and will keep for several weeks in the refrigerator. A blender gave the sauce its smooth consistency. For a milder flavor, remove the seeds and ribs from the chili. If you can find palm sugar, it would be an authentic substitute for the brown sugar.

2 lemon grass stalks, trimmed to the lower 6 inches, dry outer layers discarded, chopped

1 large shallot, chopped

3 tablespoons grapeseed or other neutral oil

1 serrano chili, stemmed and chopped

1 tablespoon tomato paste

1 tablespoon finely grated fresh ginger

2 ounces tamarind pulp, seeds removed

5 tablespoons packed light brown sugar

¼ cup fish sauce

1 tablespoon soy sauce

3 tablespoons lime juice

Ground black pepper

In a medium saucepan over medium, combine the lemon grass, shallot, oil and chili. Cook, stirring, until just beginning to brown, 3 to 5 minutes. Add the tomato paste and ginger and cook, stirring constantly, until fragrant, about 30 seconds. Add 2½ cups water, the tamarind and sugar. Bring to a boil, then reduce the heat to medium-low and simmer until the tamarind has softened, about 15 minutes. Off heat, stir in the fish sauce and soy sauce.

Let the mixture cool slightly, then transfer to a blender. Blend until smooth, about 1 minute. Strain the mixture through a fine-mesh strainer, pressing on the solids; discard the solids. Stir in the lime juice, then taste and season with pepper. Use immediately or refrigerate for up to 2 weeks.

CILANTRO-JALAPEÑO ADOBO SAUCE

Start to finish: 20 minutes
Makes about 1 cup

Spanish for marinade, adobo can be many things, but it began as a blend of olive oil, vinegar and spices that was slathered over meat and other foods to keep them from spoiling. We wanted a sauce that could go with just about anything and were inspired by a Mexican-style adobo from Rick Bayless, who blends together garlic, serrano chilies, cilantro, parsley and oil. We wanted to cut back on the oil and heat, so we chose jalapeño peppers over serrano chilies; the latter can vary widely in heat level from dud to scud. We dropped the parsley and went all in on cilantro; its fresh, clean flavor was even bolder when it didn't need to compete with another herb. Our sauce packs moderate heat; if you prefer a milder version, replace two of the jalapeños with one large Anaheim or poblano chili. Since it's blended with oil and the garlic is thoroughly cooked, the herb sauce can be refrigerated for up to three weeks.

4 jalapeño chilies

6 medium garlic cloves, unpeeled

5 cups (about 4 ounces) lightly packed fresh cilantro

6 tablespoons extra-virgin olive oil

1 tablespoon lime juice, plus more as needed

Kosher salt

½ teaspoon sugar

Heat the broiler with an oven rack 6 inches from the element. Arrange the jalapeños and garlic on a broiler-safe rimmed baking sheet and broil, turning as necessary, until the chilies are evenly blistered and the garlic skins are spotted brown, 8 to 10 minutes. Cover with foil and let sit until cool enough to handle, about 10 minutes. Peel, stem and seed the chilies and peel the garlic, trimming away any scorched bits.

In a food processor, combine the chilies, garlic, cilantro, oil, lime juice, ¼ teaspoon salt and the sugar. Process until smooth, 1 to 2 minutes, scraping the bowl as needed. Taste and adjust salt and lime juice as desired.

NƯỚC CHẤM

Start to finish: 10 minutes
Makes about 1 cup

In the Vietnamese kitchen, nước chấm is a multipurpose sauce/dressing with salty, sweet, tangy and chili notes. If you wish to moderate the spiciness, seed the chilies before mincing them. The flavors are best the day the sauce is made, but it will keep refrigerated for up to three days.

⅓ cup fish sauce

3½ tablespoons lime juice

¼ cup white sugar

3 medium garlic cloves, minced

1 or 2 serrano chilies, stemmed and minced

In a small bowl, combine the fish sauce, lime juice, sugar and 6 tablespoons water. Stir until the sugar dissolves, then stir in the garlic and chilies. Cover and refrigerate up to 3 days; bring to room temperature before serving.

ALMOND AND ROSEMARY
SALSA VERDE

Start to finish: 20 minutes
Makes about 1 cup

This quick and versatile green sauce is herbal and nutty, accented with the brightness of lemon and the brininess of capers. It's excellent with a seared or grilled steak, but is also a good accompaniment to chicken or fish, or as a sandwich spread. If convenient, make the sauce up to a day ahead and refrigerate it, but allow it to come to room temperature before serving.

1 cup lightly packed fresh flat-leaf parsley

½ cup sliced almonds, toasted and cooled

¼ cup drained capers, rinsed, drained
and patted dry

3 oil-packed anchovy fillets, rinsed
and patted dry

1 tablespoon minced fresh rosemary

2 teaspoons grated lemon zest, plus
2 tablespoons lemon juice

1 medium garlic clove, smashed and peeled

Kosher salt and ground black pepper

½ cup extra-virgin olive oil

In a food processor, combine the parsley, half of the almonds, the capers, anchovies, rosemary, lemon zest, garlic and ½ teaspoon pepper. Process until finely chopped, about 1 minute. With the processor running, slowly add the oil and process, scraping the bowl as needed, until smooth. Add the remaining almonds and pulse until roughly chopped, about 10 pulses.

Transfer to a small bowl and stir in the lemon juice. Taste and season with salt and pepper.

BAGNA CAUDA

Start to finish: 30 minutes
Makes about 1 cup

Bagna cauda, a Piedmontese sauce-like dip, is a heady mixture of butter, olive oil, lightly toasted garlic and umami-rich anchovies. We give ours a layer of herbal flavor with the addition of bay and rosemary and add some brightness with lemon juice. In traditional bagna cauda, the garlic and anchovies separate to the bottom upon standing. To avoid this, we blend the mixture after cooking to yield a silky, emulsified dip. If you're using oil-packed anchovies from a jar, you'll need about 1 ounce of drained fillets (4 teaspoons minced). Serve bagna cauda with raw or cooked vegetables, or with pieces of crusty bread. It can be refrigerated in an airtight container for up to a week; rewarm before serving.

8 tablespoons salted butter,
cut into a few pieces

¼ cup extra-virgin olive oil

12 medium garlic cloves, minced

2-ounce can oil-packed anchovy fillets
(see headnote), 2 tablespoons oil reserved,
then drained, fillets chopped

2 bay leaves

2 small sprigs rosemary

¾ teaspoon red pepper flakes

2 tablespoons lemon juice

In a small saucepan over low, combine the butter, oil, garlic, anchovies, bay, rosemary and pepper flakes. Cook, stirring occasionally, until the garlic is lightly toasted and the anchovies have disintegrated, 15 to 20 minutes.

Remove and discard the herbs and transfer the mixture to a blender. Let cool for about 5 minutes, then blend until smooth, about 30 seconds. Add 2 tablespoons of the lemon juice and the reserved anchovy oil; blend until well combined and lighter in color, about another 30 seconds.

THAI SWEET CHILI SAUCE

Start to finish: 20 minutes
Makes ½ cup

This sweet-sour, spicy and slightly syrupy sauce is called nam jim gai. It's the customary condiment for Thai grilled chicken but also is terrific with grilled or roasted pork and is an excellent dipping sauce for just about any type of fried foods, from corn fritters to egg rolls. Fresh red Thai chilies are preferable, as they bring a subtle fruitiness to the sauce, but dried red pepper flakes work, too.

3 medium garlic cloves, finely grated

2 fresh red Thai chilies, stemmed and thinly sliced or 1 to 2 teaspoons red pepper flakes

½ cup white sugar

¼ cup white vinegar

Kosher salt

In a small saucepan, combine the garlic, chilies, sugar, vinegar, ½ cup water and ½ teaspoon salt. Bring to a boil over medium-high, stirring to dissolve the sugar, then reduce to medium and simmer, stirring occasionally, until lightly syrupy and reduced to about ¾ cup, about 15 minutes.

Transfer to a jar or small bowl and cool completely. Use right away or cover and refrigerate for up to 1 week; bring to room temperature before serving.

CHILI-LIME SAUCE

Start to finish: 20 minutes

Makes about ¾ cup

This sauce strikes a balance of salty and tangy with a touch of sweet and heat. The toasted rice adds a unique flavor and gives the sauce clingability.

1½ tablespoons jasmine rice

¼ cup fish sauce

3 tablespoons lime juice

1 medium shallot, minced

2 tablespoons finely chopped fresh cilantro

1 tablespoon packed light or dark brown sugar

2 teaspoons red pepper flakes

In a small skillet over medium, toast the rice, occasionally shaking the pan, until golden brown, about 5 minutes. Transfer to a spice grinder and let cool completely, then pulse to a coarse powder, 8 to 10 pulses. Transfer to a small bowl.

Into the rice powder, stir in the remaining ingredients and 1 tablespoon water. Cover and refrigerate for at least 1 hour before using; bring to room temperature before serving. (Leftovers can be refrigerated in an airtight container for up to 3 days; the sauce will thicken slightly.)

MOJO VERDE

Start to finish: 10 minutes

Makes 1 cup

This creamy blended green sauce gets richness from toasted almonds, olive oil and avocado. Cilantro, poblano chilies and lemon zest bring fresh notes to keep the flavors bright and lively.

1 large or 2 small poblano chilies (6 ounces), stemmed, cut lengthwise into quarters and seeded

3 cups packed fresh cilantro leaves and tender stems

½ ripe avocado, pitted, peeled and chopped

¼ cup blanched slivered almonds, toasted

¼ cup extra-virgin olive oil

1 tablespoon finely grated lemon zest, plus 3 tablespoons lemon juice

1 teaspoon cumin seeds, toasted

Kosher salt

In a 10-inch skillet over medium-high, toast the chilies, flipping occasionally with tongs, until spotty brown on both sides, about 5 minutes. Let cool slightly, then roughly chop.

In a blender, combine the chilies, cilantro, avocado, almonds, oil, lemon zest and juice, cumin and ¼ teaspoon salt. With the machine running, stream in 3 tablespoons water and puree until the sauce is thick and creamy. Taste and season with salt.

MOJO PICÓN

Start to finish: 10 minutes
Makes 1 cup

To make this Canarian red sauce, we use a combination of dried chilies and roasted peppers, along with oil-packed sun-dried tomatoes. Toasted almonds and sherry vinegar lend the mixture distinctly Spanish flavor notes.

2 large New Mexico chilies, stemmed, seeded and torn into rough 1-inch pieces

¼ cup extra-virgin olive oil

½ cup drained roasted red peppers

¼ cup blanched slivered almonds, toasted

¼ cup sherry vinegar

2 tablespoons drained oil-packed sun-dried tomatoes

2 large garlic cloves

2 teaspoons honey

Kosher salt

In a 10-inch skillet over medium-high, combine the chilies and oil. Cook, stirring frequently, until the chilies are slightly darkened and the oil is reddish, 1 to 2 minutes. Remove from the heat and let cool slightly.

In a blender, combine the red peppers, almonds, vinegar, tomatoes, garlic, honey and ¼ teaspoon salt. Blend until almost smooth, about 20 seconds. Add the chilies and their oil. With the machine running, stream in 3 tablespoons water and puree until the sauce is thick and creamy, 45 to 60 seconds. Taste and season with salt.

PICKLED VEGETABLES

Start to finish: 45 minutes (30 minutes active), plus cooling
Makes about 4 cups

Salting the vegetables before pickling them enhanced their crispness and intensified their final flavor. That's because it removes water, allowing them to better absorb the brine. Once cooled, the pickled vegetables can be eaten immediately, but their flavor improves with time. We left the whole spices in the brine to infuse even more during storage; they can be removed before serving, if desired.

1 large red onion (¾ pound), halved and thinly sliced lengthwise

½ pound carrots, peeled, halved lengthwise and thinly sliced on a bias

2 jalapeños, thinly sliced crosswise

Kosher salt

1 cup distilled white vinegar

½ cup white sugar

½ teaspoon black peppercorns

½ teaspoon coriander seeds

¼ teaspoon red pepper flakes (optional)

6 allspice berries

1 bay leaf

In a bowl, toss together the onions, carrots, jalapeños and 1 tablespoon salt. Let sit for 30 to 60 minutes. Transfer the vegetables to a colander and rinse well, then set aside to drain.

Meanwhile, in a medium saucepan over high, combine the vinegar, 1 cup water, sugar, peppercorns, coriander, pepper flakes, if using, allspice and bay leaf. Bring to a boil, then reduce to medium and simmer for 5 minutes.

Transfer the vegetables to a canning jar or a heatproof, lidded container. Pour the hot brine over them, ensuring they are fully submerged. Cool to room temperature, about 2 hours, then cover and refrigerate for up to 1 month.

PICKLED CHILIES

Start to finish: 35 minutes (5 minutes active)
Makes 1 cup

These jalapeño chilies pickled in fish sauce, lime juice and a little sugar are a milder variation of the often fiery Thai dressing called nam prik. The chilies, and their sauce, add a balanced hit of heat, sweet and acid. We find them a delicious way to add bright flavor to our Thai fried rice (recipe p. 162), or any Thai or Vietnamese dish. Whisk in a little peanut oil for a quick salad, vegetable or slaw dressing. Add a spoonful to stews, or even scrambled eggs or roasted or sautéed vegetables.

4 jalapeño chilies, stemmed, seeded (if desired) and thinly sliced crosswise

¼ cup fish sauce

¼ cup fresh lime juice

1 teaspoon white sugar

In a bowl, stir together all ingredients. Refrigerate for at least 30 minutes or up to 1 week.

SLOW-ROASTED TOMATOES

Start to finish: 3½ hours
Makes about 32 halves

Tomato paste made these tomatoes more savory, while white balsamic vinegar gave them a bright, slightly sour note. Medium plum tomatoes, roughly 4 ounces each, worked best. If your tomatoes are smaller, start checking them after three hours in the oven. Slow-roasted tomatoes are a powerful pantry staple; add them to soups, sauces, pasta, polenta, sandwiches and salads.

¼ cup white balsamic vinegar

¼ cup tomato paste

Kosher salt and ground black pepper

4 pounds plum tomatoes (about 16 medium), halved lengthwise

¼ cup extra-virgin olive oil

Heat the oven to 325°F with a rack in the middle position. Line a rimmed baking sheet with kitchen parchment. In a large bowl, whisk together the vinegar, tomato paste and 1 teaspoon each salt and pepper. Add the tomatoes and toss to coat. Arrange the tomatoes cut side up on the prepared sheet. Drizzle evenly with the oil.

Roast until the tomatoes are shriveled, caramelized and lightly charred at the edges, about 3½ hours, rotating the pan halfway through. Serve immediately, or let cool, transfer to a lidded container and refrigerate for up to 1 week.

GARLIC CONFIT

Start to finish: 20 minutes
Makes ½ cup

Garlic confit is an extremely handy flavor booster to have in the refrigerator. Not only can the creamy, sweet garlic cloves be added to salad dressings, pan sauces, compound butters or simply smeared onto crusty bread, the aromatic oil is great drizzled onto soup, pasta and pizza, can be used to sauté vegetables or is a simple way to add flavor to cooked grains. Feel free to change up the flavorings in the confit— for instance, use rosemary instead of thyme, toss in a couple dried whole chilies or add a strip or two of lemon zest.

1 large head garlic (about 16 cloves), cloves separated, peeled and thinly sliced

3 tablespoons salted butter

3 tablespoons extra-virgin olive oil

1 bay leaf

4 sprigs thyme

In a small saucepan over low, heat the butter, oil, bay and thyme until butter is melted and temperature reaches 185°F. Add the garlic and stir to coat and submerge. Cook for 15 minutes, stirring occasionally, until the garlic is tender, translucent and jammy. Pour into a bowl and let cool, about 20 minutes. Use immediately or cover and refrigerate for up to 1 week.

RED CHILI AND SHALLOT SAMBAL

Start to finish: 1 hour
Makes about 1 cup

Sambal, a fiery, aromatic chili paste, is a staple condiment in Malaysia, as well as in Indonesia and Singapore. There are countless varieties, some simple, others complex; some funky with fermented seafood, others sharp with raw alliums and citrus; some are thick, while others are soupy. In this simple, jam-like version with the savory sweetness of deeply caramelized shallots and garlic, we use two kinds of red chilies: fresh Fresnos which are fruity and moderately spicy, and guajillo chilies (a type of dried Mexican chili) that feature earthy, smoky notes. The recipe makes a good amount, but the sambal keeps well in the refrigerator for up to two weeks. It's fantastic with tamarind shrimp, but also is great on grilled fish or meat, tossed onto roasted vegetables or even spooned on fried or scrambled eggs.

½ cup peanut or neutral oil

3 medium guajillo chilies, seeded and torn into rough 1-inch pieces

6 Fresno chilies (about 5 ounces), stemmed and roughly chopped

4 medium shallots, roughly chopped

2 large garlic cloves, smashed and peeled

Kosher salt

2½ teaspoons white sugar

In a 10-inch skillet, combine the oil and guajillo chilies. Cook over medium, stirring occasionally, until fragrant and the oil has taken on a golden hue, about 3 minutes. Remove from the heat and, using a slotted spoon, transfer the chilies to a food processor. Reserve the skillet with the oil.

To the food processor, add the Fresno chilies, shallots, garlic, ½ teaspoon salt and 2 tablespoons oil from the skillet. Process until finely chopped, scraping the bowl as needed, 1 to 2 minutes.

Add the chili puree to the oil in the skillet. Cook over medium, stirring occasionally, until the mixture begins to sizzle, then reduce to medium-low and cook, stirring more often as the mixture thickens and darkens, until it has a jammy consistency, a darkly caramelized appearance and a toasty aroma, 15 to 20 minutes. Remove from the heat and stir in the sugar. Transfer to a small heatproof bowl. Cool to room temperature before serving, or cover and refrigerate for up to 2 weeks. If refrigerated, bring to room temperature before serving.

GEORGIAN MINT-GREEN CHILI RELISH

Start to finish: 15 minutes
Makes about ½ cup

Adjika often is made with red peppers, but this version uses green serrano chilies with fresh mint. Spicy, herbal and savory, this adjika can be served with warm bread, offered as a condiment with meats and seafood, or turned into a dressing for vegetables. We liked the pleasant heat of the relish made with two whole chilies and two seeded. If you'd prefer a milder version, seed all four; for more heat, leave the seeds in all.

4 cups lightly packed fresh mint

4 serrano chilies, stemmed, 2 seeded, all 4 chopped

2 medium garlic cloves, smashed and peeled

1 tablespoon grapeseed or other neutral oil

1 teaspoon ground coriander

Kosher salt

In a food processor, combine the mint, chilies, garlic, oil, coriander and 1 teaspoon salt. Process until finely chopped, 1 to 2 minutes, scraping the bowl as needed. Taste and season with additional salt.

Transfer to a small bowl or jar, cover and refrigerate for at least 1 hour or up to 4 days.

SPICY COCONUT RELISH

Start to finish: 10 minutes, plus chilling
Makes about 2 cups

This condiment, a riff on the Sri Lankan coconut relish called pol sambol, is a great accompaniment to curries of almost any kind. Wide-flake coconut works best here; shredded coconut does not break down properly.

2 cups unsweetened wide-flake coconut

½ cup warm water

Kosher salt

2 tablespoons packed light brown sugar

1 tablespoon red pepper flakes

1 teaspoon sweet paprika

1 Fresno chili, stemmed, seeded and roughly chopped

½ cup lime juice

3 tablespoons fish sauce

3 tablespoons coconut milk

¼ cup chopped fresh mint

In a medium bowl, stir together the coconut, water and ½ teaspoon salt. Let stand until the coconut has softened, about 15 minutes. Transfer the mixture to a food processor; reserve the bowl. Add the sugar, pepper flakes, paprika and chili, then process until the coconut is roughly chopped, about 1 minute. Add the lime juice, fish sauce and coconut milk and process until finely chopped, about 1 minute.

Return the mixture to the bowl, cover and refrigerate for at least 1 hour or up to 3 days. Bring to room temperature before serving, then stir in the mint.

HARISSA

Start to finish: 15 minutes
Makes about 1½ cups

Our version of harissa, the spicy condiment that originated in North Africa, adds delicious punch to dips, soups, sauces and vinaigrettes. New Mexico chilies did the best job of matching harder-to-find North African chilies, bringing balanced heat. For more fire, a bit of cayenne can be added. Plenty of recipes call for either sun-dried tomatoes or roasted red peppers; we found a combination gave our harissa the sweet, ketchup-like profile Americans love and helped make it more of an all-purpose sauce, rather than simply a hot sauce. Frying the chilies, whole spices and garlic in oil is easier and works better than the traditional method of toasting in a dry skillet. And while most recipes call for rehydrating the dried chilies, we found the hot oil softened them adequately, giving the harissa a pleasant, slightly coarse texture. Adding garlic to the mix mellowed its bite, and leaving the cloves whole ensured they wouldn't burn (and meant less prep work). We favored white balsamic vinegar for its mild acidity and slight sweetness. Lemon juice or white wine vinegar sweetened with a pinch of sugar are good substitutes.

4 dried New Mexico chilies, stemmed, seeded and torn into rough pieces

½ cup grapeseed or other neutral oil

6 medium garlic cloves

1 teaspoon caraway seeds

1 teaspoon cumin seeds

1 cup drained roasted red peppers, patted dry

½ cup drained oil-packed sun-dried tomatoes, patted dry

1 tablespoon white balsamic vinegar

Kosher salt

Cayenne pepper

In a small saucepan over medium heat, combine the chilies, oil, garlic, caraway and cumin. Cook, stirring often, until the garlic is light golden brown and the chilies are fragrant, about 5 minutes. Carefully transfer the mixture to a food processor and add the red peppers, tomatoes, vinegar and ½ teaspoon of salt. Process until smooth, about 3 minutes, scraping down the bowl once or twice. Season with salt and cayenne to taste. Serve immediately or refrigerate in an airtight container for up to 3 weeks.

SMOKED PAPRIKA SPICE PASTE WITH CUMIN AND OREGANO

Start to finish: 10 minutes
Makes about ¼ cup

A combination of rich, woodsy smoked paprika, earthy cumin and herbal fresh oregano (dried oregano works well, too), this richly hued spice rub is Spanish in its inspiration. To keep the flavor profile from feeling heavy, we also include ground coriander and grated lemon zest—both add light, citrusy notes. We use cumin seeds and pulse them only a few times in a spice grinder, leaving some not fully ground so they add texture as much as flavor. This mix is ideal for mild, lean meats such as chicken or pork. It's also great tossed with cauliflower before roasting.

2 teaspoons cumin seeds

2 teaspoons ground coriander

1½ teaspoons smoked paprika

2 teaspoons grated lemon zest

**1 teaspoon minced fresh oregano
OR ½ teaspoon dried oregano**

Kosher salt and ground black pepper

2 tablespoons extra-virgin olive oil

In a spice grinder, pulse the cumin seeds until a mixture of coarsely and finely ground, about 3 pulses. Transfer to a small bowl and stir in the coriander, paprika, lemon zest, oregano, ¾ teaspoon each salt and pepper, followed by the oil. Use right away or refrigerate in an airtight container for up to 3 days (if refrigerated, bring to room temperature before use).

THYME, FENNEL AND ORANGE ZEST SPICE PASTE

Start to finish: 5 minutes
Makes about ¼ cup

Dried thyme along with coriander and licorice-like fennel evoke the flavors of Provence. We rub orange zest into the spices to release the oils and evenly distribute the citrus flavor. The inimitable taste and vibrant hue of saffron is a welcome addition, but even without it this seasoning mix still offers a well-balanced mix of savory, sweet and citrusy. It's especially good on steamed or seared seafood, and is a delicious match for pork and lamb.

2 teaspoons dried thyme OR 1½ teaspoons dried rosemary OR 1 teaspoon each

1½ teaspoons fennel seeds

1 teaspoon coriander seeds

¼ teaspoon saffron threads, crushed (optional)

Kosher salt and ground black pepper

1 tablespoon grated orange zest

½ teaspoon granulated garlic

2 tablespoons extra-virgin olive oil

In a spice grinder, pulse the thyme, fennel seeds, coriander seeds, saffron (if using) and ½ teaspoon salt until finely ground, about 6 pulses. Transfer to a small bowl and add the orange zest, granulated garlic and ¼ teaspoon pepper. With your fingertips, rub the mixture until well combined and evenly moistened. Stir in the oil. Use immediately or refrigerate in an airtight container for up to 3 days (if refrigerated, bring to room temperature before use).

BAY, GARLIC AND BLACK PEPPER SPICE PASTE

Start to finish: 5 minutes
Makes about ¼ cup

This spice rub takes inspiration from espetada, beef skewers from Madeira that are redolent of bay and garlic. And the bay doesn't just put in its usual cameo appearance; it's ground into the mix to add earthy flavor. We add subtle heat with dried red chili and some sharpness and pungency with black pepper, while brown sugar keeps the savoriness in check. This bold rub is a great match for beef or lamb, as well as a fat-rich cut of pork, such as shoulder. The recipe makes enough to season about 1½ pounds of meat.

8 bay leaves, crumbled

1 dried árbol chili OR ½ teaspoon red pepper flakes

2 teaspoons black peppercorns

2 teaspoons packed light brown sugar

1½ teaspoons granulated garlic

Kosher salt

2 tablespoons extra-virgin olive oil

In a spice grinder, combine the bay, chili and peppercorns. Process to a fine powder, 30 to 60 seconds, occasionally shaking the spice grinder. Transfer to a small bowl, then stir in the sugar, granulated garlic and 1 teaspoon salt, followed by the oil. Use immediately or refrigerate in an airtight container for up to 2 weeks (if refrigerated, bring to room temperature before use).

613

REEM KASSIS' ALL-PURPOSE NINE-SPICE BLEND

Reem Kassis, author of "The Palestinian Table," says every household has their own spice blend, a mix that is used daily. To make her family's recipe, Kassis calls for **6 tablespoons allspice, 6 cinnamon sticks** (broken in half), **3 tablespoons coriander seeds, 1 tablespoon black peppercorns, 10 whole cloves, ½ whole nutmeg** (crushed), **1 teaspoon cardamom seeds, ½ teaspoon cumin seeds** and **2 blades mace.** Toast all ingredients in a skillet until aromatic, stirring frequently. Cool, then use a spice grinder to grind to a powder. Makes about 1 cup. Keeps for three months in an airtight container. If you don't have blades of mace, stir in ½ teaspoon ground mace after grinding.

SICHUAN SEASONING

Start to finish: 10 minutes
Makes about ¼ cup

To toast the Sichuan peppercorns, heat them in a small, dry skillet over medium until fragrant, about 2 minutes. Transfer to a bowl and let cool, then finely grind in a spice grinder. Strain through a fine mesh strainer to remove any fibrous pieces.

3 tablespoons Sichuan peppercorns, toasted and ground

2 teaspoons white sugar

½ teaspoon kosher salt

In a small bowl, stir together all ingredients. Store in an airtight container for up to 1 month

FLAVORED SALTS

Start to finish: 5 minutes
Makes about ¼ cup

These flavored salts are meant to be used as finishing salts—that is, they're best sprinkled onto dishes just before serving or offered at the table for adding to taste. We use kosher salt for these recipes and our preferred brand is Diamond Crystal because the light, fluffy granules combine well with other ingredients and dissolve readily in the presence of moisture. Whole spices, as opposed to ground, offer the best flavor, aroma and texture, but they should be toasted and crushed before mixing. Toast whole spices in a small, dry skillet over medium heat, frequently shaking the pan, until fragrant, 3 to 5 minutes; let cool, then coarsely crush in a mortar with a pestle or by pulsing a few times in an electric spice grinder. The salts can be stored in an airtight container in the refrigerator for up to one week.

SPICY CURRY SALT

This salt is especially good on cooked red lentils, hearty braised greens such as collards or pureed vegetable soups. Or toss it with buttered popcorn.

1 tablespoon kosher salt, preferably Diamond Crystal

1 tablespoon curry powder

1½ teaspoons yellow mustard seeds, toasted and crushed

1 teaspoon red pepper flakes

½ teaspoon grated nutmeg

½ teaspoon ground cardamom

½ teaspoon white sugar

In a small bowl, combine all ingredients. Stir together or rub with your fingers until well mixed.

CHILI-LIME SALT

Sprinkle this salt onto corn on the cob for a take on Mexican street corn. It's also great on black beans or pinto beans, as well as on grilled steak or chicken tucked into tortillas for tacos or fajitas. When making margaritas, use it to salt the rims of the glasses for a savory-sweet accent.

2 tablespoons grated lime zest

1 tablespoon kosher salt, preferably Diamond Crystal

1 tablespoon chili powder

1½ teaspoons packed dark brown sugar

1 teaspoon smoked sweet paprika

In a small bowl, combine all ingredients. Stir together or rub with your fingers until well mixed.

HAWAIJ SALT

Hawaij is a Yemeni spice blend. We've added salt and a touch of sugar to balance the fragrant spices. Use to garnish a creamy pumpkin or cauliflower soup, or sprinkle it onto roasted sweet potatoes. The flavors also work nicely with grilled or roasted lamb.

1 tablespoon kosher salt, preferably Diamond Crystal

1 tablespoon cumin seeds, toasted and crushed

1½ teaspoons ground turmeric

1 teaspoon white sugar

½ teaspoon ground black pepper

½ teaspoon ground cloves

In a small bowl, combine all ingredients. Stir together or rub with your fingers until well mixed.

INDEX

sesame stir-fried pork with, 278–79

soup with tofu and, 85–86

L

lahmajoun, weeknight, 539

lamb

Chinese skewered, 493

Greek meatballs with, 472–73

Lebanese baked kafta with, 316–17

spiced burgers with, 545–46

stew with, 351

Turkish beans with, 133–34

Turkish skillet kebab with, 475–76

leeks

bacon and barley pilaf with, 190

chicken en cocotte with, 437

soups with, 94–95, 116–17

spicy pork with, 348–49

lemon

baharat mushrooms with, 60

broccoli with, 40–41

chicken with, 302, 339, 406

harissa mayonnaise with, 595

harissa potato salad with, 27

meatballs with, 474–75

"orzotto" with, 232–33

pesto with, 234

quinoa with, 194–95

relish with, 319

risotto with, 172–73

salmon with, 395

scallops with, 376

shrimp with, 370–71

smashed potatoes with, 63

soups with, 95–96, 110

yogurt with garlic and, 305–6

lemon grass

beef and potato curry with, 494

chicken stir-fried with, 267–68

fish with, 388

tamarind dipping sauce with, 602

Thai hot-and-sour soup with, 104–5

tofu and mushrooms with, 290–91

Vietnamese chicken with, 340, 423

Vietnamese pork with, 459–60

lentils

berbere-spiced red, 154

bulgur and, 152

dal tarka with, 154–55

salads with, 149–51

sausage and, 465

soups with, 93–94

stews with, 129–30, 151–52, 325

lettuce

fish sandwiches with, 555–56

salads with romaine, 9–10, 15

Vietnamese meatballs in, 466–67

lime

asparagus with, 39

broccoli with, 42–43

fish tacos with, 572–73

lentil and potato stew with, 325

mayonnaise with, 399

pork skewers with, 462

salads with, 18–19, 138, 478–79

salt with, 615

sauces with, 600–601, 606

Senegalese chicken with, 336

snapper with, 390

Thai hot-and-sour soup with, 104–5

Vietnamese meatballs with, 466–67

lomo saltado, 272–73

M

mango

chicken with chutney of, 414–15

shrimp with, 372

matbucha, salmon with, 386–87

mayonnaise, 594

burgers with, 548–50

chipotle-lime, 399

harissa, 595

kimchi aioli with, 595

sandwiches with, 550, 552–53, 555–56

spicy sauce with, 544

meatballs

beef and rice, 474–75

chickpea and feta, 127–28

in chipotle sauce, 471

Greek, 472–73

Japanese-style chicken, 440

kefta with tahini, 476–77

Lebanese baked (kafta), 316–17

with lemon-olive oil sauce, 474–75

Moroccan tagine with, 473–74

Neapolitan, 470

soups with, 112, 121

with spicy tomato sauce, 315–16

Vietnamese-style wraps with, 466–67

migas, cheesy Tex-Mex, 209–10

milk

four-cheese pasta with, 242

mashed potatoes with, 66

See also coconut milk; cream

mint

Georgian relish with, 610

Lebanese-style tabbouleh with, 32

salads with, 12–13, 22–23, 27, 33–35

yogurt with, 46–47, 80–81, 394

miso

broths with, 84

brown rice risotto with, 175

chicken with, 336–38, 430–31

corn chowder with, 78–79

noodles with, 84–85, 252–53

pork with, 457

salmon with, 305, 389

winter vegetables with, 60–61

mojo sauces, 606–7

mole, Oaxacan green, 576–77

molletes with pico de gallo, 561–62

muhammara (dip), 597

mujaddara (lentils and bulgur), 152

mushrooms

baharat, 60

Barolo-braised beef with, 362–64

beef tenderloin with, 501

bocadillos with, 553–54

broths with, 74, 113–14

chicken with cremini, 309–10, 437

meat-free gravy with, 601

omelet with, 211

quesadillas with, 583–84

risotto with, 175, 192

salad with fennel and, 23–24

soups with, 104–5, 109–10

Spanish beef stew with, 358–59

tofu and, 290–91

mushrooms, shiitake

barley with, 190–91

noodles with, 253, 261, 294

sesame kimchi pork with, 278–79

smothered chicken with, 337–38

soupy rice with, 88

vegetable stir-fries with, 284–86

mussels, steamed, 376–77

mustard

chicken cutlets with, 434–35

mayonnaise with, 594

omelet with, 211

sandwiches with, 558–61

tartines with, 565

vinaigrette with, 33, 190

mustard seeds

Indian rice with, 169

lemon quinoa with, 194–95

shrimp with, 372

N

nokedli (Hungarian dumplings), 335

noodles

black bean, 261

buttery udon with mushrooms, 253

Chinese hot oil, 256

chow mein traybake with, 306–7

garlicky peanut, 260

with kimchi and pork, 295

Korean spicy chilled, 257

miso ramen, 84–85

miso-walnut soba, 252–53

pad Thai with, 291–93

with scallions and pork, 259

Singapore curry, 296

Taiwanese beef soup with, 117–18

ACKNOWLEDGMENTS

Writing a cookbook is a daunting endeavor, requiring the bringing together of numerous and disparate talents to achieve one well-conceived concept, from recipe conception and development through photography, editing and design. At Milk Street, many hands and minds make this possible.

In particular, I want to acknowledge J.M. Hirsch, our tireless editorial director; Michelle Locke, our relentlessly organized books editor; our exacting food editors Dawn Yanagihara and Bianca Borges; Matthew Card, creative director of recipes; and associate editor, Ari Smolin, for leading the charge on conceiving, developing, writing and editing all of this.

Also, Jennifer Baldino Cox, our art director, and the entire design team who captured the essence of Milk Street. Special thanks to photographer Joe Murphy, our designer, Gary Tooth, and all the photographers, stylists and art directors who have worked so hard to make Milk Street look so good.

Likewise, our talented kitchen crew, including kitchen director Wes Martin, our recipe development directors, Courtney Hill and Diane Unger, and the many cooks whose talent, skill and dedication have created the thousands of recipes that are the heart of Milk Street. Also Deborah Broide, Milk Street director of media relations, has done a spectacular job of sharing with the world all we do at Milk Street.

We also have a couple of folks to thank who work outside of 177 Milk Street. Michael Szczerban, editor, and everyone at Little, Brown and Company have been superb and inspired partners in this project. And my long-standing book agent, David Black, has been instrumental in bringing this project to life both with his knowledge of publishing and his friendship and support. Thank you, David!

Finally, a sincere thank you to my business partner and wife, Melissa. She has nurtured the Milk Street brand from the beginning so that we ended up where we thought we were going in the first place.

And, last but not least, to all of you who have supported the Milk Street project. Each and every one of you has a seat at the Milk Street table.

Christopher Kimball

ABOUT THE AUTHOR

Christopher Kimball is founder of Christopher Kimball's Milk Street, a food media company dedicated to changing the way we cook. It produces the bimonthly *Christopher Kimball's Milk Street Magazine*, as well as *Christopher Kimball's Milk Street Radio*, a weekly public radio show and podcast heard on more than 220 stations nationwide. It also produces the public television show *Christopher Kimball's Milk Street*, as well as two shows produced in partnership with Roku, *Milk Street Cooking School* and *My Family Recipe*. Kimball founded *Cook's Magazine* in 1980 and served as publisher and editorial director through 1989. He re-launched it as *Cook's Illustrated* in 1993. Through 2016, Kimball was host and executive producer of *America's Test Kitchen* and *Cook's Country*. He also hosted *America's Test Kitchen* radio show on public radio. Kimball is the author of several books, including *Fannie's Last Supper.*

Christopher Kimball's Milk Street is located at 177 Milk Street in downtown Boston and is dedicated to changing the way America cooks, with new flavor combinations and techniques learned around the world. It is home to Milk Street TV, a three-time Emmy Award–winning public television show, a James Beard Award–winning bimonthly magazine, an award-winning radio show and podcast, a cooking school and an online store with more than 1,700 kitchen tools and ingredients. Milk Street's cookbooks include *Milk Street Cookish*, the IACP-winning *Milk Street Vegetables*, and the James Beard–winning *Milk Street Tuesday Nights*. Milk Street also invests in nonprofit outreach, partnering with FoodCorps, the Big Sister Association of Greater Boston and the Boys & Girls Clubs of Dorchester.